Equal in Law, Unequal in Fact

The Erik Castrén Institute Monographs on International Law and Human Rights

General Editor

Martti Koskenniemi

VOLUME 13

Equal in Law, Unequal in Fact

Racial and Ethnic Discrimination and the Legal Response Thereto in Europe

By
Timo Makkonen

MARTINUS
NIJHOFF
PUBLISHERS

LEIDEN • BOSTON
2012

This book is printed on acid-free paper.

Library of Congress Cataloging-in-Publication Data

Makkonen, Timo.
Equal in law, unequal in fact : racial and ethnic discrimination and the legal response thereto in Europe / by Timo Makkonen.
p. cm. -- (Erik Castren Institute monographs on international law and human rights, 1568-2765 : v. 13)
Includes bibliographical references and index.
ISBN 978-90-04-21705-8 (hardback : alk. paper) 1. Discrimination--Law and legislation--Europe. I. Title.
KJC5142.M35 2011
342.408'73--dc23

2011043496

ISSN 1568-2765
ISBN 978 90 04 21705 8 (hardback)
ISBN 978 90 04 21706 5 (e-book)

CONTENTS

Foreword ... ix
Acknowledgments ... xiii
Abbreviations ... xvii

PART ONE

THE CHALLENGE

1 Introduction ... 3
 1.1 The Promise – and the Practice ... 3
 1.2 About this Study ... 5
2 Diversity: Empirical and Theoretical Perspectives ... 11
 2.1 Diversity in Europe ... 11
 2.2 Difference and the Difference it Makes ... 15
 2.3 Conclusions ... 29
3 Discrimination and Equality: Theoretical Perspectives ... 31
 3.1 Tension between Equality and Discrimination ... 31
 3.2 Discrimination ... 32
 3.3 Equality ... 40
4 Discrimination: Empirical Perspectives ... 49
 4.1 Extent and Characteristics of Discrimination ... 49
 4.2 The Causes of Discrimination ... 57
  4.2.1 Racism ... 57
  4.2.2 Prejudices ... 72
  4.2.3 Stereotypes ... 76
  4.2.4 Statistical Discrimination ... 78
  4.2.5 Unintentional Biases ... 80
 4.3 The Effects of Discrimination ... 83
 4.4 Conclusions ... 90

PART TWO

THE RESPONSE

5 Anti-Discrimination Law: Preliminary Issues ... 95
 5.1 On the Sources of Law ... 95

5.2 The Hard but Basic Questions ... 96
5.3 On Instruments and Their Interpretation and Application in Practice ... 105
6 International Human Rights Law ... 113
6.1 Notes on the Development of the Principle of Non-Discrimination ... 113
6.2 Universal Declaration of Human Rights ... 118
6.3 Discrimination (Employment and Occupation) Convention ... 123
6.4 Convention against Discrimination in Education ... 127
6.5 Convention on the Elimination of all Forms of Racial Discrimination ... 128
6.6 International Covenant on Civil and Political Rights ... 149
6.7 International Covenant on Economic, Social and Cultural Rights ... 166
6.8 European Convention on Human Rights and Fundamental Freedoms ... 173
6.9 The European Social Charter (revised) ... 196
6.10 Framework Convention for the Protection of National Minorities ... 201
6.11 Other Relevant Instruments ... 208
7 European Union Law ... 215
7.1 Background ... 215
7.2 Non-Discrimination as a General Principle of EU Law ... 218
7.3 The Charter of Fundamental Rights ... 220
7.4 Directive 2000/43/EC ... 222
8 Assessment ... 237
8.1 Recapitulation ... 237
8.2 Structural Properties of Anti-Discrimination law ... 249
8.2.1 Theoretical Undercurrents – Doctrinal Perplexity within a Liberal Political Frame ... 249
8.2.2 New Problems, Old Solutions: the Capacity to Tackle Everyday Discrimination ... 263
8.2.3 The Nexus between International and Domestic Anti-Discrimination Law ... 267
8.2.4 Indirect Effects: Reinforced Essentialism and Statism ... 270
8.2.5 The Chief Mischief: Individual Litigation as the Chosen Model of Enforcement ... 272
8.3 Conclusions: Of Camouflage and Loose Cannons in the Fight Against Discrimination ... 277

PART THREE

RETHINKING THE RESPONSE

9 Rethinking the Response ... 285
9.1 Objectives ... 287
9.2 Strategies ... 291
9.3 Tactics ... 297
9.4 Conclusions ... 298
10 Collection of Equality Data ... 301
10.1 The Policy Case ... 302
10.2 Methods ... 312
10.3 Challenges ... 322
10.4 Conclusions ... 339
11 Positive Action ... 343
11.1 The Policy Case ... 345
11.2 Methods ... 350
11.3 Challenges ... 353
11.4 Conclusions ... 364
12 Positive Duties ... 367
12.1 The Policy Case ... 368
12.2 Methods ... 369
12.3 Challenges ... 379
12.4 Conclusions ... 385
13 Enforcement ... 387
13.1 The Legal Infrastructure ... 388
13.2 Strengthening Enforcement ... 392
13.3 Informal Invocation and Enforcement of the Law ... 401
13.4 Conclusions ... 404

Table of Cases ... 407
Bibliography ... 415
Index ... 433

FOREWORD

One of the most significant problems in present human rights law has to do with the move from principles and objectives to their realization. Examined abstractly, national laws, international conventions and other human rights regulation often seem excellent; just what is needed to fulfil desirable objectives. Yet it often happens that the effects of those regulations ("theory") in the lives of human beings ("practice") reveal themselves far wanting. In the workplace, say, or at school, hospital or in society at large, objectives such as equality and non-discrimination, the topic of Timo Makkonen's research, are often regarded matters of high priority. Yet the way from their declaration as such to their implementation turns out often long and difficult; the objective may even remain completely out of reach. There is no necessary reason to suspect bad faith on anybody's part. Lack of resources, competing social objectives, absence of clarity of what, in fact, the desired objective should mean in terms of administrative action intervene at surprising moments, obstructing even the most well-meaning reforms.

A "critical" view of human rights has today become a commonplace not only in the academy but also among human rights experts and professionals. There is awareness that declaring "equality" as an objective or establishing a policy of non-discrimination in some field of social action is surely necessary but insufficient as a response to demands for action. Declarations and policies are in themselves *indeterminate*, we have understood. Everything will depend on what they are chosen to mean in their context of implementation. This, again, is dependent on available resources and competing concerns for the use of those very same resources. What practical effect declarations or policies will have will be determined by concrete decisions in the competent institutions: governments, private corporations, public institutions. And they each have their preferences, their biases about desirable goals. Pointing to such problems of implementation is a necessary aspect of human rights research and activism. But it is far from sufficient. What is needed is careful study of the actual effects that legislations possess, and how they are mediated through bureaucratic biases that we sometimes may want to endorse, but often see as part of the problem to be eradicated.

Equal in Law – Unequal in Fact is precisely such a study. It examines the nature, role and effects of non-discrimination law in the national, European and international contexts. As Dr Makkonen shows, many important legislative initiatives have failed to eradicate discrimination even in the public realm, not to speak of civil society or the world of economy. Reasons for this appear to be many: the definition of prohibited discrimination is often formal, and the methods for eradicating it narrowly conceived or beside the point. The present study opens with a detailed overview of the phenomenon of racial and ethic discrimination in Europe. In so doing, it also enters the difficult terrain of what notions such as "race" or "ethnic difference" might mean, pointing to the paradox that legislation must often have recourse to essentialising definitions that are politically problematic. As the author shows, relevant instruments often do not define the notions they use (such as "discrimination" for example) and even as they cover both direct and indirect (structural) discrimination, they deal with the latter in different and often narrow ways. Makkonen identifies an individual-rights based approach to uprooting ethnic and racial discrimination that relies too much on courts and litigation as one significant source of problems. Its eradication, Makkonen correctly argues, is difficult because it is part of what he calls the "liberal political frame" within the reforms are usually conceived.

The work combines much empirical data from Europe with the shortcomings and confusions it finds in the instruments. From there it courageously moves to make recommendations on how to "rethink" current responses to racial and ethnic discrimination. Emphasis is not on more declarations but on the need of collecting data and seeking more efficient enforcement. The reader is impressed by Dr Makkonen's knowledge of the problems of European non-discrimination law as well as his commitment to proceed beyond abstract analysis or the mere identification of implementation problems. The voice of the author is that of one who has had a long-time practical involvement with the topic all over Europe, including in Europe-wide research projects. One also admires the care and moderation with which Dr Makkonen lays out his proposals, without the slightest hint of dogmatic attachment to pre-conceived strategies. No doubt, new forms of racial and other discrimination have re-emerged on the European political scene in the recent years that require new responses. This is precisely why the work brings such an invaluable contribution to the debates. Theoretically sophisticated, pragmatically oriented and undogmatic in view of its proposals, *Equal in Law – Unequal in Fact* is an indispensable instrument in the effort to push the values of solidarity back into the heart of the European project.

Martti Koskenniemi
The University of Helsinki
August 2011

ACKNOWLEDGMENTS

"A conclusion is the place where you got tired of thinking". This book is a slightly revised version of my doctoral dissertation, which I defended at the University of Helsinki in March 2010. The writing of this study has taken quite some time. A key reason for this is that I never really got tired of thinking about equality and anti-discrimination law and analysing the relationship between the two. And I really enjoyed, if not every second but most of them, of putting the pieces of this puzzle together and seeing a bigger picture starting to emerge there from. Though I can but acknowledge the fact that the resulting picture is not as perfect as I had hoped, the time inevitably had to come when this research undertaking had to be put to an end and the conclusions written.

The other reason why the writing of this study took some time is that most of it was written while working full-time on other things. What started as an ordinary research undertaking ended up more an exercise in 'learning by doing'. Luckily enough, most of these other undertakings also dealt with equality, and even better still, they dealt with it from different vantage points: At different times, I have had the opportunity to work for several government departments, my own law and consultancy firm, NGOs, university institutions, and national and transnational businesses. In these contexts, I have had the opportunity to train, in several different countries, groups such as the judiciary, teachers and police officers on equality and equality law; I have had the opportunity to conduct research on these issues; I have had the opportunity to adjudicate discrimination cases as a deputy member of the national Discrimination Tribunal of Finland; I have had the opportunity to engage in the drafting and implementation of Finnish equality policies, and evaluate the policies of other countries; I have had the opportunity to engage in the drafting and revision of the Finnish Equal Treatment Act; I have had the opportunity to represent my country in the drafting of the 'horizontal equality directive' at the Council of the European Union and in the drafting of the Durban Declaration and Plan of Action at the UN World Conference held in South Africa; and I have had the opportunity to participate in many national and international working groups, in particular the European Network of Independent Experts in the Non-Discrimination Field.

I think that the present study has benefited greatly from all these engagements and more particularly, that I benefited immensely from working with other people on these many different undertakings. I would therefore like to thank in particular the following individuals, groups and institutions: people at the Finnish League for Human Rights and its Board of Directors, in particular Kristiina Kouros, Mikko Joronen and Milla Aaltonen; people who were involved in the IOM-Helsinki's *Legal Training* –project and NetEffect Ltd's *Data Collection* –project, in particular Niklas Reuter; everyone involved in the *Making Equality a Reality* (MERA)–project, including Meri-Sisko Eskola, Flaminia Bussacchini, Mikko Cortés Téllez, Claire Herrmann, Dr. Simo Mannila, Perttu Salmenhaara, Sue Scott, Dr. Patrick Simon, Daniel Wagman and Dr. John Wrench; people working for the European Network of Independent Experts in the Non-discrimination Field, in particular Jan Niessen, Isabelle Chopin and Piet Leunis; folks at the Institute for Human Rights at the Åbo Akademi University and the Erik Castrén Institute for International Law and Human Rights at the University of Helsinki; members of the national Discrimination Tribunal of Finland, in particular Juhani Kortteinen; folks at the Legal Unit of the Ministry of the Interior, and in particular its equality team: Panu Artemjeff, Nexhat Beqiri, Sinikka Keskinen, Krista Murto, Katriina Nousiainen and Pasi Päivinen; everyone who was involved in the Equality Committee revising the Finnish Equal Treatment Act, in particular its chair Professor Matti Niemivuo, the chairs of the two sub-committees Tarja Kröger and Johanna Suurpää, and my colleagues Sini Kumpulainen, Anna-Elina Pohjolainen and Liisa Vanhala, as well as other colleagues at the Ministry of Justice, including Sami Manninen and Sten Palmgren. And many others deserve a thank-you too, including but not limited to Professor Mark Bell, Professor Sandra Fredman, Professor emeritus Lauri Hannikainen, Txomin Hernández Bediaga, Rainer Hiltunen, Dr. Inga Jasinskaja-Lahti, Professor Karmela Liebkind, Professor Kevät Nousiainen, Pirkko Mahlamäki, Professor Merja Pentikäinen, Johanna Ojala and Kirsi Tarvainen from the law firm Asianaiset, Devin "Kyösti" Rice, Dr. Reetta Toivanen and Professor Lisa Waddington. I would also like to thank Sara Norja for her most valuable help with proofreading. And yet there have been many others that perhaps should be mentioned, for instance people that I've talked with in one of the fifty or so international conferences and seminars that I've participated in during the last ten years. You know who you are: thank you too!

Four distinguished law professors deserve a special mention. First, I would like to thank Professor Martin Scheinin for his support throughout all these years and for setting such an unrivalled example with respect to how to combine many different professional engagements in the endeavour to make rights a reality. He is also to a great extent "responsible" for my engagement with human rights issues. Second, I would like to thank Professor Tuomas Ojanen, the preliminary examiner of my draft dissertation, for his many sharp and thus highly valuable comments. Third, I would like to thank Professor Christopher McCrudden for agreeing to act not just as a preliminary examiner but also as my opponent at the public defence of my dissertation. It was a tremendous privilege and pleasure, as his works have had a major impact in the field of anti-discrimination law – and also my own work. I have also taken many of the well-considered comments he made during the examination into account while preparing this slightly revised version of the study – though I must also note that I could not fully agree with each and every comment he made. Finally, I would like to thank Professor Martti Koskenniemi for supervising my doctoral work. Whatever merit that my dissertation has got is largely thanks to him, as he has – not just through his guidance but in particular through his scholarly work – challenged me to critically scrutinize not just international law but also my own analysis and conclusions. One might say that he taught me self-critical legal studies, as it were, not (just) critical legal studies. One could not hope more from a supervisor of an academic work.

Finally, I would like to thank my wife Johanna, and our children Mimosa and Nikolas, particularly for bringing so much joy into my life. I guess you are just as happy as I am that I don't have to work late hours with my doctoral thesis anymore; I promise I will never write another dissertation again! Thanks are also due to my parents, and in particular Johanna's parents Kristiina and Paavo Haapiainen, for all their support.

It is with great appreciation that I would like to acknowledge having received funding, at the initial stages of this research undertaking, from the Academy of Finland (research programme *Marginalisation, Inequality and Ethnic Relations in Finland*) and the Finnish Cultural Foundation. I would also like to thank the Erik Castrén Institute for International Law and Human Rights for providing me a workroom when I was finalizing my thesis, and the Ministry of the Interior of Finland for granting me a three weeks' leave of absence in 2008 to write the final chapters of my PhD study.

Timo Makkonen
Helsinki 17 April 2011

ABBREVIATIONS

ACFC	Advisory Committee on the Framework Convention for the Protection of National Minorities
CEACR	Committee of Experts on the Application of Conventions and Recommendations (ILO)
CEDAW	Convention on the Elimination of All Forms of Discrimination against Women
CEHR	Commission for Equality and Human Rights (UK)
CERD	Committee on the Elimination of Racial Discrimination
CoE	Council of Europe
ECHR	European Convention for the Protection of Human Rights and Fundamental Freedoms
ECJ	European Court of Justice
ECRI	European Commission against Racism and Intolerance
ECSR	European Committee of Social Rights
ECtHR	European Court of Human Rights
EU	European Union
FCNM	Framework Convention for the Protection of National Minorities
FRA	European Union Agency for Fundamental Rights
HRC	Human Rights Committee
ICCPR	International Covenant on Civil and Political Rights
ICERD	International Convention on the Elimination of All Forms of Racial Discrimination
ICESCR	International Covenant on Economic, Social and Cultural Rights
ILO	International Labour Organization
NGO	Non-governmental organisation
OECD	Organisation for Economic Co-operation and Development
TEU	Treaty on European Union
TFEU	Treaty on the Functioning of the European Union
UDHR	Universal Declaration on Human Rights
UK	United Kingdom of Great Britain and Northern Ireland
UN	United Nations
UNDP	United Nations Development Programme

UNESCO	United Nations Educational, Scientific and Cultural Organization
US	United States (of America)
VCLT	Vienna Convention on the Law of Treaties

PART ONE

THE CHALLENGE

1 INTRODUCTION

1.1 The Promise – and the Practice

The international community has embarked on a mission that is at once impressive, important and impossible. That mission is the elimination of racial and ethnic discrimination.

International commitment against racial and ethnic discrimination is indeed impressive in many respects. It has a relatively long history: the 1945 Charter of the United Nations and the 1948 Universal Declaration of Human Rights, both of which built upon philosophical and political traditions developed during the preceding centuries,[1] provided for equal rights without any discrimination on the grounds of 'race'. These initial steps by the international community have been followed by an incredible amount of action, particularly by the United Nations. This action includes a number of dedicated resolutions, action plans, declarations and a Convention; three decades have been proclaimed as a *Decade to Combat Racism and Racial Discrimination* (1973–1983; 1983–1993; 1993–2003); racism and racial discrimination were the subjects of UN World Conferences in 1978, 1983 and 2001; year 2001 was proclaimed the International Year of Mobilization against Racism, Racial Discrimination, Xenophobia and Related Intolerance; and, indeed, 21 March is the International Day for the Elimination of Racial Discrimination. Much more action indicating international commitment is undoubtedly yet to come. The commitment against racial discrimination is also widely shared: 174 countries had ratified the UN Convention on the Elimination of All Forms of Racial Discrimination (ICERD), the most significant international document in this area, by January 2011. And much action has been taken also outside the UN, for instance under the auspices of the Council of Europe and European Union.

States have wanted to manifest their commitment not only though all these actions, but also by using exceptionally strong language in these contexts. In the ICERD Convention, which was drafted in the

[1] Paul Gordon Lauren, *The Evolution of International Human Rights: Visions Seen* (Philadelphia: University of Pennsylvania Press, 1998).

1960s, states undertook "to pursue by all appropriate means and without delay a policy of eliminating racial discrimination in all its forms".[2] This promise to *eliminate racial discrimination in all its forms* is reiterated in many other documents, including the 1993 Vienna Declaration and Programme of Action, which calls for the "speedy and comprehensive elimination of all forms of racism and racial discrimination"[3] and the 2000 UN Millennium Declaration, which speaks of eliminating acts of racism and xenophobia.[4] The record in this respect, however, is set by the 2001 Durban Declaration and Programme of Action, which mentions elimination of racial discrimination more than 50 times.

The promises that states have made in the international arenas have not translated well into practical action at the domestic level, as racial and ethnic discrimination is rampant everywhere in the world. The EU Agency for Fundamental Rights (FRA) conducted victim surveys in all 27 EU member states in 2008, and found that, on the average, 30 percent of the members of the surveyed immigrant and ethnic minority groups had experienced discrimination in the course of the past 12 months.[5] Figures for particular countries and for particular groups were even more alarming: the survey found that more than 60 percent of the Roma in Czech Republic and Hungary had experienced discrimination in the past 12 months.[6] The validity of these findings based on surveys of subjective experiences is corroborated by other evidence, such as discrimination testing studies, which show beyond any doubt that on the average at least every third employer in Europe discriminates against immigrant groups or at least some of them.[7]

---

[2] Article 2(1) of the Convention.

[3] Para 15 of the Declaration.

[4] Para 25 of the Declaration.

[5] European Union Agency for Fundamental Rights, *EU-MIDIS: European Union Minorities and Discrimination Survey: Main Results Report* (Vienna: FRA, 2009).

[6] Idem. Another noteworthy research result comes from Finland, where a victim survey found that altogether 81% of those of Somali origin had experienced discrimination when applying for work. Inga Jasinskaja-Lahti – Karmela Liebkind – Tiina Vesala, *Rasismi ja syrjintä Suomessa: Maahanmuuttajien kokemuksia* (Helsinki: Gaudeamus, 2002), p. 87.

[7] In Europe, the country-specific net discrimination rates in access to employment, as found in discrimination testing research, have ranged from 33% to 41%. This means that immigrant jobseekers are discriminated against in more than every third application procedure. Discrimination testing studies involve a robust method that produces results high in validity and reliability, and there can be no doubt that racial and ethnic discrimination is widely practiced in Europe. See chapter 4.1 below for more details.

Socio-economic indicators provide further, circumstantial as it were, evidence that points towards the same conclusion. There is plenty of evidence that shows how many immigrant groups and minorities fall in disproportionate numbers to the ranks of the underemployed, the underpaid and the undereducated.[8] For instance the UNDP human development report on the situation of Roma in five European countries found Roma unemployment to average 40 percent – ranging from a high of 64 percent in Slovak Republic to a 'low' of 24 percent in Romania.[9] Though it is impossible to know the precise extent to which inequalities in the outcomes across different key life domains are the result of discrimination, there is no question that discrimination plays a major part in them, as life in deprivation is seldom a personal choice.

1.2 About this Study

Purpose of this Study and the Research Questions

This study sets out to map the gap between the promises and the practice in the field of combating discrimination. It analyses the current international and European legal response to discrimination and the reasons underlying its relative lack of success in achieving its goals. In so doing, it aims to shed light on the possible ways by which the gap may be narrowed down, and on the measures that those countries wishing to make further headway in combating discrimination could and should take. Thus this study addresses the following three sets of research questions:

(i) In light of empirical evidence, how does racial and ethnic discrimination manifest in contemporary Europe? What would appear to be its causes and consequences?

(ii) What is the current legal response to discrimination in terms of international and European law? Is it geared to tackle discrimination and its causes and consequences? All things considered, is the response effective?

[8] See e.g. Lucinda Platt, *Poverty and Ethnicity in the UK* (Bristol: Policy Press, 2007), and European Commission, *The Social Situation in the European Union 2007 – Social Cohesion through Equal Opportunities* (Luxembourg: OOPEC, 2008).

[9] United Nations Environment Programme, *Avoiding the Dependency Trap: The Roma in Central and Eastern Europe* (United Nations, 2003).

(iii) What, if anything, can be done to improve that response? Are there ways in which the anti-discrimination law can be made more effective?

The study is divided into three parts. Part I sets the scene by laying down the conceptual framework and by identifying the challenges that discrimination and its causes and consequences pose. To begin with, this part describes the nature of 'racial' and ethnic diversity in general and the scope and nature of that diversity in Europe in particular. By looking at the construction of 'racial' and 'ethnic' differences and the way they are socially attributed meaning and significance, this part lays down the foundations for the subsequent analyses. This conceptual exploration is continued through the analysis of the concept of 'discrimination'. The study introduces the different forms of discrimination, including direct, indirect, institutional and structural discrimination. It also looks at the concept of equality, which the concept of discrimination is often taken to be closely associated with. After this the study proceeds with an analysis of the extent and characteristics of discrimination in contemporary Europe. Particular attention is paid to what is called 'everyday discrimination', that is those subtle but significant and relatively frequent disadvantageous acts and practices that immigrants and persons belonging to minorities face in the course of their daily lives. This focus deliberately contrasts with popular beliefs – often spread by mass media – that depict racial and ethnic discrimination either in terms of major state-sponsored policies and practices such as Apartheid or racial segregation, or isolated violent events perpetrated by extremist hate groups.

From there Part I moves into an examination of the causes and consequences of discrimination. It shows how intimately discrimination is related to the same social and psychological processes through which we perceive and analyse the world around us and build our identities, how persistent and unconsciously activated prejudices and stereotypes can be, how even well-intending people can discriminate, and how even seemingly harmless practices of 'everyday discrimination' come to cause and sustain major social and economic disadvantages. It also shows how discrimination negatively affects also people other than its direct targets, how its effects are carried on across generations, and how knowledge of the existence of discrimination against a group can have a general demoralizing effect on the persons belonging to that group. It also shows how discrimination, the disadvantage it engenders, and the prejudices and stereotypes that disadvantages on their part feed, come to form a dangerous, self-sustaining vicious circle.

Part II provides a detailed analysis of the international and European legal responses to discrimination. It examines how these pieces of law define discrimination, whether discrimination is prohibited in such key areas of life as employment, education and provision of services, and what these pieces of law say about enforcement and remedies. It documents the diversity manifested by these instruments, the openness of the language of the pertinent provisions, the development of related legal doctrines over time, and points out that it may be difficult for a Jane or John Doe on the shop floor to know exactly which kinds of actions constitute legally challengeable discrimination and which do not. On the positive side, the study finds that anti-discrimination law has broadened its scope by means of prohibiting not just direct but also indirect discrimination and harassment, and by extending the reach of the prohibition to such areas as education and provision of services. Moreover, it argues that in particular the EU Racial Equality Directive removes many of the obstacles formerly associated with bringing legal action in discrimination cases, particularly by means of providing for the sharing of the burden of proof and by means of prohibiting retaliatory action against complainants ('victimization'). On the other hand, it is argued that international and European instruments are weak on requirements relating to enforcement and positive action, the two most important factors for making equality a reality. The study concludes that the international and European legal response relies strongly on an 'individual rights' model of enforcement, which depends on the injured individuals to bring legal action to make things right. This study joins other studies that have argued that such an approach is inadequate, *inter alia* on the grounds that in some European countries only 1–2 percent of those who have experienced discrimination take legal action, meaning that employers and service providers are under the individual rights model in practice at a liberty to discriminate without the fear of legal sanction.

Part III points out that the international and European legal instruments define only the minimum level of protection against discrimination, and that more can, and indeed should, be done to render the protection more effective. On the basis of the findings on how discrimination has a major negative impact extending beyond the direct circumstances and persons involved, and on how discrimination and disadvantage reinforce each other, the study argues that action against discrimination must be proactive rather than reactive, that it must be extensive and target not just discrimination but also its causes and effects, and that remedial action must acknowledge that the group of people harmed by discrimination extends beyond the direct victims. Different proactive approaches, including positive action, equality duties and data collection are devoted chapters of their own. Each topic is discussed from a policy point of view (what are the pros and cons involved in taking for instance positive action measures) as well as from a legal point of view (for instance which kinds of positive action measures are legally permitted). Overall, the study speaks in favour of an active, broad and reflexive approach to promoting equality, but warns that major advances may take time to take place and that it is probably the case that we will never eliminate racial and ethnic discrimination in its entirety – even if try we must.

Prior Research

This study is situated in what has fast become a fairly well-established field of law. The subject area has come to attract attention from a broad range of scholars who approach the theme from a variety angles upon which this study is able to build. There are, to begin with, text books that set out to describe and explain international, European and/or domestic anti-discrimination law.[10] Such books, which are often aimed for students and practitioners, purport mainly to describe the subject area in a manner that reflects the standard legal opinion, or is hoped to become the new standard. There are also academic publications, which

[10] Influential books in the area of international anti-discrimination law include the following: Warwick McKean, *Equality and Discrimination under International Law* (Oxford: Clarendon Press, 1983); Andrew Koppelman, *Anti-Discrimination Law and Social Equality* (New Haven: Yale University Press, 1996); and Patrick Thornberry, *International Law and the Rights of Minorities* (Oxford: Oxford University Press, 1991). What is striking, however, is the lack of in-depth legal commentaries of the main UN instrument on combating racial discrimination, the *Convention on the Elimination of All forms of Racial Discrimination*. Its individual paragraphs have been analysed in a number of articles, and have been commented upon by the CERD Committee, but there appear to be no internationally recognized monographic treatments of the Convention apart from two books by Michael Banton that came out in 1994 and 1996 and that focused as much on the politics behind the Convention as on its contents. Individual anti-discrimination provisions, as they feature in the different international and regional human rights documents, have been the subject of analysis in a high number of books and articles.

are somewhat more doctrinally oriented and consist of a deeper elaboration of the core concepts, principles and specific parts of anti-discrimination law. A relatively well-established tradition of this kind of writing about anti-discrimination law emanates particularly from the U.S., and deals with themes such as affirmative action and the concept of disparate impact discrimination.[11] A third relatively common approach is comparative anti-discrimination law, which is appropriate for a field such as this where the international and regional have strongly influenced the national, and vice versa.[12] An important and recently popular line of research deals with the theory of anti-discrimination law, particularly its purposes, functions and underlying rationales.[13] The adoption and national implementation of the EU Racial Equality Directive has prompted nothing short of an explosion of writing in the four above-mentioned genres, although it must be noted that the legal opinion is, as regards international and European law, in many respects still only at the stage of emergence.[14]

Parts of this study share some common ground with the above-mentioned traditions and build upon them. However, its overarching idea of critical assessment of the impact and effectiveness of anti-discrimination law requires recourse to a mode of analysis that is not only internal to law but also external to it. The study of racial and ethnic discrimination, in disciplines such as sociology, social psychology and political philosophy, has developed into a veritable industry of its

---

[11] See e.g. the collection of articles in Christopher McCrudden (ed.), *Anti-Discrimination Law* (Aldershot: Dartmouth, 1991).

[12] See e.g. M.H.S. Gijzen, *Selected issues in equal treatment law: a multi-layered comparison of European, English and Dutch law* (Antwerpen: Intersentia, 2006); Lynn M. Roseberry, *The Limits of Employment Discrimination Law in the United States and European Community* (Copenhagen: DJOF Publishing, 1999); Titia Loenen – Peter Rodrigues (eds.) *Non-Discrimination Law: Comparative Perspectives* (The Hague: Kluwer, 1999). See also Dagmar Schiek – Lisa Waddington – Mark Bell, *Non-Discrimination Law: Cases, Materials and text on National, Supranational and International Non-Discrimination Law* (Oxford: Hart Publishing, 2007).

[13] Key publications include another collection of articles edited by McCrudden, in Christopher McCrudden (ed.), *Anti-Discrimination Law* (Aldershot: Dartmouth, 2004) and monographic treatments of the subject by Sandra Fredman and Mark Bell: Sandra Fredman, *Discrimination Law* (Oxford: Oxford University Press, 2002); Mark Bell, *Anti-Discrimination Law and the European Union* (Oxford: Oxford University Press, 2002).

[14] See e.g. European Commission, *Critical review of academic literature relating to the EU directives to combat discrimination* (Luxembourg: OOPEC, 2004), and other thematic reports of the European Network of legal experts in the non-discrimination field.

own, and this study taps into that research within the remit of the research problem. Particular and widespread use is made of empirical studies into the extent, causes and consequences of discrimination.

Method of this Study

This study explores a complex social problem, racial and ethnic discrimination, and the equally complex matter of how the law is used, and can be used, to cope with it. It addresses a number of questions, some of which are essentially philosophical and political (what is equality?), some essentially sociological and socio-psychological (how much is there discrimination, what are its causes and consequences?), some essentially legal (what does the law say about discrimination?), whereas some are about legal politics (what should the law say about discrimination?). *Ipso facto*, the tackling of the research problem has warranted the deliberate, and for a primarily legal study perhaps somewhat unconventional and innovative, use of a multidisciplinary and multimethod approach. This study hopefully testifies, for its part, to the thesis that it is highly useful if not a *conditio qua sine non* to adopt a multidisciplinary approach to examining questions such as these.[15]

[15] Essed has quite rightly opined that when we are confronted with a problem as complex as racism, we cannot afford to let ourselves be constrained by the boundaries of specific disciplines. She has also taken note of the slow progress made in the development of interdisciplinary studies of racism. Philomena Essed, 'Everyday Racism: A New Approach to the Study of Racism', in Theo Goldberg – Philomena Essed (eds.), *Race Critical Theories* (Oxford: Blackwell, 2002), p. 176. See more generally, C. Wright Mills, *The Sociological Imagination* (Oxford: Oxford University Press, 1959).

2 DIVERSITY: EMPIRICAL AND THEORETICAL PERSPECTIVES

2.1 Diversity in Europe

Europe is, and has always been, ethnically diverse. The mainstay of ethnic diversity in Europe is due to three sources: the presence of indigenous peoples that existed before the formation of the nation-states in Europe; the existence of ethnic groups that became minorities in the struggles that led to the formation of nation-states or at some point thereafter in consequence of territorial acquisitions; and immigration. The nation-building process that led to the emergence of strong nation-states, a process that has been exceptionally powerful in Europe, is intrinsically about rendering linguistically and culturally heterogeneous populations more homogenous, thus on the one hand suppressing diversity and on the other making remaining divisions more visible. Yet it should be recognized that subtler forms of diversity permeate the entire Europe, as evidenced by the still flourishing local dialects and cultures.

The ethnic composition of Europe is not known with any great degree of precision. This is because most countries in Europe, with some exceptions, do not collect ethnic data through censuses, population registers or by any other means.[1] Where such data exists it tends to be incomplete or contested because there are no fully reliable and valid methods for recording ethnicity.

Yet it is clear that ethnic diversity is a reality in Europe today. To begin with, the indigenous people of Northern Europe, the Sami, number approximately 70 000 according to the estimate of the Swedish Sami Parliament.[2] The Roma, who are generally held to constitute the largest minority in Europe, number possibly over 10 million in Europe, a population many times the size of the total population of a number

---

[1] Lack of data concerns particularly the indigenous peoples and national minorities, which makes it impossible to give a full and reliable account of the diversity in Europe.

[2] National Sami Information Centre, *The Sami – an Indigenous People in Sweden* (Västerås: Edita, 2005), p. 4.

of EU member states.[3] Some overall estimates suggest that there are altogether 340 national minorities in Europe and that every seventh European – more than 100 million people – belongs to one of these groups.[4]

The ethnic make-up of Europe has changed substantially over the past sixty years, the main reason for this being international migration, migration being the result of a complex interplay of push and pull factors. After the Second World War and until the early 1970s the increased rates of immigration were fuelled by the demand for unskilled labour in the rapidly expanding industrialized countries of Western Europe. This labour migration to Europe took two main forms: government sponsored 'guest worker' schemes and the spontaneous immigration of 'colonial workers' to the former colonial powers. Whereas the economic recession in the early 1970s made many European states adopt stricter immigration laws, a number of individuals continued to arrive for reasons of family reunion or seeking political asylum.[5] Starting from the 1990s many countries in Europe realized that they were again in need of foreign workers, given the demographic tendencies that involve low birth rates, aging population and thus a rapidly shrinking workforce, which has led to a relatively rapid increase in labour migration. Any economic downturns that may hit the Europe in the future may slow that process down again, however, at least temporarily.

In consequence of the above-mentioned processes, the number of immigrants has grown in many countries in Europe. Data on immigrants in Europe has traditionally focused upon the percentage of foreign citizens within the population, which is an inadequate approach because naturalization renders a substantial portion of immigrant-origin persons invisible in these statistics. Only recently has data become available that indicates the actual percentage of foreign-born in the total population, showing the size of the immigrant-origin population to be appreciably higher than is usually thought. According to the data for 2005 for the EU, the percentage of foreign-born people was between 1.8 to 5.0 in Finland, Czech Republic, Hungary, Italy, Malta,

---

[3] European Commission, *The situation of Roma in an Enlarged European Union* (Luxembourg: OOPEC, 2004), p. 6.

[4] Christoph Pan – Beate Sibylle Pfeil, *National minorities in Europe. Handbook*, Ethnos Series Vol. 63 (Vienna), p. 10.

[5] David Turton – Julia González (eds.), *Ethnic Diversity in Europe: Challenges to the Nation State* (Bilbao: University of Deusto, 2000).

Poland and Slovakia; from 5.1 to 9.9 in Belgium, Denmark, Greece, Iceland, Norway, Portugal, Slovenia, Spain and United Kingdom; from 10.0 to 15.0 in Austria, Belgium, Estonia, France, Germany, Ireland, Sweden and the Netherlands; and 19.5 in Latvia, 22.9 in Switzerland, 33.9 in Liechtenstein and 37.4 in Luxemburg.[6] In absolute numbers more than 40 million foreign-born individuals lived in the European Economic Area in 2005; some 10 million lived in Germany, 6.5 million lived in France, 5.4 million lived in the UK, 4.8 million in Spain and 2.5 million lived in Italy. Austria, Sweden and the Netherlands each had between 1 and 2 million foreign-born residents.[7] Because these numbers do not include e.g. so-called second generation immigrants, born in the country of destination, the size of the immigrant-origin population is even greater than this. European countries have therefore managed to admit and absorb immigrants in considerable numbers in the past decades, more so than is usually recognized.

The growth in the numbers of immigrants has been relatively rapid. For most OECD countries the size of the foreign-born population grew by at least 20 percent in 1996–2005.[8] It is expected that Europe will grow increasingly diverse in the future, as is demonstrated by analyses conducted in different countries. For instance projections made by Statistics Norway estimate that the size of Norway's immigration population will double or triple between 2005 and 2060, leading to 20 to 31 percent of the total population being of immigrant origin.[9]

This relatively rapid increase in the ethnic diversity of Europe has not passed without notice. Immigration and integration policies have become hotly debated topics among the politicians, academics and the general public. That debate is highly polarized. The positive role of diversity is sometimes given recognition by pointing out how immigrants enrich national cultures and how the national economies

---

[6] Rainer Muenz, *Europe: Population and Migration in 2005* (Migration Information Source, June 2006). Jean-Christophe Dumont (OECD) and Georges Lemaître (OECD), *Counting immigrants and expatriates in OECD Countries: A New Perspective*, OECD Social, Employment and Migration Working Papers 25 (OECD, 2005).

[7] It is estimated that the Council of Europe member states altogether have more than 64 million migrants, representing 8.8% of the total population. Council of Europe Parliamentary Assembly, political affairs committee: 'The state of democracy in Europe: Specific challenges facing European democracies: The case of diversity and migration' doc 11623, 6 June 2008.

[8] OECD, *International Migration Outlook: Annual Report 2007 Edition* (Paris: OECD, 2007).

[9] Statistics Norway, *High growth in the number of immigrants*. Available at http://www.ssb.no (accessed 1.7.2009).

depend on their contributions, and how diversity works as a driver of innovation and collective creativity. But diversity has also brought with it anxiety. Cultural, religious and linguistic diversity has become a highly visible and therefore undeniable facet of European societies, posing a fundamental challenge for the conception and even legitimacy of the nation-state, the concept of which has to a great extent rested on the perceived homogeneity of the nation.[10] The long-term presence of 'others' among 'us' has forced all European societies to reflect upon their own identities: at what point do the 'others' that live with 'us' no longer be 'others' and become part of 'us', and what does that make 'us'? Questions relating to the recognition and accommodation of cultural and religious differences have become widely debated in Europe, as reflected in the discussions about the legitimacy of state churches and references to God or Christianity in constitutions, the wearing of veils and other religio-cultural clothing while in public office, the teaching of religion in schools, and the electoral rights of immigrants.

Another, but in many ways associated, major strand of discussion has focused on the question whether diverse societies are viable in terms of social solidarity and trust. Robert D. Putnam's empirically grounded thesis that ethnically diverse societies suffer, at least on a short and medium term, from lower rates of trust (even of one's own group), rarer altruism and community cooperation and a decreased number of friendships, has sparked much debate and undoubtedly confirmed many concerns about the deterioration of social solidarity in diverse societies.[11] Whereas these and many other debates will continue long into the future, one thing is certain: many countries in Europe are facing an identity crisis which will both impact and be impacted by the fight against ethnic discrimination. Insecurity related to the present identity crisis is bound to negatively affect inter-group relations, whereas the successful fostering of a culture of equality will

---

[10] Turton – González, *cit. supra* note 5.

[11] Robert D. Putnam '*E Pluribus Unum*: Diversity and Community in the Twenty-first Century. The 2006 Johan Skytte Prize Lecture' *Scandinavian Political Studies* Vol. 30, No 2, 2007. On the other hand, Marc Hooghe and his colleagues conclude, also on the basis of empirical evidence, that "…for Europe ethnic diversity cannot be considered as a threat for the maintenance of social cohesion." Marc Hooghe et al 'Ethnic Diversity, Trust and Ethnocentrism and Europe: A Multilevel Analysis of 21 European Countries'. Paper presented at the 102nd Annual Meeting of the American Political Science Association, Philadelphia, August 31–September 3, 2006.

necessarily have to be one of the key ingredients in resolving the present identity crisis.

2.2 Difference and the Difference it Makes

Diversity across humanity is real, multifaceted and highly tangible. People differ in terms of a high number of personal traits and capacities, colour of skin, religion, sex, occupation, interests, sexual orientation, ethical, political and moral views, health status, body shape, cultural heritage, language, hobbies, family relationships, wealth, experiences and a limitless number of other traits and qualities. As these differences do not come in ready-made bundles, every single individual is, ultimately, unique even within her most immediate social environment. However, the meeting of our personal, social, economic, cultural and political needs calls for interaction and co-operation that promotes group-formation. All the aforementioned differences have, at least in some societies, been attributed social and personal significance and have structured the formation of friendships, alliances and communities. The reality of overwhelming diversity and the drive for group-formation forces people to deal with the thorny issue of which differences matter personally, socially and politically. Over time, categorization systems have developed and continue to develop, helping people to cope with this diversity, to sort it out and to simplify and to bring order into life.[12] Once this process is set in motion, the dynamics of group formation and maintenance come into play, leading to the accentuation of in-group commonalities and their importance, and attenuation of differences and their importance.[13]

Proper analysis of the different forms of racial and ethnic discrimination and their causes and consequences, and the designing of effective counter-measures and remedies, requires an understanding of what 'racial' and 'ethnic' differences are all about and what role they play in social and personal contexts. Therefore it is of the essence to look at how these concepts originate from and are linked to real life, in the sense of fuzzy, but observable, biological, cultural and social structures. This can best be done by means of tapping into the findings

---

[12] Judith A. Howard – Daniel G. Renfrow 'Social Cognition' in John D. DeLamater (ed.), *Handbook of Social Psychology* (New York: Kluwer-Plenum, 2003), p. 262.

[13] See in general Henri Tajfel, *Human Groups and Social Categories* (Cambridge: Cambridge University Press, 1981).

and theories developed in the fields of anthropology, sociology and biology.

The Social Construction of Knowledge

Before we proceed to examining the theories about human differences and their significance, it is essential to note how changes into these theories has been brought by means of major changes in the episteme of science, in the sense of basic beliefs and presumptions that often tacitly guide the production of and interpretation of knowledge. Many 18th and 19th century scientists were inspired by the Enlightenment values that embodied the belief that there was a certain order in the universe, natural laws for both mankind and nature, laws that could be discovered by means of reason. Much of contemporary theorizing on its part embodies the belief that one should be suspicious of any attempts to look for or forge universal theories, explanations or values, and that much if not all of our received 'knowledge' is in fact socially constructed. In consequence, it is useful to understand that just like everything else, scientific theories about human nature are conditioned by slowly-changing values embedded in the deep structures of culture.[14]

In the context of intergroup relations, what people *think* there 'is' is just as important, if not more important, than what there actually 'is'. As will be seen in the following pages, ordinary peoples' understandings of these matters often bear little resemblance to those offered by contemporary science. Rather, they have much to do with the knowledge acquired through socialization and experience, mediated by the specific social and cultural setting in which people live in, the lifeworld. Over time, the lifeworld in Europe has undergone several major changes: the development of nation-states entailed a homogenisation process and the forging of an overarching national 'superethnos' that superseded smaller groups – without necessarily completely destroying them – and this process inevitably affected common but often tacit beliefs and experiences about ethnic matters; over time, modernisation and urbanisation processes have given people a chance to set themselves free from traditional social roles and ways of thinking, as these have came under the pressure of reflection, largely thanks

[14] See e.g. Peter Berger – Thomas Luckmann, *The Social Construction of Reality: A Treatise in the Sociology of Knowledge* (New York: Anchor Books, 1966). Jurgen Habermas, *Knowledge and Human Interests* (Cambridge: Polity Press, 1987).

to factors such as nation-wide and lengthy schooling;[15] and finally, the gradual emergence of post-nation-state societies, that is, societies that are self-consciously plural in ethnic and even in cultural and epistemological matters, where members of even the same family have come to have their own social networks as well as their own information sources (highly specialized education; internet; TV).[16] All these processes have affected the type, amount and content of information and misinformation that people have had – and have – access to, and on the basis of which they form their understandings of racial and ethnic issues. It is important to understand that in contemporary Europe people do not share a common worldview: the worldview and the values of a retired farmer, a businessperson, a schoolboy and an anthropology student can be worlds apart from each other, even if they are next-door neighbours, and this affects how they understand phenomena such as 'race' and 'ethnicity', and how they feel and act in intergroup situations.

Difference and What We Make of It

The most important thing in the context of intergroup relations, however, is not the real or perceived racial or ethnic differences, but the difference these differences are thought to make. The interesting issue is not just how 'race' and 'ethnicity' are perceived, but how they are perceived to explain things, and in what way they are thought to be of personal, social, political and legal significance. A key question is: is the recognition of differences, in practice, intrinsically and inevitably connected to value judgements? Some of the theories explained in chapter 4.2 of this study suggest that stereotypes, tension, prejudices and also discrimination may indeed be closely linked to our understandings of ourselves and others. At the same time, these theories also suggest ways in which the negative potential of group divisions can be substantially reduced, in particular by means of adjusting our view of ourselves and others.

The significance of 'race' and ethnicity is ambiguous in the field of politics. Nation-state ideology, which associated sovereignty with

[15] See e.g. Jurgen Habermas 'Private and Public Autonomy, Human Rights and Popular Sovereignty' in Obrad Savic (ed.) *The Politics of Human Rights* (London: Verso, 2002), pp. 57–58; Ulrich Beck, *Risk society: towards a new modernity* (London: Sage, 1992), pp. 88–94; Stuart Hall, *Identiteetti* (Tampere: Vastapaino, 1999), pp. 20–30.

[16] Cf. idem.

politicized forms of ethnicity (nationhood), has since the 19th century held a prominent foothold in Europe. Under that line of thinking, political boundaries, as represented by the boundaries of a sovereign state, should be congruent with the boundaries of a nation, represented by an ethnic group claiming sovereignty. Yet at the same time, Europe has been strongly influenced by political liberalism that emphasises such values as individual freedom, individual autonomy, tolerance and equality of rights and opportunities. It is commonly insisted by the liberal camp that the state should be neutral when it comes to choices relating to different conceptions of the good life. A liberal state, it is said, does not have its own vision of The Good; its purpose is to help its citizens realize *their* vision of The Good.[17] For liberalism, ethnic diversity and ethnic communities have, as such, no political relevance. In consequence ethnicity plays a peculiarly ambiguous role in the field of politics in Europe: on the one hand it is reified as the foundation of the nation-state, on the other its political significance is completely denied. This tension between reification and denial of ethnicity is, it is suggested, one key factor that conditions intergroup relations and debates about the meaning of equality in Europe.

'Race'

Race is one of the concepts by which people have tried to come to grips with the tangible reality of human diversity. 19th and early 20th century science, particularly physical anthropology, played a central role in the creation of the 'racial worldview'.[18] Whereas humankind has probably throughout its history shown a great interest in the differences and similarities across groups, it was these scientific theories that shaped, and still shape, popular conceptualizations of 'race'. These conceptualizations were based on externally visible traits, primarily skin colour, features of the face, and the shape and size of the

[17] See e.g. Louis Henkin, *International Law: Politics and Values* (Dordrecht: Martinus Nijhoff, 1995), p. 104.

[18] C.C. Mukhopadhay – Y.T. Moses 'Reestablishing 'Race' in Anthropological Discourse" *American Anthropologist* 99(3) (1997); American Association of Physical Anthropologists, 'AAPA Statement on Biological Aspects of Race' *American Journal of Physical Anthropology*, vol 101, 1996, pp. 569–570. It should be noted that the first 'scientific' racial taxonomies had been developed already in the 18th Century, notably by the Swedish botanist and physician Carl Linnaeus (1707–1778). Also many celebrated Enlightenment philosophers adopted and developed classifications of human races. See e.g. Immanuel Kant, *Über die verschiedenen Rassen der Menschen (On the Different Races of Man)* 1775.

head and body. A linkage between perceived racial categories on the one hand and psychological and cultural characteristics on the other was often presumed. In this scheme it was perceived natural and irreversible that different races occupy different places in a hierarchy established by God or – as those influenced by Darwin's evolution theory had it – Nature.[19] Europeans and those of European origin associated superior traits with their own 'race' and inferior traits with other 'races', and over time came to develop a deeply held racialized mindset. This mindset justified negative attitudes towards 'racial others' and legitimated their subordination and exclusion.

Scientific evidence and analyses pointing out the arbitrariness and questioning the presumed 'naturalness' of racial taxonomies and significance of racial differences from a moral point of view started to pile up at the end of the 19th century.[20] One turning point from a scientific point of view came in 1942, when Ashley Montagu published his book *Mankind's Most Dangerous Myth: The Fallacy of Race*. Montagu argued against the linking of genetics and culture and asserted that 'race' is largely a social construction and not constitutive of significant biological differences between people. He and others brought forward evidence pointing out that the physical features used to distinguish 'races' from each other were not consistently correlated with each other: for instance, dark skin colour could or could not go with other anatomical traits typically associated with 'Blacks', such as particular type of hair texture, body proportions or certain facial features.

By 1950 UNESCO decided that it was necessary to bring together some of the leading scientists of the time to speak out – and quite obviously: popularize – what was perceived to be the truth about 'race' in order to fight racism, a "major source of social tension likely to endanger peace".[21] The resulting *Statement on Race*, while not completely

---

[19] Mukhopadhayay, *cit. supra* note 18; American Anthropological Association, 'Statement on 'race" (May 17, 1998), available at: http://www.aaanet.org/stmts/racepp.htm (accessed 1.1.2010).

[20] See e.g. Mukhopadhayay, *cit. supra* note 18, p. 518. Interestingly, Charles Darwin, the father of modern evolutionary theory, wrote in 1875 that "[a]s man advances in civilization, and small tribes are united into larger communities, the simplest reason would tell each individual that he ought to extend his social instincts and sympathies to all the members of the same nation, though personally unknown to him. This point being one reached, there is only an artificial barrier to prevent his sympathies extending to the men of all nations and races". Charles Darwin, *The Descent of Man* (2nd Ed, 1875), pp. 187–8.

[21] UNESCO, *UNESCO's contribution to the struggle against racism, racial discrimination and apartheid* (Paris, 22 May 1982). Those who drafted and signed the

rejecting the idea that biological differences exist,[22] concluded that "'race' is not so much a biological phenomenon as a social myth"[23] and emphasised that "the likenesses among men are far greater than their differences"[24] and that "all men belong to the same species, *Homo Sapiens*."[25] The Statement was followed by the *Statement on the Nature of Race and Race Differences* in 1951 and by the UNESCO *Declaration on Race and Racial Prejudice* in 1978. The Declaration in particular condemned in clear terms all ideas and theories that either referred to the superiority of racial or ethnic groups or that sought to justify racial hatred and discrimination, and called for governments, the scientific community, the mass media, international organisations and all individuals to contribute towards the eradication of racial prejudices and discrimination. These and many other actions, such as comparable statements by the American Anthropological Association in 1998 and the American Association of Physical Anthropologists in 1996, were taken with a view to assaulting the still prevailing racialized mindset and its consequences.[26] Notably, the latest UNESCO statement that deals with human diversity, the 2001 *Universal Declaration on Cultural Diversity*, does not mention 'race' at all but focuses on cultural diversity instead.

Recent scientific findings particularly in the field of genomics have strengthened the view that it is not reasonable to talk of separate human races. Among humans, the same biological variations – measured for instance at the DNA level – tend to be found across all population groups, and only a small fraction of the total variation, approximately 10%, can be related to intergroup differences between so-called races.[27] This means that there is a very good chance that one has less in common genetically with the next-door neighbour than

---

document included such renowned scholars as Ashley Montagu, Claude Lévi-Strauss and Gunnar Myrdal.

[22] UNESCO, *Statement on race*, issued 18 July 1950, paras 2, 3 and 7.

[23] Para 14.

[24] Para 2.

[25] Para 1. The statement also suggests that it would be better to drop the term 'race' altogether and speak of ethnic groups instead (para 6).

[26] American Anthropological Association, *Statement on 'race'* (May 17, 1998), available at: http://www.aaanet.org/stmts/racepp.htm (accessed 1.7.2009); American Association of Physical Anthropologists, AAPA Statement on Biological Aspects of Race, *American Journal of Physical Anthropology*, vol 101, pp. 569–570, 1996.

[27] Francis Collins - Karin G. Jegalian, 'Genomics and the Future', *Scientific American*, December 1999. Chiara Romualdi et al, 'Patterns of Human Diversity, within and among Continents, Inferred from Biallelic DNA Polymorphisms' *Genome*

with any randomly chosen person living on the other side of the planet. The evidence suggests that this is because all humans share a common ancestry and most genetic variation predated the relatively recent point in time when a core group of our ancestors left Africa.[28] This has led Svante Pääbo, an eminent biologist, to remark that all humans are Africans, either residing in Africa or in diaspora.[29]

The above evidence notwithstanding, it would be premature to pronounce racial theorizing entirely dead just yet. From time to time, some members of the scientific community develop and publish ideas about genetically based racial differences, though their credibility and conclusions tend generally to be put to question. But many more in the academic world subscribe to a far more subtle presumption that racial and ethnic distinctions nonetheless capture some small but still meaningful biological differences.[30] Some population groups have been found to be more susceptible to particular diseases, an important finding that has as a by-product contributed to the re-ignition of the debate about 'racial' differences.[31] It is, however, an open question to what extent these disparities in disease risk are due to the (small) genetic variations across populations, or whether they are due to differences in environmental and other factors relevant to health, including poverty and stress caused to some population groups by experiences of pervasive racism.[32]

Res. 2002 12:602–612. Richard Lewontin, *Human Diversity* (W.H. Freeman & Co, 1995).

[28] This is likely because the gene pool in Africa contains more variation than elsewhere, and the genetic variation found outside Africa represents only a subset of that found within the African continent. Svante Pääbo, 'Genomics and Society: The Human Genome and Our View of Ourselves' *Science* Vol 291. No 5507, pp. 1219–1220 (16 February 2001). See also Collins – Jegalian, *cit supra* note 27.

[29] Idem (Pääbo).

[30] See e.g. Morris W. Foster – Richard R. Sharp, 'Classifications as Proxies of Biological Heterogeneity' *Genome Res.* 2002 12:844–850.

[31] See e.g. Neil Risch et al 'Categorization of humans in biomedical research: genes, race and disease' opinion, *Genome Biology* 2002:3 (1 July 2002). One of these diseases is sickle-cell anaemia, a genetically transmitted defect found in relatively high frequencies in certain populations in equatorial Africa, whereas it is virtually absent in North European populations. It appears that the high incidence of this condition in some populations is a result of genetic adaptation to a particular long-term environmental condition, namely malaria. See John W. Berry et al, *Cross-cultural psychology: Research and applications*, 2nd ed. (Cambridge: Cambridge University Press, 2002), pp. 260–261.

[32] See idem and Yin Carl Paradies, *Race, Racism, Stress and Indigenous Health*, PhD study, Department of Public Health, The University of Melbourne (July 2006).

Nevertheless, the bottom line clearly is that there appear to be no scientifically sound grounds or reasons for 'racialism', that is, for the view that there exists separate 'races' and major innate differences between them. Yet, this evidence and the attempts to popularize these findings have not been successful at eliminating the quasi-scientific beliefs that have remained within the general public. This appears peculiar, given the high esteem enjoyed by science as the religion of our time.

In some countries, such as the UK and the USA, the use of 'racial language' is indeed so common and widely accepted, both at the level of everyday speech and in legal and administrative practice, that they may be described as 'race-centred societies.'[33] Yet also in societies not so thoroughly permeated by racial thinking and language, such as many countries in Central and North Europe, a significant part of the population subscribes to a racialized worldview. European-wide surveys have found that some 15% of Europeans go so far as admitting that they are disturbed by the presence of people from 'other races' in their societies.[34] A survey that probed the attitudes of Finns, who were less prone than most other Europeans to have a problem with the presence of 'people from other races', found that almost one in two were of the view that people belonging to "certain races are not at all fit for living in a modern society".[35] Moreover, more than every third respondent agreed fully or in part with the view that some nations are superior to others in terms of intelligence.[36] These respondents therefore not only believed in the existence of separate 'races' or nations to begin with, but they also believed that some populations are innately superior to the others. It is highly likely that less radical forms of racial thinking are much more prevalent still today.

How is it possible that people in modern-day societies still cling to such questionable views about the existence of separate 'races' and

---

[33] John H. Stanfield II 'Methodological Reflections: An Introduction' in John H. Stanfield - M. Dennis Ruthledge (eds.) *Race and Ethnicity in Research Methods* (California: Sage Publications, 1993).

[34] According to Eurobarometer 53 report, altogether 15% of the Europeans found the presence of people of 'another race' to be 'disturbing'. The national figures ranged from 5% (Spain) to 27% (Belgium), the figure for Finland being 11%. European Commission, *Eurobarometer, Public Opinion in the European Union, Report Number 53* (October 2000).

[35] Magdalena Jaakkola, *Suomalaisten suhtautuminen maahanmuuttajiin vuosina 1987 – 2003*. Työpoliittinen tutkimus 286 (Helsinki: Työministeriö, 2005), p. 88 ff.

[36] Idem.

their superior or inferior capacities? The answer is that, to a large degree, 'race' as a concept has acquired social, ethical, political and legal relevance in our societies. Racial categorization makes it possible to articulate certain needs and positions in various fields of life, including politics, identity-building and decision-making. In societies where racial thinking is salient, explains John W. Stanfield II,

> races are created as social and cultural constructions and used as political weapons. Generations of societal residents are socialized into the belief that it is "natural" to assume that real or imagined phenotypic features predict values, personality, intellectual attributes, behaviour, moral fiber, and leadership abilities. In this sense, race is not only a category but an organising principle of everyday life, because it facilitates decision making in such matters as self-concept, concept of others, residential choice, hiring and firing in labour markets, and selection of mates and friends.[37]

A key factor that bolsters everyday racial thinking is that what looks like evidence of racial differences is everywhere: everybody knows about the vast differences in average living standard between people living in, say, Europe and Sub-Saharan Africa; they see 'racially' based social stratification in their own societies; and they see the dominance of African-origin athletes in many types of sports, and – in their ethnocentrism – the dominance of European-origin scholars in intellectual debates. For many, it is easier to attribute the source of these differences to innate abilities than to a complex interplay of environmental, cultural and social factors.

A perhaps even more important factor that explains racialism is racial discrimination itself. Racial discrimination is a massive social phenomenon; it is experienced, observed, investigated, dealt with in courts and by other competent authorities, reported by the media, fought against by governmental and non-governmental organizations in a variety of ways such as awareness raising campaigns, and politicians, philosophers and legal scholars debate how best to fight it.

Through these measures the use of racial language rather inevitably becomes part of the culture of politics, opening the door to the use of racial language in the field of law and its enforcement. Domestic statutes and constitutional provisions in many countries explicitly refer to 'race', as do several international human rights documents, such as the UN Convention on the Elimination of All Forms of Racial

[37] Stanfield, *cit. supra* note 33, p. 15.

Discrimination. Many governments and NGOs publish reports about 'race discrimination', and some countries also collect racial data through censuses and other data collection mechanisms. In the UK and USA, racial or ethnic data is collected by some employers for the purposes of complying with anti-discrimination law. All of this can have the effect of sustaining the racial mindset still prevalent in modern-day world.

At the end of the day, two conclusions regarding the existence of 'races' suggest themselves. First, we should steer clear of the perception that real biological differences belie racial distinctions; whatever biological differences there may be are of such a minor order as to be of no relevance for us.[38] Second, we should recognize that social conceptions of 'race' are alive and well and are at play in everyday situations, in good and bad. People can frame their and others' social identities in terms of race and can give these identities significance in their dealings with the other people. It is therefore not just the 'truth' about 'race' that matters; what people believe to be the truth matters as well, probably even more than the truth itself. The content and importance of racial categorisations is not determined by biological realities but by social, economic and political forces. At the same time it must be recognized that as a social construct, 'race' does not have a single essential meaning: what we have is a heterogeneous group of racial beliefs and a number of racial taxonomies reflecting skin colour, place of recent ancestral origin, parental language, religious identity of one's parents, or whatever determinant happens to be socially signified.[39]

Ethnicity

'Ethnicity' has become the most commonly used concept across various disciplines to describe human diversity, and has to a large extent displaced the concept of 'race' in Europe in the field of social sciences, although it must be noted that these two terms are usually not considered to be synonymous. Despite its popularity, or perhaps precisely

[38] This conclusion appears warranted except perhaps in the field of medical science, where 'origin' can function as a proxy for differences in environmental and other factors of relevance to health.

[39] Berry et al, *op. cit.* note 31, p. 264. Moreover, the various social conceptions of 'race', i.e. the classifications used by people in everyday situations, do not match the small biological differences across 'races'. See generally on the scientific utility of racial and ethnic identities in the construction and analysis of genomic resources, Foster – Sharp, *cit. supra* note 30.

because of it, 'ethnicity' has been conceptualized in many different ways and some scholars have even concluded that it is better to not even try to define it.[40]

From an ethnological point of view an 'ideal type' of an ethnic group would be a population group that is characterized by biological self-production and a shared culture. The people of Iceland and other peoples inhabiting relatively isolated areas come closest to this type of a group, but also there and particularly elsewhere in the world the reality is that all communities are characterized by mixed origins, intermarriages, multiple cultural influences and internal cultural and genetic diversity. Moreover, human populations that have been labelled as ethnic groups have been organized – or to be more exact, have been seen by scholars as being organized – in highly different ways. Some scholars have found 'objective' markers to be of importance: these may include cultural markers (language, religion, values, norms), territorial markers (region, land, nationality), biological markers (descent, race, tribe) and/or historical markers (oppression, war); others have pointed out that it is the group boundaries and the social idea-forces that create and maintain them that matter, not any of the 'objective' factors as such; and yet others have maintained that at the end of the day it is the subjective self-identification that matters, and that what really constitutes a community is therefore a multitude of individual acts of self-identification, no matter what prompts these identifications.[41] Moreover, the 'objective' markers are often imagined, meaning that even where a population appears to be united by common origin, it is more probably united by the *belief* in a common origin, and where a population appears to be united by a common culture, it is more probably united by the *belief* in a common culture, as the stories about

[40] See Karmela Liebkind, 'Some problems in the theory and application of cultural pluralism: the complexity of Ethnic Identity' in Juha Pentikäinen – Marja Hiltunen (eds.), *Cultural Minorities in Finland: An Overview towards Cultural Policy* (Helsinki: Sivén, 1995), p. 32.

[41] Idem (Liebkind); Fredrick Barth, *Ethnic Groups and Boundaries: The Social Organization of Culture Difference* (Bergen: Universitetsforlaget, 1969); Zygmunt Bauman, *Modernity and Ambivalence* (Cambridge: Polity Press, 1991); Timo Makkonen, *Identity, Difference and Otherness: The Concepts of 'People', 'Indigenous People' and 'Minority' in International Law*. Eric Castrén Institute Research Reports 7/2000 (Helsinki: University Press, 2000), pp. 14–31; Alan B. Anderson 'The Complexity of Ethnic Identities: A Postmodern Reevaluation' *Identity: An international journal of theory and research* 1(3) 2001, pp. 209–223.

origin tend to incorporate mythical elements and as the cultural markers are always contested.[42]

A related complicating factor is that we do not have any principles that could tell us how ethnic groups differ from nations, tribes or indeed 'races'. Gerd Baumann, in his review of the dictionary definitions of 'ethnic group' and 'nation' across 12 languages – including Arabic, Chinese, English, French, German, Spanish and Russian – found that both ethnic groups and nations are defined in terms of common descent, distinct looks, shared cultural traits (language, outlook), common destiny, and membership that is acquired from birth, the distinction being that a nation is basically one or more ethnic groups that have a responsibility for a state.[43] Another challenge is that there are no universal and absolute principles for determining which ethnic group a particular person belongs to: if your mother belongs to group x, and your father to group y, do you yourself belong to group x, y, both or neither? These kinds of questions are becoming more and more relevant in the increasingly multiethnic Europe that is characterized by intermarriages and an intermingling of cultural influences.

All these complexities do not mean, however, that there are no ethnic groups to begin with, because the kind of social group-formation does take place in real life that can usefully be described as 'ethnic'. But it means that 'ethnicity' is a descriptive label used by scholars and lay individuals to describe and explain a heterogeneous set of phenomena; 'ethnicity' is not some independent force of nature that in some principled way acts upon humankind to produce distinct communities in some orderly manner. In addition we must remember that the use of these concepts is not just theory-laden, but value-laden as well. Martin Bulmer and John Solomos sum up this well:

> Race and ethnicity are not 'natural' categories, even though both concepts are often represented as if they were. Their boundaries are not fixed, nor is their membership uncontested. Race and ethnic groups, like nations, are imagined communities. People are socially defined as belonging to particular ethnic or racial groups, either in terms of definitions employed by others, or definitions which members of particular ethnic groups develop for themselves. They are ideological entities, made

---

[42] Idem.

[43] Gerd Baumann, *The multicultural riddle: rethinking national, ethnic and religious identities* (New York: Routledge, 1999), pp. 30–31.

and changed in struggle. They are discursive formations, signalling a language through which differences may be named and explained.[44]

Ethnic Identity

Complexities relating to ethnicity notwithstanding, it tends to be an important component of the social identity of individuals. Identity can usefully be described as a tool by which individuals or groups categorize themselves and present themselves to the world.[45] Verkuyten has identified four dimensions or aspects of ethnic identity. These include *being*, which refers to the ethnic label that people use for themselves on the basis of their descent or for instance visible characteristics; *feeling*, which refers to how a person feels towards his or her ethnic identity (fundamentally, acceptance or non-acceptance); *doing*, which concerns involvement in the social life and cultural practices of the ethnic in-group; *knowing*, which is about the person's interest in and knowledgeability about the culture and history of his or her group.[46]

The different aspects of ethnic identity can combine in different ways and create unique profiles.[47] The four aspects are not only dimensions by which people's ethnic identities may be described, but they also provide the accounts or repertoires that people use when they 'negotiate' what their group is all about and who exactly should be considered its 'real' members.[48] Typically, 'being' and 'doing' are contrasted, since the aspects of 'feeling' and 'knowing' provide less practical (or less accessible) bases for determining group identity.[49]

There are thus many different ways in which individuals may identify with an ethnic group. Whether others recognize one as a member of that group is another matter. Sometimes a group is able to agree on a visible cultural marker, such as a particular type of dress or headgear,

[44] Martin Bulmer and John Solomos, 'Introduction: Re-thinking Ethnic and Racial Studies' *Ethnic and Racial Studies*, Vol. 21, No 5, 1998, p. 822.

[45] Timothy Owens 'Self and Identity', in John Delamater, *Handbook of Social Psychology* (New York: Kluwer, 2003).

[46] Maykel Verkuyten, *The Social Psychology of Ethnic Identity* (Hove: Psychology Press, 2005), pp. 198–200.

[47] Ibid, p. 200.

[48] Ibid, p. 201.

[49] To give an example, in a group of people who identify themselves as Roma, some may be of the view that to be a Roma it is enough to have parents who are Roma, whereas another part of the group may consider that in addition to having Roma parents one must also follow Roma traditions (and/or speak a Roma language) to be considered a 'real' Roma.

the wearing of which is taken as a presumptive sign of committed membership.

A certain tendency has become visible among many immigrants in Europe lately. While an overwhelming majority of immigrants continue to identify themselves in ethnic terms, and feel strongly about it, this ethnic identification is often only weakly correlated with personal participation in distinctive cultural practices, such as language, religion and dress. As for instance Verkuyten has observed, ethnic identification can persist while increasingly becoming drained of cultural content.[50] Even more fundamentally, we should note that cultural diversity is not born just out of ethnic diversity, as it is not only the interaction among members of an ethnic group that creates culture, but any community from lawyers to street gangs may become the basis of specific subcultures.[51] Indeed, as Verkuyten has pointed out, one implication of this is that all groups and societies – even nation-states – are characterized by internal cultural diversity.[52]

Yet, it must also be noted that there are people who seek to revive and maintain their distinct traditional culture. Particularly people coming from collectivist cultural contexts tend to see the maintenance of the group and its culture as a moral obligation.[53] In addition, present and aspiring community leaders often espouse essentialist and highly conservative conceptions of the culture of the group, often because their power depends on that.[54] Essentialist arguments are powerful, since they portray the group and its culture as natural and non-negotiable.[55]

The coming together of people with different cultural backgrounds can initially create tension and conflict.[56] Yet, it appears to be the norm

[50] Verkuyten, *cit. supra* note 46, p. 201. We may observe a similar process in relation to religious identity and secularization: in the Nordic countries many people have retained formal adherence to their religious identities, even though the substantive meaning of these identities has largely faded away. Pippa Norris – Ronald Inglehart, *Sacred and Secular: Religion and Politics Worldwide* (Cambridge University Press, 2004), p. 18.

[51] Harry C. Triandis, *Culture and Social Behaviour* (New York: McGraw-Hill, 1994), p. 19. For instance, most occupations have some aspects of distinct cultures, such as special vocabulary and a shared set of assumptions.

[52] Verkuyten, *cit. supra* note 46, p. 230.

[53] Idem, p. 104.

[54] Ibid, pp. 104, 124.

[55] This is also why essentialist arguments are used by groups that seek public recognition and accommodation of their cultural and religious needs.

[56] See also Putnam, *cit. supra* note 11.

and not the exception that in the long run intercultural encounters lead to cultural adaptation, through renegotiation of cultural conventions that create space for different cultural understandings. Yet this will not take place insofar as racism, prejudices and discrimination prevail to the extent that they form a barrier to successful interaction between groups. It will also not take place insofar as people cling to essentialist and exclusivist conceptions of 'race', 'ethnicity' and 'nation' that leave no room for such renegotiations.

2.3 Conclusions

Human diversity is a fascinating and peculiar phenomenon. On the one hand, diversity is a visible and tangible part of everyday life, also and increasingly in Europe. A diverse array of religions are observed (and unobserved), hundreds of languages and thousands of dialects are spoken, and endless cultural variations flourish in the context of everyday life. In short, diversity is part and parcel of daily experience.[57]

On the other hand, diversity is a deeply complex phenomenon. 'Race' and 'ethnicity' have become the key concepts by which people describe and try to cope with that reality. But it is in the nature of that diversity that it is difficult to capture by words. In effect, what we have are highly elusive, imprecise and arbitrary concepts and the kind of diversity the nature of which is far too overwhelming to yield fully to human perception and analysis.

'Races' and ethnic groups are primarily projections in the minds of individuals, projections of ideas that are socially constructed and that reflect some existing or past patterns of behaviour and create new ones. Collective identities develop in the fragile, dynamic and fuzzy shape of a decentred, even fragmented public consciousness.[58] Group

---

[57] Also Flash Eurobarometer 217, the fieldwork for which was conducted in November 2007, concludes that "[d]ay to day interaction among people belonging to different cultures is a reality in Europe" on the basis of the result that two thirds of EU citizens were able to recall interaction with at least one person either of a different religion, ethnic background or nationality than their own in the seven days prior to being questioned. European Commission, *Intercultural dialogue in Europe: Summary*. Flash Eurobarometer 217, December 2007.

[58] Jurgen Habermas, 'Private and Public Autonomy, Human Rights and Popular Sovereignty' in Obrad Savic (ed.) *The Politics of Human Rights* (London: Verso, 2002), p. 59.

formation does not precede human action but it is born out of that action, and for each group of people who interact out of a sense of community, there is a project of group formation and maintenance that creates that sense of community. Communities and ways of describing and naming them are intrinsically the results of human action, and stir up further action. Recognition of this social constructedness of group formation implies the recognition that also political and legal actors and structures participate in its making: as we will see, anti-discrimination laws and anti-discrimination policies not just reflect but affect how we perceive diversity and deal with it. It should be realized that our societies are to a great extent racialized and/or ethnicized, and that everything we do may have a positive or a negative impact on intergroup relations.[59]

Complexity tends to drive people to look for simplistic solutions that make life more manageable. There is a continuous temptation to think of 'race' and ethnicity as an essence, as something fixed, concrete, and objective. And there is also an opposite temptation, a temptation to imagine 'race' and ethnicity as mere illusions, purely ideological constructs which some ideal nonracist social order would eliminate.[60] Yet 'racial' and ethnic phenomena are *both* imaginary and real. Projects and processes – in our case laws and policies – that treat diversity as if it does not exist ('colour-blind' approaches) are out of touch with reality, just as are projects and processes that treat it as fixed and unchangeable (essentialist approaches). It must be realized that social structures and political actions contribute to the formation, maintenance and dissolution of groups and structure intergroup relations. Laws and policies therefore have a profound impact on intergroup relations, and one challenge that anti-discrimination laws and policies face is that they should embrace both the reality and fiction of diversity. This insight is of major consequence in the consideration of the legal response to discrimination in the chapters to come.

---

59 Michael Omi – Howard Winant, 'Racial Formation' in Philomena Essed – David Theo Goldberg (eds.) *Race Critical Theories: Text and Context* (Oxford: Blackwell, 2001), p. 127.

60 Ibid, p. 123.

3 DISCRIMINATION AND EQUALITY: THEORETICAL PERSPECTIVES

3.1 Tension between Equality and Discrimination

An intriguing and fundamental tension characterizes human interaction. On the one hand, all human societies have status hierarchies and make divisions between ingroups and outgroups.[1] No society is thoroughly equal, and throughout history most people have probably lived in hierarchically ordered societies. This may be the case because ingroup favouritism, and consequently subordination of outgroup members, may be functional in the course of community building since it can enhance ingroup solidarity and, in certain circumstances, contribute to the overall well-being of the group.[2] On the other hand, also aversion to inequality appears to be a human universal and has been shown to prevail in a wide variety of circumstances. Also this propensity is functional for community building, as equal reciprocal relations are critical for building cooperation and trust, and therefore during the evolution of cooperation it may have become critical for individuals to compare their own efforts and pay-offs with those of others (i.e. to diagnose whether they have been treated equally). That such sensitivity to inequality developed a long time ago in the course of evolution is suggested, *inter alia*, by some experimental studies which have shown that brown capuchin monkeys – a highly co-operative species like humans – react negatively when they are given inferior rewards than their fellow monkeys for the same efforts.[3] Both the propensity to make distinctions and the ability to feel injustice in

---

[1] Douglas Kenrick et al 'Evolutionary Social Psychology: Adaptive Predispositions and Human Culture', in John Delamater (ed.), *Handbook of Social Psychology* (New York: Kluwer, 2003), p. 113; Harry C. Triandis, *Culture and Social Behaviour* (New York: McGraw-Hill, 1994); Peter B. Smith and Michael Harris Bond, *Social Psychology Across Cultures* (Essex: Pearson Education Limited, 1998), p. 74.

[2] See e.g. John Duckitt, *The Social Psychology of Prejudice* (New York: Praeger, 1992), pp. 4–5.

[3] Sarah F. Brosnan – Frans B.M. de Waal 'Monkeys reject unequal pay' *Nature*, Vol 425, 18 September 2003, pp. 297–299.

face of unjustified distinctions, though therefore deep-seated and universally found, show substantial cultural variation in the particulars.[4]

This fundamental tension between egalitarian and inegalitarian impulses has given rise to a tremendous amount of both empirical and theoretical research, particularly in the past decades. Theoretically oriented undertakings have expanded and deepened our understanding of the political, philosophical and moral issues that are at stake when we are dealing with equality and discrimination. At the same time, empirical research has produced a wealth of information about the characteristics, extent, causes and effects of discrimination. Due to these two strands of inquiry, nowadays much more is understood about the dynamics of discrimination. This study relies heavily on both the empirical and theoretical research traditions in order to examine the basic research question, the effectiveness of the law in tackling racial and ethnic discrimination.

In the following, this study will give a general introduction to the concept of discrimination, and discuss more specific notions such as direct and indirect discrimination, and institutional and systemic discrimination. Also the relationship between the principle of non-discrimination and various conceptions of equality will be discussed. After this, chapter 4 will engage in a thorough examination of the dynamics of discrimination in practice, for the purposes of examining what it would take to combat discrimination more successfully.

3.2 Discrimination

Terms 'discrimination' and 'equality' hold prominent places in contemporary political, legal and everyday vocabularies. Most of the present discussions, particularly policy discussions, take it for granted that it is already settled if not self-evident what discrimination or equality 'is'. Yet a closer analysis reveals that it is not at all well-established what 'discrimination' and 'equality' mean. Like most other concepts, they stand for abstract, socially constructed but subjectively held ideas that do not have objective or *a priori* meanings. There is a deep truth to the aphorism that equality is not an abstract concept for those who have been denied it. But it is equally true that the subjective feeling of

[4] Idem; Duckitt, *cit. supra* note 2.

inequality can never fully be put down into words and that even if it could, it could not be operationalized into a single, precise definition capable of mustering general agreement. What represents an instance of discrimination for one person may not represent it for another. This view appears indisputable, given the many profound, apparent and ongoing disagreements about what exactly constitutes discrimination and what equality or equal treatment is all about.

Discrimination, and the associated concept of equality, can be given, and have indeed been given, a range of meanings. These concepts have been defined differently in different legal, social science, political and philosophical contexts and are used in different senses in everyday discussions. Given that there is no universal, or even general, agreement in matters of justice, no single definition of discrimination or equality can claim absolute, universal priority over the others. In consequence, the question which actions, omissions or states of affairs constitute discrimination, for instance for the purposes of the law, is and should be a matter of an ongoing debate.

The diversity of theories notwithstanding, considerable convergence in legal and public policy contexts has been achieved through the adoption and national implementation of international and European legal instruments. One of the core aims of the present study is to examine how the international and European law defines 'discrimination' and what sort of equality it (openly or tacitly) promotes. For this purpose it is useful to make here some analytical distinctions that refer to different aspects and/or conceptions of discrimination. These conceptual distinctions are meant to work as a heuristic toolkit that can help to analyze and understand the subject area. They do not represent an overall theory of what discrimination – legally, politically or philosophically – 'is' or what it should be taken to be.[5]

Discriminating between Discriminations

To begin with, it must be noted that the word 'discrimination' has two basic but broad meanings in the English language. The first one has positive connotations and refers to the ability and power to make fine distinctions between two or more things or individuals that to a less discerning eye look the same. In this sense one can speak of, for

[5] It should also be noted that the different concepts are to an extent overlapping and do not form a coherent, monolithic entity.

instance, 'discriminating readers' who are picky in terms of what they choose to read. This use of the word 'discrimination' appears however to be fading out, perhaps in part because 'discrimination' is nowadays predominantly understood in its second meaning as a reference to unfair treatment, in consequence of which the concept has acquired a predominantly negative connotation. 'Discrimination' is, in this study, used exclusively in the latter sense.

Direct and Indirect Discrimination and Everyday Discrimination

For the purposes of this chapter, racial and ethnic discrimination can be given a working definition as being about treating a person or a group of persons adversely on the basis of 'race' or ethnicity. In broad terms, discrimination can be identified by the 'but-for' test: discrimination has occurred where, but for their racial or ethnic origin, persons would not have been subjected to a disadvantage. For instance, if an employer tells an immigrant that the position she wishes to apply for has already been filled, but later on tells an applicant belonging to the ethnic majority that the post is still vacant, that is some evidence of discrimination.

It is common nowadays to distinguish between direct and indirect discrimination. In broad terms, *direct discrimination* occurs where a person or a group of persons is put at a disadvantage directly on the grounds of their origin. This takes place where, for instance, an employer tells a job applicant that she will not hire persons who belong to a certain minority because she thinks they are unreliable or because she is afraid that her business might be harmed because her clientele might not accept persons with an ethnic minority background. *Indirect discrimination* occurs where a rule, criterion or practice, which is neutral at face value, puts persons of a particular ethnic origin unduly at a disadvantage. This could take place, for instance, where an employer advertises job openings in a newspaper that is only or primarily read by people belonging to the ethnic majority, or where the employer requires a successful candidate to speak the national language as a mother tongue, a requirement which puts immigrants at a manifest disadvantage.

This study focuses on a widely neglected phenomenon that can perhaps best be called *everyday discrimination*. The term 'everyday discrimination' was coined by Philomena Essed to describe the recurrent, familiar practices of inequality that persons belonging to marginalized groups face in the course of their daily lives.[6] Such situations can be relatively minor but still be significant. Examples of everyday discrimination include name-calling, racist jokes, harassment and exclusion from social activities and networks, but can also take place in such contexts as hiring and firing or access to housing. Unlike major, overt instances of discrimination, everyday discrimination encompasses events which may for outsiders appear to be 'trivial' or even 'normal'. The difficulty in identifying this kind of discrimination arises because, as will be argued later on in more detail, prejudices and stereotypes permeate every facet of life, as they are socially constructed, culturally transmitted and subjectively and often unconsciously held, and come to inform rules, regulations, policies, practices, decisions, arrangements and conceptions. In consequence, manifestations of discrimination can be subtly intertwined with seemingly neutral or innocent social phenomena.[7]

The emphasis on everyday discrimination should not come at the cost of overlooking the threat posed by overt forms of discrimination, organized hate groups or racist violence. There is plenty of evidence of hate-based violence in Europe.[8] Rather, the purpose of emphasizing everyday discrimination is to bring to light a problem that often receives little attention from the media, scholars or the authorities, but that nevertheless affects a large number of individuals and that can have widespread damaging effects. Everyday discrimination is something that often goes under the radar, without public attention.

Institutional and Structural Discrimination

The prevailing understanding of discrimination is that it is something that occurs at a specific point in time within a particular field of life and typically involves a limited number of individuals, i.e. the direct

---

[6] See e.g. Philomena Essed 'Everyday Racism: A new approach to the study of racism' in Philomena Essed – David Theo Goldberg (eds.) *Race Critical Theories* (Oxford: Blackwell, 2002), p. 177.

[7] Even calls for colour-blindness and 'racial' and ethnic neutrality may in fact cover hidden or invisible forms and patterns of discrimination. See David Theo Goldberg – Philomena Essed, 'Introduction: From Racial Demarcations to Multiple Identifications' in Philomena Essed – David Theo Goldberg (eds.) *Race Critical Theories* (Oxford: Blackwell, 2001).

[8] See Michael McClintock, *Everyday Fears: A Survey of Violent Hate Crimes in Europe and North America* (Human Rights First, 2005).

victim(s) and the perpetrator(s). This view, which could be characterized as 'the episodic view of discrimination', quite likely derives from the field of law, where – for the purposes of determining liability – the identification of a specific legally meaningful event is crucial, as is the identification of particular individuals as 'complainants' and 'respondents'. However, the episodic and individual-centred view of discrimination hides from sight structural and institutional problems that cannot be seen by looking at individual events alone, in addition to which it strips discrimination of the wider context in which it occurs. The episodic view, just like the law, is only concerned with specific events, the fact scenarios of which meet legal or some other definition of 'discrimination', and is unconcerned with the more general mechanisms, patterns, causes and consequences that underlie or contribute to the specific events.[9] Yet discrimination, and its impact on the lives of the individuals concerned and on the society at large, cannot be properly understood unless discrimination is viewed in its broader context and as a dynamic process that functions over time in several, often unexpected, ways.

Several important philosophical, political, legal and social science contributions have lately pointed towards a need to analyze those societal, institutional and cultural structures, patterns and processes that produce or maintain disadvantages for immigrants and minorities.[10] These phenomena are usually treated under such headings as 'structural discrimination', 'institutional discrimination' or 'institutional racism'.[11] There seems to be a great variety in what different actors mean when they use such terms.[12]

For the purposes of this study, *institutional discrimination* refers to a collective failure of an organization (such as a public body, business or university) to implement the principle of equal treatment, this failure being in practice often due to a combination of factors such as

---

[9] Cf. the analysis of racist violence in EUMC, *Racist Violence in 15 EU Member States* (EUMC, April 2005), p. 186.

[10] See e.g. Paul Lappalainen, *Det blågula glashuset – strukturell diskriminering i Sverige* (Stockholm: Elanders Gotab, 2005); Mark Bell 'Combating Structural Racism through Law', *ENARgy* Issue 17; Sir William Macpherson of Cluny, *The Stephen Lawrence Inquiry: Report of an Inquiry by Sir William Macpherson of Cluny* (London: The Stationery Office 1999).

[11] For an analysis of the main terms of the debate, see John Wrench, *Diversity Management and Discrimination: Immigrants and Ethnic Minorities in the EU* (Aldershot: Ashgate, 2007).

[12] Idem.

ignorance, thoughtlessness, prejudice and racism.[13] The latter factors do on occasion become ingrained into the very culture of the organization, which means that institutional discrimination can have systemic properties that cannot be explained simply in terms of individual-level factors, even though it is always individuals that maintain it. Institutional discrimination can also be rooted in rules and procedures, meaning that it can exist independently of individual attitudes.[14] Sometimes it is appropriate to speak of *institutionalized discrimination*, namely in cases of intentional and systematic discriminatory policies, particularly if they are enforced by law as was the case in South Africa during the Apartheid system.

Because institutional discrimination is often embedded in practices and policies that represent 'business as usual' and that do not appear blatantly racist, it tends to become visible to the public only in exceptional circumstances or through specific inquiries that function as eye-openers. One such exceptional circumstance arose in 2005 when an extraordinarily deadly and costly hurricane named Katrina hit the United States.[15] As many of the areas that suffered major loss of life and economic damage were populated predominantly by ethnic minorities, and as the governmental preparation for and response to the hurricane was widely criticized as grossly inadequate, the possible role played by institutional discrimination was raised in public and scholarly discussions.[16] In the United Kingdom the existence of institutional discrimination and even institutional racism has not only been

[13] This definition owes much to the definition of institutional racism in the so-called Macpherson report, where it is characterized as "The collective failure of an organisation to provide an appropriate and professional service to people because of their colour, culture or ethnic origin. It can be seen or detected in processes, attitudes, and behaviour which amount to discrimination through unwitting prejudice, ignorance, thoughtlessness and racist stereotypes which disadvantage minority ethnic people." Macpherson, *cit. supra* note 10, para 6.34.

[14] Frank Asbrock et al 'The Road to Negative Behaviour: Discriminatory Intentions in the German Population' *International Journal of Conflict and Violence* Vol. 1(1) 2007, pp. 4–18.

[15] Katrina was the costliest and fifth deadliest hurricane to ever hit the United States. Richard D. Knabb et al, *Tropical Cyclone Report: Hurricane Katrina* (National Hurricane Center, 20 December 2005, updated in 10 August 2006).

[16] Kristin E. Henkel et al, 'Institutional Discrimination, Individual Racism, and Hurricane Katrina' *Analyses of Social Issues & Public Policy* Dec 2006, Vol. 6 Issue 1, pp. 99–124. Samuel R. Sommers et al, 'Race and Media Coverage of Hurricane Katrina: Analysis, Implications, and Future Research Questions' *Analyses of Social Issues & Public Policy* Dec 2006, Vol. 6 Issue 1, pp. 39–55. Maya Wiley – John A. Powell 'Tearing Down Structural Racism and Rebuilding Communities', *ENARgy* Issue 17, July 2006.

discussed, but has become widely and publicly acknowledged in the aftermath of the so-called Macpherson inquiry that looked into the investigation of the racist murder of a Black teenager named Stephen Lawrence. The inquiry found the British Police Force guilty of 'institutional racism', which was not attributable to individual acts of overt discrimination by police officers but stemmed instead from the occupational culture of the police.[17] This finding has had a major impact in Britain in terms of the way in which discrimination, racism and their countermeasures are conceived.[18] It is not to be thought for a second that the British Police Force is uniquely plagued by racism; it is unique only in acknowledging it.

Structural discrimination, for its part, is understood in this study as obstacles that prevent or impair the enjoyment of equal rights and opportunities by immigrants and persons belonging to ethnic minorities because of the way some part of the societal make-up (rules, policies, practices, criteria, and informal conventions) functions. Such obstacles come in many forms, but they thrive particularly well in traditionally bureaucratic branches of administration such as those in charge of immigration and immigrant matters. Examples of structural barriers include unduly complicated, costly or lengthy procedures for naturalization or obtaining residence or work permits; lack of recognition or negative evaluation of education obtained abroad; citizenship requirements for being employed as a civil servant; inadequate public funding of schools in poorer areas populated by minority groups; and loss of residence permits in the event of unemployment, a policy that in practice steers immigrants to accept jobs for lower pay and worse conditions than nationals. Clear evidence of the existence of structural discrimination comes from Sweden, where a governmental inquiry found structural discrimination in the areas of labour market, housing, politics, the legal system, education and the welfare system.[19] The result of this inquiry is all the more noteworthy because not long after the inquiry Sweden fared best in a comprehensive survey that looked at the performance of 28 countries, including all EU countries, in the

---

[17] Bob Hepple, 'Race and Law in Fortress Europe' *Modern Law Review*, Vol 67, No 1, January 2004, p. 12.

[18] See e.g. Barbara Cohen, 'The Stephen Lawrence Inquiry – lessons to be learned' *ENARgy* Issue 17, July 2006.

[19] Lappalainen, *cit. supra* note 10.

area of immigrant integration.[20] Given that even the group leader acknowledges having major problems in this area, there is reason to believe that structural discrimination is a major problem in the other countries too.[21]

It is of essence to note that the dynamics of unequal treatment extend beyond individual events, institutional discrimination and structural discrimination. This study will illustrate, in particular, (i) how discrimination experienced by victims in one field of life (e.g. employment) can cause disadvantages for them in other fields of life (e.g. housing), (ii) how the effects of discrimination may be passed on from one generation to the next, and (iii) how discrimination negatively affects not just its direct victims but also other members of the family of the discriminated-against persons, others from the same ethnic group, businesses, and even the society at large. Finally, it is argued that discrimination and its causes and effects form a vicious circle that is hard to stop once it is set in motion.

Just as it must be acknowledged that discrimination can have far-reaching effects, it must be equally acknowledged that this does not mean that discrimination could not take on very subtle forms. Indeed, as unequal treatment has increasingly become socially unacceptable and subject to more stringent anti-discrimination laws and other interventions, discrimination has began to take more covert and subtle forms than before.

In effect, it is highly challenging to investigate the nature and extent of discrimination in the society. As argued by Wrench and Modood:

> Even when racism and discrimination are conscious and intentional, they are usually difficult to identify, often subtle and hidden. Some aspects are only discovered through specific investigations. Other types of discrimination are unintended, indirect, or institutional, and these often need relatively complex investigation and theorising in order to identify the processes that lead to exclusion or disadvantage for some groups.[22]

---

[20] Jan Niessen – Thomas Huddleston – Laura Citron, *Migrant Integration Policy Index* (Brussels: British Council and the MPG, 2007).

[21] Some, but not all forms of institutional and structural discrimination fall within the scope of international and European anti-discrimination law. Bell, *cit. supra* note 10.

[22] John Wrench – Tariq Modood, *The Effectiveness of Employment Equality policies in Relation to Immigrants and Ethnic Minorities in the UK*. International Migration Papers 38 (Geneva: ILO, 2000).

3.3 Equality

Equality is one of those disturbing concepts about which almost everyone has a general theory, but no-one a theory that is generally accepted. Equality has been described as a "popular but mysterious political ideal" by Ronald Dworkin,[23] and as "at once the simplest and the most complex idea that shapes the evolution of law" by George Fletcher.[24] Political controversies over equality are usually not about whether to be in favour or against equality, but about what form of equality to favour.[25] A highly useful description of the concept of equality is provided by Amartya Sen, who writes that "equality is judged by comparing some particular aspect of a person (such as income, or wealth, or happiness, or liberty, or opportunities, or rights, or need-fulfilments) with the same aspect of another person".[26] His conceptualization, while useful, is, however, unnecessarily limited, as equality does not need to be conceived solely in individualist terms: the comparisons that equality judgments entail may also take place between groups. We can – and many think we should – be concerned not only with individual equality but also with group equality.[27]

A key challenge is that people can have equal political and other rights, enjoy equal opportunities, have equal levels of wealth, find equal satisfaction in their lives, have their community-based cultural and religious needs met equally, but they cannot have all of that at the same time. In effect, people can become equal (or at least more equal) in one way with the consequence that they become unequal (or more unequal) in others.[28] If people have equal income, for example, they will certainly differ in the amount of satisfaction they find in their lives.[29] All societies and political theories that subscribe to the ideal of

---

[23] Ronald Dworkin, *Sovereign Virtue: the theory and practice of equality* (Cambridge: Harvard University Press, 2002), p. 11

[24] George P. Fletcher, cited in M.H.S. Gijzen, *Selected issues in equal treatment law: a multi-layered comparison of European, English and Dutch law* (Antwerpen: Intersentia, 2006), p. 3.

[25] Amartya Sen, *Inequality reexamined* (Oxford: Oxford University Press, 1992); John Rawls, *A Theory of Justice* (London: Oxford University Press, 1973).

[26] Ibid (Sen), p. 2.

[27] See e.g. Christopher McCrudden, 'The New Concept of Equality' (2003) 3 ERA-Forum 9.

[28] Dworkin, *cit. supra* note 23, p. 11.

[29] Idem.

equality must therefore set out which form of equality is, in the end, prioritized over the others.[30]

Bearing the above analysis in mind, we can usefully distinguish between several possible kinds or dimensions of equality. These are termed here 'moral equality', 'civil rights equality', 'market equality', 'material equality', 'political equality', and 'cultural equality'. It should be noted that this typology is meant to be illustrative; it is not the only possible typology, nor is it necessarily exhaustive and there is a degree of overlap – and also tension – between the different enumerated dimensions of equality.[31]

Moral Equality

Moral equality is an assertion about what people are, not about what they have or should have. It conveys the idea that people are, irrespective of their particular characteristics, of equal moral worth. This assertion is at the heart of the very idea of human rights, a key motif of which is that all persons are equal in dignity and worth.[32] The Universal Declaration of Human Rights (UDHR) is particularly straightforward in articulating this vision: Article 1 of the UDHR famously proclaims that "[a]ll human beings are born free and equal in dignity and rights", in addition to which the preamble asserts that "recognition of the inherent dignity and of the equal and inalienable rights of all members of the human family" is the "foundation of freedom, justice and peace in the world." These tenets are reiterated in other key human rights instruments, including the International Covenant on Civil and Political Rights, the International Covenant on Social, Economic and Cultural Rights, and the International Convention on the Elimination

[30] Sen, *cit. supra* note 25. Although some conceptions of equality are mutually incompatible, this is not always the case, as will appear from the discussion below.

[31] For another account of the possible meanings of 'equality' as a legal concept, see Christopher McCrudden, *Buying Social Justice: Equality, Government Procurement, & Legal Change* (Oxford: OUP, 2007), pp. 512–515.

[32] This does not mean that human rights could not be viewed as grounded on some other premises or value than equal moral worth of human beings, or none at all. For instance John Rawls asserts that human rights do not depend on any particular comprehensive moral doctrine or philosophical conception of human nature such as human beings having equal worth. Instead, Rawls sees international human rights as expressing "a minimum standard of well-ordered political institutions for all peoples who belong, as members of good standing, to a just political society of peoples". John Rawls, '*The law of peoples*' in Obrad Savic (ed.) *The Politics of Human Rights* (London: Verso, 2002), p. 32. For another point of view, see Joseph Raz, *Human Rights Without Foundations* (March 2007), Oxford Legal Studies Research Paper No 14/2007.

of all Forms of Racial Discrimination.[33] These instruments stand for the doctrine that no matter what we are or do or where we come from, we are all members of the same human family, and on that basis – and on that basis alone – of equal worth.[34] In other words, they refer to an abstract and universal notion of 'a human being'.

The belief in the equal moral worth of all human beings is not a prerogative of the human rights discourse. Few, if any, modern-day major moral or political theory questions it by asserting that some people are of lesser worth simply by virtue of their origin. From a historical perspective we can also note that many religious leaders, philosophers, political figures and laywomen and laymen have developed, taught and stood for doctrines about common humanity, unique human worth and universal responsibility towards fellow human beings.[35] That said, many more have questioned and rejected such beliefs, and throughout history most people have probably lived in societies based on various kinds of hierarchical structures antithetical to any idea of equal worth.[36] Transatlantic slavery, colonialism and other forms of de facto exploitation are paradigm examples of large-scale practices that brought about major profits to members of some groups by means of inflicting major suffering on members of some other groups, and that were directly justified by theories and attitudes based on assumed inferiority of the 'racial other'.[37]

Although the idea of equal moral worth is accepted – or at least not explicitly rejected – by almost all quarters of contemporary Europe, its political, legal and social implications – beyond rejection of the most

[33] It is the UNESCO Declaration on Race and Racial Prejudice that articulates these premises most forcefully. Article 1 of the Declaration asserts that "[a]ll human beings belong to a single species and are descended from a common stock. They are born equal in dignity and rights and all form an integral part of humanity."

[34] This idea contrasts with beliefs according to which any degree of respect must be for instance earned or inherited. On the other hand, the idea only conveys equal worth as a human being; it does not postulate that all human qualities or everything that people do should be seen as equally worthy.

[35] See Paul Gordon Lauren, *The Evolution of International Human Rights: Visions Seen* (Philadelphia: University of Pennsylvania Press, 1998).

[36] Idem, p. 28 in particular; Sandra Fredman, *Discrimination Law* (Oxford: Oxford University Press, 2002), pp. 4–5.

[37] See e.g. idem (Lauren). It was indeed protests against practices like colonialism, segregation and Apartheid that, together with piling evidence demonstrating that the previously held doctrines about superiority of the 'white race' were scientifically wrong, led to the recognition of the equal worth of all human beings, and eventually, when combined with the idea of natural rights, to the conception of equal rights for all irrespective of racial origin.

blatant forms of exclusion and subordination – cannot be articulated without some further explicit or implicit theory of justice, which means that the concept of equal worth does not by itself yield anything like a set of first principles on which to found a complete political theory of equality. It is therefore necessary to examine other possible dimensions of equality.

Civil Rights Equality

One widely accepted implication of the recognition of equal moral worth of individuals is the recognition of the equal rights of individuals. International human rights instruments in particular draw an intrinsic link between equal moral worth and equal rights. This is apparent in view of the fact that the preambles of these instruments speak of the equal worth and dignity of all human beings and in that they purposively use universal terms such as 'every human being', 'everyone', and 'no-one' in framing rights and freedoms set out therein.[38] This approach was apparent already in the Charter of the United Nations, which defines one of the four purposes of the UN as being the achievement of international co-operation in "promoting and encouraging respect for human rights and fundamental freedoms for all without distinction as to race, sex, language, or religion" in the interests of "reaffirming faith ... in the dignity and worth of the human person".[39] The UDHR, as already noted, explicitly juxtaposes equality of worth and equality of rights by proclaiming that "all human beings are born ... equal in dignity and rights". The human rights instruments, for the purposes of bolstering the equal enjoyment of rights, almost without exception prohibit discrimination, *inter alia*, on the grounds of 'race' as concerns the provision and enjoyment of the rights set out in these instruments.

The contiguity of recognition of equal worth and equal rights has also been an essential quality of equality movements from the American civil rights movement to the feminist movements across the globe,

---

[38] See e.g. the International Covenant on Civil and Political Rights, Article 6 of which provides that "[e]very human being has the inherent right to life", Article 7 of which provides that "[n]o one shall be subjected to torture or to cruel, inhuman or degrading treatment or punishment", and Article 9 of which provides that "[e]veryone has the right to liberty and security of person."

[39] Preamble and Article 1(3) of the Charter, signed at San Francisco on 26 June 1945.

particularly affecting constitution-making with regard to fundamental rights and freedoms.

Market Equality
Another possible and widely endorsed dimension of equality may be termed 'market equality'. This dimension of equality is essentially about equal treatment in the markets for labour, education and commodities. It is about ensuring equal opportunities, about ensuring that discrimination based on, *inter alia*, ethnic origin does not compromise the opportunities of people to access and operate in the market place. Many countries in Europe and elsewhere have already for a number of years had, in their penal laws, employment laws and/or civil laws, provisions prohibiting discrimination in these key spheres of life.

Material Equality
Material equality is essentially about the distribution of income and wealth in a society. This *redistributive paradigm* has been a major theme in the discussions about equality in the recent decades. That discussion has in the past focused mainly on the inequalities of distribution between people belonging to different classes, with those supporting libertarian equality holding that there should be free market competition and minimal redistributive state intervention, and those supporting the equality of outcome holding that the state should actively reduce or even eliminate differences in outcomes by means of robust redistributive measures supported by heavy taxation, and with the rest by and large supporting an equality of opportunity doctrine that stands in between these two contrasting policy approaches.

We may also focus on inequalities of distribution between different ethnic groups. Again we can usefully distinguish between different major policy responses to ethnic inequalities in outcomes: (i) the state should not actively intervene in the free operation of the market and the distribution of material well-being that ensues from it (libertarian conception of equality); (ii) the state should contribute towards the creation of a socio-economic environment based on free and fair market competition secured in part by the banning of discrimination, but should not do more than that to reduce inequalities in outcomes between groups (liberal, procedural equality of opportunity); (iii) the state should actively prevent, remove and remedy unjustified disadvantages linked to racial and ethnic origin, whether or not these are directly the result of past or present discrimination, these measures presumably leading to greater equality in terms of outcomes (welfarist, substantive equality of opportunity); and (iv) the state should proactively eliminate differences in outcomes across groups, for instance through the use of robust measures such as quotas that place an emphasis on the fairness of group outcomes instead of individual procedural fairness (equality of outcome).

Cultural Equality

The redistributive paradigm as *the* dimension of equality has in recent years been somewhat displaced by what might be called the *recognition paradigm*. This paradigm is concerned with the politics of identity and culture and the unequal distribution of power in the society seen from a group perspective. This paradigm takes seriously the view that in a basic liberal democratic state, even though it guarantees political and civil rights on an equal basis ('one man, one vote') to all citizens irrespective of their origin, societal structures – as shaped by legislation, culture and market forces – are moulded to reflect and respond to the needs and values of the dominant groups. The choice of national holidays, days of rest, official languages and languages spoken at work and at the shop floor, and many other choices form a social environment that follows from and appeals to the attributes of the dominant groups.[40] If one were to put it ironically, one could say that in a basic liberal democracy both majorities and minorities are, on an equal basis, entitled to participate in the society created by the majority. But there is no irony in that this is the case in the real world and that the majority itself is blind to this cultural bias. This ethnocentric blindness develops because people are raised in particular cultures and are socialized into particular sets of local knowledge, norms and traditions, all of which come to seem normal and enduring.[41] In consequence, the majority tends to see itself as the rule, not the exception, and in effect its ideas, beliefs and attributes form the self-evident and undiscussed parameters against which it measures the behaviour of minority groups.[42] This raises a fundamental question: are people equal, irrespective of whether they belong to the majority or to the minority, in terms laid down by

[40] On this, see e.g. Will Kymlicka, *Multicultural citizenship: a liberal theory of minority rights* (Oxford: Clarendon Press, 1995).

[41] Jacob T. Levy, *The Multiculturalism of Fear* (Oxford: Oxford University Press, 2000), p. 6.

[42] Maykel Verkuyten, *The Social Psychology of Ethnic Identity* (Hove: Psychology Press, 2005), p. 59.

the majority, or should people be equal in terms laid down by themselves? Is 'equality' compatible with assimilation and nation-state values or does it call for some form of cultural pluralism?

We can present a typology of policy responses to the challenge posed by this culturalist strand of equality: (i) a *policy of monoculturalism*, which stresses the need to forge, maintain and cherish a single national identity and culture and aims at absorbing cultural minorities into the cultural mainstream; (ii) a *policy of integration*, which stresses the need to incorporate cultural minorities in the mainstream society while emphasising that it is important that they can participate in its making, without however the preservation of minority identities being valued as a goal in its own right; (iii) a *policy of recognition*, which goes beyond a policy of integration by means of positively affirming diversity and by means of adopting positive measures with a view to accommodating the practices and traits of cultural minorities; (iv) a *policy of multiculturalism*, which effectively sees the society as an ethnic mosaic, composed of a number of different ethnic groups and which asserts that each group has the right to retain its own culture and identity, however under institutions that are common to all groups; (v) a policy of *communitarian pluralism*, which is more radical in its recognition of cultural diversity than the other approaches, in that it posits that since different cultures are not necessarily compatible with each other, and since all cultures are equal, it must be recognized that all groups cannot have their needs met by common institutions, and therefore some or all communities must be granted (some form of) autonomy.[43]

Political Equality

Political or participatory equality is yet another dimension of equality. It is concerned with the various means by which immigrants and persons belonging to ethnic minorities can participate in decision-making. As a system of political democracy based on majority rule may, particularly without the accompanying 'checks and balances', in some circumstances turn into a tyranny of the majority and abuse of minorities, political equality must be concerned with the protection of the interests of the vulnerable groups. In short, political equality is

[43] This autonomy could either cover a particular geographic area or one or more material areas of law, such as family law and/or criminal law. For a discussion of the different legal models, see Ayelet Shachar, *Multicultural Jurisdictions: Cultural Differences and Women's Rights* (Cambridge: Cambridge University Press, 2001).

about giving vulnerable groups a voice especially in matters that are of particular concern to them, with a view to preventing their de facto disenfranchisement from decisions that have a profound effect on their life. The possibility to influence political and governmental decisions may be seen to require the adoption of mechanisms of participation of immigrants and minorities in the political and governmental decision-making. Particularly deliberative and communicative forms of democracy are often expected to lead to laws and policies that are, at the very least, acceptable to members of the minorities.[44] Given that the other possible dimensions of equality are determined in the various policy-making processes, it is arguable that political equality should play a primary role in the discourses about equality.

Equality and Non-Discrimination

The focus of this study is on European and international anti-discrimination law, not on equality as such. Non-discrimination law can, however, contribute towards the achievement of the different dimensions of equality. The examination of the question of to what extent it does so is one of the key themes of this study.

[44] This policy could also include some form of consensus decision-making, which not only seeks the agreement of most participants, but seeks to resolve or mitigate the objections of the minority in order to achieve the most agreeable decision.

4 DISCRIMINATION: EMPIRICAL PERSPECTIVES

4.1 Extent and Characteristics of Discrimination

Racial and ethnic discrimination have become major areas for empirical research during the past decades. Victim surveys, socio-economic statistics, discrimination testing studies and other forms of quantitative and qualitative research have been able to document and shed light on the extent, nature, causes and effects of discrimination, rendering the previously largely hidden problems more visible. Whereas it is now for the first time possible to try to paint a fairly comprehensive picture of discrimination and its dynamics, major gaps and uncertainties in our knowledge base still exist, underlining the need for further research in this area.[1]

The following sections look at the existing evidence of the extent and nature of discrimination by tapping into a variety of information sources.

Evidence from Complaints Statistics

All European countries have mechanisms in place for handling complaints about ethnic discrimination.[2] Precise statistics indicating the number of discrimination cases that are tried in the regular courts of law across Europe are, however, not available. Yet, several sources consistently point towards the finding that volume of court proceedings is low, in comparison to the extent of experienced discrimination, across Europe.[3] Somewhat more cases appear to be dealt with by specialized

---

[1] Timo Makkonen, *European Handbook on Equality Data* (Luxembourg: OOPEC, 2007).

[2] For the EU countries, the availability of judicial and/or administrative mechanisms is required by Article 7 of the EU Racial Equality Directive. All EU countries combine judicial proceedings – 'regular' civil, criminal and/or administrative proceedings – with quasi-judicial or non-judicial proceedings. Typical quasi-judicial and non-judicial bodies that are charged with the enforcement of anti-discrimination law include Equal Treatment Commissions, Ombudsmen, Human Rights Institutions and Labour inspectorates. Mark Bell et al, *Developing Anti-Discrimination Law in Europe: The 25 EU Member States compared* (Luxembourg: OOPEC, 2007), p. 66.

[3] Bell et al, *cit. supra* note 2, pp. 69–70; FRA, *Report on Racism and Xenophobia in the Member States of the EU* (Vienna, 2007), p. 20 ff. The number of claims involving

judicial bodies such as Discrimination Tribunals. For instance, of the 'race' discrimination claims handled by the UK Employment Tribunals between April 2007 and March 2008, discrimination was established in 121 cases and settlement was reached in 1 295 cases.[4]

The picture changes drastically when complaints filed with specialized bodies are focused upon, as the latter typically represent what one might call low-threshold bodies. The number of recorded cases is significantly higher, although there are major differences between the EU member states in terms of the number of complaints received by the specialized bodies. In 2007, the greatest amount of complaints was received by the specialized bodies in Belgium, France and the United Kingdom, each of which received more than 1 000 claims regarding discrimination on the grounds of racial or ethnic origin.[5] More than 900 complaints were registered in Sweden. From 100 to 500 applications were registered in Austria, Cyprus, Finland, Germany, Italy and the Netherlands. Less than one hundred complaints were registered in the other EU countries.[6] Proceedings before these bodies often end up, where discrimination is found, either in out-of-court settlement or the issuing of non-binding observations or recommendations.

The usefulness of this type of complaints data for the purposes of analyzing the extent of discrimination is severely compromised by two factors: under-recording and under-reporting. It is well documented that the relevant authorities, such as police officers, do not always record complaints reported to them or fail to do so properly; this is known as under-recording. More importantly, data on complaints only tell about *reported* cases of discrimination, whereas discrimination is an example *par excellence* of an activity that often remains hidden because it is not reported to the authorities; this phenomenon is known as under-reporting. There are two main reasons for the latter state of affairs: (i) there is evidence pointing to the fact that people may not even know it when they are being discriminated against, and cannot

indirect discrimination processed in the EU member states was surveyed and found low in Timo Makkonen, 'Measuring Discrimination: Data Collection and EU Equality Law' (Luxembourg: OOPEC, 2007).

[4] A high number of cases were also withdrawn, possibly because of out-of-court settlements. Employment Tribunals, *Employment Tribunal and EAT Statistics (GB)*. Source: http://www.employmenttribunals.gov.uk (accessed 10.1.2010).

[5] FRA, *Annual Report 2009* (Vienna: FRA, 2009), pp. 21 ff.

[6] No specialized body had been set up, or the body was not operational before the end of the year 2007, by Czech Republic, Spain and Luxemburg. Idem.

therefore be expected to file a complaint in the first place,[7] and (ii) even where a person is aware of the fact that she has been discriminated against, she may have various reasons for not pressing charges or otherwise coming forward with a formal complaint. At the end of the day, complaints data can only reveal the proverbial tip of the iceberg.

Evidence from Victim Surveys

A much more useful method for investigating the existence of discrimination in the society is to survey the people concerned directly about their experiences. With a view on this, the EU Agency for Fundamental Rights (FRA) surveyed in 2008 over 23000 individuals from ethnic minority and immigrant groups about their experiences of discrimination and racist crime in the EU.[8] People from up to three different groups were surveyed in each country.

On the average, 30 percent of the respondents reported having experienced discrimination because of their ethnicity in the course of the past 12 months. Figures for particular groups and particular countries were even more alarming: more than 60 percent of the respondents with Sub-Saharan origins in Malta or with Roma origins in Czech Republic and Hungary reported having experienced discrimination during the past year. The Roma emerged as a particularly discriminated-against group across the EU: of the Roma respondents, on the average 38 percent reported that they had experienced discrimination in access to work, 19 percent said they had been discriminated against at work, 11 percent reported that they had been discriminated against when looking for a house or apartment to rent or buy, 14 percent indicated that they had experienced discrimination by healthcare personnel and 20 percent identified discrimination when in or trying to enter

---

[7] Many researchers have argued that as a result of increased legislative and other measures in this area, discrimination is increasingly taking subtle and less easily recognizable forms. See e.g. National Research Council, *Measuring Racial Discrimination: Panel on Methods for Assessing Discrimination* (Washington DC: National Academies Press, 2004), p. 71.

[8] European Union Agency for Fundamental Rights, *EU-MIDIS: European Union Minorities and Discrimination Survey: Main Results Report* (Vienna: FRA, 2009). Other notable victim surveys in Europe include the following: European Monitoring Centre on Racism and Xenophobia, *Migrants' Experiences of Racism and Xenophobia in 12 EU Member States. Pilot Study* (EUMC, 2006); Anders Lange, *Migrants on Discrimination II* (Edsbruk, 1997); Birgit Møller – Lise Togeby, *Oplevet Diskrimination: En undersøgelse af etniske minoriteter* (København: Nævnet for Etnisk Ligestilling, 1999); and Inga Jasinskaja-Lahti – Karmela Liebkind – Tiina Vesala, *Rasismi ja syrjintä Suomessa: Maahanmuuttajien kokemuksia* (Helsinki: Gaudeamus, 2002).

a shop, during the past year. Discrimination against the Roma was intense, with those Roma who indicated that they had experienced discrimination reporting on the average eleven different incidents in the course of the preceding twelve months alone. Discrimination was however not exclusively directed against Roma or people with Sub-Saharan origins: 36 percent of respondents with origins in North Africa, 23 percent of respondents of Central and East European origin, 23 percent of respondents with Turkish origins, 14 percent of respondents of Russian origin and 12 percent of respondents of Ex-Yugoslav origin indicated that they had experienced discrimination during the past year.[9] This is some evidence for the fact that discrimination in Europe is not simply a Black and White 'race' issue.

According to the FRA's report, only 18 percent of those who had experienced discrimination had reported it to the authorities or at the place where it happened. There were major national differences in the propensity to report discrimination: in Portugal, *virtually nobody* in the Sub-Saharan and the Brazilian respondent groups filed a complaint, whereas in France more than every third victim from the Sub-Saharan group had done this.[10]

A particularly interesting line of survey research has recently focused upon the nature of contemporary discrimination. Many earlier studies focused upon egregious but apparently increasingly infrequent acts perpetrated by individuals with blatantly racist attitudes. This has had the undesired effect that the more prevalent but subtle forms of discrimination, called 'everyday discrimination' in this study, escaped attention. This also led to an underestimation of the prevalence of discrimination. Some recent empirical studies have focused particularly on everyday discrimination, and have indeed provided persuasive and disheartening evidence of the existence of such discrimination for instance in the workplace.[11] These studies have found, *inter alia*, that African American workers in the US experience substantially higher overall rates of mistreatment (not just blatant discrimination) than their ethnic majority counterparts across different types of jobs.

[9] Idem (FRA).

[10] Idem. See also European Monitoring Centre on Racism and Xenophobia, *Migrants' Experiences of Racism and Xenophobia in 12 EU Member States. Pilot Study* (EUMC, 2006).

[11] See e.g. the three studies presented in Elizabeth A. Deitch, 'Subtle Yet Significant: The Existence and Impact of Everyday Racial Discrimination in the Workplace' *Human Relations*, Vol. 56, No. 1, 1299–1324 (2003).

The findings suggest that major proportions of discrimination are subtle, ambiguous and pervasive.[12]

A further line of surveys have focused on potential discriminators instead of potential victims, with equally noteworthy results. For instance, surveys conducted among employers in the Netherlands show that approximately one third of personnel staff acknowledges that they discriminate in recruitment and selection process.[13] Given that we can presume that many people do not report engagement in socially and legally sanctioned behaviour, the actual share of discriminating personnel staff may even be higher than that.

Although victim surveys are instrumental in assessing the dark figure of discrimination, it must be underlined that they measure only the subjective experiences of the respondents. Therefore, on the one hand, the actual prevalence of discrimination may be lower than indicated by the responses, as individuals may sometimes erroneously attribute a negative event to discrimination even if discrimination played no part in it; on the other hand, the prevalence of discrimination may be higher than indicated by the responses, as the respondents may not always be aware of having been discriminated against or may at any rate not be sure enough about it to file a report. Indeed, there is evidence suggesting that victim surveys underestimate the prevalence of discrimination.[14]

Evidence from Discrimination Testing Studies

Discrimination testing is an exceptionally robust and reliable method for exposing even well-concealed forms of discrimination.[15] It is a form of social experiment in a real life situation, and involves the use of two or more individuals ('testers') that are closely matched for all relevant characteristics except for their ethnic background. The testers apply

[12] Idem.

[13] Lilian Goncalves-Ho Kang You – Louise Mulder 'Positive Action: the Dutch Experience' in Appelt, Erna –Monica Jarosch (eds.) *Combating Racial Discrimination: Affirmative Action as a Model for Europe* (Oxford: Berg, 2000), p. 173.

[14] Inga Jasinskaja-Lahti et al, *Rasismi ja syrjintä Suomessa: Maahanmuuttajien kokemuksia* (Helsinki: Gaudeamus, 2002), p. 44. Research has also found a strong, positive correlation between women's perceptions of the gender income differences they were experiencing and econometric estimates of those differences. See Mary B. Hampton – John S. Heywood 'Do workers accurately perceive gender wage discrimination?' *Industrial and Labour Relations Review*, Vol. 47, No.1 (Oct., 1993), pp. 36–49.

[15] This method is also referred to as 'audit testing', 'situation testing', 'in-situ verification testing' and 'paired testing'.

for a job, an apartment or some other good or service, and the outcomes and the treatment they receive are closely monitored. As this method allows for good control over different causal variables, there can be little if any other explanations for resulting differences in treatment than racial or ethnic origin.

The International Labour Organisation (ILO) has, since the early 1990s, sponsored discrimination testing studies in several countries, including Belgium, France, Germany, Italy, the Netherlands, Spain and Sweden, in order to study discrimination faced by immigrants in access to employment. The test group representing the immigrant testers was youngish Moroccan men in the case of Belgium, Italy, the Netherlands and Spain, youngish Turkish men in the case of Germany, immigrants from North and South Africa in the case of France, and second-generation immigrants from Middle East in the case of Sweden.[16] The majority and minority testers were closely matched in terms of human capital, and the treatment they received during the entire span of the recruitment and selection procedure (application by phone/possible personal interview/outcome of the selection) was documented across a high number of test situations in order to rule out the possibility that differences were due to sheer chance. For instance in Italy altogether 633 valid tests were performed. The studies focused on semiskilled occupations, in which it could be presumed that competition was high and where the employers were therefore more likely to be able to 'afford' to discriminate.[17]

---

[16] These groups were chosen because they constitute sizable immigrant-origin groups in these countries and because there was already evidence suggesting discrimination against them.

[17] Open vacancies were mainly found through newspaper advertisements, as the services of employment agencies could not be used since the use of these services tended to require the showing of official identity documents. Frank Bovenkerk et al, *Discrimination against migrant workers and ethnic minorities in access to employment in the Netherlands.* International Migration Papers 4 (Geneva: International Labour Office, 1995). Colectivo IOE, *Labour market discrimination against migrant workers in Spain.* International Migration Papers 9 (Geneva: International Labour Office, 1995). Goldberg et al, *Labour Market Discrimination against foreign workers in Germany. International Migration Papers 7* (Geneva: International Labour Office, 1996). Peter Arrijn et al, *Discrimination in access to employment on grounds of foreign origin: the case of Belgium.* International Migration Papers 23 (Geneva: International Labour Office, 1998). E. Allasino et al, *Labour market discrimination against migrant workers in Italy.* International Migration Papers 67 (Geneva: International Labour Office, 2004). E. Cediey – F. Foroni, *Les discriminations á raison de 'lórigine dans les embauches en France: Une enquête nationale par tests de discrimination selon la méthide du bureau international du travail* (Geneva: International Labour Office, 2007).

The net discrimination rate was found to be very high across all countries, ranging from 33% (Belgium) to 50% (France).[18] This means that immigrant jobseekers were discriminated against in more than every third application procedure in each country. The only exception to this trend was Sweden, where the net discrimination rate – for both immigrant women and men – was 16%, a high figure nevertheless but half of that of the next lowest country.[19] As in each country the testers had been matched across all employment-relevant criteria and they used the same methods for gaining employment, differences in outcomes could not be explained by such factors as inadequate education or training, lack of access to networks and connections to employers, and/or inadequate command of host country's language.

Other Evidence

Official statistics that enable comparisons between immigrants and ethnic minorities on the one hand, and ethnic majority on the other, provide further evidence, circumstantial as it were, about discrimination and other challenges that these groups face. To begin with, statistics from the EU countries show that immigrants and minorities have difficulties in accessing the labour market. This shows already in the participation rates in the labour market: statistics for 2004/2005 show that employment rate of non-EU nationals was 55%, whereas it was 65% for the EU nationals. Those non-EU nationals *in* the labour market were almost two times more likely to be unemployed (17%) than EU-nationals (9%).[20] The economic downturn of 2008/2009 hit non-EU nationals particularly hard, leaving some 20% of non-EU nationals unemployed in 2009.[21] But it seems that the Roma are even worse off in the labour market. A 2003 UNDP human development report on the

[18] The results from Germany are not included here, as the German testing procedure did not cover all the stages of the recruitment, unlike the other country studies. The results portrayed here are rather well in line with the results of respective studies from the United States, where net discrimination rate against Blacks, Asians and Arabs has never been found to be less than 25%. P. A. Riach & J. Rich, 'Field Experiments of Discrimination in the Market Place' *The Economic Journal* 2002, p. F499.

[19] International Labour Office, *Synthesis report: Discrimination Against native Swedes of immigrant origin in access to employment* (International Labour Office, 2006).

[20] European Commission, *Europe's Demographic Future: Facts and Figures on Challenges and Opportunities* (Luxembourg: OOPEC, 2007).

[21] European Commission, *Employment in Europe 2009* (Luxembourg: OOPEC, 2009), p. 40.

situation of Roma in five European countries found Roma unemployment to average 40%, ranging from a high of 64% in Slovak Republic to a 'low' of 24% in Romania.[22]

Statistics also show major disparities in educational attainment between majorities and immigrants. Whereas 35% of the EU nationals had low education, this figure was 47% for the non-EU nationals.[23] There are also disparities in domains such as health and wellbeing, and these disparities have tangible effects. For instance a 2008 European Commission report concludes that "it seems beyond any doubt that life expectancies of the Roma are some 10–15 years lower than those of majority populations".[24] It should be noted that in fact most immigrant and minority groups are, across almost all indicators of well-being, worse-off than the dominant groups.

It must nonetheless be borne in mind that minority and immigrant groups are not always and everywhere in a disadvantaged position in the society. There are immigrant and minority communities that do better, sometimes much better, in terms of employment, education and wellbeing than the majority.[25] And there are individuals within disadvantaged groups that do well in economic and other terms. It is not a natural law that immigrants and minorities are always marginalized and deprived, though persons belonging to these groups do clearly face particular challenges. Were there such a natural law, an ethnically equal society would ultimately be unattainable.

The reality behind the statistics is complex and does not allow for monocausal explanations, but unless there are groups that somehow collectively choose to be poor, to be under- and unemployed, to live in cramped conditions, to suffer ill health and to die prematurely, we must accept there must be something in the society and the way it works that advantages some and disadvantages others. Given the other

---

[22] United Nations Environment Programme, *Avoiding the Dependency Trap: The Roma in Central and Eastern Europe* (United Nations, 2003).

[23] European Commission, *cit. supra* note 20. See also European Commission, *The Social Situation in the European Union 2007 – Social Cohesion through Equal Opportunities* (Luxembourg: OOPEC, 2008).

[24] Communication from the Commission to the European Parliament, the Council, the European Economic and Social Committee and the Committee of the Regions, 'Non-discrimination and equal opportunities: A renewed commitment Community Instruments and Policies for Roma Inclusion' Brussels 2.7.2008, SEC(2008) 2172, p. 3.

[25] See e.g. Jonathan Wheatley, 'The Economic Status of National Minorities in Europe: a Four-Case Study' *Journal on Ethnopolitics and Minority Issues in Europe* 1/2007.

evidence about discrimination, it is beyond reasonable doubt that discrimination is a major source of the disadvantages experienced by immigrants and persons belonging to minorities.

4.2 The Causes of Discrimination

Having now discussed the findings related to the extent and characteristics of discrimination, it is of the essence to examine the factors that underlie that discrimination. To understand the causes of discrimination it is essential to look at what stands behind (i) intentional discrimination, including racism, prejudices, negative stereotypes and self-interested cost/benefit calculations and (ii) unintentional discrimination, including subtle stereotypes and neutral-looking business practices. Whereas the distinction between intentional and unintentional forms of discrimination is not watertight, and is of diminishing importance in the field of law, it helps to underline the point that discrimination is not always or perhaps even predominantly a matter of malicious intentions.

4.2.1 *Racism*

Racism is a relatively recent concept, as the first recorded English language usage is from the 1930s and the term became more widely used only in the 1960s.[26] That said, beliefs, practices and actions that today would be labelled racist did also occur before, but it was not until evidence questioning 'scientific' racial theories started to pile up together with reports describing how these theories were used to justify horrific Nazi campaigns against what they regarded as 'inferior races' that the use of the concept become more widespread.[27]

In its original and most well-established meaning racism refers to a more or less organized collection of beliefs and ideas. Racism in this sense is composed of two primary components:

(i) A belief according to which human beings belong to mutually exclusive races that are distinguished by innate and immutable group characteristics ('racialism'). These group characteristics are

[26] Robert Miles, *Racism* (London: Routledge, 1989); Michael Omi – Howard Winant, 'Racial Formation' in Philomena Essed – David Theo Goldberg (eds.) *Race Critical Theories: Text and Context* (Oxford: Blackwell, 2001), p. 133.

[27] Idem (Miles).

typically seen to include physical traits such as skin colour and psychological and social characteristics such as particular levels of intelligence and criminality. As these traits are perceived to be inherited, the group boundaries are held to be unbridgeable and insurmountable, making preservation of 'racial purity' a typical value held by those infected by racialist thinking.

(ii) The attribution of negative or positive value to the perceived 'racial' characteristics. The evaluation of racial differences is taken to justify the creation of a hierarchy of races, which on its part is taken to justify the discriminatory treatment of the 'inferior'. As both the belief in the existence of separate races and the value basis for their evaluation are often rather unquestionably held, this kind of racism considers inequality and discrimination to be natural and self-evident.

Pierre-André Taguieff, among others, has by means of analysing racist discourses pointed out that racist theories no longer necessarily rely on inherited biological and psychological traits in their argumentation to justify discrimination and exclusion.[28] Another form of racism has emerged which does not focus on racial difference but on cultural difference. Cultures are seen as constitutive of a nation and as mutually exclusive and incompatible. Every nation is considered to have its own, specific culture, the maintenance of which is that nation's duty. In other words, national cultures are to be protected from alien or inauthentic elements. As one comprehensive meta-analytical study concluded, this form of racist ideology often reflects awareness of basic anti-racist norms and rejects blatant expressions of racial inequality.[29] In fact, culturally oriented racism argues that all cultures are equal and important; the problem with it is that it also claims that cultures – and therefore the peoples (nations) that go with them – should preferably be kept separate.[30]

---

[28] Pierre-Andre Taguieff, 'New Cultural Racism in France' *Telos* Spring 90, Issue 83; Martin Barker, *The New Racism* (London: Junction Books, 1981); Etienne Balibar – Immanuel Wallerstein, *Race, Nation, Class: Ambiguous Identities* (London: Verso, 1992).

[29] See e.g. Jessica ter Wal 'Conclusions', in EUMC, *Racism and cultural diversity in the mass media. An overview of research and examples of good practice in the EU Member States, 1995–2000* (Vienna: EUMC, 2002).

[30] For instance one Neo-Nazi went on record at a rally in Bochum, Germany in June 2005 as stating that: "As a National Socialist, I can understand the Jews wanting to have their own nation and putting their interests first; then one must allow the same for the

Culturally oriented racism shares many features with biologically oriented racism, as both essentialize and reify group identity and see groups as homogenous and closed entities separated by insurmountable and unbridgeable differences. Empirical studies suggest that these two forms of racist argumentation are actually very close to each other and that the same people tend to accept both lines of argumentation.[31] One crucial difference exists, though: while biologically oriented racism seeks to justify discrimination and subordination, culturally oriented racism seeks primarily to justify the exclusion or full assimilation of the culturally different. But even this difference actually affirms the common core of the two lines of argumentation. We can see that both serve the same higher-level function: they are essentially and primarily ways to justify group supremacy.[32] The culturally oriented argumentation is only a more recent and presently socially acceptable justification, as speaking about 'racial inferiority' has become unacceptable in mainstream Europe. The lesson here is that people justify or disguise their discriminatory behaviour in ways that change over time under the pressure of what is considered socially acceptable.

The common core of these two conceptions of racism, among other considerations, has led a wide range of scholars to see racism more broadly as any justification or reproduction of domination and/or disadvantage or exclusion along perceived racial or ethnic lines.[33]

German people..." Federal Ministry of the Interior of Germany, *Annual Report 2005 on the Protection of the Constitution*, p. 60. Available at: http://www.verfassungsschutz.de (accessed 1.1.2010).

[31] John Duckitt, *The Social Psychology of Prejudice* (London: Greenwood, 1994), p. 21.

[32] On the nature of racism as an ideological defence of domination and subordination, see Martin Bulmer - John Solomos (eds.), *Racism* (Oxford: Oxford University Press, 1998), and Colette Guillaumin, 'Race and Nature: The system of Marks. The Idea of Natural Group and Social Relationships' *Feminist Issues* 8, No. 2 (1998), pp. 117–135.

[33] According to David T. Wellman, the essential feature of racism is not hostility or misperception, but rather the defence of a system from which advantage is derived on the basis of race. David T. Wellman, 'Toward a sociology of white racism', in Martin Bulmer - John Solomos (eds.) *Racism* (Oxford: Oxford University Press, 1999), p. 181. For Teun A. van Dijk, racism is "a specialized relation between social groups of which the dominant one has preferential access to, or control over scarce social resources, such as residence, nationality, jobs, capital, housing, education, knowledge, health or culture. Racism is the system of inequality that perpetuates this domination of one group (typically white Europeans) over others (in our case non-Europeans)." Teun A. van Dijk, 'Theoretical Background', in Ruth Wodak - Teun A. van Dijk (eds.) *Racism at the Top: Parliamentary Discourses on Ethnic Issues in Six European States* (Klagenfurt: Drava, 2000). Philomena Essed sees racism by definition as "the expression or

Under this line of thinking, what is important are not individual prejudices, hatred, bad intentions or irrational beliefs, but outcomes, the way in which it tends to be the interests of one group rather than those of the other groups that are satisfied in the society.[34] Racism can then reside not just in ideologies but in social structures, everyday practices and even in cognitions and concepts. For instance, for some critical race theorists

> Racism is viewed not only as a matter of individual prejudice and everyday practice, but as a phenomenon that is deeply embedded in language and perception. Racism is ubiquitous and inescapable feature of modern society, and despite official rhetoric to the contrary, race is always present even in the most neutral and innocent terms. Concepts such as 'justice', 'truth', and 'reason' are open to questions that reveal their complicity with power.[35]

Whereas some argue that this broader conception of racism is improperly expanded because it departs from the original usage of the term,[36] it is by no means in any way necessary or even useful to deepfreeze a concept by defining it in terms of some historical 'ideal types'.[37] In a contemporary setting it is not very useful to define racism in terms of Nazism, Apartheid or even xenophobic far-right argumentation as if they embodied timeless, absolute and exclusive forms of racism.[38] In any event it is absolutely necessary to recognize that indeed many kinds of action and practices *may* create or reproduce hierarchical ethnic structures,[39] and that it is the outcomes rather than causes that quite likely are the primary concern for most members of the disadvantaged groups. Given the evidence there is about major intergroup

---

activation of group power" and more precisely as "cognitions, actions and procedures that contribute to the development and perpetuation of a system in which Whites dominate Blacks." Philomena Essed 'Everyday Racism: A new approach to the study of racism', in Philomena Essed– David Theo Goldberg (eds.), *Race Critical Theories* (Oxford: Blackwell, 2002), pp. 179, 181.

[34] Ibid (Essed), p. 183.

[35] Citation from Dimitrina Petrova 'Racial Discrimination and the Rights of Minority Cultures' in Sandra Fredman (ed.), *Discrimination and Human Rights: The Case of Racism* (Oxford: Oxford UP, 2001), p. 46.

[36] E.g. Robert Miles describes these theories as 'inflated'. Robert Miles *Racism* (London: Routledge, 1989), pp. 41 ff.

[37] Philip Cohen 'It's Racism What Dunnit' in Martin Bulmer – John Solomos (eds.) *Racism* (Oxford: Oxford University Press, 1999), p. 271.

[38] Howard Winant, 'Racism today: Continuity and change in the post-civil rights era', *Ethnic and Racial Studies* Vol 21, No 4 (1998).

[39] This is argued e.g. by Howard Winant, *cit. supra* note 38.

differences in wellbeing across the different domains of life, there is a need for a more innovative and comprehensive analysis of the causes of these differences. A focus on institutional (macro-level) racism and everyday (micro-level) racism appears to be a useful and necessary opportunity to draw lessons about our contemporary societies,[40] much like feminism has been able to make major headway by virtue of analysing and criticising structures, social cognitions and everyday practices instead of focusing only on blatant gender stereotypes and patriarchal ideologies and practices.

Explanations of Racism
A complex phenomenon such as racism requires complex theorizing about the factors that contribute to it. A useful distinction can be made between three kinds of explanations: micro-level explanations that relate to individuals and their propensities; meso-level explanations that relate to societies; and macro-level explanations that relate to human nature and other factors that can be thought to transcend the two previous levels.

Micro-level explanations focus on the individual and what makes particular individuals susceptible to racist beliefs. These include:

(i) Prejudices. Prejudice refers to unfairly or unreasonably formed negative opinions, assumptions and/or feelings towards a group of people, and can lie behind discrimination. There are racist prejudices but not all prejudices are racist, which is why prejudices will be separately addressed below.

(ii) Other individual-level factors. Research and profiling data on offenders of racist crimes paint a fairly uniform picture of the offenders. Offenders tend disproportionately to be young males; to be unemployed or in poorly paid, low-skilled and casual employment; to suffer from educational underachievement; and to have a history of prior offending. Many offenders are also under the influence of alcohol at the time of offending.[41] Yet there are many individuals who fit the above-mentioned profile but who nevertheless do not show racist attitudes or engage in racist actions, which is why simplistic causal explanations must be avoided.

---

[40] van Dijk, *cit. supra* note 33.

[41] See e.g. EUMC, *Racist Violence in 15 EU Member States: A Comparative Overview of Findings from the RAXEN NFP Reports 2001–2004* (Wien: Floramedia, 2005).

Meso-level explanations focus upon a range of society-specific factors that are thought to contribute to the conditions in which racism can flourish. These include:

(i) The legacy of particular historical economic, cultural, political and social factors. In this analysis, slavery and the slave trade, segregation, Apartheid, imperialism, colonial conquests, economic exploitation, forced labour and genocidal practices are seen to underlie contemporary racism and racial discrimination. The precise nature of the relationship between historical events and contemporary racism is often not – and indeed probably cannot – be explained in any explicit terms,[42] but undoubtedly the history of domination, exploitation and even extermination can be presumed to create the cognitive and material conditions that form a fertile ground for intergroup animosity and racism.[43] Yet, it must be remembered that racism and discrimination thrive also in societies that have not to any major degree been involved in practices such as the trans-Atlantic slave trade or colonialism.

(ii) Present-day economic, cultural, political and social factors. Various factors are thought to create or contribute to conditions in which racism can thrive. One factor that has garnered interest is the size of the minority population. It is sometimes assumed that rapid increases in the size of the minority population increases hostility towards 'outsiders'. Whereas there is evidence that points towards this conclusion, there is also contra-evidence showing that increases in size have not had this effect and that also small minorities – such as the Jews in Europe – are a major target of racism.[44] Yet another society-specific factor that can have an effect is the degree to which the majority population feels confident in

[42] See however Daniel Goldhagen's account of how anti-Semitism that had developed in preceding centuries contributed to the Holocaust. Daniel Goldhagen, *Hitler's Willing Executioners: Ordinary Germans and the Holocaust* (London: Little, Brown and Company, 1996).

[43] United Nations, *Report of the Seminar on the political, historical, economic, social and cultural factors contributing to racism, racial discrimination and apartheid* (New York: United Nations, 1991). EUMC, *cit supra* note 41, p. 185. Ruth Wodak – Martin Reisigl, 'Discourse and Racism' in Ruth Wodak – Teun A. van Dijk (eds.) *Racism at the Top: Parliamentary Discourses on Ethnic Issues in Six European States* (Klagenfurt: Drava, 2000), p. 36 ff.

[44] EUMC, *cit supra* note 41, p. 184. Karmela Liebkind et al, 'Group Size, Group Status and Dimensions of Contact as Predictors of Intergroup Attitudes' *Group Processes & Intergroup Relations* 2004 Vol 7(2) 145–159.

itself: a confident majority can be presumed to be more tolerant towards minorities. Indeed, in established multiethnic communities, outgroup members are evaluated the more positively the more secure the ingroup members are about their own group and culture.[45] Mary E. Clark, an expert in biology and conflict resolution, has pointed towards a related society-specific circumstance that may be relevant: according to Clark, low stress levels in a society tend to lead to egalitarianism, high stress levels to hierarchy with more aggressive behaviours.[46] The meta-analysis conducted by John W. Berry and others found that the following factors tend to exacerbate the potential for intergroup violence, especially for those identifying strongly with their in-group: great relative inequalities between groups; perceived conflict between group interests; strong norms of physical retribution for perceived injustice; perceptions of group potency; deteriorating material conditions of existence; firmly entrenched scapegoating ideologies concerning the outgroups, along with dehumanizing beliefs about the values that characterize out-group members.[47] Intergroup hostilities, racism and discrimination may also be sparked by local, national or even international incidents and media reports of those incidents.[48] Indeed, the conflict between Israel and Palestinians has resurfaced around the world in many different locations, and the 9/11 attacks and the London bombings were in many places found to increase hostility towards Muslims and those that were thought to be Muslims.[49] But perhaps the most important variable is that of the general social attitude towards racism: if the local or national community actively or passively condones manifestations of intolerance and racism, then these are much more likely to occur.[50]

---

[45] Peter B. Smith – Michael Harris Bond, *Social Psychology Across Cultures* (Essex: Pearson Education Limited, 1998), p. 186; Karmela Liebkind 'Some problems in the theory and application of cultural pluralism: the complexity of Ethnic Identity' in Juha Pentikäinen – Marja Hiltunen (eds.) *Cultural Minorities in Finland: An Overview towards Cultural Policy* (Helsinki: Sivén, 1995).

[46] Mary E. Clark, *In search of human nature* (Routledge, London, 2002), particularly p. 97.

[47] John W. Berry et al, *Cross-cultural psychology: Research and applications*, 2nd ed. (Cambridge: Cambridge University Press, 2002), p. 196.

[48] See e.g. EUMC, *cit. supra* note 41, p. 186.

[49] Idem.

[50] Idem; Duckitt, *cit. supra* note 31.

Macro-level explanations explain racism more or less in terms of human nature and those human propensities that are presumed to be universal and therefore not contingent on time and place.

(i) Conflict Theory. The Conflict Theory, also known as the Competition Theory, holds that competition for scarce resources – this meaning any material or non-material good, benefit or entitlement such as career opportunities – produces conflict. People want to pursue their self-interests to the maximum extent, and because they perceive their interests generally to coincide with those of their ingroup, they react in negative ways to any real or perceived outgroup competition. There is some empirical support for the Conflict Theory: attitude surveys have found resistance to multicultural society to be stronger in countries with a high level of ethnic competition, as indicated by a relatively high level of unemployment, a relatively low GDP per capita, and a relatively high proportion of non-western non-nationals.[51] Also people on low incomes or at the fringes of the society – who can be presumed to be particularly unwelcoming to any further competition – tend to be less favourably disposed towards immigrants and minorities. Yet, support for the theory is not conclusive, as – in opposition to what would be predicted on the basis of the Conflict Theory – the data show that negative attitudes are more prevalent in rural areas where people often have little if any contact with and thereby competition from immigrants or ethnic minorities.[52] It is therefore possible that negative attitudes reflect people's generic fears and insecurities instead of actual competition.[53]

(ii) Social Identity Theory. Social identity theory, as developed by Henri Tajfel and others, is concerned with explaining why and when individuals identify themselves and others as being parts of social groups and how this affects how they behave towards members of their own groups (ingroups) and members of other groups (outgroups).[54] As Tajfel put it, although individuals deal

[51] Marcel Coenders et al, *Majorities' attitudes towards minorities in the old 15 EU Member States: results from the standard Eurobarometers 1997–2000–2003* (Vienna: EUMC, 2005), pp. 40–41.

[52] EUMC, *Majorities' Attitudes Towards Minorities: Key Findings from the Eurobarometer and the European Social Survey: Summary* (Wien: Manz Crossmedia, 2005), p. 22.

[53] Ibid, p. 23.

[54] Henri Tajfel, *Human Groups & Social Categories* (Cambridge University Press 1981).

with individuals, they are not necessarily dealing with each other as individuals.[55] Social Identity Theory proposes that there are three fundamental psychological mechanisms that lead to ingroup favouritism and outgroup discrimination. The first process is that of categorization, that is a cognitive grouping of people into categories. Categorization makes the world more manageable and offers people a foundation upon which to build the social part of their identity. The second process is that of social comparison. Categorization into distinct groups makes it possible to compare groups in terms of their attributes and relative status and power. The third process relates to achieving and keeping a positive self-esteem. As it is a general human characteristic to try to achieve and keep as much of a positive self-image as possible, one tends to value ingroup attributes more positively than those of outgroups. This biased evaluation, and perhaps even more generally the psychological need to advance the relative position of one's own group, can also inform action and motivate discrimination against members of outgroups.[56] There is ample support for the Social Identity Theory, particularly from the so-called minimal group studies. These studies have shown that even in situations where people are randomly assigned into groups, they start to show ingroup favouritism and outgroup discrimination once they are made aware of their group membership. Yet the real-life relevance of the results obtained from these controlled and oversimplified experimental situations is not fully clear. In real life, a person's social identity is derived from multiple group memberships, which in practice means that loyalties criss-cross each other and group boundaries become less meaningful. On the other hand, as the salience of any one social identity depends on the context,[57] in such societies where a particular type of categorization is highly salient, as is the case with 'race' in the United States, Social Identity Theory may have stronger explanatory value. Also the conflict of interests and previous hostility may factor in.[58]

(iii) Anxiety produced by cross-cultural encounters. Cross-cultural interaction may produce anxiety, as the immediate psychological

[55] Ibid, p. 228.
[56] Ibid, p. 174.
[57] See Maykel Verkuyten, *The Social Psychology of Ethnic Identity* (Hove: Psychology Press, 2005), p. 175.
[58] Tajfel, *cit. supra* note 54, p. 268

result of being in a new situation is lack of security.[59] Particularly ethnocentric, aggressive and insecure people appear to be affected by this.[60] Intercultural encounters may cause distressing experiences and prompt social distance particularly insofar as people do not have knowledge about each other's cultural codes.[61] The greatest shock may, however, be the encounter with one's own cultural heritage and the resulting awareness of the degree to which one is a product of it.[62]

(iv) Selfish genes. There is a genre of writing on 'selfish genes' and more generally on the theory of evolutionary biology that asserts that all organisms, including human beings, are driven by the goal of genetic self-preservation.[63] Many writings use these theories to explain kin selection, a form of natural selection that favours altruistic behaviour toward close relatives resulting in an increase in the altruistic individual's genetic contribution to the next generation. As such, these theories offer what appears a 'natural' explanation for positive ingroup and negative outgroup bias. Whereas there are findings that could perhaps be interpreted in favour of these theories,[64] the evidence is at best inconclusive and at worst contradictory, as the theory of selfish genes fails to explain many common phenomena from the use of contraceptives and the general decline of the birth rate in the affluent countries to soldiers joining up against hopeless odds in a battle.[65] Also in other species than humans one comes across behaviour that seems incompatible with direct or indirect self-interest, and for instance Berry et al conclude from all of this that genes are not a deterministic force that pre-empt moral choices.[66]

---

[59] Smith – Bond, *cit. supra* note 45, p. 232.

[60] Ibid, pp. 237, 232.

[61] Discomfort may be produced by a cycle of misattributions (people talk too much or too little, or about the wrong topics). This calls for learning, self-awareness, personal growth and cross-cultural adaptation. Ibid, p. 245.

[62] Smith & Bond, *cit. supra* note 45.

[63] See Richard Dawkins, *Selfish Gene* (Oxford: Oxford University Press, 2006).

[64] For instance, children living with a stepparent are approximately 40 times more likely to suffer physical abuse than those living with two genetic parents, and are 40–100 times more at risk of homicide. Kenrick – Ackerman – Ledlow 'Evolutionary Social Psychology: Adaptive predispositions and Human Culture' in John Delamater (ed.) *Handbook of Social Psychology* (New York: Kluwer Academic, 2003), p. 107. The authors also point out that all human cultures have systems for reckoning kinship, and norms for differential treatment of individuals according to kinship status. Ibid, p. 113.

[65] See generally on this Clark, *cit. supra* note 46.

[66] Berry, *cit. supra* note 47, p. 282

On the basis of the above analysis, it must be clear that there is no single explanation of racism, but rather that the different forms of racism are produced and reproduced by the interaction of criss-crossing social, psychological and possibly even biological factors. Any action against racism must take this into account and avoid simplistic accounts of racism and its remedies.

Who are Racist?

Biologically oriented racism is most commonly associated with openly racist movements such as Neo-Nazism and various factions of Skinheads.[67] These movements typically combine mystical ideas with pseudo-scientific argumentation about races and nations. Skinhead and Neo-Nazi groups may apparently be found all over Europe, but for most EU countries either the size of these groups is not known or this information is not released to the public by the relevant national authorities. One of the few countries where this information exists and is released is Germany, where the calculations from the Ministry of Interior shows that there were 26 600 right-wing extremists in 2009, some 9 000 of whom were considered to have a propensity to use violence.[68]

The second type of racism, cultural racism, is most often associated with extreme rightwing political movements. Political parties that have been accused of anti-immigrant and even xenophobic argumentation have gained a foothold across Europe in recent years. These include Freedom Party in Austria, Flemish Block in Belgium, Danish People's Party in Denmark, National Front in France, Northern League in Italy, and British National Party in the United Kingdom. Many of these fairly well-known parties are perhaps better described as 'ultra-nationalist' or 'populist' rather than 'extreme rightwing' parties, but they do tend either to encourage or tolerate extremist individuals among their

[67] Skinheads and Neo-Nazis should not be conflated with each other. Whereas racist attitudes and shared racist beliefs are typical elements for both movements, skinhead groups typically represent a subculture of loosely-knit young men distinguished by particular kind of clothing and music, whereas neo-Nazis typically represent a better organized group with aggressive support for extreme nationalism and/or National Socialism in some form. One should note that there are also anti-racist Skinheads in Europe, many of which identify with the SHARP (Skinheads Against Racial Prejudice) movement. See e.g. Stefan Rühl – Gisela Will, *National Analytical Study on Racist Violence and Crime*. European Forum for migration studies, Institute at the University of Bamberg.

[68] Bundesministerium des Innern, *Verfassungsschutzbericht 2009* (Berlin: Bundesministerium des Innern), p. 51.

midst. Whereas one should be very careful not to conflate the two kinds of extremist movements together – if not for any other reason but because the political extremists often denounce or at any rate distance themselves from the open racism and racist violence of Neo-Nazis and Skinheads – they are both met with open suspicion and disapproval in many quarters of the mainstream society and are monitored by state authorities and anti-racist organizations.[69] There are, of course, no guarantees that these groups will always remain at the fringes of the society, a fact that has proven itself in practice, as representatives of many extremist parties have in several countries garnered sufficient popular support to enter Parliaments and national governments.

Though they are in some respects at the margins of the mainstream society, the impact of these movements is by no means marginal. One way to assess their significance in real life is to look at the extent of right-wing extremist criminal activity recorded by the police in different countries. Whereas Austria, Germany, France and Sweden are the only EU countries that collect and publish statistics about these kinds of activities on a yearly basis, already this narrow pool of evidence shows that extremist groups are not just alive and well but highly active: the most recent data available at the time of writing shows that an extraordinary 17 176 'right-wing extremist crimes' were recorded in Germany in 2007; 387 such crimes were recorded in Sweden, 280 in Austria and 247 in France.[70] The overwhelming majority of these offences appear to have been crimes involving illegal propaganda activities or incitement to hatred and violence.[71] Qualitative information shows that the use of internet to promote racism and to facilitate communication by the right-wing extremist groups is a clear trend throughout Europe.[72] Yet another powerful indicator of the impact of

[69] Paul Gilroy, 'The End of Antiracism' in Philomena Essed – David Theo Goldberg (eds.) *Race Critical Theories: Text and Context* (Wiley-Blackwell, 2001), p. 252; EUMC, *Racist Violence in 15 EU Member States: A Comparative Overview of Findings from the RAXEN National Focal Points Reports 2001–2004* (Wien: Floramedia, 2005), p. 184.

[70] European Union Agency for Fundamental Rights, *Annual Report 2009* (Vienna: FRA, 2009), p. 27.

[71] An upward trend in extremist criminal activity since the year 2000 has been recorded in Germany (+9.8%) and Austria (+1.2%), whereas a downward trend has been recorded in France (–17.9%) and Sweden (–1.5%). Idem.

[72] Ibid, p. 127. EUMC, *Trends and Developments 1997–2005. Combating Ethnic and Racial Discrimination and Promoting Equality in the European Union* (EU Agency for Fundamental Rights, 2007), pp 37 ff.

extremist groups is the degree of support they find in the mainstream society. Research evidence from Finland shows that ten percent of the population openly accepts Skinheads' *actions* (i.e. not just arguments) against foreigners.[73]

The above evidence notwithstanding, it would be a gross mistake to attribute racism solely to Skinheads, Neo-Nazis and extreme far-right parties. The price of over-identifying racism with the activities of extremist groups is that the more mainstream racism is downplayed or even denied. The existence of mainstream racism is evident for instance in the results of the 1997 Eurobarometer survey that asked randomly chosen respondents in the then 15 EU member states to indicate how racist they felt they were. The respondents fell rather evenly into three equally large categories: those that indicated that they were 'quite' or 'very racist', those that said they were 'a little racist', and those that said they were not at all racist.[74] This point is worth rephrasing: *those who feel that they are not at all racist constitute a minority in Europe.* In another Eurobarometer survey, from the year 2000, every seventh respondent went so far as to say that they feel that the presence of people of another 'race' is 'disturbing'.[75] Other opinion surveys, such as the 2003 European Social Survey, suggest that these measures for self-assessed racism cannot be attributed to excessive self-criticism: a *majority* of the respondents in Europe expressed resistance to diversity and immigrants and perceived the existence of a collective ethnic threat.[76]

The above-mentioned findings are corroborated by the results of attitude surveys that have posed more specific questions about belief in racist statements. Such surveys have been conducted for instance in Finland and Germany. In Finland surveys have found considerable agreement with biologically oriented racism, as almost half of the population was found to agree with the view that "certain races are not at all fit for living in a modern society" and as every third person agreed

[73] Magdalena Jaakkola, *Suomalaisten suhtautuminen maahanmuuttajiin vuosina 1987–2003*. Työpoliittinen tutkimus No 286 (Helsinki: työministeriö, 2005), p. 90.

[74] European Commission, *Eurobarometer Opinion Poll no 47.1. Racism and Xenophobia in Europe* (European Commission, 1997).

[75] European Commission, *Eurobarometer No 53* (European Commission, 2000).

[76] The survey was conducted in the then 15 EU countries and selected candidate countries. EUMC, *Majorities' Attitudes Towards Minorities: Key Findings from the Eurobarometer and the European Social Survey. Summary* (Wien: Manz Crossmedia, 2005).

with the statement that some nations are more intelligent than others.[77] In Germany every seventh person agreed with such blatantly racist statements as "whites are justifiably the leading group in the world" and "there are population groups that are worth less than others".[78] There is also support for the culturally oriented racism: in Germany more than every fourth person was of the view that immigrants should be sent back home when jobs are in short supply, and that foreigners living in Germany should not be allowed to participate in any aspect of political life. Two out of three were of the view that foreigners should assimilate more with the German lifestyle.[79] In Finland every fourth person was of the view that people from different cultures should live separately and not mix, and that the practice of Islam should not be allowed because it threatens "our own culture".[80] In Germany half of the population reported that they would feel uncomfortable about moving to an area with a high percentage of Muslims.[81]

The role of mainstream racism becomes even more apparent in light of the fact that members of extremist groups account only for a small portion of all discrimination. Evidence from Finland, France, the Netherlands and Sweden – the only EU countries for which this kind of information is available – shows that members of extremist groups are responsible for 5%–18% of all racist crimes.[82] Furthermore, as the majority of racist crimes involve either propaganda, threats or assaults,

---

[77] Jaakkola, *cit. supra* note 73, p. 90.

[78] Wilhelm Heitmeyer, *Deutsche Zustände - Folge 1* (Frankfurt am Main: Suhrkamp Verlag, 2002).

[79] Statistisches Bundesamt, *Datenreport 2002* (Bonn, 2002).

[80] These findings should be interpreted in light of the results of the Eurobarometer surveys, according to which Finns tend to hold the most positive views about immigration in the EU and have more positive attitudes towards minority groups than people in the EU in the average. European Commission, *Special Eurobarometer Survey 273, European Social Reality*, p. 71. EUMC, *Attitudes towards minority groups in the European Union. A special analysis of the Eurobarometer 2000 survey* (Vienna: SORA, 2001).

[81] Frank Asbrock et al 'The Road to Negative Behaviour: Discriminatory Intentions in the German Population' *International Journal of Conflict and Violence* Vol. 1(1) 2007, p. 9.

[82] In France, only 9% of racist incidents were attributable to the extreme right in 2002; In the Netherlands, less than 5% of all discriminatory offences and racists acts that took place in 2002 could be attributed to extremists; In Sweden, 18% of "xenophobic crimes" (excluding anti-Semitism) were connected with the White Power movement. Data from Finland shows that Skinheads commit less than ten per cent of *all* racially motivated crimes, and three fourths of these cases were assaults, not acts of discrimination. Tuunia Keränen, *Poliisin tietoon tullut rasistinen rikollisuus Suomessa 2004* (Helsinki: Edita 2005).

not discrimination, it is likely that extremists are responsible for an even smaller portion of all discrimination, because profiling data for Skinheads and Neo-Nazis shows that they are not very likely even to be in a position where they could discriminate, such as being a banker or a HR director at a major company. There is therefore strong evidence for the view that it is the 'ordinary people' who are responsible for the overwhelming majority of cases of discrimination, not the extremists.[83]

The excessive focus on extremist groups serves essential social and psychological functions: one of them is that it allows for the externalization of racism and discrimination, which allows the 'mainstream society' and its members to maintain a positive, rational and tolerant self-image.[84] Racism is always located somewhere else: in the past (slavery, colonialism), abroad (Apartheid), at the margins of the political life (extreme right wing) or at the margins of the society (Neo-Nazis, Skinheads).[85] Whereas most people do formally acknowledge that they are at least somewhat racist, meaning that they recognize that they have negative feelings towards those who are ethnically different, they commonly attempt to justify these negative emotions in terms of pseudo-rational arguments, meaning that they see their own racism more in terms of 'wise caution' than prejudices. At the same time they appear to acknowledge that the truth value or persuasiveness of their arguments is questionable; otherwise they would not recognize racism in themselves.[86] Typical pseudo-rational arguments for exclusion include all-familiar statements such as "immigrants exploit the social security system", "immigrants take away employment from others", "immigrants commit more crimes than members of the mainstream

---

[83] See also EUMC, *cit. supra* note 41.

[84] The perception of racism as an anomaly in the otherwise (mostly) healthy society committed to equality often also figures in the speeches and writings of those in the anti-discrimination camp, and has long traditions there. For instance, Martin MacEwen writes about Gunnar Myrdahl's classic study "The American Dilemma" (published in 1944) that it characterises racism as "the repairable failure of the liberal, democratic practices in respect of black rights to coincide with liberal, democratic theory." Martin MacEwen, 'Promoting equal opportunity: the enforcement agency', in Martin MacEwen (ed.), *Anti-Discrimination Law Enforcement* (Aldershot: Avebury, 1997), p. 9.

[85] Cf. Teun A. van Dijk 'Denying Racism: Elite Discourse and Racism' in Philomena Essed - David Theo Goldberg (eds.) *Race Critical Theories: Text and Context* (Oxford: Blackwell, 2001), p. 310.

[86] Timo Makkonen 'Ennakkoluulojen ja jälkiviisauden välissä: Suomalaisten ulkomaalaisasenteista' *Maailmanpyörä* 3/2002.

society", "I have nothing against immigrants personally, but my employees dislike them, and therefore I can't hire them", "I am not racist, my best friend is Black, but we should not take in more immigrants".[87] Denial of racism, through these various argumentative strategies, is probably its most common form. As this denial serves to let biased practices and attitudes to go on unchecked, the society-wide failure to recognize racism and to react to it may be characterized as key elements of structural racism.

That said, it would be misleading, ethically problematic and unwise to label all or nearly all individuals and societies as 'racist'. As Dimitrina Petrova has pointed out, racist beliefs and attitudes can be present in a person's mind with varying degrees of conviction, awareness, scope and intensity.[88] Furthermore, people tend to have mixed attitudes: whereas most Europeans acknowledge that they are at least somewhat 'racist', a clear majority of two thirds is also of the view that ethnic diversity enriches national culture and that measures are needed to provide equal treatment in the field of employment.[89] A person can therefore harbour both racist and egalitarian beliefs and attitudes. Similarly, while patterns, policies and measures that disadvantage immigrants can be identified in all societies, together with a collective failure to fully remedy them, all countries in Europe have adopted legislation and policies with a view to combating racism and discrimination. There is certainly a point after which societies and individuals can be described as 'racist', but given the totalizing properties and the ultimate moral condemnation implied by the label 'racist', that point should not be reached too easily.

4.2.2 *Prejudices*

Prejudice refers to unfairly or unreasonably formed negative opinions, assumptions and/or feelings towards a group of people. It often has to

---

[87] Not only adults but also young people tend to offer these explanations for their prejudices, see e.g. Marek Fuchs - Siegfried Lamnek - Ralf Wiederer, *Querschläger. Jugendliche zwischen rechter Ideologie und Gewalt* (Leverkusen: Leske & Budrich, 2003).

[88] Dimitrina Petrova 'The Denial of Racism' in Claude Cahn (ed.) *Roma Rights: Race, Justice, and Strategies for Equality* (Amsterdam: IDEA, 2002), p. 208.

[89] European Commission, *Eurobarometer: Discrimination in the European Union*, Special Eurobarometer 263, fieldwork June-July 2006 (European Commission, 2007).

do with lack of knowledge: when faced with incomplete, inconsistent or inexistent information, people may base their actions on whatever instinctive feelings or intuitions they happen to have instead of engaging on a search for more information. Some people prefer their gut feelings even over solid information or its rational analysis. The downside of all of this is that the instincts and emotions that come into play may represent faulty or incorrect generalizations or rigid and inflexible attitudes that constitute poor bases for making judgements. Whenever they form a certain tendency or a pattern, they may be called prejudices.

One way to understand prejudices is to break the concept down into three constitutive components. These are:[90]

(i) Negative stereotypes (cognitive component). Stereotypes are standardised mental pictures held in common by members of a group about another group or phenomenon. Stereotypes typically represent oversimplified or over-generalized opinions: the perceived group characteristics are assumed to apply to each member of the group.

(ii) Negative feelings (affective component). Research indicates fear and anger to be the emotions that are the most central elements in prejudices.[91] Negative feelings may result from a negative evaluation of the stereotypes attached to a group: the more we believe outgroups are dissimilar to our ingroup standard, the more hostile we are towards them.[92]

(iii) Behavioural patterns, such as keeping social distance (behavioural component). The notion of social distance refers to the absence of, in particular, voluntary contact between the prejudiced person and members of the group against which he/she is prejudiced.[93] Contemporary social psychology has found that prejudices are reduced by voluntary intergroup contacts, especially if the contacts are of sufficient frequency, duration and

[90] See e.g. Duckitt, *cit. supra* note 31, and Berry et al, *cit. supra* note 47, p. 371 ff.

[91] Asbrock et al, *cit. supra* note 81, p. 15.

[92] Smith & Bond, *cit. supra* note 45, p. 192.

[93] Social distance can be defined as a reflection of the preferred degree of closeness in interpersonal contact and relationships with members of other group. Duckitt, *cit. supra* note 31.

> closeness and take place between people of equal status.[94] Particularly intergroup friendships have been found to be important.[95]

These three components typically reinforce each other, forming a prejudiced attitude, but the relevance of each of them probably varies from person to person and situation to situation. That said, recent research has emphasised the affective component as the core element of prejudice.[96] The three components have systemic properties, as negative feelings lead to social distance (avoidance of contact), which in its turn creates the necessary space for the development and maintenance of negative stereotypes, which again serve to reinforce negative feelings.

Early theories of prejudice, developed by Theodor Adorno and his colleagues, explained prejudices in terms of special personality types. Adorno proposed that certain family conditions, particularly the experience of excessively harsh and moralistic parenting, produce an outlook on life which is over-deferential towards authority, socially conservative, hostile towards minorities or other non-dominant groups and dominated by a simplistic and categorical perceptual and cognitive style.[97] Field research and laboratory experiments have indeed established a positive correlation between authoritarianism and prejudices.[98] A report on the European Social Survey found that so-called 'intermediate characteristics' play a part as well:

> the more people perceive decreases in their personal safety, or the more they distrust other people or distrust political leaders, or the more they consider themselves to be politically right-wing, or the more they

[94] See e.g. T. F. Pettigrew – L.R. Tropp 'Does intergroup contact reduce prejudice? Recent meta-analytic findings' in S. Oskamp (ed.), *Reducing Prejudice and Discrimination* (Hillsdale, NJ: Lawrence Erlbaum, 2000). It should, however, be noted that contact can also have negative effects: even a single experience with prejudice can have a considerable, negative impact on how group members feel in intergroup contexts, and on their expectations for future cross-group interactions. Linda R. Tropp 'The Psychological Impact of Prejudice: Implications for Intergroup Contact' *Group Processes & Intergroup Relations*, 2003 Vol 6 (2), pp. 131–149.

[95] See e.g. the special issue on intergroup contact of the journal *Group Processes & Intergroup Relations*, 2003 Vol 6(1).

[96] Asbrock et al, *cit. supra* note 81, p. 7.

[97] Theodor W. Adorno et al, *The Authoritarian Personality*, Abridged edition (New York: Norton, 1982), p. 11.

[98] Karmela Liebkind – Juha Haaramo – Inga Jasinskaja-Lahti, 'Kannattaa tutustua paremmin', in Karmela Liebkind (toim.) *Monikulttuurinen Suomi: Etniset suhteet tutkimuksen valossa* (Helsinki: Gaudeamus, 2000), pp. 56–61.

> perceive ethnic minorities to pose a collective threat, the more they favour ethnic exclusionism.[99]

Surveys often find demographic variations in the levels of prejudice: studies have quite consistently found men to be more prejudiced than women, older individuals to be more prejudiced than young adults, the less educated to be more prejudiced than the well-educated, and people living in rural areas to be more prejudiced than urban people. According to some survey results, people on low incomes and people who are in manual jobs or self-employed tend in general to have more negative attitudes.[100] Some studies, but not all, have also found a difference in the levels of prejudice between people who have different political leanings.[101]

Important findings point towards the conclusion that prejudices against different societal groups are interrelated. This means that if a typical European male, a nominally Christian middle-class heterosexual man, is prejudiced against ethnic minorities, he is also likely to be prejudiced against women, sexual minorities, religious minorities and even the homeless.[102] Studies also indicate that those who harbour intense prejudices are often not at all ashamed of it; it is the less prejudiced individuals who are self-critical about their departures from the egalitarian standards.[103]

While individual personality dynamics therefore have been found to have a considerable role to play, it is social norms rather than these personality dynamics that determine the overall levels of prejudice in particular groups and societies. This is because our opinions are strongly influenced by such factors as the opinions of those around or near us, the norms of our group, and the relationships between our group and the other groups.[104] Levels of prejudice also appear to be lower in societies that are also low on measures of hierarchy and conservatism and high on civic participation and tolerance.[105]

---

[99] M. Coenders. et al, *Majorities' attitudes towards minorities in European societies: results from the European Social Survey 2002–2003* (Vienna: EUMC, 2005), paragraph 4.0.

[100] EUMC, *Majorities' Attitudes Towards Minorities: Key Findings from the Eurobarometer and the European Social Survey. Summary* (Wien: EUMC, 2005).

[101] Asbrock et al, *cit. supra* note 81.

[102] Ibid, p. 7.

[103] Smith & Bond, *cit. supra* note 45, p. 195.

[104] Rupert Brown, *Prejudice – Its Social Psychology* (Oxford: Blackwell, 1995), p. 11.

[105] Smith & Bond, *cit. supra* note 45, p. 195.

These findings indicating the importance of social factors align well with historical experiences, ranging from Nazi Germany to the genocide in Rwanda, that have shown that levels of socially shared prejudices and hatred can skyrocket in a matter of months, even weeks, which indicates that prejudices cannot be explained simply in terms of relatively stable personality traits.

4.2.3 *Stereotypes*

Stereotypes may involve beliefs about the traits, values, behaviours, opinions or indeed beliefs of typical persons from a group.[106] It is useful and necessary to distinguish prejudices from stereotypes. The latter are not necessarily negatively loaded or completely out of touch with reality, but can also be positive and have an element of truth in them.[107] Stereotypes serve at least two functions: they facilitate the formation of social identity by making it possible to compare essentialized ingroup and outgroup traits, and they reduce uncertainty and guide behaviour by means of offering pre-established expectations.[108] Stereotypes can originate from the culture in which people are socialized, from observed intergroup differences (e.g. cultural and socio-economic differences) and also from a cognitive bias resulting from the very process of categorical differentiation between groups of people. Because of their socially constructed character, stereotypes are often culturally specific, which means that a complete analysis of prejudices in a particular context requires the taking into account of a complex mix of historical, political, economic and social structural forces that are at work in that context.

Stereotypes can be harmful because the very act of stereotyping necessarily involves and calls for intergroup comparisons and evaluation. It is particularly beliefs about the values of outgroup members that matter: a perception that benevolence and universalism are part of an outgroup's value base is associated with lower rejection of those group's members.[109] Large differences in terms of perceived values and

---

[106] Ibid, p. 185.

[107] See e.g. Duckitt, *cit. supra* note 31, p. 118.

[108] Cf. Smith – Bond, *cit. supra* note 45, pp. 186–187.

[109] Ibid, p. 193. Readiness for outgroup social contact among Jews and Arabs in Israel has been found to be positively associated with universalism and self-direction domains of values and negatively with tradition, security and conformity values. Ibid, p. 194.

perceived humanity appear to be critically dangerous for intergroup harmony; the view of the enemy as evil sustains all group conflicts.[110] On the other hand, a moderate difference in terms of perceived values may even be socially necessary for the purpose of maintaining social identities, in addition to which it has been submitted that interacting social groups often come to hold *positive* stereotypes about one another.[111]

Relationship between Attitudes and Discrimination

The relationship between attitudes (such as prejudices) and behaviour (such as discrimination) is a complex one. Research into this suggests that there is a causal connection between prejudices and discrimination: prejudices arguably determine the overall tendency of a person to discriminate, but cannot predict specific single acts with much accuracy.[112] A prejudiced person does not necessarily act in accordance with the prejudices: a prejudiced person may be barred from discriminating in an environment where discrimination is generally deemed unacceptable and where other people might come to react to it. In another environment, for instance in a peer group of like-minded individuals, or where there is no social control, or where there is impunity on part of the police or the society at large, the same person is more likely to engage in discrimination. A prejudiced person may have mixed motives, in which case the motive to discriminate is just one among many. A person who is strongly motivated to observe the law, and who knows that discrimination is illegal, may be thus precluded from taking discriminatory action.

Overall, the present mainstream scholarly opinion appears to be that the relationship between prejudices and discrimination is substantial: prejudices tend to generate discrimination.[113] Prejudices and stereotypes are dangerous also because they can be used to justify and legitimize existing imbalances in the social and power relations within a society.[114] They may therefore explain a portion of the reluctance to combat and remedy discrimination in an effective way.

---

[110] Ibid, pp. 186–187.
[111] Ibid, pp. 185–186.
[112] Duckitt, *cit. supra* note 31, p. 41.
[113] See Asbrock et al, *cit. supra* note 81, p. 8 and the references cited therein. Deitch, *cit. supra* note 11, p. 1301.
[114] Smith – Bond, *cit. supra* note 45, p. 188.

Simplistic responses such as awareness raising campaigns that aim at providing accurate, stereotype-busting information are not necessarily the right or sufficient antidote to prejudices, as people attend to, and rehearse, prejudice-consistent information more frequently than inconsistent information.[115] Instead, one useful approach is to motivate people to attend to individual differences instead of category-based stereotypes.[116]

4.2.4 *Statistical Discrimination*

Statistical discrimination is a phenomenon that has been studied particularly in the field of economics.[117] It occurs when people purposefully use overall beliefs about a group – stereotypes – to make decisions about an individual from that group. The individual may or may not correspond to the stereotype, and therefore predictions and decisions that rest on statistical discrimination carry the risk that they will prove entirely wrong. Those that engage in statistical discrimination are willing to take the risk, because they believe that they will hit the mark more often than they will miss it – hence the term *statistical* discrimination.

We all use statistical predictions every day, as they appear to make life easier. We assume, for instance, that a person with a university diploma must be of a certain intellectual capacity. Yet, even in this rather straightforward scenario we might be wrong, for instance if the diploma was forged or if, upon closer scientific examination, having a university degree does not correlate positively with intellectual capacity. When employers, service providers or for instance the police – profiling being closely related to statistical discrimination – act upon ethnic stereotypes they are on even more shaky grounds, as ethnic origin usually doesn't correlate well or at all with factors that are relevant for decision-making, unlike having a university degree.

That said, statistical discrimination can sometimes be based upon knowledge of actual distributions of characteristics within different population groups, not just beliefs about such distributions. An employer might, for instance, have observed that many immigrant

---

115 Ibid, p. 191.

116 Ibid, p. 237.

117 See e.g. David A Strauss 'The Law and Economics of Racial Discrimination in Employment: The Case for Numerical Standards' in Christopher McCrudden (ed.) *Anti-Discrimination Law* (Aldershot: Dartmouth, 2004).

groups, on average, have more children than the majority population – and be right about it – and deduce from this that an immigrant worker would be more likely than a majority worker to take time off work to take care of her children in the event of one of them falling sick, and on the basis of this analysis prefer to hire a worker with the majority background. Our employer would quite likely think that this would be a perfectly rational and legitimate decision,[118] but could be wrong because not all immigrants have large families, and many of those that do, have extended families that can take care of the children when they get sick.

The main problem with acts of statistical discrimination is not the prejudices but the fact that they often rest on shaky assumptions and unfairly disadvantage entire groups of individuals. To operate on the basis of shaky presumptions when other people's major events of life are at stake shows a high level of indifference, and suggests that there is a fine line between prejudices and incorrect statistical assumptions.[119] A further problem is that sometimes differences between groups, for instance in the average level of educational achievement, are themselves the result of discrimination, and statistical discrimination in those circumstances simply adds to the injustice. Statistical discrimination can also lead to underinvestment in education and other human capital among members of worse-off groups, because individuals adjust their aspirations and expectations in view of the fact that their individual efforts are not necessarily recognized and rewarded because of their affiliation with a particular group.[120] Because of these considerations, the use of group characteristics to make decisions about individuals, for instance in the context of employment, is usually not allowed under contemporary anti-discrimination laws.

An analogous problem arises when decision-makers have differing amounts of information about different groups. If an employer deems persons belonging to a minority to be just as talented as persons belonging to a majority, but she herself is from the majority group and

[118] Larry Alexander 'What makes wrongful discrimination wrong? Biases, preferences, stereotypes, and proxies' in Christopher McCrudden (ed.) *Anti-Discrimination Law* (Aldershot: Dartmouth, 2004).

[119] Melissa S. Williams, 'In Defence of Affirmative Action: North American Discourses for the European Context?' in Erna Appelt – Monica Jarosch (eds.) *Combating Racial Discrimination: Affirmative Action as a Model for Europe* (Oxford: Berg, 2000), p. 64.

[120] Strauss, *cit. supra* note 117, p. 311.

therefore finds it easier to identify talented members of that group, it is likely that she will seek new employees from the ranks of the majority. While the employer may find this practice rational in terms of cost/efficiency-calculation, it unfairly disadvantages persons belonging to the minority on account of their group membership, and is suspect on those grounds.

4.2.5 *Unintentional Biases*

Evidence has recently started to come in showing that not all discrimination, or perhaps even most of it, can be attributed to racism, prejudices, opportunistic 'statistical' calculations or other forms of intentional discrimination.[121] Whereas we probably still can't fully grasp the dynamics and importance of unintentional discrimination, scientific research has recently produced important findings in this respect.[122]

Contrary to what perhaps most people would expect, even well-meaning individuals who do not knowingly harbour prejudices may engage in discrimination on account of the stereotypes they have. One of the reasons for this is that people can act on internalized but unconsciously operating and subtle stereotypes. Because stereotypes are socially created and maintained, we can presume that a good portion of individuals in any given society share them. Research evidence suggests that socially learned biased cognitive categories and associations may persist and be engaged automatically, in the matter of milliseconds, and that this shapes the behavioural responses of even good-intentioned persons.[123] If a stereotype is available in the memory, relevant cues such as a job applicant's foreign name can activate it without need of awareness, intention, effort or control.[124] Stereotypes

---

[121] See e.g. National Research Council, *Measuring Racial Discrimination*. Panel on Methods for Assessing Discrimination. (Washington DC: National Academies Press, 2004), and the references mentioned therein; Matthew D Lieberman, et al 'An fMRI investigation of race-related amygdala activity in African-American and Caucasian-American individuals' *Nature Neuroscience*, Vol 8 No 6 June 2005.

[122] The different reasons that are reviewed here appear in no particular order, as we do not know the precise extent to which each one of them explains discrimination.

[123] See National Research Council, *cit. supra* note 121, and the references mentioned therein; Matthew D. Lieberman et al. 'An fMRI investigation of race-related amygdala activity in African-American and Caucasian-American individuals' *Nature Neuroscience*, Vol 8 No 6 June 2005.

[124] Susan M. Andersen et al 'Automatic Thought', in E. T. Higgins & A. W. Kruglanski (eds.), *Social psychology: Handbook of basic principles* (New York: Guilford Publications, 1996), p. 141.

are activated just too quickly, even automatically, for us to prevent them from having an effect, although it appears to be the case that if specifically and effectively primed to think about them, people internally motivated to avoid stereotypes are able to reduce their salience and effect.[125] This can take place through self-regulation of stereotyping involving deliberate corrective processes that overturn activated stereotypes or automatic processes.[126] Much also depends on the strength of the stereotype (which category dominates if a person is perceived as belonging to multiple categories) and on the social context (whether social knowledge places emphasis on a particular category).[127]

Expectation States Theory, a well-established theory in the field of social psychology, provides one explanation of how status stereotypes can come to play in group interaction situations without us being aware of their involvement. This theory holds that people align performance expectations, such as making good decisions, with status characteristics, such as being wealthy, even when the two do not in fact correlate positively. Empirical research has found, for instance, that in group interaction situations, the ideas of people who talk more in groups are often judged to be more valuable than those offered by less talkative members; that people with more prestigious jobs are more likely to be chosen leader of a group, such as a jury, even when their job has little if anything to do with the task at hand; and that ideas are often thought to sound better when offered by someone perceived to be attractive.[128] Further, group experiments have shown that the arbitrary allocation of differential pay levels to participants creates corresponding influence hierarchies among them during interaction.[129] This underlines how status differentials create performance expectations even when status is not in fact linked to actual personal performance. Given that many minority and immigrant groups suffer from a negative public image and poor socio-economic status, it is clear that their social status tends to be low and that the members of these groups are put at a disadvantage on those grounds.

---

[125] Ibid, p. 148.
[126] Ibid, p. 144.
[127] Ibid, p. 149.
[128] Shelley Correll – Cecilia L. Ridgeway 'Expectation States Theory' in John Delamater (ed.), *Handbook of Social Psychology* (New York: Kluwer, 2003), p. 29.
[129] Ibid, p. 38.

The aforementioned performance expectations shape behaviour in a self-fulfilling fashion. The greater the performance expectation of one actor compared to another, the more likely the first will be given chances to speak up and offer task suggestions, the more likely his or her suggestions will be positively evaluated, and the less likely he or she will be to be influenced when there are disagreements.[130] Therefore members of an economically better-off group gain a systematic advantage in gaining influence and esteem in the majority of situations involving individuals from several groups. Indeed, Shelley Correll and Cecilia L. Ridgeway conclude that members of ethnic minorities, due to status beliefs, must actually perform at higher levels than members of status groups to be judged as equally competent.[131] This of course flies in the face of the prevailing conception of Europe as the bastion of meritocracy, where only individual ability and ambition matter.

The concept of discrimination, also in the field of law, as will be seen, has become detached from discriminatory intentions. Indirect forms of discrimination are of particular relevance here because they encompass practices and criteria that *appear neutral* but have an unjustifiable adverse effect on members of a group. This form of discrimination can be very difficult to detect, since by definition members of all groups are treated in the same way, 'neutrally', and the disadvantage that results can often be rendered visible only through statistical means that reveal the differential impact the treatment has upon some group. For instance, informal recruitment through word-of-mouth, a widely used business practice that as such does not look suspect, can have discriminatory effects where the existing workforce consists mainly of members of the majority: immigrants are excluded from the start from the potential pool of job applicants, because they will be outside the existing contact networks and never learn about the job openings. In this way, subtle forms of discrimination can be an integral part of the very culture of an organisation without anyone ever intending it. What is at stake here is negligence or ignorance rather than prejudices or outright racism.

The extent and impact of unintentional forms of discrimination are very difficult to measure.[132] Given however the fact that many of the

---

130 Ibid, p. 31.

131 Ibid, p. 41.

132 Discrimination testing experiments can indeed reveal instances of both intentional and unintentional discrimination, but they cannot tell to what extent each form of discrimination is responsible for the overall discrimination.

psychological and social psychological mechanisms that are at work here appear to be universal, there is reason to believe that its impact is substantial and generally underestimated.

4.3 The Effects of Discrimination

Research into the dynamics of discrimination tends to disproportionately focus upon perpetrators and the causes of discrimination instead of focusing on the victims and the effects of discrimination.[133] Yet it is not possible to fully understand the factors that contribute to discrimination without looking at the impact of discrimination, as the two are connected. It is therefore absolutely necessary to investigate how discrimination affects the individuals and groups concerned and even the entire society.

Individual and Group Level Effects

Discrimination has a range of effects upon its victims. To begin with, discrimination constitutes the denial of an opportunity, benefit or some other good, such as employment. In that way, it prejudices the rights and opportunities of its victims and is intrinsically liable to produce a negative social and economic impact. Discrimination can even trigger or contribute to a downward spiral in which loss of employment leads into loss of many other things, from housing to employment-related social networks. Indeed, discrimination in one field of life can have an impact on other fields of life, and its effects may be passed on from one generation to the next.[134] As an example:

> Discrimination in access to employment, or discrimination in the conditions of work (such as the payment of a lower salary), may lead to a situation where the discriminated-against person has to relocate, with his/her family, to a less expensive neighbourhood. This neighbourhood probably has greater concentrations of people who face various degrees of deprivation, providing for a potentially hostile environment. The services in the area, including health services, are likely to be inferior to those provided in the better-off neighbourhoods. The children of the family are likely to attend a lower-quality school that has fewer teachers

[133] See e.g. Inga Jasinskaja-Lahti – Karmela Liebkind – Tiina Vesala, *Rasismi ja syrjintä Suomessa: Maahanmuuttajien kokemuksia* (Helsinki: Gaudeamus, 2002), p. 42.

[134] On the intergenerational transmission of disadvantages, see e.g. European Commission, *The Social Situation in the European Union 2007 – Social Cohesion through Equal Opportunities* (Luxembourg: OOPEC, 2008).

> and material resources and where the general attitude climate poses low expectations in terms of educational achievement. This is likely to impact their success in the school, and later on limit their employment opportunities.[135]

As this example highlights, disadvantages in general tend to reinforce each other. But it is essential to notice that discrimination not only has tangible material consequences but is also a direct assault upon the victim's identity, as it is on that basis that the person is discriminated against. Discrimination embodies, in essence, a denial of the victim's equal moral worth. A substantial amount of research has recently investigated the psychological effects that such an assault produces.[136] On the basis of a systematic meta-analysis of 138 studies Yin Paradies has concluded that experiences of discrimination are associated, on an individual level, with symptoms relating to stress and depression.[137] Further research suggests that the negative health effects of everyday discrimination are equally, if not more, profound than those of more blatant forms of discrimination.[138] The impact of perceived discrimination on psychological states has been found to be direct, strong and instant, while it is more indirect and slower on overall physical health status.[139] These negative health effects add to the negative material effects engendered by discrimination.

Yet the impact of discrimination on its victims goes even further than this. Jan Döring has theorized, on the basis of empirical findings,

---

[135] Example inspired by National Research Council, *cit. supra* note 121 and Frank Bovenkerk, *A Manual for International Comparative Research on Discrimination on the Grounds of "Race" and Ethnic Origin* (Geneva: International Labour Office, 1992). On the interrelationships between origin, discrimination and socio-economic status, see David R. Williams 'Race, Socioeconomic Status, and Health: The Added Effects of Racism and Discrimination' *Annals New York Academy of Sciences* 1999; 896: 173–188.

[136] Jasinskaja-Lahti et al, *cit. supra* note 133, p. 45.

[137] Yin Paradies 'A systematic review of empirical research on self-reported racism and health' *International Journal of Epidemiology* 2006 35(4), pp. 888–901.

[138] Deitch, *cit. supra* note 11, p. 1302. It has been suggested that everyday discrimination is a major stressor because it consists typically of events, such as exclusion from the social activities at the workplace, whose cause is not evident, unlike what is typically the case with more blatant forms of discrimination. This is because it may be easier to cope with the thought that one was mistreated because of irrational prejudices held by another person than with the thought that one was mistreated because the other person disliked one's personality. See ibid, p. 1305.

[139] Inga Jasinskaja-Lahti – Karmela Liebkind – Riku Perhoniemi, 'Perceived ethnic discrimination at work and well-being of immigrants in Finland: The moderating role of employment status and work-specific group-level beliefs' *International Journal of Intercultural Relations* 31 (2007), p. 225.

that many individuals who experience acts of racial or ethnic discrimination or violence, interpret these experiences as manifestations of more general and widespread hostility towards their group, an interpretation that is likely to trigger negative feelings towards the outgroups. His data provides strong support for the view that experiences with discrimination lead immigrants and persons belonging to minorities to perceive greater bias within public institutions and the majority group.[140] The inability of the law to prevent discrimination from taking place appears not just to erode confidence in the public authorities, but also more generally in the legal system and even the society as a whole.[141] Such experiences also engender a feeling of economic exploitation, lead to a generalized expectation of discrimination and make people less likely to identify with the mainstream society, hampering the integration of minorities into the society at large.[142] Perception of the society as racist may also lead to politicization of social identity.[143] All of this means that victims of discrimination become more aware of the existence of discrimination and more likely to grow increasingly sensitive towards racist jokes and other such signs of inequality. Discrimination also quite self-evidently fosters intergroup tensions and leads to social disintegration.

People who experience discrimination cope with it in various ways in terms of psychological reactions and behavioural responses.[144] Active behavioural responses, such as seeking professional or peer support or reporting of the incident to the relevant authorities, appear in general to be positively correlated with the mitigation of the negative health effects of discrimination, although also other factors play a role.[145] In the extreme, however, active coping may predict militant protest, especially when discrimination is perceived as widespread, the

[140] Jan Döring 'Influences of Discriminatory Incidents on Immigrant's Attitudes Toward German Society' *International Journal of Conflict and Violence* Vol 1(1) 2007, pp. 19–31.

[141] Idem (Döring); See also Kurt Salentin 'Determinants of Experience of Discrimination in Minorities in Europe' *International Journal of Conflict and Violence* Vol 1(1) 2007, pp. 32–50.

[142] Idem (Salentin); Döring, *cit. supra* note 140.

[143] Marie-Claude Gervais, *The Drivers of Black and Asian people's perceptions of racial discrimination by public services: A qualitative study* (West Yorkshire: Communities and Local Government Publications, 2008).

[144] Jasinskaja-Lahti et al, *cit. supra* note 139.

[145] The results across different studies are, however, equivocal to some extent. Idem.

majority as hostile and the own ingroup as relatively deprived.[146] This leads to poorer socio-cultural adaptation and constitutes a barrier to integration.

Many cope with their experiences more passively, however. For many discrimination is a humiliating experience that they do not want to deal with in public. Yet for others discrimination may be such a frequently recurring event that it has become an almost daily experience. Some may explain their experiences in terms other than discrimination, and may even blame themselves for their experiences. What is common for these victim groups is that they are not likely to take action, such as filing a complaint. Indeed, only a small minority of those who have experienced discrimination take legal action.[147]

The fact that victims of discrimination may not take legal action does not mean that their experiences would not affect their behaviour. One typical behavioural response is to engage in a so-called *strategy of avoidance*, by which the person concerned seeks to - knowingly or not - avoid situations in which the likelihood of ending up discriminated against is particularly high.[148] For an example, a person engaging in avoidance strategies may seek only jobs for which there is less competition - typically the less well-paid jobs - where it is thus less likely that an employer can 'afford' to discriminate. These self-imposed restrictions may be 'effective' in decreasing the likelihood of being discriminated against, but they also severely limit the opportunities of the persons concerned and are dysfunctional from the point of view of the society. Also people who have encountered forms of prejudices can be presumed to be more likely to engage in avoidance strategies, even if they have not experienced outright discrimination.[149] In addition, and

---

[146] Smith - Bond, *cit. supra* note 45, p. 281.

[147] One study, conducted by the EUMC and covering 12 European countries, found that, on average, only 14% of those who reported having experienced ethnic discrimination had reported the incidents to the competent authorities. Significant differences between countries in the propensity to report were found, being as 'high' as 37% in the UK and as low as 1% in Spain. EUMC, *Migrants' Experiences of Racism and Xenophobia in 12 EU Member States. Pilot Study* (Wien: EUMC, 2006).

[148] According to the results of the EU-MIDIS survey, one in three Roma, one in four Sub-Saharan African and one in five North African living in the EU area employ avoidance behaviour for fear of being a victim of racist crime. European Union Agency for Fundamental Rights, *EU-MIDIS at a glance: Introduction to the FRA's EU-wide discrimination survey* (Budapest: Elanders, 2009), p. 12.

[149] Linda R. Tropp 'The Psychological Impact of Prejudice: Implications for Intergroup Contact' *Group Processes & Intergroup Relations*, 2003 Vol 6 (2), pp. 131–149.

perhaps even more importantly, also people who have not themselves experienced discrimination or prejudices, but who are aware of the existence of widespread discrimination and prejudices against members of their group, may also engage in avoidance strategies. It is only rational for people who anticipate low future returns to skills to be reluctant to invest time and energy in acquiring those skills.[150]

Organization and Society Level Effects

It is increasingly recognized that ethnic and racial discrimination is bad for business. First of all, discrimination in hiring and firing practices means that the organization is not using all the available talent, as decisions are made on the basis of irrelevant factors not related to job performance. Workforce diversity is also widely believed to boost creativity and productivity, and these benefits are obviously not reaped where there is discrimination.[151] Harassment and other discrimination in workplaces, whether perpetrated by the co-workers or the employer itself, is likely to degenerate staff morale, decrease the time spent on actual work and is likely to lead to absences and to increased staff turnover when the discriminated-against individuals no longer can or will tolerate being treated in that way.[152] Businesses that are known to discriminate can also experience the deterioration of their corporate image and reputation and thereby the loss of interest on the part of some of its constituencies. Discriminating businesses may also have to become involved in costly legal proceedings. All of this is, of course, bad for business.[153]

That said, businesses and other organisations may sometimes also benefit from discrimination, particularly in the short run. As John

---

[150] See National Research Council, *Measuring Racial Discrimination*. Panel on Methods for Assessing Discrimination (Washington DC: National Academies Press, 2004), and the references mentioned therein.

[151] For instance in a survey conducted in Finland, 90% of the respondents (who were HR managers at private and public sectors) believed that workplace diversity boosts creativity, and 82% were of the view that it increases productivity. Ari Haapanen, *Monimuotoisuusbarometri 2007 – ikä ja monikultuurisuus haasteena ja voimavarana* (Espoo: Frenckell, 2007).

[152] Research indeed suggests the existence of such organizational costs. Being targeted for everyday discrimination at the workplace negatively impacts several facets of well-being (including job satisfaction), and appears to lead to absenteeism and other withdrawal behaviours and a more general lowering of organizational commitment. Deitch, *cit. supra* note 11.

[153] European Commission, *The Business Case for Diversity: Good practices in the workplace* (Luxembourg: OOPEC, 2005).

Gardner argues, immigrants and minority people are often cheaper to hire or to do business with than majority people because they have fewer valuable options to choose from, and often lower expectations.[154] This makes them vulnerable for discrimination. Abuse of cheap labour distorts competition, however, by imposing an unfair burden on law-complying businesses and therefore undermines the functioning of the market forces. The macro-economic effects do not stop there, as discrimination – because the right people are not matched to the right jobs, or may not even have jobs to begin with – leads to suboptimal use of human resources, leading to decreased tax revenues and increased social and health expenditure.[155] It is in the interests of each member of the society that immigrants and persons belonging to minorities do not remain undereducated, underemployed and underpaid. The society, as a whole, should be understood to be one of the victims of discrimination, and reversely, it should be understood to have a major stake in fighting it.

The Vicious Circle of Discrimination and Disadvantage

The above-described discussion has shown how discrimination is not just a menace to its victims but also to the society at large. It has also illustrated how discrimination at one point in time can have repercussions across several fields of life and across multiple generations. In effect, these processes limit opportunities, perpetuate stereotypes and prejudices and sustain social and economic disparities, thus multiplying the effect of the individual events of discrimination. In the worst-case scenario, on the societal level, widespread discrimination triggers a vicious circle where the different forms of discrimination lead to accumulation of material disadvantages on part of the minority and immigrant groups, which increases social distance (lack of voluntary contact) and reinforces stereotypes and negative attitudes, which then

---

[154] John Gardner 'Private Activities and Personal Autonomy' in Bob Hepple and Erika Szyszczak (eds), *Discrimination: The Limits of Law?* (London: Mansell 1992), p. 166.

[155] It is difficult to quantify in any exact terms how much racial and ethnic discrimination costs to societies. The approximate cost of disproportionately lower levels of employment of older people, resulting from structural factors and outright age discrimination, has been estimated in the United Kingdom to cost the country's economy £19–31 billion every year in lost output and taxes and increased welfare payments. National Audit Office, *Welfare to work: Tackling the Barriers to the Employment of Older People* (September 2004).

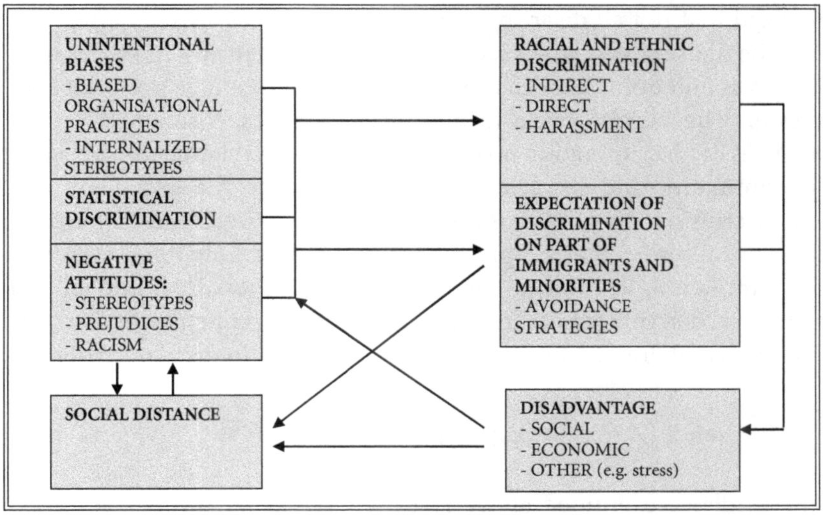

Figure 1. *Vicious circle of discrimination*

again increases the likelihood of discrimination, and so on, *ad infinitum*, as described in the following figure.

This figure is illustrative of some of the social forces that play a part in creating the circumstances in which discrimination continues to thrive. It is by no means exhaustive, in that it does not take into account the role played by intervention measures or the extent to which other factors than discrimination explain socio-economic disadvantages experienced by immigrants and persons belonging to minorities – indeed, it should be noted that disadvantages as such feed stereotypes and prejudices, irrespective of their root cause.[156] It should also be

[156] There can be, for instance, broad cultural value patterns that either favour individual achievement or commitment to collectivist goals, that may to some extent explain variations in levels of ambition on an individual level. While it may safely be assumed that discriminated-against groups are worse off than they would be if they were not discriminated against, it is remarkably difficult to tell the effect of the different factors from each other. Some researchers have used regression analyses in an attempt to control the other relevant variables, such as the average level of education, in an effort to estimate the extent to which disparities in e.g. income or employment level result from discrimination. For a case study of how immigrants' human capital and social capital are linked to their deprivation, see Perttu Salmenhaara, 'From Horizontal to Vertical Divides: Immigrant' Employment in Finland in the 1990s', *Finnish Journal of Ethnicity and Migration*, Vol. 3, No1/2008.

realized that not all discrimination leads to material disadvantages.[157] Yet, the figure shows why exactly all the efforts made by countries over the years and even decades to fight discrimination have not been successful. The vicious circle formed by the causes, forms and consequences of discrimination is simply so strong, the relationship between discrimination and disadvantages just so intimate, that racial and ethnic discrimination is hard, if not impossible, to overcome. In particular, a social order that simply concentrates upon individual events of discrimination, without taking measures to address institutional and structural discrimination and the causes and consequences of discrimination, is inherently incapable of putting an end to discrimination.

4.4 Conclusions

The evidence examined above gives rise to the following five broad conclusions.[158]

First, discrimination is highly pervasive in 21st century Europe. The evidence from a variety of discrimination testing studies, victim surveys and other forms of quantitative and qualitative research is simply too strong and consistent to allow for any other conclusions. The evidence has demonstrated the negative economic, social and health effects of discrimination, and how discrimination affects not just its direct targets, but also people who are related to them, people who come from the same social groups, businesses and the society at large. It has also shown that discrimination is not perpetrated by a few extremists that belong to fringe groups, but that it is the average Joe

[157] This would categorically be the case with some types of discrimination, such as denying access to a restaurant, which is unlikely to have a socio-economic impact. It is also true for many individuals that they increase their efforts when they experience or expect to experience obstacles. A persistent job-seeker may be repeatedly discriminated against in access to employment, except for once, and thus in the end be able to obtain a position that matches his or her qualifications. Therefore even repeated events of discrimination may not always lead to tangible differences in outcomes.

[158] Two issues need perhaps to be raised here. First, although it may be asked whether empirical findings about discrimination tell about discrimination in the sense that it is understood in the field of law, it can safely be assumed that *when examined as a whole* the empirical studies do indeed to a good extent tell about *de jure* discrimination. This is especially the case with findings that emanate from discrimination testing studies and complaints data. The 'legal validity' of individual studies, especially those that survey subjective experiences, is less obvious, unless corroborated by other evidence. Second, the conclusions presented here as well as elsewhere in this study are based upon the evidence available at the time of the writing, and will need to be reviewed when new evidence comes up.

and Jane who are responsible for the majority of instances of discrimination. It has also shown that discrimination cannot simply be explained in terms of individual racism or prejudices, as also unconscious stereotypes, organisational cultures and social structures play an important part.

Second, there is a need to recognize 'everyday racism and discrimination'. The evidence suggests that contemporary forms of discrimination are increasingly subtle and difficult to detect, which also means that they are patently difficult to prove legally. Victims are not necessarily aware of the fact that they have been discriminated against, or at any rate they may not be confident enough about it to take legal action. Perpetrators, on the other hand, are not necessarily aware of the fact that they have engaged in discrimination. It could be, for instance, that a particular neutral-looking recruitment method that an employer uses impacts a particular group negatively and thereby constitutes indirect discrimination. In effect, it can be difficult to detect discrimination.

Third, there is a need to see discrimination and unequal treatment in a broad perspective. The episodic analysis of discrimination is clearly insufficient and must be replaced with one that sees the individual episodes in their broader social, economic and historical context. The society should be concerned not only with individual events of discrimination, but also with the institutional and systemic properties of discrimination and its causes and consequences. The fight against discrimination can proceed successfully only upon a recognition of the social origin of stereotypes, prejudices and racism, and of the way in which most, if not all, members of our societies partake in them, and of the way in which many everyday practices and actions disadvantage immigrants and minorities, even if all of this does not correspond to the positive, 'civilized' self-image of Europeans.[159] There is also a need to acknowledge that not all racism and discrimination can be attributed to outright prejudices, as powerful but hard-to-identify group identity dynamics and socially learned unconscious stereotypes may influence behaviour.

---

[159] Studies conducted by Stanley Milgram and others proved, already in the 1960s, the futility of the 'civilized' self-image of the western world. Milgram and his colleagues showed through real-life experiments that people are predisposed to inflict severe pain on others, even against their own personal convictions, when told to do so by an authority figure. Stanley Milgram, *Obedience to Authority: An Experimental View* (London: Printer and Martin, 2005).

Fourth, evidence suggests that racial and ethnic discrimination cannot be eliminated, at least not in the short term. Yet that is exactly the reason why this should be attempted. The evidence shows how discrimination prejudices the rights and opportunities of its victims and assaults their health and wellbeing, places their families at risk of social and economic disadvantages, undermines the achievement, aspirations and integration of the discriminated-against groups, leads to a waste of human resources, distorts competition, causes social disintegration and unrest, and damages the public economy by compromising productivity, increasing social and health expenditure and decreasing tax revenues. Any of these reasons alone would be a sufficient reason for zero tolerance of discrimination, but their combined effect requires society to take discrimination seriously and to spare no effort in an attempt to eliminate discrimination.

Finally, the fight against discrimination requires action on a broad front and the proactive and innovative use of a wide range of measures. Perhaps the most central problem in the fight against discrimination is passivity and the narrow selection of measures used that are over-optimistically hoped to do the trick. The failure to design and implement proactive strategies to fight discrimination is quite evidently linked to the above-mentioned failure to appreciate the pervasiveness of discrimination, the failure to see racism and discrimination in their broader social, cultural and historical context, and the failure to recognize structural, institutional and everyday forms of racism and discrimination.

The finding that various forms of discrimination are so pervasive in the present-day Europe flies, of course, in the face of the widespread belief that Europe is the champion of modernism, rationalism, individualism and egalitarianism, and a bastion of meritocracy where individual achievement is based solely on individual ability and ambition. Indeed, there is palpable and widespread reluctance in Europe to recognize everyday discrimination and racism, and even more so institutional and structural discrimination, and the way they permeate our societies at all levels. This reluctance is at least partly cultural, cognitive and psychological in origin: Europeans want to see themselves as civilized, rational and tolerant – particularly when contrasted with 'others' that are supposed to be violent and intolerant, such as Arabs and Muslims – and at any rate not racist, particularly when contrasted with Neo-Nazis or the South-African Apartheid regime, the 'paradigmatic' representatives of racism.

PART TWO

THE RESPONSE

5 ANTI-DISCRIMINATION LAW: PRELIMINARY ISSUES

5.1 On the Sources of Law

The previous chapters have shown racial and ethnic discrimination to be pervasive, complex and ultimately probably ineliminable problems in contemporary Europe. The purpose of the following chapters is to examine and assess the effectiveness of the international and European legal response to these problems. The primary focus will be on international and EU law.

Sources of international law, also in the field of human rights, are generally taken to include international conventions, international custom and general principles of law.[1] The analysis will focus primarily on treaty law, given the high number of international and European conventions that deal with the subject area at hand, but occasional references will be made also to customary law and general principles of law. Also EU law will be approached both from the perspective of legal instruments and general principles.

The prohibition of discrimination has come to form an elementary part of contemporary international and European law, and is explicitly dealt with by almost every legal instrument that deals with human rights and fundamental freedoms. The main focus of this study is on these instruments and their provisions. Yet it is useful to take note of the fact that the principle of non-discrimination is not only bolstered and enforced by the specific provisions that explicitly deal with it, but implicitly by almost every single human rights provision, as these are usually worded in universal language, such as "*everyone* has the right to education" and "*no one* shall be subjected to arbitrary arrest, detention or exile". In these two ways, explicitly and structurally, the principle of equality and non-discrimination runs through all human rights treaties and declarations like a red thread.

---

[1] This is the conventional view on sources, and is based on Article 38(1) of the Statute of International Court of Justice. Article 38(1) also mentions "judicial decisions and the teachings of the most highly qualified publicists of the various nations" as subsidiary means for the determination of rules of law. The conventional view is somewhat limited, however. See Jan Klabbers, 'Constitutionalism and the making of international law' *No Foundations* No. 5, 9 April 2008.

This study will focus on eleven documents, most of which are legally binding. These are the following: Universal Declaration of Human Rights, ILO Convention No 111 on Discrimination (Employment and Occupation), UNESCO Convention against Discrimination in Education, International Convention on the Elimination of All forms of Racial Discrimination, International Covenant on Civil and Political Rights, International Covenant on Economic, Social and Cultural Rights, European Convention on Human Rights and Fundamental Freedoms, European Social Charter (revised), Framework Convention for the Protection of National Minorities, European Charter of Fundamental Rights, and EU Racial Equality Directive. Two of these legal instruments, the UN Convention on the Elimination of all forms of Racial Discrimination and the EU Racial Equality Directive, focus exclusively on racial and ethnic discrimination, whereas the other instruments are of a more general nature.

Despite the elementary character of the principle of non-discrimination, these instruments and their non-discrimination provisions differ from each other to the extent that it will be necessary to review them separately. As will be seen, the many differences do not allow us to construct a uniform, systematic approach to anti-discrimination law as if it had a single common core, although a degree of convergence has emerged in some respects particularly through scholarly and institutional interpretative practices. With a view to the differences of the various instruments, it must at this point be emphasized that an individual is always entitled to the best protection provided by any applicable instrument. The fact that another legal instrument provides for weaker protection cannot compromise the protection provided by an applicable instrument.[2]

5.2 The Hard but Basic Questions

In everyday discussions the notion of discrimination is used in a straightforward manner. It is more or less presumed that it is relatively clear and settled what the notion 'discrimination' means. Definition of discrimination as, say, 'unfair treatment', might garner a good deal of popular support. Yet, like all abstract notions, also 'discrimination' turns out to be a lot less intuitively clear and straightforward when it is

---

[2] One must also keep in mind that a particular treaty or a provision may not be binding upon a particular state because of non-ratification or a reservation.

subjected to closer scrutiny. If discrimination is taken to be about unfair treatment, then what is 'unfair'? Is making racial and ethnic distinctions always unfair? Are there situations in which making distinctions is not unfair, but allowed? More fundamentally, are there situations where reasons of fairness not only allow but *require* the making of ethnic distinctions? Equally fundamentally, is discrimination unfair because it is based on irrational or morally reprehensible motivations, or is it unfair because it causes undeserved harm to its victims – should the society, and the law, be concerned with motives or outcomes? And if discrimination is about unfair treatment, what is meant by 'treatment'? Does it encompass acts of omission as well as acts of commission? Does it encompass *practices* such as informal and haphazard recruitment methods? Does it cover the substance of laws or only their application, or both? And in which situations should the prohibition of discrimination apply? Should we consider, for instance, that there is a sphere of private life within which individuals must be left alone to act, if they so wish, upon their personal biases, however reprehensible we might think these biases to be? Most people in contemporary Europe would probably hold that anti-discrimination law should not say anything about the ethnic mix of our personal networks, but should the law say something about treating people equally when selling a house? And would it in that context make a difference if the seller was a private person or a realtor? What is discrimination and what is not? To what extent should people be protected from it by law? And how?

Whereas people engaged in everyday discussions have the luxury of choosing whether or not to address the above questions, this is not the case with those charged with applying or otherwise dealing with the law. Decisions will have to be made, questions must be answered, cases be found for the plaintiff or the respondent. Sometimes the legislator has explicitly taken (a more or less clear) stand on the above questions or some of them; often scholars have come to develop (a range of) doctrinal positions on them; but at the end of the day the individual judges have to take a stand on them. One of the key values that arguably guides the making and application of law in Europe today is the aspiration to achieve a good degree of predictability and legal certainty.[3] This value calls for a principled approach to questions of law

[3] This is clear, for instance, in the practice of the European Court of Human Rights, which requires that for a domestic law to be considered 'a law' for the purposes of the

and a measure of precision in legal matters. One of the key questions, therefore, is whether, and if yes, to what extent, international and European anti-discrimination law provides for legal certainty in the matters at hand.

The Questions

The purpose of the following chapters is to examine the international and European legal response to racial and ethnic discrimination. A structured approach is adopted and each instrument is analyzed with respect to the following five sets of questions:

(i) The concept of discrimination

The first issue to be examined with respect to each legal instrument is how it conceptualizes 'discrimination'. Under this heading the analysis will address – albeit sometimes only tacitly – three more specific questions. First, how the provision is worded; is it formulated openly, in broad and general – or even vague and confusing – terms, in which case it leaves much room for doctrinal developments, interpretations and controversies, or is it 'closed', in which case the drafters have sought to prescribe the criteria that are to be considered when the law is applied.[4] Answering this question will give us some insights about the nature of anti-discrimination law and whether that has something to do with its relative lack of success in eliminating discrimination.

Second, given the need to tackle everyday discrimination, which can come in relatively subtle forms and in acts and practices that appear neutral but are discriminatory in their effects, it must be examined whether these instruments recognize and prohibit indirect discrimination and practices such as harassment. Another important question in this respect is whether the definition of discrimination is of

---

European Convention and its many clauses that allow limitations to rights if they are "prescribed by the law" or "in accordance with the law", that 'law' must be accessible, clear and predictable in its application. See e.g. ECtHR, *Times Newspaper and others* v. *United Kingdom*, judgment of 26 April 1979. That the law, also and in particular international law, often fails to achieve predictability and legal certainty is another matter. See Martti Koskenniemi, *From Apology to Utopia. The Structure of International Legal Argument* (Cambridge: Cambridge University Press, 2005).

[4] Both the 'open' and 'closed' formulations may be problematic. Open formulations leave much room for discretion to those applying the law and remove many key questions beyond democratic decision-making and control. Closed formulations are risky in that the legislator cannot possibly foresee all the situations in which the provision in question will be applied, and therefore the application of rigid provisions may lead to results not intended by the legislator.

such a character that it manages to cope with institutional and systemic forms of discrimination. In particular, is the definition of discrimination capable of being applied not just to acts of commission but also to acts of omissions, and not just to rigid rules or decisions, but also to less formal practices?[5]

The third aspect addresses the potential weaknesses that come in the form of provisions and doctrines that provide for exceptions, derogations and justification of actions and practices that would otherwise constitute discrimination. Are they so broad or is their impact so unclear that they compromise effective protection against discrimination?

(ii) Material scope

A key factor that determines the impact of anti-discrimination law is the material scope of application of that law. Given our specific focus on everyday discrimination, it must be examined whether, and to what extent, the principle of non-discrimination applies in the fields of employment, education and provision of goods and services. In relation to this, it is crucial to examine, with respect to each scrutinized instrument, whether it requires the state to provide protection – in these fields – in relations between private parties, or whether it is confined to the exercise of public power.[6] If the law does not reach to areas such as employment and provision of services, or if it does not reach into the relations between private individuals, then the law will not be able to cope with everyday discrimination. These questions are not moot legally, as international law is primarily about legal relations between states and as treaty provisions cannot bind private individuals, and as discrimination is something that each country has to tackle with domestically.

(iii) Grounds

There are two issues that merit our attention under this heading. Firstly, and quite obviously, it must be examined whether the instruments at

[5] Another interesting set of questions relates to segregation, the provision of 'equal' services separately for different groups, also for instance with respect to *de facto* residential segregation, a phenomenon that is familiar in all the metropolises of the world.

[6] In the US, for instance, racial discrimination in the use of public powers has been forbidden since 1868, but it was long held that the Congress could not legislate against private discrimination or affirmatively to promote 'race' equality. It was only in 1964 that the Supreme Court upheld the power of Congress to reach certain forms of private conduct. Louis Henkin 'National and International Perspectives in Racial Discrimination' *Human Rights Journal* 4 (1971), p. 265.

hand prohibit discrimination on the grounds of 'race' and ethnicity. They can do that either explicitly or implicitly. In relation to this it will be examined whether these concepts have been defined (with varying degrees of authority) either in the instruments themselves, or in the practice of the supervisory organs or the pertinent legal literature relating to these instruments. This will not be done simply for the sake of satisfying academic curiosity, but for the sake of addressing the thorny problem that the law, imbued with the desire for legal certainty, has to grapple with these highly elusive concepts. There are genuine legal problems here: if the law prohibits indirect discrimination on the grounds of 'race', and defines indirect discrimination in terms of disparate impact inflicted upon (persons belonging to) a particular 'race', then demonstration of it can often only take place by means of statistics that compare the situations of persons belonging to different 'races'. But if there are no separate 'races' to begin with, or if at any rate the boundaries of such groups cannot be drawn in any even remotely objective way, as has been argued in chapter 2, how can group categories be constructed for the purposes of preparing the kind of group-based statistics that the demonstration of indirect discrimination requires?

Secondly, it should be examined whether the law is able to cope with intersectional discrimination. Evidence from different countries shows that such claims can constitute up to 50% of all discrimination claims.[7] Therefore attention will be paid to how the law takes into account the fact that 'race' and ethnicity may intersect with other factors such as gender to produce very specific types of discrimination.[8]

(iv) Enforcement and remedies

It is often simplistically assumed that for society to tackle undesirable behaviour, all it has to do is to enact a law prohibiting such behaviour, and that will be the end of it because people will abide by the law. Such a naïve belief in the power of the law to bring about social change by itself is manifestly unfounded. Evidence to this effect is abundant. For instance in the United Kingdom, the police records some five million

---

[7] Ontario Human Rights Commission, *An Intersectional Approach to Discrimination*. Discussion paper, 9 October 2001. Available at: http://www.ohrc.on.ca (accessed 1.1.2010).

[8] See generally on multiple and intersectional discrimination, European Commission, *Tackling Multiple Discrimination: Practices, policies and laws* (Luxembourg: OOPEC, 2007).

crimes – acts defined as punishable by the penal law – each year, and the British Crime Survey, whose figures can be assumed to be closer to the correct mark on the extent of actual crime, estimates that in fact approximately 11 million crimes are made each year.[9] The situation is similar in all other countries as well. It is therefore obvious that the simple enactment of a law prohibiting certain kind of behaviour is not enough to eliminate that behaviour.

The effectiveness of the law depends to a great extent on how it is enforced, on the chosen methods of ensuring or compelling observance of and obedience to that law. It is not enough to simply proclaim theoretical 'rights' and 'freedoms' that are not enforced or that possibly even cannot be enforced. In this respect it is pertinent to examine how the legal instruments under scrutiny envisage the ensuring of observance of anti-discrimination law. Do they envisage setting up special enforcement agencies, charged with overseeing the observance of the law? Do the instruments give their intended beneficiaries the right to a remedy, both in the procedural sense of availability of judicial or other mechanism for the enforcement of the law, and in the substantive sense of redress? Do they envisage specific sanctions to be imposed on perpetrators of discrimination?

This study focuses on domestic remedies, not on state responsibility in the sense of remedies that come into play when a state has breached its obligations under international law. The existence of international monitoring mechanisms – political, quasi-judicial and judicial – is important for the purposes of holding state parties accountable for the implementation of the obligations they have assumed and for the purposes of guiding the construction of legal opinion as to what, in more precise terms, is the scope and nature of these obligations. However, from the point of view of victims of discrimination, it is the existence of domestic remedies that is of chief importance. Of course, domestic remedies may not exist if the state concerned has not fulfilled its international obligations, and that is where the existence of international monitoring and complaint mechanisms is indispensable. But even then, the starting point is the existence and primacy of national remedies, and international mechanisms form only the second line of

[9] See e.g. Home Office, *Crime in England and Wales 2008/09* (edited by Alison Walker, John Flatley, Chris Kershaw and Debbie Moon, Home Office, July 2009).

defence.[10] Not focusing upon domestic remedies would be to completely misunderstand the nature of human rights and the prevalence of everyday discrimination: international monitoring mechanisms are always complementary in relation to the domestic protection of human rights.[11]

(v) Nature of state obligations

It is generally though not uncritically accepted, also in the human rights circles, that international human rights law forms part of the general regime of public international law.[12] However, unlike most other parts of international law, human rights instruments primarily create obligations towards individual right-holders rather than towards other states. This may be described as creating a vertical relationship between a state and its subjects, rather than a horizontal relationship between states.

State obligations in the human rights sphere are generally described in terms of negative obligations – what states must refrain from doing – and positive obligations – what states must do in order to comply with

---

[10] As a rule, a complainant must have exhausted domestic remedies before complaining to the international treaty bodies; this reinforces the primacy of the domestic remedies.

[11] See e.g. Allan Rosas - Martin Scheinin, "Implementation Mechanisms and Remedies" in Asbjørn Eide - Catarina Krause - Allan Rosas (eds.), *Economic, Social and Cultural Rights: A Textbook* (2nd ed, Dordrecht: Martinus Nijhoff Publishers, 2001), p. 452.

[12] For instance the Vienna Declaration puts international human rights instruments squarely within the context of general international law by stating that the protection and promotion of human rights should be conducted "in conformity with international law" (Article 7). Also the various treaty bodies have on many occasions referred to general principles of international law, as embodied for instance in the Vienna Convention on the Law of Treaties. See also the position adopted by the International Law Association in its Resolution No 4/2008 *International Human Rights Law and Practice*, adopted at the 73rd Conference of the International Law Association, held in Rio de Janeiro, Brazil, 17–21 August 2008. That said, many human rights bodies and scholars have, particularly in matters relating to the interpretation of human rights treaties and the reservations made to such treaties, seen a need to adapt the principles of general international law to better accommodate the special nature of human rights instruments. See e.g. the approach of the ECtHR, including the separate opinions, to questions of interpretation in the *Golder* case. For a systematic review of the various theoretical positions, see Martin Scheinin 'Human Rights Treaties and the Vienna Convention on the Law of Treaties - Conflicts or Harmony?' in Venice Commission (ed.), *The status of international treaties on human rights* (Strasbourg: Council of Europe Publishing, 2006). See also Louis Henkin 'Introduction' in Louis Henkin (ed), *The International Bill Of Rights: The Covenant on Civil and Political Rights* (New York: Columbia University Press, 1981), pp. 14–17.

the law.[13] Under a fairly common doctrine, rights, and in particular economic, social and cultural rights, impose three kinds of more specific obligations upon states bound by them: (i) the obligation to *respect*, which is basically a negative obligation to refrain from infringing a right; (ii) the obligation to *protect*, which is a positive obligation to protect individuals particularly from third-party infringements and may call for legislative action; and (iii) the obligation to *fulfil*, which is a positive obligation to ensure the effective enjoyment of rights through the creation and promotion of circumstances in which individuals can in fact enjoy their rights and which may call for the use of governmental means such as policy programmes.[14] However, the exact scope and nature of responsibilities varies from one treaty provision to another, and also to some extent generally from one treaty to another. Indeed, to examine the specific state obligations under each treaty or its provisions, one will have to examine those provisions instead of resorting to some generalized doctrine, which has value as a heuristic model but not as a source of state obligations.

International human rights instruments, or general principles of public international law, do not lay down any general rules regarding the specific means by which treaty obligations are to be given effect in the national legal order.[15] Only exceptionally, as will be seen, does a

---

[13] The issue of positive obligations, while nowadays widely accepted, used to be controversial. See with respect to the European Convention, Francis G. Jacobs – Robin C.A. White, *The European Convention of Human Rights*, 3rd Ed, (Oxford: Clarendon Press, 2002), p. 38.

[14] In particular the Committee on Social, Economic and Cultural Rights nowadays interprets, as a matter of solid practice, the provisions of the UN Covenant on Social, Economic and Cultural Rights in light of this model, as is clear from its General Comment 12 (1999) and several subsequent comments. See also Maastricht Guidelines on violations of Economic, Social and Cultural Rights, Maastricht, January 22–26, 1997; see also Asbjørn Eide, 'Economic, Social and Cultural Rights as Human Rights' in Asbjørn Eide et al (eds.) *Economic, social and cultural rights: A textbook* (Dordrecht: Martinus Nijhoff, 2001), pp. 23–24. By way of comparison, the UN Convention on the Rights of Persons with Disabilities, concluded in 2006, states in Article 1 that its purpose is to "*promote*, *protect* and *ensure* the full and equal enjoyment of all human right and fundamental freedoms by all persons with disabilities" (emphasis added).

[15] See e.g. J.G. Merrills – A.H. Robertson, *Human rights in Europe: A study of the European Convention on Human Rights*, 4th ed (Manchester: Manchester University Press, 2001), p. 24; Oscar Schachter, 'The obligation to implement the covenant in domestic law' in Henkin (ed.) *The International Bill of Rights: The Covenant on Civil and Political Rights* (New York: Columbia U.P., 1981); Manfred Nowak, *U.N. Covenant on civil and political rights: CCPR Commentary* (Kehl: N.P. Engel, 1993), p. 53. Although methods by which the rights and freedoms are given effect in domestic legal order are

specific treaty or a specific provision prescribe specific obligations of conduct.[16] In this sense conventions mainly set forth obligations of results rather than obligations of conduct or of means.[17] How a specific treaty is given effect in the domestic context is a matter of the constitutional norms, principles and traditions of each state. In this respect, a basic distinction can be made between 'monist' and 'dualist' countries.[18] In monist countries international rules, accepted for instance by way of ratification of a treaty, are part and parcel of the national legal order and can be directly applied and invoked in courts. In these countries treaties do not need to be 'translated' into national law. In dualist countries international law and national law are considered to be separate, and therefore international norms need to be 'translated'. This can be done in several ways: for instance, by means of incorporation, by which a treaty is made, as such, a part of the domestic law and by which the terms of the document are retained intact and given formal validity in the national legal order; or transformation, by means of which new legislation is enacted or existing legislation is amended in order to give effect to the treaty.[19]

Though international law is therefore silent on the modalities of domestic implementation, some international human rights bodies and some legal scholars working in this area are clearly is in favour of monism.[20] This is understandable, as under monist systems international law usually prevails over contradicting domestic law, whereas under dualist system more recent domestic law prevails, due to the *lex posterior* principle, over law enacted by means of incorporation or transformation. A monist state is also at a lesser risk of violating international law because its judicial and other competent bodies can, and

---

left to the discretion of the states, the means used must be appropriate in the sense of producing results which are consistent with the full discharge, in good faith, of its obligations by the state party. Article 26 of VCLT.

[16] See in particular chapter 6.5 of this study.

[17] See e.g. Nowak, *cit. supra* note 15, p. 53.

[18] The dichotomy between 'monistic' and 'dualistic' countries is largely regarded as outdated, see Martin Scheinin 'International Human Rights in National Law' in Raija Hanski – Markku Suksi (eds.), *An Introduction to the International Protection of Human Rights: A Textbook* (Turku: Åbo Akademi University Institute for Human Rights, 1999), pp. 417–428 (2nd revised edition).

[19] One should also be aware of the fact that there are also states that tend to do nothing specific at all to give effect to its international obligations in national law. See e.g. CESCR, General Comment No. 9 (1998), para 6.

[20] HRC, General Comment No.31 (2004), para 13; Rosas – Scheinin, *cit. supra* note 11, p. 452.

must, apply that law directly: in those countries where conventions are part of the domestic law, treaty provisions that are capable of direct application by the courts become in that sense 'self-executing'.[21] Because the way in which a treaty is given effect in the domestic legal order may affect the domestic remedies, these two questions will, where necessary, be examined together in the following chapters.

EU law represents, as regards the nature of obligations that it creates on the member states, quite a different story. Regulations, which are a type of secondary legislation (legislation adopted on the basis of the constitutive treaties of the EU), are directly applicable, which means that they do not need any acts of implementation by the member states, but instead automatically become part of their legal system.[22] Directives, which represent another type of secondary legislation, require national implementation, but leave to the national authorities the choice of form and methods of implementation.[23] Directives have a range of effects which will be explored in chapter 7.4 in greater detail.

5.3 On Instruments and Their Interpretation and Application in Practice

A major aspiration of this study is to analyze international and European anti-discrimination law and its effectiveness in achieving the objectives that it has set for itself. This exercise, a kind of impact assessment, calls for an analysis of how these pieces of law are interpreted and applied in practice. Yet that assessment must take into account that norms are not, for many reasons, applied in a uniform manner across, or even within, the countries that are legally bound by them. The process of putting any norms, including international and European norms, into effect is affected by both centrifugal forces, factors that work towards divergence of interpretation and application, and centripetal forces, factors that work towards uniform interpretation and application. An even-handed effort to analyse the practical impact of law ought to take both into account.[24]

---

21 See e.g. Schachter, *cit. supra* note 15, pp. 326–327.

22 Article 288 TFEU (ex Article 249 TEC). See also Sionaidh Douglas-Scott, *Constitutional Law of the European Union* (Harlow: Pearson, 2002).

23 Idem.

24 Cf. Thomas Morawetz (ed.), *Law and Language* (Aldershot: Ashgate, 2000).

A basic starting point is that international and European norms are implemented – and therefore 'used' – primarily nationally, and that members of the legislative, judicial and administrative branches in the different countries participate in the process of putting these norms into effect. This decentralized implementation, the non-existence of supranational executive and judicial institutions (with some exceptions, such as the European Court of Justice) ensuring uniform application, means that these norms *are* inevitably interpreted and 'applied' by a wide variety actors and in a wide variety of ways.

The interpretation of law, including international human rights law, is not an exact science. It is notoriously known that human rights instruments in particular tend to be couched in general, abstract and therefore inherently indeterminate language,[25] a fact which in itself does not necessarily undermine the usefulness of human rights instruments as means of achieving certain ends,[26] but which emphasizes the role of interpretation in putting these instruments and their provisions into effect.[27] The same applies to EU law, as the EU texts are often extremely vague and general in their language as well.[28] It must indeed be realized that law – both case law and statutory law – is expressed in language, and therefore the effective transmission and understanding of the law depends on the clarity and transparency of language.[29] Languages, and indeed individual words, are socially constructed and learnt particularly through imitation in processes known as primary and secondary socialization, with repeated confirmation in interaction contributing towards the emergence of shared understandings.[30] Law schools, symposia and courts of law are important places for

[25] See e.g. Martti Koskenniemi 'Human Rights, Politics, and Love' *Mennesker & rettigheter* 4/2001.

[26] David Kennedy, *The Dark Sides of Virtue: Reassessing International Humanitarianism* (Princeton: Princeton University Press, 2004), p. 8.

[27] In the words of Martin Scheinin: "Among formulations of rights, human rights tend to be rights of a higher level of abstraction. They employ notions that are connected to morality and are, hence, open to moral judgement. Within the family of rights, interpretation plays an even greater role in relation to human rights than with respect to other groups or classes of rights." Martin Scheinin, "Women's Economic and Social Rights as Human Rights" in Lauri Hannikainen and Eeva Nykänen (eds.), *New Trends in Discrimination Law: International Perspectives* (Turku: Turku Law School, 1999), p. 26.

[28] See e.g. Sionaidh Douglas-Scott, *Constitutional Law of the European Union* (Harlow: Pearson, 2002), p. 202.

[29] Tom Morawetz 'Introduction' in Tom Morawetz (ed.), *cit. supra* note 24.

[30] James Boyd White, 'Law as Expression: Thinking about our language' in Tom Morawetz (ed.), *cit. supra* note 24, p. 18.

secondary socialization in the field of law,[31] though they cannot create anything like a tightly-knit legal culture, if not for any other reason but because people attend different law schools and symposia. In addition, we are not just learners and users of our language, but its makers.[32] Each of us loads any text we write and every single expression we use with significances that derive from prior experience of language and life, significances that are not necessarily transmitted through the text, the reader of which then comes to attach her own significances to it.[33] In this way we all come to play our own variations on a common theme, and construct rather than find meanings for texts and expressions. In effect, partly due to this socially constructed nature of language, terms – including legal terms – never carry irreducibly objective, or entirely subjective, meanings.

In the field of law, the freedom of an interpreter to pick an interpretation is constrained by rules and principles that are referred to as 'canons of interpretation'.[34] Such rules and principles may be laid down in law or may have come into being through judicial and scholarly practices. When it comes to international human rights law, even the very canons of interpretation are subject to a fundamental controversy.[35] Whereas it is nowadays rather widely agreed that the general rules of interpretation of international treaties, as reflected in Articles 31 and 32 of the Vienna Convention on the Law of Treaties, constitute a point of departure for the interpretation of human rights conventions, it is also widely held that these rules do not adequately take into account the specific nature and purpose of human rights instruments.[36] At any

---

[31] Kaarlo Tuori, *Critical Legal Positivism* (Aldershot: Ashgate, 2002), pp. 172–3.

[32] White, *cit. supra* note 30, p. 5.

[33] Ibid, p. 17; David Couzens Hoy 'Interpreting the Law: Hermeneutical and Poststructuralist Perspectives', in Tom Morawetz (ed.), *cit. supra* note 24, p. 173.

[34] Stanley E. Fish, 'The Annual John Randolph Tucker Lecture - Force' in Tom Morawetz (ed.), *cit. supra* note 24, p. 273.

[35] For a discussion of these matters, see *Fragmentation of International Law: Difficulties Arising from the Diversification and Expansion of International Law*, Report of the Study Group of the International Law Commission, Finalized by Martti Koskenniemi, 13 April 2006, UN Doc. A/CN.4/L.682; Menno T. Kamminga – Martin Scheinin, *The Impact of Human Rights Law on General International Law* (Oxford: Oxford University Press, 2009); Ineta Ziemele (ed.) *Reservations to Human Rights Treaties and the Vienna Convention Regime: Conflict, Harmony or Reconciliation* (Leiden: Martinus Nijhoff, 2004).

[36] See International Law Association, Resolution No 4/2008 *International Human Rights Law and Practice*, adopted at the 73rd Conference of the International Law Association, held in Rio de Janeiro, Brazil, 17–21 August 2008. The special nature of human rights instruments was pointed at by the European Court of Human Rights in

rate it must be made clear that one cannot somehow mechanically 'extract' the practical meanings of provisions of any legal instrument, let alone a human rights instrument, with or without recourse to the Vienna Convention. The principles of the Vienna Convention have even less relevance in the field of EU law, where the European Court of Justice (ECJ) has not favoured literal or historical interpretation, which feature prominently in the Vienna Convention, but has developed its own style of teleological and contextual interpretation.[37] At any rate the controversies regarding the applicable rules of interpretation add to the indeterminacy of the law, as rules of interpretation function as one of the centripetal forces, diminishing the uncertainties of the law.[38] Yet, on the other hand, research experiments have found that legal reasoning is clearly constrained by 'common sense' in exactly the same way as everyday reasoning is.[39] The process of interpretation is, overall, neither fully determined nor fully indeterminate.

The question of *how* to interpret human rights treaties aside, it must also be asked *who* has the legitimate authority to interpret them. Theoretically speaking, the exclusive right of states to interpret the obligations they have assumed is often grounded on state sovereignty.[40] Yet, there are some institutional arrangements that surpass national autonomy in this respect. In Europe, the ECJ hands down legally binding interpretations of the Community law, and the European Commission exercises a monitoring role in that it is empowered to bring infringement proceedings against non-complying EU states. Also the judgments of the European Court of Human Rights are legally binding on the state party to the proceedings. These institutional arrangements work towards greater uniformity of interpretation and application across different countries, although it must be kept in mind

---

its oft-cited judgment in *Ireland* v. *UK* (18 January 1978, para 239): "Unlike international treaties of the classic kind, the Convention comprises more than mere reciprocal engagements between contracting states. It creates, over and above a network of mutual, bilateral undertakings, objective obligations which, in the words of the Preamble, benefit from a 'collective enforcement'".

[37] See e.g. Douglas-Scott, *cit. supra* note 28, pp. 207–224.

[38] As H.L.A. Hart observes, canons of interpretation can diminish legal uncertainties but cannot eliminate them, because these canons themselves are couched up in general terms which themselves require interpretation. H.L.A. Hart, *The Concept of* Law (Oxford: Clarendon Press, 1994), p. 123.

[39] Robert Dingwall 'Ethnomethodology and Law' in Reza Banakar – Max Travers (eds.) *An Introduction to Law and Social Theory* (Oxford: Hart, 2002), p. 231.

[40] Başak Çalı – Alice Wyss 'Authority of International Institutions: The Case for International Human Rights Treaty Bodies' (4 October 2008). Electronic copy available at: http://ssrn.com/abstract=1278582

that even the entire body of hitherto accumulated case law, dealing as it does with the application of specific norms in specific circumstances, does not authoritatively answer all or even most questions about the substance of the law.

There are institutional arrangements that work towards greater uniformity in application also in the field of international law. Most of the international human rights conventions discussed in this study include a specific type of an institutional arrangement for the monitoring of contracting states' performance of their obligations arising from that convention. These so-called treaty bodies typically have three types of functions: (i) they consider country reports that states are required to submit periodically, and give recommendations and policy advice with a view to helping each country to better fulfil its obligations; (ii) they issue General Comments (with respect to some bodies these are called 'General Recommendations'), in which they seek to develop a more fully fledged doctrinal elaboration of particular treaty provisions; and (iii) they handle individual complaints (often called 'communications' in the language of the respective conventions) and submit views as to whether the respondent state has acted in conformity with its obligations under the convention. Some of the treaty bodies are also entitled to consider state-to-state complaints, but this mechanism has hitherto not been used.

The purpose of the above-mentioned treaty body mechanisms is to assess the situation in the states parties and to encourage and help them to implement their international legal obligations. The reporting mechanism in particular may provide direct input into the development of national laws and policies, and allows national and international scrutiny of government policies. The views and comments made by the committees, while not legally binding as such,[41] are increasingly – though still only occasionally – referred to by the national and regional courts and tribunals.[42] The guiding role of the

[41] However, it has been pointed out that inasmuch as states acquiesce to these views, this acquiescence may constitute "subsequent practice in the application of the treaty which establishes the agreement of the parties regarding its interpretation" within the sense of Article 31(3)b of the VCLT, which means that these views may attain weight in interpretation. International Law Association, Committee on International Human Rights Law and Practice, *Final Report on the Impact of International Human Rights Law on General International Law*. Proceedings of the Rio de Janeiro Conference (2008).

[42] See *Concept paper on the High Commissioner's Proposal for a Unified Standing Treaty Body*, report by the Secretariat, Fifth Inter-Committee Meeting of the human rights bodies, Geneva 19–21 June 2006, HRI/MC/2006/2, para 13.

committees, in short, promotes a more uniform interpretation of international human rights instruments.[43] That said, the impact of the work of the treaty bodies is limited if not compromised in some respects. To some extent this is because many states accept the human rights treaty system on a formal level but do not engage with it, or do so in a superficial way, sometimes because of sheer lack of political will. Only a fraction of states are in full compliance with their reporting obligations, for instance.[44] It also appears that the international monitoring system is little known outside academic circles, government officials directly interacting with the system, specialized lawyers and NGOs, all of this diminishing its impact in practice. Moreover, the committees are overburdened with work, but under-resourced and composed of part-time, unremunerated experts, which means that they can't delve into each deserving question with a sufficient degree of breadth and depth.[45] It has also been suggested that there are problems with the composition of the different committees which may undermine their perceived authority.[46] All of this means that the ability of the treaty bodies to promote a more uniform interpretation of treaty obligations is, in practice, compromised to some extent.

The following chapters examine the different international and European legal instruments that pertain to racial and ethnic discrimination. The different provisions will be analyzed in light of the

[43] To give an example, the Human Rights Committee sees its role and authority, in the context of the consideration of individual petitions, as follows: "The views of the Committee under the Optional Protocol represent an authoritative determination by the organ established under the Covenant itself charged with the interpretation of that instrument. These views derive their character, and the importance which attaches to them, from the integral role of the Committee under both the Covenant and the Optional Protocol". Human Rights Committee, General Comment No. 33 (2008), para 13.

[44] As of February 2006, only 4% of states were up to date with their reporting obligations. Moreover, only 39% of the reports submitted were deemed to be in compliance with the reporting guidelines issued by the respective committees. Concept paper, *cit. supra* note 42, para 24. Some states also show disregard of the individual petition procedure; see e.g. Human Rights Committee, General Comment No. 33 (2008), paras 10 and 18 in particular.

[45] Concept paper, *cit. supra* note 42, para 18. It has been observed that treaty bodies often have insufficient information to enable them to undertake a full analysis of implementation by the state party, and that as a result the subsequent recommendations of treaty bodies may lack the precision, clarity and practical value required to enhance implementation. Ibid, para 25.

[46] Committee members are elected by states parties from candidates nominated by states from among their nationals, and it has been suggested that the composition of treaty bodies has been uneven in terms of geographical distribution, representation of the principal legal systems, gender balance, expertise and independence. Ibid, para 22.

preparatory works of the instruments, the jurisprudence of the European Court of Justice, the European Court of Human Rights and the treaty bodies, as well as legal opinions expressed in text books and other scholarly writings. These are the materials that contribute the most to the formation of the mainstream legal opinions in matters of international and European law. Some, but for reasons of space by no means all, existing or potential points of contention are explicitly addressed. This approach had to be chosen because the entire repertoire of legal opinions could not be entertained here for reasons of space.

The chosen line of approach should not overshadow the fact that in reality the pertinent norms are not interpreted and applied in a uniform manner, and that there is a continuous struggle between interpretations and for the authority to give them. It should also not be taken as implying that the opinions that are referred to are legally valid or persuasive or not, or more fundamentally, that there would necessarily have to be one, and only one, legally valid answer to each legal question. Quite vice versa, the field of human rights is, as much if not more than the other fields of law, prone to prolific and, to an extent, healthy disagreement. Reasonable lawyers often disagree about the matters of law, a fact which is also manifested by the fact that the lines of interpretation adopted by judicial and treaty bodies tend to change over time, as demonstrated by this very study, for its own part.

6 INTERNATIONAL HUMAN RIGHTS LAW[1]

6.1 Notes on the Development of the Principle of Non-Discrimination

The 1776 US Declaration of Independence famously proclaims that "[w]e hold these rights to be self-evident, that all men are created equal, that they are endowed by their Creator with certain unalienable Rights, that among these are Life, Liberty, and the pursuit of Happiness."[2] What was self-evident in the US at the time was, however, that there were free, property-owning 'White' males, that African-origin slaves were considered mere 'property' of some such males, and that any equality between the two groups was out of the question.[3] The drafters may or may not have intended the passage to be aspirational or promissory, but the fact is that it was only later on invoked in justification of the abolition of slavery and much later on in defence of equal treatment irrespective of 'race' and sex.[4] Much in the same way, the

---

[1] The term 'international human rights law' is used here without prejudice to the ongoing debate about whether human rights constitute a specific sub-field of international law or not.

[2] The Declaration continues by asserting that "to secure these rights, governments are instituted among Men", implying the conception that rights precede political decision-making and therefore that equality of men (sic) is not something a government can grant but something that people are entitled to as a birthright. On the possibility of 'pre-political rights', see Martti Koskenniemi 'Human Rights, Politics, and Love' *Mennesker & rettigheter* (4/2001).

[3] Analyses often point out that, at that time, equality and liberty were considered to be inherent in individuals only by virtue of their rationality, a conception which allowed the exclusion of many groups of people on account of their perceived lack of full capacity to reason. It has also been noted that whereas Locke, who undoubtedly was one of the persons from whom the Declaration drew inspiration, wrote that "[m]en are, by Nature, free, equal and independent", he did not see this statement to contradict hierarchical relations between a husband ("Master") and his wife, children and slaves. See John Locke, *Two treatises* (Cambridge: Cambridge University Press, 1988), p. 95. More broadly, one must consider not just the meaning but also the purpose of the passage, and in this respect one must keep in mind that the Declaration should be read in the context of the war between the American colonies and Great Britain, and particularly the challenge to the monarchy.

[4] Speaking in 1857 – more than 80 years after the adoption of the Declaration of Independence – Abraham Lincoln commented upon the passage in the following terms: "They did not mean to assert the obvious untruth that all men were then actually enjoying that equality yet or that they were about to confer it immediately upon

Declaration of the Rights of Man and of the Citizen, adopted by the National Assembly of France in 1789, proclaims in Article 1 that "[m]en are born and remain free and equal in rights." And just as the American Declaration, it was first not considered to imply the abolishment of slavery or the granting of rights to women, but was later on invoked in that purpose.

Similar phrases and references to equality before the law and equal protection of the law have since become common elements of democratic constitutions and, most essentially for our purposes, international instruments.[5] Whereas persons like las Casas in the 16th century had drawn international attention to the wrongfulness of the subjection of indigenous peoples of the Americas by colonial powers – a form of racism, in hindsight – and whereas some international treaties concluded in the 16th and 17th century sought to provide a measure of protection and rights to particular non-majority groups and/or their members,[6] it were the so-called Minority Treaties, concluded around the 1919 Treaty of Versailles and Paris Peace Conference, by which equal treatment and protection of distinct ethnic groups really entered the realm of modern positive international law.[7] However, the efforts to include the principle of non-discrimination in the Covenant of the League of Nations, drafted in 1919, were not successful.

The aforementioned Minority Treaties were designed to safeguard the rights of ethnic minorities in specific countries, particularly in Europe, for a great part in the interests of securing the maintenance of international peace.[8] Minority treaties explicitly required these countries to provide equal treatment for the minorities in question in

---

them. In fact they had no power to confer such a boon. They meant simply to declare the right so that the enforcement of it might follow as fast as circumstances permit. They meant to set up a standard maxim for a free society..." Cited in Warwick McKean, *Equality and Discrimination under International Law* (Oxford: Clarendon Press, 1983), p. 83.

[5] Some of these documents echo the US Declaration of Independence in that they also proclaim equality of all human beings to be 'self-evident'. See e.g. the preamble to the Durban declaration.

[6] See particularly the peace treaties that made up the Peace of Westphalia in 1648.

[7] See generally e.g. Nathan Lerner, *Group rights and discrimination in international law* (Dordrecht: Nijhoff, 1991), p. 7 ff; Patrick Thornberry, *International Law and the Rights of Minorities* (Oxford: Oxford University Press, 1991), p. 25 ff; Asbjørn Eide 'The Framework Convention in Historical and Global Perspective' in Marc Weller (ed.) *Rights of Minorities: Commentary on the European Framework Convention for the Protection of National Minorities* (Oxford: Oxford University Press, 2006).

[8] At the Paris Peace Conference president Woodrow Wilson stated that "nothing is more likely to disturb the peace of the world than the treatment which might in some circumstances be meted out to minorities", cited in Paul Gordon Lauren, *The Evolution*

several walks of life. For instance the Minorities Treaty concluded between the Allies and the Republic of Poland in 1919 required Poland to "undertake to assure full and complete protection of life and liberty to all inhabitants of Poland without distinction of birth, nationality, language, race or religion", proclaimed that "[a]ll Polish nationals shall be equal before the law and shall enjoy the same civil and political rights without distinction as to race, language or religion" and that "Polish nationals who belong to racial, religious or linguistic minorities shall enjoy the same treatment and security in law and in fact as other Polish nationals".[9] It also provided for linguistic and religious freedoms.[10] Similar provisions were included in the other Minorities Treaties.[11]

At that time equality was conceived broadly to include both equal treatment (non-discrimination) and what is now known as 'minority rights', that is the right of minorities to preserve their group characteristics and traditions. This conception was expressed by the Permanent Court of International Justice in its 1935 advisory opinion on the subject of (Greek) *Minority Schools in Albania:*

> The idea underlying the treaties for the protection of minorities is to secure for certain elements incorporated in a State, the population of which differs from them in race, language or religion, the possibility of living peaceably alongside that population and cooperating amicably with it, while at the same time preserving the characteristics which distinguish them from the majority, and satisfying the ensuing special needs. In order to attain this object, two things were regarded as particularly necessary, and have formed the subject of provisions in these treaties. The first is to ensure that nationals belonging to racial, religious or linguistic minorities shall be placed in every respect on a footing of perfect equality with the other nationals of the State. The second is to ensure for the minority elements suitable means for the preservation of their racial peculiarities, their traditions and their national characteristics. These two requirements are indeed closely interlocked, for there would be no true equality between a majority and a minority if the latter were deprived of its own institutions, and were consequently compelled to renounce that which constitutes the very essence of its being as a minority.[12]

---

of International Human Rights: Visions Seen (Philadelphia: University of Pennsylvania Press, 1998), p. 95.

[9] Articles 2(1), 7(1) and 8(1).

[10] Articles 2(2), 7(3) and 9.

[11] Lauren, *cit. supra* note 8, p. 95. Lerner, *cit. supra* note 7, p. 13.

[12] PCIJ, Advisory Opinion, *Minority Schools in Albania*, dated April 6th, 1935, Ser. A./B., No. 64, 1935.

Since 1920 individuals or associations acting on behalf of a minority group could submit petitions to the Council of the League of Nations in relation to the Minority Treaties.[13] Nearly nine hundred petitions were submitted.[14] Major problems confronted the League system of protection of minorities, however. First of all, the system was not of general application but was applied with respect to some countries, which raised the objection about double standards, as countries subjected to the treaty provisions complained that they were unfairly held to standards not applied to the majority of countries.[15] Another problem was that the these treaties were in the end not capable of ensuring peace and security, as the substance of the treaties did not reflect the range and gravity of threats to minorities,[16] and as they were in the end even used as a pretext for military intervention.[17] Eventually, the system of protection of minorities practically collapsed together with the League itself in 1946.[18]

Non-Discrimination in Contemporary International law

The United Nations, which was created in 1945 in the aftermath of the Second World War and the horrors of fascism and National Socialism, has since its very beginning placed the battle against discrimination in the forefront of its human rights activities.[19] Indeed, one of the purposes of the UN, as they are enunciated in the UN Charter, is to promote and encourage the respect for human rights and fundamental freedoms for all "without distinction as to race, sex, language, or religion".[20] The principle of non-discrimination, as referred to above, is actually the only clue given by the drafters of the Charter as to the substance of the rights and freedoms whose respect is to be promoted and encouraged by the UN. Notably, in Articles 55 and 56 the members of the UN "pledge themselves to take joint and separate action" for the achievement of "universal respect for, and observance of, human

[13] Lerner, *cit. supra* note 7, p. 13.

[14] Lauren, *cit. supra* note 8, p. 95.

[15] See e.g. Thornberry, *cit. supra* note 7, p. 38 ff.

[16] Thornberry, *cit. supra* note 7, pp. 50–51.

[17] See e.g. Marc Boyssuyt, 'Comprehensive examination of thematic issues relating to racial discrimination: The concept and practice of affirmative action', Commission on Human Rights 19 June 2000, para 77.

[18] Lerner, *cit. supra* note 7, 11; Thornberry, *cit. supra* note 7, pp. 46–54.

[19] Lauren, *cit. supra* note 8. Manfred Nowak, *U.N. Covenant on civil and political rights: CCPR Commentary* (Kehl: N.P. Engel, 1993), p. 460.

[20] Article 1(3) of the Charter of the United Nations.

rights and fundamental freedoms for all without distinction as to race, sex, language or religion". It is the basis of these articles that the International Court of Justice condemned, in its 1971 Advisory Opinion on Namibia, the Apartheid policy practiced by the government of South Africa in the territory of Namibia which it administered at the time:

> Under the Charter of the United Nations, the former Mandatory [i.e. South Africa] had pledged itself to observe and respect, in a territory having an international status [i.e. Namibia], human rights and fundamental freedoms for all without distinction as to race. To establish instead, and to enforce, distinctions, exclusions, restrictions and limitations exclusively based on grounds of race, colour, descent or national or ethnic origin which constitute a denial of fundamental human rights is a flagrant violation of the purposes and principles of the Charter.[21]

It is widely accepted that the principle of non-discrimination on racial grounds has acquired the status of a general principle of law.[22] This means that no state may engage in racial discrimination in violation of that principle even if it has not ratified any convention to that effect. In fact, in the 1970 *Barcelona Traction* case the International Court of Justice submitted that protection from racial discrimination is an obligation *erga omnes* of contemporary international law, an obligation of such importance that its performance is "the concern of all States" and is owed to "the international community as a whole".[23] Moreover, the principle of non-discrimination on racial grounds is often, but not

---

[21] Advisory Opinion of 21 June 1971, para 131.

[22] See e.g. Ian Brownlie, *Principles of Public International Law* (Oxford: Clarendon Press, 1990), pp. 598 ff, and the references cited therein; B.G. Ramcharan 'Equality and non-discrimination' in Louis Henkin (ed.) *The International Bill of Rights: The Covenant on Civil and Political Rights* (New York: Columbia U.P., 1981), pp. 249–250. See also Vienna Declaration and Programme of Action (adopted at the World Conference on Human Rights in June 1993, A/CONF.157/23), para 15, which states that "[r]espect for human rights and fundamental freedoms without distinction of any kind is a fundamental rule of international human rights law". One of the first analyses promoting the existence of this principle in the area of international law was made by Judge Tanaka in his dissenting opinion in the 1966 South West Africa case (Second Phase), ICJ Reports (1966), p. 299 ff. It is often also maintained that a policy of racial discrimination violates customary law, see Patrick Thornberry, *cit. supra* note 7, pp. 322–326.

[23] ICJ, *Barcelona Traction, Light and Power Company, Limited*, Judgement, I.C.J. Reports 1970, p. 3, paras 33 and 33. The Court reiterated its position in the 2006 Case Concerning Armed Activities on the Territory of the Congo (New Application: 2002): Jurisdiction of the Court and Admissibility of the Application (delivered on 3 February 2006).

always, considered to be one of the least controversial examples of a peremptory norm of international law from which no derogation is permitted (*jus cogens*).[24] The exact contours of the principle are by no means clear, but it has been argued that it extends at least to systematic state-sponsored violations of the rights and freedoms recognized in the Universal Declaration of Human Rights and the two 1966 UN Covenants.[25] Another aspect of international human rights law that underlines the fundamental importance of the prohibition of discrimination is that for instance the International Convention on Civil and Political Rights (ICCPR) expressly prohibits derogations from the principle of non-discrimination even in times of public emergency.[26]

6.2 Universal Declaration of Human Rights

Introduction

The Universal Declaration of Human Rights (UDHR), adopted by the United Nations General Assembly on 10 November 1948, is perhaps the most influential human rights document to date. Its impact on national policies and laws across the world remains inestimable, and its non-discrimination provisions have served as a model for subsequent human rights instruments.

Concept of Discrimination

The non-discrimination provision in Article 2 of the UDHR reads as follows:

---

[24] Brownlie, *cit. supra* note 22, 512 ff; Mckean, *cit. supra* note 44, p. 283; Ramcharan, *cit. supra* note 22, pp. 249–250, 269; Hernández-Truyol, "Human Rights Through a Gendered Lens: Emergence, Evolution, Revolution", in Askin - Koenig, *Women and International Human Rights* (New York: Transnational Publishers, 1999), p. 19; Marc Weller 'Conclusion: Advancing minority rights at regional and universal level' in Marc Weller, (ed.) *The Rights of Minorities: A Commentary on the European Framework Convention for the Protection of National Minorities* (Oxford: Oxford University Press, 2005), p. 616; Lauri Hannikainen, *Peremptory norms (jus cogens) in international law: Historical development, criteria, present status* (Helsinki: Finnish Lawyers' Publishing Company, 1988); For a critical view, see Thornberry, *cit. supra* note 7, pp. 326–328. *Jus cogens* norms have not been authoritatively catalogued anywhere, and there is no general agreement regarding how a norm reaches the status of *jus cogens*. For the meaning of *jus cogens*, see Article 53 of the Vienna Convention on the Law of Treaties.

[25] See Weller, *cit. supra* note 24, p. 617; and implicitly, Brownlie, *cit. supra* note 22, pp. 598–599; Thornberry, *cit. supra* note 7, pp. 322–326.

[26] Article 4(1) of the ICCPR.

> Everyone is entitled to all the rights and freedoms set forth in this Declaration, without distinction of any kind, such as race, colour, sex, language, religion, political or other opinion, national or social origin, property, birth or other status.

Article 7 on its turn provides for equality before the law:

> All are equal before the law and are entitled without any discrimination to equal protection of the law. All are entitled to equal protection against any discrimination in violation of this Declaration and against any incitement to such discrimination.

The UDHR was drafted at a time when gross and often state-sponsored racial discrimination was still rampant. Examples abound, and include lynching of African Americans and the bolstering of white supremacy through the 'separate but equal' doctrine in the United States, the Apartheid and treatment of Indians in South Africa, and the subjection of many African and Asian peoples by Western powers – who played a prominent role in the drafting of the UDHR – through colonialism.[27] This background could not but affect the drafting of the non-discrimination provisions of the UDHR, and led to many controversies.

The drafting of Articles 2 and 7 raised many difficult questions and the articles took many forms during the drafting and raised many questions.[28] To begin with, some of the delegates that participated in the drafting were unclear as to why it was necessary to have two separate articles and what the difference between them was. According to the *travaux*, they were explained that Article 2 set forth the general principle of non-discrimination, whereas Article 7 ensured individuals' protection against discrimination within their own country.[29] Article 2 is also more limited in scope than Article 7, as the latter deals with the (domestic) law in general whereas the former deals only with the rights and freedoms set out in the Declaration itself. It was also unclear whether it was of significance that Article 2 prohibits the making of any kind of *distinctions*, whereas Article 7 prohibits

[27] See Johannes Morsink, *The Universal Declaration of Human Rights: Origins, Drafting and Intent* (Philadelphia: University of Pennsylvania Press, 1999), p. 92 ff.

[28] The range of controversies was so substantial that even the *travaux préparatoires* are at times rather obscure. Jacob Th. Möller 'Article 7' in Asbjørn Eide et al (eds.) *The Universal Declaration of Human Rights: A Commentary* (Oslo: Universitetsforlaget, 1992), p. 115.

[29] Sigrun Skogly 'Article 2' in Asbjørn Eide et al (eds.) *The Universal Declaration of Human Rights: A Commentary* (Oslo: Universitetsforlaget, 1992), p. 63.

discrimination. Along this line of thinking, Article 2(1) would express the more general and rigid conviction and principle that human rights belong to everyone, without any distinctions, whereas Article 7 is more open to discussion about which kinds of distinctions in law in general constitute unequal treatment and which do not.[30] Yet the French language version, in which the Declaration was proclaimed together with the English and Russian versions, uses the words 'sans distinction' not just in Article 2 but also in the first sentence of Article 7, using the word 'discrimination' only in the second sentence of Article 7, whereas the English language version uses 'discrimination' throughout Article 7, a fact which weakens the case for such an interpretation.

Similarly it was not clear, at least for some of the delegates, whether the principle 'equal protection of the laws' required the law to be the same for everyone.[31] Since then, the interpretation that the law (particularly statutory law) should treat people in the same way except where there is reasonable justification for not doing so has become widely endorsed.[32]

However, what amounts to a reasonable justification, and what is the scope of application of that principle, is not clear. Historically, the principle of equal protection of the law had made its way into national constitutions starting with the adoption of the 14th Amendment to the US Constitution in 1868.[33] The 14th Amendment, which provides that "[n]o State shall ... deny to any person within its jurisdiction the equal protection of the laws", was motivated by the need to abolish laws, enacted by many individual states in the aftermath of the American Civil War and the abolition of slavery, that restricted the legal powers of African Americans.[34] Was Article 7 of the UDHR inspired by, or even meant to correspond to, the Equal Protection Clause of the Fourteenth Amendment? If yes, is its reach similarly limited in that relationships between private parties, for instance in the field of employment, are excluded from its scope?[35] Principles such as these

---

[30] Cf. Thornberry, *cit. supra* note 7, pp. 283 ff.

[31] Möller, *cit. supra* note 28, pp. 122 and 125.

[32] Thornberry, *cit. supra* note 7, p. 285; Mckean, *cit. supra* note 44, p. 139.

[33] Nowak, *cit. supra* note 19, p. 459.

[34] Idem.

[35] The Equal Protection Clause has indeed been interpreted, in the field of employment, as applying only to public-sector employees and to legislation governing the employment relationship. See Lynn M. Roseberry, *The Limits of Employment Discrimination Law in the United States and European Community* (Copenhagen: DJOF Publishing, 1999), p. 23.

are not self-explanatory, as is clear from the extensive, complex – and politically highly charged – jurisprudence that the 14th Amendment has spawned in the US.[36]

The central idea of the principle 'equality before the law', which originated from the American and French revolutions, appears to have been less controversial in its meaning for the drafters,[37] though it is by no means self-explanatory either. The principle is generally interpreted to mean that courts and other bodies applying law shall treat people equally except where the *law* provides otherwise.[38] This means, for instance, that persons with a minority background should not be sentenced more harshly than persons belonging to a majority for similar crimes, an ideal state of affairs that courts often fall short of.[39]

It is generally agreed that Article 7 was not intended to imply material equality in fact.[40]

Grounds

Unlike Article 1(3) of the UN Charter, the list of prohibited grounds of discrimination in Article 2 of the UDHR is relatively wide and open-ended. The expressly mentioned grounds include 'race', colour and national origin. During the drafting a controversy arose as to whether the notion of 'race' covered colour, with some delegates expressing the view that discrimination on the basis of colour was not identical to that

[36] Ramcharan, *cit. supra* note 22, p. 247. The US Supreme Court has in several cases interpreted the Equal Protection Clause; in the 1896 case *Plessy* v. *Ferguson* the Supreme Court upheld a law that required segregation of 'Blacks' and 'Whites', whereas in the 1954 case *Brown* v. *Board of Education* the Court effectively declared *de jure* racial segregation unconstitutional on the grounds that it violates the Equal Protection Clause.

[37] The studies on the drafting of Article 7 do not mention that the principle was debated by the drafters.

[38] Thornberry, *cit. supra* note 7, p. 285; McKean, *cit. supra* note 44, p. 139. For instance in *Attorney General* v. *Lavell*, the Canadian Supreme Court held that "equality before the law" in the Canadian Bill of Rights meant "equality of treatment in the enforcement and application of the laws of Canada", [1974] S.C.R. 1349, p. 1350. On the other hand, the Australian Racial Discrimination Act 1975 (as amended), which is closely linked with the ICERD Convention, defines "rights to equality before law" as having to do with "persons of a particular race, colour or national origin" as not enjoying a right that is enjoyed by "persons of another race, colour or national or ethnic origin", or enjoying it to a more limited extent, *by reason of a law or a provision thereof* (section 10 of the Act).

[39] See e.g. Lars Holmberg – Britta Kyvsgaard 'Are Immigrants and their Descendants Discriminated against in the Danish Criminal Justice System?' *Journal of Scandinavian Studies in Criminology and Crime Prevention* Vol. 4, No 2 (2003).

[40] See e.g. Ramcharan, *cit. supra* note 22, p. 253.

of race, and some others expressing the view that since the notion of 'race' had no scientific basis, people used colour as a marker of 'race' and thereby colour was covered by 'race'.[41] In the end, the term colour was included in the list of grounds, apparently to make it absolutely certain that it was covered, as there was no agreement as to whether it had a meaning distinct from the notion of race.[42] There was also considerable controversy around the meaning of the term 'national origin' and whether it should be replaced by some other term. In the end, the reference to it was retained, and it was explained as referring not to the citizenship of a state but to 'national characteristics', thus linking the notion to cultural, religious and linguistic characteristics.[43]

Material Scope of Application

Article 2 of the UDHR is not free-standing, but is, in a way, accessory to the other articles of the Declaration. Its scope is nevertheless extensive, as the rights guaranteed in the Declaration cover to a great extent the range of what are recognized as human rights and fundamental freedoms today.[44] These include "right to equal access to public service", "right to work, to free choice of employment, to just and favourable conditions of work and protection against unemployment", "equal pay for equal work", "right to education" and the right to an adequate standard of living, including in the area of housing.[45]

Complementary Equality Provisions

Several other articles of the Declaration are also relevant from the point of view of this study. Article 23 addresses pay equality separately and provides that "[e]veryone, without any discrimination, has the right to equal pay for equal work". Article 26, which provides for free elementary education, touches upon prevention of discrimination when it specifies that education shall "promote understanding, tolerance and friendship among all nations, racial or religious groups".

Article 8 declares that everyone "has the right to an effective remedy by the competent national tribunals for acts violating the fundamental

---

[41] Skogly, *cit. supra* note 29, pp. 60–61.

[42] Morsink, *cit. supra* note 27, pp. 102–103.

[43] See Morsink, *cit. supra* note 27, pp. 104–105, and the references cited therein.

[44] Asbjörn Eide - Allan Rosas, 'Economic, Social and Cultural Rights: A Universal Challenge', in Eide et al (eds.) *Economic, Social and Cultural Rights: a Textbook* (The Hague: Kluwer Law International, 1995), p. 15.

[45] Articles 21(2), 23(2), 25(1) and 26(1).

rights granted him by the constitution or by law". The formulation of Article 8 is strong, as it explicitly requires the remedies to be of judicial nature and requires that remedies are provided not just with respect to violations of rights granted by the Declaration but with respect to all rights granted by the constitution or by law, which is a demand of great intensity, keeping in mind the ever expanding number of rights provided in the national legal systems in Europe.[46]

6.3 Discrimination (Employment and Occupation) Convention

Introduction

The ILO Convention No 111 on discrimination was adopted in June 1958 and was ratified by 169 countries as of January 2011.[47] The substantive articles of the Convention are often read in light of Recommendation R111, which accompanied the Convention, as well as the comments of the Committee of Experts on the Application of Conventions and Recommendations (CEACR),[48] the task of which is to examine compliance by ILO member states with this and other ILO Conventions.[49]

Concept of Discrimination

Convention No 111 was the first international document where the term 'discrimination' was expressly defined. According to Article 1(1) discrimination refers to "any distinction, exclusion or preference made on the basis of race" that has "the effect of nullifying or impairing equality of opportunity or treatment in employment and occupation". Neither the Convention nor the accompanying recommendation define the core terms 'equal opportunities' or 'equal treatment', which brings a degree of uncertainty into the definition. Special measures are referred to in Article 5, according to which special measures designed

---

[46] See also generally on Article 8, Göran Melander 'Article 8' in Asbjørn Eide et al (eds.) *The Universal Declaration of Human Rights: A Commentary* (Oslo: Universitetsforlaget, 1992).

[47] Source: www.ilo.org/ilolex (accessed 1.1.2011).

[48] Established in 1926, and composed of 20 independent members, the Committee of Experts is a legal body responsible for the examination of the compliance by ILO member states with ILO Conventions and Recommendations.

[49] This examination takes place for instance on the basis of reports sent by governments pursuant to questionnaires prepared by the ILO Governing Body.

to meet the particular requirements of persons who are "generally recognized to require special protection or assistance" do not constitute discrimination. Distinction, exclusion or preference with respect to a particular job based on its inherent requirements does not constitute discrimination.[50]

The definition, which places an emphasis on effects and thereby on what is happening in the 'real life', is rather broad. The CEACR has come to interpret it as encompassing most situations identified as direct and indirect forms of discrimination.[51]

Scope of Application

In light of Recommendation R111, the Convention aims for the elimination of discrimination with respect to all aspects of employment, including access to employment and terms and conditions of employment and security of tenure. It is also intended to cover the benefits and welfare facilities that are provided in connection with employment.[52] Also vocational guidance and placement services are to be made available to all on an equal basis.[53] In light of the interpretative practice of the CEACR, the Convention covers both public and private sectors.[54]

State Obligations

In Article 2 states parties undertake to "declare and pursue a national policy designed to promote, by methods appropriate to national conditions and practice, equality of opportunity and treatment in respect of employment and occupation, with a view to eliminating any

---

[50] Article 1(2).

[51] CEACR, Individual Observation on Saudi Arabia, 2007, document No 062007SAU111, para 3. See also CEACR's Individual Observation on Hungary, 2007, document no 062007HUN111, where the Committee asks the Government of Hungary to provide information on the number of teaching and non-teaching staff, disaggregated by sex, which were dismissed due to the 1995 austerity measures. The Committee points out that whenever public employment must be reduced due to budgetary constraints, an assessment of the *impact* of measures needs to be made "in order to avoid dismissals contrary to the principle of equality of opportunity and treatment", in de facto recognition of the concept of indirect discrimination.

[52] ILO, R111 Discrimination (Employment and Occupation) Recommendation, 1958. CEACR, Individual Observation, India, 2007 (document no. 062007IND111). CEACR, Individual Observation on Saudi Arabia, 2007 (document no 062007SAU111).

[53] R111, para 2(b)(i).

[54] See e.g. CEASR, Individual Observation on Lithuania, 2007 (document no 062007LTU111), para 6.

discrimination in respect thereof." What is particularly noteworthy is that the undertaking is not couched in terms of individual rights, but in terms of a national *policy* that the contracting states undertake to declare and pursue with a view to eliminating any discrimination with respect to employment and occupation. Recommendation R111 specifies that the national policy "should be applied by means of legislative measures, collective agreements between representative employers' and workers' organisations or in any other manner consistent with national conditions and practice."

Article 3 sets out further and more detailed obligations for the contracting states. Under the said article governments undertake, inter alia, to seek the co-operation of the social partners in promoting the acceptance and observance of the national policy; to enact such legislation and to promote such educational programmes as may be calculated to secure the acceptance and observance of the policy; and to repeal any provisions and modify any administrative instructions or practices that are inconsistent with the policy. They also undertake to report, in their respective country reports, on the action they have taken.

At least *prima facie*, Article 2 leaves the contracting states much room for discretion in the choice of measures by which to pursue the national equality policy. This is counterbalanced by the fact that the obligations are demanding, as the Convention is ambitious in that the required policies are to aim at the elimination of discrimination, and in that it and the Committee place an emphasis on securing *observance* of anti-discrimination laws and policies *in practice*. In its dialogue with the states parties, the Committee has taken the opportunity to advocate the adoption of legislative measures. In view of the Committee,"legal protection from discrimination through effective mechanisms and procedures is an important element of any national policy to promote and ensure equality of opportunity in employment and occupation, as envisaged by the Convention".[55] Furthermore, the Committee is of the view that governments should take the necessary steps to ensure that anti-discrimination and equality provisions are properly enforced and that the legislation is "known, understood and observed in practice".[56]

[55] CEACR, Individual Observation concerning Croatia, 2007 (document no 062007HRV111). Emphasis added.

[56] Idem, and CEACR, Individual Observation concerning Lithuania, published 2007 (document no 062007LTU111).

It has also recommended that effective means of redress be provided.[57] It should also be noted that the Committee has, in its individual observations, called for the adoption of a "flexible complaints mechanism that takes into account the difficulties that the worker has in producing evidence of discrimination and the need to protect complainants, so as to guarantee the effectiveness of the procedure."[58]

The Committee has in fact made it clear that in its view, for a country to be in compliance with its obligations, it is not sufficient for it simply to adopt anti-discrimination legislation. It has called for comprehensive measures, including the following: adoption of "concrete and proactive measures" such as educational and awareness-raising programmes;[59] measures that seek, *inter alia*, to promote equal access to vocational training;[60] measures that address stereotyped behaviours and prejudicial attitudes and promote respect and tolerance for ethnic minorities;[61] and monitoring of the progress made in the implementation of domestic policies through the collection of statistics disaggregated by race, ethnicity and sex.[62] For the Committee, the ultimate test is whether equal opportunities and equal treatment are enjoyed in practice.[63] To assess whether this is the case, it is customary for the Committee to ask the governments to report information, such as information relating to judicial decisions and statistics, which allows it to appreciate the application of the Convention in practice.[64]

---

[57] See e.g. CEACR, Individual Observation concerning Saudi Arabia, 2007 (document no 062007SAU111), para 3.

[58] See CEACR, Individual Observation concerning Uruguay, 2007 (document no 062007URY111), para 2.

[59] CEACR, Individual Observation concerning Cameroon, 2007 (document no 062007CMR111), para 1.

[60] See R111 Article 2(b)(i). See also CEACR, Individual Observation concerning El Salvador, 2007 (document no 062007SLV111, para 4), in which the Committee expressed its hope that the Government would pay "particular attention to equal access to vocational training, which is key to gaining access to the labour market."

[61] See e.g. CEACR, Individual Observation concerning Saudi Arabia, 2007 (document no 062007SAU111); CEACR, Individual Observation concerning Senegal, 2007 (document no 062007SEN111); CEACR, Individual Observation concerning Bulgaria (document no 062007BGR111), para 6.

[62] See e.g. CEACR, Individual Observation concerning Chad, 2007 (document no 062007TCD111), para 3; CEACR, Individual Observation concerning Mauritania, 2007 (document no 062007MRT111), para 1.

[63] See e.g. CEACR, Individual Observation concerning Morocco, 2007 (document no 062007MAR111), para 5; CEACR, Individual Observation concerning Poland, 2007 (document no 062007POL111), para 5.

[64] General Report of the CEACR, 2007, para 45. CEACR, Individual Observation concerning Germany, 2007 (document no 062007DEU111); CEACR, Individual Observation concerning Greece, 2007 (document no 062007GRC111).

6.4 Convention against Discrimination in Education

Introduction

The Convention against Discrimination in Education was adopted by the General Conference of the United Nations Educational, Scientific and Cultural Organization (UNESCO) in December 1960. By January 2011 it had been ratified by 98 countries.[65]

Concept of Discrimination

Discrimination is defined in Article 1 of the Convention as follows:

> For the purposes of this Convention, the term 'discrimination' includes any distinction, exclusion, limitation or preference which, being based on race, colour, sex, language, religion, political or other opinion, national or social origin, economic condition or birth, has the purpose or effect of nullifying or impairing equality of treatment in education.[66]

This definition bears a degree of resemblance with the definition of discrimination included in the ILO Convention, but speaks of 'limitations' in addition to distinctions, exclusions and preferences, and is broader in that it covers also actions, the purpose – not just effect – of which is to impair equality of treatment.

An important clarification is made in Article 2 of the Convention, which provides that the establishment and maintenance of religious educational institutions is not to be considered discrimination, provided that attendance at such institutions is optional and that the education provided confirms to applicable official standards.

Grounds and Material Scope

The Convention prohibits discrimination on the grounds of 'race', colour and national or social origin. These terms are not defined or explained in the Convention. Consequently, it is not clear in what way 'race' is different from 'colour' or whether national origin refers to minorities, immigrants, to both or neither.

---

[65] Source: http://portal.unesco.org (accessed 1.1.2011).

[66] The definition sets out in more detail an exemplary list of situations that constitute discrimination. These include: (a) depriving any person or group of persons of access to education of any type or at any level; (b) limiting any person or group of persons to education of an inferior standard; (c) subject to the provisions of Article 2 of the Convention, establishing or maintaining separate educational systems or institutions for persons or groups of persons; or (d) inflicting on any person or group of persons conditions which are incompatible with the dignity of man.

The Convention specifies that the term 'education', for the purposes of the Convention, refers to all types and levels of education, and includes access to education, the standard and quality of education, and the conditions under which it is given.[67]

State Obligations

The Convention requires states parties to abrogate any provisions, instructions and practices which involve discrimination in education and to ensure, "by legislation where necessary, that there is no discrimination in the admission of pupils to educational institutions."[68] The Convention acknowledges, albeit in soft terms, the importance of special measures by stating that the contracting states undertake to "formulate, develop and apply a national policy which, by methods appropriate to the circumstances and to national usage, will tend to *promote* equality of opportunity and of treatment".[69] The Convention envisages that this is to be done, in particular, by means of making primary education free and compulsory and by ensuring that the standards of education are equivalent in all public institutions of the same level.[70] There is no obligation for the state to provide financial or other assistance to minorities to carry out their own educational activities.[71]

6.5 Convention on the Elimination of all forms of Racial Discrimination

Introduction

The Convention on the Elimination of All forms of Racial Discrimination (ICERD), concluded in 1965, is widely regarded to be the principal international instrument concerning racial discrimination.[72] The Convention has also become one of the most widely ratified

[67] Article 1(2) of the Convention.

[68] Article 3.

[69] Article 4. Emphasis added.

[70] Article 4(a) and (b).

[71] Thornberry, *cit. supra* note 7, p. 290.

[72] The paramount importance of the CERD Convention is recognized e.g. in the Durban declaration and plan of action. See also e.g. Michael O'Flaherty 'The UN Committee on the Elimination of All forms of Racial discrimination as an implementation agency' in Martin MacEwen (ed.), *Anti-Discrimination Law Enforcement* (Aldershot: Avebury, 1997), p. 210. The future importance of ICERD was anticipated also in the drafting phases of the Convention: Thornberry notes that "[i]t is clear from

human rights instruments in the world: by January 2011, altogether 174 countries had ratified the Convention.[73] By virtue of these two facts the Convention and its provisions will be examined here in some detail.

Preparations for the Convention started in the 1960s, prompted primarily by a wish to respond to an epidemic of anti-Semitic incidents taking place in Europe at that time.[74] The broader backdrop for the Convention was the recognition of the need to condemn also some other particularly topical forms of discrimination, in particular colonialism and the discrimination associated therewith, and apartheid, segregation and other "government policies based on racial superiority or hatred", the latter term expressing concern over Nazism and fascism and their possible re-emergence.[75] The *raison d'être* of the Convention was therefore twofold: first, to secure international condemnation of systematic, often state-sponsored, expressions of racism, racial superiority and related phenomena including colonialism, and second, to curb the actions of individuals, groups and organisations that were spreading racial hatred and acting on that basis. At the time of its adoption, discrimination was viewed by many states as a social pathology that afflicted states other than their own, and the struggle against racial discrimination was seen as belonging primarily within their foreign policy.[76] It has been observed that it was widely thought that racism was solely about the consequences of Western imperialism, an

the history of the preparation of the Convention that it received a thorough consideration at various levels in the United Nations hierarchy and constitutes as near an authentic expression as possible of the general view at the United Nations in 1965. Thornberry, *cit. supra* note 7, p. 259.

73 Source: http://treaties.un.org (accessed 1.1.2011).

74 Lerner, *cit. supra* note 7, p. 46.

75 Preamble to the Convention. Also noteworthy are Article 3, which condemns segregation and apartheid, and Article 15, which envisages a mechanism under which the CERD was to give opinions and recommendations to petitions submitted by inhabitants of Trust and Non-Self Governing Territories. See also Michael Banton, *International action against racial discrimination* (Oxford: Clarendon Press, 1996), p. 68. The UN Declaration on the Elimination of All Forms of Discrimination, which was adopted in 1963, i.e. just a few years before the CERD Convention, and to which the latter explicitly refers to in its preamble, expressly – though not exhaustively – links racial discrimination with state-sponsored practices including colonialism, "apartheid, segregation, and separation" and "promotion and dissemination of racial superiority and expansionism". In this context it is also noteworthy that Article 5 of the Declaration requires that "An end shall be put without delay to governmental and other public policies of racial segregation and especially policies of apartheid, as well as all forms of racial discrimination and separation resulting from such policies".

76 Banton, *cit. supra* note 75, pp. 68 and 306.

assumption which inevitably placed the Convention in a fraught political environment.[77] The Convention is a child of its time also in the sense that it is strongly integrationist, almost assimilationist, in its spirit and does not expressly provide for cultural rights, a fact that is alleviated only to a small degree by the recent references by its monitoring committee to such rights.[78]

The Committee on the Elimination of Racial Discrimination (CERD) monitors the domestic implementation of the ICERD in particular through the following three facets of its work: (i) consideration of periodic reports submitted by states parties, (ii) consideration, under the optional individual complaints system, of complaints (called "communications" in the Convention), and (iii) by means of issuing general recommendations on thematic issues, in which the Committee has the opportunity to outline its interpretations of the content of the provisions of the treaty in a more systematic fashion.

By January 2011, 54 states parties, including 20 Member States of the European Union,[79] had recognized the competence of the Committee to consider complaints (called "communications" in the Convention) against them. Such communications may be submitted, after having exhausted available domestic remedies, by groups or individuals who consider that their rights have been violated by a state party under whose jurisdiction they are. The number of communications has remained peculiarly low: since 1982, when the communication system became operational, until January 2011, only 45 communications had been submitted; 10 had been found to disclose a violation of the Convention, 14 had been found not to disclose a violation, 17 were considered inadmissible and 4 were pending ('living').[80] Despite the low volume of complaints, the procedure has allowed the CERD committee the opportunity to build up its jurisprudence.

---

[77] Kevin Boyle - Anneliese Baldaccini 'A Critical Evaluation of International Human Rights Approaches to Racism' in Sandra Fredman (ed.) *Discrimination and Human Rights* (Oxford: Oxford University Press, 2001), p. 150.

[78] The Committee urges, in its General Recommendation on self-determination (a right that the ICERD does not deal with as such), governments to be sensitive towards the rights of persons belonging to ethnic groups, particularly the right to preserve their culture.

[79] These were: Austria, Belgium, Czech Republic, Denmark, Estonia, Finland, France, Hungary, Ireland, Italy, Luxembourg, Malta, Netherlands, Poland, Portugal, Romania, Slovakia, Slovenia, Spain and Sweden. Source: http://treaties.un.org (accessed 1.1.2011).

[80] OHCHR, *Statistical survey of individual complaints*. Available at www.ohchr.org (accessed 1.1.2011). Interestingly, nearly half of the communications have originated from Denmark.

Concept of discrimination
Racial discrimination is defined in Article 1(1) of the Convention as follows:

> In this Convention, the term 'racial discrimination' shall mean any distinction, exclusion, restriction or preference based on race, colour, descent, or national or ethnic origin which has the purpose or effect of nullifying or impairing the recognition, enjoyment or exercise, on an equal footing, of human rights and fundamental freedoms in the political, economic, social, cultural or any other field of public life.

This definition is based on the definitions of the previously mentioned ILO and UNESCO documents. Although Article 1(1) is careful to point out that the definition was adopted only for the purposes of the Convention itself, it has become an almost standard definition of racial discrimination in the field of international human rights. The definition is broad, complex and imbued with illusory precision, in that it consists of several different elements and is couched in general terms, which render both its analysis and application a challenging exercise. In consequence, the definition is at least in theory capable of being applied in a relatively wide range of situations, but its application in those situations is not straightforward because of the openness of its language.

The reference to enjoyment of rights 'on an equal footing' contains the comparative element that is often taken to be at heart of discrimination: to constitute racial discrimination, an infringement must have put an individual or a group at a disadvantage on 'racial' grounds. It also emphasises the fact that what is at issue here is not a requirement of identical or similar treatment, but equal treatment, which allows a measure of differential treatment in order to accommodate genuine individual or group-based characteristics and needs. In examining whether discrimination has taken place, the Committee generally uses the legitimation test: differentiation of treatment is taken to constitute discrimination if the criteria for such differentiation, judged against the objectives and purposes of the Convention, are not considered legitimate.[81] This approach, of course, leaves the Committee much discretion.

---

[81] CERD, General Recommendation XIV (1993), para 2.

In any case, the concept of discrimination in the Convention is broad in that the taking of action that is deliberately aimed at infringing the rights of an individual or a group, on racial grounds, constitutes racial discrimination even if the intended results never materialize. The making of a distinction, exclusion, restriction or preference may also constitute an act of racial discrimination even if the resulting infringement of rights or freedoms was not purposeful.[82] The Committee has in its practice eventually moved beyond what is perhaps the most obvious literal reading of Article 1(1), and interpreted the Convention to also prohibit indirect discrimination, defined as *any action* (i.e. not just distinction, exclusion, restriction or preference *based on* race, colour, descent, or national or ethnic origin) that has an unjustifiable disparate impact upon a group distinguished by race, colour, descent, or national or ethnic origin.[83] In its General Recommendation No XIV the Committee stated that in its view

> particular actions may have varied purposes. In seeking to determine whether an action has an effect contrary to the Convention, it [the Committee] will look to see whether that action has an unjustifiable disparate impact upon a group distinguished by race, colour, descent, or national or ethnic origin.[84]

The Committee used this kind of an approach in *B.M.S.* v. *Australia*, where it set out to examine Australia's policy of setting a quota for medical doctors trained overseas, in order to determine whether it was possible to "reach the conclusion that the *system works to the detriment*

---

[82] Under the terminology adopted in this study, this (an act based on e.g. 'race' but without *mens rea* that has a disparate impact upon the members of a group) does not constitute indirect discrimination, but direct discrimination, as the latter is about the making of distinctions on the grounds of 'race' which do not need to have been committed with *mens rea* whereas indirect discrimination is about acts that appear neutral (do not use 'race' as a criterion) but that nevertheless unjustifiably disadvantages the members of a group.

[83] E.g. Nathan Lerner, a specialist in the drafting history of the Convention, submits that "distinction, exclusion, restriction and preference" are four types of acts prohibited by the Convention, and adds that "the intention of the drafters of Article 1 was to cover in its first paragraph all kinds of acts of discrimination among persons, as long as they were based on motivations of a racial nature, in the broad sense of the word". See Lerner, *cit. supra* note 7, pp. 48–49 (emphasis added).

[84] See also CERD, General Recommendation No. 20, paragraph 2, where the Committee interprets Article 5 of the Convention and submits that "Whenever a State imposes a restriction upon one of the rights listed in article 5 of the Convention which applies ostensibly to all within its jurisdiction, it must ensure that neither in purpose nor effect is the restriction incompatible with article 1 of the Convention". General Recommendation No. 20 (1996).

of persons of a particular race or national origin".[85] In *L.R. et. al. v. Slovakia* the Committee elaborated upon its view and opined that "the definition of racial discrimination in Article 1 expressly extends beyond measures that are explicitly discriminatory, to encompass measures that are not discriminatory at face value but are discriminatory in fact and effect, that is, if they amount to indirect discrimination."[86] The Committee has stated that when it is assessing whether indirect discrimination has taken place, it will take full account of the particular context and circumstances of the petition, as "by definition indirect discrimination can only be demonstrated circumstantially".[87] The Committee's approach, the rejection of the formalistic approach according to which discrimination must be linked to acts which in one way or the other single out (by means of a distinction, exclusion, restriction or preference) members of a particular group, significantly expands the scope of the definition of discrimination in the ICERD.

Although the definition of discrimination encompasses also preferences based on 'race', such preferences are allowed if they constitute special measures envisaged in Articles 1(4) and 2(2). Indeed, one of the innovations of the ICERD was the incorporation into the very definition of discrimination of a provision allowing special measures targeted at particular groups; in this way, special measures cannot be construed as narrowly-interpreted exceptions to the principle of non-discrimination.[88] Article 1(4) spells out the legitimacy and limits of special measures:

> Special measures taken for the sole purpose of securing adequate advancement of certain racial or ethnic groups or individuals requiring such protection as may be necessary in order to ensure such groups or individuals equal enjoyment or exercise of human rights and fundamental freedoms shall not be deemed racial discrimination, provided, however, that such measures do not, as a consequence, lead to the maintenance of separate rights for different racial groups and that they shall not be continued after the objectives for which they were taken have been achieved.

This Article has caused much confusion: some commentators have been concerned over the question of whether it prohibits minority

[85] CERD, *B.M.S.* v. *Australia*, Communication No. 8/1996. Emphasis added.
[86] CERD, *L.R. et. al.* v. *Slovakia*, Communication No. 31/2003.
[87] Ibid, para 10.4.
[88] McKean, *cit. supra* note 44, p. 159.

rights, i.e. standing rights that aim at guaranteeing minorities the opportunity to preserve and develop their cultural, linguistic and religious identity and heritage.[89] This concern arises because minority rights inherently target particular ethnic groups and are not of a temporary nature, as is required by Article 1(4). On the other hand, other commentators have hailed the said article as an express recognition of the legitimacy of such rights.[90] While the literal reading of Article 1(4), when read alone, might indeed seem to rule out minority rights, it is plausible to interpret Article 1 as implying that minority rights do not constitute discrimination to begin with, as the purpose or effect of special measures is not to nullify or impair the recognition, enjoyment or exercise of human rights or fundamental freedoms within the meaning of Article 1(1) but to ensure them.[91] State practice and the practice of the Committee also support the interpretation that minority rights and related action are by no means in breach of the Convention.[92] Indeed, the Committee has explicitly stated that special measures should not be confused with minority rights or other specific rights pertaining to certain categories of person.[93] 'Special measures' as a term used in the Convention merely refers to such measures that aim to eliminate inequalities that jeopardize the full and equal enjoyment of all human rights and fundamental freedoms.[94]

Grounds and the Personal Scope of Application

The grounds covered by the ICERD are exhaustively enumerated; these are race, colour, descent, and national or ethnic origin. Despite the fact that these notions therefore in a crucial manner delimit the scope of application of the Convention, the Convention itself does not define them and no definitions have been formulated by the CERD Committee either.

---

[89] See e.g. the debates reviewed by Thornberry, *cit. supra* note 7, p. 266 ff.

[90] Mckean, *cit. supra* note 44, p. 159.

[91] Although Article 5 of the Convention mentions several civil and political rights guaranteed by the ICCPR, but not the right of minorities to maintain and develop their identities laid down in Article 27 of ICCPR, there are no apparent legal grounds for arguing that Article 27 would not be one of the rights that come within the purview of the CERD Convention, including Articles 1 and 5.

[92] See also Ryszard Cholewinski, 'The Racial Convention and the Protection of Cultural and Linguistic Ethnic Minorities', *Revue de Droit International* (69) 1991.

[93] CERD, General Recommendation No. 32 (2009), para 15.

[94] Ibid, para 11 ff.

Whereas 'race' or the other terms have not been defined in the Convention, it defines '*racial* discrimination' as discrimination based on race, colour, descent or national or ethnic origin.[95] The Convention, including its preamble, reflects popular conceptions of its time, and treats 'races' as distinct, real entities. This is evident in the frequent and unqualified references to 'races' and 'racial groups' in the text of the Convention.[96] Moreover, the Convention is clear to condemn only doctrines of racial superiority, not racial thinking as such, its very *raison d'être* being the elimination of discrimination linked to such doctrines.[97] The drafters had been reminded of the fact that scientifically speaking there was no such thing as 'race',[98] which suggests that either they were unconvinced of the truth value of that statement or that they nevertheless chose to use that term as a kind of useful legal fiction.

Banton, a long-time member of the CERD Committee, has made an effort to interpret what the Convention means by 'race'. In his view the notion of 'race' should not be understood along the lines of biological objectivism, because the Convention addresses actions that are based on *assumed race* or some other group-related ascription of a person or a group of persons.[99] In his vocabulary, 'race' is a way of defining otherness, a generic idiom for structures of social differentiation.[100] Indeed, the Convention prohibits "distinction, exclusion, restriction or

[95] Some commentators are of the view that the Convention defines 'race' as 'race, colour, descent or ethnic or national origin', but this reasoning is manifestly erroneous, if not for any other reason but for its circularity. Yet other commentators a bit more cautiously submit that the concept of race under the Convention 'encompasses' colour, descent and national or ethnic origin, a statement which can be misunderstood to convey the same idea. See e.g. Nowak, *cit. supra* note 19, p. 47; Kristin Henrard 'The Impact of International Non-Discrimination Norms in Combination with General Human Rights for the Protection of Minorities: The European Convention on Human Rights', Strasbourg 25 October 2006, DH-MIN(2006)020, p. 5.

[96] For instance Article 2(1) (e) speaks of eliminating "barriers between races", Article 4(a) requires states to criminalize acts of violence "against any race" and Articles 1(4), 2(2) and 7 speak of "racial groups".

[97] The Convention nowhere condemns racial thinking as such, but the preamble to it famously proclaims that the states parties to the Convention are "[c]onvinced that any doctrine of superiority based on racial differentiation is scientifically false, morally condemnable, socially unjust and dangerous, and that there is no justification for racial discrimination, in theory or in practice, anywhere". Therefore the Convention took a different stand than the preceding Declaration, the preamble of which condemned "*any doctrine of racial differentiation* or superiority" (emphasis added).

[98] Lerner, *cit. supra* note 7.

[99] Banton, *cit.* supra note 75, p. 52; Banton 'The causes of, and remedies for, racial discrimination', E/CN.4/1999/WG.1/BP.6, para 1.

[100] Banton, *cit. supra* note 75, pp. 76–79.

preference *based* on race", not for instance actions targeted at individuals or groups "distinguished by race". Again, it is relevant that the drafters had been reminded of the fact that there are no such things as 'races', and that they nevertheless deemed it necessary to use that concept in the Convention.[101] Under that view, discriminatory action is based on social and/or personal, not natural or 'real' conceptions of 'race'. The same conclusion could also be reached with regard to the other grounds enumerated in the Convention. Along that line of thought, it should usually not be necessary, for the purposes of establishing that racial discrimination has taken place, to prove that the aggrieved person actually belongs to a particular 'racial' or ethnic group – a task that would scientifically speaking be rather senseless in case of the second term and entirely senseless in the case of the first.

Of the enumerated grounds, the notion of 'descent' does not appear in comparable international instruments of the time, for instance the UN Declaration on Race, but was apparently taken aboard in order to cover caste-type arrangements.[102] Care must be taken to distinguish between 'citizenship' and 'national origin': differential treatment on the basis of citizenship is not as such prohibited by the Convention, whereas differential treatment on the basis of national origin is. That said, there were major differences of opinion during the drafting stages as to the meaning of the term 'national origin'. For some, the term referred to groups that were distinct from the majority population in terms of mother tongue and culture; For others, the term referred to groups that were associated with another country through past citizenship. In all cases, however, it was clearly understood that the term 'national origin' did not refer to current citizenship status.[103] Article 1(2) expressly provides that the Convention "shall not apply to distinctions, exclusions, restrictions or preferences made by a State Party to this Convention between citizens and non-citizens". The Convention is also without prejudice to domestic laws concerning nationality, citizenship and naturalization, provided that such laws do not discriminate against any particular nationality.[104]

---

[101] The point that there is no such thing as race but that the notion would nevertheless have to be used in the convention was made by the Finnish delegate. See Lerner *cit. supra* note 7, p. 49, particularly footnote 19.

[102] See CERD, General Recommendation No. 29 (2002); McKean, *cit. supra* note 44, p. 156; Thornberry, *cit. supra* note 7, p. 262.

[103] Thornberry, *cit. supra* note 7, pp. 262–263.

[104] Article 1(3).

Distinction based on nationality was at issue in the 1991 case of *Diop* v. *France*, where the CERD took the view that a French law which stipulated that only citizens of France could accede to the legal profession in France did not violate the Convention because the refusal to admit the petitioner was based on nationality and not on any of the grounds enumerated in Article 1.[105] This said, the Committee has reminded through its case law and general comments that also non-citizens are to be protected from racial discrimination as it is defined in the Convention, and that distinctions based on citizenship should not be allowed to be used as a pretext for racial discrimination as that would undermine the basic prohibition of discrimination as defined in the Convention. In the 1999 case of *Ziad Ben Ahmed Habassi* v. *Denmark* the Committee took the view that nationality was not the most appropriate criterion for assessing the petitioner's will or capacity to repay a loan, and proceeded to examine whether the real reasons for the refusal to grant a loan to the petitioner constituted discrimination on the grounds of racial or ethnic origin.[106]

Furthermore, the Committee has construed Article 1(2) narrowly on the grounds that the ICERD should not be interpreted to detract in any way from the rights and freedoms recognized and enunciated in other human rights conventions, since human rights are, in principle, to be enjoyed by all persons, irrespective of nationality, which means that States parties are under an obligation to guarantee equality between citizens and non-citizens in the enjoyment of human rights.[107] In view of the CERD, states should also take into consideration that in some cases denial of citizenship for long-term or permanent residents could result in creating disadvantages for them in access to employment and social benefits, in violation of the Convention's anti-discrimination principles.[108] On these grounds the Committee has concluded that differential treatment based on citizenship or immigration status may also constitute discrimination under the Convention.[109]

---

[105] CERD, *Diop* v. *France*, Communication No 2/1989.

[106] CERD, *Ziad Ben Ahmed Habassi* v. *Denmark*, Communication No. 10/1997.

[107] CERD, General Recommendation No. 30 (2004).

[108] Idem.

[109] Ibid, paragraph 4. However, a general reference to 'foreigners' is not at present considered to single out a group of persons on the basis of a specific race, ethnicity, colour, descent or national or ethnic origin within the meaning of Article 1. CERD, *Kamal Quereshi* v. *Denmark*, Communication No. 33/2003.

Despite the fact that specific anti-Semitic events occurring in Europe were a major factor behind the adoption of the ICERD, the Convention does not prohibit discrimination on the basis of religion, which means that such discrimination is left to be dealt with by other international instruments.[110] The same applies to language. Given the close linkage between ethnic or national origin and linguistic and religious differences, difficult issues relating to drawing boundaries inevitably arise. It is clear, though, both in light of Article 1 and CERD's practice, that multiple discrimination, involving discrimination on the grounds of religion, language, sex, age or any other grounds, falls within the scope of the Convention insofar as discrimination on the grounds of race, colour, descent, or ethnic or national origin is also involved. The Committee has indeed lately recognized, both in its case law and its general recommendations, the interface between the grounds recognized in the Convention and the other grounds.[111] In *A.W.R.A.P.* v. *Denmark*, the Committee expressly pointed out that "it would be competent to consider a claim of 'double' discrimination on the basis of religion and another ground specifically provided for in Article 1 of the Convention", although in that specific case the Committee was forced to conclude that the case was outside its competence because it involved exclusively discrimination on the basis of religion.[112] The fact that racial discrimination can have another dimension such as gender or age discrimination does thus not in any way inhibit the Committee from addressing such discrimination.[113] As long as the difference in treatment is in any way connected to 'race' or the other grounds explicitly mentioned in the ICERD, it is considered 'racial discrimination'.

The implementation of the Convention, for instance in the context of implementation of special measures, may give rise to a need to

---

110 Thornberry, *cit. supra* note 7, p. 264. Boyle and Baldaccini, *cit. supra* note 77, pp. 148–9.

111 For instance in its General Recommendation on gender-related forms of racial discrimination, the Committee noted that "racial discrimination does not always affect women and men equally or in the same way. There are circumstances in which racial discrimination only or primarily affects women, or affects women in a different way, or to a different degree than men." CERD, General Recommendation No. 25 (2000), para 1. See also CERD, General Recommendation No. 30 (2004), para 8, and Banton, *cit. supra* note 75, pp. 191–2.

112 CERD, *A.W.R.A.P.* v. *Denmark*, Communication No. 37/2006.

113 See also CERD, Concluding observations on Austria (CERD/C/60/C/1, 21 May 2002), para 9; CERD, General Comment No. 32 (2009), para 7.

identify which racial or ethnic group a person belongs to. In this connection the CERD Committee has opined that it is not up to the state or third parties to determine this: in its General Recommendation No 8 it submitted that "the identification shall, if no justification exists to the contrary, be based upon self-identification by the individual concerned."[114] The Committee has reiterated its position in subsequent recommendations, but it has not elaborated upon the reasons underlying its opinion or the circumstances in which it would be justified to depart from the principle of self-identification.[115]

The Committee has also been of the view that it is not up to the state to determine which groups are to be regarded as racial or ethnic groups for the purposes of the Convention: this is to be determined by objective criteria.[116] In this regard the Committee has noted that the recognition of some groups and the exclusion of others may give rise to a violation of the Convention.[117]

Material Scope of Application

One of the main ambiguities of the Convention relates to its material scope of application. By the wording of the definition of discrimination, its sphere of application is limited to the political, economic, social, cultural and other fields of "public life", and more particularly to the enjoyment of "human rights and fundamental freedoms" in those fields. Unfair treatment outside these fields, or treatment that prejudices the enjoyment of some right not considered to be a human right,[118] does not constitute discrimination for the purposes of the Convention. The express reference to 'public life', which does not appear in the otherwise similar definition of gender discrimination in the CEDAW Convention adopted more than a decade after ICERD, would seem to exclude from the scope of the Convention

---

[114] CERD, General Recommendation VIII (1990).

[115] See, in particular, CERD, General Recommendation No. 32 (2009), para 34.

[116] CERD, General Recommendation XXIV, para 3. For a point of comparison, Article 1, subsections 1 and 2, of the ILO Convention No 169 (Indigenous and Tribal Peoples Convention), defines 'indigenous peoples' in both objective (descent from certain populations) and subjective (self-identification as indigenous) terms.

[117] CERD, General Recommendation XXIV, para 3.

[118] The question which rights qualify as human rights has not been authoritatively and exhaustively defined anywhere. Presumably the list of rights and freedoms mentioned in Article 5 was developed exactly because of this.

discrimination that takes place in the sphere of private life. Indeed, according to Banton, this was the intention of the drafters.[119]

The material scope of application of the ICERD is dealt with in more detail in Article 5 of the Convention which enumerates a broad but non-exhaustive list of civil, political, economic, social and cultural rights, to the enjoyment of which the prohibition of discrimination applies. The list enumerates, *inter alia*, the following rights:

- the right to equal treatment before organs administering justice;
- the right to security of person and protection by the State against violence or bodily harm;
- political rights, in particular the right to participate in elections (to vote and to stand for election);
- right to freedom of movement;
- the right to housing;
- the right to education and training;
- the rights to work, to free choice of employment, to just and favourable conditions of work, to protection against unemployment, to equal pay for equal work, to just and favourable remuneration;
- the right to marriage and the choice of spouse;
- the right of access to any place or service intended for use by the general public, such as transport, hotels, restaurants, theatres and parks; and
- the right to inherit.

As is clear from the last three rights in particular – last two of which are not recognized in the UDHR, the ICCPR or the ICESCR[120] – the

[119] Also some governments have read the Convention this way. For instance the reservation made by the United States of America upon its ratification of the CERD Convention supports this reading by referring on the one hand to its "extensive protections against discrimination" and its protections of individual privacy and freedom from governmental interference in private conduct on the other, and submitting that it "understands that the identification of the rights protected under the Convention by reference in article 1 to fields of 'public life' reflects a similar distinction between spheres of public conduct that are customarily the subject of governmental regulation, and spheres of private conduct that are not". The reservation goes on to submit that to the extent that the Convention calls for a broader regulation of private conduct, the United States does not accept any obligation under the Convention to enact legislation or take other measures under it.

[120] The UDHR (Article 16) and the ICCPR (Article 23) recognize the right to marry, but do not explicitly mention the right to the choice of spouse, even though both instruments underline that marriage shall only be entered into with the consent of the intending spouses. The right to choose one's spouse is explicitly referred to in the preamble of the UN Convention on Consent to Marriage, Minimum Age for Marriage

Convention goes a long way into what is often considered the realm of private life. At least *prima facie*, this stands in direct contrast to the reference to 'public life' made in Article 1. That said, the idea of Article 5 has been interpreted to be not the creation of new rights, but the acknowledgement of rights as they have been set forth in the core human rights documents and constitutional traditions of the states parties. This view is held by the CERD, for instance, which has submitted that "[i]t is not within the Committee's mandate to see to it that these rights are established; rather, it is the Committee's task to monitor the implementation of these rights, once they have been granted on equal terms."[121] If Article 5 is interpreted in this way, then the contradiction with Article 1 is softened somewhat, as the reference to 'public life' would then simply convey the idea that whenever a country provides for a particular right, then that right comes within the purview of 'public life' for that particular country, and thereby also within the purview of the Convention in respect to that country.[122] The Committee, in its General Recommendation No. 32 (2009), took this view and submitted that "[t]he list of human rights to which the principle [of non-discrimination] applies under the Convention ... extends to any field of human rights regulated by the public authorities in the State party."[123]

Article 5, explicitly and in an unqualified manner, refers to employment, housing and provision of services, the areas of life that are of particular interest from the point of view of this study. The Convention requires states to not only refrain from discrimination in these areas, but to take action to prohibit and bring to an end discrimination perpetrated by private parties. This is clear in light of Article 1(d) of the

---

and Registration of Marriages, concluded in 1962. The reference in the ICERD to the right to choose one's spouse was apparently added by way of reference to the laws that banned marriages between persons who were considered to be of different races. Such laws had existed in Nazi Germany (the so-called Nuremberg laws) and continued to exist, at the time of the adoption of the ICCPR, in many parts of the USA and South Africa.

[121] CERD, *Yilmaz-Dogan* v. the *Netherlands*, Communication No. 1/1984, para 6.4. It should also be noted that Article 5 does not delimit the competence of the Committee to consider individual complaints: In *The Jewish Community of Oslo et al* v. *Norway*, Communication No 30/2003, paragraph 10.6, the Committee noted that it "considers that its competence to receive and consider communications under article 14 is not limited to complaints alleging a violation of one or more of the rights contained in article 5."

[122] Cf. Banton, *cit. supra* note 75, p. 195; Boyle – Baldaccini, *cit. supra* note 77, p. 159 ff.

[123] CERD, General Recommendation No. 32 (2009), para 9.

Convention, which explicitly requires each state party to "prohibit and bring to an end … racial discrimination by any persons, group or organisation." The Committee has also had no difficulties in finding that a state had not fulfilled its duties in a case where the authorities had not taken due action in a situation involving discrimination perpetrated by a private employer, or to consider that a "condition of racial segregation" which states are obliged to eradicate under Article 3 of the Convention "can also arise without any initiative or direct involvement by the public authorities".[124] The reference to public life in Article 1 appears redundant and confusing also from this perspective.

State Obligations

The Convention lays down a wide array of both negative and positive obligations.

Article 2 is the main operative paragraph of the Convention and sets out the key obligations that states undertake by means of ratification. Under Article 2(1), contracting states agree to condemn racial discrimination and to pursue "*by all appropriate means* and *without delay* a policy of eliminating racial discrimination in all its forms and promoting understanding among all races" and to take a variety of measures in order to give the Convention effect.[125] In subparagraphs (a)–(e) they specifically undertake (a) to refrain from engaging in racial discrimination, (b) not to sponsor, defend or support racial discrimination by any person or organisation, (c) to review policies and amend, rescind or nullify laws and regulations which have the effect of creating or perpetuating racial discrimination, (d) to prohibit and bring to an end racial discrimination by any persons, groups or organisations, by all appropriate means, including legislation as required by circumstances, (e) to encourage, where appropriate, integrationist multiracial organisations and to discourage anything which tends to strengthen racial division. The thrust of sub-paragraph (d), the subject area of which is of the outmost importance for our purposes, is somewhat compromised by the references indicating that the means used should be 'appropriate' and that there is an obligation to adopt anti-discrimination legislation only where circumstances so require, as these two qualifications allow states to defend their choice not to enact legislation by claiming that legislation would not be the appropriate response

[124] CERD, General Recommendation No. 19 (1995), para 3.
[125] Emphasis added.

to the situation or that the situation is not so grave as to warrant its adoption. In this context the CERD Committee has simply opined that the bottom line is that the equal enjoyment of rights and freedoms referred to in Article 5 "shall be protected" by each state party and that protection may be achieved "in different ways".[126] The Committee has nevertheless called for "comprehensive anti-discrimination legislation ... in particular in the fields of housing, health care, social security (including pensions), education and access to public services".[127] Like subparagraph (d), subparagraph (e) is compromised by the addition of the phrase 'where appropriate' and vague language; factors that can potentially "strengthen racial division" are many and there is no general agreement as to what they may be.

Article 2(2), which deals with special measures, is closely associated with Article 1(4) despite many subtle differences in wording between the two.[128] It is an original and even radical provision in that it expressly makes taking special measures one of the fundamental obligations of the Convention. It requires state parties to take, "when the circumstances so warrant ... special and concrete measures to ensure the adequate development and protection of certain racial groups or individuals belonging to them, for the purpose of guaranteeing them the full and equal enjoyment of human rights and fundamental freedoms." It further specifies that these measures "shall in no case entail as a consequence the maintenance of unequal or separate rights for different

[126] CERD, General Recommendation No. 20 (1996), para 5.

[127] It has done this particularly in the context of the consideration of periodic state reports. CERD, Concluding observations on Estonia, (19 October 2006), CERD/C/EST/CO/7, para 11. See also CERD, Concluding observations on Ukraine (8 February 2007), CERD/C/UKR/CO/18. Theo van Boven, a former member of the CERD Committee, observes that the Committee "has repeatedly called upon States Parties to enact comprehensive anti-discrimination legislation, not only in the criminal sphere to suppress incitement to racial hatred and discrimination and acts of racial violence, but also in the area of civil and administrative law". Theo van Boven, 'The Committee on the Elimination of Racial Discrimination: Trends and Developments' *Roma Rights* 1–2, 2003.

[128] Some of the terminological differences – which are not explained – between Article 1(4) and Article 2(2) are the following: 'special measures' v. 'special and concrete measures', 'securing adequate advancement' v. 'ensuring adequate development and protection', 'separate rights' v. 'unequal or separate rights', 'racial or ethnic groups' v. 'racial groups', and 'equal enjoyment or exercise of human rights and fundamental freedoms' v. 'equal enjoyment of human rights and fundamental freedoms'. The CERD Committee has opined that these "nuances of difference... do not disturb [the] essential unity of concept and purpose" of the two provisions. CERD, General Recommendation No. 32 (2009), para 29.

racial groups after the objectives for which they were taken have been achieved".

The meaning of Article 2(2) has remained unclear and its impact modest, both in light of academic doctrines and state practice. One might be tempted to explain this in terms of the complex wording of the Article, which the CERD Committee and the academic commentators have done little to elucidate until lately.[129] Article 2(2) indeed has its share of compromissary phrases and obscurities,[130] but even a basic literal reading appears to suggest primarily two things. The Article recognizes that to be able to enjoy their rights and freedoms in practice, (i) 'racial groups' must be protected by the state from anything and everything that endangers their enjoyment of those rights, such as vigilante groups trying to interfere with their right to freedom of assembly, and (ii) that 'racial groups' must be targeted for positive/affirmative action in so far as any condition, for instance poor material conditions or below-average educational attainment levels, effectively prevents members of these groups from the enjoyment of their rights or freedoms. What has made it so difficult for states to embrace this article might therefore not be its obscure wording; the reason may also be political and doctrinal. Article 2(2) poses difficulties for many states, because it comes close to recognition of group rights and because it places positive obligations upon them. Article 2(2) may be experienced as problematic also from a doctrinal point of view, because the general thrust of the other articles of the Convention is to prohibit the making of distinctions on the basis of 'race' and the other associated criteria, whereas the implementation of Article 2(2) in practice may indeed require the making of such distinctions.

The ICERD condemns racial segregation and apartheid in Article 3. That article obliges states parties to "prevent, prohibit and eradicate all practices of racial segregation", and the Committee has in its respective General Recommendation No 19 opined that a condition of racial

[129] Lerner, *cit. supra* note 7, p. 163 ff; Boyle - Baldaccini, *cit. supra* note 77, pp. 156 ff. It was only in 2009 that the CERD issued a General Recommendation on Articles 1(4) and 2(2), viz. General Recommendation No. 32.

[130] Article 2(2) employs some open phrases, such as "when the circumstances so warrant" and "adequate development". It is not entirely clear from the Convention whether, and if yes why, the obligation to take special measures was deliberately restricted only to "racial groups". In view of the CERD, special measures should as a matter of principle be available to any group or person covered by Article 1 of the ICERD, not just "racial groups". See CERD, General Recommendation No. 32 (2009), para 24.

segregation can also arise without any initiative or direct involvement by public authorities, for instance as an unintended by-product of the actions of private individuals linked with residential patterns influenced by group differences in income.[131] Accordingly the Committee has invited states to monitor all trends that can give rise to segregation and to work for the eradication of any negative consequences that ensue.

Article 4 requires states to "condemn all propaganda and all organizations which are based on ideas or theories of superiority of one race or group of persons of one colour or ethnic origin or which attempt to justify or promote racial hatred and discrimination in any form"; the specific actions to be undertaken are enumerated in subparagraphs a–c. The Committee has sought to clarify the obligation under Article 4, and has considered that state parties are required to penalize four categories of conduct: (i) dissemination of ideas based upon racial superiority or hatred; (ii) incitement to racial hatred; (iii) acts of violence against any 'race' or group of persons of another colour or ethnic origin; and (iv) incitement to such acts.[132] Article 4 was an outcome of a difficult compromise after long discussions,[133] and some of its aspects have been viewed as an infringement of the fundamental rights of freedom of speech and freedom of association, which is why several countries made reservations in this respect upon the ratification of ICERD.[134] These critical positions have been challenged by the Committee, according to which the prohibition of the dissemination of ideas based upon racial superiority or hatred is compatible with the right to freedom of opinion and expression.[135]

Article 7 places an obligation upon states parties to adopt "immediate and effective measures, particularly in the fields of teaching,

---

[131] CERD, General Recommendation No. 19 (1995).

[132] Threats and remarks were deemed to constitute incitement to racial discrimination and to acts of violence contrary to Article 4(a) in CERD, *L.K.* v. *The Netherlands*, Communication No. 4/1991.

[133] Lerner, *cit. supra* note 7, p. 53.

[134] USA is one of these countries.

[135] See further CERD, General recommendation XV (1993), where the Committee also emphasized that provisions of Article 4 are of mandatory character and should be effectively enforced. What is also of legal relevance in this dispute is that Article 4 specifies that the actions enumerated in subparagraphs a–c are to be undertaken "with due regard to the principles embodied in the Universal Declaration of Human Rights and the rights expressly set forth in article 5 of this Convention", including therefore freedom of expression and freedom of assembly and association.

education, culture and information", with a view to "combating prejudices", "promoting understanding, tolerance and friendship among nations and racial and ethnical groups" and "propagating the purposes and principles of the Charter of the United Nations, the Universal Declaration of Human Rights, the United Nations Declaration on the Elimination of All Forms of Racial Discrimination, and this Convention". This educative obligation is wide-reaching and theoretically speaking of high importance, but has been largely neglected in practice.[136]

Domestic Enforcement and Remedies

Article 6 of the Convention requires states to provide effective national remedies for acts of racial discrimination:

> States Parties shall assure to everyone within their jurisdiction effective protection and remedies, through the competent national tribunals and other State institutions, against any acts of racial discrimination which violate his human rights and fundamental freedoms contrary to this Convention, as well as the right to seek from such tribunals just and adequate reparation or satisfaction for any damage suffered as a result of such discrimination.

Article 6 requires the availability, nationally, of judicial mechanisms. Any judicial avenue, whether of criminal, civil or administrative nature will presumably do, provided that individual complainants have the right to seek just and adequate reparation or satisfaction for any damage incurred and that protection and remedies can be deemed to be effective.[137] The Committee seems to implicitly favour a legal system where several different types of legal avenues are available.[138] To assess the effectiveness of national remedies, the Committee routinely asks

---

[136] Many academic commentators deal with Article 7 in passim, and for instance McKean describes Article 7 as "mere hortatory portmanteau clause of little normative importance", *cit. supra* note 44, p. 165. The CERD has also noted that only few states have reported of the measures they have adopted to give effect to Article 7, and has emphasised the importance of Article 7 by opining that measures envisaged therein are "important and effective means of eliminating racial discrimination". CERD, General Recommendation V (1977). To complete the picture, Boyle and Baldaccini have recorded an "almost total neglect of Article 7" also on part of the CERD, *cit. supra* note 77, p. 154.

[137] van Boven, *cit. supra* note 127.

[138] The Committee has, for instance, called states parties to consider giving victims of racial discrimination the opportunity to use parajudicial procedures for conflict resolution, including mediation and conciliation. General Recommendation 31 (2005), para 16. See e.g. CERD, Concluding observations on Finland, CERD/C/304/Add. 107 (1 May 2001), para 15.

states parties to report on the number of complaints and prosecutions processed, and where it finds a low number of proceedings, it usually requests the state party to consider whether the lack of formal complaints may be result of victims' lack of awareness of rights, lack of confidence in police or judicial authorities, or the authorities' lack of attention, sensitivity, or commitment to cases of racial discrimination.[139] With respect to civil proceedings the Committee has increasingly begun to recommend that states provide for a shift in the burden of proof in order to alleviate the difficulties associated with establishing discrimination.[140] Whereas a literal reading of Article 6 would result in the absurd view that an act of racial discrimination would already have to be legally established before a petitioner would be entitled to protection and a remedy, the Committee has taken the position that Article 6 provides protection to alleged victims if their claims are 'arguable' under the Convention.[141]

A considerable number of communications submitted to the Committee have dealt with the requirements posed by Article 6 and the nature of state obligations in this respect. In the case of *Gelle* v. *Denmark* the CERD noted the following on the nature of state obligations:

> The Committee observes that it does not suffice, for purposes of article 4 of the Convention, merely to declare acts of racial discrimination punishable on paper. Rather, criminal laws and other legal provisions prohibiting racial discrimination must also be effectively implemented by the competent national tribunals and other State institutions. This obligation is implicit in article 4 of the Convention, under which State parties "undertake to adopt immediate and positive measures" to eradicate all incitement to, or acts of, racial discrimination. It is also reflected in other provisions of the Convention, such as article 2, paragraph 1(d), which requires States to "prohibit and bring to an end, by all appropriate means," racial discrimination, and article 6, guaranteeing to everyone "effective protection and remedies" against acts of racial discrimination.[142]

---

[139] See e.g. CERD, Concluding observations on Czech Republic CERD/C/63/CO/4 (2003), para 11; CERD, Concluding observations on Bahrain CERD/C/BHR/CO/7 (14 April 2005), para 18.

[140] See CERD, General Recommendation XXX, para 24. See also CERD, Concluding observations on Australia, CERD/C/AUS/CO/14, 14 April 2005, para 15.

[141] CERD, *Durmic* v. *Serbia and Montenegro*, Communication No. 29/2003, para 9.6.

[142] CERD, *Gelle* v. *Denmark*, Communication No 34/2004, *para* 7.3. See also CERD, *L.K.* v. *The Netherlands*, Communication No. 4/1991, paras 6.4 – 6.7; CERD, *Yilmaz-Dogan* v. *Netherlands*, Communication No. 1/1984; CERD, *Adan* v. *Denmark*, Communication No. 43/2008, paras 7.1.-7.8.

In several cases the Committee has emphasized the duty of states to investigate claims of discrimination, where a matter falls under the purview of national criminal law, promptly, thoroughly, effectively and with due diligence and expedition.[143] It has also pointed out that there is a duty to ensure the impartiality of the judicial process and of the juries in particular, and has submitted that there is a need to have simple enough procedures to deal with complaints of racial discrimination, in particular where more than one recourse measure is available.[144]

The Committee has, in the interests of promoting the effectiveness of domestic remedies, also called for states parties to take following measures: to offer procedural status for associations for the protection of the rights of victims; to grant victims legal aid and an interpreter free of charge; to protect victims and their families against any form of victimization (intimidation or reprisals); to supply the requisite legal information to persons belonging to most vulnerable social groups, and to promote centres that provide free legal help and/or conciliation and mediation services.[145]

The Committee has, in no uncertain terms, been of the view that states also have more general enforcement duties (in *sensu lato*) that are linked to their general obligation to eliminate discrimination. It has, for instance, been of the view that where there is evidence of disproportionate levels of unemployment among migrant and minority groups, the state concerned should assess the extent to which the disproportionate level of unemployment is the result of discrimination, and then take measures to combat this phenomenon.[146] With regard to housing, it has asked states to provide information on measures taken to prevent ghettoization/segregation in housing.[147] These examples suggest that in view of the CERD there exists a pattern of responsibility

[143] CERD, *Jama* v. *Denmark*, Communication No. 41/2008, para 9; *CERD*, *Durmic* v. *Serbia and Montenegro*, Communication No 29/2003, para 10; CERD, *Ms. M.B* v. *Denmark*, Communication No. 20/2000; CERD, *Ziad Ben Ahmed Habassi* v. *Denmark*, Communication No. 10/1997; CERD, *L.K.* v. *The Netherlands*, Communication No. 4/1991.

[144] CERD, *Z.U.B.S.* v. *Australia*, Communication No. 6/1995.

[145] CERD, General Recommendation 31 (2005), paras 6–9, 17.

[146] See e.g. CERD, Concluding observations on Denmark (19 October 2006), para 16.

[147] CERD, Concluding observations on Denmark (19 October 2006), para 17; CERD, Concluding observations on Portugal (19 August 2004), para 12; CERD, Concluding observations on Luxemburg (18 April 2005), para 17.

where each state has to monitor the realisation of a particular right in practice and to investigate any imbalances that are found, and if the investigation forecloses that the imbalance is due to discrimination, then there is an obligation to take measures with a view to eliminating discrimination.

6.6 International Covenant on Civil and Political Rights

Introduction

After the proclamation of the UDHR, preparations were started with a view to making the rights and freedoms enunciated in it legally binding. In that process there were intense debates about whether to have a single, comprehensive instrument, or whether it would be better to have two separate instruments, one dealing with civil and political rights and the other with economic, social and cultural rights. In the end the latter opinion prevailed, primarily because some state representatives viewed at that time that the two sets of rights were of a different nature.[148] The standard argument evoked in support of this view was that the rights in the first group are absolute and immediate, justiciable (capable of being applied by courts and other relevant bodies) and relatively inexpensive to implement, whereas the latter set of rights are programmatic, to be realized gradually, not justiciable and having more substantial financial implications.[149] Many human rights documents and academic commentaries have since challenged this view, in the interests of promoting the principle that all human rights are indivisible and interrelated,[150] though it is often also acknowledged that differences remain.[151] In any case the reality is that the 'international

[148] See Asbjørn Eide, 'Economic, Social and cultural rights as Human Rights' in Asbjørn Eide et al (eds.), *Economic, social and cultural rights: A textbook* (Dordrecht: Martinus Nijhoff, 2001); See also Eide – Rosas, *cit supra* note 44.

[149] See e.g. idem (Eide), p. 10.

[150] For instance the Vienna Declaration proclaims, in Article 5, that "[a]ll human rights are universal, indivisible and interdependent and interrelated".

[151] E.g. Eide and Rosas submit that one cannot deny that there are some significant differences of emphasis between the typical civil rights on the one hand and some of the economic, social and cultural rights on the other, particularly as regards the role of the state and justiciability of some of the latter rights. Asbjørn Eide – Allan Rosas, *cit supra* note 44, pp. 4–6. According to Scheinin the underdeveloped justiciability of international treaties is due to the vague wording of many of the provisions and the relatively weak international monitoring mechanisms under the treaties in question. Scheinin, 'Economic and Social Rights as Legal Rights', in Asbjørn Eide et al (eds.) *Economic, social and cultural rights: A textbook* (Dordrecht: Martinus Nijhoff, 2001).

bill of rights' consists of the UDHR and two separate instruments, the International Covenant on Civil and Political Rights (ICCPR) and the International Covenant on Social, Economic and Cultural Rights (ICSECR).

The ICCPR was concluded in 1966 and it had been ratified by 167 countries as of January 2011.[152] The opinions issued by the Human Rights Committee (HRC), established to monitor the implementation of the Covenant, have gained considerable authority, at least within the human rights circles and most of the academic world. The practical importance of the ICCPR and the HRC is further emphasised by the existence of the individual complaint mechanism provided for in an Optional Protocol. More than one hundred countries have recognized the competence of the Committee to receive and consider individual complaints. An individual can submit a communication after having exhausted all available domestic remedies, which emphasizes the primacy of domestic remedies. More than 1 800 communications have been filed.[153] The inter-state complaint procedure, set out in the ICCPR, has never been used.

Concept of Discrimination

Much like the UDHR, the ICCPR contains two main provisions on non-discrimination, in addition to which several articles underline the equal enjoyment of particular rights.[154] The first main provision is Article 2, which relates to the obligation to ensure the rights recognized in the Covenant to all individuals without any distinction:

> Each State Party to the present Covenant undertakes to respect and to ensure to all individuals within its territory and subject to its jurisdiction the rights recognized in the present Covenant, without distinction of any kind, such as race, colour, sex, language, religion, political or other opinion, national or social origin, property, birth or other status.

The reality in any case is, that many states do still make a distinction between the two sets of rights. For instance Christopher McCrudden has recorded "continuing unease" in the UK over socio-economic rights, see McCrudden, 'Mainstreaming Human Rights' in Colin Harvey (ed.) *Human Rights in the Community: Rights as Agents of Change* (Oxford: Hart, 2005).

152 Source: http://treaties.un.org (accessed 1.1.2011).

153 Report of the Human Rights Committee (Sessional/Annual report of the Committee, Vol. 1, 2009), A/64/40.

154 These include Articles 3, 4(1), 14(1 and 3), 23(4), 24 and 25.

Article 26, for its part, provides for equal protection of the law and a prohibition of discrimination:

> All persons are equal before the law and are entitled without any discrimination to the equal protection of the law. In this respect, the law shall prohibit any discrimination and guarantee to all persons equal and effective protection against discrimination on any ground such as race, colour, sex, language, religion, political or other opinion, national or social origin, property, birth or other status.

The fundamental role of the prohibition of discrimination is underlined by Article 4, which provides that under no circumstances, even in times of a public emergency, is it allowed to pursue measures which "involve discrimination solely on the ground of race, colour, sex, language, religion or social origin".[155]

Article 2 requires that the rights recognized in the Covenant are to be respected and ensured without 'distinction' of any kind, whereas Article 26 requires states to prohibit 'discrimination'. A disagreement broke out in the drafting of Article 2 as to whether it should prohibit 'distinctions' or 'discrimination'.[156] Those who favoured the term 'distinction' argued that this more rigid term be used because the term 'discrimination', for which there was no generally adopted test at the time, would open the door to legal arguments defending arrangements such as Apartheid on the grounds that they do not constitute discrimination but are legitimate distinctions that for instance simply take into account the distinct nature of different groups.[157] In this view it was therefore necessary to prohibit all 'distinctions'. Those who favoured

---

[155] See HRC, General Comment No 29 (2001) for the Committee's interpretation of Article 4.

[156] See e.g. Ramcharan, *cit. supra* note 22, p. 258 ff; Nowak, *cit. supra* note 19, pp. 43–44.

[157] This argument was indeed made by the government of South Africa on numerous occasions. In its submissions to the International Court of Justice in the *South West Africa* cases, South Africa defended its policy of differentiating between groups on the grounds that the different groups were at completely different stages of development and on the grounds of the "desire of the various groups to retain their separate identities". See International Court of Justice, *South West Africa Cases*, Volume II (1966), Section B. Pleadings, 5. *Counter-Memorial filed by the Government of the Republic of South Africa*, submitted on 10 January 1964, para 22 ff. Similarly, in its written statements to the International Court of Justice in *Advisory Opinion on Namibia* the government of South Africa contended that the Apartheid policy was pursued in the interests of the inhabitants of Namibia. See International Court of Justice, *Legal Consequences for States of the Continued Presence of South Africa in Namibia (South West Africa) notwithstanding Security Council Resolution 276 (1970)*, Advisory Opinion of 21 June 1971, paras 128–131.

the term 'discrimination' argued that the use of the term 'distinction' would close the door not just from Apartheid and other unjust arrangements, but also from positive special measures such as affirmative action that may involve the making of distinctions. In the end the term 'distinction' was chosen for the purposes of Article 2, possibly in order to align it with Article 2 of the UDHR,[158] but with the majority opinion favouring the view that the use of the term nevertheless did not rule out special measures but only arbitrary or unjust distinctions.[159] *Travaux préparatoires*, the practice of the HRC, and academic literature all support the reading that the difference in wording between Articles 2 and 26 is in this respect of no great relevance, and that both provisions are to be interpreted as prohibiting only arbitrary or otherwise unjust distinctions.[160]

Article 26 of the ICCPR and its reference to the principles 'equality before the law' and 'equal protection of the law' derive from Article 7 of the UDHR.[161] These principles were again debated during the drafting stages in "long, controversial discussions" that "not infrequently climaxed in a crucial vote."[162] One of the points not fully clear from the start was again whether the two principles preclude the making of any distinctions on the mentioned grounds.[163] It was explained that these principles deal with equality, not identity of treatment, and that they therefore do not rule out reasonable differentiation between individuals and groups.[164] There were also debates about the meaning of the two principles, and it was explained that they are directed on the one hand on those who apply the law, such as judges and administrative officials, and the legislature on the other.

---

[158] Skogly, *cit. supra* note 29, p. 63. The word 'distinction' is also used in the Constitution of France, a fact which might also have played a part, as the French Constitution was often regarded as a model for the drafting of the ICCPR. See Ramcharan, *cit. supra* note 22, pp. 258–259 and the references cited.

[159] Dominic McGoldrick, *The Human Rights Committee: Its Role in the Development of the International Covenant on Civil and Political Rights* (Oxford: Clarendon Press, 1991), p. 275; Thornberry, *cit. supra* note 7, p. 281 ff; Ramcharan, *cit. supra* note 22, pp. 258–259.

[160] See e.g. HRC, General Comment 18 (1989), para 8 in particular; Dominic McGoldrick, *cit. supra* note 159, p. 275; Thornberry, *cit. supra* note 7, pp. 281–286; Ramcharan, *cit. supra* note 22.

[161] See HRC, *Zwaan-de Vries*, Communication No.182/1984; Ramcharan, *cit. supra* note 22, p. 254.

[162] Nowak, *cit. supra* note 19, p. 462.

[163] Thornberry, *cit. supra* note 7, pp. 284–285; Ramcharan, *cit. supra* note 22, p. 254.

[164] Ramcharan, *cit. supra* note 22, p. 254; Nowak *cit. supra* note 19, p. 464.

The specific meaning of the second sentence of Article 26, which provides that "the law shall prohibit any discrimination and guarantee to all persons equal and effective protection against discrimination", has also raised questions.[165] By its wording it appears to include an obligation to prohibit discrimination by enacting special laws and an obligation to afford effective protection against discrimination.[166] These very broad lines of interpretation are supported by the *travaux*, the practice of the HRC and the legal commentaries.[167] By way of an example, the HRC submitted in *Zwaan-de Vries* that Article 26 "prohibits discrimination in law or practice in any field regulated and protected by public authorities" and that Article 26 is "thus concerned with the obligations imposed on States in regard to their legislation and the application thereof."

As mentioned, Article 26 employs the concept of 'discrimination', a notion that is not self-explanatory or defined in the Convention itself. The Human Rights Committee, finding itself in need to clarify that term, elaborated a definition in its General Comment No 18 (1989). Under the apparent influence of the CERD Convention, the CEDAW Convention, and implicitly also the ILO and UNESCO Conventions, it submitted that

> the Committee believes that the term "discrimination" as used in the Covenant should be understood to imply any distinction, exclusion, restriction or preference which is based on any ground such as race, colour, sex, language, religion, political or other opinion, national or social origin, property, birth or other status, and which has the purpose or effect of nullifying or impairing the recognition, enjoyment or exercise by all persons, on an equal footing, of all rights and freedoms.[168]

In this General Comment, the Committee went on to reiterate that the enjoyment of rights and freedoms "on an equal footing" does not mean identical treatment in every instance.[169] In its opinion "not every differentiation of treatment will constitute discrimination, if the criteria for such differentiation are reasonable and objective and if the aim is to achieve a purpose which is legitimate under the Covenant."[170] The

---

[165] Nowak, *cit. supra* note 19, p. 475.

[166] Ibid, p. 476.

[167] See Ramcharan, *cit. supra* note 22, pp. 254–256; Nowak, *cit. supra* note 19, pp. 464–465.

[168] HRC, General Comment No. 18 (1989), para 7.

[169] Ibid, para 8.

[170] Ibid, para 13.

Committee has followed this broad and flexible line of reasoning, which leaves it a considerable amount of discretion, also in its case law. For instance in the 2010 decision in *Drda* v. *Czech Republic* it stated that "[t]he Committee reiterates its jurisprudence that not all differentiations in treatment can be deemed to be discriminatory under Article 26. A differentiation which is compatible with the provisions of the Covenant and is based on objective and reasonable grounds does not amount to prohibited discrimination within the meaning of Article 26."[171]

The above considerations apply best where direct discrimination is at issue. The HRC has eventually, after long and complicated developments, come to embrace the concept of indirect discrimination. The complications and inconsistencies in the HRC's approach are probably at least partly attributable to the vagueness of the above-mentioned definition of discrimination that it borrowed from the other instruments.[172] The General Comment No. 18 on non-discrimination, adopted in 1989, did not explicitly refer to indirect discrimination, though it did note, as mentioned above, that a distinction can violate Articles 2 and/or 26 even if it was not made for the purposes of discriminating against a particular group or individual but was discriminatory in its effects. In its decision in *Bhinder* v. *Canada*, which was adopted by the Committee at the same session as the General Comment, the HRC refused to directly address the question whether a general measure – in that case a hard hat requirement issued by a rail road company on its employees – could possibly constitute *de facto* discrimination against Sikh men who are required to wear a turban for religious reasons and who in consequence could not wear a hard hat.[173]

---

[171] HRC, *Drda* v. *The Czech Republic*, Communication No. 1581/2007, para 7.2. See also HRC, *Süsser* v. *The Czech Republic*, Communication No 1488/2006, para 7.2; HRC, *Vjatseslav Tsarjov* v. *Estonia*, Communication No. 1223/2003; HRC, *Zwaan-de Vries* v. *The Netherlands*, Communication No.182/1984, paragraph 13; HRC, *X* v. *Colombia*, Communication No. 1361/2005. Sometimes the HRC uses a slightly different wording, and requires that for a distinction not to constitute discrimination, it "must be justified on reasonable and objective grounds, in pursuit of an aim that is legitimate under the Covenant." HRC, *Haraldsson and Sveinsson* v. *Iceland*, Communication No 1306/2004.

[172] See Sarah Joseph – Jenny Schultz – Melissa Castan, *The International Covenant on Civil and Political Rights: Cases, Materials and Commentary* (Oxford: Oxford University Press, 2000), p. 533 ff.

[173] In para 6.2 the Committee said that "[i]f the requirement that a hard hat be worn is seen as a discrimination de facto against persons of the Sikh religion under article 26, then … the legislation requiring that workers in federal employment be protected

In *Simunek et al* v. *The Czech Republic*, adopted in 1995, the HRC expressed its view that intent "is not alone dispositive in determining a breach of Article 26" and that "an act which is not politically motivated may still contrive Article 26 if its effects are discriminatory", a conceptualization that does not however indicate that it had fully embraced the concept of indirect discrimination yet.[174] Finally, in 2003, in the case of *Althammer* v. *Austria* (no 2.), the HRC expressly recognized the concept of indirect discrimination by noting that indirect discrimination occurs when a rule or a measure that is neutral at face value or without the intent to discriminate has detrimental effects that exclusively or disproportionately affect persons having a particular 'race'. It reiterated this position in the 2004 case *Derksen* v. *the Netherlands* in the following way:

> The Committee recalls that article 26 prohibits both direct and indirect discrimination, the latter notion being related to a rule or measure that may be neutral in its face without any intent to discriminate but which nevertheless results in discrimination because of its exclusive or disproportionate adverse effect on a certain category of persons. Yet, a distinction only constitutes prohibited discrimination in the meaning of article 26 of the Covenant if it is not based on objective and reasonable criteria.[175]

The *travaux préparatoires* to Articles 2 and 26 clearly indicate that these articles were not meant to preclude positive or affirmative action.[176] The HRC has pursued the same line of interpretation and has stated that the prohibition of discrimination in Article 26 does not rule out positive action measures, not even relatively far-reaching ones. In *Jacobs* v. *Belgium* the Committee considered that a domestic rule that required at least four of the eleven 'non-justice members' of the national High Council of Justice to be women and four men was in accordance with the ICCPR, as was the use of gender as a tie-breaker between equally qualified job applicants in a situation where equality between men and women was still lacking.[177]

---

from injury… is to be regarded as reasonable and directed towards objective purposes that are compatible with the Covenant". HRC, *Karnel Singh Bhinder* v. *Canada*, Communication No. 208/1986.

[174] HRC, *Simunek, Hastings, Tuzilova and Prochazka* v. *The Czech Republic*, Communication No. 516/1992.

[175] HRC, *Derksen* v. *The Netherlands*, Communication No 976/2001, para 9.3.

[176] Ramcharan, *cit. supra* note 22, pp. 259–261.

[177] HRC, *Jacobs* v. *Belgium*, Communication No. 943/2000.

The Committee has actually not just acknowledged the legitimacy of positive action, but has opined that states are *obliged* to take such action in order to diminish or eliminate conditions which cause or help to perpetuate discrimination prohibited by the Covenant:

> For example, in a state where the general conditions of a certain part of the population prevent or impair their enjoyment of human rights, the state should take specific action to correct those conditions. Such action may involve granting for a time to the part of the population concerned certain preferential treatment in specific matters as compared with the rest of the population. As long as such action is needed to correct discrimination in fact, it is a case of legitimate differentiation.[178]

Furthermore, in General Comment No 4 on Article 3 (on gender equality), the HRC said that

> article 3, as articles 2(1) and 26 in so far as those articles primarily deal with the prevention of discrimination on a number of grounds, among which sex is one, requires not only measures of protection but also affirmative action designed to ensure the positive enjoyment of rights. This cannot be done simply by enacting laws.

Despite its potential importance, this aspect of the HRC's jurisprudence is surprisingly underdeveloped and unclear.[179] One of the unresolved questions is whether any obligation to take 'specific action' and 'preferential treatment' to correct discrimination in fact is of an immediate or progressive nature.[180] The tactic of the HRC in this respect appears to be one of persuading state parties rather than condemning them for having failed to take the necessary action, implying a measure of flexibility.[181]

Personal Scope and Grounds

The beneficiaries of the Convention rights and freedoms include all individuals within the territory of a state party and subject to its jurisdiction, and are thus not restricted to nationals of that state.[182] The lists

---

[178] HRC, General Comment No. 18 (1989), para 10.

[179] Similarly Martin Scheinin 'Experiences of the application of article 26 of the International Covenant on Civil and Political Rights' in Council of Europe, *Non-discrimination: A human right*, Proceedings of the Seminar marking the entry into force of Protocol No 12 to the European Convention on Human rights, Strasbourg, 11 October 2005 (Council of Europe, 2006).

[180] McGoldrick, *cit. supra* note 159, p. 275.

[181] Idem.

[182] This is without prejudice to the fact that several rights guaranteed in the Covenant are in themselves restricted in one way or the other.

of prohibited grounds of discrimination in Articles 2 and 26 are identical, and include 'race', 'colour', religion and 'national or social origin'. A motion made during the drafting that proposed to replace the words 'race' and 'colour' with the term 'ethnic origin', on the grounds that 'race' was considered to be imprecise and unscientific, was defeated on the grounds that 'race' and 'colour' were perceived to be more easily understood in their general usage.[183] The lists are not exhaustive, as is indicated by the words 'such as' and 'other status'. It is not entirely clear what other grounds should be taken to be covered in addition to those that are explicitly mentioned. Some authors have suggested that the 'other' grounds must logically be *materially similar* to those listed, that is, distinctions unrelated to an individual's merit, abilities or efforts.[184] Yet other authors suggest that every conceivable distinction that cannot be objectively justified is, in the final analysis, impermissible.[185]

The Human Rights Committee has considered in its practice that sexual orientation, nationality, age, place of residence, and employment/unemployment and a number of other factors can count as 'other statuses' protected by Articles 2 and 26.[186] Determination of impermissibility has been made on a case-by-case basis. The HRC, in *Kavanagh* v. *Ireland*, actually adopted the view that the first sentence of Article 26 ("[a]ll persons are equal before the law and are entitled without any discrimination to the equal protection of the law") can be evoked without any reference to a particular ground of discrimination – and without reference to any particular comparator.[187] This suggests that the HRC is disposed to take a liberal attitude towards the issue of grounds, though at the same time it appears that differentiation on grounds not explicitly mentioned is likely to be tested less strictly than

---

[183] Nowak, *cit. supra* note 19, p. 46.

[184] Thornberry, *cit. supra* note 7, p. 281.

[185] Nowak, *cit. supra* note 19, p. 45. Indeed, the Covenant does not speak of "other such status" or of "other similar status", but only of "other status", which is wider in scope and does not seem to require that the other protected grounds are materially similar to those explicitly mentioned. Therefore, and given also that the aim of the Article 2 is to ensure to "all individuals" fundamental human rights "without distinction of any kind", the view that basically any ground of distinction can be considered under Articles 2 and 26 appears well-founded.

[186] HRC, *Toonen* v *Australia*, Communication No 488/1992; *Gueye et al.* v *France*, Communication No. 196/1985; *Love et al* v. *Australia*, Communication No. 983/2001; *Lindgren et al* v. *Sweden*, Communication No 298/1988; *Calvancati Araujo-Jongens* v. *The Netherlands*, Communication No 418/1990. See also Joseph et al, *cit. supra* note 172, p. 530.

[187] HRC, *Kavanagh* v. *Ireland*, Communication No 819/1998.

differentiation on grounds that are explicitly mentioned.[188] While none of the individual communications examined by the HRC have so far dealt with *ethnic* discrimination, it is clear also from its comments on country reports that ethnicity is considered to be one of the grounds on which it is not permissible to discriminate, and that it indeed is a ground that the HRC takes a special interest in, although it is less clear whether in analytical terms ethnicity should be considered to form a ground of its own or whether it should be considered to be subsumed under the notion of 'race'.

The HRC has lately recognized intersectional discrimination and has called states to address it.[189] Its decision in *Kavanagh* that equal treatment cases do not always need to proceed by means of rigid comparisons – which has been perhaps the single most difficult, sometimes prohibitive, issue in intersectional discrimination cases – also shows one possible way of dealing with such discrimination.

Material Scope

Article 2 provides for an accessory right, meaning that it can only be violated in conjunction with some other substantive provision of the Covenant.[190] Under the case law of the HRC, the accessory nature of Article 2 does not mean that a violation of it can only be established when another provision of the Covenant has been violated together with Article 2.[191] If a state party to the Covenant provides, with respect to some right covered by the Covenant, for a higher level of protection than what is explicitly required, but does so in a discriminatory manner, then that is considered to violate Article 2.[192] Article 2 therefore provides protection with respect to the rights and freedoms enshrined in the Convention, including right to life, freedom of movement, right

---

[188] Joseph et al, *cit. supra* note 172, p. 532. Irene P. Asscher-Vonk "Towards One Concept of Objective Justification", in Loenen – Rodrigues (eds.), *Non-Discrimination Law: Comparative Perspectives* (The Hague: Kluwer Law International, 1999), p. 50. However, Scheinin advises that "great caution" must be exercised if one is tempted to draw any conclusions that some grounds of discrimination are more suspect than others, see Martin Scheinin "Economic and Social Rights as Legal Rights" in Asbjørn Eide et al (eds.) *Economic, social and cultural rights: A textbook* (Dordrecht: Martinus Nijhoff, 2001), p. 33.

[189] HRC, General Comment 28 (2000), para 30.

[190] Nowak, *cit. supra* note 19, p. 34.

[191] Ibid, p. 35.

[192] See HRC, *Shirin Aumeeruddy-Cziffra and 19 other Mauritian women* v. *Mauritius*, Communication No. 35/1978, para 9.2 (b) 2(i)8.

to privacy, freedom of religion, freedom of association, political rights and minority rights.

Article 26, on the other hand, is not similarly limited, which is one of the reasons why it is sometimes considered to be one of the most important international provisions on discrimination.[193] The scope of this article is mainly delimited by the notions of "equality before the law" and "equal protection of the law".[194] In its General Comment on Article 26 the HRC submitted that the Article

> prohibits discrimination in law or in fact in any field regulated and protected by public authorities. Article 26 is therefore concerned with the obligations imposed on States parties in regard to their legislation and the application thereof. Thus, when legislation is adopted by a State party, it must comply with the requirement of article 26 that its content should not be discriminatory. In other words, the application of the principle of non-discrimination contained in article 26 is not limited to those rights which are provided for in the Covenant.[195]

In *Haraldsson and Sveinsson* v. *Iceland* the HRC asserted that under Article 26, "States parties are bound, in their legislative, judicial and executive action, to ensure that everyone is treated equally and without discrimination".[196]

In 1987 the HRC came, in the consideration of *Zwaan – De Vries*, *Broeks*, and *Danning* v. *the Netherlands* cases, after long discussions, to the conclusion that Article 26 also applies in the sphere of social security. This move, which was not universally applauded at the time and which is of far-reaching consequences,[197] has now become a solid part of the Committee's jurisprudence.

The scope of Article 26, interpreted this way, is thus sweeping. First, the fields "regulated and protected by public authorities" have expanded over time, a development which has brought new areas within the purview of the Article. All countries in Europe regulate the field of

[193] Nowak, *cit. supra* note 19, p. 465. Nowak asserts that the broad interpretation of Article 26 follows unambiguously from a grammatical, systematic interpretation of Articles 2 and 26. See also HRC, General Comment No. 18 (1989); HRC, *Broeks*, Communication No 172/1984; HRC, *Zwaan-de Vries*, Communication No. 182/1984.

[194] Nowak, *cit. supra* note 19, p. 469.

[195] Para 12 of the General Comment 18 (1989).

[196] HRC, *Haraldsson and Sveinsson* v. *Iceland*, Communication 1306/2004, para 10.2.

[197] Martin Scheinin, "Women's Economic and Social Issues of Practical Implementation" in Hannikainen & Nykänen, *New Trends in Discrimination Law – International Perspectives* (Turku: Grafia, 1999), p. 20.

employment, and at least some aspects of provision of goods and services, including banking and public housing, and these areas that are of key interest to us therefore also come within the purview of the prohibition of discrimination.[198] Second, Article 26 contains a positive obligation on states to take steps to provide protection against discrimination, irrespective of whether it is perpetrated by public or private actors.[199] This has been taken to follow from the second sentence, which provides that the law shall prohibit any discrimination and guarantee to all persons equal and effective protection against discrimination in the areas covered by the first sentence, i.e. all matters dealt with by law. Indeed, in its General Comment 31 the HRC confirmed that in its view Article 26 requires that individuals are to be protected from discrimination "in fields affecting basic aspects of ordinary life such as work or housing".[200] At the end of the day, any discrimination in the application of law, whether by courts, tribunals or the public administration, is therefore prohibited,[201] as is any discrimination between private parties in the areas covered by law. Drafters and commentators, however, have been keen to emphasize that protection of privacy lays down the outer limits for the scope of application of the principle of non-discrimination.[202]

Domestic Enforcement and Remedies

Article 2(3) of the Convention provides that

Each State Party to the present Covenant undertakes:

(a) To ensure that any person whose rights or freedoms as herein recognized are violated shall have an effective remedy, notwithstanding that the violation has been committed by persons acting in an official capacity;

(b) To ensure that any person claiming such a remedy shall have his right thereto determined by competent judicial, administrative or

---

[198] See also Nowak, *cit. supra* note 19, p. 478.

[199] This appears also to have been the intention of the drafters, although the matter was not considered self-evident from the beginning, see Ramcharan, *cit. supra* note 22, pp. 261–263. Nowak, *cit. supra* note 19, p. 478.

[200] HRC, General Comment No 31 (2004), para 8.

[201] See also Nowak, *cit. supra* note 19, pp. 466–469, and Thornberry, *cit. supra* note 7, p. 285.

[202] Nowak observes that"[d]uring the drafting of Art. 26, it was repeatedly emphasised that discrimination in private relations was a matter of legitimate, personal decision-making, which is protected against State interference by the right to privacy." Nowak, *cit. supra* note 19, p. 477.

legislative authorities, or by any other competent authority provided for by the legal system of the State, and to develop the possibilities of judicial remedy;
(c) To ensure that the competent authorities shall enforce such remedies when granted.

This article provides for the overarching framework towards remedies under the ICCPR. It is complemented by other articles that require the provision of more specific remedies with respect to violations of certain rights and freedoms such as those laid down in Articles 9(5) and 14(6), the right to equal treatment not being among them. Read together, subsections (a)–(c) of Article 2(3) basically require the existence of an effective, accessible and enforceable remedy. Subsection (b), specifying that the right to a remedy can be determined by "any competent authority", has been interpreted to bring into the scope of remedies for instance investigations by parliamentary committees and ombudsmen.[203] The apparent open-endedness of the provision is qualified in view of the express emphasis laid on judicial remedies and in view of the requirement placed by subsection (a) that states must ensure that the remedy is effective, considering that the drafters expressed a strong sentiment in favour of judicial remedies as the most effective means of protection within a national system.[204]

The HRC has, through the consideration of periodic reports, engaged in a wide-reaching examination of the available domestic remedies in the different countries. It has posed questions, *inter alia*, about the provision of legal aid, possible doctrinal limitations conditioning the exercise of remedies, types of evidence that are admissible under domestic laws and the independence and impartiality of the competent authorities.[205] In its case law the HRC has drawn state parties' attention particularly to the need to pay adequate compensation and to take measures, over and above any victim-specific remedy, to ensure that similar violations do not reoccur.[206] In its jurisprudence under Article 5(2)(b) of the first optional protocol, which requires that individuals complaining to the HRC must have exhausted "all available domestic remedies" to have their communications considered, the

203 See e.g. Nowak, *cit. supra* note 19, p. 59.
204 Regarding the last point, Schachter, *cit. supra* note 15, p. 326; Nowak, *cit. supra* note 19, pp. 32, 58–59.
205 See McGoldrick, *cit. supra* note 159, pp. 279–280.
206 McGoldrick, *cit. supra* note 159, p. 285; HRC, *Blaga* v. *Romania*, Communication No 1158/2003.

HRC has indicated that it is judicial remedies that are most likely to be considered effective in that context as well.[207]

The drafting and adoption by the HRC, in 2004, of General Comment No. 31, entitled *Nature of the General Legal Obligation Imposed on States Parties to the Covenant*, allowed the Committee to elaborate its views on Article 2(3) in a more systematic manner. In this comment the HRC put particular emphasis on three matters. First, it submitted that it "attaches importance to" – but did hence not go as far as to submit that it would make the ICCPR require – "States parties' establishing appropriate judicial and administrative mechanisms for addressing claims of rights violations under domestic law".[208] Second, it stated that "[a]dministrative mechanisms are particularly required to give effect to the general obligation to investigate allegations of violations promptly, thoroughly and effectively through independent and impartial bodies", notably with respect to acts that are recognized as criminal under domestic or international law, though it did not specify where exactly this "general obligation" stemmed from.[209] Third, it submitted that Article 2(3) "requires that States parties make reparation to individuals whose Covenant rights have been violated" and said that it "considers that the Covenant generally entails appropriate compensation".[210] The Committee went on to observe that reparation can take the form of, *inter alia*, restitution, rehabilitation and measures of satisfaction, such as public apologies, public memorials, guarantees of non-repetition and changes in relevant laws and practices, as well as bringing to justice the perpetrators of human rights violations.[211] The Committee also reiterated the obligation to take measures to prevent, where a violation of a right has been established, the reoccurrence of such violations.[212]

Towards the end of General Comment No 31, the HRC interestingly and realistically observes that violations of the Covenant rights still

---

[207] See *R.T.* v. *France*, Communication No 262/87, para 7.4, where the HRC observed that the reference "all available remedies" "clearly refers in the first place to judicial remedies." See also HRC, *Vicente et al* v. *Colombia* Communication No 612/95, where the HRC considered that "purely administrative and disciplinary measures cannot be considered adequate and effective" where violations of basic human rights, such as the right to life, are at stake.

[208] Para 15.

[209] Paras 15 and 18.

[210] Para 16.

[211] Para 16.

[212] Para 17.

take place even when a State party has provided for the remedies envisaged in Article 2(3), but proceeds to make the – perhaps less realistic – assumption that this is "presumably attributable to the failure of the remedies to function effectively in practice".[213]

Complementary Equality Provisions

A number of other provisions of the ICCPR are also relevant from the equality point of view. These include in particular Article 27, which touches upon cultural equality. Article 27 guarantees individuals belonging to minorities a measure of protection by requiring that they "shall not be denied the right, in community with the other members of their group, to enjoy their own culture, to profess and practise their own religion, or to use their own language".[214] Article 27 is formulated in an extremely cautious way, one example of which is that it is couched in negative and indirect ("shall not be denied") rather than positive and direct ("has the right to") terms. This undoubtedly has to do with the fact that many differences of opinion emerged during the drafting of Article 27. In particular, it was not clear which minorities should be protected, whether it was a collective or an individual right that was at issue, and whether state obligations should go beyond mere toleration of the particular characteristics of minority groups.[215] The contemporary interpretation of Article 27, both by academic commentators and the HRC, has settled for the view that it requires states to refrain from a policy of assimilation and from any action that threatens the very existence of minorities. It is also generally considered that Article 27 requires the state to take positive measures to protect the identity of a minority against infringements by non-state actors.[216] Moreover, the HRC has opined that Article 27 may require the state to take positive measures "to ensure the effective participation of members of minority communities in decisions which affect them", thus calling for measures that provide for greater political equality.[217] Yet, the legal opinion is undecided as to what extent Article 27 might be interpreted as having

[213] Para 20.

[214] Freedom of religion, also for immigrants and persons belonging to minorities, is bolstered in Article 18.

[215] Louis B. Sohn, 'The Rights of Minorities' in Louis Henkin (ed.) *The International Bill Of Rights: The Covenant on Civil and Political Rights* (New York: Columbia University Press, 1981), pp. 273, 284–285; Nowak, *cit. supra* note 19, p. 484.

[216] HRC, General Comment No. 23 (1994), para 6.1.

[217] Idem, para 7; HRC, *Länsman et al* v. *Finland*, Communication No 671/95, para 10.4.

a programmatic effect, requiring the state to take active measures to create the kind of conditions in which minority cultures can thrive.[218] The HRC has advocated the view that positive measures by states are necessary whenever the ability of a group to maintain its identity is in jeopardy.[219] The existence of programmatic duties beyond that point is unclear, and it would seem a bit far-fetched to interpret Article 27 to require, for instance, the provision of cultural and religious accommodation in the workplace.

The ICCPR also envisages the provision of a measure of *preventive* protection, particularly through Article 20(2), which provides that "[a]ny advocacy of national, racial or religious hatred that constitutes incitement to discrimination, hostility or violence shall be prohibited by law". The HRC has interpreted the requirement to 'prohibit' to imply that the domestic law should provide for an appropriate sanction in case it is violated.[220]

Nature of State Obligations

The principal article governing the scope of state obligations under the ICCPR is Article 2. As mentioned, state parties undertake in Article 2(1) "to respect and to ensure to all individuals within its territory and subject to its jurisdiction the rights recognized in the present Covenant, without distinction of any kind". Article 26 poses more specific obligations, and expressly requires that the law shall prohibit discrimination and that states shall provide "all persons equal and effective protection against discrimination." The HRC has interpreted that this requires the adoption of non-discrimination legislation.[221]

---

[218] For instance Nowak has argued that Article 27 cannot be interpreted as having any kind of a programmatic effect. Nowak, *cit. supra* note 19, pp. 502–505. In view of Nowak, Article 27 was deliberately formulated in a *laissez faire* spirit. On the other hand, Thornberry submits that Article 27 should be interpreted as requiring that states should "take such measures as are necessary in order to assist the minority to preserve its values". See Thornberry, *cit. supra* note 7, pp. 178–186.

[219] The Committee opined in General Comment 23 (1994), para 6.2. as follows: "Although the rights protected under article 27 are individual rights, they depend in turn on the ability of the minority group to maintain its culture, language or religion. Accordingly, positive measures by States may also be necessary to protect the identity of a minority and the rights of its members to enjoy and develop their culture and language and to practise their religion, in community with the other members of the group."

[220] HRC, General Comment No 11 (1983), para 2.

[221] HRC, *Zwaan-de Vries* v. *The Netherlands*, Communication No. 182/1984, para 12.4.

The obligation to 'respect' and to 'ensure' is generally taken to imply both a negative and a positive obligation.[222] States are obliged both to refrain from violating the rights guaranteed in the Covenant, as well as to take positive steps to give effect to these rights. The latter aspect relates to Article 2(2), which provides that "[w]here not already provided for by existing legislative or other measures, each State Party to the present Covenant undertakes to take the necessary steps, in accordance with its constitutional processes and with the provisions of the present Covenant, to adopt such legislative or other measures as may be necessary to give effect to the rights recognized in the present Covenant". The means by which a state gives effect to these rights has therefore been left up to the state to be decided in accordance with its constitutional processes. The HRC in its General Comment 31 interpreted subsection 2 and the requirement to take necessary measures to mean that it imposes on states parties an obligation to "adopt legislative, judicial, administrative, educative and other appropriate measures in order to fulfil their legal obligations".[223]

The obligation to 'ensure' also means that the state party must take effective measures to secure that the rights in question are protected in relation to all violations, including those that result from actions by private individuals or other private actors. In this respect the HRC has observed that, whereas the Covenant does not have direct horizontal effect as a matter of international law and is not a substitute for domestic criminal or civil law,

> the positive obligations on States parties to ensure Covenant rights will only be fully discharged if individuals are protected by the State, not just against violations of Covenant rights by its agents, but also against acts committed by private persons or entities that would impair the enjoyment of Covenant rights insofar as they are amenable to application between private persons or entities.[224]

The interpretation that states parties are obliged by Article 26 to put a stop to discriminatory practices among private parties in sectors such as employment, education, transportation, hotels, and theatres is also supported by the *travaux*.[225]

---

[222] See e.g. Nowak, *cit. supra* note 19, pp. 36–37; Thomas Buergenthal, 'State obligations and permissible derogations' in Louis Henkin (ed.) *The International Bill Of Rights: The Covenant on Civil and Political Rights* (New York: Columbia University Press, 1981), pp. 77–78.

[223] General Comment 31 (2004), para 8.

[224] Idem.

[225] Nowak, *cit. supra* note 19, p. 478.

6.7 International Covenant on Economic, Social and Cultural Rights

Introduction

The International Convention on Economic, Social and Cultural Rights (ICESCR) was adopted in 1966. As of January 2011 it had been ratified by 160 states.[226] As already mentioned, a distinction is often made between civil and political rights on the one hand, and economic, social and cultural rights on the other, the distinction being that only the former are seen as readily justiciable rights, meaning rights that can be enforced through courts of law. While it is true that economic, social and cultural rights (ESC rights) are often framed as state obligations aiming at progressive realization and also acknowledging the constraints due to the limits of available financial resources, some ESC rights or aspects thereof are considered to impose obligations which are of immediate effect. The clearest example of a justiciable right in this context is considered to be the right to enjoy ESC rights without any discrimination.[227]

However, it is the case that there is very little legal guidance in the area of ESC rights, which places a great demand on the Committee on Economic, Social and Cultural Rights (CESCR), the body that monitors implementation of the ICESCR, and the community of legal scholars, to elucidate on the Convention's often vaguely-worded provisions. The CESCR has produced a volume of legal opinions through its General Comments and the observations that it has made in the course of the examination of periodic country reports. In particular, its General Comment No. 20 on non-discrimination, adopted in 2009, answered a number of questions about how the Committee understands the principle of non-discrimination. Moreover, an optional protocol to the ICESCR was adopted in 2008, by virtue of which states may recognise the competence of the Committee to receive and consider individual complaints, providing the Committee a new important avenue for developing and communicating its views.[228] A source of legal opinions that has gained a position of some *de facto* authority

[226] Source: http://treaties.un.org (accessed 1.1.2011).

[227] CESCR, General Comment No. 3 (1990). See also Martin Scheinin, 'Economic and Social Rights as Legal Rights', in Asbjørn Eide et al (eds.) *Economic, social and cultural rights: A textbook* (Dordrecht: Martinus Nijhoff, 2001).

[228] As of January 2011, only Ecuador, Mongolia and Spain had ratified the Optional Protocol. The entry into force of the Protocol requires ten ratifications.

with respect to the interpretation of ESC rights consists of two consensus documents, the Limburg Principles and the Maastricht Guidelines, drafted by two groups of experts to elaborate upon the Convention.[229]

The Concept of Discrimination
Article 2(2) of the Covenant reads:

> The States Parties to the present Covenant undertake to guarantee that the rights enunciated in the present Covenant will be exercised without discrimination of any kind as to race, colour, sex, language, religion, political or other opinion, national or social origin, property, birth or other status.

Unlike its counterpart Article 2(2) of the ICCPR, Article 2(2) of the ICESCR explicitly employs the term 'discrimination' instead of 'distinction'. The *travaux préparatoires* to the two Covenants, prepared at the same time, clearly suggest that the two provisions and two concepts were meant to be understood in the same way, namely as excluding only arbitrary or unjust distinctions.[230] The ICESCR itself does not define what it means by 'discrimination'. The CESCR has on several occasions indicated that it conceives discrimination along the lines set out in other international human rights conventions, in particular the ICERD and CEDAW.[231] The Limburg Principles, the Maastricht Guidelines and many individual experts support this interpretation.[232] From this point of view discrimination is conceived as any distinction,

[229] David L. Martin, in his survey of the relevant academic literature, concludes that Limburg Principles "have been largely accepted by the human rights community". David L. Martin 'The Limburg Principles Turn Ten: An Impact Assessment' *Sim special* 20, p. 200.

[230] Ramcharan, *cit. supra* note 22, p. 259.

[231] CESCR, General Comment No. 20 (2009), para 7; CESCR, General Comment No. 16 (2005), para 11 and General Comment No. 5 (1994), para 15. See also para 18 of the CESCR, General Comment No. 18 (2005), where the Committee implies that the prohibition set out in Article 2(2) of the Covenant corresponds to the prohibition of discrimination set out in Article 7 of the International Convention on the Protection of the Rights of All Migrant Workers and Members of Their Families. See also CESCR, General Comment No. 13 (1999), para 31, where the Committee interprets Article 2(2) in light of the UNESCO Convention against Discrimination in Education.

[232] Limburg Principles on the Implementation of the International Covenant on Economic, Social and Cultural Rights (UN Doc. E/CN.4/1987/17, annex; *Human Rights Quarterly*, Vol 9 (1987), pp. 122–135), para 41; Maastricht Guidelines on violations of Economic, Social and Cultural Rights (Human Rights Quarterly, vol. 20 (1988), pp. 691–705), para 12; Katarina Frostell – Martin Scheinin, 'Women' in Asbjørn Eide – Catarina Krause – Allan Rosas (eds.), *Economic, Social and Cultural Rights: A Textbook*, 2nd revised Edition (The Hague: Kluwer Law International, 2001).

exclusion, restriction or preference, based on a prohibited ground, which has the intention or effect of nullifying or impairing the recognition, enjoyment or exercise, on an equal footing, of economic, social or cultural rights.[233]

The Committee expressly distinguished between direct and indirect discrimination in its 2005 General Comment No. 16 on gender equality, and further elaborated upon its approach in the 2009 General Comment No. 20 on non-discrimination, where it provided the following definitions:

> Direct discrimination occurs when an individual is treated less favourably than another person in a similar situation for a reason related to a prohibited ground.
>
> Indirect discrimination refers to laws, policies or practices which appear neutral at face value, but have a disproportionate impact on the exercise of Covenant rights as distinguished by prohibited grounds of discrimination.[234]

In view of the Committee, special measures that involve differentiations between persons or groups of persons are legitimate in so far as they are aimed at redressing *de facto* discrimination and are discontinued when *de facto* equality is achieved.[235] This interpretation, which is in line with the above-mentioned instruments and their interpretation by the respective bodies, is supported, *inter alia*, by the Limburg Principles.[236] In fact, the Committee has over time come to take the view that states are in some cases under an *obligation* to adopt special measures for the purposes of ensuring effective enjoyment of Covenant rights.[237] It has also pointed out that some types of special measures, such as interpretation services for linguistic minorities, need to be of permanent nature.[238]

---

[233] CESCR, General Comment No. 20 (2009), para 7; CESCR, General Comment No. 5 (1994), para 15.

[234] CESCR, General Comment No. 20 (2009), para 10.

[235] CESCR, General Comment No. 16 (2005), para 15. See also General Comment No. 13 (1999), para 32.

[236] Limburg Principles, para 39.

[237] CESCR, General Comment No. 20 (2009), paras 8 and 9. For instance, in the context of disability discrimination the Committee has submitted that there is an obligation to take positive action to reduce structural disadvantages and to give appropriate preferential treatment to people with disabilities in order to achieve the objectives of full participation and equality within society, considering that people with disabilities constitute a vulnerable and disadvantaged group. CESCR, General Comment No. 5 (1994), paras 9 and 18. See also General Comment No. 3 (1990), para 12.

[238] CESCR, General Comment No. 20 (2009), para 9.

Grounds and Personal Scope of Application

The list of prohibited grounds of discrimination in Article 2 of the ICESR is the same as in Articles 2 and 26 of the ICCPR, and includes 'race', 'colour' and 'national origin'. The list is not exhaustive, meaning that other grounds can qualify under the 'other status' category, and the Committee has submitted that for instance disability and age qualify as other statuses within the meaning of Article 2(2).[239] The Committee took the stance in its 2009 General Comment on non-discrimination that the ground of 'race' includes 'ethnic origin', finally clarifying that issue after having before that been almost silent about ethnic discrimination in its comments.[240] In the same instance the CESCR also opined that multiple discrimination "merits particular consideration and remedying".[241]

As regards the personal scope of application and discrimination on the basis of nationality, the Committee has taken the view that "[t]he Covenant rights apply to everyone including non-nationals, such as refugees, asylum-seekers, stateless persons, migrant workers and victims of international trafficking, regardless of legal status and documentation."[242] One must however take note of Article 3, which provides that "[d]eveloping countries, with due regard to human rights and their national economy, may determine to what extent they would guarantee the economic rights recognized in the present Covenant to non-nationals". The applicability of this provision is restricted in three respects: 1) it applies only to such developing countries whose national economy could not adequately bear the fulfilment of these rights, 2) it applies only to economic and not social or cultural rights, and 3) it is without prejudice to rights guaranteed in other international human rights documents. Hence the possibilities to justify distinctions on the basis of nationality are limited indeed, in Europe in particular.

---

239 CESCR, General Comment No. 20 (2009), paras 28 and 29. We may note an interesting development with respect to the recognition of age discrimination, as in 1995 the Committee opined that "it may not yet be possible to conclude that discrimination on the grounds of age is comprehensively prohibited by the Covenant", though it did soften that conclusion by adding that "the range of matters in relation to which such discrimination can be accepted is very limited." CESCR, General Comment No. 6 (1995), paras 11–12.

240 The Committee did however refer to 'minorities' in its General Comment No. 18 (2005), para 23.

241 CESCR, General Comment No. 20 (2009), para 17.

242 Ibid, para 30.

Material Scope of Application

The non-discrimination clause of Article 2(2) of the Covenant is not self-standing but is accessory to the other rights enunciated in the Covenant. Of the latter, especially the rights included in Articles 6, 7 and 13 are particularly relevant in the present context.

In Article 6 the states parties "recognize the right to work, which includes the right of everyone to the opportunity to gain his living by work which he freely chooses or accepts". To this end they assume the obligation to take "appropriate steps to safeguard" that right.[243] In Article 7 the states parties recognize the right of everyone to the enjoyment of "just and favourable conditions of work" which ensure, in particular, equal remuneration for work of equal value without distinction of any kind, as well as "equal opportunity for everyone to be promoted in his employment."[244] In its General Comment on Article 6 the CESCR opined that protection from discrimination is an essential part of the right to work. Accordingly, states should refrain from "denying or limiting equal access to work" and should "adopt legislation or to take other measures ensuring equal access to work and training".[245] In the view of the Committee, the right to work has several components, notably the right of the worker to just and favourable conditions of work, in particular to safe working conditions, the right to form trade unions and the right not to be unfairly deprived of employment.[246] It has underlined that the right to work should not be understood as an absolute and unconditional right to obtain employment.[247]

In Article 13 the states parties recognize the right of everyone to education. The article further provides that education shall be directed to the "full development of the human personality and the sense of its dignity, and shall strengthen the respect for human rights and fundamental freedoms", and that education shall enable all persons to participate effectively in a free society and promote "understanding, tolerance and friendship among all nations and all racial, ethnic or religious groups". Article 13(2) provides that primary education shall be compulsory and available free to all and that higher education be

[243] Article 6.
[244] Article 7(a)(i) and (c).
[245] Para 12 ff.
[246] Paras 6 and 12.
[247] Para 6. More generally on the right to work, see Krzysztof Drzewicki 'The Right to Work and Rights in Work' in Asbjørn Eide et al (eds.), *Economic, Social and Cultural Rights: A textbook* (Dordrecht: Martinus Nijhoff, 2001).

made equally accessible to all, on the basis of capacity. By virtue of that right states should repeal any discriminatory legislation and "take measures" to address de facto educational discrimination.[248]

It is notable that the Committee has drawn attention to the fact that discrimination is frequently encountered in the private sphere, for instance in private housing, and that it has called the states to adopt measures to ensure that individuals and entities in the private sphere do not engage in discrimination.[249]

Given that Article 2 of the ICESCR is not self-standing but accessory to the other rights enunciated in the Covenant, situations might arise where discrimination in the social, economic and cultural *sphere* does not amount to discrimination in the enjoyment of any of the rights enshrined in the CESCR. Paradoxically, under the prevailing interpretations and practices of the respective committees, such discrimination would thus be prohibited under Article 26 of the ICCPR but not the ICESCR itself.[250]

Enforcement and Remedies

The ICESCR contains no direct counterpart to Article 2, paragraph 3 (b), of the ICCPR, which obliges States parties to, *inter alia*, "develop the possibilities of judicial remedy". The CESCR has, however, inferred a right to an effective remedy on the one hand from Article 2(1) of the Covenant, which requires the achievement of a full realization of the rights enunciated in the Covenant "by all appropriate means", and from Article 8 of the UDHR, which requires the provision of "effective remedies", on the other. This interpretation is shared by the Limburg Principles and the Maastricht guidelines.[251] In the view of the CESCR the right to an effective remedy does not always require the existence of a judicial remedy; administrative remedies will in many cases be

[248] CESCR, General Comment 13 (1999), para 59. More specifically on the right to education, see Manfred Nowak 'The Right to Education', in Asbjørn Eide et al (eds.) *Economic, Social and Cultural Rights: A textbook* (Dordrecht: Martinus Nijhoff, 2001).

[249] CESCR, General Comment No. 20 (2009), para 11.

[250] For more on how the ICCPR and other human rights instruments can be evoked for the protection of economic and social rights, see Martin Scheinin "Economic and Social Rights as Legal Rights", in Asbjørn Eide et al (eds) *Economic, social and cultural rights: A textbook* (Dordrecht: Martinus Nijhoff, 2001).

[251] Limburg Principles, paras 18 and 19 state that legislative measures alone are not sufficient to fulfil the obligations of the Covenant and that states parties should provide for effective remedies including, where appropriate, judicial remedies. Maastricht guidelines, para 22 states that victims should have access to effective judicial or other appropriate remedies at both national and international levels.

adequate.[252] It has however been of the view that there are some obligations, such as those concerning non-discrimination, in relation to which the provision of some form of judicial remedy would "seem indispensable in order to satisfy the requirements of the Covenant".[253]

State Obligations

Article 2(1) of the Covenant states that each state party to the Covenant

> undertakes to take steps ... to the maximum of its available resources, with a view to achieving progressively the full realization of the rights recognized in the present covenant by all appropriate means, including particularly the adoption of legislative measures.

The interpretation of this broad and flexible provision, particularly as regards "progressive realization of rights", has generated much legal commentary into which there is no need to go into here, as it goes beyond the scope of this study.[254] The formulation of Article 2(2) on non-discrimination, cited above, has more absolute and practice-oriented overtones, as is implied by terms "guarantee" and "will be exercised". Indeed, the CESCR and many authors have emphasised that Article 2 taken as a whole imposes on state parties some obligations that are of immediate effect, in particular the undertaking to guarantee that the relevant rights will be exercised without discrimination.[255] In effect, a state is considered to be in breach of the Covenant if it has not taken all measures needed to effectively ensure that all ESC rights can be enjoyed in practice without any discrimination. The CESCR has noted that also non-public entities, such as private employers and private suppliers of goods and services, should be made subject to non-discrimination norms under the Covenant.[256] In this context it is interesting to note that the preamble to the CESCR explicitly refers to the duties of individuals, as it proclaims that the contracting states realize "that the individual, having duties to other individuals and to the community to which he belongs, is under a responsibility to strive for the promotion and observance of the rights recognized in the present Covenant"; the nature of that responsibility or the legal

---

[252] CESCR, General Comment No. 9 (1998), para 9.

[253] Idem; CESCR, General Comment No. 3 (1990), para 3.

[254] See e.g. the articles in Asbjørn Eide et al (eds.), *Economic, Social and Cultural Rights: A textbook* (Dordrecht: Martinus Nijhoff, 2001).

[255] See e.g. CESCR, General Comment 3 (1990), para 1.

[256] CESCR, General Comment No. 5 (1994), para 11.

significance of the statement are left unclear, but at the very least this observation is not at odds with the interpretation that the prohibition of discrimination should apply also in relations between private parties. The view that the CESCR has indirect horizontal effects in relations between private parties is supported by the Limburg Principles and the Maastricht Guidelines.[257]

Article 2(1) foresees that the Covenant is to be given effect nationally by "all appropriate means, including particularly the adoption of legislative measures". In this connection the CESR has opined that in some instances "legislation is desirable and even indispensable".[258] In particular, in its view it would be impossible to "combat discrimination effectively in the absence of a sound legislative foundation for the necessary measures".[259]

6.8 European Convention on Human Rights and Fundamental Freedoms

Introduction

The European Convention on Human Rights and Fundamental Freedoms (ECHR) was concluded in 1950. As of January 2011, it had been ratified by all 47 member states of the Council of Europe, which includes all EU member states.[260] It has been observed that the Council of Europe was prompted to take up the cause of human rights primarily for the purposes of affirming and preserving the rule of law and the principles of democracy in Europe, particularly in contrast to the totalitarianism exhibited both by the Nazis and communists.[261]

---

[257] Para 40 of the Limburg Principles state that de facto discrimination should be "brought to an end as speedily as possible" and that Article 2(2) demands from states parties that they prohibit private persons and bodies from practicing discrimination in any field of public life. Maastricht Guidelines, para 6, notes that the obligation to protect ESC rights means that for instance a failure to ensure that private employers comply with basic labour standards may amount to a violation of the right to work or the right to just and favourable conditions of work.

[258] CESCR, General Comment No. 3 (1990), para 3; CESCR, General Comment No. 20 (2009).

[259] Idem.

[260] Source: http://conventions.coe.int (accessed 1.1.2011).

[261] J.G. Merrills – A.H. Robertson, *Human rights in Europe: A study of the European Convention on Human Rights*, 4th ed (Manchester: Manchester University Press, 2001), pp. 3–5. See also Steven Greer 'What's Wrong with the European Convention on Human Rights' *Human Rights Quarterly* 30 (2008), pp. 680–702.

It is widely considered that the European Convention has been something of a success story among the family of human rights instruments, particularly because of its relatively robust international enforcement system. An individual claiming to be a victim of a violation of the Convention may, after exhausting domestic remedies, directly lodge an application alleging a breach by a state of one of the Convention rights with the European Court of Human Rights (ECtHR) in Strasbourg. More than half a million applications have been lodged with the Court by now,[262] and the high number of judgments delivered has allowed the Court the opportunity to develop a fairly systematic approach to the interpretation of the Convention.[263] At the same time, the interstate complaint mechanism – originally envisaged to be the *modus operandi* of the Convention – has remained almost a dead letter.[264]

The Concept of Discrimination

The ECHR contains a non-discrimination provision in Article 14. The ECtHR has on several occasions underlined the fundamental importance of this article. In its 2004 decision *Nachova and others* v. *Bulgaria*, which was the first case ever in which it found discrimination on the grounds of 'race' or ethnicity, it took the opportunity to proclaim that "the prohibition of discrimination in general, and of racial and ethnic discrimination in particular, under Article 14 reflect basic values of the democratic societies that make up the Council of Europe."[265]

Article 14 reads:

> The enjoyment of the rights and freedoms set forth in this Convention shall be secured without discrimination on any ground such as sex, race, colour, language, religion, political or other opinion, national and social origin, association with a national minority, property, birth or other status.

---

[262] By the end of the year 2007 more than 490 000 applications had been filed with the Court. European Court of Human Rights, *Annual Report 2007* (Registry of the European Court of Human Rights, Strasbourg, 2008). This massive caseload has overburdened the Strasbourg Court, bringing it at the verge of an acute crisis.

[263] See however the excellent account of Merrils regarding how different judicial ideologies have come to play in the Strasbourg court. J.G. Merrills, *The development of international law by the European Court of Human Rights* (Manchester: Manchester University Press, 1993).

[264] Greer, *cit. supra* note 261, pp. 681–682.

[265] See ECtHR, *Nachova and others* v. *Bulgaria*, chamber judgment of February 2004, para 155. The case was referred to the Grand Chamber [GC], which delivered

As Article 14 or the other articles of the Convention do not define 'discrimination', the interpretation of the very meaning of the concept becomes crucial. The English text version of Article 14 explicitly uses the word 'discrimination', whereas the French text, which is equally authentic,[266] uses the words 'sans distinction aucune'. The Court resolved the discrepancy between these two language versions in favour of the English version already in the 1968 *Belgian Linguistics* case, in which it submitted that:

> In spite of the very general wording of the French version ("sans distinction aucune") Article 14 does not forbid every difference in treatment in the exercise of the rights and freedoms recognized. This version must be read in the light of the more restrictive text of the English version ("without discrimination").[267]

In the Belgian Linguistics case the Court went on give its interpretation of the notion of discrimination by noting that certain differences in treatment exist in many democratic countries, and that some legal inequalities (distinctions in law) tend only to correct factual inequalities. It continued by observing that

> … the principle of equality of treatment is violated if the distinction has no objective and reasonable justification. The existence of such a justification must be assessed in relation to the aim and effects of the measure under consideration, regard being had to the principles which normally prevail in the democratic societies. A difference of treatment in the exercise of a right laid down in the Convention must not only pursue a legitimate aim: Article 14 is likewise violated when it is clearly established that there is no reasonable relationship of proportionality between the means employed and the aims sought to be realized.[268]

The Court adopted this broad and flexible approach by "following the principles which may be extracted from the legal practice of a large number of democratic States", without specifying what those countries were.[269] This approach has proved to be durable and the ECtHR has,

judgment in the case on 6 July 2005. The GC, for its part, declared that racial violence "is a particular affront to human dignity", para 145 of the judgment.

[266] Article 59 of the Convention.

[267] ECtHR, Case 'Relating to Certain Aspects of the Laws on the Use of Languages in Education in Belgium', judgement of 23 July 1968, p. 34. The Court's reasoning was based on the argument that literal application of the French text would lead to "absurd results" (para B.10).

[268] Idem.

[269] Idem.

broadly speaking, followed it ever since. For instance in the 2010 judgment in the *Yiğit* case, the Court [Grand Chamber, GC] reiterated that

> According to the Court's settled case-law, discrimination means treating differently, without an objective and reasonable justification, persons in relevantly similar situations. A difference in treatment has no objective and reasonable justification if it does not pursue a legitimate aim or if there is not a reasonable relationship of proportionality between the means employed and the aim sought to be realized.[270]

The Court has in different cases focused upon the different components of this definition: In *Gaygusuz* the focus was on the examination of the justification; in the cases of *Zarb*, *Willis* and *Okpisz* the court concentrated on the comparative element of Article 14, by focusing on whether the difference in treatment took place between persons in relevantly similar or analogous situations;[271] and in the cases of *Andrejeva, Rainys and Gasparavicius* and *Yiğit* it focused particularly upon the proportionality of the challenged measure.[272]

The ECtHR grants the contracting states a 'margin of appreciation' – essentially a conceptual device that allows states a measure of discretion in the way the Convention rights are implemented nationally[273] – in assessing whether and to what extent differences in otherwise similar situations justify different treatment in law, the scope of this margin varying according to the circumstances, the subject matter and the background of the case.[274] For instance in the *Burden* case, the Court stated that the margin of appreciation is "usually wide when it comes

---

[270] ECtHR, *Yiğit* v. *Turkey*, GC judgment of 2 November 2010, para 67. See also ECtHR, *Andrejeva* v. *Latvia*, GC judgment of 18 February 2009, para 81.

[271] ECtHR, *Zarb Adami* v. *Malta*, judgment of 20 June 2006, para 71. In the *Lithgow* case the Court stated that the Article 14 "safeguards persons…who are placed in analogous situations against discriminatory differences of treatment", see *Lithgow and others* v. *United Kingdom*, judgement of 8 July 1986. In the *Fredin* case the Court stated that for a claim to succeed, it has to be established, inter alia, that the situation of the alleged victim can be considered similar to that of persons who have been better treated. ECtHR, *Fredin* v. *Sweden*, judgment of 18 February 1991.

[272] ECtHR, *Andrejeva* v. *Latvia* [GC], judgment of 18 February 2009, paras 87–89; ECtHR, *Rainys and Gasparavicius* v. *Lithuania*, judgment of 7 April 2005, para 36; ECtHR, *Yiğit* v. *Turkey*, GC judgment of 2 November 2010, paras 83–88.

[273] See e.g. Merrills – Robertson, *cit. supra* note 261, pp. 222–224.

[274] See ECtHR, *Andrejeva* v. *Latvia* [GC], judgment of 18 February 2009, para 82, in which the Court opined that "[t]he Contracting States enjoy a certain margin of appreciation in assessing whether and to what extent differences in otherwise similar situations justify a different treatment." See also ECtHR, *Inze* v. *Austria*, 28 October 1987, para 41; ECtHR, *Sheffield and Horsham* v. *United Kingdom*, judgment of 30 July 1998; ECtHR, *Yiğit* v. *Turkey*, GC judgment of 2 November 2010, para 70.

to general measures of economic or social strategy".[275] Some commentators have criticized this and have opined that the doctrine of margin of appreciation should play a role only in the consideration of the other substantive article that is applied in conjunction with Article 14, not Article 14 itself.[276]

The consideration of the justification of differential treatment leaves considerable room for the Court to develop its doctrines, in the development of which the ECtHR has shown a great interest in the trends prevalent in Europe, including individual countries, the European Union and the other organs of the Council of Europe.[277] The Court has only rarely been called upon to elaborate on the legitimacy of positive/affirmative action,[278] but on those occasions it has actually gone as far as to hold that in certain circumstances states have an *obligation* to engage in it.[279]

The ECtHR has recently broadened its understanding of the concept of discrimination. In *Thlimmenos* v *Greece*, adopted in 2000, it famously held that it is not just differential treatment of similarly situated persons that may constitute discrimination, but also similar treatment of persons in dissimilar situations:

> The Court has so far considered that the right under Article 14 not to be discriminated against in the enjoyment of the rights guaranteed under the Convention is violated when States treat differently persons in analogous situations without providing an objective and reasonable justification. However, the Court considers that this is not the only facet of the prohibition of discrimination in Article 14. The right not to be discriminated against in the enjoyment of the rights guaranteed under the Convention is also violated when States without an objective and reasonable justification fail to treat differently persons whose situations are significantly different.[280]

---

[275] ECtHR, *Burden* v. *The United Kingdom*, judgment of 29 April 2008, para 60. See also ECtHR, *Andrejeva* v. *Latvia* [GC], judgment of 18 February 2009, paras 81–92.

[276] Aart Willem Heringa, 'Standards of review for discrimination: The scope of review by the Courts' in Loenen – Rodriquez (eds.), *Non-Discrimination Law: Comparative Perspectives* (The Hague: Kluwer, 1999), p. 31.

[277] See e.g. Merrills – Robertson, *cit. supra* note 261, p. 202. See the ECtHR cases *Inze* v. *Austria*, judgment of 28 October 1987; *Sheffield and Horsham* v. *United Kingdom*, judgment of 30 July 1998; *D.H. and others v. The Czech Republic*, judgment of 7 February 2006; *Oršuš and others* v. *Croatia*, GC judgment of 16 March 2010.

[278] Marc de Vos, 'Beyond Formal Equality: Positive Action under Directives 2000/43/EC and 2000/78' (Luxembourg: OOPEC, 2007), p. 51.

[279] ECtHR, *Andrejeva* v. *Latvia* [GC], judgment of 18 February 2009, para 82.

[280] ECtHR, *Thlimmenos* v. *Greece*, judgment of 6 March 2000, para 44.

Thus failure on part of a state to treat differently persons whose situations are significantly different may constitute discrimination in the absence of an objective and reasonable justification.[281] Despite the fact that the Court has used similar reasoning in several subsequent cases, *inter alia* in the 2001 case of *Chapman* v. *The United Kingdom* [GC][282] and in the 2005 case *Nachova and others* v. *Bulgaria* [GC],[283] and despite its huge potential importance and radical ramifications, this aspect of the principle of non-discrimination has theoretically speaking remained rather underdeveloped and unclear in the ECtHR's jurisprudence. The Court itself has been cautious in applying the principle, and for instance the outcome of the *Chapman* case seems to suggest that there is a certain threshold for the Court to condemn a state party for a failure to accommodate the characteristics and needs of minorities in their general policies.[284]

The Thlimmenos doctrine has given rise to theoretical controversies. Commentators disagree for instance upon the question whether the type of failure involved in Thlimmenos constitutes direct or indirect discrimination.[285] It could also be understood as a third type of

---

[281] See also ECtHR, *Yiğit* v. *Turkey*, GC judgment of 2 November 2010, para 69; ECtHR, *Oršuš and others* v. *Croatia*, GC judgment of 16 March 2010, para 150. Also some cases decided before *Thlimmenos* suggested that discrimination may be found where essentially different groups are treated in an identical way. See Geoff Gilbert, 'The protection of minorities under the European convention on human rights' in Janet Dine - Bob Watt (eds.), *Discrimination Law: Concepts, Limitations, and Justifications* (London: Longman, 1996); Nicholas Grief, "Non-Discrimination under the European Convention on Human Rights: a critique of the United Kingdom Government's refusal to sign and ratify Protocol 12", *27 E.L.Rev. Human Rights Survey*, 2002, HR/5.

[282] ECtHR, *Chapman* v. *The United Kingdom*, judgment of 18 January 2001.

[283] In paragraph 160 the Grand Chamber approvingly quotes the following passages from the Chamber judgment in the same case: "when investigating violent incidents and, in particular, deaths at the hands of State agents, State authorities have the additional duty to take all reasonable steps to unmask any racist motive and to establish whether or not ethnic hatred or prejudice may have played a role in the events. Failing to do so and treating racially induced violence and brutality on an equal footing with cases that have no racist overtones would be to turn a blind eye to the specific nature of acts that are particularly destructive of fundamental rights. A failure to make a distinction in the way in which situations that are essentially different are handled may constitute unjustified treatment irreconcilable with Article 14 of the Convention." This position is reiterated also in ECtHR, *Stoica* v. *Romania*, judgment of 4 March 2008, para 119.

[284] ECtHR, *Chapman* v. *The United Kingdom*, judgment of 18 January 2001, paras 126–130.

[285] See Mark Bell, 'Direct discrimination' in Dagmar Schiek - Lisa Waddington - Mark Bell, *Non-Discrimination Law: Cases, Materials and text on National, Supranational and International Non-Discrimination Law* (Oxford: Hart Publishing,

discrimination, failure on part of the state to take positive measures with a view to accommodating specific characteristics and needs linked to religion, ethnicity or other such grounds. International human rights documents and doctrines have until now conceptualized discrimination mainly in terms of prohibition of differential treatment, where it is assumed that instances where it is legitimate to treat people differently on grounds of 'race' or ethnicity are few and can be reviewed under the 'legitimacy test' and where the question of positive state obligations to differentiate on the basis of 'ethnicity' falls within the ambit of an entirely different set of rights, namely minority rights.[286] However, it does not appear that Article 14 could, given its limited material scope, extend to a full recognition of minority rights.[287]

The Court has broadened its understanding of the concept of discrimination also by coming, after a long development,[288] and clearly influenced by the EU equal treatment directives,[289] to explicitly embrace the concept of indirect discrimination. Thus in its 2001 judgement in the *Hugh Jordan* v. *United Kingdom* case,[290] and later in the 2007 *D.H. and others* case, the Court accepted that a general policy or measure that has disproportionately prejudicial effects on a particular group may be considered discriminatory, notwithstanding that it is not specifically aimed at that group.[291] This corresponds to its understanding of indirect discrimination.[292] In the *D.H.* case the Court held that a

2007); Olivier de Schutter, *Prohibition of discrimination under European Human Rights Law* (Luxembourg: OOPEC, 2005).

[286] See e.g. Kristin Henrard, *Devising an Adequate System of Minority Protection: Individual Human Rights, Minority Rights, and Self-Determination* (The Hague: Kluwer, 2000).

[287] This is because such differential treatment is warranted only when it is called for by the Convention, for instance in the interests of ensuring equal enjoyment of the Convention rights in practice. See for instance the *Zarb* case, where the Court submitted that "in other words, the notion of discrimination includes in general cases where a person or group is treated, without proper justification, less favourably than another, even though the more favourable treatment is not called for by the Convention." ECtHR, *Zarb Adami v. Malta*, judgment of 20 June 2006, para 73.

[288] Heringa, *cit. supra* note 276, p. 28. Already in the above mentioned *Belgian Linguistics* case the Court distinguished between the aims and effects of a measure and in the *Building Societies* case it recognized that allegations of discriminatory effect are covered by Article 14. ECtHR, *Building Societies* v. *The United Kingdom*, judgment of 23 October 1997.

[289] See e.g. ECtHR, *D.H. and others* v. *The Czech Republic*, judgment of 13 November 2007, para 184.

[290] ECtHR, *Jordan* v. *United Kingdom*, judgement of 4 April 2001, para 154.

[291] ECtHR, *D.H. and others* v. *The Czech Republic*, judgment of 13 November 2007, para 175.

[292] Ibid, para 184.

schooling system where Roma pupils in disproportionate numbers ended in special education of inferior quality constituted indirect discrimination. The decision of the Court in that case was somewhat controversial. In it, the Grand Chamber quashed, by a majority of thirteen votes to four, an earlier Chamber judgement that had not found any discrimination. The four dissenting Grand Chamber judges annexed exceptionally strongly worded opinions to the majority judgment.[293]

The ECtHR has recognized that discrimination contrary to the Convention may result from a 'practice' or a 'de facto situation', not just from a law, decision or the like.[294] This, and the recognition of the concept of indirect discrimination, enables the Court to deal with many types of discrimination that occur in the context of everyday life.

The Convention or the Court have not laid down rules regarding burden of proof or admissibility of evidence applicable in domestic contexts, other than the general requirement laid down in Article 13 that the domestic remedies must be effective. Whereas these matters are therefore for the national authorities to determine, the ECtHR's praxis with regard to its own procedures may influence the national practice, given that a mismatch detrimental to a contracting state arises where its procedural rules are less favourable to the complainants than those applied by the ECtHR, as this would lead to more complaints being submitted to the ECtHR and being resolved in favour of the applicants.[295] In view of this it is useful to take a look at the ECtHR's approach in this respect.

Regarding the burden of proof, the basic rule applied by the ECtHR in cases involving alleged discrimination is that once the applicant has shown a difference in treatment, it is for the Government to show that

---

[293] For instance the dissenting opinion of Judge Zupančič holds the majority opinion to"border on the absurd" and adds that"[n]o amount of politically charged argumentation can hide the obvious fact that the Court in this case has been brought into play for ulterior purposes, which have little to do with the special education of Roma children in the Czech Republic." Judge Jungwiert, for his part, submits that the "abstract, theoretical reasoning" which he saw to underlie the majority decision "render the majority's conclusions wholly unacceptable". Judge Borrego Borrego submits that he is "somewhat saddened by the judgment in the present case" and suggests that the Court departed from its judicial role in the decision.

[294] ECtHR, *Zarb Adami v. Malta*, judgment of 20 June 2006, para 76; *D.H. and others* v. *The Czech Republic*, judgment of 13 November 2007.

[295] Whereas a mismatch would result also in the case where the national rules applied by a state party would be more favourable to the complainant than those applied by the ECHR, this is not likely to be experienced as a problem, as domestic cases would be less likely to make it to the ECtHR or be successful there.

it was justified.[296] In the *D.H. and others* case the Court, after referring to this basic principle, went on to refer to the specifics of the case and to the EU equal treatment directives and their provisions on shifting of the burden of proof, and submitted that "where an applicant alleging indirect discrimination thus establishes a rebuttable *presumption* that the effect of a measure or practice is discriminatory, the burden then shifts to the respondent State, which must show that the difference in treatment is not discriminatory".[297] In *Nachova* the Court held that it can, in cases involving alleged discrimination, shift the burden of proof to the respondent Government, particularly where the events lie wholly, or in large part, within the exclusive knowledge of the authorities.[298] Whereas the Court's approach to the burden of proof has not yet consolidated into a rock solid doctrine, these cases show that the Court is willing to ease the applicant's burden of proof particularly where indirect discrimination is at issue or where the evidence is wholly or in part in possession of the respondent.

The – though possibly tentative – conceptualization of indirect discrimination in terms of a general policy or a measure that has "disproportionately prejudicial effects on a particular group" readily raises the question how such group effects can – or should – be demonstrated to the satisfaction of the Court. The Court has answered this question by clarifying that, in proceedings before it, there are "no procedural barriers to the admissibility of evidence or pre-determined formulae for its assessment" and that it "adopts the conclusions that are, in its view, supported by the free evaluation of all evidence".[299] Whereas in *Jordan* it concluded that it "does not consider that statistics can in themselves disclose a practice which could be classified as discriminatory within the meaning of Article 14",[300] in *Hoogendijk* and *Zarb Adami* cases it came to declare that it was prepared to accept statistical

[296] See e.g. ECtHR, *D.H. and others* v. *The Czech Republic* [GC], judgment of 13 November 2007, para 177; ECtHR, *Andrejeva* v. *Latvia* [GC], judgment of 18 February 2009, para 84. The burden of proof is obviously different in cases that involve alleged discrimination by way of similar treatment of people that are in different situations, as in *Thlimmenos*. In such cases, the burden of proving that the difference in treatment is not discriminatory falls upon the responding state as soon as the applicant produces *prima facie* evidence that the *effect* of a measure or practice is discriminatory. ECtHR, *Oršuš and others* v. *Croatia*, GC judgment of 16 March 2010, para 150.

[297] Ibid, para 189. Emphasis added.

[298] ECtHR, *Nachova and others* v. *Bulgaria*, GC judgment of 6 July 2005, para 157.

[299] Ibid, para 147.

[300] ECtHR, *Hugh Jordan* v. *The United Kingdom*, judgment of 4 May 2001, para 154.

evidence, clarifying finally in *D.H. and others* that it "considers that when it comes to assessing the impact of a measure or practice on an individual or group, statistics which appear on critical examination to be reliable and significant will be sufficient to constitute the prima facie evidence the applicant is required to produce."[301] Indeed, in *D.H. and others* the Court acknowledged that the evidence marshalled by the applicants, namely ethnic statistics compiled on the basis of a survey, while not necessarily "entirely reliable", was capable of revealing "a dominant trend", particularly as the statistics were corroborated by evidence obtained from independent supervisory bodies such as the CERD and ECRI. On these grounds the statistics were taken to be "sufficiently reliable and significant to give rise to a strong presumption of indirect discrimination" and in the end, a finding of a violation of Article 14.[302] The Court was, however, careful to underline in its reasoning that indirect discrimination can also be proved by other means than statistics.[303] In *Oršuš* the Court found the statistical evidence presented to it to be inadequate, and inferred indirect discrimination from the facts of the case when the broader circumstances of the case were taken into account. The Court relied, in its consideration of these broader circumstances, on the reports of the Council of Europe Commissioner for Human Rights and the European Commission against Racism and Intolerance (ECRI).[304]

Grounds and Personal Scope

Article 14 prohibits discrimination on "on any ground such as sex, race, colour, language, religion, political or other opinion, national or social origin, association with a national minority, property, birth or other status". The list of grounds is non-exhaustive, as is indicated by the words 'such as' and 'other status', and is not limited to in-born characteristics as is clear especially from the inclusion of the ground of 'property'.[305] The Court has in its practice considered alleged

---

[301] *D.H. and others* v. *The Czech Republic* [GC], judgment of 13 November 2007, para 188.

[302] Ibid, paras 190 and ff.

[303] Idem.

[304] ECtHR, *Oršuš and others* v. *Croatia*, GC judgment of 16 March 2010, paras 152–155.

[305] Again there is a difference between the French and English texts, as the French text reads "toute autre situation" where the English text reads "other status" and thereby the French text would seem to take an even more liberal position towards the "other" prohibited grounds of discrimination.

discrimination on the basis of for instance sexual orientation, marital status, transsexuality and even military rank.[306] Some authors have suggested that any criterion of differentiation may be potentially examined under Article 14.[307]

In *Timishev* the ECtHR confirmed that ethnic discrimination falls within the scope of Article 14, but, under the explicit influence of the definitions of racial discrimination in Article 1(1) of the ICERD and ECRI's General Policy Recommendation No 7, it came not to treat it as an autonomous ground but as a form of racial discrimination.[308] The Court did distinguish between the notions of 'ethnicity' and 'race' in the said case, however, proceeding even to outline what it takes these notions to mean:

> Ethnicity and race are related and overlapping concepts. Whereas the notion of race is rooted in the idea of biological classification of human beings into subspecies according to morphological features such as skin colour or facial characteristics, ethnicity has its origin in the idea of societal groups marked by common nationality, tribal affiliation, religious faith, shared language, or cultural and traditional origins and backgrounds.[309]

Under the practice of the Court, it is for the applicant to show that there has been a difference of treatment, which quite readily calls for a comparison between individuals or groups that are placed in analogous or otherwise comparable situations but that differ in terms of a ground on which it is prohibited to discriminate under Article 14.[310] Under cases involving indirect discrimination the applicant will

---

[306] ECtHR, *Salgueiro Da Silva Mouta* v *Portugal*, judgement of 21 December 1999; ECtHR, *S.L.* v. *Austria*, judgment of 9 January 2003 and ECtHR, *L. and V.* v. *Austria*, judgment of 9 January 2003. See also ECtHR, *B.B.* v. *the United Kingdom*, judgment of 10 February 2004 and *Sheffield and Horsham* v. *The United Kingdom*, judgment of 30 July 1998. In the 2010 case of *Yiğit* the Court explained that a "status" within the meaning of Article 14 refers simply to a "personal characteristic by which persons or groups of persons are distinguishable from each other", see ECtHR, *Yiğit* v. *Turkey*, GC judgment of 2 November 2010, para 77.

[307] De Schutter, *cit supra* note 285, p. 13.

[308] ECtHR, *Timishev* v. *Russia*, judgment of 13 December 2005, para 56. The Court took a similar position in *D.H. and others*, judgment of 13 November 2007, para 176; *Stoica* v. *Romania*, judgment of 4 March 2008, para 117 ff, and ECtHR, *Sejdić and Finci* v. *Bosnia and Herzegovina*, GC judgment of 22 December 2009, para 43.

[309] Ibid (*Timishev*), para 55. This passage was with some modifications reiterated in ECtHR, *Sejdić and Finci* v. *Bosnia and Herzegovina*, GC judgment of 22 December 2009, para 43.

[310] See Francis G. Jacobs – Robin C.A. White, *The European Convention of Human Rights*, third ed. (Oxford: Clarendon Press, 2002), pp. 355–356.

presumably need to show – depending on the exact burden of proof – that the challenged measure or practice had, in fact, had a disproportionate impact upon a particular group, which again entails inter-group comparisons. Thus much turns on comparing, for instance, individuals or groups that differ in terms of ethnicity.

In the non-discrimination jurisprudence of the ECtHR, some grounds are held to be intrinsically more suspect – to borrow a notion from the American equal protection jurisdiction – than others, requiring 'very weighty reasons' or even 'compelling reasons' to be forwarded to justify differential treatment on those grounds.[311] It has been submitted that very weighty reasons are required to justify differences based on, *inter alia*, nationality, race, religion and sex.[312] In *Timishev* the Court confirmed that differential treatment on the basis of ethnicity warrants strict scrutiny, and went on record to say that "[r]acial discrimination is a particularly invidious kind of discrimination and, in view of its perilous consequences, requires from the authorities special vigilance and a vigorous reaction" and furthermore that the "Court considers that no difference in treatment which is based exclusively or to a decisive extent on a person's ethnic origin is capable of being objectively justified in a contemporary democratic society built on the principles of pluralism and respect for different cultures."[313] In the *D.H. and others* case it adopted a slightly less absolute opinion, stating that "[w]here the difference in treatment is based on race, colour or ethnic origin, the notion of objective and reasonable justification must be interpreted as strictly as possible".[314] It is unclear whether such strict scrutiny applies also to the failure to treat people differently outlined in the *Thlimmenos* case.

---

[311] See e.g. ECtHR, *Van Raalte* v. *The Netherlands*, judgment of 21 February 1997; ECtHR, *Abdulaziz, Cabalez and Balkandi* v. *United Kingdom*, judgment of 18 May 1985, para 78.

[312] Jacobs – White, *cit. supra* note 310, pp. 355–356. Nicholas Grief, "Non-Discrimination under the European Convention on Human Rights: a critique of the United Kingdom Government's refusal to sign and ratify Protocol 12", *27 E.L.Rev. Human Rights Survey*, 2002, HR/5. Heringa, *cit. supra* note 276, p. 30.

[313] ECtHR, *Timishev* v. *Russia*, judgment of 13 December 2005, paras 56 and 58.

[314] *D.H. and others* v. *The Czech Republic* [GC], judgment of 13 November 2007, para 196. See also ECtHR, *Oršuš and others* v. *Croatia*, GC judgment of 16 March 2010, para 149, where the Court is of the view that "very weighty reasons" would have to be put before it could regard a difference based exclusively on the ground of ethnic origin as compatible with the Convention.

Material Scope

As the wording of Article 14 indicates, it is not an independent prohibition of all kinds of discrimination, but is limited to the enjoyment of the rights and freedoms set forth in the Convention, including its protocols.[315] The reason why the drafters chose not to frame the Article in broader terms, such as the principle of equal protection of the law, was apparently that they felt that the meaning of such broader terms would be too uncertain.[316]

Article 14 is complementary to the other substantive provisions in the sense that it can be applied only where the facts at issue fall within the ambit of one or more of the substantive provisions of the Convention.[317] Article 14 has independent meaning, though, in the sense that under ECtHR's jurisprudence it is unnecessary to show that there has been a breach of another Convention provision.[318] It suffices to demonstrate that another provision has been applied in a manner which is discriminatory, even in situations in which the national law implementing the right goes *beyond* the obligations expressly provided by the Convention. The Court summed up its practice in *Okpisz*:

> As the Court has held on many occasions, Article 14 comes into play whenever "the subject-matter of the disadvantage ... constitutes one of the modalities of the exercise of a right guaranteed", or the

[315] Matti Pellonpää, *Euroopan ihmisoikeussopimus* (Helsinki: Lakimiesliiton kustannus, 1996), p. 435. See e.g. ECtHR, *Krasnov and Skuratov* v. *Russia*, judgment of 19 July 2007, para 69.

[316] Jeroen Schokkenbroek 'A New European Standard Against Discrimination: Negotiating Protocol 12 to the European Convention on Human Rights' in Stéphanie Lagoutte (ed.), *Prohibition of discrimination in the Nordic Countries: The Complicated fate of Protocol No. 12 to the European Convention on Human Rights* (Copenhagen: the Danish Institute for Human Rights, 2005), p. 20.

[317] See e.g. ECtHR, *Abdulaziz, Cabalez and Balkandi* v. *United Kingdom*, judgment of 18 May 1985; ECtHR, *Burden* v. *The United Kingdom*, judgment of 29 April 2008, para 58; ECtHR, *Sejdić and Finci* v. *Bosnia and Herzegovina*, GC judgment of 22 December 2009, para 39.

[318] See e.g. ECtHR, *Yiğit* v. *Turkey*, GC judgment of 2 November 2010, para 55. Where a substantive Article of the Convention has been relied on both on its own and in conjunction with Article 14 and a separate breach has been found of the substantive Article, the Court does not usually consider separately the allegation of a violation under Article 14, unless discrimination is a fundamental aspect of the case. See e.g. ECtHR, *Oršuš and others* v. *Croatia*, GC judgment of 16 March 2010, para 144; ECtHR, *Dudgeon* v. *United Kingdom*, judgment of 22 October 1981. See also Francis G. Jacobs – Robin C.A. White, *The European Convention of Human Rights*, third edition (Oxford: Clarendon Press, 2002), p. 353.

> measures complained of are "linked to the exercise of a right guaranteed".[319]

This interpretative approach, which has developed over the years, somewhat expands the otherwise limited scope of application of Article 14. Yet the fact remains that the Convention provides only for a limited range of rights and freedoms. None of the provisions in the Convention address, as such, access to employment or occupation, or access to goods and services available to the public, including housing.[320] Of the fields that are of particular interest to this study, only education is covered. Article 2 of the first additional protocol provides:

> No person shall be denied the right to education. In the exercise of any functions which it assumes in relation to education and to teaching, the State shall respect the right of parents to ensure such education and teaching in conformity with their own religious and philosophical convictions.

Though drafted in negative terms, the Court's interpretation of the first sentence is that there is a right to education, a right that applies to primary, secondary, and further or higher education.[321] The second sentence has been interpreted as aiming at safeguarding a degree of pluralism in education, and to require states to ensure that the content of the education is free from any indoctrination and that information and knowledge included in the curriculum is conveyed in an "objective, critical and pluralistic manner".[322] The Court has opined that the rights enshrined in the Article involve a duty on the state to regulate the provision of education, although the state has a wide margin of appreciation as to its organization and as to the resources it devotes to the educational system.[323]

---

[319] ECtHR, *Okpisz* v. *Germany*, judgment of 15 February 2006, para 31. See also Case 'Relating to Certain Aspects of the Laws on the Use of Languages in Education in Belgium', judgment of 23 July 1968, para 9.

[320] The Convention does, in Article 11, provide for the right to form and join trade unions, which must therefore be secured without any discrimination.

[321] Jacobs - White, *cit. supra* note 318, pp. 320–1. For instance in *Folgerø* the Court opined that by binding themselves not to deny the right to education, "the Contracting States guarantee to anyone within their jurisdiction a right of access to educational institutions existing at a given time and the possibility of drawing, by official recognition of the studies which he has completed, profit from the education received." ECtHR, *Folgerø and Others* v. *Norway*, judgment of 29 June 2007.

[322] Idem.

[323] Jacobs - White, *cit. supra* note 318, pp. 321–4.

Several important cases considered by the Court have dealt with discrimination in the field of education. In the *Belgian Linguistics* case the Court, though noting that Article 2 of Protocol 1 does not include a right to be taught in the language of parents' choice, found the Belgian legislation to be discriminatory as it led, in fact, to a situation where certain linguistic communities, depending on their place of residence, had an unequal access to education in their own language. In *Folgerø and Others* v. *Norway* the Court held that the compulsory school subject 'Christianity, Religion and Philosophy', which laid a quantitative and qualitative emphasis on Christianity, coupled with an exemption system the use of which was considered to pose a heavy burden, violated Article 2 of Protocol No 1.[324] In *D.H. and others* v. *The Czech Republic*, the applicants successfully challenged a schooling system whereby a disproportionate amount of Roma children were placed in schools for children with mental disabilities.[325] The placement of Roma children in Roma-only classes was similarly considered to be discriminatory in *Oršuš and others* v. *Croatia*.[326]

A measure of protection against discrimination, for instance in the field of working life, may also result from the Court's habit of broad interpretation of the Convention rights, the right to respect for private life in particular. In *Sidabras and Dziautas* v. *Lithuania*, the Court, while reiterating that the Convention does not as such guarantee access to a particular employment, stated that a ban to pursue professional activities may have effects on the enjoyment of the right to respect for private life within the meaning of Article 8 of the Convention, and be prohibited on those grounds.[327] States may even have positive obligations to adopt measures designed to secure equal treatment between private parties, in so far as a failure to do so would amount to a failure to provide effective respect for private or family life *sensu lato*.[328] Whereas cases may therefore arise in which the ECtHR requires states parties to take action to counteract discrimination in various fields of life, this requires that a link can be made between that field and one of the Convention rights or freedoms. However, it is impossible to outline

[324] ECtHR, *Folgerø and Others* v. *Norway*, judgment of 29 June 2007.

[325] ECtHR, *D.H. and others* v. *The Czech Republic* [GC], judgment of 13 November 2007.

[326] ECtHR, *Oršuš and others* v. *Croatia* [GC], judgment of 16 March 2010.

[327] ECtHR, *Sidabras and Dziautas* v. *Lithuania*, judgment of 27 July 2004, paras 42–50.

[328] See ECtHR, *Phinikaridou* v. *Cyprus*, judgment of 20 December 2007, para 47.

the scope of each of the Convention rights, as the Court has on many occasions emphasised that for instance Article 8 obligations cannot be laid down in any abstract way and that the Court will decide cases on a one-by-one basis.

Discrimination, also outside the field of education, may sometimes be so severe as to constitute degrading treatment that is prohibited in Article 3 of the Convention. In *Cyprus* v. *Turkey* the Court found that the Greek-Cypriots living in the Karpas area were compelled to live in a situation where they were "isolated, restricted in their movements, controlled and with no prospect of renewing or developing their community". Restrictions of freedom of movement were of such nature that they were considered to weigh heavily on the group's enjoyment of private and family life and their right to practice their religion. The Court concluded that the Karpas Greek Cypriots had been subjected to discrimination amounting to degrading treatment.[329] That severe forms of discrimination may amount to degrading treatment has been recognized also in other cases.[330]

The ECHR and the Court's jurisprudence under it are not clear whether and to what extent there is a positive duty to act against discrimination committed by private parties.[331]

At the end of the day the conclusion is warranted that the Convention as such, as interpreted by the Court, requires states to provide protection against discrimination in the areas of working life and provision of goods and services only in rather exceptional circumstances.[332]

---

[329] The Court reasoned as follows: "For the Court it is an inescapable conclusion that the interferences at issue were directed at the Karpas Greek-Cypriot community for the very reason that they belonged to this class of persons. The treatment to which they were subjected during the period under consideration can only be explained in terms of the features which distinguish them from the Turkish-Cypriot population, namely their ethnic origin, race and religion … The conditions under which that population is condemned to live are debasing and violate the very notion of respect for the human dignity of its members. In the Court's opinion, and with reference to the period under consideration, the discriminatory treatment attained a level of severity which amounted to degrading treatment." *Cyprus* v. *Turkey*, judgment of 10 May 2001, paras 302–311.

[330] See also e.g. European Commission of Human Rights, *East African Asians* v. *United Kingdom*, decision of 14 December 1973, and ECtHR, *Petropoulou – Tsakiris* v. *Greece*, judgment of 6 December 2007.

[331] See also Henrard, *cit supra* note 95, p. 17.

[332] This is the conclusion also of Gerards, in Janneke Gerards, 'Protocol No. 12 – the Dutch Debate' in Stéphanie Lagoutte (ed.) *Prohibition of Discrimination in the Nordic Countries: The Complicated Fate of Protocol No. 12 to the European Convention on Human Rights* (Copenhagen: The Danish Institute for Human Rights, 2005), p. 39.

Enforcement and Remedies
Article 13, which deals with remedies, provides as follows:

> Everyone whose rights and freedoms as set forth in this Convention are violated shall have an effective remedy before a national authority notwithstanding that the violation has been committed by persons acting in an official capacity.

Whereas this is not fully clear from its wording, it is now generally accepted, by the ECtHR as well as legal scholars, that Article 13 must be understood as dealing with the domestic implementation and enforcement of the Convention rights; it is not about state responsibility or the remedies that should be available when the ECtHR has established that a state party has breached the Convention.[333] The Court reiterated its position on this for instance in the 2007 case of *Cobzaru* v. *Romania*, where it said that "Article 13 of the Convention guarantees the availability, at the national level, of a remedy to enforce the substance of Convention rights and freedoms in whatever form they might happen to be secured in the domestic legal order".[334] Insofar as the Convention requires state parties to provide protection from discrimination, also in relations between private parties, there must therefore be a domestic remedy.

Yet this line of interpretation presents a further problem: if remedies – understood to include access to justice – come into play only after rights and freedoms as set forth in the Convention have been found to be violated, which is what the article says, how is the remedy-triggering violation itself to be established, as that would require the availability of a procedural remedy?[335] The Court has resolved this issue by holding in several cases that the right to a national remedy arises "where an individual has an *arguable* claim to be the victim of a violation".[336] This 'arguable claim' test, while generally accepted by legal scholars,[337] is inherently imprecise and necessarily leaves a measure of discretion both to the national authorities and the Strasbourg Court.

Whereas the early case law on Article 13 set only relatively low-level requirements upon states, mainly requiring the existence of some

---

[333] See e.g. Merrills, *cit. supra* note 261, p. 194; Jacobs – White, *cit. supra* note 318, pp. 386–387.

[334] ECtHR, *Cobzaru* v. *Romania*, judgment of 26 July 2007.

[335] Merrills, *cit. supra* note 261, pp. 194–195.

[336] See e.g. ECtHR, *Silver* v. *United Kingdom*, judgment of 25 March 1983. Emphasis added.

[337] Merrills, *cit. supra* note 261.

mechanism that might lead to a remedy, ECtHR's jurisprudence has since evolved and has now remained rather static over the last years.[338] The starting point is still that the Court acknowledges that contracting states are free to choose how to secure the Convention rights and freedoms in the domestic legal order and that they also have "some discretion as to the manner in which they confirm to their Convention obligations" under Article 13.[339] Remedies must, however, be understood both in the procedural and substantive sense, and must be effective.[340] Article 13 indicates that procedural remedies need not always be judicial; ombudsman procedures and other non-judicial procedures may therefore qualify, depending on the nature of the complaint.[341] The Court has also pointed out that "as a general rule, if a single remedy does not by itself entirely satisfy the requirements of Article 13, the aggregate of remedies provided for under domestic law may do so".[342]

These interpretations were summed up in the 2007 case of *Cobzaru* v. *Romania*:

> The effect of Article 13 is thus to require the provision of a domestic remedy to deal with the substance of an "arguable complaint" under the Convention and to grant appropriate relief, although Contracting States are afforded some discretion as to the manner in which they conform to their Convention obligations under this provision. The scope of the obligation under Article 13 varies depending on the nature of the applicant's complaint under the Convention. Nevertheless, the remedy required by Article 13 must be "effective" in practice as well as in law; in particular, its exercise must not be unjustifiably hindered by the acts or omissions of the authorities of the respondent State.[343]

As the Court pointed out in the above case, the scope of states' obligations under Article 13 varies depending on the nature of the applicant's complaint, and the Court has expressed its view that in certain situations the Convention requires a particular remedy to be provided. Thus in cases that implicate Articles 2 (right to life) or 3 (prohibition of

---

338 Jacobs – White, *cit. supra* note 318, pp. 386 ff.

339 See e.g. ECtHR, *Keenan* v. *United Kingdom*, judgement of 3 April 2001.

340 See e.g. idem, where the Court said that the domestic remedy must be provided for the purposes of (i) dealing with the substance of an arguable complaint, and (ii) granting appropriate relief.

341 Jacobs – White, *cit. supra* note 318, p. 390.

342 ECtHR, *Cobzaru* v. *Romania*, judgment of 26 July 2007, para 81.

343 Ibid, para 80, references omitted. See also ECtHR, *Bazorkina v. Russia*, judgment of 27 July 2006, paras 160–161; and ECtHR, *Aydin* v. *Turkey*, judgment of 25 September 1997, para 103.

torture), the Court has interpreted Article 13 to require, "in addition to the payment of compensation where appropriate, a thorough and effective investigation capable of leading to the identification and punishment of those responsible for the acts of ill-treatment".[344] Where the suspicion arises that such acts were induced by racial attitudes, the authorities have "an additional duty to take all reasonable steps to unmask any racist motive and to establish whether or not ethnic hatred or prejudice may have played a role in the events" and to be particularly careful to pursue the official investigation with vigour and impartiality, as otherwise Article 14 may have been infringed as well.[345]

In a number of cases the ECtHR has consistently held that Article 13 does not amount to a requirement of judicial review, meaning that it does not go so far as to guarantee a remedy allowing a contracting state's primary legislation to be challenged before a national authority on grounds that it is contrary to the Convention.[346]

Protocol No. 12 to the European Convention

Protocol No. 12 was adopted in November 2000 and it entered into force in April 2005. By January 2011 it had been ratified by 18 out of 47 Council of Europe member states, and by 6 of the 27 EU countries.[347] Since there is little case law under Protocol No. 12 at the time of writing, the following analysis will rely strongly on the Explanatory Report that accompanied the Protocol.[348]

Article 1 of the Protocol sets out a general prohibition of discrimination:

> 1. The enjoyment of any right set forth by law shall be secured without discrimination on any ground such as sex, race, colour, language,

---

[344] ECtHR, *Cobzaru* v. *Romania*, judgment of 26 July 2007, para 81; ECtHR, *Bazorkina v. Russia*, judgment of 27 July 2006, para 161.

[345] See ECtHR Grand Chamber judgment in *Nachova and others* v. *Bulgaria*, judgment of 6 July 2005, para 160. With regard the obligation to ensure equal treatment in the administration of justice, see also ECtHR, *Moldovan and Others* v. *Romania*, judgment of 12 July 2005, paras 139 and 140.

[346] See e.g. ECtHR, *Roche* v. *The United Kingdom*, judgment of 19 October 2005, para 137.

[347] These were Finland, Luxemburg, the Netherlands, Romania, Slovenia and Spain. The number of ratifications, particularly by the EU member states, is remarkably low.

[348] As is a usual practice for the Council of Europe, the Explanatory Report is not legally binding, but is intended to shed light on the intended meaning of the adopted instrument. It should be noted, in any case, that the ECtHR has at times given the Report considerable weight. See e.g. *Savez crkava "Riječ života" and Others* v. *Croatia*, judgment 9 December 2010 (not final).

religion, political or other opinion, national or social origin, association with a national minority, property, birth or other status.
2. No one shall be discriminated against by any public authority on any ground such as those mentioned in paragraph 1.

Article 1 explicitly uses the term 'discrimination', as does Article 14. This time the French text reads 'sans discrimination aucune' instead of 'sans distinction aucune', aligning it with the English text and the ECtHR's practice.[349] In the 2009 case of *Sejdić and Finci* v. *Bosnia and Herzegovina*, which was the first case decided under Protocol No. 12, the ECtHR held that it interprets the concept of discrimination in the Protocol along the lines of its case law under Article 14.[350] This follows the intention of the drafters.[351]

The operative paragraphs of Protocol No. 12 do not expressly refer to special measures. However, the preamble to Protocol 12 reads that:

> the principle of non-discrimination does not prevent States Parties from taking measures in order to promote full and effective equality, provided that there is an objective and reasonable justification for those measures.

The central notions at play here, 'full and effective equality' and 'objective and reasonable justification' are not defined in the Protocol or the Explanatory Report. Though the existing case law from the ECtHR provides some leads, particularly with respect to assessment of justifications, that case law is limited in scope and therefore the permitted scope of special measures is left open. What seems clear under a literal interpretation is that taking special measures is in any case allowed but not required.[352]

---

[349] See also para 18 of the Explanatory Report.

[350] ECtHR, *Sejdić and Finci* v. *Bosnia and Herzegovina*, GC judgment of 22 December 2009, para 55.

[351] See the Explanatory Report, para 18. See also Jeroen Schokkenbroek, 'A New European Standard Against Discrimination: Negotiating Protocol 12 to the European Convention on Human Rights' in Stéphanie Lagoutte (ed.), *Prohibition of discrimination in the Nordic Countries: The Complicated fate of Protocol No. 12 to the European Convention on Human Rights* (Copenhagen: The Danish Institute for Human Rights, 2005).

[352] The preamble also has regard to the "fundamental principle according to which all persons are equal before the law and are entitled to the equal protection of the law". The legal implications of this reference on Article 1 are not wholly clear either – why were these principles not incorporated into the operative paragraphs?

The list of grounds is identical with Article 14. The inclusion of additional grounds was considered during the drafting process, but deemed unnecessary since the list is not exhaustive and the explicit inclusion of some new grounds was anticipated to give rise to *e contrario* - arguments that some other grounds were thus excluded.[353] Given that the Court has already considered discrimination on the grounds of ethnicity under Article 14, it appears warranted to expect that it will be prepared to do the same under the Protocol as well.

The *ratio* of Protocol 12 was to extend protection from discrimination to areas not covered by Article 14, the scope of which is limited to the enjoyment of the rights and freedoms set forth in the Convention.[354] The scope of application of the Protocol is indeed defined in broader terms: Article 1(1) requires state parties to secure the enjoyment of "any right set forth by law" without discrimination and Article 1(2) provides that "no one shall be discriminated against by any public authority". While it is generally accepted that the Protocol indeed goes further than Article 14 in terms of material scope, scholars and representatives of states are puzzled about how far it actually goes.[355] One unresolved question is whether the term 'law' should be taken to cover not just national law but also international law; would the European Court have jurisdiction to examine whether a right emanating from another international instrument, say the UN Covenant on Civil and Political Rights, is applied in a discriminatory manner by a state party to the Protocol?[356]

The Explanatory Report goes to some lengths to explain the scope of application of Article 1, but fails to alleviate many of the uncertainties in this respect. According to the Report, the Protocol provides added protection, in comparison to Article 14, where a person is discriminated against:

- in the enjoyment of any right specifically granted to an individual under national law;
- in the enjoyment of a right which may be inferred from a public authority's clear obligation under national law to behave in a particular manner;

[353] Para 20 of the Explanatory Report.

[354] See the Explanatory Report; Jeroen Schokkenbroek, *cit. supra* note 351.

[355] See the articles in Stéphanie Lagoutte (ed.), *cit. supra* note 351.

[356] The Explanatory Report indeed suggests that this might be the case, see para 29 of the Report.

- by a public authority in the exercise of discretionary power (for example, granting subsidies);
- or by any other act or omission of a public authority (for example, the behaviour of police officers when controlling a riot).[357]

The principal objective of Article 1 is clearly to protect individuals from discrimination by public authorities, the latter notion including the courts, legislative bodies and the administrative bodies.[358] Authorities, particularly in light of the second subparagraph, must refrain from any discrimination in their role as employers and service-providers, which extends protection at least to some types of education, social services, medical care and public transportation. However, from the point of view of protecting individuals from discrimination, it does not matter much whether the employer or a service-provider is a public authority or a private company. The question therefore arises whether the Article imposes a positive obligation on the states parties to take measures to prevent or remedy discrimination also in relations between private parties.

The Explanatory Report is remarkably ambiguous in this respect. It states that the inclusion of a general obligation to take legislative or other action to prevent or remedy all instances of discrimination in relations between private persons "would not have been suitable" because the Convention contains justiciable individual rights, whereas such an obligation would have been of "programmatic character", and the report concludes that "the extent of any positive obligations flowing from Article 1 is likely to be limited".[359] Yet it notes that in some instances the failure of a state to provide protection from discrimination in relations between private persons might be so "clear-cut and grave" that it engages Article 1.[360] This could occur where interpersonal relations concern "relations in the public sphere normally regulated by law, for which the State has a certain responsibility".[361] Access to work and access to services which private persons make available to the

[357] Explanatory Report, para 22. The ECtHR affirmed the importance of the guidance provided by the Explanatory Report in *Savez crkava "Riječ života" and Others v. Croatia*, judgment 9 December 2010, paras 104–105 (not final).

[358] On the last point see ibid, para 30.

[359] Ibid, paras 24–27.

[360] See ibid, paras 26–29.

[361] Ibid, para 28.

public are mentioned as areas implicated by Article 1, whereas "purely private matters" are taken to fall outside its scope in the interests of protecting "the individual's right to respect for his private and family life."[362] Many countries, including Finland, have been of the view that the existence of positive obligations is not apparent under the Protocol.[363]

In the *Sejdić* case the Court addressed this matter in passim. It noted that "Article 1 of Protocol No. 12 extends the scope of protection to any rights set forth by law", and that it "thus introduces a general prohibition of discrimination."[364] This would seem to support the interpretation that states must provide protection from discrimination also in the private sphere, at least in areas that are regulated by law and where individuals therefore can have rights.[365] Interestingly, in *Sejdić* the Court noted in *obiter dictum* that Article 1 of the Protocol is similar - although not identical - to Article 26 of the International Covenant on Civil and Political Rights.[366] Keeping in mind the sweeping scope of the latter provision, it appears that the Court is indeed prepared to interpret the material scope of the Protocol broadly.

The Protocol's relationship with the Convention is governed by Article 3 of the Protocol, which provides:

> As between the States Parties, the provisions of Articles 1 and 2 of this protocol shall be regarded as additional articles to the Convention, and all the provisions of the Convention shall apply accordingly.

Thus, Protocol No 12 does not amend or abrogate Article 14, which will continue to apply with respect to states party to the Protocol. Any questions regarding the relationship between these two provisions will be within the Court's jurisdiction.[367]

---

362 Explanatory Report, para 28.

363 As for Finland see the report of the Constitutional Law Committee of the Parliament of Finland, PeVL 4/2004 vp.

364 ECtHR, *Sejdić and Finci* v. *Bosnia and Herzegovina*, GC judgment of 22 December 2009, para 53.

365 It must be noted that rights may derive not just from legislation but also from contractual relationships. Given the express reference in Article 1 to rights "set forth by law", the Protocol probably does not apply to contractual relationships that are not governed by e.g. employment or tenancy laws.

366 ECtHR, *Sejdić and Finci* v. *Bosnia and Herzegovina*, GC judgment of 22 December 2009, para 55.

367 Explanatory Report, para 33.

6.9 The European Social Charter (Revised)

Introduction

The European Social Charter was adopted in 1961. As of January 2011 the Charter had been ratified by 27 member states of the Council of Europe.[368] Despite the official rhetoric within the Council of Europe stressing the indivisibility of civil and political rights on the one hand, and social, economic and cultural rights on the other, the conviction that the latter set of rights are not of justiciable character in the same way as the first set of rights played a key part in the process that led to the adoption of the Charter. One consequence of this was that whereas compliance with the ECHR is supervised by a Court handing out legally binding decisions, no complaints procedure was initially available under the Charter.[369] This, the open-ended language of the Charter, and the politicized supervision of the Charter, together with other factors, led some commentators to characterize the Charter, particularly when contrasted with the ECHR, as little known, rarely referred to and often ignored in practice.[370] Starting from the late 1980s a number of additional protocols, supplementing existing Charter rights and modifying the supervision machinery, were adopted with a view to reinvigorating the Charter. Finally, the revised European Social Charter was adopted in 1996. As of January 2011 the revised Charter had been ratified by 30 countries.[371] The following analysis will focus upon the revised Charter.

The implementation of the legal obligations contained in the Charter is subject to supervision by the European Committee of Social Rights (formerly known as the Committee of Independent Experts). The contracting states submit to a routine reporting mechanism whereby the Committee is to "assess from a legal standpoint the compliance of national law and practice with the obligations arising from the Charter".[372] The Charter now also provides for a system of collective

---

[368] Source: http://conventions.coe.int (accessed 1.1.2011).

[369] See generally on this Tonia Novitz, 'Remedies for violation of Social Rights within the Council of Europe: The Significant Absence of a Court' in Claire Kilpatrick, Tonia Novitz and Paul Skidmore (eds.) *The Future of Remedies in Europe* (Oxford: Hart, 2000).

[370] Ibid, p. 244 and the references cited therein.

[371] Source: http://conventions.coe.int (accessed 1.1.2011).

[372] Part IV, Article C of the revised Charter, Article 24 of the original Charter as modified by the 1991 Amending Protocol (CETS No: 142).

complaints, whereby trade unions, employers' organisations and NGOs may lodge complaints with the Committee.[373]

The Concept of Discrimination

Whereas the original Charter did not feature an operative paragraph on non-discrimination but simply declared in its preamble that the rights provided therein should be secured without discrimination,[374] Article E of the revised Charter reads as follows:

> The enjoyment of the rights set forth in this Charter shall be secured without discrimination on any ground such as race, colour, sex, language, religion, political or other opinion, national extraction or social origin, health, association with a national minority, birth or other status.

Article E draws its inspiration from Article 14 of the ECHR, as did the principle of non-discrimination enunciated in the preamble to the original Charter. The Committee has observed that the function of Article E is to help secure the equal effective enjoyment of all the rights concerned regardless of the specific characteristics of certain persons or groups of persons.[375] The Appendix to the Charter specifies that differential treatment based on an objective and reasonable justification shall not be deemed discriminatory.

The Committee has interpreted Article E as requiring the prohibition of both direct and indirect discrimination.[376] It considers that discrimination may take the form of a rule, act or practice.[377] Direct discrimination is understood by the Committee as "a difference in treatment between persons in comparable situations where it does not pursue a legitimate aim, is not based on objective and reasonable grounds or is not proportionate to the aim pursued."[378] Whether a

---

[373] Part IV, Article D of the revised Charter, Article 8 of the 1995 Additional Protocol.

[374] The preamble states that contracting states considered "that the enjoyment of social rights should be secured without discrimination on grounds of race, colour, sex, religion, political opinion, national extraction or social origin". This principle, inspired by Article 14 of the ECHR, is accessory in nature in that its application is limited by the scope of the Charter.

[375] ECSR, *Autisme-Europe* v. *France*, decision of 4 November 2003, para 52.

[376] ECSR, *Centre on Housing Rights and Evictions (COHRE)* v. *Italy*, decision of 25 June 2010, para 35.

[377] ECSR, *Sud Travail et Affaires sociales* v. *France*, decision of 16 November 2005, para 33. See also ECSR, Conclusions on France 2002, p. 24

[378] ECSR, *Syndicat national des Professions du Tourisme* v. *France*, decision of 10 October 2000, paras 24–25.

difference in treatment pursues a legitimate aim and is proportionate is assessed in light of Article G of the Charter, which provides that the material provisions of the Charter shall not be subject to any restrictions or limitations not specified in those provisions, except where "prescribed by law" and "necessary in a democratic society for the protection of the rights and freedoms of others or for the protection of public interest, national security, public health, or morals."[379]

The Committee sees indirect discrimination as arising when a measure or practice without a legitimate aim disproportionately affects "persons having a particular ethnic origin" or "persons belonging to a particular race".[380] Influenced by the ECtHR's decision in the *Thlimmenos* case, the Committee has recognized that indirect discrimination may also arise where a state party fails, without an objective and reasonable justification, to treat differently persons whose situations are different: indirect discrimination may arise by failing to take due and positive account of all relevant differences or by failing to take adequate steps to ensure that the rights and collective advantages that are open to all are genuinely accessible by and to all.[381] For instance, in the *European Roma Rights Centre* v. *Italy* case, the Committee was of the view that the state party had failed "to take into consideration the different situation of Roma or to introduce measures specifically aimed at improving their housing conditions, including the possibility for an effective access to social housing", and on those grounds it found a violation of Article 31 together with Article E.[382]

In the *Centre on Housing Rights and Evictions (COHRE)* v. *Italy* case, the Committee held that the use of xenophobic political rhetoric against particular ethnic groups, by public actors, constitutes a violation of Article E taken in conjunction with Article 19 of the Charter.[383]

The Committee has recognized that exceptions to the general prohibition of discrimination may be made for the purposes of recognising

[379] ECSR, Conclusions XVI-1, Greece, pp. 279–280.

[380] ECSR, *European Roma Rights Centre* v. *Bulgaria*, decision of 18 October 2006, para 57.

[381] ECSR, *ERRC* v. *Italy*, decision of 7 December 2005, para 36; ECSR, *Autisme-Europe* v. *France*, decision of 4 November 2003, para 52; ECSR, *Centre on Housing Rights and Evictions (COHRE)* v. *Italy*, decision of 25 June 2010, para 35.

[382] Para 46.

[383] ESCR, *Centre on Housing Rights and Evictions (COHRE)* v. *Italy*, decision of 25 June 2010, paras 139–140.

genuine occupational requirements and for the sake of positive action measures.[384] It has also submitted that to make the prohibition of discrimination effective, state parties should provide protection against retaliatory action by the employer against an employee who has lodged a complaint or taken legal action.[385]

Grounds

The list of expressly prohibited grounds of discrimination includes, among others, race, colour, and national extraction. The list is not exhaustive, and is comparable with the list in Article 14 of the ECHR, although for some reason the Charter mentions 'national extraction' where the Convention mentions 'national origin'.[386] The Committee has interpreted the Charter also to prohibit discrimination on the grounds of membership of an ethnic group.[387] It has indicated that it regards membership of a 'race' or ethnic group as particularly suspect grounds of discrimination.[388]

Material Scope

Article E is accessory in nature in that its application is limited to the enjoyment of the rights set forth in the Charter. In terms of material substance, part I of the Charter lays down 31 broadly formulated "rights and principles" that range from the "opportunity to earn living in an occupation freely entered upon" to "right to housing". Part I specifies that the state parties "accept as the aim of their policy, to be pursued by all appropriate means ... the attainment of conditions" in which these rights and principles may be "effectively realised". In Part II, states undertake a number of more specific obligations with a view to ensuring the effective exercise of each one of the rights laid down in Part I. However, pursuant to Part III, state parties do not need to consider to be bound by all of the rights and principles set out in the Charter, but can choose, within the limits specified in Article A of Part III, which obligations to assume. Article E on non-discrimination is placed in Part V, and its observance is not optional.

[384] ECSR, Conclusions 2006, Bulgaria.

[385] ECSR, Conclusions XVI-1, Iceland, p. 313.

[386] It is also noteworthy that the Charter does not mention 'property' as a prohibited ground of discrimination, unlike the Convention.

[387] ECSR, Conclusions XVI-1, Austria, p.25.

[388] Idem.

The Charter reaches into the areas of employment, education and housing. In Part II, under Article 1 entitled 'the right to work', the parties undertake:

(i) to accept as one of their primary aims and responsibilities the achievement and maintenance of as high and stable a level of employment as possible, with a view to the attainment of full employment;
(ii) to protect effectively the right of the worker to earn his living in an occupation freely entered upon;
(iii) to establish or maintain free employment services for all workers;
(iv) to provide or promote appropriate vocational guidance, training and rehabilitation.

The Committee has interpreted that paragraph 2, when read together with Article E, prohibits all discrimination which may occur in connection with recruitment and employment conditions in general, including remuneration, training, promotion, transfer and dismissal.[389] In fact, it has interpreted the Charter to require adoption of legislation that prohibits discrimination in employment.[390] It has further suggested that the domestic legal order should provide the means by which any discriminatory provision which appears in collective labour agreements, in employment contracts or in companies' own regulations, may be declared null or be rescinded, abrogated or amended.[391] Besides Article 2, also other provisions of the Charter seek to provide added protection from particular types of harm, including harassment, experienced in the working life. For instance Article 26 of Part II, entitled 'the right to dignity at work', requires states to promote awareness, information and prevention of "recurrent reprehensible or distinctly negative and offensive actions directed against individual workers" and to take all "appropriate measures to protect workers from such conduct".

In Article 17 of Part II, concerning "the right of children and young persons to social, legal and economic protection", parties assume, *inter alia*, the obligation to "take all appropriate and necessary measures designed to ensure that children and young persons … have … the education and the training they need". In Article 31, entitled "the right

389 Idem.
390 Idem.
391 ECSR, Conclusions XVI-1, Iceland, p. 313.

to housing", the parties undertake to take measures designed, *inter alia*, to "promote access to housing of adequate standard". These activities are to be pursued with regard to Article E on non-discrimination.

Domestic enforcement and remedies

The Committee has repeatedly emphasized the role of effective remedies, both in the procedural and substantive sense. It has called for "appropriate and effective remedies" in the event of an allegation of discrimination,[392] specifying that the remedies must be adequate, proportionate and dissuasive.[393] It has further opined that sufficiently deterring sanctions should be imposed for instance in cases of discriminatory dismissals, and that in such cases the victim should be entitled to adequate compensation that is proportionate to the damage suffered.[394]

As regards procedural remedies, the Committee has opined that the domestic law should provide for the alleviation of the burden of proof in favour of the plaintiff in discrimination cases.[395] It has also recommended that state parties should recognize the right of trade unions to take action in cases of employment discrimination, including action on behalf of individuals, and that they should establish special, independent bodies which promote equal treatment particularly by providing victims with the support they need to take proceedings.[396]

6.10 Framework Convention for the Protection of National Minorities

Introduction

Immediately after the adoption of the European Convention on Human Rights, which does not include a provision on minority rights, initiatives were brought forward to remedy the situation.[397] Yet it took more than 40 years for these efforts to bear fruit, as the Framework

---

392 Idem.

393 ECSR, Conclusions 2006, Albania. It therefore considers that the imposition of predefined upper limits to compensation that may be awarded are not in conformity with the Charter, as in certain cases upper limits may preclude damages from being awarded which are commensurate with the loss and damage actually sustained.

394 ECSR, Conclusions Albania, 2008.

395 ECSR, Conclusions France, 2002, p. 24

396 ECSR, Conclusions XVI-1, Iceland, p. 313.

397 Explanatory Report to the Framework Convention.

Convention for the Protection of National Minorities (FCNM) was adopted in 1995. By January 2011 the Convention had been ratified by 39 out of the 47 Council of Europe member states, making it one of the most widely ratified treaties of the Council of Europe.[398]

The Convention is the first ever legally binding multilateral instrument devoted to the protection of national minorities in general. The Convention states that its aim is to ensure "the effective protection of national minorities and of the rights and freedoms of persons belonging to those minorities",[399] and it sets out a number of provisions that deal with equal treatment, protection of identity and culture, and promotion of good inter-group relations. Implementation of the Convention by states parties is monitored by the Committee of Ministers of the Council of Europe which is assisted by an Advisory Committee.[400] Monitoring principally takes place by means of consideration of periodic state reports.[401]

Concept of Discrimination

Article 4(1) of the Convention provides:

> The Parties undertake to guarantee to persons belonging to national minorities the right of equality before the law and of equal protection of the law. In this respect, any discrimination based on belonging to a national minority shall be prohibited.

Neither the Convention nor its Explanatory Report explain what is meant by 'right of equality before the law' or by the 'right of equal protection of the law'. The Explanatory Report simply states that Article 4(1) takes "the classic approach to these principles", suggesting that these principles are self-explanatory or that at any rate their meaning is settled.[402] The Advisory Committee has, in the context of the consideration of country reports, interpreted these principles to require

---

[398] Source: http://conventions.coe.int (accessed 1.1.2011).

[399] Preamble to the Convention.

[400] Hoffmann has observed that the conclusions and recommendations of the Committee of Ministers have in fact been guided by the Advisory Committee opinions, and that the country-specific resolutions adopted by the former have clearly reflected the findings of the Committee. Rainer Hoffmann 'The Framework Convention For the Protection of National Minorities: An Introduction' in Marc Weller (ed.) *The Rights of Minorities: A Commentary on the European Framework Convention for the Protection of National Minorities* (Oxford: Oxford University Press, 2005), pp. 6–12.

[401] See section IV of the Convention.

[402] Explanatory Report, para 39.

"effective remedies against acts of discrimination by public authorities and private entities in a number of societal settings, such as education, job-advertisements and housing" and equal application of law by state authorities.[403]

The Convention and the Explanatory Report are also silent as regards the meaning of the concept of 'discrimination'. The Advisory Committee has, again in the course of consideration of country reports, taken the view that discrimination should be conceived as encompassing both direct and indirect discrimination.[404] That said, it has been observed that the Committee has been cautious in concluding that indirect discrimination has actually taken place.[405]

In its comments to country reports, the Advisory Committee has welcomed or recommended a series of measures in connection to the performance of their obligations under Article 4 by the state parties, including adoption of comprehensive anti-discrimination legislation in public law, criminal law and civil law with effective means of implementation; active roles for the courts, tribunals, and independent national institutions in combating discrimination; dissemination of information, education, and other efforts "to ensure that individuals are informed of their rights in this sphere and that they have the confidence in the relevant authorities to seek remedy when they consider that these rights have been violated".[406]

Article 4(2) deals with special measures, by providing that "[t]he Parties undertake to adopt, where necessary, adequate measures in order to promote, in all areas of economic, social, political and cultural life, full and effective equality between persons belonging to a national minority and those belonging to the majority." Two issues in particular merit attention. First, the Article is couched in terms of a positive recognition of the need to take measures to promote equality in fact. This makes it a not-so-distant relative of Article 2(2) of the ICERD.

---

403 ACFC, Hungary, 22 September 2000.

404 ACFC, Switzerland, 20 February 2003, paras 28 and 86; ACFC, Former Yugoslav Republic of Macedonia, 27 May 2004; See also Rainer Hoffman 'The Impact of International Norms on the Protection of National Minorities in Europe: The Added Value and Essential Role of the Framework Convention for the Protection of National Minorities' Strasbourg, 5 December 2006.

405 See Henrard, *cit supra* note 95, p. 26.

406 Gudmundur Alfredsson, 'Article 4' in Marc Weller (ed.) *The Rights of Minorities: A Commentary on the European Framework Convention for the Protection of National Minorities* (Oxford: Oxford University Press, 2005), p. 150; ACFC, Russian federation, 11 May 2006, paras 48–49.

The Advisory Committee has opined that the Article, through its reference to full and effective equality, implies the need for the authorities to take specific measures in order to overcome past or structural inequalities.[407] Second, this recognition is circumscribed in several ways. Measures are to be taken "where necessary"; the Convention nowhere defines when measures are to be considered necessary or who is to make the decision that certain measures are necessary. It is clear that subjective appreciation will necessarily be involved. The obligation does not consist of an obligation to take measures to *bring about* de facto equality; it consists of an obligation to take measures to *promote* such equality. Measures to be taken are to be "*adequate*", an open term which does not indicate whether it should be understood in the sense of "fully sufficient" or in the sense of "barely sufficient". The Explanatory Report sets out to interpret the meaning of the term "adequate", and explains that it means that the measures in question must be in accordance with the "proportionality principle" and avoid "discrimination against others".[408] It further specifies that the principle requires, among other things, that such measures do not extend, in time or in scope, beyond what is necessary in order to achieve the aim of full and effective equality.[409]

Grounds and Personal Scope

The effect of the Convention is to a degree compromised by the fact that it does not define its intended beneficiaries, that is national minorities and their members, and no definition has been formulated by the monitoring bodies either. According to the Explanatory Report no definition was adopted because the drafters "decided to adopt a pragmatic approach, based on the recognition that at this stage, it is impossible to arrive at a definition capable of mustering general support of all Council of Europe member States."[410] In response to the lack of definition several states have added declarations to their instruments of ratification by which they have usually sought to limit the breadth of their FCNM obligations to groups typically referred to as 'historic'

[407] ACFC, Commentary on the effective participation of persons belonging to national minorities in cultural, social and economic life and in public affairs (Strasbourg, 5 May 2008), para 14.
[408] Explanatory Report, para 39.
[409] Idem.
[410] Ibid, para 12.

or 'traditional' minorities[411] – to the exclusion of 'new' minorities. The Advisory Committee, for its part, has adopted a pragmatic and flexible approach to the definitional issue and has opined that states have a 'margin of appreciation' in this respect but must avoid arbitrary or unjustified distinctions.[412] This approach goes well with the Committee's general tendency to avoid unnecessary confrontation with governments.[413]

Material Scope

The prohibition of discrimination in Article 4(1) relates to the obligation to guarantee 'equality before the law' and 'equal protection of the law', and therefore its scope of application is determined by the scope of application of the two principles. Insofar as the two principles are understood as relating to the substance of domestic legislation and its application, which is the standard reading of the two principles, then any discrimination on the grounds of membership in a national minority is prohibited in these respects. The scope of the prohibition of discrimination will therefore vary to some extent from one country to another, but will be limited to the exercise of public powers, specifically legislative, administrative and judicial powers.

Complementary Equality Provisions

The Convention, in separate provisions, addresses also the issues of cultural and political equality for national minorities. The most relevant articles in this respect are Articles 5 and 15 of the Convention.

Article 5(1) touches on cultural equality, and provides as follows:

> The Parties undertake to promote the conditions necessary for persons belonging to national minorities to maintain and develop their culture, and to preserve the essential elements of their identity, namely their religion, language, traditions and cultural heritage.

---

411 Hoffmann, *cit. supra* note 400, p. 16; Tove H. Malloy 'The Title and the Preamble' in Weller (ed.), *cit. supra* note 400, p. 50.

412 Hoffmann, *cit. supra* note 400, p. 16; Hans-Joachim Heintze, 'Article 1' in Weller, (ed.) *cit. supra* note 400, p. 111. For a good example of the Committee's pragmatic and flexible approach, see ACFC, Hungary, 17 September 2010, paras 32–36.

413 Gudmundur Alfredsson 'A Frame with an Incomplete Painting: Comparison of the Framework Convention for the Protection of National Minorities with International Standards and Monitoring Procedures' *International Journal on Minority and Group Rights* 7:291–304, 2000. Hoffmann, *cit. supra* note 400, p. 17.

The second paragraph of Article 5 furthermore specifies that states shall refrain from policies or practices aimed at assimilation of persons belonging to minorities, and shall protect them from any action aimed at such assimilation.

The modalities by which states may fulfil their obligations under Article 5 are ostensibly diverse. The Advisory Committee has mainly drawn states' attention to the need to involve minority groups in the process of determining what the state has to do to "promote the necessary conditions" for those groups to flourish, and has indicated that Article 5 may impose a financial obligation in certain circumstances.[414] The Explanatory Report and commentators have by and large refrained from elaborating on how states should, or even could, go about fulfilling Article 5, and whether it for instance calls for cultural and religious accommodation at the workplace.[415]

Article 15 deals with participation, and provides:

> The Parties shall create the conditions necessary for the effective participation of persons belonging to national minorities in cultural, social and economic life and in public affairs, in particular those affecting them.

Article 15 has been hailed as a provision of fundamental importance. The Explanatory Report describes that its aim is no less than to "encourage real equality", and Marc Weller explains it in terms of "genuine integration" and "co-governance".[416]

Its theoretical importance notwithstanding, the Report and the Advisory Committee have refrained from laying down specific guidelines as to how states should "create the conditions necessary for effective participation", choosing instead to highlight what measures can be considered as good practices.[417] The Committee has opined that Article

---

[414] See Geoff Gilbert 'Article 5' in Weller (ed.), *cit supra* note 400.

[415] See e.g. idem. There are, of course, theoretical explorations of how states may pursue multicultural policies, see e.g. Will Kymlicka, *Multicultural citizenship: a liberal theory of minority rights* (Oxford: Clarendon Press, 1995).

[416] Explanatory Report, para 80; Marc Weller 'Article 15' in Weller (ed.), *cit. supra* note 400.

[417] The report, for instance, mentions the following mechanisms: consultation with institutions representing minorities whenever states are contemplating legislation or administrative measures likely to affect them directly; involving persons belonging to minorities in the preparation, implementation and assessment of national and regional development plans and programmes likely to affect them directly; impact assessment studies; effective participation of persons belonging to national minorities in the decision-making processes and elected bodies both at national and local levels; and decentralized or local forms of government. Explanatory Report, para 80. The Advisory

15 calls for the setting up of effective channels of communication that facilitate "continuing and substantive dialogue" both between persons belonging to national minorities and the majority population, and between persons belonging to national minorities and the authorities.[418] With respect to the latter aspect, it has emphasised that mere formal participation is not sufficient, but participation must have a substantial influence on decisions taken and that on these grounds mere consultation is, as such, not sufficient.[419] There has also been an emphasis on equal participation in the electoral process and on adequate representation in parliament and other elected bodies.[420]

State Obligations, Domestic Enforcement and Remedies

The Convention deals with a subject area that is politically highly sensitive, a fact which led to great difficulties on the part of the drafters with agreeing upon acceptable language and, eventually, to many compromises in the text.[421] The specific nature of the FCNM as a *framework* convention has also given rise to some confusion and much legal commentary.[422] Indeed, as its title says, it is a framework treaty, which readily indicates that states are left discretion – within the confines of the framework set out – regarding how to give effect to its provisions. The text mentions in many places that it sets out 'principles', not rights or freedoms as such, which is also reflected in that the provisions are framed in general and open terms.[423] Most of the substantive provisions of the Convention are programmatic in nature, not meant to be invoked as such in courts of law. In a rather unceremonious and candid way, the Explanatory Report explains that the purpose of the last

Committee, in its *Commentary on the effective participation of persons belonging to national minorities in cultural, social and economic life and in public affairs* [ACFC/31DOC(2008)001, Strasbourg 5 May 2008, para 10] lists and comments upon a number of possible initiatives, and explains its approach as follows: "Article 15, like other provisions contained in the Framework Convention, implies for the State Parties an obligation of result: they shall ensure that the conditions for effective participation are in place, but the most appropriate means to reach this aim are left to their margin of appreciation. This Commentary aims to provide the State Parties with an analysis of existing experiences so as to help them to identify the most effective options".

418 Ibid (Advisory Committee), paras 11–12.

419 Ibid, paras 19 and 71.

420 Weller, *cit. supra* note 416.

421 Hoffmann, *cit. supra* note 400, p. 5.

422 See the articles in Weller (ed.), *cit. supra* note 400; Weller 'Conclusion' in ibid, p. 633.

423 See e.g. Article 19, where the contracting states agree to "undertake to respect and implement the principles enshrined in the present framework Convention…".

recital of the Preamble, which proclaims that the contracting states are "determined to implement the principles set out in this framework Convention through national legislation and appropriate governmental policies", is to indicate that the provisions of the Convention are not directly applicable.[424] All in all, the Explanatory Report and many commentators have concluded that the Convention does not create directly enforceable rights for individuals, that its implementation will be left to the states concerned in terms of their internal legislation and practice, and that it allows the contracting states an unusually wide measure of discretion in implementation.[425] Yet, it has been observed that states have generally taken seriously the commitments made when ratifying the Convention, and that a growing respect for the achievements of the Convention has emerged.[426]

6.11 Other Relevant Instruments

The most essential international and European human rights instruments relating to non-discrimination, for the purposes of this study, have been discussed above. Yet a number of other documents merit our attention as well, and will be briefly discussed below.

Instruments by the United Nations and its Agencies

International Convention on the Protection of the Rights of All Migrant Workers and Members of Their Families (ICRMW). This Convention was concluded in 1990. It had been ratified by 44 countries, only four of which were Council of Europe member states and none of which was a member of the European Union, by January 2011.[427] The low number of ratifications by immigrant-receiving countries in particular

---

[424] Paragraph 29 of the Report. Weller, *cit. supra* note 422, p. 634.

[425] Indeed, the Explanatory Report, paragraph 11, underlines that that "these provisions, which will not be directly applicable, leave the States concerned a measure of discretion in the implementation of the objectives which they have undertaken to achieve, thus enabling them to take particular circumstances into account." See also Malloy, *cit. supra* note 411, pp. 49 ff; Hoffman, *cit. supra* note 400, p. 5; Alfredsson, *cit. supra* note 413.

[426] See e.g. Marc Weller 'Preface' in Weller (ed.), *cit supra* note 400, p. vii, and the contributions in Council of Europe, *Filling the Frame: Five years of monitoring the Framework Convention for the Protection of National Minorities* (Strasbourg: Council of Europe Publishing, 2004).

[427] The four Council of Europe member states that are parties to the Convention are Albania, Azerbaijan, Bosnia and Herzegovina and Turkey.

is likely associated with the broad scope and very ambitious nature of the Convention: the number of articles that deal with substantive rights is as high as 64, which is compounded by the fact that many of these articles have up to nine paragraphs. The Convention establishes a Committee for the purpose of reviewing the application of the Convention by the state parties. This review is to take place by means of the examination of periodic country reports and by means of the examination of individual complaints (called 'communications' in the Convention) with respect to those countries that have recognized the competence of the Committee to that effect.[428]

As already mentioned, the scope of the ICRMW is extraordinarily wide, which together with the low number of ratifications in Europe, means that it will only be necessary to review some of its most relevant paragraphs here. Article 25(1) of the Convention deals specifically with employment, and provides that migrant workers "shall enjoy treatment not less favourable than that which applies to nationals of the State of employment in respect of remuneration and: (a) Other conditions of work, that is to say ... termination of the employment relationship and any other conditions of work which, according to national law and practice, are covered by these terms; (b) Other terms of employment". Article 25(2) specifically underlines that it shall not be lawful to derogate from the principle of equality of treatment referred to in Article 25(1) in private contracts of employment. Article 7 provides that states parties undertake to "respect and ensure" the rights provided for in the Convention for all migrant workers and members of their families without distinction of any kind such as to race, colour or national, ethnic or social origin. States shall also ensure "respect for the cultural identity of migrant workers and members of their families".[429] Article 43 provides that migrants shall enjoy equality of treatment with nationals of the state of employment, *inter alia*, in relation to access to educational institutions and services; access to vocational guidance and vocational training; and access to housing, including housing schemes. Article 45 requires states to provide many of the same rights to members of the family of the migrant.[430]

---

[428] Articles 72–78 of the Convention.

[429] Article 31.

[430] This applies to migrants and members of their families who are 'documented' or in a 'regular situation'. Article 30 applies to all migrants and the members of their families, and provides that each child of a migrant worker shall have the basic right of access to education on the basis of equality of treatment.

ILO Indigenous and Tribal Peoples Convention (Convention No 169). Convention No 169 was concluded in 1989 and was, as of January 2011, ratified by 22 countries, including three EU countries.[431] The Convention is of relevance in Europe, particularly in those parts of Northern Europe that are inhabited by the Sami people. In Article 2 of the Convention, the governments of states parties undertake to take measures to ensure that members of indigenous and tribal peoples benefit on an 'equal footing' from the rights and opportunities which national laws and regulations grant to other members of the population. Furthermore, the Convention goes beyond this formal approach and emphasizes throughout the need to respect these groups' identities and the need to take special measures for the purposes of alleviating de facto disadvantages and challenges faced by the peoples concerned. In Article 20 the governments undertake to "do everything possible to prevent any discrimination between workers belonging to the peoples concerned and other workers", in particular as regards admission to employment and equal remuneration for work of equal value. Governments are to take positive measures to ensure that members of the peoples concerned have the opportunity to acquire education at all levels "on at least an equal footing" with the rest of the national community.[432] They are also obliged, somewhat vaguely, to "assist" members of the peoples concerned to "eliminate socio-economic gaps that may exist between indigenous and other members of the national community".[433]

Convention against Torture or other Cruel, Inhuman or Degrading Treatment or Punishment (CAT). This Convention was concluded in 1984, and as of January 2011 it had been ratified by 147 countries. Implementation of the Convention is supervised by the Committee against Torture, which carries out its duties through consideration of periodic country reports and individual communications submitted under an optional procedure laid down in Article 22 of the Convention. Though CAT does not directly deal with the kind of discrimination focussed upon in this study, it is a good example of a legal instrument which indirectly requires provision of a measure of protection to

---

[431] Source: http://www.ilo.org/ilolex/ (accessed 1.1.2011). The EU countries concerned were Denmark, the Netherlands and Spain. Of the remaining Council of Europe member states only Norway has ratified the treaty.

[432] Article 26.

[433] Article 2(2)c.

minorities and immigrants. *Hajrizi Dzemajl et al.* v. *Yugoslavia*[434] is a case in point, as an example of the way in which the Convention provides protection from acts that involve racist motives. In that case the Committee against Torture held that the burning down of Roma homes by a mob of non-Roma neighbours constituted acts of cruel, inhuman and degrading treatment. The failure of the police authorities to take appropriate steps to protect the Roma amounted to acquiescence to these acts, since the police authorities were informed of the immediate risk facing the Roma and were even present at the scene of events. Accordingly the Committee found a violation of Article 16, paragraph 1 of the Convention by the state party.

A number of other instruments – some of which are legally binding and some of which are not – similarly directly or indirectly require the provision of a measure of protection from discrimination within their specific fields of application. These include the Convention on the Rights of the Child; Convention on the Rights of Persons with Disabilities; UN Millennium Declaration; Declaration on Race and Prejudice; Declaration on the Rights of Persons Belonging to National or Ethnic, Religious and Linguistic Minorities; Declaration on the Human Rights of Individuals Who are not Nationals of the Country in which They Live; and Declaration on the Elimination of All Forms of Intolerance and of Discrimination Based on Religion or Belief.

Council of Europe Instruments

Council of Europe documents that are relevant in this context include the Convention on Cybercrime, in particular its Additional Protocol concerning the criminalization of acts of a racist and xenophobic nature committed through computer systems,[435] and the European Charter for Regional or Minority Languages.[436] A high number of documents dealing directly with racism and racial discrimination have been adopted by the European Commission against Racism and

---

[434] CAT, *Hajrizi Dzemajl et al.* v. *Yugoslavia*, case No. 161/1999.

[435] The Protocol provides that each Party to the Protocol shall adopt such legislative and other measures as may be necessary to establish as criminal offence the distribution, when committed intentionally and without right, of any material that advocates, promotes or incites hatred, discrimination or violence against any individual or group of individuals based on 'race', colour, descent or national or ethnic origin (exceptions apply). Paras 1–3 of the Protocol.

[436] Adopted on 5.11.1992, CETS No.:148.

Intolerance (ECRI). ECRI, established in 1993, is the Council of Europe body entrusted with the task of combating racism and racial discrimination.[437] ECRI has adopted a number of so-called General Policy Recommendations, including one on national legislation to combat racism and racial discrimination, and another on combating racism and racial discrimination in and through school education.[438] By 2010, ECRI had started its fourth round of so-called country-by-country analyses, within the confines of which it visits each country under study and publishes country reports in which it presents its analyses and recommendations for improvements.

Organization for Security and Co-operation in Europe (OSCE) instruments

The OSCE has adopted a significant number of so-called soft law instruments in the area of human rights that are relevant to the topic at hand.[439] For instance in the Final Act of the Conference on Security and Co-operation in Europe the participating states pledged to "respect human rights and fundamental freedoms ... for all without distinction as to race, sex, language or religion".[440] Similar pledges were made in the Concluding Document of Vienna.[441] In the document of the Copenhagen meeting of the Conference on the Human Dimension,

[437] ECRI is charged with pursuing the following four objectives: (i) reviewing member states' legislation, policies and other measures to combat racism, xenophobia, anti-Semitism and intolerance and their effectiveness; (ii) to propose further action at the local, national and European level; (iii) to formulate general policy recommendations for member states; and (iv) to study international legal instruments applicable in the matter with a view to their reinforcement where appropriate. Council of Europe, Committee of Ministers Resolution Res(2002)8 on the statute of the European Commission against Racism and Intolerance, and its Appendix.

[438] ECRI, General Policy Recommendation No 7 on national legislation to combat racism and racial discrimination, adopted by ECRI on 13 December 2002; ECRI General Policy Recommendation No 10 on combating racism and racial discrimination in and through school education, adopted by ECRI on 15 December 2006.

[439] On the highly problematic concept of 'soft law', see e.g. Jan Klabbers, *The Concept of Treaty in International Law* (The Hague: Martinus Nijhoff, 1996).

[440] Final Act of the Conference on Security and Co-operation in Europe, adopted in Helsinki on 1 August 1975.

[441] In the Vienna document, the participating states pledged to "ensure human rights and fundamental freedoms to everyone within their territory and subject to their jurisdiction, without distinction of any kind such as race, colour, sex, language, religion, political or other opinion, property, birth or other status". The Third Follow-Up Meeting, Vienna 15.1.1989, para 13.7.

the participating states "solemnly declared" that "all persons are equal before the law and are entitled without any discrimination to the equal protection of the law. In this respect, the law will prohibit any discrimination and guarantee to all persons equal and effective protection against discrimination on any ground".[442]

[442] Document of the Copenhagen meeting of the Conference on the Human Dimension of the CSCE, 29 June 1990, paras 5 and 5.9.

7 EUROPEAN UNION LAW

7.1 Background

The track record of the European Union[1] (EU) in the field of combating racial and ethnic discrimination was, for a long time, not very impressive. The 1957 Treaty of Rome prohibited discrimination on the grounds of nationality (banning discrimination of nationals of other member states, not nationals of third countries) and sex (albeit only in the area of equal pay), but it did not prohibit discrimination on the grounds of racial or ethnic origin.[2] Indeed, the EU began to regulate discrimination on the grounds other than sex and nationality only recently, being for a long time satisfied with the adoption of 'soft law' instruments in these areas.[3] This had to do with the fact that the basic imperatives behind the formation and operation of the Union were of an economic nature and had to do with the creation of the common market, not social policy.[4] Combating racism and racial

[1] The term 'European Union" is used here also in reference to the organisational forms that preceded it, the European Communities in particular.

[2] See, in particular, Articles 7 and 119 of the original Treaty establishing the European Economic Community (EEC).

[3] For racial discrimination, the soft law instruments included Council Resolution on the fight against racism and xenophobia [1990] OJ C157/1, and Council Resolution on the Fight Against Racism and Xenophobia in the fields of Employment and Social Affairs [1995] OJ C296/13. Relevant instruments include also the following European Parliament documents, better known as the *Evrigenis report* and the *Ford report*: European Parliament, 'Committee of Inquiry into the Rise of Fascism and Racism in Europe' (Luxembourg: OOPEC, 1985), European Parliament, 'Report of the Committee of Inquiry into Racism and Xenophobia' (Luxembourg: OOPEC, 1991). See generally e.g. Damian Chalmers 'The Mistakes of the Good European' in Sandra Fredman (ed.) *Discrimination and Human Rights* (Oxford: Oxford University Press, 2001), pp 204 ff.

[4] Niessen notes that although some – including notably the Council of Ministers and the European Commission – were of the opinion that the European Treaties did not provide a legal basis for the European institutions to act on racial discrimination, such action could possibly have been taken on the basis of Article 235 (later 208), according to which actions could be taken, by unanimous vote, as long as they are necessary for the attainment of the objectives of the Community. Jan Niessen, 'Making the Law Work. The Enforcement and Implementation of Anti-Discrimination Legislation' *European Journal of Migration and Law* 5 (2003): 249–257. See also Erika Szyszczak, 'Race Discrimination: The Limits of Market Equality?' in Bob Hepple and Erika Szyszczak (eds.), *Discrimination: The Limits of Law?* (London: Mansell 1992).

discrimination was, in many quarters and for a long time, held to be a matter for national, not EU action.[5] There was also little pressure for action before the number of migrant workers from third countries started to increase in the 1960s and 1970s.

The bottom line is that EU intervention in employment regulation used to be regarded as justified only where it was considered necessary in order to prevent unfair competition that could disrupt the smooth functioning of the internal market.[6] For instance, the equal pay provision was originally inserted into the Treaty of Rome upon the insistence of those member states that already domestically observed that principle, in order to rule out the possibility that other member states could gain an unfair competitive advantage in intra-Community competition by relying heavily on cheap female labour.[7] Also the prohibition of discrimination on the basis of nationality was enacted primarily for economic reasons, as it served the purpose of facilitating free movement of workers between the member states. Racial and other forms of discrimination were addressed only in the form of non-binding soft law instruments. This traditional approach of the EU was clearly intrinsically linked with its competition and employment agenda.

During the 1990s, however, there were signs that the EU was developing a 'social agenda' that entailed an expanded role for the Union in guaranteeing a range of fundamental social rights, in the course of which the idea of European citizenship evolved from mere 'market citizenship' towards 'social citizenship'.[8] These developments formed a background which was increasingly favourable to the anti-discrimination initiatives presented by a broad cross-country lobby consisting of a range of migrants' rights groups, churches and human

---

[5] See e.g. Mark Bell, *Anti-Discrimination Law and the European Union* (New York: Oxford University Press, 2002), pp. 61–63.

[6] Bell, *cit. supra* note 5, p. 2.

[7] This of course means that Article 119 was not motivated primarily by fundamental rights considerations but by economic interests. Bell, *cit. supra* note 5, p. 8; Paul Craig - Gráinne de Búrca, *EU law: text, cases, materials* (Oxford: Oxford University Press, 2007), p. 879. See however ECJ, *Defrenne* v. *Sabena* [1976] ECR 455, where the ECJ states that article 119 pursued a *double* aim: First, the prevention of competitive disadvantage resulting for those countries that have actually implemented the principle of equal pay and second, ensuring of "social progress" and "the constant improvement of the living and working conditions" of the peoples of the Community, paras 8–10.

[8] Sionaidh Douglas-Scott, *Constitutional Law of the European Union*, (Harlow: Person, 2002), pp. 479–514; Bell, *cit. supra* note 5, p. 2 ff.

rights organisations.[9] The growing pressure towards Community action led to an important opening in the form of the adoption of the Article 13 in the 1997 Treaty of Amsterdam. Article 13, which was slightly revised by the Treaty of Lisbon and which is now Article 19, read originally as follows:

> Without prejudice to the provisions of this treaty and within the limits of the powers conferred by it upon the Community, the Council, acting unanimously on a proposal from the Commission and after consulting the European Parliament, may take appropriate action to combat discrimination based on sex, racial or ethnic origin, religion or belief, disability, age or sexual orientation.

As is clear from its wording, this Article is an enabling provision, and cannot be applied directly. Its significance lies in providing the legal basis for the adoption of further EU law on discrimination, and indeed it provided the basis for the adoption of two directives on equal treatment in 2000. The Racial Equality Directive, which will be in focus here, dealt with discrimination on the grounds of racial or ethnic origin, whereas the Employment Equality Directive dealt with discrimination on the grounds of religion or belief, disability, age and sexual orientation.

The adoption in 2000 of the Charter of Fundamental Rights of the European Union, which also includes a non-discrimination provision, was yet another step towards the recognition of fundamental rights, despite the fact that the Charter did not have major legal effect before the coming into force of the Treaty of Lisbon in 2009. Importantly, the Treaty of Lisbon also requires the Union to accede to the European Convention for the Protection of Human Rights and Fundamental Freedoms.[10]

The following subchapters focus on three sources of EU law in the area of equal treatment irrespective of racial or ethnic origin. These are the general principles of EU law, the Charter of Fundamental Rights and the Racial Equality Directive. As will be seen, the non-discrimination provisions in the EU instruments constitute a complex fabric of obligations that make them rather difficult tools to apply in the Member States. Moreover, case law from the ECJ regarding the interpretation of

---

[9] This lobby was known as the Starting Line Group. See e.g. Ibid (Bell), p. 68; Bob Hepple, 'Race and Law in Fortress Europe' *The Modern Law Review*, Vol 67 January 2004, No 1, p. 3.

[10] New Article 6(2) of TEU.

the Racial Equality Directive has only started to emerge, which is why many commentators have relied upon its case law in the area of gender equality for guidance also in the area of ethnic equality, given the many similarities between these two areas of law. That said, there are also significant differences between them, a fact which makes it difficult to give reliable predictions about the ways in which the interpretation of the EU anti-discrimination law is going to evolve.

7.2 Non-Discrimination as a General Principle of EU Law

Fundamental rights, including the principle of non-discrimination, constitute part of the general principles of law which the Union has to respect in its activities, even in the absence of specific provisions to that effect. The European Court of Justice (ECJ) took this position in 1969 in response to concerns that arose in some member states regarding the Court's case law, according to which EU law must be regarded as superior to conflicting national legal provisions.[11] Some countries feared that as a consequence fundamental rights guaranteed by the national constitutions would become subordinated to the market interests embedded in the Community law.[12] The ECJ sought to absolve these fears by incorporating fundamental rights considerations as an unwritten part of the primary law of the EU. This incorporation of fundamental rights by the Court as "part of general principles of law" is subject to two limitations, however: first, measures may be challenged only if they fall within the scope of EU law; second, the Court determines the nature and extent of fundamental rights on a case-by-case basis, meaning that there is a good degree of uncertainty with regard to the exact scope and content of those rights.

This role of the fundamental rights finds an express legal basis in Article 6(3) of the revised TEU[13]:

---

[11] See Craig – de Búrca, *cit. supra* note 7, pp. 381–382. The primacy of Community law in relation to domestic law was established for the first time in the ECJ's landmark case of *Costa* v. *ENEL* [1964] ECR 585. In that case the Court submitted that "... the law stemming from the treaty, an independent source of law, could not, because of its special and original nature, be overridden by domestic legal provisions, however framed, without being deprived of its character as community law and without the legal basis of the community itself being called into question."

[12] Craig – de Búrca, *cit. supra* note 7, p. 381; Tuomas Ojanen, *Johdatus perus- ja ihmisoikeusjuridiikkaan* (Helsinki: Yliopistopaino, 2009), pp. 95–97.

[13] Former Article 6(2).

> Fundamental rights, as guaranteed by the European Convention for the Protection of Human Rights and Fundamental Freedoms and as they result from the constitutional traditions common to the Member States, shall constitute general principles of the Union's law.

The Court, for its part, has established that it draws inspiration not just from the constitutional traditions of member states, but also from "international treaties on which the Member States have collaborated or of which they are signatories."[14] It has noted that the European Convention on Human Rights has special significance in this respect, and has stated that for instance the International Covenant on Civil and Political Rights is one of the international instruments which it "takes into account" in applying the principles of EU law.[15] Article 7 of the TEU provides a mechanism for sanctioning those member states which in a "serious and persistent" manner breach the fundamental rights referred to in Article 6.[16]

In its case law, the Court has consistently held that all the sources of fundamental rights support the existence of a strong principle of equality and non-discrimination.[17] In *Defrenne* III, the Court drew on the provisions of the 1961 European Social Charter and ILO Convention No 111 in support of its view that

> respect for fundamental personal human rights is one of the general principles of Community law, the observance of which it [the Court] has a duty to ensure. There can be no doubt that the elimination of discrimination based on sex forms part of those fundamental rights.[18]

It is generally held that also other grounds explicitly mentioned in the European Convention on Human Rights are protected as well, including 'race'.[19] The exact content of the non-discrimination principle is not

---

[14] See e.g. ECJ, *European Parliament* v. *Council of the European Union*, Case C-540/03, 27 June 2006, para 35.

[15] Ibid, paras 35–37.

[16] Article 7 was amended by the Nice treaty in 2000 to provide for the possibility to act before a breach has occurred, partly in response to the controversial Haider affair, which began when a series of diplomatic sanctions were adopted by fourteen of the then fifteen Member States against Austria after the far-right Freedom party entered into the coalition government in 2000. See Craig – de Búrca, *cit. supra* note 7, p. 403.

[17] This general principle remains in effect even after the adoption of the more specific equal treatment directives, as is implied e.g. in ECJ, *Werner Mangold v. Rüdiger Helm*, Case C-144/04, 22 November 2005, paras 74–75.

[18] ECJ, *Defrenne* v. *SABENA (III)*, Case 149/77, 15 June 1978, paras 26–27.

[19] See e.g. Bell, *cit. supra* note 5, p. 21 and the references cited therein; Christopher McCrudden and Haris Kountouros submit that the principle of non-discrimination

clear, as the Court has generally confined itself to explaining the principle in very general and formalistic way, for instance as requiring "that comparable situations not be treated differently and different situations not be treated alike unless such treatment is objectively justified".[20]

7.3 The Charter of Fundamental Rights

On 7 December 2000, the Council, Parliament and Commission solemnly proclaimed the Charter of Fundamental Rights of the European Union. It came into effect, in a slightly amended form, upon the entry into force of the Treaty of Lisbon on 1 December 2009. The Charter now has the same legal value as the European Union Treaties.[21] The Charter sets out a wide range of rights, clarifying to an extent which fundamental rights are protected in the context of the EU. Article 51 of the Charter determines its scope of application:

> The provisions of this Charter are addressed to the institutions and bodies of the Union with due regard for the principle of subsidiarity and to the Member States only when they are implementing Union law. They shall therefore respect the rights, observe the principles and promote the application thereof in accordance with their respective powers.[22]

Articles 20 and 21 of the Charter deal with equal treatment.[23] Article 20, in its entirety, simply proclaims that "[e]veryone is equal before the

---

"presumably applies" to all statuses listed in Article 13, including racial and ethnic origin. Christopher McCrudden – Haris Kountouros, 'Human Rights and European Equality Law' in Helen Meenan (ed.) *Equality Law in an Enlarged European Union* (Cambridge: Cambridge University Press, 2007). The ECJ recognized the principle of non-discrimination with respect to age in ECJ [GC], *Werner Mangold v. Rüdiger Helm*, Case C-144/04, 22 November 2005.

[20] ECJ, *Spain* v. *Council*, Case 203/86, 20 September 1988, paragraph 25; *EARL de Kerlast v. Union régionale de coopératives agricoles (Unicopa) and Coopérative du Trieux*, Case C-15/95, 17 April 1997, para 35; *Test-Achats ASBL* v. *Belgium*, GC Case C-236/09, 1 March 2011, para 28. The Court has also opined that member states must observe the principle of proportionality whenever they impose restrictions on the exercise of fundamental rights. Therefore a restriction must not constitute, "having regard to the aim pursued, disproportionate and unreasonable interference undermining the very substance of [fundamental] rights". ECJ, *Wachauf v. Bundesamt für Ernährung und Forstwirtschaft*, C5/88, 13 July 1989, para 18; *Kjell Karlsson and Others*, Case C-292/97, 13 April 2000.

[21] Article 6(1) of the Treaty of European Union as amended by the Treaty of Lisbon.

[22] The Charter also reads that it does not establish or modify the powers or tasks of the Union (Article 51).

[23] In addition, Article 23 deals with equality between women and men.

law". This is not explained or specified in any manner. Yet, the fact that this principle was given an article of its own, is often taken to underline not just its importance but also its 'constitutive' role in view of the prohibition of discrimination.[24]

Article 21(1), for its turn, provides for a sweeping prohibition of all forms of discrimination:

> Any discrimination based on any ground such as sex, race, colour, ethnic or social origin, genetic features, language, religion or belief, political or other opinion, membership of a national minority, property, birth, disability, age or sexual orientation shall be prohibited.

Article 21(1) contains innovative features. First of all, its scope of application has not been restricted in any apparent way. It is expected, for instance, to apply also in relations between private parties.[25] Second, its list of expressly prohibited grounds is not just extensive but unprecedented among international instruments, following a trend of proliferation of the expressly mentioned grounds of discrimination.[26] In addition, the list is not exhaustive. Altogether seventeen grounds are explicitly mentioned, and these include many that are not mentioned in the European Convention on Human Rights or any other major human rights document. Discrimination based on race, colour, ethnic origin and membership of a national minority are each expressly and separately prohibited. There is nothing to suggest how colour might be different from 'race' and why membership of a national minority would not already be covered by 'ethnic origin'.

Discrimination on the basis of nationality is dealt with in a separate provision, namely paragraph 2 of Article 21. The scope of application of the prohibition in Article 21(2), which is based on the EU Treaty, is considerably narrower than that of Article 21(1). Distinctions based on nationality laid down in the EU Treaty are expressly excluded from coming within the scope of the prohibition of discrimination. As the EU Treaty confers special rights to citizens of the EU-countries, this means that third-country nationals are in practice put at a disadvantage in comparison with EU nationals in many respects without this being challengeable under the Charter. This situation, where all are equal but some are more equal than others, is one of the embodiments

---

[24] EU Network of Independent Experts on Fundamental Rights, *Commentary of the Charter of Fundamental Rights of the European Union*, 20 June 2006, pp. 183–187.

[25] Ibid, p. 193.

[26] Ibid, p. 191.

of the asymmetric development of Community non-discrimination law on the different grounds.

Article 21(1) is expressly couched in terms of 'discrimination'. The drafters made it extraordinarily clear that Article 21(1) "draws from" Article 14 of the ECHR and that *insofar as the former corresponds to the latter* it is to be interpreted in accordance with it.[27] Yet the exact relationship between Article 21 of the Charter and Article 14 of the ECHR is ambiguous at best, as it is not at all clear whether Article 21 comes within the purview of Article 52(3) of the Charter, which provides that "[i]nsofar as this Charter contains rights which correspond to rights guaranteed by the [ECHR], the meaning and scope of those rights shall be the same as those laid down by the [ECHR]". The Explanatory note produced by the drafters of the Charter provides a list of the Charter articles that are meant to be covered by Article 52(3), but Article 21 is not among them.[28] This would seem to suggest that Article 14 of the ECHR was considered to be the reference point as regards the meaning of the concept of discrimination in Article 21 of the Charter, but that the scopes of the two articles were considered to differ from each other, particularly as concerns protection from discrimination on the grounds of nationality. This may be problematic and confusing from the point of view of protection of fundamental and human rights.[29]

Of significance in the present context is also Article 47 of the Charter, which provides that everyone whose "rights and freedoms guaranteed by the law of the Union are violated has the right to an effective remedy before a tribunal".

7.4 Directive 2000/43/EC

Introduction

The Council Directive 2000/43/EC, implementing the principle of equal treatment between persons irrespective of racial or ethnic origin (generally known as the 'Racial Equality Directive'), was adopted on 29 June 2000. EU member states were to adopt the laws, regulations and administrative provisions necessary to comply with the Directive

[27] Praesidium, Explanations for the Draft Charter of Fundamental Rights of the European Union, Brussels, 11 October 2000 (18.10) (OR. fr) CHARTE 4473/00.

[28] Ibid, pp. 48–50.

[29] Tuomas Ojanen, *Johdatus perus- ja ihmisoikeusjuridiikkaan* (Helsinki: Yliopistopaino, 2009), p.104.

by 19 July 2003. As of January 2009, almost all 27 member states of the EU had taken legislative action to transpose the Directive into their national laws, although doubts remained with respect to some of them as to whether they had done so correctly.[30]

The speed with which the Directive was adopted was remarkable, as was in many respects the substantive content of the Directive.[31] Whilst the Directive was built, to a great extent, on the concepts of EC legislation prohibiting discrimination on grounds of sex and nationality, the final text adopted by the Council was at times stronger than many expected.[32] Paradoxically, it was the entry of Jorg Haider's populist Freedom Party into the Austrian government that helped to create the momentum for the then draft directive, as the Directive was seen as one channel for expressing the condemnation of both racial discrimination and the Freedom Party's agenda.[33]

Concept of Discrimination

Article 2 of the Directive defines what it means by 'equal treatment' and 'discrimination'. Equal treatment is defined in negative terms, as absence of direct or indirect discrimination based on racial or ethnic origin.[34] The Directive expressly distinguishes between four types of discrimination: (i) direct discrimination, (ii) indirect discrimination,

---

[30] Because member states have had some difficulties in transposing correctly the Racial Equality Directive into domestic legislation, one should keep in mind the principle of direct applicability of Directives as one possible way for domestic courts to apply the directives in cases of nonadherence in domestic legislation. One should however also keep in mind that under the current ECJ doctrine there is no horizontal direct applicability of directives *between individuals*. In any case, it is the responsibility of the domestic courts to interpret domestic legislation in accordance with the Directives. If it is not possible to reach the result aimed at with the Directive through interpretation, the principle of supremacy of Community law overrides the conflicting national norm.

[31] See e.g. Adam Tyson, 'The Negotiation of the European Community Directive on Racial Discrimination' *European Journal of Migration and Law* 3, 2001, p. 201; Kevin Boyle–Anneliese Baldaccini, 'A Critical Evaluation of International Human Rights Approaches to Racism', in Sandra Fredman (ed.) *Discrimination and Human Rights* (Oxford: Oxford University Press, 2001). And indeed, as pointed out by Damian Chalmers, the Directives were adopted at a time when many member states were pressing for less EC legislation, not more. Damian Chalmers 'The Mistakes of the Good European' in Sandra Fredman (ed.) *Discrimination and Human Rights* (Oxford: Oxford University Press, 2001).

[32] See e.g. Tyson, *cit. supra* note 31.

[33] Ibid, p. 218.

[34] In this context it is interesting to note that the preamble to the Directive recognizes 'equality before the law' and 'protection against discrimination' as 'universal rights', but does not mention equal protection of the law.

(iii) harassment and (iv) instruction to discriminate. Each of these will be analyzed separately below.

Article 2(2) (a) defines direct discrimination in the following way:

> direct discrimination shall be taken to occur where one person is treated less favourably than another is, has been or would be treated in a comparable situation on grounds of racial or ethnic origin.

This definition is based on a comparative rationale, and for instance the motives or intentions that led to the less favourable treatment play no role in it.[35] Although the provision requires a comparison to be made in order to identify less favourable treatment, the standard is flexible in that the comparison can be made not just against an actual individual in a comparable situation (actual comparator), but also against an individual who has previously been in a comparable situation (past comparator) and also against a 'hypothetical individual' in a comparable situation (hypothetical comparator).[36] The latter option allows those applying the law to engage in speculation about whether a person would have been treated more favourably had he or she been of a different ethnic origin. This definition of direct discrimination is essentially based on the concept of equality as consistency, and is as such primarily a relative one: as long as there is consistency, the outcome is irrelevant.[37]

A distinct feature of this definition is its rigid nature: direct discrimination cannot be 'justified', except in *lex specialis* situations where positive action as envisaged in Article 5 of the Directive is at stake, or where a person's racial or ethnic origin constitutes a "genuine and determining occupational requirement" within the meaning of Article 4. That said, the application of the definition is not always straightforward, as it does not prohibit the making of all distinctions but only distinctions that constitute *less favourable* treatment. The rule cannot therefore be comprised into a straightforward maxim "thou shalt not make distinctions on the grounds of racial or ethnic origin", as a more qualitatively oriented assessment is called for.

---

[35] This notwithstanding, a showing of a prejudice or discriminatory intent on part of the respondent may be useful evidence in establishing a *prima facie* case of discrimination.

[36] This is apparent in light of the wording: discrimination occurs where one person is treated less favourably than another (i) is, (ii) has been or (iii) would be treated.

[37] Sandra Fredman, *Discrimination Law* (Oxford: Oxford University Press, 2002), p. 92 ff.

Indirect discrimination is defined as follows:

> indirect discrimination shall be taken to occur where an apparently neutral provision, criterion or practice would put persons of a racial or ethnic origin at a particular disadvantage compared with other persons, unless that provision, criterion or practice is objectively justified by a legitimate aim and the means of achieving that aim are appropriate and necessary.

The definition of indirect discrimination is also based on a comparative logic. For a finding of indirect discrimination it first has to be demonstrated that a provision, criterion or practice *would* put persons of a racial or ethnic origin at a disadvantage, which means that it is sufficient to show that the provision, criterion or practice serves to produce a disadvantageous effect compared with other persons. The comparison is to be made at a group level, as is indicated by the use of the word 'persons' in the plural. Discrimination must, broadly speaking, be attributable to a provision, criterion, or more flexibly, practice. Therefore the provision may be able to encompass some forms of institutional or even structural discrimination; for instance the kind of educational disadvantages complained of in the *D.H. and others* case may potentially come within the purview of the Directive.

The definition of indirect discrimination incorporates an open justification defence. Instead of laying down a predefined list of allowed exceptions, the Directive allows the use of provisions, criterions and practices that, even though disadvantageous for the members of a group, are "objectively justified by a legitimate aim", provided that the means used to achieve that aim are "appropriate and necessary". The terms at hand are of course open, and therefore it remains unclear as to what exactly can constitute objective justification.[38] The practical impact of the prohibition of indirect discrimination will therefore depend, to a very large degree, on the future case law of the European Court of Justice regarding the interpretation of said terms. It seems likely that the ECJ will leave the member states a measure of discretion

---

[38] This is so also under the Gender Equality Directives. See Craig – de Búrca, *cit. supra* note 7, p. 888, where the authors note that in equal pay claims the ECJ often leaves the matter for the national court to decide, only giving some guidance by declaring some grounds of justification to be too general and indicating that others may be sufficient. The authors observe more generally that under the ECJ's case law the commercial objectives of the undertaking or an employer can 'relatively easily' defeat a claim of indirect discrimination, and that the ECJ gives member states a margin of appreciation where social policy objectives are at issue. Ibid, p. 894 ff.

in this regard, particularly where social policy is at issue. That said, the requirement that the means used be 'necessary' suggests that not just any measure that appears legitimate on its face will do, because if there are alternative measures that do not disadvantage members of a group, then it will not be 'necessary' to use a measure that does.

Does proving indirect discrimination require the production of statistical evidence? To begin with it must be noted that some parts of the definition of indirect discrimination ('would put', 'disadvantage') imply that to prove indirect discrimination one does not need to prove actual disparate impact, the proving of which intrinsically calls for statistical breakdowns.[39] Instead, it appears that 'a particular disadvantage' can, where applicable, also be inferred from facts that are generally known.[40] This reading is supported by the Directive, where Recital 15 acknowledges that rules of evidence are a matter of national rules or practice, but reminds that such rules "may provide in particular indirect discrimination to be established by any means including on the basis of statistical evidence".[41] The use of the word 'may' clearly indicates that the drafters envisaged that indirect discrimination may be demonstrated also by means other than statistical evidence.[42] In this way, the definition of indirect discrimination compares favourably with the older definition of indirect discrimination that prevailed in the field of EU gender equality law prior to the adoption of the Directive 2004/113/EC. That definition called, as a rule, for statistical evidence, as it required the showing of evidence that a neutral provision, criterion, or practice disadvantages a "substantially higher proportion of the

---

[39] In the sphere of EU gender equality law, indirect discrimination used to be couched in terms of 'unfavourable impact', and the question has often arisen what kind of statistical evidence is needed to establish such discrimination. See e.g. ECJ, *Regina* v. *Secretary of State for Employment*, C-167/97, 9 February 1999.

[40] One does not need to produce statistical evidence to show that an unconditional rule requiring all police officers to wear a particular type of headgear puts Sikh men at a particular disadvantage because it is common knowledge that they wear turbans for religious reasons and are on those grounds unable to comply with that rule. Perhaps also a company rule requiring cleaning personnel to speak the national language fluently, a requirement that is usually excessive and not based on the requirements of the work in question, can simply be assumed to constitute a prima facie case of discrimination against immigrant workers, as it is general knowledge that immigrants seldom speak the national language fluently.

[41] Recital 15 of the Preamble, emphasis added. Similarly, de Schutter, 'European Union Legislation and the Norms of the Framework Convention for the Protection of National Minorities' Strasbourg 23 October 2006, DH-MIN(2006)019.

[42] According to Tyson this was indeed the intention of the drafters. See Tyson, *cit. supra* note 31, pp. 202–204.

members of one sex".[43] In practice, however, in many situations it will be difficult to prove indirect discrimination without statistics, as the disadvantageous effects of a provision, criterion or practice usually cannot simply be 'known'. How can one for instance demonstrate that the apparently neutral recruitment practices of a company discriminate against immigrants, other than by showing how many immigrants have applied but not been selected, or by showing that there is a mismatch between the proportion of such persons employed by the company and the proportion of such persons living in the relevant catchment area? Or how will it be known, without statistical comparisons, that the pay scheme adopted by a company puts certain groups at a disadvantage?

The third type of discrimination, harassment, is defined in the Directive as taking place "when an unwanted conduct related to racial or ethnic origin takes place with the purpose or effect of violating the dignity of a person and of creating an intimidating, hostile, degrading, humiliating or offensive environment".[44] The references to 'conduct' – a way of acting – and to 'environment' were deliberately chosen in order to set the bar rather high and to exclude, as a rule, isolated incidents from being considered harassment.[45] The Directive further stipulates that "in this context, the concept of harassment may be defined in accordance with the national laws and practice of the Member States". As the formulation "in this context" indicates, the national latitude provided cannot undermine the substance of the right altogether, but the provision does seem to leave into national discretion matters such as whether employers should be made liable for harassment they did not directly initiate, for instance harassment against an employee by another worker or a customer.[46]

Article 1(4) provides that an instruction to discriminate constitutes discrimination *an sich*. This means that employers who instruct employment agencies not to send them workers from certain ethnic groups are engaging in discrimination, irrespective of whether the instruction was acted upon.

Article 4 provides for a limited exception to the prohibition of discrimination, and allows a difference of treatment where a characteristic related to racial or ethnic origin constitutes 'a genuine and

---

43 Burden of Proof Directive.
44 Article 2(3) of the Directive.
45 Tyson, *cit. supra* note 31, pp. 205–206.
46 Cf. Bell, *cit. supra* note 5, pp. 75–76.

determining occupational requirement', provided that the objective of the differential treatment is legitimate and the requirement is proportionate. The situations in which a particular 'racial' or ethnic origin would constitute such an occupational requirement are subject to some debate. It is likely that courts in most countries would accept reasons related to 'authenticity'. A director of a historical play would therefore not have to hire a white actor to play the role of Martin Luther King Jr., even if that person would be considered to be the best actor overall, and the manager of a Chinese restaurant could prefer Chinese-origin applicants over others. Yet it can be asked whether this should be so.[47] In any case, the Directive instructs that the exception written down into Article 4 shall apply only in very limited circumstances.[48]

Article 5 deals with positive action and follows the conventional EU anti-discrimination doctrine in that it merely allows but does not require such action: member states are allowed, "with a view to ensuring full equality in practice", to maintain or adopt "specific measures to prevent or compensate for disadvantages linked to racial or ethnic origin". The justification for positive action can therefore lie either in past, present or anticipated discrimination, and positive action measures can be taken as long as 'full equality in practice' has not been achieved. The fact that the European Court of Justice has interpreted the notion 'positive action' in the context of gender equality law in a way that has been somewhat restrictive and unpredictable, casts a shadow of uncertainty also upon the practical impact of Article 5.[49]

---

[47] Would it be legitimate to hire a person of Chinese origin, for reasons of 'authenticity', to work as the chef of a Chinese restaurant, even if the person concerned had never lived in China and even if he was hired instead of a person who is a known specialist in Chinese cuisine but of 'wrong' ethnic origin? Is it legitimate to hire a person of Chinese origin to work as a waiter in a Japanese restaurant over a better qualified person of German origin? It is clear that the application of the 'genuine and determining occupational requirement' exception raises difficult questions to which legal rules and principles provide little directly applicable guidance. See also the critique posed in Gwyneth Pitt, 'Madame Butterfly and Miss Saigon: Reflections on Genuine Occupational Qualifications', in Janet Dine & Bob Watt (eds.), *Discrimination Law: Concepts, Limitations, and Justifications* (London: Longman, 1996).

[48] Recital 18 of the Preamble specifies that a difference of treatment where a characteristic related to racial or ethnic origin constitutes a genuine and determining occupational requirement is justified only in very limited circumstances.

[49] See chapter 11 below.

Grounds and the Personal Scope of Application

The Directive prohibits discrimination 'on grounds of racial or ethnic origin'. The latter terms are used without further precision. The drafters however felt compelled to remind their audience, through recital 6 of the Directive, that the notion of 'race' should not be understood along the lines of biological objectivism:

> The European Union rejects theories which attempt to determine the existence of separate human races. The use of the term 'racial origin' in this Directive does not imply an acceptance of such theories.

In *Chacón Navas* the ECJ held that the notions defining the grounds of discrimination – in that case the notion of disability under the Framework Directive – are to be given "an autonomous and uniform interpretation".[50] This means that national approaches to these matters will not be decisive. At the time of the writing the Court has not been called to interpret the notions of racial origin or ethnic origin. Should the issue arise, the Court may be influenced by Article 10 of the Council Directive 2004/83/EC which contains a rare definition of 'race' in the context of EU law, the said Article providing that "the concept of race shall in particular include considerations of colour, descent, or membership of a particular ethnic group".[51] Yet it is fully possible that the Court will take some other approach.

It is notable that the Directive prohibits discrimination on the grounds of racial or ethnic *origin*, not 'race' or 'ethnicity' as such. This shifts the focus from the present status of a person or a group of persons to their past. But how far back in time should one go? If one goes back 250 years in time, which makes approximately ten generations, everyone has up to 1024 ancestors. How many of them should have been from Africa for a modern-day European to be considered to be of African origin? And does the reference to ethnic origin instead of

---

[50] ECJ, *Chacón Navas*, GC, C-13/05, 11 July 2006, para 42. In para 40 the Court explained its reasoning as follows: "It follows from the need for uniform application of Community law and the principle of equality that the terms of a provision of Community law which makes no express reference to the law of the Member States for the purpose of determining its meaning and scope must normally be given an autonomous and uniform interpretation throughout the Community, having regard to the context of the provision and the objective pursued by the legislation in question."

[51] Article 10 also defines 'nationality' by noting that it "shall not be confined to citizenship or lack thereof but shall in particular include membership of a group determined by its cultural, ethnic, or linguistic identity, common geographical or political origins or its relationship with the population of another State."

ethnicity, the latter term usually presuming the existence of a living community dimension with a distinct cultural identity, whereas 'origin' does not contain that idea as such, have an impact on the range or nature of protection provided for by Directive? In particular, does it mean that the Directive was not at all, or only to a small extent, meant to give protection against infringements of cultural identity? The legal opinion on these questions is only beginning to emerge.

In *Feryn*, the ECJ held that the existence of direct discrimination is not dependent on the identification of a complainant who claims to have been the victim. In that case a Belgian association was able to bring *actio popularis* proceedings against an employer that had publicly stated that it would not recruit employees of immigrant origin.[52]

In *Coleman* the ECJ addressed another key question and ruled that the equal treatment directives prohibit 'discrimination by association'. In this case the claimant, who did not have a disability herself, had allegedly been treated unfavourably on the grounds that she was the primary carer of her son who did have a disability. The Court held that this unfavourable treatment, if substantiated in the national court, constitutes discrimination on the grounds of disability, irrespective of the fact that the person discriminated against did not have a disability herself. According to the Court, "the principle of equal treatment enshrined in the directive applies not to a particular category of person but by reference to the grounds mentioned" in the Directive. Insofar as the same rationale applies to racial and ethnic discrimination, and there are no apparent reasons to assume that it would not, then this means that for instance harassment and other types of discrimination that ethnic majority partners of immigrants and persons belonging to minorities are subjected to also come within the purview of the Directive and are therefore prohibited by it.[53]

Article 3(2) of the Directive provides that it does not cover difference of treatment based on nationality and is without prejudice to the entry into and residence of third-country nationals and to any treatment which arises from the legal status of the third country nationals concerned.[54] This exception is broad and the scope of its applicability unclear. Given that differential treatment allegedly taking place on the

---

[52] ECJ, *Feryn*, Case C-54/07, 10 July 2008.

[53] ECJ, *Coleman*, GC, C-303/06, 17 July 2008. The Court's reasoning would however not seem to apply to indirect discrimination as defined in the EU directives.

[54] Article 3(2) of the Directive.

grounds of 'nationality' may constitute indirect or even direct discrimination on the basis of racial or ethnic origin, the question arises whether Article 3(2) renders such discrimination untouchable.[55]

The Directive doesn't cover 'pure' religious discrimination, since that ground is addressed in the Framework Employment Directive. It has to be reiterated, though, that religion can constitute one of the most important elements of ethnicity, and thus the delimitation of the borderline between ethnic and religious discrimination can be a difficult one. The Directive does not address the problems inherent in intersectional and multiple forms of discrimination.[56] Indeed, EU's chosen policy line has been to regulate the different grounds separately, with the result that legal protection against discrimination is different with respect to different grounds, a policy that is unfavourable for fighting multiple and intersectional discrimination. Given that the ECJ has in several cases ruled that for a treatment to be considered discrimination on a particular ground it is sufficient that the treatment was 'essentially' based on a factor directly linked to that ground, it can however be expected that it would be ready to treat intersectional discrimination that has got an ethnic dimension as discrimination on the grounds of ethnic origin.[57] That said, the fact that the definition of discrimination is based on comparisons can complicate things, as ground-specific comparisons cannot always identify situations where discrimination is not based on a single ground. At the end of the day, the extent to which people are provided protection from intersectional discrimination depends on the content and structure of the domestic law.

Material Scope of Application

Article 3 defines the material scope of the Directive and hence the areas in which the prohibition of discrimination is to apply. The scope

---

[55] This question has been posed by e.g. Bell, *cit. supra* note 5, p. 71.

[56] Recital 14 does, however, refer to multiple discrimination as follows: "In implementing the principle of equal treatment irrespective of racial or ethnic origin, the Community should, in accordance with Article 3(2) of the EC Treaty, aim to eliminate inequalities, and to promote equality between men and women, especially since women are often the victims of multiple discrimination."

[57] For instance in the case of *P* v. *S and Cornwall County Council*, C-13/94, 30 April 1996, the ECJ held that discrimination against transsexuals is in fact based, "essentially if not exclusively", on the sex of the person concerned, i.e. is sex discrimination. See also ECJ, *Mayr* v. *Bäckerei und Konditorei Gerhard Flöckner OHG*, Case C-506/06, [GC] 26 February 2008.

is wide and laid down in relatively detailed but not necessarily precise terms,[58] and covers all aspects of employment, including selection criteria and employment and working conditions; access to self-employment and occupation; access to vocational guidance and training; membership of and involvement in an organisation of workers or employers; social protection including social security and health care; social advantages; education; and access to and supply of goods and services which are available to the public, including housing. The application of the provision is subject to a general limitation doctrine, however, which prescribes that the Directive may only deal with matters that fall within the powers conferred upon the Community, a doctrine that may diminish the applicability of the Directive in some specific but limited instances.[59]

Article 3 further makes it explicitly clear that it shall apply to all persons, as regards both the public and private sectors, including public bodies. Its thrust is to put into effect the principle of equal treatment both in relations between private parties as well as in relations where the other party is a public authority, in so far as the matter falls within the material scope defined in Article 3. This extensive scope of the Directive has reportedly been difficult for some member states to accept due to traditional doctrines concerning the distinction between the public and private sphere, and because of the perception that the Directive interferes with the freedom of contract.[60]

Enforcement and Remedies

The general EU law and ECJ case law have tended to emphasise, as a starting point, the principle of national procedural autonomy and the primary responsibility of the state in the field of remedies.[61] Yet, the ECJ has, in the interests of ensuring the effective implementation of the EU law, made some significant inroads into this area. It has, in its

---

[58] See e.g. the observations that Craig and de Burca make with respect to similar provisions in the gender equality directives, Craig - de Búrca, *cit. supra* note 7, pp. 919 ff.

[59] Article 3, which defines the material scope of application of the Directive, starts with the clause "[w]ithin the limits of the powers conferred upon the Community, this directive shall apply to..." See also Bell, *cit. supra* note 5, pp. 76 and 131–136.

[60] Commission of the European Communities, *Communication from the Commission to the Council and the European Parliament*, (Brussels, 30.10.2006) COM(2006) 643 final.

[61] For a fuller discussion, see Sionaidh Douglas-Scott, *cit. supra* note 8, pp. 312–339.

case law, developed several principles in the field of remedies, two of which are particularly relevant here: the effectiveness principle (the national remedy must provide a real deterrent against the unlawful act) and the equivalence principle (the national remedy must be comparable to the remedy available in national law for infringement of comparable national rights).[62] Several sectoral pieces of law, including the Racial Equality Directive, have provisions which complement these principles.

The Directive features a number of relatively specific and even innovative provisions that deal with enforcement and remedies. First, Article 7 requires the availability of "judicial and/or administrative procedures".[63] Such procedures must be available "to all persons who consider themselves wronged by the failure to apply the principle of equal treatment to them", a standard that appears to be more favourable to potential complainants than the 'arguable claim' standard applied with respect to many other instruments.

Second, the Directive provides for a shifted burden of proof.[64] Thus, when a complainant establishes "facts from which it may be presumed that there has been direct or indirect discrimination, it shall be for the respondent to prove that there has been no breach of the principle of equal treatment".[65] What is at issue is a shared, not reversed burden of proof, as the complainant still has to make a *prima facie* case of discrimination and to rebut the counter-claims made by the respondent to succeed. Shifting of the burden of proof does not apply to criminal procedures.[66]

---

[62] The meaning of these principles is, of course, not fully clear. By way of an example, in ECJ, *Edis* v. *Ministero della Finanze*, C-231/96, 15 September 1998, the Court stated that the observance of the principle of equivalence implies that "the procedural rule at issue applies without distinction to actions alleging infringements of Community law and to those alleging infringements of national law, with respect to the same kind of charges or dues", para 36. See also Craig – de Búrca, *cit. supra* note 7, p. 305 ff, and Barry Fitzpatrick, 'The Effectiveness of Equality Law Remedies: A European Community Law Perspective' in Bob Hepple – Erika Szyszczak (eds.), *Discrimination: The Limits of Law?* (London: Mansell, 1992).

[63] Recital 20 appears to prefer judicial remedies, as it declares that "[t]he effective implementation of the principle of equality requires adequate judicial protection against victimisation."

[64] The partial reversal of burden of proof would seem to apply not just to claims that involve direct or indirect discrimination, but also to instructions to discriminate and harassment, but not victimization (cf. Articles 1, 8 and 9).

[65] Article 8(1).

[66] Article 8(3).

Third, member states are to ensure that organisations with a "legitimate interest … may engage, either on behalf or in support of the complainant, with his or her approval, in any judicial and/or administrative proceedings provided for the enforcement of obligations under [the] Directive".[67] Taken at face value, the wording is ambiguous as to whether each member state is required to allow organisations to act on behalf of (potential) complainants, which would for instance include the right to initiate proceedings, or whether it is sufficient for the organisations in question to simply be allowed to act in support of the complainant. The preamble is not helpful in resolving this question, and the ECJ has not yet had the opportunity to rule on the matter, but the legal opinion seems to favour the interpretation that it is sufficient that obstacles are removed from the way of the organisations in question so that they can support victims.[68]

Fourth, states are required to introduce into their legal systems such measures as are necessary to protect individuals from victimization, which is defined as "adverse treatment or adverse consequence as a reaction to a complaint" of discrimination.[69] It is not just the victims themselves, but also their families, legal representatives and other individuals related to the issue who are protected from victimization.

Fifth, Article 9 requires member states to lay down the rules on sanctions applicable to infringements of the national provisions adopted pursuant to the Directive and to "take all measures necessary" to ensure that they are applied.[70] These sanctions must be effective, proportionate and dissuasive.[71] It is for the domestic courts to determine, in accordance with the relevant rules of domestic law, which remedies are appropriate. However, purely token sanctions are not sufficiently dissuasive. It has been submitted that for instance a court order that simply prohibits particular type of discriminatory behaviour qualifies as an 'appropriate remedy', at least in some circumstances.[72]

---

[67] Article 7(2).

[68] Mark Bell et al, *Developing Anti-Discrimination Law in Europe: The 25 EU Member States compared* (Luxembourg: OOPEC, 2007).

[69] Article 9.

[70] Article 15.

[71] Idem.

[72] Opinion of Advocate General Poiares Maduro, delivered on 12 March 2008, Case 54/07, *CGKR* v. *Firma Feryn*, para 28.

Last but not least, member states are to designate a body or bodies for the promotion of equal treatment of all persons irrespective of racial or ethnic origin. These bodies are to provide independent assistance to victims of discrimination in pursuing their complaints, to conduct surveys concerning discrimination and make recommendations on any issue relating to discrimination.[73]

In many respects the Directive leaves considerable room for interpretation. At the end of the day, the ECJ will have the last word in infusing the rules with greater specificity. Given the rather slow pace with which rulings in this area have emerged from the Court, it will take some time before substantial progress is made in the clarification of the legal obligations under the Directive.

Complementary Equality Provisions

The Directive focuses primarily on equality of treatment in the spheres of life specified in Article 2, thus providing for market equality in the spheres of employment, education and provision of goods and services, and for equality of rights in the sphere of social protection and social advantages. The focus on these forms of equality is however not exclusive, as the Directive also touches upon political equality and participation. Article 12 of the Directive requires member states to encourage, with a view to promoting the principle of equal treatment, dialogue with non-governmental organisations with an interest in fighting ethnic discrimination. They are, by virtue of Article 11, also to promote a dialogue between the two sides of the industry with a view to fostering equal treatment. There is, in other words, at the very least recognition of the desirability of having a broad debate about equality and of the ways in which it can be achieved.

State Obligations

A directive shall, under Article 288 of the TFEU (ex Article 249 TEC), "be binding as to the result to be achieved, upon each Member State to which it is addressed, but shall leave to the national authorities the choice of form and methods". Eventual implementation need not be uniform in every member state. Provisions of binding EU law which are clear, precise and unconditional enough to be considered justiciable can be invoked and relied on by individuals before national courts.[74]

---

[73] Article 13.

[74] These criteria were formulated by the ECJ in *Van Gend en Loos*, Case 41/74.

Though directives cannot impose obligations on individuals of themselves and individuals can only claim the rights conferred by a directive against the state or emanations of the state (directives do not therefore have what is called 'horizontal direct effect'), there is a broad obligation on national courts to interpret domestic law, as far as possible, in conformity with directives ('indirect effect', both in the vertical relationship between an individual and the state and in the horizontal relationship between individuals) after the time limit for their implementation has expired.[75] Indeed, the ECJ has through its case law increasingly put pressure on national courts to play the lead role in the enforcement of the EU law, to the benefit of right-holders.[76]

[75] ECJ, *Von Colson and Kamann* v. *Land Nordhein-Westfalen*, Case 14/83, 10 April 1984. In *Von Colson*, para 26, the ECJ submitted that the member states' obligation arising from a directive to achieve the result envisaged by the directive and their duty to take all appropriate measures to ensure fulfilment of that obligation is binding on all authorities, including the courts, meaning that national courts are required to interpret their national law in light of the wording and the purpose of the directive. See also Andrew Clapham, *Human rights and the European Community: A Critical Overview* (Baden-Baden, Nomos, 1991).

[76] See e.g. Damian Chalmers – Adam Tomkins, *European Union Public Law: Text and Materials* (Cambridge: Cambridge UP, 2007), pp. 365 ff; ECJ, *Defrenne* v. *Sabena*, C-43–75, 8 April 1976.

8 ASSESSMENT

8.1 Recapitulation

The preceding chapters have analysed both the contemporary problem of discrimination and the legal response to it. The time has come to assess the contribution of international and European anti-discrimination law and to examine its strengths and weaknesses from the point of view of combating discrimination. How does the legal response, explored in chapters 6–7, respond to the problems outlined in chapters 3–4? Are people protected from discrimination, in particular everyday forms of discrimination, and if they are, to what extent? In particular, are they protected from indirect discrimination and harassment, and is the law capable of dealing with structural and intersectional discrimination? Does the protection extend to spheres of everyday life such as employment, education and provision of goods and services? What is the effect of all these instruments and all the jurisprudence on the lives of victims of discrimination in practice? What are the overall strengths and weaknesses of the prevailing legal regime?

Answering these questions is of course anything but straightforward and simple. International and European anti-discrimination law has developed into a complicated and technical labyrinth of instruments, doctrines and case law. All Council of Europe countries, EU countries in particular, are parties to a high number of substantively overlapping conventions and other instruments. On the one hand the high number of instruments and ratifications arguably indicates that the principle of non-discrimination finds major support across the world, also in Europe. On the other hand, the fact that the relevant pieces of law overlap to a great extent, when combined with the fact that the relevant provisions are by no means identical, means that it has not been straightforward to operationalize this support into clear and unambiguous provisions. The following analysis focuses on the net effect of all the law.

The Concept of Discrimination

Most of the instruments examined, including the UDHR, ICCPR, ICESCR and the FCNM prohibit discrimination without defining it.

Express definitions have only been laid down in the ICERD and the Racial Equality Directive. Interestingly, these two definitions are different in many respects. Whereas the Directive expressly defines discrimination in terms of direct and indirect discrimination, harassment and instructions to discriminate, these elements are not apparent in the case of the ICERD. In fact, the definition provided in the ICERD is inoperational to the extent that it has been imperative for the CERD to develop an entirely different approach to determining what constitutes discrimination for the purposes of the application of the ICERD in practice.

There are areas where the approaches of the ICERD, the Directive and the interpretative practices of the ECtHR, HRC and the other bodies share common ground. First, it is clear in light of the relevant provisions, the preparatory works and the interpretative practices of the different bodies, that the purpose has never been to ban the making of any kinds of distinctions on the basis of 'race' or ethnic origin ('colour-blindness'). This is so even despite the fact that several human rights instruments rather peculiarly confuse 'distinction' and 'discrimination' and use them almost interchangeably.[1] Second, intention is not an essential part of any definition or conceptualization of discrimination. This means that it is not necessary, for instance, for a complainant to show that the respondent intended to discriminate, although demonstration of intent may help to build the case in a court.

A degree of common ground can also be identified in the interpretative practices of the international human rights bodies. The ECtHR, HRC, CERD and ECSR all agree, by and large, that differentiation constitutes discrimination if the criterion used has no objective and reasonable justification or if there is no reasonable relationship of proportionality between the means employed and the aim sought to be realized.[2] This formulation follows the logic of the Aristotelian maxim

---

[1] A similar conclusion is drawn by Marc Bossuyt, *The concept and practice of affirmative action*, preliminary report by Mr. Marc Bossuyt, Special Rapporteur to the Commission on Human Rights, 19 June 2000, para 48.

[2] For the CERD, differentiation constitutes discrimination if the criteria for such differentiation, judged against the objectives and purposes of the Convention, are legitimate. For the HRC, differentiation constitutes discrimination if the criteria for such differentiation are reasonable and objective and if the aim is to achieve a purpose which is legitimate under the ICCPR. For the ECtHR, differentiation constitutes discrimination if the criteria have no objective and reasonable justification or if there is no reasonable relationship of proportionality between the means employed and the aim sought to be realized.

'treat equal cases equally' and is ultimately about assessment of rationality: are there good and valid reasons for determining that the two cases at hand are equal or not? The Racial Equality Directive explicitly deals with one situation where it is deemed rational – and therefore legitimate – to treat people differently on the grounds of ethnic origin, by stipulating that a distinction based on 'racial' or ethnic origin does not constitute discrimination where a characteristic related to origin constitutes a "genuine and determining occupational requirement". As we have seen, the application of this exception is not straightforward.

The 'objective and reasonable justification' test has its merits and demerits. On the one hand, it is flexible and allows the bodies concerned to develop their doctrines in response to changing circumstances and, in particular, changing social values. It allows judges and others charged with applying the law to respond to changes in the nature and forms of discrimination. On the other hand, it is almost void of fixed substance and provides little if any guidance for national authorities, judges, employers and service providers, victims of discrimination and other stakeholders. Moreover, reliance on this test does not contribute to legal certainty, as decisions as to what is discrimination and what is not are bound to evolve on a case-by-case basis and are bound to reflect subjective appreciation and the particular judicial ideologies and values of those who make the decisions.[3] Moreover, there is always the immanent danger that the social or personal values are those held by the ethnic majority, which may well be very different from the values held by the minorities, particularly on an issue such as this which is of great importance to the minorities. In consequence the extent of the protection that the minorities enjoy from discrimination perpetrated by the majority may become determined by the latter.[4]

Particularly the ECtHR, and following it the ECSR, have moved on to recognize the second limb of the Aristotelian maxim, to require that

[3] With regard to the role played by the judicial ideologies of judges, see J.G. Merrills, *The development of international law by the European Court of Human Rights* (Manchester: Manchester University Press, 1993).

[4] This interpretation is not far-fetched when one examines the case law of the ECtHR and the ECJ with respect to discrimination against transgender people and sexual minorities. See e.g. ECtHR, *Sheffield and Horsham* v. *United Kingdom*, judgment of 30 July 1998, where one of the key motivations for the narrow interpretation of Convention rights was that transsexualism raises "complex moral and social issues", an explicit acknowledgement of the fact that there is (was) no adequate support for rights for transsexuals among the general public.

'different cases be dealt with differently'. The second limb is more difficult to apply than the first, as its application requires the elaboration of a positive theory of equality and not just the application of the 'harm principle' that disallows measures that unfairly disadvantage particular groups or individuals. One obstacle for the implementation of the second limb has been the tradition of suspicion towards distinctions based on ethnicity, a tradition that was born because differential treatment has historically speaking almost always meant adverse treatment, and in retrospect manifestly so, as was the case in South Africa during the Apartheid regime, in Germany during the Nazi rule and in the United States under the so-called Jim Crow laws. There is also a more general distaste in Europe towards group rights, which an obligation to differentiate on the basis of group membership rather inevitably comes close to. All of this is compounded by the fact that the ECtHR's jurisprudence in this respect is not extensive, and the standards that it will apply in future cases are respectively unclear. In effect, the legal opinion regarding the second limb is only starting to take its shape.

All the bodies examined in this study, the CEACR, CERD, HRC, ECtHR, ECSR and the ACFC, have, starting from the 1990s, come to recognize the phenomenon of indirect discrimination. Yet they, and the EU Directive, have come to conceptualize indirect discrimination in different ways: whereas the Directive defines indirect discrimination in terms of putting persons of a particular ethnic origin at a "particular disadvantage", the ECtHR speaks about "disproportionately prejudicial effects", the CERD about "unjustifiable disparate impact", the HRC about "disproportionate adverse effect not based on objective and reasonable criteria" and the ECSR about "disproportionate effect". These differences are legally significant, because terms 'disparate impact' and 'disproportionate impact' readily call for statistical evidence showing the existence of such an impact on a particular group, whereas 'particular disadvantage' is a more relaxed standard in this respect. That said, on the one hand the relevant bodies have been careful to point out that a disparate/disproportionate impact can be shown also by other means than statistics, and on the other hand the Directive is clear on the fact that statistical evidence is also one of the methods by which the existence of a 'particular disadvantage' may be demonstrated. The fact remains that in practice it will be difficult to demonstrate indirect discrimination, however defined, without statistical evidence, unless the causal connection between the impugned 'neutral' measure and the harm inflicted is so self-evident and based on facts that are generally so well-known that it is unnecessary to have recourse to any other evidence. This, coupled with the fact that across Europe there is great reluctance to collect ethnic data – without which the statistics cannot be compiled in the first place – effectively means that protection against indirect discrimination is presently compromised to a great extent, and that instances of indirect discrimination are not detected except in the most extreme cases.[5]

The definition of indirect discrimination, both under the Directive and practice of the different bodies, incorporates an 'objective justification' defence. Under the Directive, an apparently neutral provision, criterion or practice which puts persons of a particular ethnic origin at a particular disadvantage compared with other persons does not constitute discrimination provided that it is "objectively justified by a legitimate aim and the means of achieving that aim are appropriate and necessary". Again, the use of open terms such as these ('legitimate aim', 'appropriate', 'necessary') has both its pros and cons: on the one hand, it allows the bodies concerned to develop their doctrines in accordance with changing social circumstances and values; on the other hand, it introduces a great deal of legal uncertainty, as the addressees of the legislation have little guidance as to how the law will be applied in practice, particularly before the emergence of a solid amount of case law. It has been observed that the justification allowed for indirect discrimination has "proved fatal" in practice for some types of cases, and it has been suggested that the assessment of the 'objective justification' should be interpreted to incorporate a necessity test, so that a justification could be considered to be 'objective' only where no other measure, that would be more favourable from the point of view of equal treatment, could have been used to achieve the same objectives.

One welcome feature of the contemporary international and European anti-discrimination law is that the range of situations that can give rise to a finding of discrimination has broadened up. It is general practices, and not just rigid provisions or the use of certain criteria, that can constitute discrimination. In this way anti-discrimination law can, at least in theory, be used to challenge some forms of institutional and structural discrimination, as was done in the case of *D.H. and others*, decided by the ECtHR.

---

[5] This seems to be the experience also outside Europe, see e.g. Meredith Wilkie, 'Australia's Human Rights and Equal Opportunity Commission' in Martin MacEwen (ed.), *Anti-Discrimination Law Enforcement* (Aldershot: Avebury, 1997), p. 85.

The EU Directive is the only piece of law that expressly prohibits harassment and defines it as a form of discrimination. The Directive's definition of harassment is not particularly clear or inclusive, as harassment is defined in terms of a violation of dignity and the creation of a hostile or degrading environment, considering that the first term is vague and the second elevates the bar rather high. In consequence, the effect of the prohibition of harassment remains not just uncertain but also limited, at least for the time being.

It is important to note that the ICCPR, ICERD and the UDHR prohibit incitement to discrimination, and that the Directive prohibits instructions to discriminate. It is therefore not only actual instances of discrimination that are prohibited by the law.

There is a good degree of conceptual and substantive diversity – or, less euphemistically, confusion – when it comes to measures aiming to promote the achievement of de facto equality. Essentially the same idea, though with different emphases and standards, is variously called 'positive action', 'temporary special measures' or 'affirmative action'. These measures are crucial for the success of the fight against discrimination. The common ground across the different instruments is that taking such measures is allowed, either expressly or in light of the preparatory works and/or the interpretative practices of the different bodies.

Beyond that common basic platform there are two major areas of uncertainty. First, Article 2(2) of the ICERD expressly *requires* states to take special measures "where the circumstances so warrant". Article 4(2) of the FCNM requires states parties to adopt "where necessary, adequate measures" to promote full and effective equality for their national minorities, and Article 2(2)c of the ILO convention 169 requires states to "assist" indigenous peoples to achieve the same goal. The ECtHR, the HRC and the CESCR have interpreted that the non-discrimination provisions of the instruments whose implementation they supervise also *require* taking specific action and preferential treatment to correct discrimination in fact. Yet the legal opinion, under all these conventions, is remarkably ambiguous, underdeveloped, and unclear when it comes to the more exact nature and scope of these obligations. This is very unfortunate from the point of view of fighting discrimination, and probably has something to do with the fact that the issue of special measures/positive action is a politically highly charged subject, as is demonstrated by the heated debates that have taken place in all countries that have policy programmes or legal provisions requiring such action.[6] Second, there is presently not only uncertainty as regards the very existence of an obligation to take positive action measures, but also as regards the lawful scope of such measures under the various pieces of law. Is the use of rigid quotas allowed, for instance in the field of employment? If not, what about aspirational targets, or policies that favour the selection of candidates belonging to under-represented groups in tie-break situations where two or more candidates have equal qualifications?[7] The above-mentioned uncertainties notwithstanding, it is clear that the different documents do not go so far as to hold states responsible for ensuring the achievement of material equality between minorities and the majority.

Minority rights (in *sensu stricto*) have by and large come to be separated from anti-discrimination law.[8] The most relevant provisions that deal with the right of persons belonging to minorities to maintain and develop their cultural, religious and linguistic identities and to cherish their traditions are Article 27 of the ICCPR and Article 5 of the FCNM. That said, also non-discrimination instruments and provisions go some way in the direction of accommodating the particular needs and characteristics of minorities and immigrants. First, as already mentioned, the *Thlimmenos* doctrine developed by the ECtHR requires a measure of accommodation – but exactly how much, remains an open question. Second, the prohibition of indirect discrimination may also require the accommodation of some of the needs and characteristics of minorities and immigrants. This is so even though the relevant pieces of law do not expressly refer to a duty to accommodate cultural, linguistic and religious differences, unlike with respect to disability discrimination under the Framework Employment Directive, which expressly requires employers to provide "reasonable accommodation" in order to "guarantee compliance with the principle of equal treatment".[9] By virtue of

[6] One only needs to think about the issue of affirmative action in the United States, and the high number of controversial court decisions, policies and legal and political commentaries that the subject area has given rise to.

[7] These questions are examined in greater detail in chapter 11.

[8] See Kristin Henrard, *Devising an Adequate System of Minority Protection: Individual Human Rights, Minority Rights and the Right to Self-determination* (The Hague: Kluwer, 2000).

[9] Article 5 of the Directive provides as follows: "In order to guarantee compliance with the principle of equal treatment in relation to persons with disabilities, reasonable accommodation shall be provided. This means that employers shall take appropriate measures, where needed in a particular case, to enable a person with a disability to have access to, participate in, or advance in employment, or to undergo training, unless such measures would impose a disproportionate burden on the employer."

the prohibition of indirect discrimination, rigid language requirements and dress codes imposed by employers may be challenged on the grounds that they put members of particular groups at a disadvantage or have a disparate impact upon them, in which case the legitimacy of such requirements depends on the assessment of the justification of the measure. Insofar as no acceptable justification can be presented, such requirements must effectively be abolished or modified in order to accommodate the groups in question. It would obviously have been a preferable and clearer solution to have a separate provision directly clarifying the extent of the obligation to provide accommodation rather than having to infer the existence of such a requirement indirectly through the prohibition of indirect discrimination, as the latter solution inevitably involves technical complexities and uncertainties.

Grounds and Personal Scope of Application

All instruments under study that prohibit discrimination on multiple grounds expressly mention 'race' as one of the prohibited grounds. Race is actually mentioned first in the list of grounds in all the documents concluded under the auspices of the UN or its specialized agencies, and is placed second in the list in the European documents right after sex, with the exception of the Social Charter (revised), which mentions 'race' first. This, as well as the fact that there are several instruments that deal exclusively with racial discrimination, together with the widespread tendency among judicial and quasi-judicial bodies to consider 'race' to be a particularly suspect ground for making distinctions, reflects the general agreement that racial discrimination is considered to constitute a particularly invidious form of discrimination.

The approach to the issue of 'grounds' in international and European instruments raises several issues, three of which will be discussed here. First, the concepts used are not strictly distinct from each other. Peculiar ambiguity underlies all of this. On the one hand, international and European human rights documents expressly mention 'race', 'colour', 'national origin' and 'religion', notions that overlap to the extent that it appears that the only logical explanation for including all of them is that the preferred strategy has been to add as many concepts as possible in order to avoid any lacunae. On the other hand, 'ethnicity' or 'ethnic origin' is mentioned only in the EU Directive and the European Social Charter (revised). If the idea has been to be absolutely certain that all forms of discrimination based on origin are prohibited, why has 'ethnicity' been left out? There can be no doubt that ethnicity as a notion is farther removed from the notion of 'race' than the notion of 'colour'. If colour is expressly mentioned, why is ethnicity not?

Second, these core concepts are not defined anywhere. This is perhaps understandable in the case of instruments that prohibit discrimination on a number of grounds, but the same observation applies also with respect to the ICERD and the Racial Equality Directive. The only issue that is relatively settled is that under the ICERD and the practice of the ECtHR, ethnic discrimination is taken to be one form of racial discrimination. This approach is not without its problems.[10] But what is more worrying is the fact that the terms 'race' and 'ethnicity' are used in the legal instruments and in the practice of the different bodies in a straightforward and unqualified manner.[11] The ICERD and its monitoring body in particular have no problems with speaking about 'different races' as if such things really existed.[12] This all probably springs from, and contributes to the maintenance of, prevailing objectivist and essentialist understandings of 'race' and 'ethnicity'. That said, it would of course be even more problematic to expressly define these terms, given that there can be no single scientifically acceptable definition of 'race' or 'ethnicity'. The question of the exact definition of the terms at hand, and the question of whether a specific individual 'really' belongs to a particular group or not, have seldom been touched upon in the practice of the international and European bodies. It appears that the different bodies have by and large taken a pragmatic approach to the role played by the particular ground involved in an allegedly discriminatory event. Where an individual claims that she has been discriminated against on the grounds of her ethnic origin, the focus of the

---

[10] The notion of 'race', unless its meaning is significantly stretched from its current everyday usage, is generally understood to refer to biological, not cultural, religious and/or linguistic differences, unlike is the case with ethnicity. But if 'ethnicity' is stripped of cultural, religious and linguistic meanings and reduced simply to biological differences, then the question arises whether this by implication means that persons belonging to an ethnic group are not protected from discrimination that is based on (typical) cultural, religious and linguistic characteristics of the group.

[11] Occasional statements such as that made in recital 6 of the Racial Equality Directive, stating that the use of the term 'racial origin' in the Directive does not imply an acceptance of theories which attempt to determine the existence of separate human races, are far too rare and lacking in legal strength to offset the unqualified objectivist use of the terms 'race' and 'ethnicity' in these documents.

[12] See e.g. CERD, General Recommendation XXIV (1999).

proceedings is usually primarily on whether she was put at a disadvantage in comparison to others, and the existence of a 'racial' or ethnic difference is usually acknowledged without much ado or further examination, unless the claim is contested or manifestly unfounded.

Third, the fact that the terms used are overlapping but undefined and therefore imprecise means that it will often not be a straightforward matter to determine on which ground(s) a person was discriminated against or whether a particular event or practice comes within the scope of a particular instrument.[13] If the police's stop-and-search practices disproportionately target young men with Mid-Eastern looks, does that constitute discrimination on the grounds of ethnicity or discrimination on the grounds of (presumed) religion? If a shopkeeper refuses to let in Roma women, who in some countries typically wear distinctive and voluminous traditional velvet dresses, on the grounds that he believes that they might steal from the shop and hide goods under their dresses, is that discrimination on the grounds of ethnicity or is it discrimination on the grounds of sex, both or neither?

The latter example brings us to a fourth issue, which is that the existence of the problem of intersectional and multiple discrimination is currently acknowledged but the legal problems involved have not by any means been resolved.[14] None of the instruments at hand explicitly addresses this issue by providing for means by which to cope with such forms of discrimination, nor have any legal solutions in this regard been developed by the monitoring bodies. Indeed, the chosen – though

[13] For instance the CERD has encountered situations where the Committee members have been uncertain whether a particular situation comes within the scope of the ICERD. In his letter of 18 August 1995 to the Secretary-General of the UN, the chairman of the CERD stated the following: "In many conflicts sentiments of ethnic belonging are mixed with sentiments of a religious or political character. The text of the Convention provides little guidance on the differentiation of ethnic from political motivation, while the position is further complicated by its definition of racial discrimination as covering distinctions which are racial either in their purpose or their effect. In several of the situations considered during 1995, Committee members were uncertain whether the ethnic elements in the apparent tensions were sufficient to bring the situation within the scope of the Convention." Report of the Committee on the Elimination of Racial Discrimination, *Elimination of Racism and Racial Discrimination*, A/50/18, 22 September 1995.

[14] For instance, recital 14 of the Racial Equality Directive provides that"[i]n implementing the principle of equal treatment irrespective of racial or ethnic origin, the Community should, in accordance with Article 3(2) of the EC Treaty, aim to eliminate inequalities, and to promote equality between men and women, especially since women are often the victims of multiple discrimination."

not exclusive – policy line within the UN and the EU has been to develop ground-specific instruments, a policy which in itself is unfavourable for the purposes of fighting intersectional and multiple discrimination, as the applicable definitions of discrimination and scopes of application differ from one instrument to another, and therefore the outcome of a case may greatly depend on the ground on which the claim is based. Insofar as the international and European examples have led countries to adopt ground-specific anti-discrimination laws with strict comparison-based definitions of discrimination à la the EU Directive, victims of intersectional discrimination are likely to experience major difficulties in proving their cases. This is because complainants in such cases are in practice often forced to present their cases as if they are linked only with a single ground, a factor that privileges the respondents because they therefore have the opportunity to rebut the *prima facie* case by presenting 'comparators' that share the single identified ground but have not been put at a disadvantage. Indeed, protection against intersectional discrimination requires innovative legal solutions that are presently in great demand and short supply. This is unfortunate in view of the fact that intersectional discrimination, and particularly the proving thereof, presents particular challenges that must be tackled for the protection against discrimination to be effective in practice.[15]

Material Scope of Application

The primary focus of the international anti-discrimination law is on guaranteeing equality of rights, on prohibition of discrimination in the exercise of public powers, and on banning Apartheid and other manifest forms of discrimination. The EU law focuses on equality of treatment in the market place, and on equality with respect to some areas of social policy. Taken together, the international and European anti-discrimination law has come to cover many of those areas of life where discrimination, including everyday discrimination, typically takes place. These areas include employment, education and provision of goods and services. That said, almost all of the human rights documents, whether international or European, are unclear about the reach of their non-discrimination provisions. This is particularly and

[15] Paola Ucellari, 'Multiple Discrimination: How Law can Reflect Reality' *The Equal Rights Review*, Vol One (2008).

manifestly so with the ICERD and Protocol No 12 to the ECHR. The material fields of application are not laid down in most of the instruments in any express terms, but have been left to be inferred by means of interpretation, a solution that brings with it a good measure of legal uncertainty. The only exception in this regard is the EU Directive, which expressly defines its scope of application, although it also has its grey areas and uncertainties.

State Obligations, Domestic Enforcement and Remedies

Countries are under a wide array of both negative and positive obligations under the international and European conventions and other instruments. A short list of the core obligations include the following: the obligation to amend, rescind or nullify any incompatible domestic legislation; the general obligation to pursue a policy of eliminating racial discrimination 'by all appropriate means' and 'without delay'; obligation to penalize dissemination of ideas based upon racial superiority or hatred, incitement to hatred, incitement to acts of violence and incitement to discrimination; and the obligation to promote understanding, tolerance and friendship among nations and to combat prejudices, through the fields of education, culture and information. The EU Directive is the only document that expressly requires the enactment, nationally, of comprehensive anti-discrimination legislation where such does not already exist. That said, the different committees, the CERD in particular, have called for concrete, comprehensive and proactive measures to combat discrimination and have recommended the adoption of anti-discrimination legislation.

ICCPR, ICERD and ECHR, as well as the UDHR, require states to provide for an 'effective remedy' in discrimination cases. There is wide agreement that the notion 'remedy' is to be understood both in the procedural and substantive sense. The ICERD goes further than the other documents and specifically requires, in Article 6, the provision of judicial mechanisms, without, however, specifying whether these should be of criminal, civil or administrative nature. That Article also requires that victims must be provided with the right to seek "just and adequate reparation or satisfaction for any damage suffered as result of discrimination" through those mechanisms. The EU Racial Equality Directive, for its part, requires member states to ensure that "judicial and/or administrative procedures" are in place for the defence of the rights of victims of discrimination. The bottom line appears to be that a victim of discrimination must have access to the general judicial system or at least to an administrative body such as an equality tribunal, ombudsman, a national commission for equality or some other comparable body with competence to deal with complaints about discrimination. The Directive expressly requires that the burden of proof be shared and that protection be provided from victimization. In addition, it goes a few steps beyond the traditional individual-rights based legal approach to remedies, and requires that specialized bodies be established for the purposes of promoting equal treatment, and that these bodies, and collective actors such as the social partners and NGOs, must be engaged in the endeavour to combat ethnic discrimination.

8.2 Structural Properties of Anti-Discrimination Law

On the basis of the above analysis, it is possible to analyse at a deeper level the structural properties of contemporary international and European anti-discrimination law. These properties will be discussed in the following with an eye on how they either contribute to, or compromise, the cause of fighting discrimination and promoting equality in an effective manner. The different properties of the law will be subjected to a SWOT analysis, which highlights the strengths, weaknesses, opportunities and threats involved in the law. As will be apparent, it will oftentimes be the case that the different structural properties of anti-discrimination law have both their positive and negative implications.

8.2.1 *Theoretical Undercurrents – Doctrinal Perplexity within a Liberal Political Frame*

Anti-discrimination law, as it now stands, does not have a single theoretical foundation, as many historical factors and political, religious and philosophical convictions have contributed to its formation. Although we can observe certain developments in the substance of the law and discern analytical models which the different pieces of law correspond to,[16] anti-discrimination law, taken as a whole, does not

[16] See e.g. the typology presented by McCrudden in 'The New Concept of Equality' (2003) 3 ERA-Forum 9.

spring from or follow a single totalizing theory.[17] There is no general agreement as to what exactly constitutes discrimination, why it should be prohibited, what the ultimate purposes of the law are and whether it should provide for – or at least promote – material and cultural equality. The different pieces of law and their interpretations have developed in an ad hoc manner without a clear overarching vision or set of first principles.

This should not be a matter of surprise or even concern, as the very search for ultimate theoretical foundations, in matters of social justice, is itself without a foundation.[18] Classical principles such as 'equality' do not have fixed contents awaiting discovery.[19] Meanings are constructed rather than found, which is why conflicting convictions about social justice issues are part and parcel of legal provisions, theories, doctrines and interpretations. Whereas there is nothing abstract or theoretical about the hurt and disadvantage that victims of discrimination experience, the fact remains that – just like other concepts – equality and equal treatment are abstract and *an sich* empty or at the very least contested and open-ended concepts, which is why anti-discrimination law cannot self-evidently be founded on some particular theory that would explain what exactly should be prohibited and why. Numerous different theories have of course been formulated, but even their abundance only testifies to the lack of general agreement.[20] Major parts of anti-discrimination law are intrinsically linked to general international human rights law, and therefore share some of its theoretical problems. Both are an offspring of conflicting and inherently imperfect philosophical theories and historical accidents of untheorizable suffering to which they constitute a response to, and as such they are both theoretically ambiguous and beyond apparent theoretization.[21]

---

[17] This conclusion should not be taken as precluding any attempts to achieve a common understanding and theory of anti-discrimination law. See e.g. the opinion of Advocate General Poiares Maduro in *Coleman* v. *Attridge Law*, 31 January 2008, Case C-303/06, where he argues that the aim of the EU anti-discrimination law is to protect human dignity and personal autonomy.

[18] Martti Koskenniemi, 'Human Rights, Politics, and Love' *Mennesker & rettigheter* 4/2001.

[19] Roberto Mangabeira Unger, *The critical legal studies movement* (Cambridge: Harvard University Press, 1986).

[20] See e.g. the theoretical approaches presented in Christopher McCrudden (ed.), *Anti-Discrimination Law* (Aldershot: Dartmouth, 2004).

[21] Indeed, the law attempts the impossible when it tries to construe absolutes from conflicting ideological and political premises of the lawmakers and the accidents of experience that gives rise to its adoption.

This said, the compatibility of the current regime of anti-discrimination law with the central tenets of political liberalism is remarkably clear, suggesting a close linkage between the two. To a great extent, anti-discrimination law reflects and, for its part, upholds – and even enforces – the core doctrines and values of liberalism. Akin to liberalism, anti-discrimination law is markedly individualist in its orientation. Discrimination is couched in terms of harm inflicted by individuals on one another and the law is mostly unconcerned with problems that cannot be conceptualized in that way. Protection from discrimination is – clearly for dogmatic, not empirical reasons – provided equally and 'universally' to all individuals, though people do not suffer from it equally, and therefore the law fails to recognize that it is some people rather than others that are affected. The law provides for individual justice, not group justice that would require attention to be paid to material, political and cultural equality. The whole idea of anti-discrimination law, as it stands, is to protect the enjoyment of individual rights and freedoms and equality of opportunity from unwarranted governmental or private intervention, and thereby to protect individual liberty and autonomy. It bolsters an apparent culture of rationalism by means of seeking to remove irrational elements from decision-making, one example of which is the deployment of the 'principle of merit' in the field of employment.[22] Anti-discrimination law also reflects the so-called harm principle, according to which the state is entitled and even required to intervene in order to prevent one person from inflicting harm on another,[23] as well as the doctrine that there are public affairs where public power may be exercised over individuals and private affairs where it may not.[24] Individualism, individual autonomy, individual liberty, rationalism, the harm principle and the distinction between public and private affairs are all central to the classical theory of political liberalism as formulated by J.S. Mill.[25]

Yet it would be incorrect to conclude that anti-discrimination law is simply, necessarily or exclusively an embodiment of classic political liberalism. The law is flexible enough to accommodate different strands

---

[22] That the content of the principle of merit is controversial and that it can be deployed in order to mask irrational or morally repulsive actions is another matter, and will be considered below.

[23] The harm principle (or 'doctrine' as he himself described it) was formulated by J.S. Mill in his *On Liberty* (London: John W. Parker and Son, 1859), pp. 21–23.

[24] Ibid, p. 27 ff.

[25] Idem.

of liberalism, including welfare liberalism which advocates a greater role for the state in the reduction of *de facto* inequalities. This is reflected in that the law allows taking positive action/special measures, but does not require it or requires it only to a modest and unclear extent, leaving the decision whether to work towards material equality to governments. The present focus of the law on formal equality and on processes, instead of substantive equality and outcomes, has a definite liberal twist to it. Major parts of the international law, which show restraint in imposing obligations upon states that go beyond elimination of openly discriminatory laws and policies, may even satisfy libertarians. The EU Directive, which staunchly requires state intervention in the fields of employment and provision of goods and services, is less accommodating of libertarian aspirations, but may find some appeal not just among classical and welfare liberals but also among communitarians, given that it takes some steps towards the recognition of the collective aspects of the fight against discrimination.[26] The close linkage between liberalism and current regime of international and European anti-discrimination law is perhaps also showcased by the fact that traditionalist legal and political elites in post-socialist countries have had difficulties in accepting that anti-discrimination law, and with it individual rights, liberal values and genuine rule of law, could prevail over collective interests and political expediency.[27]

Anti-discrimination law is not only wrought with tensions arising from the competing political orientations that it tries to accommodate, but also tensions and other problems that are internal to these orientations, including political liberalism, which it is closely associated with. Some of these tensions have to do with the liberal conception of individual rights. There are tensions between anti-discrimination law on the one hand, and with the right to privacy, freedom of contract,

[26] The EU Directive arguably recognizes group aspects in several ways. To begin with, the concepts of indirect discrimination and positive action involve recognition of the group dimensions of discrimination. In addition, the Directive recognizes the important role played by the social partners and the collective bargaining system, as well as the NGOs representing the interests of the different groups victimized by discrimination.

[27] See e.g. Margarita Ilieva, *The Bulgarian Draft Anti-Discrimination Law: An Opportunity to Make Good on the Constitutional Promise of Equality in a Post-Communist Society* (European Roma Rights Centre, 2003), available at: http://www.errc.org/cikk.php?cikk=1444 (accessed 1.1.2010).

freedom of speech and individual autonomy on the other.[28] These tensions and even conflicts that occur at the level of principles (and rules laid down on the basis of them) have to a large extent not been resolved by the law (or at the very least the question *how* they have been resolved is in dispute), nor do they absolve by themselves. These unresolved tensions bring doctrinal indeterminacy to anti-discrimination law, pinpointing areas of controversy that are ultimately political in nature. Yet another structural property of the present regime of anti-discrimination law is that its excessive individualism hides from sight problems that are collective, social and/or cultural in nature. This individualism is undoubtedly related to the unwillingness of the theory of liberal democracy to recognize entities other than the individual and the state, and hampers the ability of the law to reduce inequalities.

The drafters' and legislators' apparent wish to make anti-discrimination law compatible with several types of political theories and orientations, while probably a precondition for its general acceptability, necessarily imbues the law with profound indeterminacy. The very objectives of the law are open, and therefore open to dispute, which also affects how the different elements of the law are interpreted, given that laws are often interpreted, or at least expected to be interpreted, in light of their (stated or presumed) objectives and purposes.[29] If the objective of the law is taken to be the achievement of formal equal opportunity, then any exception to the principle of equal treatment should be read narrowly, including the taking of positive action/special measures. If the objective of the law is taken to be the achievement of substantive equal opportunity, then the law should be read expansively so as to maximize the role played by positive action/special measures. Reading the law from libertarian, socialist or collectivist positions would have other, but equally fundamental, implications. The thing, then, about doctrinal controversies over questions of substance in the field of anti-discrimination law, is that they are at the end of the day political and moral controversies not *a priori* solved by the law itself.

[28] Sometimes the anti-discrimination instruments themselves refer to these other principles as limiting the applicability of the principle of non-discrimination. See e.g. recital 4 of the Racial Equality Directive and its reference to protection of private and family life.

[29] Vienna Convention on the Law of Treaties, Article 31.

Indeterminacy of the law and its theoretical premises is not necessarily a weakness; once recognized, it can also be a strength, as it allows and even invites the development of a range of theoretical and doctrinal models, forcing us to think harder and deeper about the social justice matters involved.

Equal Treatment Rather than Treatment as Equals

As theorized in chapter 3, there are a number of possible dimensions to equality: we can speak of material, cultural, political, civil rights and market equality. As already noted, contemporary anti-discrimination law focuses primarily on two types of equality: civil rights equality and market equality. *Ipso facto*, that law must be a disappointment for anyone who hopes that it would define and guarantee some other dimension of equality.

As concerns material equality, it can be observed that the central thrust of the present legal regime is the defence of formal equal opportunities of individuals. Law comes into play for instance whenever a person is not hired because of the colour of his or her skin. The focus is on equal treatment and equality of opportunities, on the formal flawlessness of the *process* of distribution of jobs and social goods. The focus is not, or is only to a modest extent, on the *actual* distribution of jobs and social goods, or on the factors that brought it about. The extent to which any society should be concerned with material equality between groups is – under contemporary law – up to that society itself, any such concern being subject, however, to the requirement that the practical implications of such a policy must not violate the aforementioned requirement of procedural fairness. Accordingly, the present law poses limits on the extent to which a society may pursue a policy of equal outcomes in practice.

As concerns cultural equality, international and European anti-discrimination law is markedly obscure with respect to the question whether, and if yes, to what extent, it recognizes, embraces or endorses cultural diversity and pluralism. As has been established in previous chapters, the present regime of anti-discrimination law does not directly address the question whether the non-accommodation of cultural or religious characteristics may constitute direct or indirect discrimination on the grounds of origin. Case law in this regard is only starting to emerge.[30] The deliberate use in law of the terms equal

[30] See e.g. ECtHR, *Thlimmenos* v. *Greece*, judgment of 6 April 2000.

treatment and equal opportunity, instead of such terms as 'identical treatment' or 'similar treatment', suggests that a measure of differentiation may at the very least be *allowed* insofar as it does not constitute unfavourable treatment. Given the openness of the formulation of the definition of indirect discrimination in particular, which gives courts and other competent bodies much leeway in this area, it is clear that the extent to which the anti-discrimination law protects expressions of other than the majority identity in various contexts of everyday life remains uncertain.[31] Ultimately, the law's *ratio* appears to be that people are alike, irrespective of origin, or that at the very least they should, irrespective of origin, be taken to be alike and by and large be treated alike. In this way, the law partakes in the social invention of the autonomous individual detached from any group affiliations. The legislator's reluctance to confront and resolve the tension between what we might call the "assimilationist" and "pluralist" conceptions of anti-discrimination law is again probably due to its wish to accommodate different political views and conceptions of justice, as choices in this area necessarily have discernible political implications. It is also not far-fetched to assume that the ambiguity shown by the law towards recognition of cultural pluralism reflects the present identity crisis of European nation states – and quite likely contributes to it too.

Material and cultural equality have come to be dealt with by other parts of the law, including other parts of the international human rights law. Indeed, social and economic rights set out a number of minimum living standards, and minority rights (and freedom of religion) set out minimum standards with respect to the protection of minority identities. The relationship between these areas of the law on the one hand, and anti-discrimination law on the other, is by no means clear or resolved.[32] It is not too far-fetched to speak of a disjunction between the different areas of human rights law or of fragmentation of that law. Legally speaking it is not irrelevant which part of the law deals with these matters: economic and social rights as well as minority rights are mostly formulated as rights that are not directly enforceable, whereas this is not the case with anti-discrimination law. In consequence,

[31] At present, protection of (minority) identity comes down to an assessment of whether a contested rule, criterion or practice reflecting majority standards is (with some generalisation) "objectively justified" and "proportionate in view of the ends".

[32] See generally on this subject matter, Martin Scheinin – Reetta Toivanen (eds.), *Rethinking non-discrimination and minority rights* (Turku: Institute for Human Rights, Åbo Akademi University, 2004). See also Dimitrina Petrova, 'A Right to Equality Integral to Universal Human Rights' *The Equal Rights Review*, Vol. One (2008).

the incorporation into anti-discrimination law of considerations relating to material and cultural equality would carry significant legal benefits.

The bottom line is that the focus of the law is not on economic, social or cultural inequality. The crux of the contemporary anti-discrimination law is on equal treatment, not on treatment as equals, with all the attendant legal, political and social consequences. The threat in all of this is that focusing the law on particular dimensions of equality may serve to steer public and legal attention away from the other dimensions. Dubbing equal treatment law – essentially protecting market equality – as 'equality law' is not therefore politically innocent.[33] This conclusion is not as damning as it could be, because many minority groups themselves do give market equality a high priority.[34] And again, the openness of the theoretical premises of anti-discrimination law mean that the market equality focus is not merely a weakness: had the states drafting international and European conventions tried to reach an agreement on each state's obligations in the areas of material and cultural equality, they would most likely have settled for very low standards, given the exigencies of international negotiation, the diversity of national traditions and policies, and the consequent drive towards compromises. Indeed, prevailing theoretical openness provides an opportunity for international, European and national debate about how the law could be made more responsive to the different equality concerns. In effect, one of the challenges for the future is the uneasy task of formulating and debating contesting theories and legal doctrines about how our conflicting ideas about equality can be connected to our conflicting ideas about ethnic difference, in a manner that better promotes the achievement of the different dimensions of ethnic equality.

---

[33] See also Nico J. Beger, 'Putting Gender and Sexuality on the Agenda: Queer Theory and Legal Politics', in Reza Banakar – Max Travers (eds.), *An Introduction to Law and Social Theory* (Oxford: Hart, 2002), p. 175.

[34] For instance a survey conducted among Muslims living in Great Britain, France, Germany and Spain found out that Muslims were more worried about unemployment (46%–56% very worried per country) than decline of religion (18%–45% very worried) or Muslim women taking on modern roles in society (9%–22%). The Pew Global Attitudes Project, *Muslims in Europe: Economic worries top concerns about religious and cultural identity*, July 2006. Available at: http://pewglobal.org/reports/pdf/254.pdf (accessed 1.1.2010).

Standards and Their Abundance: On Legal Evolution and Legal Uncertainty

Anti-discrimination law has grown in importance and breadth, and has come to pose a major restraint on the actions of both public and private actors in a variety of domains of life.[35] Yet the regulatory impact of that law in the actual behaviour of those actors is obscure at best, and not just because of the openness and diversity of its theoretical premises.

Already the sheer volume of the law presents major challenges. Each EU country is party to at least a dozen human rights treaties, all of which prohibit discrimination either in their specific fields of application or more generally. Some of these treaties are remarkably complex and lengthy, such as the revised Social Charter, the substantive articles of which number 31, or the Migrant Convention, which has 93 articles. A conscientious interpreter of international human rights law would also take into account the numerous international declarations that deal with this subject area, as well as the jurisprudence and comments of the different supervisory and monitoring bodies, as well as the general recommendations and country-specific comments submitted by the latter bodies. This effectively creates an insuperable barrier for mastering the subject area in question. Many of the relevant declarations are considerably lengthy, such as the Durban Declaration and Plan of Action, which has no less than 341 articles. The general recommendations, which usually seek to explain only one article or just a single paragraph, tend to be several pages in length. The CERD alone had issued 33 general comments by January 2011, the longest of them being 13 pages.[36] Their length notwithstanding – and without prejudice to the assessment of their overall quality – these documents tend to be couched in technical and open language, which means that these interpretative texts themselves need interpretation. Given these circumstances, is it rational, or reasonable, to expect even the well-intending members of the judicial, legislative and administrative branches – not to mention the average employer or school principal,

[35] At this point it should be reiterated that it is not just the judiciary that needs to be aware of the substance of the law; also the legislative and administrative branches of the state must know the law in order to comply with the negative and positive obligations set forth by that law.

[36] CERD, General Recommendation No. 31 (2005).

the 'end users' of the law – to master the entire field of international and European anti-discrimination law? That the answer must be in the negative is suggested by the fact that books, research reports and articles that deal with this body of law are, without exception, more than less selective, indicating that even the experts in this field are exhausted by the insurmountable amount of relevant materials. Even this study, though it covers much ground, has had to concentrate on the main legally binding international and European materials to the exclusion of non-binding materials, many of which provide valuable guidance and suggest best practices that may well work in practice.[37]

At the same time, that law – particularly international law – is couched more in terms of general and flexible standards than rigid rules. Rules provide for precision and certainty, but their rigidity may in practice lead to results that the lawmaker did not intend.[38] Standards, on the other hand, provide for less precision and certainty, but are flexible and allow evolution.[39] Recourse to standards in the area of anti-discrimination law poses both threats and opportunities. On the one hand, addressees of the law are not always clear as to what their rights and obligations are, and there is always the danger that the arbitrary value judgments of those applying the law come into play, compromising the effectiveness of that law. The latter aspect is of high importance, given the spread of prejudices and stereotypes throughout society, including the judiciary, public administration and others who are obliged to comply with the law. On the other hand, the use of standards leaves room for creativity, teleological reasoning (which is highly prevalent in human rights reasoning) and the evolution of doctrines, making it possible that doctrines and case law are when necessary brought to bear on new forms of inequality. Indeed, all international monitoring bodies discussed in this study have shown a degree of willingness and ability to develop their doctrines, and this has had a positive effect in terms of securing greater legal protection from discrimination.

---

[37] This concerns e.g. the recommendations of ECRI.

[38] This is because of the under- or overinclusiveness of rules in view of the lawmakers' purposes. See Frederick Shauer, *Playing by the Rules: A Philosophical Examination of Rule-Based Decision-Making in Law and in Life* (Clarendon Press, 1992).

[39] Yet, the certainty of rules is often illusory, given the subjectivity of legal interpretation, whereas standards may over time and with the accumulation of experience lead to the setting of a more precise rule either through sedimentation of case law or new legislation. Duncan Kennedy, 'Form and Substance in Private Law Adjudication' *Harvard Law Review* Vol 89:1685, pp. 1701–1713 in particular.

The generality and openness of the law is apparent in the different aspects of the law, including the very definition of discrimination, the legitimate scope of positive action/special measures, and the precise material scope of the prohibition of discrimination. To take an example, discrimination is conceptualized by the ECtHR, CERD, HRC and ECSR, and indirect discrimination by the EU Directive, as (with some generalisation) differentiation or disadvantage that lacks 'objective and reasonable justification' or that violates the proportionality principle. These tests are highly general and their ability to guide the application of the law in practice is consequently weak. Consider for instance the merits and demerits of the 'objective and reasonable justification' test. On the one hand, this test is flexible and allows the interpreting bodies to develop their doctrines in response to changing circumstances, such as changes in the nature and forms of discrimination. It also allows them to take into account changes in social values. On the other hand, it is almost void of substance and provides little or no real guidance for national authorities, judges, employers and service providers, victims of discrimination and other stakeholders. Moreover, reliance on this test does not contribute to legal certainty, as decisions as to whether there has been discrimination or not are bound to depend highly on subjective appreciation and the particular judicial ideologies and values at play in decision-making. In particular, there is always the immanent danger that the values that come into play are either those social values that are predominant in the particular society in question, which would mean that the extent of the protection that a minority enjoys from discrimination perpetrated by the majority would become determined by the latter,[40] or personal values held by the decision-maker, which makes legal protection depend on whimsical factors. What this means is that the 'objective justification test' – as well as the proportionality test, for that matter – is so general that it can be used as an empty place-holder for other less presentable reasons for finding or not finding discrimination. Those charged with interpretation and enforcement of the law are therefore vested with considerable authority and responsibility.

[40] This interpretation is not far-fetched when one analyses the case law of the ECtHR and the ECJ with respect to discrimination against transgender people and sexual minorities. See e.g. ECtHR, *Sheffield and Horsham* v. *United Kingdom*, judgment of 30 July 1998.

Indeed, the open and obscure language and complexity of international and European anti-discrimination law underlines the role and importance of judicial interpretation of that law. The fact, however, is that the international courts and treaty bodies have hitherto dealt only with a handful of cases that concern racial or ethnic discrimination. Their jurisprudence, even if combined, does not help to resolve the many basic but hard questions, as the case law is not by any means comprehensive or even well-established in the sense that a solid legal tradition would emerge from it. The low number of cases brought before these bodies supports the conclusion drawn earlier that the international supervision and enforcement structures are, at the end of the day, only the second line of defence, and in practice national interpretative practices are foremost in importance.

Of course the situation is not so grim that everything is up for grabs and that any interpretation, no matter how unprecedented or aberrant, is accepted as legally valid by higher courts, legal scholars or members of the society at large. Probably most of those who interpret and apply the law do so in good faith, do their best to consider all relevant factors and try to suppress their prejudices from influencing their judgment. Many judges and legal scholars in countries that do not have a well-established body of case law in these matters, which is the case with the majority of European countries today, will look to those jurisdictions (UK, USA, Canada) that do, which will serve to bring down the number of the most egregious interpretations, though at the same time borrowed interpretations replicate the weaknesses of the initial interpretations.[41] But none of this does away with legal uncertainty, and the fact remains that potential or actual victims of discrimination, and potential or actual perpetrators of discrimination, have legal questions that they will not have answers to without resorting to litigation, the outcome of which will oftentimes be unpredictable. Legal uncertainty also means that there are major risks associated with bringing legal action through litigation, a fact which may serve as a disincentive for legal resolution of problems.

[41] Borrowing from other jurisdictions, though an ordinary practice, may indeed have its problems. A solution arrived at in a single case in some other legal context is not necessarily the best one or transferable as such to another legal context. In fact, the search for legal precedents from other jurisdictions may give rise to a snowball effect, where suboptimal solutions spread from court to another and from country to another, causing much unnecessary damage.

Unresolved problems in the theoretical undercurrents of anti-discrimination law, the fact that the law does not address many key questions in any direct manner, the open language of the law and the more general problems that relate to treaty interpretation in the field of international human rights law in particular, place formidable responsibilities upon bodies whose task is to apply, interpret and/or monitor the implementation of that law. It is of course a truism that courts and other competent bodies can never simply 'apply' the law and that interpretation is always called for, whatever the field of law in question. But it may be the case that the challenges are extraordinarily present in the field of international human rights law, a challenge which it is important to be aware of, because it calls for further theoretical and doctrinal elaboration and transparency of judicial reasoning that allows the evaluation of judicial decisions.

Openness of Standards: The Merit Principle as an Example

The open nature of legal standards is often not visible, let alone widely recognized. Take the merit principle, which has a central place in the liberal conception of equality of opportunity, and which in popular discourse harbours positive connotations about neutral, objective and rational assessment of the qualifications of individuals who are looking for work. It is generally accepted that differentiation on the grounds of 'merit' in recruitment is legitimate and does not constitute discrimination. The reality is, however, that whereas people mostly speak about 'merit' as if there was nothing controversial about it, there is no single 'merit principle' but a number of different conceptions, the application of which to any particular fact scenarios lead to different outcomes in practice.[42] What constitutes merit and what weight merit, however conceived, should carry in decision-making are very much in dispute.[43] The measuring and 'weighting' of the different elements of a chosen conception (say, "competence, capability and availability to perform the essential functions of the post concerned"[44]) and the comparison of

---

[42] McCrudden has distinguished between five conceptions (or models) of merit: (i) Merit as absence of intentional discrimination, (ii) general common sense merit, (iii) strict job-relatedness conception of merit, (iv) merit as the capacity to produce particular job-related results, and (v) merit as the capacity to produce beneficial results for the organisation. Christopher McCrudden, 'Merit Principles' *Oxford Journal of Legal Studies*, Vol 18, Winter 1998.

[43] Idem.

[44] This is the formulation used in the EU Framework Employment Directive, recital 17.

the merits of two or more persons, cannot therefore be performed in any straightforward and objective manner.

Take the concept of competence, for instance. Is it allowed under the law and the principle of merit to take into consideration the kind of social, cultural and linguistic competence that helps people to get along with fellow workers and customers – and those in charge of hiring and firing – but which immigrants and persons belonging to minorities are less likely to have because such competence is culture specific?[45] The content of notions such as 'competence' is not self-evident nor is the choice between the different conceptions value-free. The choice of a particular conception and its application in practice requires recourse to values, which makes the whole exercise a subjective if not political one, which is precisely what principles such as 'merit' claim not to be. The reality is that the 'merit principle' leaves employers and other decision makers so much room for discretion and tinkering of the criteria for merit that courts will have a hard time reaching the conclusion that a particular decision, made nominally on the basis of considerations of merit, in fact involved discrimination. In fact, recourse to the merit principle may indeed help employers and other decision makers mask their real but less presentable motives, as they may easily decide to 'weigh' certain criteria more at the expense of others so as to achieve the desired outcome without getting into trouble, since differentiations on the basis of 'merit' are *a priori* considered to be legitimate. Moreover, employers sometimes hire 'promising' individuals irrespective of consideration of their merits in terms of prior experience, but this route to employment may not be accessible to persons belonging to minorities because of the status harms that they experience.[46] The undesirable effect of all of this is that victims of prejudice are led to believe that the real reason for which they were denied employment, promotion or some other good were their inferior merits, and in consequence they will not only be denied the good in question but will be left with damaged self-esteem.[47] We may well be

---

[45] 'Social competence' refers here to the knowledge of social norms prevalent in a particular context.

[46] See chapter 4.2 of this book.

[47] For instance Jennifer L. Pierce, in her study of law firms, observed that 'unqualified' had become the code word for racial and ethnic minority employees. Jennifer L. Pierce 'A Raced and Gendered Organisational Logic in Law Firms', in Reza Banakar – Max Travers (eds.), *An Introduction to Law and Social Theory* (Oxford: Hart, 2002).

justified in concluding that merit arguments are more trouble than they are worth.[48]

8.2.2 *New Problems, Old Solutions: The Capacity to Tackle Everyday Discrimination*

One of the key features of the current state of play in the area of non-discrimination law is the number of high profile human rights treaties and other documents that address this issue. Indeed, racial discrimination has prompted more action within the UN and Council of Europe than any other 'human rights issue',[49] with the possible exception of gender equality.[50] The high number of these legally binding documents, the most important of which are exceptionally widely ratified across the world and particularly Europe, testifies positively to the fact that racial discrimination has become an anathema in contemporary international relations.

In substantive terms, despite its grey areas, international law condemns gross racial discrimination in no uncertain terms. At the core of the international law approach is the recognition of any discrimination in consequence of which individuals or groups are deprived of the full enjoyment of their rights on the grounds of 'race' or 'ethnicity'. Genocide, segregation, and other forms of manifest exclusion or subjugation grounded in law and/or public policies come within the purview of the law without a question. The same applies to incidents perpetrated by extremists motivated by racial hatred. The prohibition of systematic discrimination by way of an official policy may even amount to a *jus cogens* norm under international law, and must be observed also in times of public emergency.

These achievements are somewhat compromised, however, in two respects.

First, the apparent resoluteness of the international legal instruments does not necessarily mean that people would, everywhere and at all times, be protected even from gross breaches of the law. The international response to racial discrimination has undoubtedly helped to

---

[48] McCrudden, *cit. supra* note 42, p. 546.

[49] Whether anti-discrimination law should be classified exclusively, necessarily or primarily as a matter of human rights is a question that is not addressed here in more detail.

[50] This is clear in a quantitative and qualitative assessment of the substance of international conventions, declarations, plan of actions, conferences and other actions.

cut down manifestly discriminatory domestic laws and policies, and individuals have by virtue of it come to enjoy legal protection against the most egregious forms of discrimination. However, the impact of international obligations depends, in practice, primarily upon the level and sincerity of commitment of each government. The international system as such is not necessarily capable of preventing, stopping or constraining even gross forms of racial or ethnic discrimination. History teaches realism in this respect: the ICERD was adopted in 1966, but the Apartheid policy practiced in South Africa was not really dissolved before the first free elections held in 1994, which was also the year when a genocide took place in Rwanda despite it having acceded to the ICERD in 1975.

Second, legal protection against the most egregious forms of discrimination appears to have had the effect of driving underground those overt expressions of racism that were current in the past. The vast majority of employers and shop-keepers know better than to engage in explicit racial and ethnic discrimination; signs indicating "No gypsies" are not as prevalent nowadays as they used to be. Yet, discrimination itself, particularly in the fields of employment and provision of services and goods, has not disappeared. Discrimination testing studies have shown beyond any doubt that employers and service providers keep on discriminating, albeit possibly at lower levels than before. Those who engage in discrimination just do not do it openly anymore, as the fear of legal and/or social sanction has led them to learn how to mask their actions so as to make them appear neutral. Indeed, as the forms of discrimination targeted by the international human rights instruments are primarily ones based on state policies or propelled by open racial hatred, it is pertinent to ask whether the legal approaches that were deemed most desirable forty years ago are capable of addressing problems that are present today. This is what we shall turn to next.

Capacity to Tackle Contemporary Discrimination

The previous chapters have suggested that to be able to deal with everyday discrimination effectively the law should possess the following qualities: it should be able to recognize indirect discrimination, harassment and other subtle forms of discrimination; it should address discrimination that arises not just from the application of rigid rules and criteria, but from more general practices, bringing at least some forms of institutional and structural discrimination within the scope of the law; it should recognize discrimination that takes place between private parties; it should recognize and redress harms inflicted not just on direct victims but also on indirect victims of discrimination, the other members of the victimized groups in particular; and it should address not just discrimination but its causes and effects as well. Anything less than that will not stop the vicious circle of discrimination, where discrimination and disadvantage reinforce each other.

International law has, mainly through doctrinal developments, come to recognize the notion of indirect discrimination and the applicability of the law in relations between private parties. The focus of the law is now more on victims instead of perpetrators, and discrimination is increasingly conceptualized in terms of the harm inflicted upon the (direct) victims, not in terms of racism or other motivations behind it.[51] The law has also come to recognize that discrimination may arise not just from rules or criteria but also from more general practices, and the different monitoring bodies have been able to draw attention to structural problems through their dialogue with states under the reporting procedures.[52] Accordingly, international law has, to some extent, been brought to bear on systemic, institutional and subtle forms of discrimination. Yet, its main weakness in terms of combating everyday discrimination is that its predominant focus is on equality of rights, and that it does not expressly and clearly enough require states to take effective action to combat all forms of discrimination in such fields as employment and provision of goods and services. At any rate it is clear that only a few countries, even in Europe, have adopted wide-ranging equality laws to give effect to their treaty obligations in this respect.

---

[51] This shift in perspective is evident in the recognition of the concept of indirect discrimination, in the recognition of the concept of harassment (which is not based on a comparative rationale – even if an employer harasses everyone on a equal basis, that is harassment) and in the move away from an approach based in criminal law as the model for enforcing anti-discrimination law.

[52] Particularly the HRC, the CESCR, the CERD and ECRI have the possibility to draw attention to broader issues, including structural discrimination, even where no individual victim comes forward, through the consideration of state reports. This is one mechanism through which these bodies can address discrimination and act as catalysts in the process of development of domestic protection. That said, these bodies' country analyses are bound to be somewhat superficial, as they seldom have the requisite evidence and time to address the pertinent problems in their full scope and depth. For instance Banton has made the observation that many states use the dialogue with the CERD as an opportunity to publicize the government's activities, and the situation is the same for the other bodies as well. See Michael Banton, *International action against racial discrimination* (Oxford: Clarendon Press, 1996), p. 114.

Within the EU, most of the above-mentioned positive developments find a solid legal basis in the Racial Equality Directive. The Directive, moreover, does not focus simply on equality of rights but on securing equal treatment in the various fields of everyday life.

Yet the reality is that both sets of law have major difficulties when it comes to tackling certain aspects of everyday discrimination, such as discrimination embedded in an organisational or occupational culture,[53] or subtle harassment that manifests for instance as avoidance or unfriendly verbal and nonverbal communication.[54] Discriminatory disadvantage that arises out of complex structural, systemic and institutional factors often also escapes legal attention because it cannot be attributed to the acts of one individual against another.[55] Both sets of law also fail in that they address discrimination, not so much its causes or effects. There is little or no understanding of the broader harm inflicted by discrimination upon the society, the economy, individual businesses and the indirect victims. The law does not require structural remedies such as positive action, or do so in too obscure a way for states to get the message.[56] The provisions in international human rights conventions that require awareness raising and other such preventive measures that are supposed to generate a positive change in attitudes are opaque, little enforced, and questionable in their practical impact. The conclusion is warranted that the law, as it stands, is not capable of breaking the vicious circle of discrimination, a conclusion that is clear also in view of the empirical findings that demonstrate the persistence of discrimination.

There is still some room for further doctrinal development with regard to tackling some of the issues identified above; yet other aspects call for further legislation. The past doctrinal developments have been

---

[53] This has been suggested by Bob Hepple in the context of the Macpherson report and institutional racism in the police forces. Bob Hepple, 'Race and Law in Fortress Europe' *Modern Law Review*, Vol 67, No 1, January 2004, p. 12.

[54] Indeed, subtle forms of discrimination are often not considered a 'practice' because such incidents are of a more abstract and general nature, subjectively experienced and not necessarily patterned. See e.g. Birgitta Lundström et al, *Yhdenvertaisuuslain toimivuus*, Työ- ja elinkeinoministeriön julkaisuja 11/2008, pp. 114, 126.

[55] Ucellari, *cit. supra* note 15, p. 37.

[56] A few states do, however, provide for structural remedies. Such remedies may for instance require an employer found to have engaged in discrimination to pursue a policy of positive action in order to obtain a more balanced workforce, or call an educational establishment to pursue a policy of desegregation. See Mark Bell et al, *Developing Anti-Discrimination Law in Europe: The 25 EU Member States compared* (Luxembourg: OOPEC, 2007), pp. 60–63.

gradual, by no means easy or self-evident, and based on international and/or domestic experiences and influences. That international anti-discrimination law has taken the course towards recognising other than discrimination motivated by racism and other forms of intolerance is not self-evident in view of the fact that it undoubtedly was the strong moral condemnation passed on racism and other forms of intentional discrimination that initially built the momentum for international action in this area. That courts and other bodies applying the law develop their interpretations and doctrines is business as usual for them and there is nothing inherently extraordinary or suspect about that. Yet there may become a point at which these bodies are subjected to criticism for engaging in judicial activism, a charge which may negatively affect the persuasiveness and impact of their decisions as well as the public image of these bodies. The first warning signs, indicating that we may be approaching this stage, whether right or wrong, have already appeared.[57]

8.2.3 *The Nexus between International and Domestic Anti-Discrimination Law*

International and European anti-discrimination law has played a major role in shaping domestic laws and policies across Europe. It is clear that international co-operation has prompted many states to take domestic action in this field that they would not have otherwise taken, although it is also clear that experiences from some countries (particularly the US and the UK) have influenced international and European law. It appears, perhaps somewhat non-intuitively, to be the case that foreign policy considerations have played a major, if not decisive part in bringing states to negotiate, adopt and ratify international conventions, declarations and plans of action with regard to non-discrimination, as a by-product of which they have had to make an effort to live up to the standards domestically. For instance the inclusion of reference to non-discrimination on the grounds of 'race' in the UN Charter and the UDHR had much to do with the aspiration to formally recognize the equality of nations in the 'inter-national' relations, as well as with the condemnation of Nazism and the aspiration

[57] See the dissenting opinions attached to ECtHR's decision in *D.H. and others* [GC], judgment of 13 November 2007.

to prevent similar ideologies from resurfacing.[58] The adoption of the ICERD, for its part, was a reaction to a series of anti-Semitic incidents taking place in certain parts of Europe and to Apartheid policy practiced by the then South African government.[59] Condemnation of far-right political parties, the Austrian Freedom Party in particular, figured strongly behind the adoption of the EU Racial Equality Directive. In addition to these specific impulses, international and regional action against racial and ethnic discrimination has most likely also been motivated by a broader aspiration (conscious or not) to reduce inter-state tensions that would occur if migrants, diplomats, tourists and other people with close ties to one country were systematically subjected to racism and discrimination in another country.[60] There has also been a tendency in international relations to take some interest in how countries (or some of them) treat their minorities more generally, visible for instance in the Minority Treaties, and this has also underlined the need for international action in this area.[61] In the EU in particular one of the underlying motives has undoubtedly been the need to ensure the smooth functioning of the common market, which would be disrupted if immigrant-receiving countries were allowed to take the opportunity to extract the labour resources of foreign workers for less by means of allowing unequal pay and unequal employment security. These transnational issues related to foreign, security and economic

[58] See e.g. Johannes Morsink, *The Universal Declaration of Human Rights: Origins, Drafting and Intent* (Philadelphia: University of Pennsylvania Press, 1999). The connection between racism and equality of states (and 'civilizations') is made for instance in the 1978 UNESCO Declaration on Race and Racial Prejudice, Article 3 of which condemns "[a]ny distinction, exclusion, restriction or preference based on race, colour, ethnic or national origin or religious intolerance motivated by racist considerations, which destroys or compromises the sovereign equality of States and the right of peoples to self-determination".

[59] Kevin Boyle–Anneliese Baldaccini, 'A Critical Evaluation of International Human Rights Approaches to Racism' in Sandra Fredman (ed.), *Discrimination and Human Rights* (Oxford: Oxford University Press, 2001), pp. 148–9.

[60] One of the preambular paragraphs of the ICERD stresses that the States Parties to the Convention reaffirm "that discrimination between human beings on the grounds of race, colour or ethnic origin is an obstacle to friendly and peaceful relations among nations and is capable of disturbing peace and security among peoples and the harmony of persons living side by side even within one and the same State."

[61] At the Paris Peace Conference, US president Woodrow Wilson said that "nothing is more likely to disturb the peace of the world than the treatment which might in some circumstances be meted out to minorities." Cited in Paul Gordon Lauren, *The Evolution of International Human Rights: Visions Seen* (Philadelphia: University of Pennsylvania Press, 1998), p. 95

policies, although not an exhaustive explanation for international co-operation in this area, are indeed of such a nature that they could not satisfactorily have been left to national solutions, and hence international action in this field has come about.[62]

Perhaps a bit paradoxically, the primary way by which states have been able to take action against racial and ethnic discrimination internationally has been by means of committing themselves, through adoption and implementation of international instruments, to take action domestically.[63] The impetus given by international action to domestic efforts is clear in view of the fact that many states had to adopt new legislation to give effect to their obligations under the ICERD, and that domestic anti-discrimination laws in the EU member states were brought to an entirely new level in the course of the transposition of the EU Directive into national laws, as only a few EU countries had anything like comprehensive anti-discrimination laws prior to the adoption of the Directive. The conclusion that the focus of action has been on perceived problems in countries other than one's own appears warranted also in view of the fact that many states have not been particularly forthcoming or progressive in taking domestic measures to combat discrimination even after becoming legally bound by international and European norms. This is clear from the country reports produced by the CERD and ECRI, which without exception criticise states for insufficient and/or inappropriate domestic action, as well as from the number of infringement proceedings initiated by the European Commission for the failure of some EU member states to take the requisite action to transpose the EU Racial Equality Directive.

That there has been this international interest in co-operation can be considered a strength for the fight against discrimination, in view of the fact that a domestic political system based on majoritarian decision-making is not necessarily a great defence for the interests of a minority. In a democracy based on majoritarian decision-making, a self-interested majority can easily walk over the interests of a minority

[62] Cf. Henkin, who argues that much, particularly of the early, standard-setting in the field of international humanitarian law had political-economic rather than humanitarian motivations. Louis Henkin, *International Law: Politics and Values* (Dordrecht: Martinus Nijhoff, 1995), p. 168.

[63] In a sense this partially follows also from Article 2(7) of the UN Charter, which excludes UN intervention into "matters which are within the domestic jurisdiction of any state", except in specific situations envisaged in chapter VII of the Charter.

unless effective constraints are in place.[64] Moreover, in most countries of the world only citizens are entitled to vote and to stand as candidates at national elections, which means that immigrants are automatically excluded from participation in the construction of the body politic to begin with. In consequence, protection against racial and ethnic discrimination is seldom high on the political agenda, as the majority does not need such protection. These considerations suggest that without international action and pressure, the level of protection against ethnic discrimination would quite likely be considerably weaker across the world today.

On the other hand, the fact that international and European law has in many countries driven the development of domestic law means that the domestic laws replicate its shortcomings too. Whereas the international and European anti-discrimination law is clear in that it defines only the minimum standards of achievement that states have to comply with, the reality is that instead of being the floor, it may have become the ceiling.[65] The number of infringement proceedings initiated by the European Commission for the failure to implement the EU Directive properly or at all, and the recurrent criticism directed by the CERD, HRC, ACFC, ECRI and other bodies at the contracting states for failure to live up to their obligations, indicates that states have not been particularly eager to implement even the minimum standards. This is not the whole picture though, as many countries have also gone beyond their minimum obligations in some respects.[66] But more important than that is that the established but in many respects obscure and insufficient standards laid down in international and European law may have inadvertently steered attention away from new, creative solutions or from other forms of inequalities than those now addressed.

8.2.4 *Indirect Effects: Reinforced Essentialism and Statism*

Legal remedies often have their undesired side-effects.[67] In fact, just like in the field of medicine, there may even be cases where the

---

[64] Such constraints could provide for, *inter alia*, effective participation of the target groups in all decision making that is of concern to them, or a secured Constitutional status.

[65] That this may often be the case with human rights was suggested by David Kennedy in *Dark Sides of Virtue: Reassessing International Humanitarianism* (Princeton University Press, 2004).

[66] Bell et al, *cit. supra* note 56.

[67] See generally on this Kennedy, *cit. supra* note 65.

cure is worse than the disease. There are two types of negative side-effects related to anti-discrimination law that in particular merit our attention.

First, anti-discrimination law and related discourse may inadvertently have come to reinforce prevailing essentialist conceptions of 'race' and ethnicity. The different instruments and the practice of their monitoring bodies reflect common-sense understandings of 'race' and 'ethnicity'. As the preceding analysis has revealed, these notions are used in a straightforward, unqualified and essentialist manner, meaning that these notions are by and large treated as if in reality there really were distinct 'races' and monolithic ethnic groups. This is most pronounced in the case of the ICERD and the work of its monitoring committee. The Convention itself refers in many places to the existence of separate races, and the Committee – instead of challenging this – 'confirms', *inter alia*, in its General Recommendation No. 24 that "the Convention relates to all persons who belong to different races".[68] The unqualified and straightforward use of such language in official contexts and in the legal vocabulary in particular undoubtedly contributes to, reinforces and legitimizes racial thinking (racialism), which as theorized in chapter 4, is a critical component of racism itself. The timid disclaimers found in some instruments,[69] stating that the use of these notions should not be taken as an acceptance of theories that attempt to determine the existence of separate races, are of little avail in offsetting the negative side-effects, as these disclaimers remain hidden underneath a pile of racial language and are seldom if ever brought to public attention. Whereas a degree of essentialism may for practical reasons be useful in the designing and implementation of for instance positive action schemes, there is absolutely no reason to use outright racialist language in any context. A peculiar tension currently exists between the universalist language and universalist aspirations of international human rights law and movement, and the overt use of inherently divisive racial language in the ICERD and other instruments. At the very least a distinction should be made between the existence of racial discrimination, and the existence of 'races'; whereas there are no

[68] CERD, General Recommendation No 24, para 1.

[69] Cf. recital 6 of the Racial Equality Directive. Also one of the 38 preambular paragraphs of the Durban Declaration states that the participating states strongly reject "any doctrine of racial superiority, along with theories which attempt to determine the existence of so-called distinct human races".

'races' as such, there is discrimination based on the assumed existence of 'races'. The two issues should be kept clearly separate.

Second, the fact that international and European conventions, declarations and action plans are designed, adopted and implemented by states or intergovernmental bodies reinforces and almost reifies the role of the state in combating discrimination. It creates a statist culture which emphasises the role of legislation, policy programmes and other centrally coordinated action, and sustains the utopia that governments can effectively prevent people from engaging in discrimination and thereby eliminate all forms of discrimination. Such statism may inadvertently or even openly discourage non-state action and broader mobilization and campaigning against discrimination – unless of course such action is backed up by the government of the day. This need not be the case, and indeed the range of instruments available to a government (legislation, policy programmes, and awareness raising campaigns) cannot and should not replace the more grass-roots oriented work best carried out by NGOs and independent equality bodies. Judging by the numbers, the anti-racist movement is strong in Europe: the European Network Against Racism, an EU-wide network of NGOs, has more than 700 active member organisations.[70] Yet the reality appears to be that NGOs are an under-resourced, undervalued and underused resource in the fight against discrimination, and therefore their capacity to complement state action is presently somewhat compromised.

8.2.5 *The Chief Mischief: Individual Litigation as the Chosen Model of Enforcement*

International and European law, including anti-discrimination law, poses few requirements when it comes to enforcement and remedies. This deliberate choice to "respect national procedural autonomy" effectively defeats the promise that states have made to eliminate discrimination in all its forms. Most international and European instruments

---

[70] http://www.enar-eu.org/ (accessed on 1.3.2011). There are also organisations other than NGOs that are active in this field. One particularly active organisation is the European Roma Rights Centre (ERRC), which is an international public interest law organisation that engages in a range of activities aimed at combating anti-Romani racism and the human rights abuse of Roma. The approach of the ERRC involves, in particular, strategic litigation, international advocacy, research and policy development, and training of Romani activists.

are content with the abstract requirement that there must exist an 'effective remedy', which is usually interpreted as requiring the existence of some kind of a procedural (and substantive) remedy, but not necessarily a judicial one. The ICERD and the EU Racial Equality Directive go a bit further, and explicitly require that victims of discrimination have access to a judicial or administrative mechanism.

One of the core characteristics of international and European anti-discrimination law is that it is conceptualized in terms of individual rights.[71] For there to be 'discrimination' there generally has to be an identifiable complainant who has suffered some legally provable disadvantage. That there may be more than one person who has been discriminated against in one and the same instance does not detract from this conclusion; the individual rights of all of them have been violated. The right to a remedy is an individual right as well: the law requires that mechanisms be available by which individuals can vindicate their rights when these have been violated. And it is indeed individuals who stand as respondents in courts and tribunals, although on occasion also corporations and other legal persons may be held responsible as well.

Is individual litigation an effective mechanism for the enforcement of anti-discrimination law? Does it help to prevent discrimination from taking place? Does it bring the people concerned and the society where they would be if there was no discrimination – or anywhere near there? The effectiveness of the individual litigation system has in recent years been improved in many ways. The EU Directive, and also the other pieces of law as interpreted by the monitoring bodies, requires states to remove many of the obstacles formerly associated with bringing legal action in cases of discrimination. Key aspects in this respect include lowering the burden of proof in other than criminal cases; the prohibition of victimization; the requirement of effective and proportionate sanctions; and the requirement that there must exist, nationally, a body for the promotion of equal treatment with a competence to provide independent assistance to victims of discrimination. Surely at least these advances have rendered the system effective?

These improvements notwithstanding, the answer to the questions posed above must be a resounding "no". Whatever the possible merits

[71] The discussion here is without prejudice to any domestic arrangements, such as class actions, which go beyond the minimum requirements of international and European law.

of the individual rights-based model in 'empowering the victims' (it might also be a source of stress) and in releasing pressures by at least providing for an opportunity to take legal action, the fact is that only a few individuals who consider themselves discriminated against ever take legal action. An EU-wide survey conducted among immigrant and minority groups found that, on average, only 18% of those who considered that they have been discriminated against had reported the matter to the competent authorities or at the place where it happened.[72] In some countries virtually no-one had done so.[73] The real numbers are likely to be even lower than that, because people are not necessarily aware of the fact that they have been discriminated against, given the oftentimes subtle or structural nature of contemporary discrimination.

All of this has a number of consequences. Discriminating employers and shopkeepers are basically assured that the likelihood of being brought to court are minimal, and the likelihood of being convicted is smaller still, as the complainant or the public prosecutor will seldom have evidence that will satisfy the courts. Comprehensive, fully reliable and up-to-date cross-European data on the success rates of discrimination claims in courts does not presently exist, but the evidence there is indeed strongly suggests that discrimination claims are seldom successful. The evidence gathered by the EU Fundamental Rights Agency shows that not a single discrimination case resulted in the award of compensation or in the imposition of a penalty in no less than 12 EU Member States during 2006–2007.[74] In 11 Member States there had been less than ten such cases. Of the remaining four countries only the UK had had a fairly significant number of successful cases.[75] Yet also in the UK only a fraction – in 2008/2009 some 3% to be more exact – of for instance employment-related 'race' discrimination claims were successful, as 38% resulted in a specific type of conciliated settlement, 28% were withdrawn, 17% were unsuccessful at a hearing, and

[72] European Union Agency for Fundamental Rights, *EU-MIDIS: European Union Minorities and Discrimination Survey: Main Results Report* (Vienna: FRA, 2009).

[73] Idem.

[74] These countries were the following: Czech Republic, Cyprus, Denmark, Lithuania, Germany, Luxembourg, Estonia, Poland, Greece, Portugal, Spain and Slovenia.

[75] European Union Agency for Fundamental Rights, *Annual Report 2008* (Budapest: Elanders Hungary Kft., 2008), pp. 17–21. See also European Union Agency for Fundamental Rights, Report on Racism and Xenophobia in the Member States of the EU (Budapest, Elanders Hungary Kft, 2007), pp. 20–22.

13% were either struck out before a hearing or dismissed at a preliminary hearing.[76] It therefore appears clear that claimants are seldom successful in discrimination cases when it comes to civil litigation. Data from the United States points to the same direction: almost half of the federal race discrimination cases are settled, in some 40% of the cases the plaintiffs have their cases dismissed or they lose on summary judgment, whereas only some 5% of the cases result in trial. In addition, plaintiffs prevail in less than one-third of those trials.[77]

The success rates are not necessarily much better when it comes to criminal law proceedings. Research evidence from Finland suggests that only one in four discrimination crimes reported to the police in the end lead to a 'guilty' verdict in the court.[78] From a European perspective, the chance that a discriminator faces legal sanctions would therefore appear to be less than 5%, considering that only 18% of the victims report their cases to begin with.[79] This figure is only indicative, but certainly suggests that businesses are in practice free to discriminate without much fear of legal sanction. For the same reasons the law is not just ineffective in preventing discrimination, it is also ineffective in redressing discrimination that has already taken place: no legal action, no redress. More fundamentally, even where a victim pursues a case and is successful, the redress is (usually) limited in scope in that it will be aimed at making good the harm suffered by the individual complainant, not at remedying the harm inflicted on other direct or indirect victims. Moreover, there is research that has found no sign of litigation having a major, let alone lasting impact on respondent

[76] Tribunals Service, *Employment Tribunal and EAT Statistics (GB) 1 April 2008 to 31 March 2009*. Available at: www.employmentribunals.gov.uk (accessed 1 June 2010).

[77] Laura Beth Nielsen et al, *Contesting Workplace Discrimination in Court: Characteristics and Outcomes of Federal Employment Discrimination Litigation 1987–2003* (Chicago: American Bar Foundation, 2008).

[78] A study that examined all cases of suspected crimes with racist characteristics that were reported to the police in Helsinki in 2006, found the following: in less than half of the cases the investigation was completed successfully and the case was sent to the prosecutor; the prosecutor took two out of three suspects to the court; and the court reached a 'guilty' verdict in less than half of the cases brought before it. The foremost reason why cases were not successful at the different stages of the judicial process was lack of evidence. See Laura Peutere, *Rasistisia piirteitä sisältävät rikosepäilyt rikosprosessissa* (Tampere: Poliisiammattikorkeakoulu, 2008).

[79] It is presupposed here, on the grounds of research evidence that suggests this, that people who report in surveys that they have been discriminated against do indeed have legitimate grounds for believing so.

employers, for instance.[80] Simple individual litigation as a model of enforcement therefore has its fundamental limits, because of which it fails to overcome the broader detrimental effects of discrimination and break the cycle of disadvantage.

There are a number of reasons that explain why people do not take legal action, some of these explanations being general in nature and some specific to the subject area at hand. Litigation is slow, expensive and stressful for the complainant. People who have experienced subtle types of everyday discrimination are often unlikely to be aware of that or feel confident enough about that, *and* have the requisite evidence, to go to the court. They might also feel insecure because they do not know the content of the law and the vagaries of judicial processes (particularly relevant in the case of immigrants[81]), they may lack institutional support (both legal and psychological), and there may be insufficient safeguards against retaliation.[82] There are also groups, such as *sans papiers* and trafficked persons, for whom legal remedies remain theoretical because coming forward would put them at the risk of deportation.

One must also take note of the fact that people are generally not very eager to go to the court. For example, figures from the 2008/2009 British Crime Survey (BCS) show than more than half (59%) of crimes were never reported to the police.[83] The likelihood of reporting crime varied considerably by the type of offence: thefts of vehicles were most

---

[80] Michael Selmi, 'The Price of Discrimination: The Nature of Class Action Employment Discrimination Litigation and its Effects' *Texas Law Review* Vol 81 (2003); Christopher McCrudden et al, 'Affirmative Action without Quotas in Northern Ireland' *The Equal Rights Review*, Vol. Four (2009).

[81] Indeed, it may well be the case that immigrants are, on the average, and because of linguistic and other barriers, less likely to file a claim on experienced discrimination than members of ethnic minorities. Consider the case of Finland, for example, where the number of Roma (a traditional minority) is thought to be around 10 000 and where the number of foreigners (foreign citizens) is around 132 600 (situation as of 1.1.2008). A comprehensive impact assessment study that reviewed the domestic anti-discrimination case law concluded that the *majority* of crime reports about discrimination in access to and provision of goods and services were submitted by persons of Roma origin, a fact that is in stark contrast with the relatively small size of the community. Whereas persons of Roma origin may be more likely than immigrants, on the average, to be discriminated against, this factor cannot plausibly explain the discrepancy in its entirety. Lundström et al, *cit. supra* note 54, p. 128.

[82] See e.g. Mark Bell, *Anti-Discrimination Law and the European Union* (Oxford: Oxford University Press, 2002), pp. 49–50.

[83] Alison Walker et al (eds.), *Crime in England and Wales 2008/09*, Home Office, July 2009, p. 25.

likely to be reported (89%), whereas reporting rates were lower for crimes such as assault without injury, theft from the person and vandalism (30%–35%).[84] The results of the BCS also indicate that victims were not inclined to report crimes that they considered to be a private matter, too trivial, or of such a nature that they believed that the police would do nothing about them.[85] All of the above factors may indeed explain the low volumes of legal action in the subject field at hand. This reinforces the conclusion that individual litigation is not a particularly effective mechanism for the enforcement of anti-discrimination law.

The emphasis on individual litigation as the model of enforcement of anti-discrimination law may well spring from the prevalent episodic understanding of discrimination. Enforcement through individual litigation might suffice if equality really was the rule and discrimination the exception, if racial discrimination was a curable anomaly within the otherwise healthy society, if it only were a few very unfortunate individuals who were discriminated against. But in a society permeated by everyday discrimination it cannot plausibly be expected that every time someone is harmed she or he will bring legal action. As mentioned, litigation takes time, energy and money, thus being a major burden. All this leads to the following question: is there not something fundamentally unfair about a system that puts the burden on the aggrieved individuals to take action to correct the wrongs done unto them? Should not the burden rest on the side that engages in discrimination?

Chapters 9–13 of this study present and analyze the strengths and weaknesses of a variety of approaches that go beyond the individual rights and individual litigation based approach to anti-discrimination law.

8.3 Conclusions: Of Camouflage and Loose Cannons in the Fight Against Discrimination

Activities in the subject area at hand are frequently referred to as "fight against discrimination", "combating discrimination" or "mobilization against discrimination".[86] The use of military metaphors gives the

---

[84] Idem.

[85] Idem; Sian Nicholas et al (eds.), *Crime in England and Wales 2006/2007*, Home Office, July 2007, p. 26.

[86] See e.g. the Durban declaration.

impression that decisive action and large-scale interventions and campaigns are underway and that these operations are based on carefully planned strategies and clear objectives. It appears to be only a matter of time when discrimination is defeated once and for all, and indeed promises to that end are made.

Prima facie, there indeed appears to be much action. There have been numerous dedicated decades, well-known and well-ratified conventions, detailed declarations and ambitious action plans. Important bodies have been set up for the purposes of monitoring the conduct and activities of states in this area. Different bodies and most of their individual members have undoubtedly done what they could to advance the good cause. A high number of individuals have fought the good fight in the roles of activists, lobbyists, legal counsellors, judges, prosecutors, scholars, advisers, campaigners, policy officers, teachers, artists and so on, and deserve our praise for that. Significant advances have been made, a high number of cases have been won, and the egalitarian agenda is more widely accepted today than probably ever before. There is no reason to belittle the impact or importance of any of that. Yet the strides made cannot overshadow the impression that something is still seriously wrong. Seen from the perspective of victims of discrimination, the protection offered by the law amounts to not much more than a camouflage. There are several reasons for this state of affairs.

The demands posed by international and European anti-discrimination law are intense. The law sets out structures which not so much dictate that one should not oppress strangers, but that one should treat strangers as brothers and sisters.[87] In view of the prevalence of discrimination in contemporary Europe and the wide variety of factors that explains it (racism, prejudices, stereotypes, unconscious motives) this is, frankly speaking, a demand of great intensity. The obligation to *eliminate* discrimination, imposed by states parties on themselves, is a demand of even greater intensity; as a matter of fact, it demands too much, as no state can possibly live up to it. In effect, progress towards the meeting of these demands does not come without a real fight and it is clear that any progress in tackling these challenges is bound to be incremental and slow to emerge.

---

[87] Damian Chalmers, 'The Mistakes of the Good European' in Sandra Fredman (ed.) *Discrimination and Human Rights* (Oxford: Oxford University Press, 2001), p. 194.

There is little evidence that governments have really grasped, or perhaps even wanted to grasp, how drastic measures they would have to take to keep the promise to eliminate discrimination. This is evident for instance in that they have been slow to adopt comprehensive and effective anti-discrimination laws. This state of affairs is at least partly the result of a mindset according to which racism and racial discrimination are exceptional phenomena that bedevil only a few unfortunate societies. The ICERD itself is greatly influenced by this mindset, stating as it does in its preamble that the states parties to the Convention are "[a]larmed by manifestations of racial discrimination *still* in evidence in *some* areas of the world".[88] This mindset has by no means disappeared. Thus, the majority of governments, sixteen out of thirty, that were invited to respond to an inquiry by a UN Special Rapporteur in 1994 – almost thirty years after the adoption of the ICERD – replied that racism, racial discrimination, xenophobia or related intolerance does not exist in their country.[89] No progress in elimination of any problem can be made if there is widespread denial about the existence of that problem.

There has also been a more general reluctance to confront some of the difficult but basic questions involved. Drafters of international and European documents have either been unwilling, or unable because of lack of general agreement, to really address what equality should be taken to mean and how it could be achieved. The existing legal regime is less the result of the gradual unfolding of some great vision, theory or a set of first principles, than a reaction to *particular* human catastrophes and a non-monolithic bundle of a number of theoretical, philosophical and political influences, economic interests, interstate compromises, legal models adopted from particular countries, and lately also interest group lobbying. Yet between the lines, the different documents set formal equality of opportunity, national unity and political liberalism as 'default positions'. There is, in a sense, a bias towards social order rather than social justice.

[88] Emphasis added. The UN Declaration on Elimination of All forms of Racial Discrimination contains a similar paragraph, in addition to which it proclaims that "although international action and efforts in a number of countries have made it possible to achieve progress in that field, discrimination based on race, colour or ethnic origin in certain areas of the world continues none the less to give cause for serious concern."

[89] Report on contemporary forms of racism, racial discrimination xenophobia and related intolerance prepared by the Special Rapporteur of the Commission on Human Rights, 23 November 1994, UN doc. A/49/677, paras. 40–45.

One of the key characteristics of the law is its open language and wide use of terms and principles such as 'objective justification' and 'proportionality'. Open language does not necessarily have to be suspect or a weakness; it does also provide opportunities. Yet the reality is that terms such as these leave those charged with interpreting and applying the law much room for manoeuvre, meaning also that various subjective – individual or social – values, beliefs and prejudices can come into play. Given the pervasive nature of prejudices and stereotypes, which are often not consciously held, this can be highly problematic. Open terms are loose cannons – sometimes hitting the mark, often missing it – in that they can be used to justify almost any subjective moral assessment: sometimes nothing is more subjective than what a person considers to be objective. International bodies and legal scholars aspire to contribute to the formation of a more systematic and coherent legal opinion, but the impact of these efforts is always limited. The reality is that judges and other persons and bodies charged with applying the law tend to prefer rigid rules instead of provisions couched in open language, because they do not have the time to read through the relevant analyses and materials, which moreover may not be applicable in the specific circumstances of the case and can be obscure, equivocal or inconsistent with some other part of the law. There is no doubt that an empirical inquiry into judicial practice, particularly the practice of courts of first instance, would in any jurisdiction reveal a stunning diversity of approaches and interpretations in questions of law (and also of interpretations of fact in comparable circumstances).[90] In consequence there is always the danger that the open terms used in law may backfire in practice and lead to disappointing results from the point of view of victims of discrimination.

The greatest single obstacle for making major advances in the fight against discrimination is the individualist orientation of the law and the consequent individualization of the fight. The battle is fought in single, usually relatively minor episodes that will not have broader impact. It is fought by a few isolated and aggrieved individuals who face major legal and de facto hurdles (building up a case, gathering

---

[90] To take the example of Finland again, specialized training courses and text books on anti-discrimination law are available for judges, prosecutors, legal counsels and other legal professionals. Yet, decisions rendered by courts and tribunals in these fields often surprise scholars and create controversy. The existence of the same phenomenon can be observed at the international level, as is clear for instance from the great number of scholarly critiques of the decisions of the ECJ in the field of gender equality and positive action in particular.

evidence, general personal deprivation) and who mostly lack sufficient institutional support. The massive mobilization suggested by the use of military language is simply not there. The fight is passive, reactive, backward-looking and defensive, not proactive or future or results oriented. The dissuasive effect of the law is poor,[91] and the law ignores the collateral damage inflicted on indirect victims of discrimination, the society at large and those direct victims who lack the means, will or awareness to pursue legal action.

The individualist orientation of the law comes with a high price, but is no surprise, as that law is embedded in a broader legal and social culture that takes individuals and individual rights as its exclusive rallying point. The individualist orientation may come at the expense of social action, collective remedies, and duties to promote equality. The language of individual rights possesses rhetorical force, but the danger is that the fundamentally important interests 'protected' by means of rights remain nothing but rhetorical for the individuals concerned. Rights, if actively relied upon, can be powerful weapons in one-to-one legal fights, but they will not help to win the broader war against contemporary forms of racism and discrimination. The existence of rights creates the impression, if not illusion, that all is well and problems are tackled, when in fact problems are rampant and little progress is made. This, it is suggested, might also more generally be a problem with human rights.[92]

Anti-discrimination law is caught in a Catch-22 situation. On the one hand, the blindness of the liberal paradigm to collective or group level problems prevents it from identifying the real problems and consequently, better responses to discrimination. On the other hand, group-based remedies and other measures are highly problematic, given that there are no uncontroversial answers to questions such as "which groups are entitled to particular remedies such as positive action?" and "on the basis of which criteria can we determine whether a person belongs to such a group?"[93] Racism and racial discrimination operate in an arbitrary manner and are based on a variety

---

[91] This appears clear given the empirical evidence on the prevalence of discrimination.

[92] The observation that rights are actually put to use only when they are evoked is not new. This state of affairs is, however, not always seen as a problem. See e.g. Jack Donnelly, *Universal Human Rights in Theory and Practice*, (2nd ed., Ithaca, N.Y.: Cornell University Press, 2003).

[93] See Timo Makkonen, *Identity, Difference and Otherness: The Concepts of 'People', 'Indigenous People' and 'Minority' in International Law*. Eric Castrén Institute Research

of unscientific and mutually contradictory racial beliefs and ways of categorization. Whereas the law should ideally remedy the harms inflicted, no conceivable law can replicate the unscientific and contradictory beliefs and ways of categorization that brought the harm in the first place. This fact alone results in a kind of imbalance which makes redress difficult. Moreover, also other kinds of categorization systems – even those that appear scientific – are problematic, as they can never be fully objective, and therefore risk increasing the levels of racial awareness and essentialism that in turn can reinforce discrimination and levels of racism. The solution, then, lies in strategies that take the collective aspects involved fully in account without falling victim to an essentialist approach to 'race' and ethnicity in hope that one could render these subjects 'governable': it is for the law to fit to the facts, not for the facts to fit to the law.

Any final verdict about the effectiveness of present anti-discrimination law in bringing about the desired social change must necessarily be mixed and cautious. On the one hand the law poses some intense demands; on the other hand, it is weak in enforcing those demands. These two viewpoints are, naturally, connected: one could not, up until now, have had anti-discrimination law that was both ambitious in its content and enforcement. Feminism and many other social movements have shown that positive social development is painstakingly slow to take place, especially where a change of attitudes and socially prevalent and culturally transmitted beliefs is called for. Any progress is therefore likely to be gradual, and the imposition of staunch enforcement measures at an early stage of the process could even have been counterproductive. Yet, the level of ambition should rise with the progress that is made, and the time has come to take the fight against discrimination to the next level.

It is difficult and perhaps unnecessary to assess whether the failure on part of the states to keep the promise to eliminate all forms of racial discrimination is due to ignorance, indifference or unfounded optimism. Quite likely all of these factor in. The ineffectiveness of the present legal response has in any case not escaped the attention of the main actors in the international human rights arenas. For instance one of the first preambular paragraphs of the 2001 Durban Declaration

Reports 7/2000 (Helsinki: University Press, 2000); Dwora Yanow, *Constructing "Race" and "Ethnicity" in America: Category-Making in Public Policy and Administration* (New York: M.E. Sharpe, 2003).

laments the fact that "despite the efforts of the international community, the principal objectives of the three Decades to Combat Racism and Racial Discrimination have not been attained and … countless human beings continue to the present day to be victims of racism, racial discrimination, xenophobia and related intolerance." But the response of the international community, socialized into international rights talk, has been to dedicate more decades and declarations for the individual rights based fight against discrimination, as the Durban Declaration and Programme of Action with its 341 articles so amply testifies to. But this course of action is flawed in that the problem is not so much quantitative as it is qualitative, and in that measures need to be taken nationally, not just internationally; there is a need to fundamentally rethink the response to discrimination. Within the EU area the adoption and national implementation of the Racial Equality Directive represents new openings, in that there are elements in the Directive that go some way in rendering the national legal protection against discrimination more effective. But it does not go long enough, because the problem is not just that of effectiveness. There is not just a gap between theory and practice; the theory itself is flawed in that it cannot achieve its stated purposes. In consequence, as things stand, any country that wishes to make further headway in combating racial and ethnic discrimination must necessarily go beyond the existing international and European requirements.

PART THREE

RETHINKING THE RESPONSE

9 RETHINKING THE RESPONSE

The previous chapters have identified and analyzed the problems with discrimination, the present international and European responses thereto, and the problem with these responses. The present legal response was found to be severely limited, and in consequence there is a need to rethink the response. The following chapters examine key legal and policy tools that can help to narrow down the gap between the promises and the practice.

Envisioning strategies for dealing with social problems is a tricky business. It is difficult to assess the scope and nature of complex social problems to the full, and to devise effective remedies. There is always also the risk of just bypassing these key stages of problem-solving by resorting simply or primarily to personal preferences, the influence of which can of course never be fully avoided anyway. Idealists think that everything should – and therefore can – be changed; conservatives think that nothing can – and therefore should – be changed. The kind of critical pragmatism advocated in this study would, on the other hand, suggest that we should be as clear as possible about what should be changed and what can be changed (as these are not always the same), and concentrate our efforts on the areas where these two overlap. Bearing this in mind, we can usefully rethink the response by engaging in a holistic analysis and by distinguishing – as in military and business parlance – between the objectives, strategies and tactics of the fight against discrimination. *Objectives* are fundamental and set out the desired outcomes, *strategies* are broad means for achieving the objectives, and *tactics* are more specific means for implementing and supporting the strategies. The following subchapters develop a framework of principles that provide guidance in the setting out of these aspects in the subsequent chapters, and perhaps also in the broader societal debate about the means and objectives of the law, this study being but one contribution to that debate.

9.1 Objectives

Equality through Rights or Politics – or Both?

There is a tendency in mainstream legal and political discourse not to put to question the objectives and means of law, particularly insofar as that law deals with matters that are perceived to belong to the realm of human rights. This is of course linked to the fact that disrespect of law and particularly of human rights has brought about intolerable suffering in the past. But even this should not overshadow the fact that these rights and the associated pieces of law are the result of political processes, inter-state compromises reached by what after all is a small number of state representatives, and particular political, philosophical and religious projects. The meaning of the concept of 'equality' is contested, and the way the law defines it, privileges some conceptions of it to the detriment of others.

The previous chapters have examined the nature and objectives of the present anti-discrimination law. The main thrust of international and European anti-discrimination law was found to be on equality of rights and on market equality. That law does touch upon other possible dimensions of equality, such as material, political and cultural equality, but only somewhat lightly and vaguely. It would certainly not be unfair – at least from some vantage points – to conclude that the present international anti-discrimination law has not realised its full potential, as it allows injustices of recognition, distribution, and representation by not really engaging those themes as it could.

Not only is the content – to the extent that we can speak of it in such essentialist terms – of the law socially and politically constructed, but so is its judicial and scholarly interpretation, including the terms in which those interpretations are framed, in our case 'race', 'disadvantage', 'merit' and so on. What this means is that the law is formulated and interpreted in *this* way although it could also be formulated and interpreted in *that* way, and that there is a structural bias in that only some people and thereby some interests have been and are engaged in these processes.[1] It should be acknowledged that laws, institutions and other major social arrangements are the end result of a competition of different socio-political interests and usually reflect the prevailing distribution of power, and that the competition continues after this in the struggles about the interpretations of law and the operations of institutions.[2] In particular and most importantly, it appears that the people most directly affected by the different forms of exclusion, that is

[1] On the concept of structural bias, see Martti Koskenniemi, *From Apology to Utopia: the structure of international legal argument* (Cambridge: Cambridge University Press, 2005, reissue with new epilogue).

[2] Idem.

immigrants and persons belonging to minorities, are by and large excluded also from the legislative and judicial processes in which their very exclusion is addressed.

If it is accepted that the practical implications of equality cannot simply be deduced from some universal principles, then that concept must be opened up for a society-wide and -deep dialogue. That dialogue should, as a matter of principle, be open, inclusive and permitting maximum contestation. That said, it should be recognized that – again with a necessary degree of generalization – states, and the powerful economic, political and other elites behind them, have until now dominated the discussions. It is now time for the 'international community' and each state to pay attention to those whose voices and interests have hitherto been excluded.[3] What is needed is a more inclusive, reflective and transparent notion of equality and justice.

It is not to be expected that the previously silenced will speak with one voice, and even less that their points of view would not often clash with those of 'the establishment'. But conflict is desirable, because it forces us to deliberate more deeply about the moral and political choices involved. Some may find it difficult or undesirable to criticize the present arrangements, the present legal instruments and institutions upholding them, for they are – often with good justification – perceived to do good, to be on the right side. Yet, these instruments and institutions cannot be elevated above criticism, for they might well be made to do a better job. Indeed, there is a need to keep the existing arrangements under review at all times, because all progress stops the very second people are satisfied with the existing achievements. The lack of constructive criticism also leaves the deliberative arenas to those who criticise the existing arrangements for all the wrong, say purely racist, reasons.

Acknowledging the social and political constructedness of law, also that dealing with fundamental rights, and of the *de facto* diversity and pluralism of values, again also in matters of fundamental rights, emphasizes the fundamental role of the political sphere (in *sensu lato*) as the arena for settling these issues.[4] Yet, the matter is not that

---

[3] See e.g. Anne Phillips, 'Multiculturalism, Universalism and the Claims of Democracy', in M. Molyneux and S. Razavi (eds.) *Gender Justice, Development and Rights* (Oxford: OUP, 2002).

[4] See also Andrea Baumeister, *Liberalism and the 'Politics of Difference'* (Edinburgh: Edinburgh University Press, 2000).

straightforward. To begin with, we should not naively assume that the controversies will be resolved through open confrontation in the context of political deliberation, and that the process somewhat miraculously leads to a rationally motivated consensus either through the prevailing of 'the best argument' or through a negotiated compromise that can be generally accepted. The criterion of consensus is unrealistically demanding; people do not rely only upon reason but also their biases, and there are power differentials in consequence of which bargaining positions are not by any means equal. It is simple mathematics that majorities enjoy a privileged position in a representative democracy, whereas minorities can be out-numbered and out-voted. And inasmuch as majorities are not free from biases, prejudices and negative stereotypes, as we have reason to believe, then the outcomes of democratic processes cannot be presumed to be without bias either. The many examples of ethnic persecution in – at least nominally – democratic societies is all the reason that is needed for putting in place strict, enforceable and ultimately 'non-negotiable' legal safeguards for persons belonging to minorities. There are perhaps no fully satisfactory solutions for resolving the dilemma between democratic policymaking and rights that protect minorities by 'trumping' the possible damaging outcomes of such policymaking,[5] but these considerations would seem to support constitutional democratic systems where there are legal guarantees for minorities and an opportunity to adjust those guarantees through inclusive democratic deliberative processes.[6]

Objectives of Equality Law for the Purposes of the Present Discussion

Whereas there is thus a need for a deeper and broader debate about the meaning of 'equality', it is not desirable or even possible to try to pre-empt that discussion by anticipating the outcomes of that debate for the purposes of the present study. In consequence, the rest of the chapters focus upon how the objectives outlined in the now prevailing international and European anti-discrimination law can best be met. In effect, the rest of the study examines possible answers to the question

---

[5] For the theory of rights as trumps, see Ronald Dworkin, *Taking Rights Seriously* (London: Duckworth, 1978).

[6] At the time of the writing many European countries, including United Kingdom, are reviewing their equality policies and laws, and particularly the objectives thereof, through broad consultative processes. See e.g. Equalities review, *Fairness and Freedom: The Final Report of the Equalities Review* (Crown, 2007).

"what should be done to achieve the kind of social change anticipated by the contemporary anti-discrimination law?"

9.2 Strategies

Methodological Notes

The following chapters present four broad categories of measures that are geared towards helping to close the gap between the rhetoric of the law and the reality on the ground. These measures are subjected to a strict scrutiny so as to assess their potential effectiveness and the circumstances in which they can be presumed to work. Too often these or some other measures are optimistically and even naively presented as off-the-shelf panacea sure to deliver, without any consideration of the challenges that they bring or the negative side-effects that they have. The presentation of this or that solution as a cure-all to discrimination creates high but false expectations, and may bar the further development of more effective tools to fight discrimination. Equally often these solutions are dismissed on the grounds of (supposed or real) incompatibility with some political vision, or as too costly, without any real consideration of the viability or benefits of the action in practice. There is therefore a need to steer clear of any such abstracted approaches.

Methodically, the following analysis combines theoretical considerations with empirical research and experiences from different countries where available. The approach is multidisciplinary, as singular approaches are inherently insufficient for capturing and analysing the subject areas at hand. This study does not claim to present conclusions that are certain to work everywhere and every time. Societies are not the same, and no society is a machine, the problems of which can be identified and fixed by means of some socio-technical engineering. Often it will be true that even with the best application of tools of multidisciplinary analysis and research, it is not possible to project all the foreseeable consequences of a far-reaching and complex policy or legal tool, and at the end of the day any policy advice and policy decisions rest in part on hunch and guesswork.[7] Yet, our advice and decisions can only be as good as is the information that they are based

[7] See e.g. Robert K. Fullinwider, *The Reverse Discrimination Controversy* (New Jersey: Rowman and Littlefield, 1981), p. 19.

on, meaning that it is necessary to make full use of all relevant experience and research, and in the future to review existing policies whenever new evidence comes up.

No Mechanical Legal or Policy Transplantation

The roots of the European legal and policy response to racial and ethnic discrimination can to a large extent be traced to the United States. But Europe, as heterogeneous as it is, is demographically, politically and historically different from the US. For Europe – with a highly necessary degree of generalization – the problem is not a binary Black and White problem of major socio-economic differences that are to a significant extent due to history of slavery and other forms of 'white supremacy' and economic exploitation, but a more theoretically complex situation of high number of heterogeneous 'old' minorities and 'new' immigrant groups living within what are still perceived as nation states, with many of these groups doing worse economically than the ethnic majorities but some doing better than them. Furthermore, for many individuals and groups living in Europe, 'equality' is not just about equal opportunities and inclusion but also about appreciation and respect for the diversity of cultures, languages and religions, in contrast to the 'melting pot' ideology prevailing in the US.

The latter aspect is relevant, because the nationalist idea-forces operating in Europe, building on Europe's nation-statist traditions, oppose the recognition of ethnic, cultural and religious diversity. As an empirical fact, nation states are largely a thing of the past, but they still exist as political ideals that have a hold of public imagination and many societal institutions. Minorities and immigrants, with their own traditions and cultures, fit badly into that picture. The upholding of strong social identity-based boundaries between 'us' and 'them', is one of the barriers that inhibit 'them' from being fully included in the society supposedly consisting just of 'us'.

Insofar as social identities are part of the problem, they must also be part of the answer. A consistent theme in much social-psychological writing on prejudices, for instance in the seminal works of John Duckitt and Rupert Brown, is that our policies should attempt to minimize the destructive potential of category divisions by decreasing the salience of those divisions.[8] This does not mean that, for instance, national

[8] John Duckitt, *The Social Psychology of Prejudice* (London: Greenwood, 1994), p. 260; Rupert Brown, *Prejudice – Its Social Psychology* (Oxford: Blackwell, 1995), p. 269.

identities should be rendered empty of meaning or somehow culturally neutral. Rather, it could for instance mean updating that identity by means of discarding the myths of a single, overriding and essential ethno-national identity, narrative and future. A national identity, a kind of 'super-identity', may be formed around common citizenship, inclusive civic participation, common economic interests, and the recognition of a range of ethnically or otherwise more specific 'supraidentities'. Indeed, both Brown and Duckitt hold that it is not just possible but also necessary both to recognize cultural and ethnic diversity and the associated group dynamics, and to work towards decreasing the salience of group boundaries by means of fostering an overarching, common civic identity.[9] Also the fact that we all have multiple identities (based on gender, age, religion, profession, hobbies and so on) should be recognized: research evidence suggests that the recognition of multiple group memberships and of crisscrossing loyalties is a key factor in having good intergroup relations.[10] In consequence, whatever measures are taken to combat discrimination, they should be based on, or at least be compatible with, the recognition of deep cultural and social diversity, but steer clear of divisive identity politics. The American 'melting pot' cultural policy, which is also reflected in the theoretical premises of its anti-discrimination law tradition, should not as such be imported to Europe.

A certain necessary break with the American model of anti-discrimination law and policy arises also from the fact that most of the Europe is not as 'racially aware' as is the US. For many in Europe, their 'racial identity' is not their primary social identity, and even talk of 'races' is found repulsive in some societies. This has the consequence that strategies that require a high level of racial awareness to be operational, in particular those that involve the collection of personal racial data, may not be viable for most parts of Europe. Europe should therefore rethink anti-discrimination law and policy with fresh,

[9] Idem. This also calls for facilitation of cross-cultural adaptation, which in this context refers to encounters with different people, different norms, different standards, and different customs. What sustains individuals in this process is a willingness to open oneself up to new cultural influences, a willingness to face obstacles head-on by the use of instrumental strategies, and a resolve not to run away. These motivations require time and peer support for their sustained deployment. Peter B. Smith–Michael Harris Bond, *Social Psychology Across Cultures* (Essex: Pearson Education Limited, 1998), pp. 269–270.

[10] Brown, *cit. supra* note 8, p. 78.

unprejudiced eyes, and perhaps decide what the best course of action is by learning from others and then forgetting about it.

The Proper Role of Anti-Discrimination Law

Any legal-political strategic planning should involve the consideration of the proper role of the law in achieving policy ends. One starting point is that laws are often imperfect means for achieving social policy goals such as equality in its different dimensions.[11] Ample evidence comes from the field of gender discrimination: the principle of equal pay has been part of the international and EU law since the 1950s, but there still isn't a single country in the EU where women's wages are equal to those of men.[12] It has also been observed that anti-discrimination law has grown in complexity to such a degree that the enforcement of legal obligations has become somewhat impractical.[13] Disappointment with the capacity of the law to induce social change has led policy makers, particularly at the EU level, to look for new forms of governance, based not on command and control but on facilitating and encouraging change through less hierarchical and coercive mechanisms. Some characteristics of this approach include guidance by information – that is by means of identification and spreading of 'best practices' through research, benchmarking, validation and peer learning – and inclusive participation by all the stakeholders concerned in the formulation of the ends and means of a policy.[14] Some mechanisms, including data collection and mainstreaming, that are linked with these approaches will be discussed in the following chapters. Yet, as that discussion shows, also these mechanisms are of limited efficiency in affecting social change. This means, among other things, that the role of 'hard', enforceable law should not be forgotten.[15]

[11] See e.g. Roger Cotterrell, *The Sociology of Law*, 2nd ed. (London: Butterworths, 1992), p. 44 ff.

[12] Commission of the European Communities, Report from the Commission to the Council, the European Parliament, the European Economic and Social Committee and the Committee of the Regions on equality between women and men 2006. Brussels 22.2.2006, COM(2006) 71 final.

[13] Dagmar Schiek, 'From European Union non-discrimination law towards multidimensional equality law for Europe' in Dagmar Schiek – Victoria Chege (eds.), *European Union Non-Discrimination Law: Comparative perspectives on multidimensional equality law* (Oxon: Routledge-Cavendish, 2009), p. 11.

[14] See e.g. Tanja A. Börzel et al, *Conceptualizing New Modes of Governance in EU Enlargement* (Free University of Berlin, 7 February 2005).

[15] See also Kevät Nousiainen, 'Utility based equality and disparate diversities – from a Finnish perspective' in Schiek – Chege (eds.), *cit supra* note 13.

Indeed, it appears that the pursuance of a dual-track approach, based on the utilization of both legal and policy tools, is the most viable way to combat discrimination.

When considering the role of law, one should keep in mind that some of the objectives that *anti-discrimination* law is hoped to achieve, say material equality and cultural equality, may perhaps better be met by social protection laws and/or laws providing for cultural and religious rights. And at all times one should keep in mind that the law can be used not just to prohibit and punish, but to allow, encourage and/or to facilitate. This is an all the more relevant consideration in the field of combating discrimination, given that much of discrimination does not arise from a 'guilty mind' but from unconsciously activated stereotypes and unreflective application of established organisational practices.

Problem-Centred Approach

Discrimination is not, as the preceding chapters have hopefully made clear, a problem; it is a whole bunch of problems. Any response to it that purports to be effective must acknowledge the full range of inequalities and their causes and effects. The response must therefore address subtle and unsubtle forms of discrimination, and individual, structural and institutional discrimination. It must recognize the collateral damage inflicted by discrimination on its indirect targets, including the victims' families, individuals from the same group, businesses, and the society at large. It must recognize that it is not just racism and prejudices that explains discrimination, but unconscious stereotypes, opportunistic cost/benefit calculations, (often discreetly) biased organisational cultures, and unequal social structures and realities. It must also be based upon the recognition that there is nothing on the basis of which we can expect prejudices, stereotypes, racism and discrimination to disappear all of a sudden, or to expect that victims of discrimination suddenly start to take their cases to the courts in high numbers. In part this means that we must start to think about how to *redistribute the costs* arising from discrimination. The response must also be based upon the recognition that discrimination is highly pervasive in contemporary societies and is part of the daily social reality and the mainstream society, not a matter of seldom-occurring episodes taking place at the fringes of the society or in some distant unfortunate countries. In short, action against discrimination must be brought from the fringes to the mainstream.

A Focus on Behaviour and Attitudes

Anti-discrimination policy is currently almost exclusively oriented on the idea that it is possible to affect a change in people's behaviour but that it is not possible to affect a change in people's attitudes.[16] This idea, which fits squarely into the framework of mainstream liberal political philosophy and therefore resonates well among large audiences, is unsatisfactory in two respects.

First, as we have seen time and again, the means – primarily legal means – that European countries have used for affecting a sea change in behaviour have not worked. There may be fewer acts of discrimination today in Europe than there were twenty-thirty years ago – we do not have the statistical data to know this for a fact – but what we do know is that discrimination is a widespread and serious problem today.[17] While there is both room and reason for increasing the efficiency of anti-discrimination legislation and its enforcement, it would quite likely take extraordinary enforcement mechanisms coupled with unduly harsh sanctions for the individual litigation –based approach to really affect a profound change in our societies. This is not at the radar at the moment, nor should it be.

Second, the idea that it is not possible, or at any rate desirable, to try to affect a change in people's attitudes is too cautious, to say the least. To say this is not to suggest any kind of direct influencing of individual people's attitudes. Quite vice versa, top-to-bottom awareness raising and sensitising campaigns using leaflets, advertisements and diversity training schemes may be counter-productive, for instance because many people may find such direct attempts at changing attitudes repulsive.[18] Information-based campaigns risk only reinforcing the faith of the already converted, as people are selective in that they tend not to be

---

[16] That law cannot, partly for reasons of burden of proof, attempt to control attitudes and beliefs but only observable behaviour, was influentially argued by Roscoe Pound in his seminal article 'The limits of effective legal action' 27 *Int'l J. Ethics* 150 (1917).

[17] The evidence that there is about progress made in combating racial and ethnic discrimination is neither comprehensive nor particularly reassuring. With regard to the latter aspect, evidence from the UK, a country that has been rather active in fighting discrimination, shows that ethnic minorities were 17.9% less likely to find work than those belonging to the ethnic majority in 1997, whereas some ten years later the gap was still 15.5%. British Government Equalities Office, *Framework for a Fairer Future – The Equality Bill* (The Stationary Office, June 2008).

[18] There is, indeed, empirical evidence that suggests that for instance diversity training schemes may have, if anything, counterproductive effects. Alexandra Kalev – Frank Dobbin – Erin Kelly, 'Best Practices or Best Guesses? Assessing the Efficacy of Corporate Affirmative Action and Diversity Policies' *American Sociological Review*, August 2006, Vol. 71, pp. 589–617.

receptive to information that does not fit into their existing world view. Instead, we should recognize that the way the society and social relations are organized affects people's perceptions, values and behaviour, inevitably, in good and bad, irrespective of whether we want it or not or are even aware of it. Negative stereotypes and prejudices are socially constructed and culturally transmitted, and an enormous amount of social psychological literature and research has shown how to reduce intergroup biases and tensions through affecting a change in those *social structures* and other factors that play a central part in the creation and maintenance of those biases. The two most important means in this respect, as discussed in this study, are the reduction of intergroup distance and the reduction of intergroup differences in material wellbeing. Not to realise this is not just to miss an opportunity to work towards equality but to be complicit in the maintenance of inequality.

9.3 Tactics

By far the most important, though not exclusive, tactical move that those promoting equality can make is to engage, head-on, in all debates that have a bearing on equality, whether of a political, judicial, scholarly or popular nature. Conversely, the worst mistake one can make is to remain passive, particularly considering that the hundreds of European human rights groups and associations representing minorities seldom enjoy the kind of powerful position that ensures that their voice is really heard by the right audiences unless these groups use every opportunity to speak out loud. In contrast, there are other stakeholders, such as the social partners, that do wield considerable political power and that can ensure that their intended audience is listening whenever they speak, but who have interests that do not always coincide with those of the immigrant and minority groups.

The proactive equality measures discussed in the rest of the book are resource-intensive. It cannot be presumed that states are willing to invest in them to the extent that it would take to achieve major social change towards a more equal society, unless policy makers begin to demonstrate real leadership. For them to do that, it is up to those who are discriminated against to demand such leadership.[19] At any rate it is

[19] Paul Lappalainen, 'Stimulating leadership to promote positive action' in European Commission, *Putting Equality to Practice: What role for positive action?* (Luxemburg: OOPEC, 2007).

highly likely that the different stakeholders with an interest in promoting equality – ranging from NGOs to equality bodies to government departments in charge of equality issues – will have to continue to struggle with limited resources. There is constant pressure for minimizing public expenditure, and the cause of combating ethnic discrimination is just one of the infinite number (or so it seems) of 'good causes' that compete for public funding. Accordingly, the stakeholders concerned must think hard about how to deploy the resources they have, and must be clever in assessing what is possible in given political and social circumstances so as not to waste scarce resources available on endeavours that will not pay off.[20]

Yet it should not be hard to make the case for substantial increases of funding. If there is a consensus that discrimination is a social problem, a matter of justice, then what follows is that the fight against discrimination cannot be reduced into something that its victims have sole responsibility for. As our analyses have revealed time and again, discrimination is not the kind of an interpersonal dispute that the present anti-discrimination law would have us to believe. Rather, it is a matter for the society, something that public resources should be devoted for. Any other approach to this issue simply aggravates the injustice of the perverse economics of discrimination, where the costs of adverse treatment are borne by its direct and indirect victims, not by the perpetrators. In short, the principle should be 'the discriminator pays', not 'discrimination pays'.

9.4 Conclusions

There is a need to affect a paradigm shift from static *non*-discrimination policies to more proactively attuned *anti*-discrimination policies, and beyond that, to positively attuned *policies for the promotion of equality*. Presently dominating strategies, such as providing the direct victims the opportunity to bring legal action does not prevent discrimination from taking place, and cannot remedy it, given the low rates of legal action. Proactive deployment of a broad spectrum of preventive and remedial measures is therefore called for.

[20] Colm O'Cinneide, 'The Racial Equality Directive as a Basis for Strategic Enforcement' in Janet Cormack (ed.) *Strategic Enforcement and EC Equal Treatment Directives* (Migration Policy Group, 2004), p. 52.

Whatever policies are adopted and whatever measures are taken, they must respond to the real problems on the ground. On this basis it is necessary to build to a knowledge base on discrimination. The response itself must be as multifaceted as is the problem, and must be directly targeted at the particular problems: for instance, negative stereotypes and collateral damage should be addressed by means of positive action and redistributive measures; subtle, structural and institutional forms of discrimination should be made visible by means of research and investigations, and remedied by means of placing pro-active duties on organisations to identify these problems and to make the necessary adjustments; and opportunism based on cost/benefit calculations should be discouraged by increasing the likelihood and intensity of costs of discrimination.

Taken together, these viewpoints support the conclusion that it will be necessary to incite action on a broad front and with a long time-span, and to mobilize a comprehensive range of strategies: the many dimensions of inequality have built up over a long period of time, and will take a long time to bring down. As Christopher McCrudden has put it, a "wise policy maker, therefore, will not want to put all her eggs in one basket, and will want instead to keep a range of tools available with which to attempt to achieve the desired changes in behaviour."[21] It is also crucial to recognize that the forms of inequality and discrimination will not stay the same permanently but will change, which means that also measures that are aimed at countering them must change accordingly: our policies must be reflexive at all times.

These conclusions are, at this time and age, already rather widely shared. The 2008 Declaration of Principles on Equality, which was developed for the purposes of "modernising and integrating legal standards related to the protection against discrimination", comes as close to achieving a consensus among the experts in this field as it is possible to get, as it was developed and signed by 128 prominent human rights experts and advocates from 44 countries. Similarly with the conclusions of this study, the Declaration calls for action on a broad front and underlines that "the right to equality requires positive action", that states should "[p]romote equality in all relevant

---

[21] Christopher McCrudden, *Buying Social Justice: Equality, Government Procurement, & Legal Change* (Oxford: OUP, 2007), p. 128.

policies and programmes", and that "States must collect and publicise information, including relevant statistical data" to uncover and remedy inequalities.[22]

There is therefore a need to examine in more detail the modalities by which the proactive initiatives identified above can be implemented. This is done in the following chapters.

[22] Declaration of Principles of Equality, principles 3, 11 and 24 in particular. The Declaration is available at the website of the Equal Rights Trust, www.equalrightstrust.org (visited 1.1.2010).

10 COLLECTION OF EQUALITY DATA

Evidence suggests that each year millions, quite possibly tens of millions people living in Europe experience discrimination on the basis of their racial or ethnic origin.[1] Yet most of this discrimination remains invisible, under the radar. In consequence of this we have difficulties with assessing the nature, prevalence, causes and consequences of discrimination and designing countermeasures. At the same time, anti-discrimination law has widened its focus from an emphasis on individual prejudice to one which addresses also organizational and societal patterns and practices. Group outcomes are emphasised, both in order to diagnose discrimination, and to discover whether remedial measures have been effective. This in turn makes it important to have access to statistical data and to be in a position to utilize that data in a way that is relevant for fighting discrimination and promoting equal treatment. In short, there is a need to collect and utilize so-called 'equality data'.

The notion of equality data is used in this study in reference to any piece of information that is useful for the purposes of analyzing the state of equality. The information may be quantitative or qualitative in nature. The main focus is on equality statistics, by which are meant aggregate data that reflect inequalities, their causes or effects in the society. All EU countries have taken some measures in order to produce equality data in relation to ethnicity, but only a few countries have developed anything like a systematic or institutionalized framework for doing this.[2] The existing data tends to be good as far as it goes, but it just does not go very far.[3] This state of affairs can be contrasted with

---

[1] This conclusion appears warranted, considering that immigrants and members of national minorities number possibly around 140 million in Europe and that in the MIDIS-survey conducted by the FRA some 30% of the respondents reported that they had been discriminated against on the grounds of their ethnic origin in the course of the last 12 months.

[2] Lack of data collection on ethnic discrimination was clearly demonstrated in the course of the work carried out by the now defunct European Monitoring Centre on Racism and Xenophobia (EUMC). See e.g. EUMC, *Racism and Xenophobia in the EU Member States – trends, developments and good practice. Annual Report 2005 – Part 2* (EUMC, 2005).

[3] Timo Makkonen, *European Handbook on Equality Data* (Luxembourg: OOPEC, 2007).

the widespread collection and use of equality data in the field of gender equality, where it is already widely accepted that commitment to equality requires measuring of progress made towards achieving it.

Some methods of producing equality data involve the collection and other processing of ethnic data. The idea of collecting such sensitive data raises many concerns and fears. This is because the data are, by themselves, capable of being used for both legitimate and illegitimate purposes, as experiences with past misuses show. Because of this some people are of the view that ethnic data should not be collected, not even for the purposes of combating discrimination. It is also widely believed that collection of sensitive data is prohibited by international, EU and/or national laws relating to the protection of personal data. The following discussion will therefore discuss these matters and make a distinction between those data collection methods that involve the collection of ethnic data, and those that do not.

10.1 The Policy Case

A survey conducted by the European Commission in 2004 found that 93 % of the respondents, most of whom were experts in the field of anti-discrimination, were of the view that data collection was 'important' or 'very important' to the development of effective policies to promote equality and tackle discrimination.[4] Also governments have on several occasions recognised the need to compile equality statistics.[5] This widespread recognition of the need for data collection reflects the many and absolutely vital roles that statistical data can play in this context, as outlined below.

Evidence-Based Policy Development and Implementation

Data can be highly useful for the purposes of policy development and implementation both at the national and European levels. Decisions can only be as good as the information on which they are based, which means that decision-makers need to have access to a rich knowledge-base in order to arrive at the right decisions. It will be hard to arrive at

[4] European Commission, *Response statistics for Green paper on anti-discrimination and equal treatment*. Available at: http://ec.europa.eu. It is however not clear what kind of data collection the respondents had in mind.

[5] See for instance the Durban Declaration and Plan of Action and the Vienna Declaration and Programme of Action of 12 July 1993, A/CONF.157/23.

the right decisions if they have to be made in the dark or be arrived at through trial and error. Making the right analyses and decisions right at the start helps to better secure equal opportunities of the individuals and groups concerned, being cost-effective in addition. Equality considerations are relevant for all policy areas, including employment, education, health care and provision of services and goods. Data is indispensable for identifying and overcoming inequalities in these fields of life, and can help to identify the best course of action to take, although they cannot *an sich* guarantee the quality of actions. In any case, research and statistics on the extent and nature of discrimination are the key to overcoming the common 'no problem here' attitude, and to provide an explanation for the public for the need to take more effective anti-discrimination measures.[6] The integral role played by

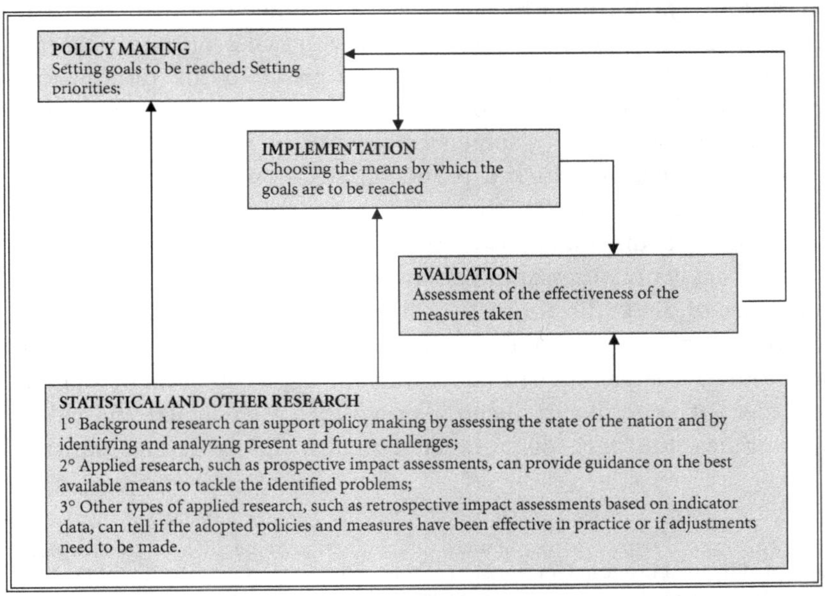

Figure 2. *The role of data in evidence-based decision-making*

[6] The 'no problem here' attitude has been documented e.g. by Wrench, see John Wrench, 'Combating Employment Discrimination in Europe: National Variation and the Dawn of 'Good Practice" in Erna Appelt –Monica Jarosch (eds.) *Combating Racial Discrimination: Affirmative Action as a Model for Europe* (Oxford: Berg, 2000), p. 275.

research in the formation of European and national anti-discrimination laws and policies in different countries is well documented.[7]

Ideally, in a knowledge-based society, information emanating from statistical and other research feeds into every stage of the decision-making process.

Judicial Decision-Making

Statistical data is sometimes a *conditio qua sine non* for the judicial assessment of whether discrimination has taken place. To the extent that modern forms of discrimination are subtle and covert, they are also less easy to prove. Direct evidence of discrimination is rare, and where such evidence exists, corroboration is even rarer.[8] Problems of evidence are present in both criminal and civil proceedings, and although shifting the burden of proof in civil cases, brought about by the EU Directive, eases that burden somewhat, complainants still have to establish "*facts* from which it may be presumed that there has been direct or indirect discrimination" in order to make a *prima facie* case resulting in the shift of the burden of proof to the respondent.[9] Empirical evidence can help to build such a case, either by demonstrating the adverse nature of some treatment or by forming the broader background against which a particular decision or practice can be assessed. In any event, statistics typically constitute circumstantial, as opposed to documentary, evidence.[10]

It is usually not necessary to provide statistical data to make a *prima facie* case of direct discrimination. This is because it should suffice to show that only one individual has been treated unfairly in comparison to another, whereas statistics deal with the aggregate level of analysis and do not as such conclusively prove that a particular individual has, or has not, been discriminated against. In particular, statistics

---

[7] Existence of more evidence of racial discrimination in the different spheres of life was cited by the European Commission as one of the reasons why the Racial Equality Directive went further than the Framework Employment Directive in terms of material scope of application. See Communication COM [19999] 564 of 25 November 1999, and Jan Niessen, 'The Starting Line and the promotion of EU anti-discrimination legislation: The role of policy-oriented research' *Journal of International Migration and Integration* Vol. 1, No 4, December 2000.

[8] Fitsum Alemu, *Testing to prove racial discrimination: methodology and application in Hungary*. An internet article available at: http://www.errc.org/cikk.php?cikk=1016 (accessed 1.10.2009).

[9] Article 8 of the Racial Equality Directive.

[10] See e.g. Joseph L. Gastwirth, 'Statistical Evidence in Discrimination Cases' *J. R. Statist. Soc.* A (1997).

produced by the respondent, showing e.g. a balanced workforce, should not suffice – at least not alone – to rebut a case made by the complainant. The fact that an employer does not discriminate as a matter of regular practice does not prove that he or she did not do so in a particular instance.

There is a very important exception to the above-stated main rule, however. Judicial bodies know that it may be difficult for a complainant to bring even *prima facie* evidence of discrimination, and may allow the use of statistical evidence to infer direct discrimination. In particular, statistical evidence may be used to establish a regular pattern of treatment of a particular group: regular failures by the members of a group to obtain appointment or promotion, or clear evidence of under-representation in particular grades, may give rise to an inference of discrimination. In such situations, statistical evidence may in practice be a *conditio qua sine non* for successful pursuance of a case, especially if no other evidence is available or if it is too weak.[11] For instance, in the British case *Marshall v F Woolworth & Co. Ltd.*, the complainant considered that she had not been offered a job because she was Black, i.e. that direct racial discrimination was involved. An employment tribunal inferred the existence of *direct* discrimination from the fact that there was no Black person working at the store in question, even though there is a sizeable Black community living in the local area and half of the job applicants were black.[12] In Britain a court may use the monitoring records of an employer, showing an imbalance in e.g. the ethnic profile of the workforce, to draw an inference of discrimination.[13] Statistics may also play an important role in showing

---

[11] The situation prevailing under the EU law can be contrasted with the situation prevailing under the US federal law. In the US, statistics are often admissible in individual disparate treatment cases, but they are rarely determinative without additional anecdotal evidence, because of the need to show the intent to discriminate. See Jay W. Waks. et al, 'The Use of Statistics in Employment Discrimination Cases' *The Trial Lawyer*, Vol. 24 (2001), p. 261.

[12] *Marshall* v *F Woolworth & Co. Ltd*, COIT 1404/80, ET.

[13] For instance in *West Midland Passenger Transport Executive v Singh*, Balcombe LJ in the Court of Appeal stated that "statistics obtained through monitoring are not conclusive in themselves, but if they show racial or ethnic imbalance or disparities, then they may indicate areas of racial discrimination.... In the absence of a satisfactory explanation in a particular case, it is reasonable to infer that the complainant as a member of the group has been treated less favourably on grounds of race. Indeed, evidence of discriminatory conduct against the group in relation to promotion may be more persuasive of discrimination in the particular case than previous treatment of the applicant which may be indicative of personal factors peculiar to the applicant and not necessarily racially motivated." *West Midland Passenger Transport Executive v Singh* [1988] ICR 614 at 619.

that the justification proffered by the respondent is merely a pretext.[14] The respondent can in turn introduce statistical evidence that challenges the relevancy, accurateness or completeness of the statistics relied on by the complainant.

The concept of indirect discrimination, as it has been conceived in the EU law and in the case law of the various monitoring bodies, rests, as discussed, on a comparative approach. Indirect discrimination is concerned more with substantive outcomes than with any formal consistency of treatment.[15] Indeed, it recognizes that sometimes formally consistent application of seemingly neutral criteria may in fact have discriminatory effects. All of this quite readily calls for identification and measurement of possible gaps in achievement that may exist between two groups of people.

In the employment context comparisons can be drawn in a number of ways. Comparisons can be drawn for instance between those who have applied and those who have been selected, between those who are in employment and those who live in the relevant catchment area and so on.

Consider the following case from Britain:

> In *Aina* v *Employment Service*, a Black African employee applied for the post of equal opportunities manager in his organisation. He was assessed as having the skills and ability for the job. However, his application was rejected because, unknown to him, the post was open only to permanent staff at higher grades than his. Monitoring data showed that the organisation had no permanent Black African employees at the grades in question. The employment tribunal held that there was no justification for the requirement, and that it amounted to indirect discrimination on racial grounds.[16]

As in direct discrimination cases, respondents are allowed also in these cases to submit data of their own that challenges the relevancy, accurateness or completeness of the statistics relied on by the complainant.

While the comparative rationale of the concept of indirect discrimination invites the use of statistical evidence, such evidence is in

---

[14] Waks, *cit. supra* note 11.

[15] For a general discussion of this, see Sandra Fredman, *Discrimination Law* (Oxford: Oxford University Press, 2002), p. 106 ff.

[16] *Aina* v *Employment Service* [2002] DCLD 103D.

practice not required in all, or perhaps even in most cases.[17] In some circumstances the competent bodies may take 'generally known facts' into account, and make assumptions about ordinary behaviour without requiring statistical evidence. For example in the British case of *Panesar v Nestlé Co Ltd* it was accepted that those with Pakistani ethnic origins were more likely than others to have beards, and therefore a claim for indirect discrimination could be made out against a rule that prohibited employees from having beards.[18] In two other British cases, *Mandla v Lee*[19] and *Singh v British Rail Engineering*,[20] bans on the wearing of turbans were treated as making out a claim for indirect race discrimination against Sikhs. Importantly, the European Court of Justice has confirmed in its case law in the field of gender discrimination that there are circumstances where it is not necessary to analyze the specific consequences of the application of a criteria or practice in order to find indirect discrimination.[21]

Despite the potential usefulness of statistical evidence in deciding discrimination cases, the overwhelming majority of the EU countries so far has none, or only very limited experience of it. This situation can be contrasted with the widespread use of statistics in the field of sex discrimination cases in Europe,[22] and with the equally widespread use of statistics in the field of racial discrimination cases in the USA.

---

[17] Cf. the European Parliament, which has submitted that it considers that indirect discrimination becomes impossible to prove in the absence of statistical data. European Parliament Resolution on non-discrimination and equal opportunities for all - a framework strategy /2005/2191(INI)), adopted on 14 June 2006, para 18.

[18] *Panesar* v *Nestlé Co Ltd*, [1980] IRLR 482.

[19] *Mandla* v *Lee*, [1983] IRLR 209.

[20] *Singh* v *British Rail Engineering*, [1986] ICR 22.

[21] See e.g. the case of *Schnorbus*, where the selection procedure regarding access to practical legal training discriminated against women because of the preference accorded to applicants who had completed compulsory military or civilian service, which could be done only by men. The court said: "...it is not necessary in this case to analyse the specific consequences of the application of the [selection criteria]. It is sufficient to note that, by giving priority to applicants who have completed compulsory military or civilian service, the provisions at issue themselves are evidence of indirect discrimination since, under the relevant national legislation, women are not required to do military or civilian service and therefore cannot benefit from the priority accorded by the abovementioned provisions of the JAO to applications in circumstances regarded as cases of hardship." ECJ, *Schnorbus* v. *Land Hessen*, case C-79/99, 7 December 2000, paragraph 38.

[22] ERRC - Interights - MPG, *Strategic Litigation in Europe: From Principles to Practice* (Nottingham: Russell Press ltd, 2004), p. 82.

The lack of experience in this regard appears to be directly linked to the present lack of ethnic data in Europe. It must also be noted that the compilation and use of statistical evidence involves many difficult and technical obstacles, particularly with respect to the identification of the correct pools of comparison. In effect, even if ethnic monitoring was introduced across Europe, it may take some time before the legal cultures of the EU member states become accustomed to the use of statistical data in the present context.[23]

Monitoring by Specialized Bodies

One of the reasons why equality data is needed is because the national specialized bodies and international monitoring bodies need it in order to perform their monitoring and supervisory functions. As appears from the examples below, the international bodies have frequently asked the states parties to furnish them with the necessary equality data. It should be recalled that all EU member states are parties to the main human rights conventions, and are thus under a direct legal obligation to report periodically on the human rights situation in their countries and to include in these reports quantitative and qualitative information, also in relation to discrimination.[24]

- The UN Human Rights Committee, in its guidelines for state reports, reminds the contracting states that their reports should include "sufficient data and statistics" in order to enable the Committee to assess progress in the implementation of human rights by states parties.[25]
- The UN Committee on the Economic, Social and Cultural Rights, in its guidelines for state reports, calls states to provide "[s]tatistical

[23] Timo Makkonen, *Measuring Discrimination: Data collection and EU Equality Law* (Luxembourg: OOPEC, 2007).

[24] The reporting system is being reformed at the time of the writing with a view to rationalizing it. The new instructions for state reports included in the *Harmonized guidelines on reporting under the international human rights treaties, including guidelines on a core document and treaty-specific documents* (see HRI/GEN/2/Rev.5, 29 May 2008) underlines the importance of data collection, and provides that states should develop an efficient system for the collection of all statistical and other data relevant to the implementation of human rights (para 15). The *Indicators for assessing the implementation of human rights*, listed in Appendix 3 to the Guidelines, further requires that all social, economic, cultural, demographic, political, and justice system statistics be disaggregated by "main population groups".

[25] HRC, *Consolidated guidelines for state reports*. CCPR/C/66/GUI/Rev.2 (26.02.2001), paragraph C.6.

data on the enjoyment of each Covenant right, disaggregated by … ethnic origin" on an annual comparative basis. In relation to Article 2 on non-discrimination, the Committee asks states to "provide disaggregated and comparative statistical data on the effectiveness of specific anti-discrimination measures and the progress achieved towards ensuring equal enjoyment of each of the Covenant rights by all."[26]

- The UN Committee on the Elimination of All Forms of Racial Discrimination, in its guidelines for state reports, calls states to collect information on the ethnic characteristics of the population. In view of the Committee, "[i]f progress in eliminating discrimination based on race, colour, descent, or national or ethnic origin is to be monitored, some indication is needed … of the number of persons who might be treated less favourably on the basis of these characteristics." The Committee also calls states to monitor all trends that can give rise to racial segregation; to provide statistics on complaints filed, prosecutions launched and sentences passed in relation to discrimination; to provide information on whether persons of minority origin are proportionately represented in all State public service and governance institutions; to indicate whether persons belonging to protected groups are over- or underrepresented in certain professions or activities, and in unemployment; to indicate any variations in the level of education and training between the different population groups; to indicate whether the protected groups are concentrated in particular localities; and to describe different needs for health and social services. The Committee also requests state parties to describe, "as far as possible in quantitative and qualitative terms, factors affecting and difficulties experienced in ensuring the equal enjoyment by women of rights under the Convention", and specifies that they "should provide data by race, colour, descent and national or ethnic origin, which are then disaggregated by gender within those groups".[27]
- The Advisory Committee on the Framework Convention for the Protection of National Minorities, in its outline for country reports,

[26] CESCR, Guidelines on treaty-specific documents to be submitted by states parties under articles 16 and 17 of the International Covenant on Economic, Social and Cultural Rights (E/C.12/2008/2, 24 March 2009), paras 3 and 10 in particular.

[27] CERD, Guidelines for the CERD-specific document to be submitted by states parties under article 9, paragraph 1, of the Convention (13 June 2008), CERD/C/2007/1, paras 11 and 19 in particular.

> also calls for the collection of necessary data. According to the outline, states should provide "factual information ... such as statistics and the results of surveys." The document also points out that "where complete statistics are not available, governments may supply data or estimates based on ad hoc studies, specialized or sample surveys, or other scientifically valid methods, whenever they consider the information so collected to be useful."[28]

An express treaty obligation to monitor the realization of human rights through data collection mechanisms has been a long time coming. That idea was, in the context of ethnic equality, introduced in the Durban Declaration, which urges states to

> collect, compile, analyse, disseminate and publish reliable statistical data at the national and local levels and undertake all other related measures which are necessary to assess regularly the situation of individuals and groups of individuals who are victims of ... racial discrimination.[29]

The Declaration also invites states to "improve concepts and methods of data collection and analysis" and to "develop indicators of progress and participation of individuals and groups of individuals in society", and endorses quantitative and qualitative research.[30] There are also other instruments calling for the collection of data in relation to discrimination.[31]

It should also be kept in mind that the national bodies for the promotion of equality, which all EU Member States are required under Article 13 of the Racial Equality Directive to have, are under the Directive to "conduct independent surveys concerning discrimination" for the purposes of analysing the problems involved and

---

[28] ACFC, Outline for reports to be submitted pursuant to Article 25 paragraph 1 of the Framework Convention for the protection of national minorities. Adopted by the Committee of Ministers on 30.09.1998. ACFC, Commentary on the effective participation of persons belonging to national minorities in cultural, social and economic life and in public affairs [ACFC/31DOC(2008)001, Strasbourg 5 May 2008], paras 30–31.

[29] Paragraph 92.

[30] Paragraphs 93 and 94.

[31] Article 31 of the UN Convention on the Rights of Persons with Disabilities, entitled "Statistics and data collection", provides that "States Parties undertake to collect appropriate information, including statistical and research data, to enable them to formulate and implement policies to give effect to the present Convention".

studying possible solutions.[32] Whereas the term used ("surveys") is generic to the extent that member states seem to have a wide discretion as to how to go about fulfilling this requirement, Article 13 underlines in general the need to build to a national knowledge-base on discrimination.

Workplace Monitoring

Data can be an indispensable tool for organizations, such as business enterprises and government agencies, which want to make sure that their firing, hiring and other policies and practices comply with the equal treatment laws. They can do this by monitoring the composition of their workforce and applicants by ethnic origin. The resulting aggregate internal data can be used to track down how people with different origins are treated for instance with respect to promotion and retention, to ensure that there are no biases in this respect. The data may also be compared with external benchmark data showing the composition of the general population for the purposes of detecting possible under-representation in the organization as a whole. In a similar vein, an organization that provides services to the public may want to monitor its service delivery. For instance, a housing agency may want to monitor its service delivery to ensure that it provides equal housing on equal terms for everyone. For all this to be possible, the organizations in question need to collect the necessary internal data, in addition to which they would benefit from the availability of suitable external benchmark data, such as census data, against which it can compare its internal data. Ethnic monitoring is currently practiced in Britain, Canada and the United States. Monitoring is practiced also on other grounds: for instance, in Northern Ireland designated authorities and all employers with ten or more employees are required to monitor the composition of their workforce in terms of (religious) community background and sex.

Awareness Raising

Qualitative and quantitative data can be a major asset for sensitizing and awareness-raising activities. Reliable evidence on the extent and nature of discrimination can serve as a compelling, factual baseline for national discussion on discrimination, benefiting governments and

---

[32] Article 13 and recital 24 of the Racial Equality Directive.

NGOs alike, as they use this information for the purposes of advocacy, awareness-raising and education. Indeed, there is evidence suggesting that that this kind of information is frequently used for these purposes and is perceived to be an effective tool in this respect.[33]

Resource for Researchers

In many ways, researchers and statisticians are the eyes and the ears of the society. Equality data is an indispensable resource for researchers seeking to improve our understanding of discrimination as a phenomenon. Research, again, is a prerequisite for developing and implementing more effective policies to fight discrimination. Given that discrimination is a complex and often subtle social phenomenon, it can often be rendered visible only by means of rigorous research efforts.

Other Uses

In addition to these rather practical functions, the compilation of equality statistics can be seen to have more symbolical functions. Already the mere existence of a data collection system sends a message to the actual and potential perpetrators, actual and potential victims, and the general society, signalling that the society disapproves of discrimination, takes it seriously, and is willing to take the steps necessary to fight it. This can have a general dissuasive effect.

It should also be noted that the fight against discrimination requires broad-based mobilization and action, and this is facilitated by data collection, as data renders discrimination visible and helps to make inequality a societal concern instead of being a concern just to its victims.

10.2 Methods

The data needs, identified above, are substantial. No single data source alone can meet all these needs. Discrimination is a complex social phenomenon, which makes it is a tricky subject to study and analyze. A single data source usually throws light into one aspect of

[33] Niklas Reuter – Timo Makkonen – Olli Oosi, *Study on Data Collection to measure the extent and impact of discrimination in Europe*. Final Report 7.12.2004. Available at http://ec.europa.eu/social (accessed 1.10.2009).

discrimination (typically either its causes, nature, extent or effects) from a single point of view (the victim's, society's, or perpetrator's), in addition to which the different data sources vary, as will be discussed, in terms of their validity and reliability. These challenges mean that it is essential to adopt a multi-source and a multi-method approach to the investigation of discrimination.[34] It is only when a mutually consistent pattern of results across different analyses emerges that we can achieve a reasonably valid picture of discrimination as a social problem. It is therefore necessary to set up and support several mechanisms by which equality data is compiled.[35] The different mechanisms, their uses, and their advantages and disadvantages, are discussed below.

Official Statistics

Official statistics are, by definition, produced by government agencies, and form an integral part of society's infrastructure. All countries in Europe produce population-wide statistics on employment, level of education, income, health and wealth. Such statistics provide all-important information of the socio-economic status of the population, and if broken down by ethnicity, they provide a relatively solid point of entry for the analysis of the situation of the different population groups. There are three possible primary sources of social, economic and demographic data: population censuses, household surveys and administrative records. Different countries have adopted different approaches in this respect.

The compilation of equality data through official statistics has two major advantages. First, the necessary data is often produced by the state on a regular basis, which allows for the steady development of longitudinal data, enabling trend analysis. Second, socio-economic data provides an important insight into the effects of direct, indirect and structural discrimination as well as all other causes of disadvantage. This is important, as it is patently difficult to measure indirect and structural discrimination in particular.

While this source of information has its benefits, it has its limitations as well. First, not all discrimination leads to observable differences in outcomes, which means that some forms of discrimination

[34] Makkonen, *cit. supra* note 3.

[35] National Research Council, *Measuring Racial Discrimination. Panel on Methods for Assessing Discrimination* (Washington DC: National Academies Press, 2004).

are not visible in socio-economic statistics.[36] Second, it is challenging to establish clearly the portion to which the disadvantaged position of a group, as shown by outcome statistics, is the result of discrimination. While it may safely be assumed that members of groups that are discriminated against are worse off than they would be if they were treated equally, it is extremely difficult to establish the extent to which their socio-economic disadvantage results specifically from discrimination. Some researchers have used multivariate analyses[37] in an attempt to control the other relevant variables, such as average level of education, in order to estimate the extent to which disparities in, for instance, income and employment level result from discrimination. The ability to effectively carry out regression analysis poses further demands on data collection, as it requires the availability of a wide range of ethnic data, for instance with regard to educational achievements. Such data is currently not often available. In addition, the method itself has also been subject to some criticism.[38] In consequence, statistics based on official data sources perhaps best function as indicators: they pinpoint differences in outcomes but do not explain them.

At any rate, however, it is highly valuable also from the point of view of other policy goals to establish if there are differences in socio-economic situations of different groups, even if it cannot be positively established to what extent the disparities result from discrimination. The existence of disparities calls for closer investigation of the matter and possibly also the adoption of appropriate remedial measures. This is especially the case where the statistics disclose

[36] This would categorically be the case with some types of discrimination, such as denial of access to a restaurant, which is unlikely to lead to differences in socio-economic status. A person may also be repeatedly discriminated against in access to employment, except for once, and thus be able to obtain a position that matches her qualifications. Therefore even repeated events of discrimination do not always lead to observable differences in outcomes.

[37] Under a multivariate analysis, discrimination is found through the unexplainable residual gap that remains between two groups even after all the variables that can be reasonably assumed to have factored in have been taken into account and controlled for.

[38] See P.A. Riach – J. Rich, 'Field Experiments of Discrimination in the Market Place' *The Economic Journal* 112, November 2002, p. F481. From a theoretical perspective, one limitation of the method is that it does not take into account the extent to which the variables that are controlled for reflect discrimination in themselves.

disparities in outcomes across multiple areas of life, such as employment, housing and health.[39]

Complaints Data

Another type of baseline data on discrimination is provided for by so-called 'complaints data'. Complaints data is generated as a by-product of the work carried out by those bodies that, in one way or another, handle discrimination complaints. Complaints data typically includes information on the numbers and types of complaints filed with a particular body within a particular timeframe, typically a year. Also other data may be available, such as aggregate profiles of offenders/respondents and complainants, broken down by variables such as age and gender. The primary source of complaints data is the justice system. Such sources of data include tribunals, regular and specialized courts, and specialized bodies such as equality commissions and ombudsmen. In those countries where discrimination is a criminal offence, complaints data can also be compiled on the basis of police crime report registers and prosecution registers. Complaints data, in the broad sense of the notion, may also be available through non-governmental organizations that provide direct services (for instance advice and assistance) to victims of discrimination.

As useful as statistics on complaints are for some purposes, particularly for highlighting the nature of reported discrimination, they constitute poor indicators of any actual levels of discrimination. Cases that are reported to the police or taken to the courts represent but the proverbial tip of the iceberg – exactly how small the tip is, is difficult to estimate unless some other data is available, such as victim survey data.

Research

Several types of research methods are available for the purposes of studying inequalities. These include the following.

Victim surveys. Victim surveys refer to studies whose purpose is, as the name suggests, the gathering of information about the experiences of people at a particular risk of discrimination. Victim surveys

[39] Here it needs to be reiterated that for instance the EU Directives link the adoption of positive action measures to the existence of disadvantages, not just discrimination.

provide a good overview of the extent, nature and effects of discrimination as experienced by the people concerned. Surveys can provide detailed information, such as information relating to the experienced obstacles in access to justice, and the effects, psychological and other, of discrimination. While victim surveys can be instrumental in assessing the dark figure of discrimination, it should be underlined that victim surveys can measure only the subjective experiences of the respondents: the actual prevalence of discrimination may be higher than indicated by the responses, as the respondents may not always be aware that they have been discriminated against; on the other hand, the prevalence of discrimination may be lower than indicated by the responses, as individuals may sometimes erroneously attribute a negative event to discrimination even if discrimination played no part in it. In any case, results from victim surveys can provide highly important insights into the operation of discrimination and how people cope with it.

Self-report surveys. Self-report surveys focus on the attitudes, opinions and/or behaviour of respondents. These surveys are usually directed at the general public, or a specific target group, such as employers. Attitude surveys in the context of anti-discrimination work are usually used to map out the prevalence and type of prejudices and stereotypes within a specific population. Attitude surveys, when conducted at regular intervals, give information on changes in attitudes, and can thus function as an early warning system: while there is no straightforward correspondence between negative attitudes and discriminatory behaviour at an individual level, increased social acceptability of prejudices signals a danger of increasing levels of discrimination in the society in general. Surveys can also set out to inquire about behaviour and practices that are questionable from the point of view of equal treatment. While people may be reluctant to report such behaviours (the same applies to negative attitudes), they are more likely to do so if their responses remain fully confidential.

Discrimination testing. Testing is a form of social experiment in a real-life situation. In discrimination testing, two or more individuals are matched for all relevant characteristics other than the one that is expected to lead to discrimination, in our case ethnic origin.[40] The testers apply, for instance, for a job or an apartment, usually on

[40] Michael Fix – Margery Turner 'Testing for Discrimination: The Case for a National Report Card' *Civil Rights Journal*, Fall 1999.

numerous different occasions, and the outcomes and the treatment they receive are closely monitored.[41] The method was originally developed as a tool for checking compliance with the law, and may be used as a means of evaluating the effectiveness of anti-discrimination legislation.[42] The discrimination testing method has been applied in many different contexts, such as employment, housing and provision of services and goods. Despite its robust nature in exposing discrimination, it does have its limitations: it has some inherent limitations such as that it cannot be used to study discrimination beyond a certain stage – for example, it can be used to study the first stages in access to employment but not necessarily the subsequent stages, and it cannot at all be used to study differences in wages, progression or redundancy. There has also been some debate over the ethical acceptability of the method, but the conclusion appears warranted that there are no major problems in that respect, especially insofar as minimal inconvenience is caused to those involved in the study.[43]

Other types of research. A considerable number of other research methods are available for the purposes of studying inequalities. These include qualitative research strategies, such as in-depth interviews, theme interviews and case studies. Qualitative analyses can provide important insights and unique perspectives on the victims, perpetrators and circumstances of discriminatory events, the historical and social contexts of these events and more particularly on the motives and other reasons behind the events. Qualitative research is an essential companion to quantitative research; it brings the analysis from the macro-level to the micro-level and helps to see the people behind the numbers. Qualitative research methods are an essential part of any research programme that aims to study discrimination, but they are even more important in studying such types and forms of discrimination that are difficult to study by means of more quantitatively oriented research.

Overall, the different forms of research constitute indispensable tools for examining the causes, extent and effects of discrimination with any precision. They have all been used for several decades,

---

[41] Idem.

[42] Colectivo IOE, *Labour market discrimination against migrant workers in Spain*, International Migration Papers 9 (Geneva: International Labour Office, 1995).

[43] P.A. Riach – J. Rich 'Deceptive Field Experiments of Discrimination: Are they Ethical?' *Kyklos*, Vol. 57, 2004, pp. 457–470.

meaning that the related methodologies are already well-developed and refined, and have been used to study discrimination in many areas of life. Victim surveys and discrimination testing in particular have been found to constitute effective means for measuring the prevalence of discrimination, whereas qualitative research methods have proved to provide important insights about the causes, nature and effects of discrimination. However, research projects are all too often 'one-off' exercises, meaning that the use of these methods needs to be systematized in order to obtain information that is up-to-date and capable of showing trends.

Ethnic Monitoring

Ethnic monitoring refers to situations where an organization collects data on the ethnic make-up of its workforce and/or its clientele in order to track down any imbalances. The purpose of monitoring is to allow an organization to obtain an overall, statistically valid picture of the way in which its policies and practices affect persons belonging to different groups.

Monitoring is perhaps the most robust measure an organization can take to ensure it is in compliance with the equality laws. It can help organizations to highlight possible inequalities, investigate their underlying causes, remove any unfairness or disadvantage, and send a clear message to employees, job applicants, customers and shareholders that the employer takes equal opportunities seriously.[44] Moreover, monitoring is indispensable for tracking down the effects of any positive action schemes. Experiences from countries where monitoring is practiced have often been positive.[45] In particular, it is evident that in Northern Ireland, monitoring and other duties imposed on employers by the Fair Employment and Treatment (NI) Order 1998, have together with other public policy interventions resulted in substantial remedying of the earlier imbalances in participation in employment

[44] Commission for Racial Equality, *Ethnic Monitoring: A Guide for public authorities* (CRE, 2002), p. 3. Equality Commission for Northern Ireland, 'Sexual Orientation Discrimination in Northern Ireland. The Law and Good Practice' (Belfast: Equality Commission for Northern Ireland, 2004), p. 32 ff.

[45] B. Hepple – M. Coussey and T. Choudhury, *Equality: A new framework*. Report of the Independent Review of the Enforcement of UK Anti-Discrimination Legislation (Cambridge: University of Cambridge, 2000). Commission for Racial Equality, *cit. supra* note 44. Shirley Dex and Kingsley Purdam, *Equal Opportunities and Recruitment. How Census data can help employers to assess their practices* (York: York Publishing Services, 2005), p. 10. Christopher McCrudden et al, 'Affirmative Action without Quotas in Northern Ireland' *The Equal Rights Review*, Vol. Four (2009).

for members of the different community groups.[46] This development can be contrasted with the modest effects of the earlier, standard non-discrimination law.[47]

In employment, monitoring lets employers examine the make-up of their workforce in terms of ethnic origin, and compare this with benchmark data where such exist. It also lets them to analyze how their personnel practices and procedures affect different groups.[48] In service delivery, monitoring can tell which groups are using the services, and how satisfied they are with them. Organizations can then consider ways of reaching underrepresented groups and make sure that the services meet the specific needs of each group, and that the services are provided fairly.[49]

Obtaining information with regard to the representation of the different equality groups within the workforce can be useful in and of itself, especially when monitoring is carried out on an on-going basis or repeated at regular intervals, as the development of longitudinal data allows the assessment of trends. However, when the internal data of an organization can be compared with some external benchmark data – that is, data on the expected participation rates of these groups as disclosed by for instance official statistical data or data gathered by other organisations operating under similar circumstances – the internal data becomes even more useful.

Monitoring can be carried out in two ways, either through the collection of personal data (data related to identifiable individuals) coupled with associated record-keeping, or through the collection of anonymous data. The data can be collected directly from the persons concerned, by means of using self-classification, or indirectly through third-party observation, by means of using other-classification.

Conclusions

The following table illustrates and summarises the purposes for which data is needed, by whom, what kind of data is needed, and how it can be obtained:

---

[46] Equality Commission for Northern Ireland, *2008 Monitoring Report - Monitoring Report No 19: A Profile of the Monitored Northern Ireland Workforce* (Belfast: Equality Commission for Northern Ireland, 2009).

[47] Christopher McCrudden has observed that the earlier anti-discrimination legislation had "little effect on employers' practices". See McCrudden, *Buying Social Justice: Equality, Government Procurement, & Legal Change* (Oxford: OUP, 2007), pp. 72–73.

[48] Commission for Racial Equality, *cit. supra* note 44.

[49] Idem.

Type of action	Body	What data is needed	Methods/ mechanisms
Policy-making	Political and administrative bodies at the national, European and international levels	– Baseline data, such as demographic data and socio-economic data – Data on nature, extent, causes and consequences of discrimination	– Official statistics, broken down by origin or a proxy variable such as language or place of birth – Research data
Monitoring (external)	International monitoring bodies (e.g. CERD, ECRI, FRA); national monitoring bodies (e.g. ombudsmen)	Same as above	Same as above
Monitoring (internal)	Public and private organisations	– Monitoring data on the composition of workforce and/or recipients of services (ethnic data/qualitative data) – Benchmark data	– Ethnic monitoring (anonymous or non-anonymous) – Benchmark data (census or register data, data from major surveys or from comparable organisations)
Judicial proceedings	Complainants, respondents, courts	– Context-specific data, such as data on hiring and firing practices of the organisation – Baseline data	– Ethnic monitoring – Ad hoc investigations – Census or register data, data from major surveys)

(*Contd.*)

Type of action	Body	What data is needed	Methods/ mechanisms
Awareness raising and sensitizing activities	National and international public and private bodies, NGOs	- Accessible, compelling information	- Victim surveys, discrimination testing, self-report surveys and other research
Research	The scientific community	- Baseline data - Data on nature, extent, causes and consequences of discrimination	- Official statistics - All kinds of research - Monitoring data

An all-important distinction must at this point be made between those data collection mechanisms that involve the processing of ethnic data, and those that do not. The more robust mechanisms involve the collection and other processing of personal ethnic data. Here it is important to be aware of the fact that data can be used not just to secure and promote rights, but to breach them. Examples of past misuse of sensitive data have shown that there are real and significant dangers involved in collection of sensitive data, ethnic data in particular. On this basis, many feel that ethnic data should not be collected. Many also believe that collection of ethnic data runs against privacy laws and data protection laws. These two issues merit closer consideration and will be discussed in the following subchapters.

As the data protection laws apply only where processing of personal data is involved, an elementary distinction must be made between those operations that involve processing of personal data and those that do not. Typically, the latter group includes most forms of discrimination testing, anonymous surveys and anonymous workplace monitoring.

Many other forms of data collection however require the processing of personal data and therefore also engage data protection laws. These include the collection of ethnic data through censuses or non-anonymous workplace or service delivery monitoring, and the collection of data for the purposes of various kinds of administrative records maintained by central or local authorities or for instance schools.

10.3 Challenges

Information is Power, and Power can be Abused

That the concept of collecting ethnic data, often perceived as 'sensitive data', raises many concerns and fears is understandable in light of the many historical and some contemporary examples related to misuse of data in the context of human rights abuses. There have been several well-known situations where population data systems have been used, or attempted or planned to be used, to target vulnerable groups within the population. Selzer and Anderson have identified 17 cases where population data systems have either been used to target individuals or population subgroups, or where such efforts were initiated, or where such targeting has been seriously contemplated.[50] Examples include the extermination and forced migration of Jews, Roma and other groups during the Second World War in altogether six European countries, the internment and forced migration of Japanese Americans during 1941–1945, the Apartheid in South Africa, the Cultural Revolution in China and the 1994 Rwandan genocide.[51]

The research shows that the misuse or attempted misuse of population data have occurred in both totalitarian and democratic countries, although in democratic societies such misuses tend to occur primarily in times of national stress.[52] The targeted groups have included 'racial' and ethnic minorities, linguistic minorities, indigenous populations and subjected populations such as the African, 'Indian' and 'Coloured' populations in South Africa. In terms of geographical scope, all regions of the world are represented, except Latin America and Western Asia, though the latter factor may be attributable to the lack of information concerning these areas. While almost all of the examples of misuse or suspected misuse of population data systems are historical, the use

[50] William Selzer, 'On the use of Population Data Systems to Target Vulnerable Population Subgroups for Human Rights Abuses' *Coyuntura Social* No. 30, 2005.

[51] Idem. See also William Selzer – Margo Anderson 'After Pearl Harbor: The Proper Role of Population Data Systems in Time of War (2000).' A research paper available at: http://www.uwm.edu/~margo/govstat/newpaa.pdf (accessed 1.1.2010).

[52] Idem.

or contemplated use of surveys and administrative data to investigate and prosecute suspected terrorists after 9/11 in the United States is also included in the list of the 17 cases.[53]

These historical experiences advise extreme caution in relation to those forms of data collection that lead to the maintenance of large datasets that contain data on nationality, ethnicity, religion and their possible proxies such as language and place of birth. The existence of such datasets poses a threat in a situation where things go seriously wrong and some group that wishes to target some other groups for abusive purposes has been able to wield power, and where the ordinary legislative and institutional safeguards for the protection of fundamental rights are no longer capable of precluding or stopping the abuse.

But a number of other viewpoints also merit our consideration. First of all, it should be recognized that the collection of ethnic data (in *sensu lato*) is already widespread in the context of census-taking. Many countries in the world, including USA, Canada, UK and many Central and Eastern European countries, already gather data on racial or ethnic origin through their censuses.[54] And even those countries that do not collect ethnic data do have extensive datasets containing such personal information as that pertaining to nationality, mother tongue and place of birth, factors that can work as proxy indicators for ethnicity. And at any rate, in the context of everyday life, people know or assume they know the ethnic origin of the people they meet, meaning that lack of ethnic data is no guarantee against abusive targeting.

It should also be noted that many institutions, including the European Parliament, are of the view that data collection is just so critical for combating discrimination, that it should be undertaken notwithstanding historical and cultural considerations.[55]

These viewpoints suggest that priority should perhaps be given to securing the confidentiality of data. Modern data protection technology provides useful means by which any data set can be protected from unauthorized access and by which the data can be rendered useless (by way of obscuring or masking individual data) even if accessed

[53] Idem. Processing of ethnic data may also be highly problematic in the context of ethnic profiling, see EU Network of Independent Experts on Fundamental Rights, *Ethnic Profiling*. CFR-CDF, Opinion No 4/2006, December 2006.

[54] Makkonen, *cit. supra* note 23.

[55] European Parliament resolution on non-discrimination and equal opportunities for all – a framework strategy (2005/2191(INI)), para 14.

by unauthorized third parties.[56] But even these mechanisms cannot render each system entirely watertight, and the question remains whether the risk involved in introducing the collection of ethnic data, however remote it may feel, is worth taking. That is a question that cannot be answered in the abstract, and at the end of the day that question should primarily be answered by the representatives of minorities and immigrants due to the fact that they are the groups that would on the one hand stand to benefit from the introduction of ethnic monitoring, and on the other they would have to stand the risk of possible misuse.

Protection of Individuals with Regard to Privacy and the Processing of Personal Data

International and European instruments relating to the right to privacy and protection of personal data regulate the manner in which ethnic data may be collected, registered, used or disseminated. Whereas the protection of personal data was initially treated as a dimension of the right to respect for private life, it is nowadays increasingly conceived of as a fundamental right in and of itself.[57] Yet, instruments protecting both sets of rights are relevant in this context.

These instruments are engaged whenever personal information, that is information relating to identified or identifiable natural persons, is collected or otherwise processed.[58] Whereas statistics, when released, regularly do not disclose information with regard to any particular individual,[59] this does not mean that the carrying out of statistical operations would not engage the rules that relate to the protection

[56] It must equally be kept in mind, however, that also the techniques used to gain unauthorized access to such data and to link anonymized data to specific identifiable individuals (re-identification of data) are constantly developing as well.

[57] The Charter of Fundamental Rights of the European Union was the first international document that had separate provisions with regard to respect for private and family life (Article 7) and protection of personal data (Article 8). See Makkonen, *cit. supra* note 23, pp. 52–72; Maria Tzanou – Tuomas Ojanen, *Thematic EU/International Legal Study on assessment of data protection measures and relevant institutions* (EU Fundamental Rights Agency, forthcoming).

[58] David Bainbridge, *EC Data Protection Directive* (London: Butterworths, 1996), p. 2.

[59] A key element of data protection laws and laws regulating statistical activities are the rules and principles that prohibit and prevent the connecting of a particular – in itself 'anonymous' – data to any particular individual through direct or indirect means ('re-identification').

of personal data. This is because statistics are based on the processing of microdata, in our case personal ethnic data.[60]

A particular challenge for any attempt to analyze the concrete implications of the international and national instruments relating to data protection and the right to privacy arises from the fact that they often take the form of framework instruments. Instead of directly addressing for instance the permissibility of ethnic monitoring, they set down rather diffusely formulated, general rules whose application to particular circumstances is quite challenging, given also the almost complete absence of legal analyses or case law.[61]

Right to Privacy

All EU member states have ratified the European Convention on Human Rights (ECHR). Article 8 of the ECHR provides for the protection of privacy. Article 8(1) provides that "[e]veryone has the right to respect for his private and family life, his home and his correspondence". It is a well established interpretation of the ECtHR that the right to respect for private life encompasses the right to respect for information relating to private life.[62] Therefore the processing of personal data, including ethnic data, falls within the ambit of Article 8. The collection or other processing of personal data without the knowledge or consent of the data subject, especially if the data is capable of being used in ways that are harmful to the data subject, may amount to an interference with the rights provided in Article 8. Also the subsequent use or disclosure of voluntarily submitted personal data may engage Article 8 if the data is used for purposes other that those that the data subject was informed of, or if the data is disclosed to unauthorized third parties, or stored in a way that fails to guarantee security of the data.

The right to respect for private life is not absolute: interference thereof may be justified under Article 8(2) of the ECHR. If it is not to contravene Article 8, an interference must (i) have been in accordance

---

[60] See e.g. Explanatory memorandum to the Council of Europe Recommendation No. R(97) 18 on the protection of personal data collected and processed for statistical purposes (30 September 1997).

[61] See ibid, p. 3.

[62] European Commission on Human Rights, *X* v. *UK* 30 DR 239 1982; ECtHR, *Amann* v. *Switzerland*, judgment of 16 February 2000; ECtHR, *MS* v. *Sweden*, judgment of 27 August 1997.

with the law, (ii) pursue a legitimate aim, and (iii) be necessary in a democratic society in order to achieve that aim. These requirements are to be interpreted narrowly.[63] While the first two requirements should not be difficult to meet in the context of collecting ethnic data, the third requirement, that is whether the activity can be considered 'necessary in a democratic society', is critical. Under the case law of the ECtHR, for the answer to be in the affirmative, there should be a pressing social need justifying the interference, in addition to which the interference must be proportionate to the aim pursued.[64] Article 8 therefore requires strict evaluation of which data collection operations are 'necessary', one element of which is the principle of proportionality that requires that one should always employ those data collection methods that pose the least threat to privacy.

Also other international treaties are relevant here, the International Covenant on Civil and Political Rights (ICCPR) in particular. Article 17 of the ICCPR prohibits "arbitrary and unlawful interferences" of privacy. In that context the UN Human Rights Committee has opined that "the competent public authorities should only be able to call for such information relating to an individual's private life the knowledge of which is essential in the interests of society as understood under the Covenant."[65] While it should be uncontroversial that collection of personal data for the purposes of guaranteeing equal treatment is "in the interests of the society as understood under the Covenant" – given, for instance, the fact that the very same Committee has encouraged the collection of this kind of data – it is clear that each data collection operation must also meet the test of being essential for those interests.

The guidance provided by the ECHR and the ICCPR is of a very general nature, leaving many questions unanswered. It can, however, be safely submitted that they do prohibit, for instance, the use of voluntarily submitted ethnic data for such purposes as ethnic profiling by the police, unless the data subject has given her consent thereto. To that extent, they do require the provision of some protection against the misuse of ethnic data.

---

[63] See e.g. ECtHR, *Rotaru* v *Romania*, judgment of 4 May 2000, paragraph 47.

[64] ECtHR, *Smith and Grady* v. *United Kingdom*, judgment of 27 September 1999; *Chassagnou* v. *France*, judgment of 29 April 1999.

[65] HRC, General Comment 16 (1994).

Protection of Individuals with Regard to Processing of Personal Data
More specific guidelines on the permissibility of collecting ethnic data are provided by data protection instruments such as the EU Data Protection Directive. The importance of the latter is underlined by the fact that the ECJ has tended to interpret the Directive in a generous manner with a view to ensuring a high level of protection of personal data.[66]

Processing sensitive data is prohibited by Article 8(1) of the Directive, which provides that "Member States shall prohibit the processing of personal data revealing racial or ethnic origin".[67] This prohibition implies the legislator's general distaste towards the collection of ethnic data.

Exceptions to Article 8(1) are laid down in Article 8(2), however. These provide, first of all, that the processing of ethnic data is allowed where the data subject – the person to whom the data relates to – has explicitly and freely expressed his or her informed consent thereto.[68] The requirement that the consent has to be freely given means that the data subjects must be given a real choice and no penalty may be imposed in case one decides not to co-operate: individuals from whom information is requested must not be subject to any kind of duress, influence or pressure, whether direct or indirect.[69] There is some disagreement as to whether an employee can ever be considered to be acting out entirely freely when an employer asks her to disclose some personal information, even if the employee is told that disclosure is voluntary.[70] The condition that the consent given must be 'informed'

---

[66] Maria Tzanou – Tuomas Ojanen, Thematic EU/International Legal Study on assessment of data protection measures and relevant institutions (EU Agency for Fundamental Rights, forthcoming). See also ECJ, *Tietosuojavaltuutettu* v. *Satakunnan Markkinapörssi OY, Satamedia*, C-73/07, 16 December 2008.

[67] Note however that the Directive does not actually use the concept 'sensitive data', but uses the phrase 'special categories of data' instead.

[68] See also Article 2(h) of the Directive.

[69] See also Council of Europe Recommendation No. R(97) 18 on the protection of personal data collected and processed for statistical purposes, and it's Explanatory Memorandum, p. 69.

[70] In Belgium, an Executive Decree issued by the government (Executive Decree of 13 February 2001 implementing the Federal Law of 8 December 1998 on the protection of the right to private life with respect to the processing of personal data) provides that consent cannot constitute a justification for the processing of sensitive data where the consent cannot be considered to have been given 'freely'. This is taken to be the case in the context of the employment relationship, as it is considered that a power imbalance exists between the employer and the employee. The Belgian government took this position despite two prior contrary opinions issued by the Belgian

means that it must be clear to the person whose consent is being sought what exactly she is consenting to. The party requesting the sensitive data must make it clear that disclosing sensitive information is not obligatory, and must inform the data subject of the purposes for which the information is being requested, and to what kind of use the information will be put, and if it will be disclosed to third parties. Moreover, the paragraph leaves it to the each member state to decide whether it considers that the giving of consent constitutes a sufficient condition for justifying the processing of sensitive data.[71] This is an important restriction, as opinions in the EU countries are mixed in this respect.[72]

Article 8(2) allows processing of ethnic data also where it is "necessary for the purposes of carrying out the obligations and specific rights of the controller in the field of employment law in so far as it is authorized by national law providing for adequate safeguards".[73] Whereas it is clear that ethnic monitoring can be useful, even highly useful, for employers for the purposes of complying with employment law, it is doubtful whether it can be considered 'necessary'.[74]

Article 8(2) allows the processing of ethnic data also where the processing relates to data that is necessary for the "establishment, exercise or defence of legal claims". Where a court or other competent body has the power to require an organization to produce documents or other information for the purposes of finding out whether equal treatment laws have been breached, the necessary processing of data can be justified under this subparagraph. Employers are also allowed to carry out the necessary data collection activities in order to defend their legal rights. It is doubtful, or at any rate not clear, whether organisations are allowed to keep records for monitoring purposes even before a claim has been filed, as a sort of precautionary measure.[75]

Commission for the protection of private life (Commission for the protection of private life, Opinion Nos 8/99 and 25/99).

[71] Article 8(2) of the Directive.

[72] See Douwe Korff, *EC Study on Implementation of Data Protection Directive. Comparative Summary of National Laws* (Cambridge: Human Rights Centre, September 2002).

[73] Article 8(2)b.

[74] Rosemary Jay - Angus Hamilton, *Data Protection Law and Practice* (2nd ed, London: Sweet & Maxwell, 2003), p. 192; Makkonen, *cit. supra* note 23, pp. 59–60.

[75] See Makkonen, *cit. supra* note 23, p. 61.

Processing of ethnic data may also be allowed under Article 8(4), which provides that

> Subject to the provision of suitable safeguards, Member States may, for reasons of substantial public interest, lay down exemptions in addition to those laid down in paragraph 2 either by national law or by decision of the supervisory authority.

Article 8(4) provides yet another avenue for ethnic monitoring. Processing of ethnic data is allowed under this subparagraph provided that three conditions are met. First, there has to be a 'substantial public interest'. It should go without further argument that the guaranteeing and promotion of equal treatment meets this requirement. Second, the processing of the data must be provided for in national law, or be authorized by the national supervisory organ where it has been given the necessary powers. Third, suitable safeguards must be in place to protect the rights and freedoms of individuals. This may require the taking of appropriate technical and organizational measures, particularly in order to maintain the security of the data and thereby to prevent any unauthorized transmission or access to the data.[76] One of the objectives of Article 8(4) is to facilitate scientific research and government statistics, making it legitimate to process and store sensitive data in central population registers, tax registers, census registers and the like. Ethnic monitoring in the UK has been justified under this article.[77]

Any collection of sensitive data must not just be allowed under Article 8, but must also meet a set of qualitative principles laid down in Article 6. The first requirement put forth by Article 6 is that personal data must be processed 'fairly and lawfully'. The conditions under which sensitive data can 'lawfully' be processed are laid down in Article 8, as discussed before. Secondly, all personal data must be processed 'fairly'. Fairness is somewhat less obvious in meaning, but is potentially a broader notion. At a very general level, the notion of fairness means that, in striving to achieve their data-processing goals, data controllers must take account of the interests and reasonable expectations of data subjects.[78] The notion of fairness brings with it

[76] See recitals 34 and 46 of the Directive.

[77] Jay – Hamilton, *cit. supra* note 74, p. 190 ff.

[78] Lee A. Bygrave, *Data Protection Law: Approaching its Rationale, Logic and Limits* (The Hague: Kluwer, 2002), p. 58.

requirements of balance and proportionality: the collection and further processing of data must be carried out in a manner that does not, in the circumstances, intrude unreasonably upon the data subject's privacy nor interfere unreasonably with their autonomy and integrity.[79] The requirement of fairness is also seen to imply that a person must not be unduly pressured into supplying her personal data or to accept that the data are used for particular purposes.[80] It has also been interpreted to favour, as a point of departure, an approach where personal data is collected directly from data subjects.[81] Fairness also implies that where data subjects have a right to be informed of a particular data processing activity, they are to be informed in such a language and in such a manner that is intelligible for them, a condition that is important especially for foreigners.

Article 6 further provides that data must be "collected for specified, explicit and legitimate purposes and not further processed in a way incompatible with those purposes". This requirement is really a cluster of four principles: 1) the purposes for which data are collected shall be specified; 2) these purposes must be explicit, i.e. fully and clearly expressed; 3) the purposes must be legitimate; and 4) the purposes for which data are further processed shall not be incompatible with the purposes for which the data were first collected. Importantly, the subsection expressly recognizes that the further processing of data for statistical or scientific purposes is not considered incompatible, on the condition that 'appropriate safeguards' are in place.[82] It should be pointed out that some EU Member States have been found to provide too weak safeguards or none at all in this respect.[83]

---

[79] Idem.

[80] Idem.

[81] Ibid, p. 59. This principle is also supported by Article 9.2 of the Council of Europe *Recommendation No. R(97) 18 on the protection of personal data collected and processed for statistical purposes*. The Recommendation, as interpreted in its Explanatory Memorandum, actually goes as far as to require that sensitive data may not be collected by any other means than by collecting it directly from the data subjects. See p. 58 of the Explanatory Memorandum.

[82] Such safeguards may consist of for instance the following measures: the legal requirement that the data must not be used to take decisions on data subjects; the obligation to notify the national data protection authority or an ethics committee of the planned operations; obligation to obtain prior authorization from the national data protection authority; the requirement that a particular balance test be met; the requirement that the data should be pseudonymized or anonymized whenever possible. Korff, *cit. supra* note 72.

[83] Ibid, p. 66 ff.

Article 6 furthermore requires that the data must be "adequate, relevant and not excessive in relation to the purposes for which they are collected and/or further processed." This lays down the principle of proportionality, which specifies that only those personal data may be collected that are necessary to achieve the purposes of the data collection operation. Insofar as doing so does not put the objectives of a particular operation in jeopardy, the controller should opt for secondary rather than primary data collection,[84] anonymous rather than nominal surveys, sampling rather than full-scale surveys, and for voluntary rather than compulsory surveys.[85] The requirement of adequacy may be seen to favour, as a point of departure, data collection methods that proceed from the basis of self-classification; however, if the utilization of the self-classification method leads in a particular instance to a situation where a high number of people choose not to classify themselves, or categorize themselves along lines that clearly do not match the 'objective reality', methods employing third-party identification may be applied as they may in fact better meet the adequacy requirement.[86]

The data must also be 'accurate'.[87] All reasonable steps should be taken to ensure that the data is not factually misleading. This speaks in favour of obtaining the data directly from the data subjects, as in general it can be assumed that data obtained in this way is accurate.[88] Personal data is to be erased or rendered anonymous once it is no longer required for the purposes for which it has been kept.[89] Where the design of a scientific or statistical project so requires, the necessary identification data may be retained, provided that specific, 'appropriate' domestic safeguards are in place. Privacy-enhancing technologies should be used where possible.[90]

---

[84] *Primary data collection* refers to 'original' collection of data, while *secondary data collection* refers to the usage of some dataset consisting of data that has already been collected.

[85] See Council of Europe Recommendation No. R(97) 18 on the protection of personal data collected and processed for statistical purposes and the Explanatory Memorandum, p. 62.

[86] CRE, *cit. supra* note 44, p. 69.

[87] Subparagraph d.

[88] Idem.

[89] Subparagraph (e); Bygrave, *cit. supra* note 78, p. 60.

[90] On the concept of Privacy-Enhancing Technologies, see e.g. John Borking 'Privacy-Enhancing Technologies (PET) - Darf es ein Bitchen weniger sein?' *Datenschutz und Datensicherheit*, Volume 25, Number 10, October 2001.

Processing of personal data is also regulated by the Council of Europe Convention for the Protection of Individuals with regard to Automatic Processing of Personal Data. The Convention, which was adopted in 1981, is the only international treaty dealing specifically with data protection, and has been ratified by all EU member states. The Convention corresponds in many respects with the EU Directive, being however somewhat more generally formulated. A key requirement of the Convention is that "appropriate safeguards" must be in place for any processing of ethnic data to be legitimate.[91]

Other Fundamental Rights Considerations

The principle that no-one can, as a rule, be obliged to disclose his or her ethnic origin, is rather well-established in the field of international human rights law. The Framework Convention for the Protection of National Minorities recognizes in Article 3(1) that "[e]very person belonging to a national minority shall have the right to choose to be treated or not to be treated as such".[92] This provision leaves it to every such person to decide whether or not she wishes to come under the protection flowing from the principles of the Convention. This has been interpreted as implying that each person shall be entitled to require not to be treated as belonging to a minority, and that no-one may be obliged to disclose his or her possible affiliation with a minority.[93] As the Advisory Committee on the Framework Convention put it in its report on Bosnia and Herzegovina: Identification with an ethnic group, for instance in the context of a population census, must be optional.[94] Concurrently, the Committee of Ministers of the Council of Europe has on several occasions confirmed the existence

[91] Makkonen, *cit. supra* note 23, pp. 62–64.

[92] The OSCE Copenhagen document of 1990 provides for a related right in Article 32: "To belong to a national minority is a matter of a person's individual choice and no disadvantage may arise from the exercise of such choice".

[93] See Opinion of the ACFC on Cyprus, 6 April 2001, ACFEC/OP/I(2002)004, para 18, Opinion on Azerbaijan, 22 May 2003, ACFC/OP/I(2004)001, para. 21, Opinion on Ukraine, 1 March 2002, ACFC/OP/I(2002)010, para 22, and Opinion on Bosnia and Herzegovina, 9 October 2008, ACFC/OP/II(2008)005, paras 50–52.

[94] Idem, para 50. See also the opinion of the ACFC on Poland, where it noted that "[w]hile recognising the need for quality data in this area, the Advisory Committee considers that the right not to be treated as a person belonging to a minority also extends to a census and that a compulsory answer to a question on ethnic origin or a question on language used is not compatible with that principle". ACFC, Opinion on Poland, 27 November 2003, ACFC/INF/OP/I(2004)005, para 24.

and importance of the principle of free self-identification.[95] That the principle is not without its exceptions has been recognized in the specific context of Northern Ireland.[96]

The Human Rights Committee has for its part given indications that in its view no-one can be compelled to reveal his or her adherence to a religion or belief, and it is likely that it would opine similarly with respect to ethnic origin, given the close connection between the two.[97]

The CERD Committee has also emphasized the right of an individual to be in control of information that relates to her person. This is clear in view of the Committee's General Recommendation VIII, which reads as follows:

> *The Committee on the Elimination of Racial Discrimination,*
>
> *Having considered* reports from States parties concerning information about the ways in which individuals are identified as being members of a particular racial or ethnic group or groups,
>
> *Is of the opinion* that such identification shall, if no justification exists to the contrary, be based upon self-identification by the individual concerned.

---

[95] Committee of Ministers (Council of Europe), Resolution CM/ResCMN(2009)5 on Albania, Resolution CM/ResCMN(2008)5 on Cyprus and Resolution CM/ResCMN(2007)10 on Ireland.

[96] In Northern Ireland employers are under fair employment legislation encouraged to determine the community background of their employees, even where some employees have not submitted this information. The Advisory Committee, while noting that restrictions on the right to free self-identification "are not consistent with Article 3 of the Framework Convention", submits that this practice "may be relevant", "in the specific context of Northern Ireland ... at this particular moment in time", considering the aims of the practice and the fact that the data remain anonymous and may only be used for statistical purposes. Opinion of the ACFC on United Kingdom, 26 October 2007, ACFC/OP/II(2007)003, paras 47–49. Indeed, it could be argued that since the employee data is collected only for statistical purposes and is rendered anonymous, it cannot be used for purposes that could have a direct impact on the rights or responsibilities of the employees, and thus the practice does not constitute 'treatment' within the sense of Article 3(1) of the FCNM. Interestingly, the Committee of Ministers did not comment this matter in any way in its corresponding Resolution CM/ResCMN(2008)7 on the United Kingdom. For a fuller discussion of the Northern Ireland case, see Christopher McCrudden 'Consociationalism, Equality and Minorities in the Northern Ireland Bill of Rights Debate: The Role of the OSCE High Commissioner on National Minorities" in John Morison – Kieran McEvoy – Gordon Anthony (eds), *Judges, Transition and Human Rights Culture* (Oxford: Oxford University Press, 2007).

[97] See HRC, General Comment No. 22 (1993), para 3. It should be noted, however, that in the consideration of state reports the HRC has never drawn any attention for instance to the question of the lawfulness of the Northern Irish fair employment monitoring system, so hasty conclusions should be avoided.

The Committee has not further elaborated upon its opinion, for instance with regard to its underlying rationale, nor has it explained in what situations it would consider it 'justified' to use other methods than self-identification for the purposes of identification.

It should be noted that the principle of self-identification has also been endorsed by the CESCR, the ECRI and the Durban Declaration and Plan of Action, and is explicitly laid down in some national laws.[98]

Domestic Data Protection Laws

All EU countries have adopted domestic legislation on data protection. Their laws closely follow the substance of the international and European instruments.[99] This is of significance, because the latter instruments allow states parties to provide for a higher level of protection of personal data than what is provided for by the international instruments, meaning that they can forbid the collection of ethnic data altogether if they so wish. Yet, state parties have not used this opportunity beyond the introduction of some rather technical requirements by some of them.[100]

Socio-Political Considerations

Given that it is legally possible – provided that a number of quite specific criteria are met – to collect ethnic data, the next stage in the assessment of whether ethnic data collection should be introduced for the purposes of fighting discrimination is to consider the social and political questions involved. Is there popular support for monitoring, considering that for ethnic monitoring to work, people would need to

[98] CESCR, General Comment No. 20 (2009); Isil Gachet 'The Issue of Ethnic Data Collection From the Perspective of Some Council of Europe Activities' in Andrea Krizsan (ed.), *Ethnic Monitoring and Data Protection: The European Context* (Budapest: Central European University Press, 2001), p. 54; Article 92(a) of the Durban Declaration and Plan of Action; Article 7 of the Hungarian Minority Act.

[99] Makkonen, *cit. supra* note 23.

[100] See Idem (Makkonen). However, in Belgium, an Executive Decree issued by the government (Executive Decree of 13 February 2001 implementing the Federal Law of 8 December 1998 on the protection of the right to private life with respect to the processing of personal data) provides that consent cannot constitute a justification for the processing of sensitive data where the consent cannot be considered to have been given 'freely'. This is taken to be the case in the context of the employment relationship, as it is considered that a power imbalance exists between the employer and the employee. The Belgian government took this position despite two prior contrary opinions issued by the Belgian Commission for the protection of private life (Commission for the protection of private life, Opinion Nos 8/99 and 25/99).

co-operate in it on a voluntary basis? What do the persons most directly concerned, immigrants and persons belonging to minorities, think about ethnic monitoring? Would the introduction of ethnic monitoring be counterproductive in some way? If so, would the benefits still outweigh the disadvantages?

To find answers to the first two questions, the European Commission commissioned two Special Eurobarometer surveys, the results of which were published in 2007 and 2008. To begin with, 75% of the respondents to the 2007 Eurobarometer said that they are in favour of providing information about one's ethnic origin as part of a census, on the condition of anonymity, with 19% opposing disclosure of such data.[101] On average, there is therefore a broad degree of acceptance among the European public to provide ethnic information as part of a census, for the purposes of fighting discrimination. Respondents to the 2008 survey were asked to indicate whether they support or oppose ethnic monitoring in the field of employment, either in the context of monitoring the composition of the work-force in order to evaluate the representation of people from ethnic minorities, or to monitor recruitment procedures to ensure that candidates from ethnic minorities have the same chance of being selected for an interview or hired as other candidates with similar skills and qualifications. According to the results, 57% of the respondents supported monitoring the composition of the workforce, whereas 33% opposed it, the rest being undecided. Major differences in opinion between the EU member states appeared, as more than 70% of the respondents in Ireland, Denmark, Greece and Cyprus were in favour of workplace monitoring, whereas only a minority of respondents supported monitoring in Germany, Latvia, Slovakia, and Austria. There was considerably greater support for monitoring *applicants* than monitoring the actual *workforce*, as 71% of all European respondents were in favour of the first type of action. There was also less variation between countries with respect to this question, as a clear majority in all countries was in favour of monitoring in this context.

Significantly, those who self-identified themselves as part of an ethnic minority were *more favourable* towards both kinds of monitoring,

[101] The condition of anonymity is probably to be understood, in this context, as referring to an arrangement where the ethnic data is not permanently associated with any identifiable individual. European Commission, *Discrimination in the European Union*. Special Eurobarometer 263 (European Commission, January 2007), p. 28.

as 67% of these respondents supported workplace monitoring and 77% supported monitoring recruitment procedures. This suggests that the overwhelming majority of persons belonging to minorities and immigrants do not perceive that any risk of misuse would arise from the introduction of monitoring, or that at any rate they are not held back by it. Yet, it must be kept in mind that many still do have reservations.

For the majority of the countries there would appear to be substantial, perhaps even adequate, popular support for the introduction of mechanisms for collecting ethnic data. Moreover, experience from those countries that have already introduced ethnic monitoring regimes indicate that the residual public resistance often turns into acceptance once monitoring is introduced and people get first-hand experience of how the system works. For instance in Northern Ireland, the concept of monitoring on a religious basis was an anathema to both public and private sector employers, but after the introduction of the regime of monitoring in the civil service, it was generally asked why it should not also be applied in the private sector and, after pressure was exerted to strengthen the domestic fair employment legislation, the legislation was amended to require monitoring from all employers with more than 10 employees.[102]

Yet things are not at all this simple and straightforward. To be operational, data collection schemes – and particularly workplace monitoring – require the co-operation of basically every individual whose data is requested. Less than close to perfect co-operation leads to skewed results that are not of much use. For instance in the context of recruitment, in small to medium size businesses there may only be few minority-origin persons within the pool of applicants, even on a yearly account, and the resulting statistics will not be of much use if one or more of these persons choose not to disclose their ethnic origin. Keeping in mind the principle that no-one may be obliged to reveal his or her ethnic origin, and the fact that there is opposition to disclosure of ethnic data, this is a difficult equation to solve, particularly in countries where opposition to monitoring is high.

There is always also the problem with the construction of categories for the purposes of monitoring. Given that social construction is strongly and inevitably involved in all 'racial' and ethnic distinctions

---

[102] Bob Cooper 'The Fair Employment Commission in Northern Ireland', in Martin MacEwen (ed.), *Anti-Discrimination Law Enforcement* (Aldershot: Avebury, 1997), pp. 203–204.

and classifications, and that there is no scientifically valid basis for these practices, there can be no objective way of constructing ethnic classifications and assigning people into the available categories. The choices made will be subjective, and countries that practice ethnic data collection use classifications that are specific to their history, perceptions prevalent in the popular culture, bureaucratic practices, their current demographic structure and prevailing legal system. The year 2001 British census questionnaire, to give an example, asked "What is your ethnic group?" and gave five broad, quite interestingly essentially 'race'-based, categories to choose from: "White", "Mixed", "Asian or Asian British", "Black or Black British" and "Chinese or other ethnic group".[103] To give a somewhat contrasting example, the Hungarian 2001 census form asked the respondent the question "Which of these nationalities do you think you belong to", and gave 14 different choices such as 'Bulgarian', 'Roma' and 'Hungarian'.[104] These contrasting approaches aptly demonstrate the lack of universally applicable principles and the influence of socio-historical factors. The difficulties that people have in placing themselves in 'racial' or 'ethnic' boxes such as these is often exacerbated by the fact that classification schemes tend to provide only for a few broad categories to choose from, and do not necessarily accommodate persons with 'mixed backgrounds'. Moreover, the reporting of the census results – "Whites live like this, Blacks like that" – contributes to ethnogenesis, the social construction of essentialized ethnic and 'racial' divisions and identities.[105] The simplicities of data collection, in short, do not do justice to the diversity and complexity of the social reality.

There is always also the problem that self-identification procedures may lead to over- or underestimation of the numbers of individuals who belong to ethnic minorities, as some persons belonging to majorities may falsely identify as members of minorities, for instance for the

[103] Much in the same vein, the year 2000 US census questionnaire posed the question "What is your race?" and asked the respondent to indicate if she was of, inter alia, 'White', 'Black, African American or Negro', 'American Indian or Alaska Native', 'Asian Indian' or of 'Some other race'. An entirely different question asked whether the respondent is "Spanish/Hispanic/Latino", which aptly shows the ambiguity of designing taxonomies.

[104] Census questionnaires from the different countries are available at the website of the United Nations Statistics Division, http://unstats.un.org (visited 1.1.2010).

[105] Dvora Yanow, *Constructing "Race" and "Ethnicity" in America: Category-Making in Public Policy and Administration* (New York: M.E. Sharpe, 2003).

purposes of benefiting from some social programme aimed at the minorities; this phenomenon is known as the problem of 'false positives'. On the other hand, some persons belonging to the minorities may choose to identify as members of the ethnic majority for instance in order to avoid stigmatization; this phenomenon is known as the problem of 'false negatives'.[106] For example, in some censuses conducted in Central and Eastern Europe, it appears that even fewer than one in ten Roma persons identified themselves as such.[107] In consequence of these phenomena, census-taking and monitoring exercises may lead to distorted results even if there nominally is full co-operation on part of all the persons concerned.

It must be realized that the collection of ethnic data may have the counter-productive effect of increasing the salience of ethnic identities. When people answer ethnic questions they are obviously reminded of their ethnic identity, its implications and its importance. As argued in chapters 2–4 above, a strong case can be made that even mere acts of distinction-making on the basis of group affiliations produce ingroup favouritism and outgroup bias.[108] Increasing racial awareness is liable to increase 'racial' and ethnic divisions, unless it is counterbalanced by effective measures that underline the existence of a broader, overarching 'intergroup identity'.[109] As the meeting of the latter condition is far from straightforward, the introduction of ethnic data collection always carries the risk of increasing group divisions, and therefore even risk breaching Article 2(1) of the CERD Convention, in which each contracting state "undertakes ... to discourage *anything* which tends to

---

[106] For instance in Hungary, the application of the self-identification rule in determining who are eligible to participate in minority self-government elections as voters and as candidates has reportedly led to an abuse of the system by non-minority people. On the other hand, in many countries, including Canada, there is clear evidence of ethnic minority people reporting as belonging to the majority. See Makkonen, *cit. supra* note 23, p. 77 and the references cited therein.

[107] For an example, in the 1991 Czechoslovak census only some 33 000 people declared themselves as Roma, whereas most unofficial estimates show a Roma population of between 250 000 – 300 000. Barbora Bukovska, 'Ethnic Statistics and Data Protection: The Czech Case' in Krizsán, Andrea (ed.), *Ethnic Monitoring and Data Protection* (Budapest: CPS Books, 2001). See also European Commission, *The Social Situation in the European Union 2007 – Social Cohesion through Equal Opportunities* (Luxembourg: OOPEC, 2008), p. 92.

[108] See e.g. Henri Tajfel, *Human Groups and Social Categories* (Cambridge: Cambridge University Press, 1981).

[109] See e.g. Richard J. Crisp – Sarah R. Beck 'Reducing Intergroup Bias: The Moderating Role of Ingroup identification', *Group Processes & Intergroup Relations*, 2005 Vol 8 (2), p. 182.

strengthen racial division".[110] It must, however, be considered that ethnic data collection will not have the same effect in all societies, because there are major cultural differences in the prevalent levels of 'racial' and ethnic awareness. In those countries where levels of that awareness are already high, such as the USA and the UK, the introduction or further extension of data collection mechanisms cannot therefore be presumed to pose the kind of a problem as it would in many other countries.

Many of the apparent problems with ethnic data collection could be circumvented if the data were collected by means of third-party observation instead of self-identification. This would involve the employer or a census interviewer filling in the ethnic data for the data subjects without consulting them about it, on the basis of visual observations or some other cue such as the surname or mother tongue of the person concerned. There are three major problems with this approach, however: First, it is in tension with the legal instruments on privacy, data protection and human rights, which are in favour of the self-identification method. Second, the idea of third-party observation rests on the highly problematic thought, reflecting scientific positivism, that ethnicity and 'race' are fixed, objective and therefore observable facts.[111] Third, census questionnaires are nowadays in almost all countries filled in by the data subjects themselves, and it is not likely that countries will – simply for the sake of introducing an ethnic question that can be filled in a particular way – switch back to the older method where census returns were filled in by the interviewer. In effect, even if monitoring based on third-party observation would be introduced at workplaces, a mismatch would rather inevitably result between the monitoring data and the census data, because the two sets of data would be collected in different ways.

10.4 Conclusions

European countries should step up their activities when it comes to collecting equality data. This is clear in view of the number of benefits that an evidence-based approach can bring, and in view of the presently meagre performance of EU countries in this area. Currently

---

[110] Emphasis added.
[111] Yanow, *cit. supra* note 105, p. 106.

discrimination mostly remains in the dark, and authorities and other stakeholders do not have a clear picture of the realities of everyday life for immigrants and persons belonging to minorities. One consequence of this is that they also put inadequate effort to solving these, for them invisible, problems.

The question remains what is the best way to collect data about discrimination, its causes and effects. A distinction may be made between a 'sociological approach', which involves the conducting of quantitative and qualitative surveys and other types of research, and which can reveal inequalities and their causes and consequences in the society, and 'ethnic monitoring', which involves the collection of ethnic data, and which can expose specific discriminatory practices. These two approaches are not mutually exclusive, but can be used in conjunction. The choice whether to pursue the sociological approach does not so much involve matters of principle, it involves more matters of finance, as a fully fledged and continuing research programme can be costly to run. The pursuance of this line of action depends therefore primarily on political will.

The pursuance of ethnic monitoring, on the contrary, raises several issues of principle. It is a fascinating and much-promising tool in that it can at least in theory render particular instances of discrimination visible and help to achieve fairer outcomes. The international, European and national rules on protection of privacy and data do not categorically prohibit the collection of ethnic data, though they are suspicious towards it and lay down conditions that must be strictly observed whenever such data is collected. States that are interested in the introduction of ethnic monitoring must above all provide 'suitable safeguards' for the protection of the data subjects. From a practical point of view it is not clear whether the provision of such 'suitable safeguards' is enough, as the available safeguards can never be entirely watertight. The risk of abuse cannot be assessed in the abstract, as it is only immigrants and persons belonging to minorities, that is those individuals whose interests data collection might put at (however distant) risk and in whose interests such data would be collected, who should be entitled to answer the question of whether the existence of that risk is sufficiently great so as to preclude collection of ethnic data. Policy-makers, on the other hand, must consider whether the introduction of ethnic data collection is counterproductive, as it may increase the levels of divisive ethno-racial awareness and identification. At any rate, a monitoring regime that would guarantee the necessary degree of accuracy and reliability would take years to develop, as it would take some time before people would grow used to it and show confidence in it. At the end of the day, the decision about ethnic data collection must therefore depend on the particular socio-political circumstances and particularly on the views of the groups directly concerned. What is good for one society may not be good for another.

11 POSITIVE ACTION

Anti-discrimination law does not, as pointed out, prohibit measures that are aimed at improving the social and economic status of groups that are socially at a disadvantage. This general principle, manifested in the different instruments and pieces of case law, hides significant disagreement behind it. To begin with, the different pieces of anti-discrimination law use different terms, sometimes referring to this type of measures as 'positive action', 'affirmative action' or 'special measures'. In this chapter the term 'positive action' is used as an umbrella term for the sake of convenience, not, for instance, because of any assumed superiority of the concept. Secondly, the substantive content of the principle is couched in several different ways. Perhaps most importantly, it is sometimes suggested that states have an obligation to take positive action, whereas most pieces of anti-discrimination law are generally interpreted only to allow, not require, such action. There are also manifest differences in terms of the legitimate scope of positive action, as will be shown a bit later on. In short, the applicable legal standards exhibit conceptual and substantive diversity.

For the purposes of the present discussion, positive action is broadly speaking used to refer to a policy or a specific operation that directly or indirectly helps to diminish or eliminate particular disadvantages suffered by a group or the members thereof in terms of opportunities or resources, over and above those measures that need to be undertaken to identify and eliminate discriminatory practices and criteria.[1] Positive

[1] For other conceptualizations, see Marc de Vos, 'Beyond Formal Equality: Positive Action under Directives 2000/43/EC and 2000/78' (Luxembourg: OOPEC, 2007), p. 11; Anita Allen 'Can Affirmative Action Combat Racial Discrimination? Moral Success and Political Failure in the United States' in Appelt, Erna – Monica Jarosch (eds.) *Combating Racial Discrimination: Affirmative Action as a Model for Europe* (Oxford: Berg, 2000), p. 25; Olivier de Schutter 'Chapter Seven: Positive Action' in Dagmar Schiek – Lisa Waddington – Mark Bell, *Non-Discrimination Law: Cases, Materials and text on National, Supranational and International Non-Discrimination Law* (Oxford: Hart Publishing, 2007), p. 759. De Schutter, for instance, considers that positive action is about differences in treatment on the basis of otherwise suspect grounds. This study, however, proceeds from the understanding that already equal treatment sometimes requires that "suspect grounds" are taken into account, and that on the other hand, positive action is not about using "suspect" criteria but about the impact of such measures on the target groups.

action can, at least in theory, be distinguished from positive, active measures taken in order to track down and eliminate discrimination, in that positive action goes beyond such measures.[2] What is characteristic of positive action is that it is oriented towards *accelerating* and even ensuring the achievement of a more equal distribution of opportunities or other social goods, seen from a group perspective. It is about taking into account the very characteristic – ethnic origin – that puts people at a disadvantage in our societies. There is, however, not necessarily even a fine line between positive action on the one hand, and policies of equal opportunity and general welfare policies on the other.[3] For an example, an employer may train the staff on equal treatment law, and may review selection, recruitment and other employment criteria and practices to track down factors that slow down the hiring of minority persons. These measures may well lead to an increase in the number of minority employees, and one could well argue both that they constitute plain anti-discrimination work and that they constitute positive action.[4] General welfare programmes and policies are by definition aimed at the least well-off, which means that in an ethnically stratified society many immigrant and minority groups do benefit from them in a particular way. Again, it is largely a matter of opinion whether this is seen as positive action or not. The above examples suggest that positive action should perhaps not be conceptualized as a deviation from general equal opportunity policies or general welfare policies. In fact, there may be significant overlap between these approaches.

The diversity of legal standards and the fact that they mostly stop short of requiring positive action express the plurality of political views on this subject matter. Positive action goes into the heart of theories and sentiments about social justice, as it deals with the distribution of

[2] See e.g. Nathan Glazer, 'Affirmative Action and "Race" Relations: Affirmative Action as a Model for Europe' in Erna Appelt–Monica Jarosch (eds.), *Combating Racial Discrimination: Affirmative Action as a Model for Europe* (Oxford: Berg, 2000), p. 140. International and European anti-discrimination law emphatically point out, that the prohibition of discrimination does not preclude positive action measures. Such a clarification would not be necessary if positive action was simply about measures taken to eliminate discriminatory practices.

[3] See e.g. Melissa S. Williams 'In Defence of Affirmative Action: North American Discourses for the European Context?' in Erna Appelt – Monica Jarosch (eds.) *Combating Racial Discrimination: Affirmative Action as a Model for Europe* (Oxford: Berg, 2000), p. 70.

[4] This is the case particularly if one operates within the conceptual framework of substantive equality of opportunity.

goods such as opportunities and resources. It forces the society to take a stand on tough and ultimate questions such as "what is equality" and "how can and should equality be achieved". In consequence it is not at all surprising that positive action is an issue that engenders controversy, and that legislative and judicial caution is exercised in this area, particularly with respect to international and European law.

Yet the lack of overall agreement over positive action should not become prohibitive for taking such action. As the next subchapter will show, positive action is the key to unlocking a positive development and must necessarily form a part of an effective anti-discrimination policy where there are major intergroup differences in wellbeing, as in modern-day Europe. This basic point of departure is fairly widely acknowledged.[5] In addition, Europe has not seen anything like the controversies that have vexed the US, where affirmative action policies have in recent decades been both fiercely opposed and defended. One must also note that the opposition to affirmative action in the US appears to stem to a large extent from a belief that such action is primarily about preferential treatment that leads to less-qualified African Americans being hired over better-qualified whites.[6] Such a belief is, particularly in the present European context, entirely misplaced. In consequence, positive action need not be the divisive and political issue it has become or is perceived to have become.[7]

11.1 The Policy Case

This subchapter aspires to make a general argument for the adoption of positive action measures, without prejudice to the kinds of positive action that should be pursued.

Positive action is, broadly speaking, aimed at eradicating or reducing group-wide socio-economic disadvantages. This is a laudable aim,

[5] For instance the European Commission, in its 2008 Communication on *Non-discrimination and equal opportunities*, declares that it "will use the permanent dialogue with Member States to promote the full utilisation of the possibilities for positive action, in particular in access to education, employment, housing and health care." See Commission of the European Communities, Communication from the Commission to the European Parliament, the Council, The European Economic and Social Committee and the Committee of the Regions, *Non-Discrimination and equal opportunities: A renewed commitment*, 2.7.2008 COM(2008) 420 final, pp. 7–8.

[6] See e.g. Allen, *cit. supra* note 1, pp. 26–27.

[7] Vos, *cit. supra* note 1, p. 5.

also and particularly from the point of view of promoting market equality and material equality. People's socio-economic status, and even their *assumed* socio-economic status, affects how others perceive them and behave towards them. Intergroup differences seem to generate or reinforce intergroup prejudice, they appear to influence the salience of group identities and intergroup distinctions, and they structure interpersonal contacts and stimulate the attribution of negative traits and inferiority to the less advantaged group.[8] This simple dynamic between status and the treatment one receives conditions relationships and plays into the construction of inequality in a variety of ways, as discussed in this study. Perhaps most importantly, major intergroup disparities feed and sustain negative stereotypes, because people tend to explain these disparities in ways that confirm their prejudices. People are sensitive not just to group divisions, but also to the status patterns that appear to go with them, and draw inferences from that.[9] In effect, there is a short step from a particular group being visibly overrepresented in second-class jobs to that group being labelled second-class workforce and its members second-class citizens. Seen from the point of view of minorities and immigrants, the vicious circle of discrimination and deprivation may foster the kind of dissatisfaction and social unrest that many in Europe so much fear. One key lesson that decision-makers in Europe and elsewhere should learn is that if a group of people have nothing, they have nothing to lose, and vice versa: the more they have, the more they have to lose too. There appears to be, indeed, a link between general wellbeing and security.

It is also possible to set in motion an upward spiral, and this is where positive action measures step in. Upward social mobility helps to dismantle negative stereotypes, and the increased integration and visibility of immigrants and minorities helps the general public to reconsider and reshape its identity in a manner that acknowledges the society's full ethnic and cultural diversity. This will have major positive social-psychological effects and can foster the emergence of a more inclusive

[8] John Duckitt, *The Social Psychology of Prejudice* (London: Greenwood, 1994), p. 125.

[9] A theory known as illusory correlation explains how this takes place. This theory holds that people tend to see a stronger (and possibly more natural) relationship between two relatively unusual but attention-capturing phenomena that to certain extent appear to go together (such as being an immigrant and being deprived), even if the correlation is in reality slight or even entirely illusory. In consequence, people can come to overestimate the link between being an immigrant and being deprived.

and accepting public culture that is more appealing also to the persons belonging to minorities. The 'give and take' role of mutual assistance and dependence that equal participation (for instance as tax payers) in the society promotes, helps to create a sense of common endeavour, a 'we-ness' not based on origin but common interest.[10]

Positive action will also bring about minority role models and is likely to reinforce target communities' trust in the society at large and its fairness.[11] We may also presume that increased participation in the labour life, on equal terms, promotes integration and active commitment to the society in general. Fostering such commitment is of the outmost importance, since particularly newcomers lack the kind of deep roots and social networks in the host society that help them feel like integral parts of that society. Participation in the labour market, the political life and other public domains fosters a sense of control over one's life and boosts one's self-respect.

The benefits to the society at large and the target groups aside, what about businesses and other organizations the efforts of which the successfulness of positive action to a great extent depends on? Why would they undertake such measures, unless of course they were legally obliged to do that? The answer is that businesses can be expected to benefit in a range of ways from engaging in positive action. To the extent that positive action helps to prevent discrimination, it helps to save financial and public image costs linked with discrimination litigation and other enforcement measures. Businesses may also experience an improvement in their public image, making them more appealing to minority jobseekers and customers, which would help them to tap into a broader pool of talent and customer base. On the cost side, positive action requires some advance planning and therefore the use of human resources, entailing costs. Yet, its implementation does not necessarily have to be costly, as the typology of positive action measures set out in the next subchapter demonstrates. Whatever costs there are may well be offset by the benefits.

---

[10] John Duckitt, in his seminal work on prejudices, concludes that positive action is needed to break entrenched cycles of exclusion and to redress the often severe social and economic inequities that result from the histories of injustice and discrimination, and holds that positive action ultimately lessens negative stereotyping. Duckitt, *cit. supra* note 8, p. 253.

[11] Erna Appelt 'Affirmative Action: a Cross-National Debate' in Erna Appelt–Monica Jarosch (eds.) *Combating Racial Discrimination: Affirmative Action as a Model for Europe* (Oxford: Berg, 2000), p. 9; Allen, *cit. supra* note 1, p. 30.

So far the policy case has been developed on fairly practical and broad social utility terms. Indeed, the impact of upward social mobility of disadvantaged ethnic groups on both the attitudes and wellbeing of those groups themselves and the attitudes – and indirectly also the wellbeing and sense of security – of the ethnic majority is so strong that the case for positive action may be considered compelling on those grounds alone. However, the case for positive action can be made, and is usually made, not on the grounds of social utility but on the grounds of justice. In the United States a major, if not the main, rationale for affirmative action policies has been the desire to redress negative effects of past discrimination, including segregation, slavery and other forms of 'white supremacy'.[12]

In Europe, the case for using positive action to redress the present effects of past gross injustices is perhaps not as strong as in the US, although one must keep in mind that colonialism, racism and other forms of subordination and exclusion constitute an undeniable part of the history of Europe as well. This means that also in Europe there is a legacy of disadvantage that is attributable to past discrimination. The kind of systematic, institutional, widespread and often subtle discrimination that operates in Europe *today*, with all its repercussions, is, however, all the reason that is needed to support positive action. The moral duty to compensate for undue disadvantages imposed upon persons and groups victimized by discrimination is strong. Even if anti-discrimination law (as presently conceived) was enforced to the full extent, which it surely is not, the disadvantages would not be eliminated, as that law cannot cope with the broad effects of past and present discrimination. The existing group-structured inequalities respond only to group-based remedies, such as positive action.[13]

Material inequalities and disparities may, however, also arise from factors other than discrimination, and it is difficult if not impossible to tell to which extent existing disadvantages can be attributed to discrimination. In this respect it is important to remember that international and European law allows the use of positive action to ameliorate disadvantages in general, irrespective of their source. This is reflected

[12] See e.g. Robert K. Fullinwider, *The Reverse Discrimination Controversy* (New Jersey: Rowman and Littlefield, 1981), p. 26.

[13] Similarly, Williams *cit. supra* note 3, p. 66.

in the language of the relevant provisions, which are couched in terms of "ensuring adequate *development* and *protection* of certain groups and individuals belonging to them" and "prevention and compensation of *disadvantages* linked to ethnic origin".[14]

The reality is that no matter how convincing a theoretical case for positive action is made in terms of social utility or in terms of justice, the decision to engage in such action often hinges, in practice, on popular support – or the lack of it, as political decision-makers may be unwilling to support positive action out of fear of losing voters. The example of the United States has demonstrated how positive action can become an overly politicized and controversial issue, with attendant cautiousness to engage with it. The attitude climate in Europe is presently much more hospitable towards positive action than is the attitude climate in the US. In a 2008 survey conducted in the EU, 72% of the respondents – almost three out of four – said that they were in favour of positive action, defined as "specific measures … adopted to provide equal opportunities for everyone in the field of employment".[15] This is a remarkably high figure, because one cannot automatically expect the dismantling of privileges to be popular among the privileged. The fact that such an overwhelming majority supports positive action would indeed seem to suggest that the case for positive measures is compelling in Europe. As people may sometimes support some general idea but oppose its practical implications,[16] a distinct feature of the survey was that it specified that positive action encompasses, for instance, "special training schemes" and "adapted selection and recruitment processes", two relatively strong and practical lines of action. Importantly, opposition towards positive action was found to be rather low, ranging from 9% (Spain) to 36% (Austria) and averaging 22% in the EU. In light of these findings, lack of popular support cannot be used as an excuse for not taking positive action measures in Europe.

---

[14] ICERD and the Racial Equality Directive, respectively (emphasis added).

[15] European Commission, *Discrimination in the European Union: Perceptions, Experiences and Attitudes*. Special Eurobarometer 296 (July 2008), p. 28.

[16] For instance the very same Eurobarometer survey found that whereas "only" 6% of the respondents said that they would feel uncomfortable with having a neighbour of a "different ethnic origin" (a general statement), altogether 24% said they would feel uncomfortable with having a Roma neighbour (a more specific statement). Ibid, pp. 120–127.

11.2 Methods

Positive action can be accomplished and implemented in a variety of ways. It can be engaged in by both public and private organizations, including businesses, schools and public bodies.[17]

As previously noted, in an ethnically stratified society, 'general' social policy measures tend to have an ethnic impact. For instance, measures such as increases in the human and material resources of schools in areas inhabited predominantly or disproportionately by immigrants and persons belonging to minorities have a positive action dimension to them. Employment policies and tax policies may also be geared towards helping the least well off groups, which often disproportionately consist of immigrants and persons belonging to minorities. Measures such as these cannot go all the way in eliminating group-wide disadvantages, as they usually benefit only the least well-off without helping the majority of these population groups. Targeted policy measures such as language courses, socio-cultural competence courses and further education courses for immigrants have got a more direct positive action quality to them and can be expected to have a broader effect.

Positive action is most often associated with policies and measures undertaken by public or private organizations in the context of employment. Different measures can be helpful at different stages of the recruitment and selection process, and engagement in positive action at one stage does not exclude engagement in it at others. A typology of positive action measures is developed below. At this point, this typology is presented without prejudice to the assessment of their legal acceptability or socio-political feasibility, as both issues will be discussed at a later stage.

The different individual measures vary in intensity, starting with measures that harbour on general anti-discrimination measures.

---

[17] There can also be third-party positive action, for instance by public employment services that are not themselves the final employers, and that provide for instance subsidized learning opportunities for a fixed period of time. This kind of third-party action may be the only way to bring positive action to small and medium size enterprises that would not individually have the capacity or know-how to engage in it. Elisabeth Strasser – August Gächter – Mariya Dzhengozova, *The Benefits of Positive Action: Thematic Discussion Paper*. Discussion paper prepared by the International Centre for Migration Policy Development for the FRA (Vienna, March 2008), p. 22.

Commitment to an explicit equal opportunities policy. This kind of a policy should first of all aim at elimination of discrimination from all the operations of the organization. This would involve consciously and comprehensively examining, identifying and eradicating any discriminatory or distorting practices. Secondly, the policy could have a more proactive component, such as training personnel in equality law.[18]

Outreach. This category consists of encouragement measures to attract minority applicants and increase their proportion in the pool of applicants. Possible outreach measures include advertising open vacancies in minority or local media and placing advertisements in community and intercultural centres; using minority languages and images in advertisements and in other company communication, including on the internet; promoting better intercultural relations through sponsoring events that are of interest to the target groups; and appointing or designating a diversity recruitment officer in charge of outreach measures.

Pre-employment support. This category includes measures designed to help the target groups to better compete for jobs or other opportunities, and can come close to outreach measures. Potential support measures include training and specialist advice on issues such as CV writing, interview techniques and presentation skills. Labour agencies can also appoint counsellors to support migrants and members of minorities during the interview.[19] Special preparatory classes for new employees may also be helpful. Courses aimed at improving employability may be targeted particularly at immigrants and persons belonging to minorities.

Adaptation of merit, skill and selection criteria. This category includes measures by which one reviews and redefines the criteria that are relevant for recruitment and selection. Once we realize and accept that there are no inherently neutral or self-evident employment criteria and that any criteria will be advantageous for some and disadvantageous for others, then a review of these criteria appears not just possible but

---

[18] Paul Taylor 'Positive Action in the United Kingdom' in Erna Appelt – Monica Jarosch (eds.) *Combating Racial Discrimination: Affirmative Action as a Model for Europe* (Oxford: Berg, 2000).

[19] During one campaign carried out in the Netherlands, 250 counsellors were hired to support migrants during job interviews. This tactic proved effective in overcoming ethnic stereotyping. See Ravinder Singh Dhami – Judith Squires – Tariq Modood, *Developing positive action policies: learning from the experiences of Europe and North America*. Department for Work and Pensions, Research Report No 406 (Corporate Document Services, 2006), p. 45 and the references cited therein.

necessary.[20] For instance, skills and experience more likely to be found among persons belonging to minorities may be considered an asset or a requirement for a job. Language skills, or social skills such as familiarity with a particular culture or an intercultural environment, can be considered a merit and made relevant and favourable selection criteria for many types of positions. In several countries ethnic origin does, for instance, constitute a legitimate criterion for employment in the hiring of police officers to work with youth from minority communities.[21] A further type of measure is the adjustment of standardized employment tests or their results in order to take into account their cultural biases, considering that these tests do not always reflect the knowledge, skills and competence of minorities.

Positive recruitment measures. This category includes recruitment measures that may be considered a form of indirect positive action. An employer may, for instance, reach the target population by focusing on those geographical areas with substantial concentration of immigrant families or by focusing on the long-term unemployed if the target groups are overrepresented in that category.

Preferential treatment in recruitment. A particularly useful measure would be a decision to invite at least one immigrant or minority origin person, who meets the minimum requirements, to be interviewed whenever there is a job opening. This policy has been used in Norway, with notable success.[22]

Preferential treatment in selection. This category of measures gives members of underrepresented groups some kind of preference in the actual selection decision. The purpose of preferential employment is to

[20] Frank Cunningham, 'Positive Action and Democracy' in Erna Appelt - Monica Jarosch (eds.) *Combating Racial Discrimination: Affirmative Action as a Model for Europe* (Oxford: Berg, 2000), p. 56

[21] There is experience in this respect at least in Great Britain, the U.S. and Germany. See e.g. Allen, *cit supra* note 1, p. 26. An academically and legally interesting question is whether - or more precisely: when - these types of measures should be considered as falling under the category of positive action and when under 'genuine occupational requirements'. See Fullinwider, *cit supra* note 12, p. 17, who holds that "[i]f a black is hired because he is black but being black is a job-related qualification, then this is not a case of preferential hiring as I have defined it." See also Schutter, *cit. supra* note 1, p. 771. One possible answer to this question is to pose another question: is tweaking employment-related criteria made in the interests of the social policy aim of promoting more equal representation in the workforce, or is it made in the interests of selecting the best person for a particular job? See Vos, *cit. supra* note 1, pp. 34–35.

[22] See Timo Makkonen 'Good as far as it goes, but does it go far enough? A report on Norway's Anti-discrimination laws and policies' (Migration Policy Group, 2008).

achieve an ethnically balanced workforce. This purpose makes it necessary to assess, in some way, what the present composition of the workforce is and what a balanced workforce would look like, using the distribution of groups in the national or local population as a point of comparison. Such assessments are often used in connection with soft targets, the attainment of which need not necessarily lead to actual preferential treatment, or with more rigid quotas, the attainment of which may more readily call for robust use of preferential treatment.

Preferential treatment may vary in intensity, depending on the threshold rule that is used to trigger the treatment:

- 'the other things being equal rule', that is, under-representation is used as a decisive criterion in tie-break situations where there are two or more equally qualified candidates;
- 'the high threshold of qualification rule', that is, under-representation is used as the decisive criterion where the nominally best candidate is only marginally more qualified;
- 'the minimum threshold of qualification rule', that is, under-representation is used as the decisive criterion where the person belonging to the underrepresented group meets the minimum level of competence, irrespective of whether there are candidates who are better qualified.[23]

In-service positive action. This group of measures is aimed at those who are already in employment, and include training to increase the potential for career advancement; early intervention to ensure retention; mentoring; and cultural and religious accommodation, where not already required by the law.

11.3 Challenges

The policy case for positive action was argued above at a general level, without prejudice to the assessment of the socio-political desirability and legal acceptability of any individual types of measures. The latter perspectives call for our attention, however, as they set the parameters within which positive action can be carried out in practice. For the purpose of the following discussion, a general distinction is made here between 'hard measures', which involve outright preferential treatment on the basis of origin, and 'soft measures', which promote inclusion without engagement in direct preferential treatment.

---

[23] Williams, *cit. supra* note 3, p. 73.

Legal Perspectives

There is remarkably little international or European judicial or even quasi-judicial guidance on positive action in the area of combating ethnic discrimination, considering the outstanding practical and legal importance of the subject area at hand.[24] The most basic principle is rather clear, though: anti-discrimination law does not preclude positive action, and appears even to require it in order to guarantee the effective and equal enjoyment of human rights. But major legal questions remain unresolved, such as "what exactly constitutes positive action", "what is the legitimate scope of positive action" and "when exactly is the taking of positive action required and not just allowed"? For instance the ECtHR has yet to rule on these issues. By far the most authoritative and detailed case law in relation to positive action has been developed by the European Court of Justice in the context of gender equality law. Scholars are divided on the issue of whether we can expect the *acquis* developed in the field of gender equality law to apply *mutatis mutandis* also in the field of racial equality.[25] Therefore that case law will be reviewed here only briefly, as a general illustration of the Court's approach in this area.

The ECJ's approach with regard to positive action in the field of gender equality has developed incrementally, and we can note changes in its approach over time.[26] But the red thread for the Court, as seen from today's perspective and in the perspective of cases such as *Kalanke*, *Marschall*, *Badeck* and *Abrahamsson*, is that selection rules and processes, that give automatic and unconditional preferences to those belonging to the underrepresented sex, and that do not include an objective assessment of specific personal situations of all the candidates, are inconsistent with the EU law and its provisions on positive action in particular.[27] *Automatic* and *unconditional* preferences are precluded even between candidates having equivalent or substantially equivalent merits.[28] The *ultima ratio* of the Court's reasoning appears

[24] There is a wealth of case law in the US, but it is not applicable as such to international or European law.

[25] For two contrasting opinions, see Vos, *cit. supra* note 1, pp. 31 and 68 and the references cited therein, and de Schutter, *cit. supra* note 1, pp. 821–825.

[26] See Vos, *cit. supra* note 1; de Schutter, *cit. supra* note 1.

[27] ECJ, *Kalanke* v. *Freie Hansestadt Bremen*, C-450/93, 17 October 1995; ECJ, *Hellmut Marschall* v. *Land Nordrhein-Westfalen*, C-409/95, 11 November 1997; ECJ, *Badeck*, C-158/97, 28 March 2000; ECJ, *Abrahamsson and Anderson* v. *Elisabet Fogelqvist*, C-407/98, 6 July 2000. The Court summarised its conception in *Abrahamsson*, para 43.

[28] Idem (*Abrahamsson*).

to be that the goal of "ensuring full equality in practice", referred to both in Article 157(4) (ex Article 141(4)) of TFEU and the Racial Equality Directive, is about ensuring the full equal opportunities of individuals, that is, about compensating for the negative baggage (effects of past or present discrimination in particular) that a particular social background may bring to the competition for opportunities, but not about ensuring any particular outcomes.[29] The Court put this emphatically in the *Lommers* case, in which it stated that a "group of measures designed to eliminate the causes of women's reduced opportunities in access to employment and careers and intended to improve the ability of women to compete on the labour market and pursue a career on an equal footing with men" are not precluded by EU law.[30] It appears that in view of the Court, the purpose of positive action is 'merely' to correct irregularities that obstruct the optimal operation of the market and the principle of equal opportunities. Indeed, the Court has said that in its view *a procedure for the selection of candidates for a post involves, as a rule, simply the assessment of their qualifications by reference to the requirements of the vacant post or of the duties to be performed*, and nothing else.[31] From this it follows that positive action is conceptualized more as an exception to the principle of equal treatment, than an integral element of it. In line with this approach, the ECJ has emphasised that any positive action measure has to have due regard for the principle of proportionality, and that any such measure must remain within the limits of what is appropriate and necessary in order to achieve the aim in view.[32] On that account, the Court is of the view that a measure that gives priority to a person belonging to an under-represented group, who meets the minimum qualifications but who does not have qualifications equivalent to those of the person who would otherwise be selected, is disproportionate and thus precluded by EU law on that ground alone.[33]

---

[29] The Court explains in *Abrahamsson* that the legitimate positive action criteria "aim … to achieve substantive, rather than formal, equality by reducing de facto inequalities which may arise in society and, thus … to prevent or compensate for disadvantages in the professional career of persons belonging to the under-represented sex.". See also ECJ, *H. Lommers* v. *Minister van Landbouw, Natuurbeheer en Visserij*, 19 March 2002, para 33.

[30] ECJ, *Lommers, cit. supra* note 29, para 33.

[31] ECJ, *Abrahamsson, cit. supra* note 27, para 46.

[32] ECJ, *Lommers, cit. supra* note 29, para 39; ECJ, *Abrahamsson, cit. supra* note 27, para 55.

[33] Idem (*Abrahamsson*).

In light of this analysis it appears likely that the ECJ would allow, as a rule, measures that simply facilitate and improve the ability of under-represented groups to pursue, and to progress in, their careers.[34] It is, however, questionable whether the ECJ would be ready to accept outright preferential treatment measures. Perhaps only a rule or a scheme that favours a person belonging to an underrepresented group (how ever that under-representation would have to be demonstrated), in situations where that person and some other candidate have got the best and substantially equivalent qualifications, would survive the Court's scrutiny, provided that this rule or scheme is not applied unconditionally or automatically, and that the situations of both candidates are fully and equally taken into account.

At the end of the day, ECJ's current conceptualization of positive action favours formal equality and equality of opportunities over substantive equality and equality of outcome.[35] This point of view can be contrasted with the point of view adopted in the sphere of international human rights law, particularly the ICERD, where positive action to ensure the effective enjoyment of rights is considered, albeit vaguely, an integral part of anti-discrimination law. This is, however, not an instance of inconsistency, as with some simplification, international anti-discrimination law is primarily about *equal* and effective enjoyment of *rights*, whereas EU law is primarily about *equal opportunities* in the market place. The two share common ground in that neither set of laws guarantees any kind of equality of outcome in terms of material equality. Yet, the presumption that equality of opportunities can be achieved without any concern whatsoever to outcomes appears flawed in the analysis of this study. Major socio-economic differences generate and sustain negative stereotypes and prejudices and generate further disadvantage through fertilizing the root causes of discrimination. To achieve equality of opportunity we must therefore pay attention to any socio-economic gulfs that persist between groups.

Socio-Political Perspectives

Would positive action schemes, if widely adopted and implemented, have the kind of counter-productive effects that substantially compromise, or even surpass, their benefits? The literature on positive action,

---

[34] See also ECJ, *Lommers*, *cit. supra* note 29, para 38.

[35] de Schutter, *cit. supra* note 1, p. 824.

which is substantial, has brought up several kinds of concerns about the potential negative impact that such policies may have. Yet, what must be made clear from the start is that these debates have focused almost exclusively on preferential treatment, not the other types of positive action. Preferential treatment rests on ethnic distinctions and therefore increases the salience of group membership, and is to that extent a legitimate concern for the efforts to reduce intergroup divisions. The following discussion will therefore pay attention to these concerns particularly in the context of preferential treatment.

Would positive action schemes, if more widely deployed, promote racial stereotypes, by means of sending the message that immigrants and members of minorities need special attention to make it in the modern competition-based society?[36] The scenario that positive action schemes could indeed foster negative stereotyping does not seem entirely implausible, *insofar* as positive action relies on preferential treatment *and* the adoption of such measures arouse major public attention.[37] As things stand, positive action has not aroused any major public interest in Europe and any reliance on outright preferential treatment seems to be without political, popular and legal support. The softer methods, while calling for employers to pay attention to ethnic diversity and the 'ethnic impact' of the measures they take, do not involve the making of rigid distinctions on the basis of origin, and are unlikely to increase the salience of group divisions in the society in any substantial manner. Moreover, the softer positive action measures do enjoy general support according to opinion polls, meaning that the general public appears convinced that such measures are not just legitimate but necessary. Given these circumstances there is no reason to be concerned about *soft* positive action measures having the unintended effect of reinforcing negative stereotypes. Quite vice versa, to the extent that such action contributes to the upward social mobility of the target groups, it will help to dismantle the existing negative stereotypes.

Would the adoption and implementation of '*hard*' preferential treatment schemes, if such were found necessary and legally acceptable, then have counterproductive effects? In other words, would preferential treatment schemes be taken by the public as an indication that the beneficiary groups are in some way inferior, thus reinforcing and

[36] See e.g. Fullinwider, *cit. supra* note 12, p. 20.
[37] Dhami et al, *cit. supra* note 19.

reinvigorating vulgar beliefs about 'racial' superiority and inferiority?[38] Would preferential treatment promote group divisions? Asking these questions may appear theoretical, given that preferential treatment on the grounds of ethnic origin does not currently appear to be practiced in Europe. Asking these questions may also appear somewhat premature, given that it would be fully possible to capitalize on the current popular support for positive action, to pursue preferential treatment, and to reconsider the continuance of this line of action if preferential treatment would start to show the kind of undesirable effects that outweigh its benefits. And answering these questions involves an inevitable, active and uncomfortable engagement in speculation. Yet, the issue will continue to be debated, and therefore the matter cannot be ignored here either.

Preferential treatment could indeed trigger further negative stereotyping if there was major public debate about it, and if sizable portions of the general public would be persuaded that the reason for the need for preferential treatment is some fault or failure on the beneficiaries' part, not the unfair disadvantages imposed upon them. As preferential treatment involves the making of ethnic distinctions and distributes advantages and burdens on the grounds of these distinctions, it is prone to generate intergroup rivalry insofar as the public becomes aware of it and is not of the opinion that such policies promote 'the common good'. It would certainly not be a surprise if populist and far-right argumentation would draw attention to preferential treatment policies and reinterpret them in terms of 'unjust benefits' and 'discrimination against the majority', in an effort to turn the public opinion against such treatment and the target groups in general. But the possible reinforcement of the beliefs of the already prejudiced is no argument against redressing the damage that these same individuals have inflicted and continue to inflict upon the victims; perhaps vice versa. What matters are popular perceptions, and these could turn either way, given the pre-existing general propensity both to support egalitarian values and to hold negative stereotypes. In effect, if public discussion over preferential treatment and its rationale would arise, politicians and interest groups and individuals would need to be ready not just to support and pursue such action but to actively engage in the public discussions, equipped with the data that show why that action needs to

[38] On this debate, see Allen, *cit. supra* note 1, p. 33.

be taken.[39] Indeed, much of the early success of affirmative action in the US can be credited to a strong Black protest movement and the case it made for preferential treatment.[40]

That said, no stereotype-forming public discussion will necessarily even arise, nor will the general public necessarily take preferences to indicate inferiority instead of discrimination and disadvantage, in which case the upward social mobility of immigrants and persons belonging to minorities would simply serve to dismantle existing negative stereotypes and prejudices. Be that as it may, the impact of preferential treatment on the public opinion is hard to predict, and much will depend on how well the case for preferential treatment is made in the public.

A second thing to consider in this context is whether preferential treatment compromises the self-esteem or self-respect of members of beneficiary groups.[41] It should be underlined that this risk is feared to materialize in the context of preferential treatment only. It hurts one's self-esteem to be selected for employment over a more competent person simply for the sake of one's ethnic origin, so the argument goes. The merits of this argument look questionable on three counts at least. First, those supporting it have not come up with any empirical evidence.[42] Second, the argument supposes that the preferred persons would be convinced (a) that some other candidate really was more qualified, *and* (b) that it is morally wrong to compensate for disadvantages in this way. Usually people will not know about the qualifications of the other candidates, let alone be fully aware of all selection criteria, so the merits of that argument look at least dubious. Alternatively, one could of course expect damage to the minorities' self-esteem to result not from their own assessment of the situation but from other people's assessment of it. But if that argument was correct, if the members of

[39] Indeed, the experiences from the US and Canada suggest that government, when promoting positive action, should do so robustly and should communicate with the public effectively regarding the rationale and nature of the policies. See Dhami – Squires – Modood, *cit. supra* note 19, pp. 114–116.

[40] Melinda Chateauvert 'Using Historical and Sociological Evidence to Defend Anti-Discrimination Policies' in Appelt, Erna – Monica Jarosch (eds.), *Combating Racial Discrimination: Affirmative Action as a Model for Europe* (Oxford: Berg, 2000), p. 114.

[41] This has been suggested e.g. by Thomas Sowell, in *Affirmative Action Reconsidered: Was it Necessary in Academia* (Washington: American Enterprise Institute for Public Policy, 1975).

[42] Williams, *cit. supra* note 3, p. 78; Harry Holzer – David Neumark 'Assessing Affirmative Action' *Journal of Economic Literature*, Vol 38, No 3 (Sep. 2000).

the beneficiary groups would be generally harassed with claims that they have been hired not on the basis of merits but group privileges, then one could expect them to feel at the very least ambivalent about preferential treatment. This brings us to the third point: if it were true that positive action, preferential treatment in particular, hurts its beneficiaries' self-esteem or self-respect, then it would be logical to expect them to oppose such measures or at any rate be ambivalent about them. But the evidence does not support this, as surveys from the US show that beneficiaries support these measures substantially more often than other people.[43] This means, at the very least, that the beneficiaries tend to think that the benefits of positive action outweigh the costs. In effect, if the beneficiaries are not concerned about positive action damaging their self-esteem, why should other people be?

A third, and most serious, issue to consider in this context is whether preferential treatment raises levels of group division. Preferential treatment policies – the connection of tangible benefits to the possession of particular characteristics – advantage some and disadvantage others on the grounds of their 'racial' or ethnic origin, and therefore run against prevailing liberal ideas about neutrality and equal treatment. It would, in other words, be felt to violate the basic sense of formal justice, making people to feel strongly about it. Indeed, there are elements in the public perceptions in the US about preferential treatment that suggest that resistance to it is not just about pragmatic, 'rational' assessment of its pros and cons.[44] Preferential treatment would be bound to increase both the number of groups seeking the status of a disadvantaged group and the number of individuals seeking recognition as a member of such a group. This kind of signification of origin and the associated competition for benefits can indeed be expected to contribute to the essentialisation of group identities, raise the levels of 'racial' and/or ethnic consciousness and thereby increase group divisions, unless the levels of such consciousness are already at a high level in the society concerned. The potential impact of preferential treatment therefore depends on the values and perceptions prevalent in each society. In most parts of contemporary Europe the impact would quite likely be negative at this time.

---

[43] Charlotte Steeh – Maria Krysan 'The Polls – Trends: Affirmative Action and the Public, 1970–1995' *Public Opinion Quarterly* Vol 60 (1996), pp. 135–137.

[44] Ibid, pp. 139–140.

At this point one has ample reasons for asking why the public debate – conducted mainly in the US, not Europe – has been so overly concerned with the possible counterproductive effects of positive action. For most forms of positive action – the softer measures – these concerns appear to be entirely unfounded, and for preferential treatment they appear to be speculative and context-dependent at the least. Why is it that 'no-one' is concerned about the effects of positive action on women in context of gender equality? Why is it that 'no-one' is worried about the negative impact that the existing preferences and privileges enjoyed by individuals belonging to the majority have on *their* self-esteem, for it should be manifestly evident that discrimination inflicted upon members of minorities – a phenomenon which the members of the majority are well aware of in light of surveys[45] – must by definition unjustly privilege members of the majority? Why is it that any plans to confer limited preferences to immigrants and minorities raise so many concerns?

Research conducted in the US has demonstrated that there exists a major discrepancy between the experienced threat of 'reverse discrimination' and its actual incidence: a *vast majority* of the respondents in the US believe that it is likely that an African American will get a job instead of an equally or more qualified 'White American' whereas only a *small fraction* of 'Whites' say that they have actually been in a situation where an 'African American' was preferred over them because of preferential treatment.[46] Evidence from the US also suggests that people may attribute minorities' advances in the field of employment to positive action rather than their merits.[47] Why so? The answer may lie in the self-interest of the majority; for it, 'racial preferences' are a problem as soon as it is no longer in the receiving end, irrespective of whether social justice or utility considerations would demand support for preferential treatment in favour of the presently disadvantaged. Research has also found that old-fashioned racial thinking and racial divisions explain much of 'White' opposition to affirmative action.[48]

---

[45] Again, one might keep in mind that 62% of Europeans – almost two out of three – say that they think that ethnic discrimination is 'very widespread' or 'fairly widespread' in their country. See European Commission, *cit. supra* note 15, p. 35.

[46] Steeh – Krysan, *cit. supra* note 43, pp. 139–140.

[47] Allen, *cit. supra* note 1, p. 32.

[48] R. Michael Alvarez – Lisa García Bedolla 'The Revolution against Affirmative Action in California: Racism, Economics, and Proposition 209, *State Politics and Policy Quarterly*, Vol 4, No 1 (Spring 2004), pp. 1–17.

Given the social prevalence of negative stereotypes and prejudices, it would indeed be unexpected if these factors would not influence what the public thinks about the matters at hand. Indeed, the contemporary calls for colour-blindness, neutrality and formal equality of opportunity, and not for positive action and preferential treatment, may cover hidden forms of racism and exclusion.[49] In effect, whereas it is fully legitimate – and indeed necessary – to consider the socio-psychological consequences of particular courses of action, the excessive concern for the prejudicial effects of positive action appears not just unwarranted but morally suspect.[50]

Effectiveness

Whereas the case for positive action can rather confidently be made at a theoretical level, this does not mean that we should expect all kinds of positive action programmes to be successful everywhere and every time. Indeed, there is evidence to the effect that positive action programmes have not always delivered or been as effective as has been expected.[51] It is therefore crucial to delve into the assessment of the effectiveness of the different positive action measures and the conditions that affect their successfulness. This is a tricky business, however, as the assessment of the impact of particular measures in the highly complex settings of the real world is really demanding, which is the reason why there are so few comprehensive studies in this area.

Under these circumstances, the uniquely comprehensive research report by Dhami, Squires and Modood, in which they review the research conducted on positive action in Canada, the Netherlands, Northern Ireland and the United States, is highly welcome. In their report the authors posed the obvious question about the effectiveness of positive action policies in general, and reached the overall conclusion that there can be "clear benefits" from a programme of positive action, a finding which led the authors to recommend stronger positive action policies.[52] Perhaps the main merit of the report, however,

---

[49] David Theo Goldberg–Philomena Essed, 'Introduction: From Racial Demarcations to Multiple Identifications' in Philomena Essed - David Theo Goldberg (eds.) *Race Critical Theories* (Oxford: Blackwell, 2001).

[50] This conclusion should not be surprising, considering the evidence on the prevalence and intensity of prejudices.

[51] See e.g. Dhami et al, *cit. supra* note 19, p. 97; Frank Cunningham, *cit. supra* note 20, p. 42.

[52] Dhami et al, *cit. supra* note 19, pp. 6–8. Their study, including the recommendations, is made with the UK in mind in particular.

was the study of the experiences from different countries of conditions under which positive action appears to be effective. In their conclusions, the authors point out that positive action schemes are effective where these measures are supported by adequate levels of political will; are applied in a flexible manner; are subject to periodic review; are accompanied by a more general cultural shift that results in broader support for such programmes also among employers; are vigorously enforced and adequately resourced; do not involve too much red tape and bureaucracy; and where supply-side issues of education and skills training (for the immigrants and persons belonging to minorities) are addressed.[53] Their conclusions clearly demonstrate that it is not enough simply to adopt positive action measures and then sit still and wait for positive results; rather, a well-considered, long-term and reflexive engagement is called for.

What kinds of positive action measures or programmes appear effective? The evidence is incomplete at best, but suggests that both soft and hard measures may lead to positive results. For instance the policy of inviting at least one qualified immigrant to interview whenever there is a job opening, implemented in Norway in the public sector, has led to an increase in the representation of immigrants.[54] There is also evidence of the effectiveness of many other types of 'soft positive action' measures, including pre-employment counselling.[55] A study that focused on Northern Ireland found that schemes whereby employers voluntarily concluded agreements with equality authorities were more effective than legally-enforceable agreements in terms of achieving a more balanced workforce. The results of the study also speak in favour of monitoring and the setting of numerical goals, as well as for the use of outreach methods in recruitment.[56]

The evidence also suggests that affirmative action, particularly preferential treatment, has increased the opportunities of African Americans in the United States and has decreased their wage inequalities.[57] This has come with little or no cost in terms of business

---

[53] Idem.

[54] See the evaluation report regarding the National Action Plan to Combat Racism and Discrimination 2002–2006, Arbeids- og inkluderingsdepartementet, *Handlingsplan mot rasisme og diskriminering* (Arbeids- og inkluderingsdepartementet, November 2006).

[55] Dhami et al, *cit. supra* note 19.

[56] Christopher McCrudden et al, 'Affirmative Action without Quotas in Northern Ireland' *The Equal Rights Review*, Vol. Four (2009).

[57] Dhami et al, *cit. supra* note 19.

efficiency.[58] Indeed, because of its robustness, one could expect the 'hard' positive action measures to be a particularly effective means of promoting equal opportunities.

The efficiency of preferential treatment is however circumscribed in two ways. First, it appears that preferential treatment only helps individual better-off members of minorities, not those who are most in need of it.[59] Second, preferential treatment schemes appear to fail if they are poorly defined and do not involve ethnic monitoring and numerical goals or possibly even quotas.[60] In effect, preferential treatment can best be pursued in those countries where the general attitude climate and the vulnerable groups in particular are favourable to monitoring.[61]

11.4 Conclusions

Entrenched inequalities, in terms of opportunities and outcomes, call for positive action to redress current discrimination and the legacy of past discrimination. The power of positive action lies in that it appears to be the only, or at the very least main, method for breaking down the vicious cycle of disadvantage and discrimination. Yet positive action is no miracle cure; it does not come without sustained and well-planned efforts, and its positive impact is by no means automatic, immediate or strong enough to *always* affect tangible social change. Much depends on the extent to which the proponents of positive action are able to mobilize themselves, on the extent of political will, on the extent to which employers and other stakeholders are willing to put their time, energy and resources into implementing it. And even then, not all methods of positive action suit all societies at all times.

A general challenge in the incorporation of positive action as a key element of equal treatment policies involves a change in the mindset

---

[58] Holzer and Neumark, in their extensive economic investigation of the issue, conclude that "all in all, the evidence suggests to us that it may be possible to generate affirmative action programs that entail little sacrifice of efficiency" and add that there may even be *overall* efficiency gains, *cit. supra* note 42, p. 559.

[59] See e.g. the arguments and statistics presented in Thomas Sowell 'From Equal Opportunity to "Affirmative Action" in Francis J. Beckwith – Todd. E. Jones (eds.) *Affirmative Action: Social Justice or Reverse Discrimination* (New York: Amherst, 1997). See also Allen *cit. supra* note 1, p. 33.

[60] Strasser et al, *cit. supra* note 17, p. 23; Dhami et al, *cit. supra* note 19.

[61] Indeed, if preferential treatment cannot be systematically applied, then the question whether the pros still outweigh the cons becomes increasingly legitimate.

with regard to what it means to treat people equally. A break in the practice of the prevailing non-discrimination approaches that are inherently unable to affect a positive change is called for. This means that now that the general public has by and large learned – some the hard way – that 'racial' or ethnic origin are not relevant criteria in today's societies, the public is asked to re-acknowledge these criteria and to accept that inequalities cannot be addressed unless these factors *are* taken into account. Also legal professionals, the judiciary in particular, will need to re-examine their doctrines about equal treatment and the permissible scope of positive action. These changes in the mindset may not be impossible to achieve, as they fit rather well into the recent broad cultural change in values in Europe.[62]

It is perhaps somewhat ironic that preferential treatment, arguably the most effective means of positive action, bears the greatest risk of being counterproductive. Due to its intrinsic quality of signifying group membership and the necessity to engage in ethnic monitoring to implement it in a satisfactory way, it can perhaps only be successfully implemented in countries where the levels of 'racial' and ethnic consciousness are high to begin with and where the general public and the vulnerable groups in particular are favourably disposed towards collection of ethnic data. This perspective renders preferential treatment policies inapplicable in practice for many parts of contemporary Europe, if not most.

The need to engage in preferential treatment is perhaps to some extent diminished by the fact that basic welfare guarantees, often also for immigrants, are fairly substantial in Europe, particularly in comparison to the rest of the world. Moreover, the case for preferential treatment for the needy immigrant and minority groups is diminished also in view of the fact that there are other groups, such as people with disabilities, women, sexual minorities, religious minorities and senior people that currently suffer from discrimination and that would also 'deserve' preferential treatment and benefit from it. The most deserving individuals would presumably be those suffering from multiple discrimination. But if preferential treatment schemes would encompass these individuals and groups as well, then these schemes risk becoming too burdensome to manage. In effect, class- or

[62] Ronald Inglehart, 'Globalization and Postmodern Values' *The Washington Quarterly*, 23:1 Winter 2000.

income-based welfare policies that are applied universally across the society and irrespective of membership in any group have much to speak for them. That said, we should not be under the illusion that class- or income based policies would lead to the same outcome as ethnically-based preferential treatment; they are simply not as effective in promoting inclusion.[63]

[63] Holzer–Neumark, *cit. supra* note 42, p. 561.

12 POSITIVE DUTIES

Dissatisfaction with the individual rights based approach to combating racial and ethnic discrimination has led to theoretical and legislative innovations, particularly after the turn of the 21st century. A particularly influential idea has been that of introducing positive equality duties as a means of accelerating the achievement of de facto equality. There is no generally agreed definition for positive duties, but for the purposes of the present context, it can be defined as *an overarching obligation, placed by law upon an organisation, to take active measures to promote the achievement of equality.*[1]

At its broadest, the duty means that its bearers are required to take account of equality considerations in everything they do. This kind of a duty encompasses the role of the organization concerned in its dual capacity of an employer and provider of goods and/or services. In its employer role, the organization is required to mainstream equality considerations into its decisions and practices that deal with, *inter alia*, recruitment and selection, training, promotion and retention. In its role as a provider of goods and services, the organization is required to ensure that it provides services of equal quality at equal value and on equal terms for all groups. A broad duty would also require an organization to take equality into account in its decisions and practices that concern its public image, external and internal communication, procurement, and relations with other stakeholders, including the different communities.[2]

Positive duties can in principle be placed both upon public and private bodies, but up until now there is mainly experience of public sector duties. Authorities are indeed uniquely placed to affect a change in the society, given their role as providers of public services in areas such as education, employment, housing, the justice system, and health and social care. The private sector plays however a much greater role in the

---

[1] See also Discrimination Law Review, 'A Framework for Fairness: Proposals for a Single Equality Bill for Great Britain', June 2007, p. 79. Available at: http://www.communities.gov.uk (accessed 1.1.2010).

[2] See e.g. CRE, *Towards Racial Equality: An evaluation of the public duty to promote race equality and good race relations in England and Wales* (2002), p. 13.

field of employment, as private sector jobs account for some 70 percent of all jobs in Europe.[3]

12.1 The Policy Case

The idea of positive duties has got much to speak for itself, particularly against the backdrop of the failures of the individual rights based approach to equality. Firstly, and perhaps most importantly, it promises to affect a broader and more lasting change, whereas the changes brought about by the latter are patchy and concern only a few individuals at best.[4] The reality is that often equality concerns are experienced as significant only if one is in some way responsible for tackling them. Under the individual rights model, this happens when one is sued to the court, which means infrequently, if ever. In contrast, the duty to promote equality is a lasting, on-going duty. It is proactive, not reactive in nature. Moreover, and again in contrast to the individual rights based approach, duties require a more systematic and broad approach to guaranteeing and promoting equality. In effect, it stands a better chance of identifying and removing indirect, institutional and structural discrimination in particular.[5]

Secondly, the former approach places obligations and burdens on the side which is creating the problems, not on the side upon which problems are inflicted. To that extent, it is certainly more in line with predominant understandings of fairness, and is practical in that it is organizations that are better able than the disadvantaged individuals to shoulder the burdens involved in ensuring that equality laws are complied with. The above said, the approach based on duties is not about blaming anyone, it bypasses the need to find fault and to identify individual complainants and respondents, as well as the problems of proof and the need to take potentially lengthy and costly legal action.

---

[3] Situation for the EU-27 for 2007. Source: Eurostat, *European Union Labour Force Survey - Annual Results 2007*, Eurostat Data in Focus 27/2008. The private sector is here defined broadly as consisting of agriculture, industry and market services and excluding non-market services provided by the public and non-profit institutions.

[4] See also Alexandra Kalev–Frank Dobbin, 'Enforcement of Civil Rights Law in Private Workplaces: The Effects of Compliance Reviews and Lawsuits Over Time', *Law & Social Inquiry*, Volume 31, Issue 4, 855–903, Fall 2006.

[5] See also Fredman - Spencer, "Beyond Discrimination: It's Time for Enforceable Duties on Public Bodies to Promote Equality Outcomes" *E.H.R.L.R.* Issue 6 (2006), p. 600.

Thirdly, duties are anticipatory in nature, in that they aim at preventing harm from being inflicted, whereas individual rights aim at remedying the harm already done, being retrospective in nature. In other words, whereas the predominant anti-discrimination framework primarily aims at putting things right after they have gone wrong, positive duties aim at getting things right in the first place. Instead of being about sitting down and waiting for the complaints to arrive, it is about the active compensation of past wrongs and prevention of new ones.

The fourth benefit of positive duties is that it is a goal-oriented approach. The action taken can be given a clear direction, the precise formulation of the goal of course depending on the domestic legislator. Indeed, it need not just to be about market equality, it can also be about the other dimensions of equality.

Overall, positive equality duties promise to set in motion a kind of domino effect whereby a change in the legal parameters brings about an institutional and cultural change that on its turn contributes to a social change.[6] This is some promise, and warrants a closer look at the methods by which the positive duties can be implemented, as well as a closer examination of the conditions under which positive duties can be presumed to be effective.

12.2 Methods

The idea of positive equality duties is a relatively recent innovation and is still in its infancy, particularly in terms of theoretical development and even more so in terms of practical implementation. Finland, Sweden and United Kingdom offer three, rare at the time of writing, examples of imposition of positive equality duties in law, and will be reviewed in the following.

United Kingdom

The general statutory equality duty was introduced in Great Britain in 2000, and was revised in 2010 by the Equality Act. The revised equality duty requires an extensive list of public bodies to have, in the exercise

[6] For instance the British Discrimination Law Review report notes that positive duties are intended to help to bring about a culture change so that promoting equality becomes part and parcel of public authorities' core business. Discrimination Law Review, *cit supra* note 1, p. 79.

of their functions, "due regard" to the need to (i) eliminate unlawful discrimination, harassment and victimisation, (ii) advance equality of opportunity, and (iii) foster good relations between people who share a protected characteristic and those who do not.[7] The duty covers eight so-called protected characteristics, of which 'race' is one. Whereas the first arm of the duty is rather self-explanatory, the Act helpfully gives examples of the kinds of actions that the implementation of the second and third arms may involve. Having due regard to advancing equality of opportunity involves, for instance, removing or minimising disadvantages suffered by people belonging to the protected groups, taking steps to meet the needs of people from these groups, and encouraging such people to participate in the public life and in other areas. Fostering of good relations is explained as involving tackling of prejudices and promotion of understanding between people from different groups.

Complementary specific duties have been introduced in secondary legislation. These apply to most public authorities bound by the general duty, and are designed to help to meet the general duty.[8] The specific duties are under revision at the time of the writing, but will likely incorporate (i) the duty to prepare and publish one or more equality objectives, and (ii) the duty to publish information to demonstrate compliance with the general equality duty.[9] Whereas the old set of duties required the development of a specific 'race equality scheme', this is no longer the case with the new duties.

Under the first specific duty, each authority would have to prepare and publish equality objectives that it thinks it should achieve. These objectives would have to be specific and measurable. These measures must be taken at least every four years.

Under the second specific duty each authority would have to publish, at least once a year, information to demonstrate its compliance with the three aims of the general equality duty. This information would have to include, in particular, information on the effect that its equality policies and practices are having on service users from the protected groups. Public authorities with 150 or more employees

[7] Section 149 of the Equality Act 2010.

[8] The original specific duties were set out in the Race Relations Act 1976 (Statutory Duties) Order 2001.

[9] Government Equalities Office, *Equality Act 2010: The public sector Equality Duty: reducing bureaucracy*, Policy review paper 17 March 2011. These draft specific duties concern England and non-devolved public bodies in Scotland and Wales.

would also be required to publish information relating to employees from the protected groups.[10]

The purpose of the duty to have and use this information is to embed equality-related, evidence-based policy-making into the work of the public bodies. The publishing of the required information is expected to make decision-making more transparent and accountable. Whereas authorities with 150 or more employees would be required to produce information relating to workforce diversity, no express requirement to carry out ethnic monitoring is envisaged.[11]

A specialized agency, the Commission for Equality and Human Rights, has been empowered to publish statutory and non-statutory Codes of Practice that elaborate upon these duties and provide guidance on how to meet them. The Commission is also chiefly responsible for ensuring compliance with the duty. Authorities not meeting the duty may be given a 'compliance notice' by the Commission, requiring them (i) to comply with the duty and (ii) to provide the Commission information about the steps that will be taken to comply with the duty. Those failing to comply with a requirement of the notice may be taken by the Commission to a High Court under a judicial review procedure.[12]

A specific set of duties exist in Northern Ireland under Section 75 of the Northern Ireland Act 1998. The Act places duties upon designated authorities, which include for instance government departments, universities and local councils. These authorities are required, in carrying out of their functions, to "have due regard to the need to promote equality of opportunity" and to have "regard to the desirability of promoting good relations" across a number of equality grounds, including "racial group". The Equality Commission for Northern Ireland is charged with a number of responsibilities in respect of ensuring the fulfilment of these duties.

Each designated authority is required to produce an 'equality scheme' setting out how it proposes to fulfil the duties. The scheme must be submitted to the Equality Commission for approval. The schemes must conform to any guidelines, as to form and content, issued by the Commission with the approval of the Secretary of State.

---

[10] Idem.

[11] Equality and Human Rights Commission, *Equality information and the equality duty: A guide for public authorities*, (EHRC, 2011).

[12] Equality Act 2006, Sections 30–32.

Each authority must furthermore conduct a review of the scheme within five years of submission of the scheme to the Commission, and the Commission must be informed of the outcome of that review. Furthermore, the legislation requires authorities to conduct equality impact assessments. The results of equality impact assessments must be published and the equality scheme must state the authority's arrangements for this. The legislation also requires that persons likely to affected are consulted in the course of the policy-making process. The duty to ensure equality of opportunity is also to be taken into account in public procurement.[13]

Finland

In Finland, Section 4(1) of the Equal Treatment Act (21/2004) places a general obligation on all public authorities

> to promote equality, in all their functions, in a goal-oriented and planned manner, and to consolidate such administrative and operational practices that will ensure promotion of equality in the making and preparation of decisions. In particular, authorities shall address the circumstances that prevent the realization of equality.[14]

This duty is basically about mainstreaming equality considerations into all public decision-making, whether governmental, municipal or local. This general equality duty, applicable with respect to all grounds of equality, is supplemented by a specific duty to promote equality on the grounds of ethnic origin. This specific duty requires each authority to adopt an 'equality plan', in which they are to set out the measures regarding how they will go about fulfilling the general duty with respect to ethnic equality.[15] The nature of the functions of the authority in question determines the required extensiveness of the plan, introducing an element of proportionality into the equation. The plan may involve positive action measures, which is why Section 7(1) of the Act specifically provides that action taken in pursuance of an equality plan does not constitute discrimination.

The law charges the Ministry of the Interior to issue General recommendations in relation to the content of the plan. The prevailing

---

[13] See e.g. Equality Commission for Northern Ireland and the Central Procurement Directorate, *Equality of Opportunity and Sustainable Development in Public Sector Procurement* (May 2008).

[14] Unofficial translation by the author.

[15] Section 4(2) of the Equal Treatment Act.

General recommendations specify, *inter alia*, that each plan shall cover the authority's role both as an employer and as a provider of public services. It also urges each authority to draw up the plan in cooperation with the representatives of the groups concerned. While both the general and specific duties are legally binding, the law does not attach any hard and fast sanctions or mechanisms of enforcement to these duties.

Sweden

In Sweden, Chapter 3 of the Act on Discrimination (567/2008) places detailed duties on employers in particular. A general obligation is placed on each employer to promote, in a goal-oriented manner and in the framework of its activities, the achievement of equal opportunities and equal rights. This general duty is complemented by a range of specific duties including the following: an employer must take reasonable accommodation measures to ensure that the working methods and the work environment are fit for everyone irrespective of origin; it must take measures to prevent harassment and victimization; it must take measures with a view to promoting the opportunity of each individual, irrespective of origin, to apply for work opportunities; and once in every three years it shall prepare an equality plan that sets out the measures that the employer intends to undertake in order to comply with the specific duties. The subsequent plan must include a report on the measures actually taken to implement the previous plan. The reporting duty concerns only employers with 25 or more employees. Education providers are under a different set of duties, including a duty to adopt an equality plan on a yearly basis.[16]

Compliance with these duties is overseen by the Discrimination Ombudsman and the Discrimination Tribunal. The Ombudsman has effective investigative powers, and can take an employer to the Tribunal in case of suspected non-compliance. The Tribunal is empowered to order the employer to comply with its duties under the threat of a fine.[17]

Instruments of Implementation

A general equality duty, as also the examples of the three states show, typically requires the duty-bound organizations to pay attention to

[16] *Disrimineringslag*, Sections 3–16.

[17] Chapter 4, Sections 1–5 of the Act.

both the contents of decision-making and the processes that lead to it. In effect, positive equality duties generally have three partly overlapping characteristic components: they involve the equality mainstreaming ethos, consultative policy-making processes, and impact assessment of the effects of policy decisions.[18] An obligation to set them out in an equality plan supports the sustained, coherent and effective design and implementation of each of these elements.

There is a considerable amount of experience of mainstreaming in the context of gender equality, where the idea of placing equality considerations at the heart of all decision-making has by and large become accepted throughout Europe, with the Nordic countries leading the way.[19] Mainstreaming can be conceptualized in a variety of ways,[20] but many definitions reflect the idea of systematic inclusion of equality considerations into all organizational processes and the examination of the equality impact of the various parts of those processes, as reflected in the following definition adopted by the European Commission:

> Gender mainstreaming involves not restricting efforts to promote equality to the implementation of specific measures to help women, but mobilising all general policies and measures specifically for the purpose of achieving equality by actively and openly taking into account at the planning stage their possible effects on the respective situation of men and women (gender perspective). This means systematically examining measures and policies and taking into account such possible effects when defining and implementing them.

Mainstreaming strategies respond to the common experience that questions of equality and non-discrimination may easily become sidelined.[21] Substantive mainstreaming of equality issues should not be

---

[18] Etienne Mclaughlin, 'From Negative to Positive Equality Duties: The Development and Constitutionalisation of Equality Provisions in the UK' *Social Policy & Society* 6:1, p. 115.

[19] European Commission, *Gender mainstreaming of employment policies. A comparative review of thirty European countries* (Luxembourg: Office for Official Publications of the EC, 2007). For a look at the historical development of the concept, see Panu Artemjeff, 'Mainstreaming Equality: Conceptual Development and Mainstreaming Model of the Join In Project' in Panu Artemjeff – Kirsi Henriksson (eds.), *Mainstreaming Equality and Non-discrimination in Theory and Practice* (Helsinki: Cosmoprint, 2006), p. 19 ff.

[20] Idem (Artemjeff), pp. 20–22.

[21] Christopher McCrudden, 'Regulating Discrimination: Advice to a Legislator on Problems Regarding the Enforcement of Anti-Discrimination Law and Strategies to Overcome Them' in Titia Loenen – Peter Rodrigues (eds.) *Non-Discrimination Law: Comparative Perspectives* (The Hague: Kluwer, 1999), p. 311.

achieved simply through the technical introduction of pertinent discussion items into decision-making; rather, and perhaps more importantly, it calls for the consultation of the groups concerned about what equality requires in each specific context at hand.[22] As such, it suggests building a new relationship between the citizens and the government, a relationship where responsibility for making decisions and tackling problems is not just on government officers and other 'experts' but also on the affected groups.[23] In effect, *inclusive mainstreaming* may be defined as *systematic incorporation of non-discrimination and equality considerations into all decision-making in co-operation with the groups concerned*. Reviews suggest that equality concerns should be taken into account throughout the whole decision-making lifecycle, from design through to implementation, monitoring and evaluation.[24] For public bodies, mainstreaming entails the incorporation of non-discrimination objectives into all policies, legislation and programmes, and is also linked to principles of good governance. The idea of shared and systematic responsibility across a wide range of governmental and non-governmental organizations contrasts positively, because of reasons of scale, with the previously dominant idea of charging one government department or agency with equality issues.

Mainstreaming also has got its more indirect benefits. The objective of promoting equal treatment is intrinsically connected to other major social objectives, such as the promotion and guaranteeing of human rights and democratic decision-making. Non-discrimination is also linked to such all-important societal goals as high level of employment and of social protection, the raising of the standard of living and quality of life, economic and social cohesion, and solidarity. The more efficiently anti-discrimination efforts are embedded in policies aimed at achieving these other goals and objectives, and the more efficiently they are seen to be essential for these policy goals, the higher the chance that the efforts are effective and embraced by the population at large.[25]

---

[22] See also Artemjeff, *cit. supra* note 19, pp. 20–2.

[23] See generally on shared governance, Matt Leighninger, *The Next Form of Democracy: How Expert Rule is Giving Way to Shared Governance... and Why Politics Will Never Be the Same* (Nashville, Vanderbilt University Press, 2006).

[24] Centre for Strategy & Evaluation Services, *Non-discrimination mainstreaming – instruments, case studies and way forwards* (April 2007). Available at http://ec.europa.eu.

[25] Jan Niessen, 'Making the Law Work: The Enforcement and Implementation of Anti-Discrimination Legislation' *European Journal of Migration and Law* 5: 249–257, 2003, p. 2.

How exactly can the mainstreaming of equality concerns then take place, for instance in the context of review of a policy? At the level of an 'ideal model for mainstreaming' we can distinguish four main stages.[26] The first step of the process is 'a preparatory phase', which involves preparatory work such as the identification and involvement of the different stakeholders and definition of their responsibilities, the formulation of objectives and targets, and drawing up a budget if necessary. The next step is 'baseline review', conducted on the basis of all available data for the purposes of identifying present inequalities relevant to the policy. Use should be made of existing evaluation procedures and data, such as different indicators, customer surveys, consultation with affected communities, research, and where such exists, ethnic monitoring data.[27] This review also forms the starting point for later evaluation. The third step is 'impact assessment', which is often taken to be at the very heart of effective mainstreaming of equality.[28] The idea is to use prospective impact assessments, a special type of social analysis, to predict potential equality impacts of policies and laws. Consultation of the groups affected by the policy can be highly useful at this point, particularly in order to identify potential indirect adverse effects. Impact assessments can be demanding in terms of time and resources, which is why it would be a sensible strategy to use screening techniques to determine if a full assessment is warranted and what its scope should be.[29] The fourth step is 'redesign of policy', which involves adjustment of the policy in light of the materials gathered and views presented. Again, involvement of the representatives of the groups in question is called for. The policy-making cycle should be concluded by a retrospective assessment of the equality impact of the adopted policy. Consultation can be an important source of feedback in assessing the impact of policies, but where available, the real test of progress will be the extent to which key outcomes are delivered on the ground, as measured by indicators such as satisfaction levels of ethnic minority users of public services, educational attainment

[26] European Commission, *cit. supra* note 18; Artemjeff, *cit. supra* note 18.

[27] Artemjeff, *cit supra* note 18, p. 25.

[28] CRE, *cit supra* note 2, p. 10.

[29] The High Court of England and Wales commented in the *Elias* case on the British equality duty, set out in section 71 of the Race Relations Act, as follows: "No doubt in some cases it will be plain even after a cursory consideration that section 71 is not engaged, or at least is not relevant. There is no need to enter into time consuming and potentially expensive consultation exercises or monitoring when discrimination issues are plainly not in point". [2005] EWHC 1435 (Admin), para 96.

levels of ethnic minority youths at school or college, and the representation of ethnic minorities at all levels in the public sector.[30] For the mainstreaming strategy to be comprehensive, this process must be repeated with respect to all relevant policies and processes.

Mainstreaming may or may not lead into the adoption of positive action measures. Mainstreaming can also be seen to be about reviewing and challenging the status quo, as a way of recognizing that all policies, institutional structures and laws, as neutral as they may appear, may in fact reinforce disadvantages. It can bring under discussion how particular decisions and arrangements may serve the needs and aspirations of some groups rather than others; that decisions about who participate in decision-making, or how resources are distributed, can and do have an impact on equality. For instance, a public housing programme reflecting the dominant demand for small starter homes, accommodating the needs of typical priority groups such as single parent families, may respond poorly to the needs of immigrants, many of whom have larger families. In the area of city planning, a decision to build a sports arena instead of an intercultural contact point similarly reflects and responds to particular preferences and interests to the detriment of others. In all policy-making, some social interests and some groups win, others lose, and the end result conveys a message to the public as to what is held important in that society. Mainstreaming is, in effect, ultimately about bringing the situation and needs of minorities from the margins of organizational culture to its centre. This does not mean that the interests of these groups will prevail at all times; rather it means that their interests will prevail at least at some times.

A comprehensive equality duty, imposed on public authorities, would require them to take equality into account in public procurement. This is a potentially powerful instrument, given that public authorities do business with private companies on a large scale: in the EU, public procurement represents some 16 percent of EU gross domestic product.[31] Procurement contracting represents a unique opportunity for the public authorities to use the power of the public purse in the interest of promoting the implementation of social justice

[30] CRE, *cit. supra* note 2, p. 10.

[31] Fabienne Ilzkovitz et al, *Steps towards a deeper economic integration: the Internal Market in the 21st century: A contribution to the Single Market Review*, European Commission Economic Papers No 271, January 2007, p. 62.

in the private sector.[32] This can take place, roughly speaking, in two ways.[33] Firstly, and presumably more effectively, this would involve a contract compliance programme, in which public authorities specify certain social criteria that a contractor who wants to obtain government contracts must meet. By means of integrating equality considerations into public procurement, public authorities can gently pressure businesses into embracing equality and diversity policies. In practice, the integration of equality considerations into public procurement entails that companies that provide goods and services to the public are required to take action to promote the achievement of *de facto* equality. This may involve, for instance, drawing up equality plans, signing otherwise voluntary Diversity Charters, setting up goals to achieve a representative workforce, and/or conducting workplace monitoring.[34] This kind of public procurement is used as an instrument to promote equality *inter alia* in the UK and the USA, and it has been suggested that it should be more widely applied across Europe.[35] The second approach would be to have a programme under which public authorities are required to disqualify a contractor from tendering for a contract if he or she has seriously breached anti-discrimination laws in the course of his or her business or profession.

The existing empirical research shows that under right conditions, taking equality into account in public procurement can have considerable beneficial effects.[36] Effects have however been reduced where enforcement, monitoring and compliance efforts have been inadequately funded or resourced, or where previous support for such a policy has been withdrawn, or where those administering the policy have seen that function as secondary or peripheral to their work.[37]

---

[32] Christopher McCrudden, *Bying Social Justice: Equality, Government Procurement, & Legal Change* (Oxford: OUP, 2007).

[33] For more elaborate distinctions, see idem.

[34] A number of EU member states have promoted (France, Belgium and Germany) voluntary Diversity Charters, through which companies commit themselves to non-discrimination and diversity.

[35] For further information on public procurement, see McCrudden, *cit. supra* note 32; PLS Ramboll Management, *Study of the Use of Equality and Diversity Considerations in Public Procurement: Final Report.* Available at: http://ec.europa.eu (visited 1.1.2009).

[36] The empirical research is reviewed by McCrudden in ibid, pp. 594–617.

[37] Ibid, p. 595.

12.3 Challenges

The experiences of Finland and United Kingdom – sufficient practical experiences have not been gained in Sweden yet – of the introduction of positive duties are mixed but encouraging. On the one hand, it is widely agreed that this approach has been useful, but on the other hand, it is also widely agreed to have been less useful than had been hoped.

In Britain, there is experience with respect to the former set of equality duties, which broadly speaking correspond to the new ones with respect to the general duty but which put more emphasis on processes, such as the adoption of the 'race equality scheme', in the specific duties. The review of the old set of duties found that there was "encouraging evidence that, to an extent, it [positive duties] has had a positive influence on public authorities' practices", particularly in relation to compelling them to pay greater attention to ensuring fair treatment of all their employees.[38] But there has been, and still is, recurrent criticism as well. The general duty has been criticised for being too weak in the extent to which it requires action to be taken. It has been pointed out that the duty only requires the authorities concerned to "have due regard to the need" to act, rather than really requiring them to act.[39] Indeed, it appears that for many duty-bound public bodies, the focus has so far excessively been on processes and bureaucracy, and too little on achieving tangible equality outcomes.[40] For some public bodies it appears that the making of the equality scheme has been seen as the main component of the equality duty, not the implementation of that scheme.[41] This is one of the reasons cited by the British government behind the move towards a new set of specific duties that cut down many process-based requirements such as the making of the equality scheme.[42] Overall, there has also been dissatisfaction with the relative

[38] Discrimination Law Review, *cit. supra* note 1, p. 83. Moreover, in a survey conducted in 2002, 69% of the responding authorities felt that their work on the public duty had produced positive benefits.

[39] This is perhaps the mainstream reading, see e.g. Fredman – Spencer, *cit. supra* note 5, p. 600. For a different interpretation see Rupert Harwood, 'Race Back from Equality: Has the CRE been breaching race equality law and has race equality law been working?' Public Interest Research Unit, 2007, pp. 18–19.

[40] See e.g. Harwood, *cit. supra* note 39, pp. 149–166.

[41] Great Britain Government Equalities Office, *The Equality Bill – Government response to the Consultation* (Stationary Office Limited, July 2008), p. 22.

[42] Government Equalities Office, *Equality Act 2010: The public sector Equality Duty: reducing bureaucracy*, Policy review paper 17 March 2011.

lack of clarity of the ends sought by means of the imposition of the duties, which is at least partly attributable to the vague terminology used (the concept of 'equality of opportunity' in particular).[43] The system, with its general and specific duties and statutory and non-statutory codes of practice, is also widely perceived as too complex.

In Northern Ireland, the Equality Commission for Northern Ireland conducted in 2008 a comprehensive review of the effectiveness of public sector duties. The report, which was drawn on the basis of a number of research undertakings and consultation processes, concludes that the duties have over a relatively short period of time effected a substantial change in how policy is made.[44] The result has been a more informed and evidence-based policy that reflects the needs of individuals in terms of equality of opportunity and good relations. According to the report, effective consultation has been a particular success, giving rise to an inclusive policy making process. The report identifies several shortcomings as well, in particular with regard to identifying and measuring inequalities and the actual impact that policies are having in terms of reducing or removing those inequalities. It was also found that the public authorities were not always certain about such concepts as 'good relations' or 'screening', and that they exercised caution in going beyond non-discrimination towards promotion of equality of opportunity. Authorities were not always sufficiently aware of the needs of the different groups in terms of equality of opportunity and good relations, which might to some extent be explained by the levels of capacity, skills and resources among the voluntary and community sector organisations concerned.[45]

In Finland, almost two out of three respondents to an impact assessment study of the Equal Treatment Act were of the view that the Act has in fact promoted the achievement of equality and has had a positive impact on the attitude climate.[46] In lieu of ethnic monitoring or other systematic evidence about the outcomes it is impossible to say whether this perception is correct.

---

[43] Fredman – Spencer, *cit. supra* note 5, pp. 600–601; Harwood, *cit. supra* note 39, pp. 21–22.

[44] Equality Commission for Northern Ireland, *Section 75 – Keeping it Effective. Reviewing the Effectiveness of Section 75 of the Northern Ireland Act 1998*. Final Report, November 2008, p. 4.

[45] Idem.

[46] Birgitta Lundström et al, *Yhdenvertaisuuslain toimivuus. Tutkimusraportti viranomaisten käsityksistä sekä oikeus-, laillisuusvalvonta- ja lainvalvontakäytännöstä*. Työ- ja elinkeinoministeriön julkaisuja 11/2008, p. 66 ff.

Quantitative and qualitative assessment of the equality plans may serve as one indicator of the successfulness of the Finnish system. The results are somewhat discomforting: in 2007, more than three years after the duty to adopt an equality plan had come into effect, only 53% of the responding public bodies had adopted an equality plan, 12% said that they were in the process of drafting it, and 35% had not even began the preparations for producing it.[47] If anything, this shows a widespread lack of enthusiasm if not outright disregard of the equality law. There was also great diversity in the scope of the already adopted plans, with one third being regarded as too limited in scope or drawn in too general terms to be of much practical benefit. The authorities clearly had difficulties in putting in concrete terms what it means to 'promote equality', whereas the concept of non-discrimination was much more familiar.[48] Even those plans that were classified as 'comprehensive' were lacking or vague in terms of timetables and attribution of responsibility, two central factors that affect success. Moreover, four out of five authorities had not in *any* manner involved representatives of the target groups in the preparation of the plan. On the positive side, almost all plans included a design for follow-up and review.[49]

The Finnish experience clearly shows that the introduction of a legally binding equality duty may be a necessary but not sufficient element of a proactive strategy. Where enforcement and sanctions are absent or unclear, many organizations will ignore their duties or adopt nominal compliance policies and not really reconsider their policies and practices.[50] The trade-off between enforcement and effectiveness may not be as straightforward as it may first appear, however. The British experience shows that it takes more than duties and their enforcement to achieve any real transformation of institutional structures and policy making, and that enforcement may play an ambivalent part in that. In order to be practical, enforcement must be linked to tangible, 'material' outcomes such as the production of an equality scheme, because a broad and vague general duty does not in itself easily lend to any form of enforcement. This, however, carries with it the risk of minimal, formal compliance and may encourage focusing on

---

47 Ibid, p. 74.
48 Idem.
49 Ibid, pp. 66–88.
50 See also Lowri Griffiths 'Positive Duties to Promote Equality' in Soraya Obura – Fiona Palmer (eds.) *Strategic Enforcement: Powers and Competences of Equality Bodies* (Brussels: Equinet, 2006).

the kind of action by which one is *seen* to comply with the letter of the duty, rather than action by which one is actually complying with the *spirit* of the duty. Also considering the wide variety of public bodies and their functions, the diversity of their work environments and the need to avoid the imposition of unnecessary burdens, any duties must be laid down in law in rather general terms and the organizations concerned must retain a degree of autonomy in their implementation. Too specific duties and/or too specific guidance may be counterproductive for organizational learning, forming a barrier to any real transformation. On the other hand, general duties that are not supported by any guidance will be hard to implement, as few organizations can be expected to have the time, expertise and resources necessary to work their way from the abstract principles to successful and thorough implementation thereof in practice,[51] as there is no fail-safe toolbox of implementation measures that deliver without exception. The sheer number of public bodies that are subject to the duty – for instance in Britain the duty-bound authorities number around 44 000 – makes the systematic monitoring of compliance difficult or impossible in practice, unless enormous investments are made in establishing enforcement agencies across the country. The other option, the enabling of judicial review in which an individual or group can ask a court of law to scrutinize whether an organization has complied with its duties, may equally be a no-starter, if not for any other reason but because individuals seldom have the time, money and/or interest to pursue such action. All of this makes the efficient enforcement of equality duties difficult.

Taking into consideration of the situation and needs of immigrants and minorities, through participation of the target groups, are often taken to be at the heart of equality duties and mainstreaming in particular. This raises major challenges, however: first, resorting to stereotyping should be avoided when minorities' and immigrants' interests are being considered, lest the action reinforces those stereotypes instead of eliminating them. For instance a Finnish study that compared immigrants' preferences and needs in the housing market, and the *housing authorities' perceptions* of their preferences and needs, found the two to be diametrically opposite in some respects: the authorities were under the impression that immigrants wanted to live

[51] Discrimination Law Review, *cit. supra* note 1, p. 101 ff.

in close proximity to other immigrants and to their places of worship, whereas immigrants themselves preferred to live in 'ordinary' neighbourhoods and to have neighbours who were from the ethnic majority.[52] The need to steer clear of stereotypes speaks for active involvement of the target groups, as otherwise it is *assumed* as opposed to *real* interests that are mainstreamed into decision-making.[53] But this brings us to the second challenge: *Which groups* should be given a voice and *who* within each group? How to promote inclusion without engaging in identity politics and essentialism? There is a need to steer clear from a presumption of homogeneity, from the perception that "any immigrant can represent all immigrants". Immigrants and minorities are not homogenous groups, let alone *a* homogenous group. It must also be recognized that there are other social divisions and other types of group-based injustices than 'race' and ethnicity – for instance those based on gender, age, sexual orientation, religion or disability – which criss-cross the former types of divisions and injustices.[54] The radical plurality of identities and experiences mean that any consultation should be inclusive. Indeed, those organizing consultations with a view to developing equality policies should be aware of the need to avoid indirectly silencing dissenting voices through their choice of participants.[55] These viewpoints suggest that careful consideration should go into the planning of the modalities of consultation and inclusion mechanisms, and that broad consultation is called for in any case. The groups concerned might also benefit from being democratically and otherwise well-organized.

Organizations seldom welcome new burdens being placed upon them, and this is particularly the case with private businesses operating in the competitive market economy environment. In addition, the private sector cannot perhaps be assumed to bear the same responsibility as the public sector in implementing social justice. That said, the private sector, given its weight in the areas of employment and delivery

---

[52] Nexhat Beqiri, *Toiveena monipuolinen asukasrakenne*. Sisäasiainministeriön julkaisuja 30/2008.

[53] Martin MacEwen 'Concluding remarks' in Martin MacEwen (ed.), *Anti-Discrimination Law Enforcement* (Ashgate 1997), p. 242.

[54] See e.g. Reza Banakar – Max Travers, 'Critical Approaches' in Reza Banakar – Max Travers (eds.), *An Introduction to Law and Social Theory* (Oxford: Hart, 2002), p. 98.

[55] Paola Ucellari 'Multiple Discrimination: How Law can Reflect Reality' *The Equal Rights Review*, Vol One (2008), pp. 42–43.

of goods and services, is also to a great degree if not chiefly responsible for bringing about the disadvantages experienced by the groups vulnerable to discrimination, and should therefore have a role in the eradication of those disadvantages. Businesses do not operate in some apolitical, amoral and asocial space, nor is their social impact neutral. In consequence, if the private sector is not part of the solution, it is part of the problem. The impact of the turn from a passive anti-discrimination strategy to a proactive equal treatment strategy will be highly limited unless the private sector takes part in it.[56] As the present system relying on individual rights is a no-starter in terms of affecting change, also the private sector should be given a more proactive role in achieving equality. Furthermore, we should take into account the unique experience from Northern Ireland, where all employers with more than ten employees are required to register with the Equality Commission, to monitor the community background composition of the workforce, to conduct periodic reviews of the workforce and of employment practices and, where reasonable and appropriate, to take affirmative action. That experience is encouraging, as the earlier imbalances in fair participation in employment were to a substantial extent remedied in the course of 2001–2008.[57]

That said, the imposition of positive duties on the private sector could at least in theory have a chilling effect on activity in general. Moreover, increases in the 'costs' related to employment risk leading some employers to invest not in employees, but in machinery capable of substituting them, or may encourage businesses to relocate to countries where there is less employment regulation. In light of these and other similar considerations, the question of whether private sector should be imposed an equality duty, or whether a contract compliance or some other programme would suffice, should perhaps be left for further and wider debates. For the time being there does not appear to be any broad-based support for the introduction, across Europe, of

[56] In this context it should be noted that evidence from the USA suggests that only a few firms engage entirely voluntarily (i.e. where not required by federal contract compliance programs) in some affirmative action policy. See e.g. Alexandra Kalev – Frank Dobbin – Erin Kelly 'Best Practices or Best Guesses? Assessing the Efficacy of Corporate Affirmative Action and Diversity Policies' *American Sociological Review*, 2006, Vol. 71 (August 589–617).

[57] See Equality Commission for Northern Ireland, *2008 Monitoring Report: Monitoring Report No. 19: A profile of the Monitored Northern Ireland Workforce*, p. 20. Due to constraints of data, it is not possible at the time to give a conclusive answer to the question whether the earlier imbalances have entirely been corrected.

positive equality duties upon the private sector. On the other hand, it is clear in light of practical experience that simple voluntary measures will not be sufficient. Measures such as signing diversity charters will be undertaken mostly by 'best practice' private sector employers who are already inclined to comply with the equality laws, which means that some further arrangements are necessary if the all-important private sector is to be engaged in the proactive work towards equality.[58]

12.4 Conclusions

The idea of positive equality duties is a promising innovation that links up with the recent call for new forms of governance to deal with social problems.[59] The different individual strands of the duty promise many benefits: mainstreaming challenges the status quo of 'business as usual' and forces the organizations in question to ask the right questions; impact assessments uncover the disadvantaging properties of rules, practices and structures that appear neutral on their face; consultation and inclusion brings empowerment to the target groups, facilitating a shift from expert rule towards shared governance; and linking public procurement with promotion of equality helps to engage the private sector in the quest for a more equal society. The implementation of the duties, and the drafting, implementation and monitoring of equality plans in particular, call for such organizational structures establishing responsibility (diversity committees, diversity staff positions) that empirical studies have found to be the key to unlocking a positive development in workforce diversity.[60] Overall, the imposition of duties

[58] The argument against relying on voluntary action might run like this: "We should assume…that organisations will only modify disapproved-of behaviour if faced with sufficient incentives. Where an organisation expects to benefit from infringing the law by continuing to act in a certain way, it is unlikely to change its behaviour unless the costs of doing so outweigh the anticipated benefits." Christopher McCrudden, 'International and European Norms Regarding National Legal Remedies for Racial Inequality' in Sandra Fredman (ed.) *Discrimination and Human Rights* (Oxford: Oxford University Press, 2001), pp. 304–305.

[59] On new modes of governance and the protection of human rights, see Gráinne de Búrca 'New Modes of Governance and the Protection of Human Rights' in Philip Alston – Olivier de Schutter (eds.) *Monitoring fundamental rights in the EU: the contribution of the fundamental rights agency* (Oxford: Hart, 2005).

[60] Alexandra Kalev – Frank Dobbin – Erin Kelly 'Best Practices or Best Guesses? Assessing the Efficacy of Corporate Affirmative Action and Diversity Policies' *American Sociological Review*, 2006, Vol. 71 (August 589–617).

promises to affect the kind of long-term cultural and structural change in organizations that mere lawsuits are inherently incapable of achieving.

Yet the introduction of duties is subject to challenges that risk circumscribing much of their effectiveness. The more stringent these duties are, and the more effectively they are enforced, the more likely such duties will generate resistance. There are political constraints linked to any introduction of new 'regulatory burdens' in particular on the private sector, the mobilization of which would be of high importance, as otherwise the impact of the approach is limited. Also other, more specific challenges abound. Mechanisms and modalities of target group inclusion require careful advance planning, lest they be counterproductive by means of reinforcing identity politics and stereotyping. The identification of problems and the measuring of the progress made in their elimination – two aspects that are integral to equality duties – call for ethnic data collection, but this may not be an option in many countries, a fact which may to an extent undermine the potential effectiveness of certain kinds of duty-based approaches. And most importantly, there is always the risk that without real commitment, particularly from the top of the organization, implementation of the duty collapses into one more bureaucratic routine aimed at meeting the minimum conditions of compliance, with no organizational learning or real transformation.

In effect, the future of positive duties depends primarily on two things: first, the extent to which the interested organizations and communities are able to put pressure on and persuade politicians and other key stakeholders to take the necessary action to impose duties; second, the extent to which workable solutions to the above-identified challenges are found. Even if these two conditions are met, social change will not take place overnight.

13 ENFORCEMENT

The introduction of the above-mentioned proactive strategies by no means has to come at the price of the exclusion of strategies based on litigation and other means of enforcement. Indeed, it should not come at that price, because no reasons have come up in light of which it could be expected that the proactive strategies could eliminate all forms of discrimination. Any progress that will be made by means of introduction of data collection, positive duties, positive action and other policies will be incremental and slow to emerge. These policies may, over time, affect a cultural change at the organizational and societal levels, and reduce stereotypes by means of promoting the opportunities, inclusion and material well-being of the target groups and by decreasing social distance between groups. Positive strategies will however be unlikely to affect a change in the mindset and behaviour of those who hold the most egregious forms of prejudices; some strategies may even be counterproductive by increasing the perceptions that immigrants and minorities are to an unjust extent at the receiving end of various public policy measures. The persistence of racism from a historical perspective, and its ability to take new forms under social pressure and legal and policy interventions, suggests that positive interventions may go some way towards achieving a more equal society, but they will hardly go all the way. Subtle, indirect and structural forms of discrimination will also be as hard to identify and combat as ever. In view of all of this we must proceed from the prediction that discrimination on the grounds of racial and ethnic origin will not be eliminated in any near future. There will therefore always be individuals in need of legal protection against discrimination, which is why there is a need to strengthen the enforcement of the related law. In effect, it is not just possible but also desirable to pursue a two-track strategy, to strengthen the enforcement of the law in addition to the pursuance of proactive policy measures.

Specialized bodies, meaning bodies established to promote equal opportunities and/or to secure their enjoyment through judicial or quasi-judicial functions, play a crucial role in this. Such bodies have been established across Europe. Article 13 of the EU Racial Equality

Directive requires EU member states to designate one or more equality bodies and to charge them with three functions: (i) to provide independent assistance to victims of discrimination in pursuing their complaints about discrimination, (ii) conduct independent surveys concerning discrimination, and (iii) publish independent reports and make recommendations on any issue relating to such discrimination. The wording of the Article is notoriously imprecise,[1] but it does provide a basis for further institutional development. This chapter suggests some specific arrangements, including several that have to do with the functions of the specialized bodies, that can be used to strengthen the legal protection. Mere redesign of the functions of these bodies may however not be sufficient. In light of the limited resources of the existing bodies,[2] additional funding may be called for, though prioritization may also lead to more effective use of the existing resources.

13.1 The Legal Infrastructure

In drafting equality legislation, the legislator has to make a decision with regard to which branch of law to rely upon. Choices include constitutional law, criminal law, civil law, labour law and administrative law.[3] The use of each of these has its positive and negative aspects, which are – in broad terms – summed up in the following table:

---

[1] See e.g. Gay Moon, 'Chapter Eight: Enforcement Bodies' in Dagmar Schiek - Lisa Waddington - Mark Bell, *Non-Discrimination Law: Cases, Materials and text on National, Supranational and International Non-Discrimination Law* (Oxford, Hart Publishing, 2007), p. 890; Colm O'Cinneide, 'The Racial Equality Directive as a Basis for Strategic Enforcement' in Janet Cormack (ed.) *Strategic Enforcement and EC Equal Treatment Directives* (Migration Policy Group, 2004), p. 49.

[2] The financial and human resources of existing bodies are summarised in the Appendix of Rikki Holtmaat, *Catalysts for Change: Equality bodies according to directive 2000/43/EC – existence, independence and effectiveness* (Luxembourg: OOPEC, 2007).

[3] NB: The titles of the different areas of law vary between countries, especially between common law and civil law countries.

Branch of Law	Positive Aspects	Negative Aspects
Constitutional law	- Carries authority, has symbolical value, defines core values of the society; - Frames, constrains and guides the actions of the legislator, the judiciary and the public administration; - Normally enjoys supremacy over ordinary laws.	- Can hardly suffice on its own, as it is usually not directly applicable in situations not involving public authorities; - Is rigid in its content in the sense that chancing it often requires an extraordinary process.
Criminal law	- Expresses the society's condemnation of discrimination; - Has a general dissuasive effect, the degree of which however depends upon the probability with which perpetrators are brought to justice; - Evidence is collected by the police and/or public prosecutor; - Usually low financial risk for the victim.	- Criminal proceedings are seldom brought about: in some European countries only 1–2% of victims of discrimination file a complaint; this can generate an impression that legal action is futile; - Higher threshold for proving discrimination i.e. it is harder to win cases; - Victims have little or no control over the proceedings; this may contribute to the reluctance to bring cases; - Individual misconduct is usually at issue: a finding of discrimination often has little effect outside the particular circumstances; - Use is limited to situations involving criminal liability (*mens rea*); - The persons accused (employers, banks etc) often do not fit into the profile of a typical offender, which may make it harder for the police

(Continued)

(*Contd.*)

Branch of Law	Positive Aspects	Negative Aspects
		and prosecutors to see the crimes committed.[4]
Civil law[5] and Labour law	- Shifted burden of proof; Civil law is best placed to impose positive duties; - The complainant has better control of the proceedings, and settlement is possible; - The available remedies (such as compensation for pecuniary and non-pecuniary damages) are often appreciated by the victims.[6]	- Responsibility for proving the case i.e. gathering evidence, is upon the complainant; This responsibility can be alleviated to an extent by shifting the burden of proof and/or by providing a right to obtain evidence; - Risk of potentially high litigation costs.

Whereas EU member states typically have anti-discrimination legislation that spans all branches of law, most member states transposed the EU equality directives through civil and/or labour law, with a minority also having introduced or amended criminal law provisions.[7] Considerably many states opted for a type of equality legislation that covers different types of discrimination (ethnic, religion, age, gender, disability) in a single law. The traditional approach in the Nordic countries has been to opt for a combination of criminal law and labour law,[8] but lately the tendency has been towards generally applicable

[4] Paul Lappalainen 'The challenges posed by the EU anti-discrimination directives' Working paper presented at the Sixth International Metropolis Conference, 27 November 2001.

[5] In this context the term 'civil law' is used to mean the law that governs relations between private individuals.

[6] If damages are limited to mere compensation, this may be taken as a signal that the lawmaker is actually indifferent as to whether discrimination is a moral wrong. On the other hand, if damages are not limited to compensation, then this may have a deterrent or chilling effect on activity in general. Duncan Kennedy 'Form and Substance in Private Law Adjudication' *Harvard Law Review* Vol 89, p. 1694.

[7] Mark Bell et al, *Developing Anti-Discrimination Law in Europe: The 25 EU Member States compared* (Luxembourg: OOPEC, 2007), p. 14.

[8] Reliance on criminal law has in a historical perspective often resulted from pursuing the fulfilment of international obligations, such as those set by the CERD Convention.

legislative frameworks.[9] The European Commission against Racism and Intolerance (ECRI) has, in its General Policy Recommendation No. 7 on *national legislation to combat racism and racial discrimination*, recommended that anti-discrimination legislation should include provisions in all branches of law, as "only such an integrated approach will enable member States to address these problems in a manner which is as exhaustive, effective and satisfactory from the point of view of the victim as possible".[10] In light of the above table, which clearly shows how the use of each branch does have its particular advantages, this is sound advice.[11] That said, civil law should arguably play the leading role, because it is necessary for the law to reach beyond situations that involve criminal liability, just as it is necessary for the law to reach beyond the actions of the public sector.[12] Moreover, the imposition of positive duties can best take place in the context of civil law. In view of this, some of the views and recommendations made in the following subchapters specifically concern civil law arrangements.

Upon considering a reform of the equality law, a national (or European) legislator should also consider whether to opt for *rules*, the application of which to factual circumstances is more straightforward, or for more flexible *standards*, the application of which leaves more room for discretion.[13] Rules appear to offer precision, certainty and compulsiveness, but suffer from mechanical over- and under-inclusion from the point of view of the lawmaker's purposes. Standards, on the other hand, appear to leave more room for evolution and creativity, but their flexibility may also bring along arbitrariness and uncertainty. At the end of the day, real-life experience is the final arbiter as to what

---

[9] Indeed, many experts are of the view that it is important to include broad civil law procedures and remedies to the framework of anti-discrimination law. See e.g. Michael Banton, *Discrimination* (Buckingham: Open University Press, 1994), p. 54 ff.

[10] ECRI, General Policy Recommendation No 7, adopted on 13 December 2002; see also the Explanatory Memorandum to the Recommendation, p. 11.

[11] Note however, that it has been warned that the multiplicity of pieces of law and institutions tackling discrimination may lead to disintegration of the efforts to fight discrimination. EU Network of Independent Experts on Fundamental Rights, *Combating Racism and Xenophobia through Criminal Legislation: The Situation in the EU Member States*. Opinion No 5-2005, 28 November 2005, p. 9.

[12] The use of civil law has other benefits too, see e.g. Peter R. Rodrigues 'The Dutch experience of enforcement agencies: current issues in Dutch anti-Discrimination law' in Martin MacEwen (ed.), *Anti-Discrimination Law Enforcement* (Ashgate 1997), pp. 55–57.

[13] The legislator should also consider what role voluntary arrangements, such as codes of practice or diversity declarations, could play.

approach fits best a given society at a given time. That said, judges and other legal professionals are not immune from having prejudices and stereotypes, and there is indeed research evidence suggesting that these factors do play a role in judicial decision-making.[14] And as John Griffiths argues, "if we start from the assumption that in discrimination cases the victim will generally be less highly organised, less wealthy, and more socially marginal than the defendant, then a large body of literature tells us that, despite the legal system's pretence of formal legal equality, the tactical advantage with regard to a whole range of matters will be strongly with the defendant."[15] Active review of court decisions by individuals and organizations committed to promoting equality, a form of informal social control, is also weak in Europe. These considerations speak for the use of rules as opposed to standards at this point of time in Europe.

13.2 Strengthening Enforcement

Individual Litigation

Whereas the limits of a strategy based on individual litigation are clear, particularly as a means of ensuring general compliance with equality laws, this is no reason for not allowing individuals to take legal action. What is wrong with the present individual rights and individual litigation based approach is that it perceives legal action not as the last resort, as it perhaps should be, but as the *only* resort. Indeed, insofar as the proactive and preventive measures are not capable of curbing discrimination, victims of discrimination should be encouraged, not discouraged, to take their cases to courts, as that is necessary in order for them to obtain a remedy for the particular wrongs suffered – provided, of course, that the available remedies are adequate in terms of offsetting the harms and motivating the victim to seek the aid of the legal system.[16]

---

[14] See e.g. Cyndi Banks, *Criminal Justice Ethics: Theory and Practice* (Sage 2004); Lars Holmberg – Britta Kyvsgaard, 'Are Immigrants and their Descendants Discriminated against in the Danish Criminal Justice System?' *Journal of Scandinavian Studies in Criminology and Crime Prevention* Vol. 4, No 2 (2003), pp. 125–142.

[15] John Griffiths 'The Social Working of Anti-Discrimination Law' in Titia Loenen – Peter Rodrigues (eds.) *Non-Discrimination Law: Comparative Perspectives* (The Hague: Kluwer, 1999), p. 326.

[16] Roger Cotterrell, *The Sociology of Law*, 2nd ed. (London: Butterworths, 1992), p. 53.

Whether individual claimants are able to enforce their rights in practice depends on a number of factors. Individuals may, first of all, not have adequate information about equal treatment law and may not have access to legal help, or if they do have the access, the lack of trained and motivated lawyers may be a problem. They may, in addition, not know whether they have been discriminated against, or may be unsure about that because they do not have the requisite information about the reasons underlying the actions of the alleged discriminator. Judicial proceedings can be costly, lengthy and emotionally strenuous, and an individual who believes that she has for instance been denied employment on discriminatory grounds would have good reasons to arrive at the conclusion that it will take less time, money, effort and emotional engagement to find employment from some other place than to sue the discriminator, pursue the case in the court, win the case and finally obtain compensation – provided, of course, that all goes well. Potential complainants may also be subject to victimization or fear becoming subject to it. Taken together, the different challenges can effectively debar access to justice.[17]

There are two broad and complementary groups of measures by which these challenges can to some extent be tackled. The first one involves training and the dissemination of information on anti-discrimination law, the provision of support to victims of discrimination, adjustments of procedural rules, and the establishment of low-threshold specialist tribunals and/or bodies charged with alternative dispute settlement functions. In short, the first group of measures aims at enabling individuals to pursue legal action in practice. The second group of measures, on the contrary, consists of measures that aim at strengthening enforcement carried out by specialized agencies charged with that function, without necessarily requiring the involvement of individual victims of discrimination.

Support Structures for Individual Legal Mobilization

There are a number of general supporting measures that are essential for helping the anti-discrimination law to be properly enforced.

[17] See also Peter R. Rodrigues, *cit. supra* note 12, pp. 56–57; Christopher McCrudden 'Regulating Discrimination: Advice to a Legislator on Problems Regarding the Enforcement of Anti-Discrimination Law and Strategies to Overcome Them' in Titia Loenen – Peter Rodrigues (eds.) *Non-Discrimination Law: Comparative Perspectives* (The Hague: Kluwer, 1999), p. 302.

Useful measures include, first of all, the dissemination of information about anti-discrimination law to a broad range of stakeholders, including groups vulnerable to discrimination; businesses and other public and private organizations, particularly gatekeepers (for instance human resources personnel) within them; and the general public. A second useful measure is capacity-building for legal professionals, particularly judges, prosecutors and attorneys. This entails the arrangement of training in anti-discrimination law and its inclusion in law school curricula, and the availability of legal materials on anti-discrimination law.

Specialist legal assistance is obviously a major asset wherever available, particularly if available free of charge. The EU Directive, as noted, requires each member state to have an equality body that provides "independent assistance to victims of discrimination in pursuing their complaints". The Directive does not set out the nature or form of this 'assistance', but it is generally thought that the provision of advice for instance over telephone is probably sufficient to meet its requirements, and that the Directive by no means requires the relevant body to provide legal representation to each individual claiming to be a victim.[18] That said, there is nothing in the Directive or in any other document to stop an equality body or some other organization from providing such services, and indeed many countries in Europe and elsewhere have bodies that give legal assistance through providing help with writing of complaints and in some cases representation in courts. However, it is a general experience that bodies offering legal assistance soon become overwhelmed with requests for assistance.[19] Their resources, even if substantial which is often not the case, will inevitably be insufficient in face of the huge demand. In practice, bodies that offer legal assistance, particularly in the form of representation, will have to be selective and

---

[18] See e.g. Moon, *cit. supra* note 1, p. 892.

[19] See e.g. Eilís Barry, 'Strategic Enforcement - From Concept to Practice' in Janet Cormack (ed.) *Strategic Enforcement and EC Equal Treatment Directives* (Migration Policy Group, 2004), p. 6. Colm O'Cinneide reports that the Canadian Human Rights Commission, which used to be required to investigate each case referred to it in order to decide whether it should be sent forward to conciliation or to a tribunal or whether it should be rejected, used to have a considerable backlog and a high complaint rejection rate (possibly driven by an administrative desire to reduce the backlog), which gave rise to "serious credibility issues and low staff morale". He also reports that the US Equal Employment Opportunities Commission, to which employment equality cases commenced under the US federal equality law must first be filed for investigation, has developed major backlogs which peaked at 111 000 cases in 1995. O'Cinneide, *cit. supra* note 1, p. 51–52.

thus engage in strategic litigation. Strategic litigation, while not of immediate help to the majority of potential claimants, does have its benefits too, in that the case work can be focused on those cases that stand out as likely to lead to the clarification of an important legal issue or lead to the adoption of a judgment which will affect large numbers of people.[20] The selectiveness of strategic enforcement can result in claims, on part of the discriminated against groups, and particularly where flagrant discrimination is rampant, that the specialized body is not really of assistance to them; many may experience this as another broken promise on part of the mainstream society.[21] In light of this it would be sensible to offer at least *some* help to all potential claimants, particularly in the form of advice. But at the end of the day, strategic litigation is better than no litigation at all, and the availability of low-threshold judicial or quasi-judicial avenues that require no specialist legal representation can do much to alleviate the problems of the non-availability of specialist legal help.

Domestic rules on legal standing that allow for *representative actions* (also known as class actions) and/or *public interest actions* (also known as *actio popularis*) offer two more examples of ways in which enforcement can be strengthened. Representative actions allow an organization, such as a trade union or an equality body, to bring a discrimination claim on behalf of a number of individuals who been harmed in a similar way. This would be the case, for instance, where an employer systematically pays its foreign workers less than its 'domestic' workers for work of equal value. Representative actions are cost-efficient in that the cases of all potential complainants can be handled at once. In a public interest action, an organization brings a discrimination claim not in the interests of named individuals, but in the interests of the public or some section thereof. An interested organization might, for instance, have legal standing where an employer has publicly stated that it will not hire immigrants, and where no identifiable victim exists because immigrants have not applied for work knowing that their applications would not be successful.[22] The threat of representative actions and

---

[20] Individual cases can be expensive, especially if lost and the agency ends up having to pay the legal fees for the other party. Litigation may also prove not to have the desired strategic outcome. Razia Karim 'A legal Strategy to Combine and coordinate Different Tools Available' in Janet Cormack (ed.) *Strategic Enforcement and EC Equal Treatment Directives* (Migration Policy Group, 2004), pp. 31–32.

[21] Moon, *cit. supra* note 1, p. 892.

[22] This was at issue in ECJ, *Feryn*, judgment of 10 July 2008.

public interest actions can provide a further incentive to employers to get their policies and practices right. Despite the potential usefulness of these two legal devices, they are currently grossly underused in Europe.[23]

A viable way to bypass the perceived and real complexities of legal proceedings brought before ordinary courts of law is to create specialized judicial or quasi-judicial bodies to resolve complaints. Specialist tribunals and quasi-judicial bodies have many advantages. First of all, access to justice comes without a great cost, as there are usually no court fees and, as at least in some jurisdictions, there is no risk of having to pay the other party's expenses if one's case fails.[24] Processing before these bodies is usually informal, which makes legal representation unnecessary and which may be experienced as less strenuous emotionally. These bodies also have the kind of specialist expertise and experience that ordinary courts of law tend to lack in an area of relatively unpractised law.[25] Indeed, complainants may be more assured that that their cases will be taken seriously in a Discrimination Tribunal or an Equal Treatment Commission than in a regular court of law where discrimination cases seldom enjoy priority.

Mediation and other forms of alternative dispute resolution (ADR) have become increasingly popular tools for resolving complaints in Europe. ADR refers to any means of settling disputes outside of the courtroom, including mediation and arbitration.[26] Most European equality bodies are empowered to use this tool, and for some equality bodies there is a legal requirement to try to reach a voluntary settlement before taking any other action.[27] Alternative dispute settlement

---

[23] At the time of the writing, no EU country has introduced rules on representative actions in the field of discrimination law, though the issue is under consideration in the UK. Public interest actions are in use only in Belgium, Hungary and Romania. Bell et al, *cit. supra* note 7, pp. 88–90. Communication from the Commission to the European Parliament, the Council, The European Economic and Social Committee and the Committee of the Regions, *Non-discrimination and equal opportunities: A renewed commitment Community Instruments and Policies for Roma Inclusion*, Brussels 2.7.2008, SEC(2008) 2172, p. 6.

[24] This is the case for instance in Finland with respect to the national Discrimination Tribunal.

[25] Martin MacEwen 'Promoting equal opportunity: the enforcement agency', in Martin MacEwen (ed.), *Anti-Discrimination Law Enforcement* (Aldershot: Avebury, 1997), p. 6 and MacEwen 'Concluding remarks', in idem, p. 239.

[26] Mediation is a type of procedure that is resolved by an agreement between parties facilitated by a third party (the mediator), whereas arbitration is a type of procedure that is resolved unilaterally by a third party acting as a judge.

[27] Bell et al, *cit. supra* note 7, p. 67; Moon, *cit. supra* note 1, pp. 897–899.

mechanisms have their benefits particularly when contrasted with legal proceedings, as they may be less disruptive of the relations between parties, require less legal expertise, and take less money and usually also less time. Excessive use of these mechanisms does have its drawbacks, however, as the impression may arise that equal treatment is negotiable and as pertinent confidentiality requirements keep problems under the radar of decision-makers and the wider society. Moreover, systematic recourse to these processes does not allow the development of case law that clarifies to the different stakeholders what the law actually requires. Sometimes the use of these mechanisms may also lead to early or unbalanced settlement, particularly where disputants have unequal skills and are under mediator pressure.[28]

Adjustment of certain procedural rules concerning the discovery of documents may also significantly improve the chances of individuals to bring legal action in practice. One of the key challenges in bringing legal action is that to the extent that modern forms of discrimination are subtle and covert, they are also less easy to prove. Direct evidence of discrimination is rare, and where such direct evidence exists, corroboration is even rarer.[29] In criminal proceedings the burden of an individual litigant to produce evidence is not a major problem, as it is typically up to the police, prosecutor or the court to investigate the facts. But the processes brought under civil and labour law are adversarial in nature, where the onus of proving a fact is upon the party wishing to rely upon it.[30] A particular problem emerges in that context: in discrimination cases the factual evidence, or important parts thereof, is usually in the possession of the respondent, not the complainant – provided, of course, that the necessary information exists in the first place. Proper application of the shift in the burden of proof, as provided for by the EU Directive, may on occasion make it unnecessary

---

[28] Jenny Goldschmidt 'Enforcement of equal treatment: The role of the Equal Treatment Commission in the Netherlands' in Martin MacEwen (ed.), *Anti-Discrimination Law Enforcement* (Aldershot: Avebury, 1997), p. 148.

[29] Fitsum Alemu, *Testing to prove racial discrimination: methodology and application in Hungary*. An internet article available at: http://www.errc.org/cikk.php?cikk=1016 (visited 1.1.2006).

[30] It is sometimes suggested that this difference between criminal and civil proceedings with regard to the need to produce proof has led to a situation where victims of discrimination prefer to bring criminal proceedings instead of civil proceedings. See e.g. Sophie Latraverse, *Report on Measures to Combat Discrimination. Country Report – France*. December 2004. European Network of Legal Experts in the non-discrimination field. Available at: www.non-discrimination.net (visited 1.1.2010).

for the complainant to rely on the information that is in the possession of the respondent, but this is not always the case as the complainant will still have to prove facts sufficient to make a *prima facie* case. The overwhelming majority of the EU countries address this problem through rules concerning discovery of documents, whereby a court may, on its own initiative or upon the request of one of the parties, order the other party to submit information that is in her possession and of relevance to the case.[31] Where the respondent refuses to furnish the court with the requested information, without providing a satisfactory justification thereto, the court is usually entitled to freely appreciate the inferences it draws from that. The existence of this kind of arrangement is crucial, as otherwise an imbalance results in that the respondent can in practice decide to use the information in the proceedings only where it is to her own benefit.

However, the rules concerning discovery only provide a partial answer to the problem. The civil procedure is not concerned with the process by which a potential complainant can discern whether he or she might have a legal claim. In consequence, complainants need as much information as possible already *before* commencing legal action, in order to assess whether a *prima facie* case of discrimination can be made. Some jurisdictions have adopted specific solutions to deal with this problem. In Sweden, a person who applies for a job, promotion or training opportunity but is not selected has a right to request and receive written information from the employer regarding the education, work experience and other qualifications of the person who was selected, in order to be able to compare qualifications. A different type of arrangement exists in the UK, where an alleged discriminator can be asked for information, including statistical data, through the 'questionnaire procedure' before or after proceedings have been commenced ('pre-litigation discovery'). Under this procedure, if the respondent does not fill in the questionnaire, or gives unreasonable answers, the court may find sufficient grounds to draw inferences and shift the

[31] The respondent, e.g. an employer, is usually not required to provide material where it is not readily available, or where an employer would be required to begin a process of data collection that would add unnecessarily to the length and cost of a hearing. This is the case for instance in Britain, see *Carrington v Helix Lighting Ltd* [1990] ICR 125. Furthermore, in the case of criminal proceedings the principle against self-incrimination provides that a person charged with a criminal offence cannot be compelled to provide self-incriminating evidence. In some countries the scope of the obligation to submit documents or information is also in some specific circumstances limited by the domestic data protection laws.

burden of proof to the respondent. Though they do not have official standing, many discrimination cases have been won in the UK because of inadequately answered questionnaires, and specialized equality bodies routinely use them.[32] Discrimination lawyers in other European countries have adopted similar, though less formulaic, questionnaires.[33] Pre-litigation discovery mechanisms, along these or some other lines, can therefore be highly valuable.

Agency Enforcement

Some of the problems associated with the individual enforcement-oriented processes can be addressed by powers given to a specific body to conduct investigations into cases of suspected discrimination and/or conduct inquiries that are of a more general nature.[34] This is particularly so where the process may be initiated without a formal complaint, and the body has strong information gathering powers, including the enforceable power to demand written or oral evidence and the discovery of documents, thereby overcoming difficulties arising from lack of access to information. A major benefit of inquiries in particular is their ability to address discriminatory patterns and structures instead of just individual incidents.

Ombudsmen, or broadly speaking equivalent institutions that have been set up in many EU countries, are generally empowered to conduct investigations on the basis of specific complaints and/or on their own initiative.[35] Usually these bodies are entitled to impose a fine, or to take some other enforcement action, if their request for appropriate information is not met. A finding of discrimination typically leads to the issuing of recommendations or advice and is without prejudice to the victim's right to initiate legal proceedings, for instance with a view to obtaining compensation.[36]

Labour inspectorates or equivalent bodies have been entrusted with the task of supervising compliance with the equality legislation in the

---

[32] ERRC – Interights – MPG, *Strategic Litigation in Europe: From Principles to Practice* (Nottingham: Russell Press ltd, 2004), p. 72. For critical comments see Sandra Fredman, *Discrimination Law* (Oxford: Oxford University Press, 2002), p. 165.

[33] Idem (ERRC et al).

[34] See generally Fredman, *cit. supra* note 32, p. 175.

[35] These countries include e.g. Cyprus, Estonia, Finland, Greece, Lithuania, Slovenia and Sweden. For an analysis of the existence, independence and effectiveness of these bodies see Holtmaat, *cit. supra* note 2.

[36] Bell et al, *cit. supra* note 7, p. 67.

field of employment in a number of countries.[37] These authorities usually have broad powers to conduct on-site investigations and demand documentation that is in the possession of the employer. Usually labour inspectorates carry out their general supervisory tasks on an ongoing basis, conducting more specific investigations where they surmise that such might be needed or where they have been prompted to do so, usually by way of a non-formal complaint.

Yet other types of bodies and procedures exist. For instance in the UK, the Commission for Equality and Human Rights (CEHR) has the power to conduct 'inquiries' and 'investigations'. Inquiries are of a general nature, may target a branch or a sector, and may not involve the consideration of whether one or more persons have breached the law. Investigations, on the other hand, focus on finding out whether or not a legal or natural person has in fact complied with the equality laws. Investigations must be based on a suspicion that the equality laws have not been complied with, arising possibly, but not necessarily, out of the findings made in the course of an inquiry. If satisfied that unlawful acts of discrimination have occurred, the Commission can issue 'an unlawful act notice' to the respondent, requiring it to prepare an action plan for the purpose of avoiding repetition or continuation of the unlawful act and to recommend action to be taken for that purpose. In carrying out an investigation or an inquiry, the Commission may order, by way of giving a notice, a respondent to provide information in his possession, to produce documents in his possession or to give oral evidence. Non-compliance with a notice is considered an offence. The Commission shall publish a report of its findings on an inquiry or investigation, and can make recommendations as part of the report. A court or Tribunal may have regard to a finding of a report, but it shall not treat it as conclusive.[38]

While the investigations can provide a significant means of fact-finding, and represent an important weapon in the armoury of equality bodies,[39] experiences, especially from the UK, have shown that effectively carrying out investigations requires not just the existence of formal powers, but especially the availability of considerable amounts

---

[37] These countries include e.g. Belgium, Finland, Hungary, Malta, Poland and Portugal.

[38] Schedule 2 to the Equality Act 2006, Sections 9–17.

[39] Brian Doyle 'Disability discrimination and enforcement in Britain: future prospects' in Martin MacEwen (ed.), *Anti-Discrimination Law Enforcement* (Aldershot: Avebury, 1997), p. 78

of financial resources, in the absence of which the coverage of the work can never be adequately comprehensive.[40] Investigations can be complex and therefore resource-intensive. Their impact can also be mixed. Investigations and inquiries may not immediately benefit individuals who have been discriminated against, and may not have effects outside their direct targets if a wider audience is not listening.[41] They may also be experienced by their targets as confrontational, therefore inhibiting any promotional work that the same agency may be undertaking. On the positive side, any changes made in response to the results of an investigation or inquiry carry long-term and wide benefits, provided that the audience *is* listening. Experience particularly from the UK suggests that formal investigations may be particularly effective where the discriminator is a repeat offender, meaning that litigation has not brought about a change in its practices or procedures, or where there is evidence of institutional and systemic discrimination that is not easy to reach by means of litigation, or where there is evidence of discriminatory practices but no identifiable victim to bring proceedings.[42] At the end of the day, the use of investigations and inquiries, given the often limited resources and the consequent need to prioritize, calls for the use of careful consideration as to when their deployment is best warranted.[43]

13.3 Informal Invocation and Enforcement of the Law

The aim of all regulation is, it is said, to modify the behaviour of those subject to regulation in order to generate a desired outcome.[44] But how exactly does this 'modification of behaviour' take place? Those subject to anti-discrimination law include most people, from bus drivers to social workers to teachers to each and every person employed in the

---

[40] It should also be noted that the UK commissions have been hampered by the fact that a 'named person investigation' cannot take place without the Commission suspecting that unlawful discrimination is occurring.

[41] Des Hogan 'Inquiries within a wider functional strategy' in Janet Cormack (ed.) *Strategic Enforcement and EC Equal Treatment Directives* (Migration Policy Group, 2004).

[42] Karim, *cit. supra* note 20, p. 33–34.

[43] For some of the considerations that may need to be taken into account, see Des Hogan, *cit. supra* note 41.

[44] Karen Yeung 'Private Enforcement of Competition Law' in Christopher McCrudden (ed.) *Regulation and Deregulation: Policy and Practice in the Utilities and Financial Services Industries* (Oxford: Clarendon Press, 1999), p. 40.

public or private sector. In the social context, the totality of situations in which anti-discrimination norms are relevant is infinite in number, day in and day out. If anti-discrimination law is to do what it is supposed to do, then basically each and every person should know what exactly the law requires from them in these different situations of everyday life, and they should be willing to do what the law requires.

Lawyers, policymakers and members of the public are always at the risk of a failure to appreciate that most of the use of legal norms is really by ordinary people in the course of their daily activities, not by legal professionals in the course of formal legal proceedings.[45] But people seldom know (or even really want to know) about the intricacies of the law or how a particular provision should be applied in this or that particular circumstance. Even less frequently do they have the opportunity to consult a legal expert every time they are in a situation where the law is relevant. For most of people law proper is something that is outside the context of their ordinary lifeworld, something that is perceived to belong to the realm of the extraordinary world of lawyers and legal institutions. In consequence, for most people most of the time, the law of law books and precedents is not much more than an irrelevance.

In practice, legal rules are of relevance to 'non-professionals' only indirectly, through social norms and social control. Social norms reflect culturally transmitted perceptions and beliefs about appropriate behaviour in particular circumstances. Due to their nature as social constructs, they may be specific to a society, group or organization, and any single person can be under the influence of a number of possibly conflicting sets of social norms. The connection between legal norms and social norms is not clear or simple.[46] For legal rules to be effective in social life, they must have become transformed into social norms, into widely shared beliefs about appropriate ways of behaviour. For legal norms to transform into social norms they must be known to the public (or the more specific group in question) and be embraced by it, meaning that these norms cannot deviate much from what is considered reasonable within this group. Precision is lost by way of transformation, as social norms usually need to be clear and simple.[47] There

---

[45] Griffiths, *cit. supra* note 15, p. 321. Cotterrell, *cit. supra* note 16.

[46] See generally on this Cotterrell, *cit. supra* note 16, pp. 44–45. Much depends, for instance, on cultural evaluation of the law, whether strict obedience to legal norms itself is one of the social norms.

[47] Griffiths, *cit. supra* note 15, p. 327.

may also be distortion, as what people think that the law requires has been transmitted by non-specialist information sources such as the media, workmates, family members, and so on.[48] At the end of the day, popular understandings of the law's requirements may differ to a great extent from what the legislator has intended.[49]

Progress towards the reduction of discrimination can take place through informal invocation of the pertinent social norms, by persons who feel that they are being discriminated against. A protest indicating that the treatment that one is being subjected to is illegal serves to remind the offender about normative aspects of the incident, repeated successful protests contributing to the vitality of the social norm. There can also be informal social enforcement, in the form of negative reactions by third parties to a breach of a social norm. This kind of informal social control of the observance of social norms can be an effective mechanism for de facto enforcement of social justice. Indeed, Griffiths argues that "when rules are effective, this is often likely to be due to enforcement by informal social control than enforcement by legal officials".[50] These observations call for active engagement by those members of the society who believe that unequal treatment should not be tolerated, to intervene whenever and wherever they encounter discrimination. The practical effectiveness of equality norms, given the economics of scale, can best be promoted through the fostering of a public culture that does not tolerate intolerance and discrimination.[51] A promising factor is that opinion polls indicate that the principle of equal treatment enjoys a high degree of popular support, a fact which can significantly enhance the effectiveness of the related legislation.[52] Capitalization of this support requires widespread mobilization, however, turning a critical mass of people into everyday activists. Whether this can and will happen remains to be seen, but high hopes should not be raised in this respect, as the reality is that many individuals – struggling with the tangible and immediate realities of their

---

[48] See also ibid, p. 317.

[49] Social norms can, however, also be more progressive – from the point of view of promotion of equality – than the law, for example by means of requiring one to observe the principle of equal treatment even where the law does not require it.

[50] Griffiths, *cit. supra* note 15, p. 330.

[51] See e.g. Jan Niessen, 'Making the Law Work: The Enforcement and Implementation of Anti-Discrimination Legislation' *European Journal of Migration and Law* 5: 249–257, 2003.

[52] See also Cotterrell, *cit. supra* note 16, pp. 59–63.

everyday life – do not have the time, energy or interest for matters of social justice.

13.4 Conclusions

There is no evidence before us on the basis of which it could be predicted that racial and ethnic discrimination are about to disappear. It rather looks as though we are only beginning to understand and appreciate the multidimensional and complex nature of inequality and its many causes and consequences. The perverse economics of discrimination, where for the discriminator discrimination pays (in one way or the other), and where the costs are borne by the victim and the rest of the society, are not going to wither away on their own.

The belief that the law possesses power that by itself transforms the society into its image may be popular but is fundamentally mistaken. The best of laws is not worth the paper it is written on if it is not enforced; and in the case of frequently occurring infringements, frequently enforced. Effective access to justice is an empty slogan until the time when the people concerned are confident that it is worthwhile to bring about legal claims. This may call for legislative reform of procedural rules and the establishment of specialized procedures and bodies to deal with claims, and most of all, for the establishment of specialized bodies with the competence to provide legal help. Enforcement agencies may also come to play a major role. All of this requires substantial public funding. Indeed, a key measure of any government's sincerity in keeping its promise to eliminate all forms of discrimination is the number of investments it makes in improving enforcement of the pertinent law.

Yet this is just one side of the story. Banton made a point when he claimed that "[t]he best protections against discrimination are those in the hearts of people who believe discrimination to be wrong".[53] The arm of the law, no matter how long, simply cannot reach all places at all times. This speaks for the invigoration of informal social control, where people who believe discrimination to be wrong make it known whenever they come across it. The problem with this, however, is that we need laws against discrimination so desperately precisely because it is so widely practiced, because the prevailing social norms are not able

[53] Banton, *cit supra* note 9, p. 36.

to constrain it. And even more importantly, we don't just need to engage in informal social control and develop (international, European and national) laws that are more effective in practice, but we also need to expose and remedy those social structures that contribute to the sustenance of the vicious circle of disadvantage and discrimination. We have a problem not just with prejudiced attitudes and ineffective laws and legal structures, but also with social structures and realities that feed those attitudes and hinder further development.

At the end of the day, the goal of eliminating discrimination is likely to continue to be as important, impressive and ultimately impossible to reach as ever. For many individuals it will be the case that they remain equal in law – at least in some respects – but unequal in fact. But for how many, it depends on us.

TABLE OF CASES

Permanent Court of International Justice

Minority Schools in Albania, Advisory Opinion, PCIJ Series AB, No. 64 (1935), 4

International Court of Justice

Barcelona Traction, Light and Power Company Limited (Belgium v. Spain) (Second Phase) ICJ Reports (1970) 3

South West Africa Cases, (Ethiopia v. South Africa; Liberia v. South Africa) (Second Phase) ICJ Reports (1966) 4

European Court of Justice

Abrahamsson (Katarina) and Leif Anderson v. *Elisabet Fogelqvist*, 6 July 2000, C-407/98, ECR 2000, page I-5539

Badeck (Georg) and others, 28 March 2000, C-158/97, OJ C 149 27.5.2000, p. 10–11

Chacón Navas (Sonia) v *Eurest Colectividades SA*, GC 11 July 2006, C-13/05, OJ C 224, 16.9.2006, p. 9

Centrum voor gelijkheid van kansen en voor racismebestrijding v *Firma Feryn NV*, 10 July 2008, C-54/07, OJ C 223, 30.8.2008, p.11–12

Coleman (S.) v. *Attridge Law, Steve Law*, GC 17 July 2008, C-303/06, OJ C223 30/08/2008, p. 6–7

Costa v. *ENEL*, 3 of June 1964, Case 6/1964, ECR 1964, 585

Defrenne (Gabrielle) v. *Société anonyme belge de navigation aérienne Sabena*, 8 April 1976, C-43–75, ECR 1976, p. 455

Defrenne (Gabrielle) v. *Société anonyme belge de navigation aérienne Sabena* (III), 15 June 1978, Case 149/77, ECR 1978, p. 1365

EARL de Kerlast v. *Union régionale de coopératives agricoles (Unicopa) and Coopérative du Trieux*, 17 April 1997, Case C-15/95, ECR 1997 I-1961

Edis v. *Ministero della Finanze*, 15 September 1998, C-231/96, ECR 1998 I-4951

European Parliament v. *Council of the European Union*, 27 June 2006, Case C-540/03 ECR 2006 p. I–0576

Kalanke (Eckhard) v. *Freie Hansestadt Bremen*, 17 October 1995, Case C-450/93, ECR 1995, p. I–3051

Kingdom of Spain v. *Council of the European Communities*, Court of 20 September 1988, Case 203/86, ECR 1988, p. 4563

Kjell Karlsson and Others, 13 April 2000, Case C-292/97, OJ C 192, 8 July 2000, p. 4

Lommers (H.) v. *Minister van Landbouw, Natuurbeheer en Visserij*, 19 March 2002, Case C-476/99, ECR 2002, page I–2891

Mangold (Werner) v. *Rüdiger Helm*, 22 November 2005, Case C-144/04, OJ C 036, 11 February 2006, p. 10–11

Marschall(Hellmut) v. *Land Nordrhein-Westfalen*, 11 November 1997, C-409/95, ECR 1997, p. I–06363

Mayr v. *Bäckerei und Konditorei Gerhard Flöckner OHG*, [GC] 26 February 2008, Case C-506/06, OJ C 92, 12 April 2008, p. 7

P. v. *S. and Cornwall County Council*, 30 April 1996, Case C-13/94, ECR 1996, page I-02143

Regina v. *Secretary of State for Employment, ex parte Nicole Seymour-Smith and Laura Perez*, 9 February 1999, Case C-167/97, ECR 1999, page I–623

Schnorbus (Julia) v. *Land Hessen*, 7 December 2000 (1), Case C-79/99, ECR 2000, p. I-10997

Test-Achats ASBL v. *Belgium*, C-236/09, 1 March 2011

Tietosuojavaltuutettu v. *Satakunnan Markkinapörssi OY and Satamedia*, C-73/07, 16 December 2008, ECR 2008, p. 0000

Von Colson and Kamann v. *Land Nordhein-Westfalen*, 10 April 1984, Case 14/83, ECR 1984, p. 1891

Wachauf v. *Bundesamt für Ernährung und Forstwirtschaft*, 13 July 1989, Case 5/88, ECR 1989, p. 2609

European Commission on Human Rights

East African Asians v. *United Kingdom*, *inter alia* nos. 4403/70-4419/70, 14 December 1973, (1981) 3 EHRR 76

X v. *UK* 30 DR 239 1982

European Court of Human Rights

Abdulaziz, Cabales and Balkandali v. *United Kingdom*, 28 May 1985, Series A, No. 94; (1985) 7 EHRR 471

Amann v *Switzerland* [GC], no. 27798/95, 16 February 2000, ECHR 2000-II

Andrejeva v. *Latvia* [GC], no. 557707/00, 18 February 2009

Aydin v. *Turkey*, no.23178/94, 25 September 1997, (1997) 25 EHRR 251

B.B v. *the United Kingdom*, no. 5376/00, 10 February 2004, (2004) 39 EHRR 635

Bazorkina v. Russia, no.69481/01, 27 July 2006, ECHR 2006 751

Beard v. *The United Kingdom*, no. 24882/94, (2001) 33 EHRR 442

Building Societies (The National & Provincial Building Society, The Leeds Permanent Building Society and The Yorkshire Building Society) v. *United Kingdom*, nos. 21319/93; 21449/93; 21675/93, 23 October 1997, Reports 1997-VII, p. 2363

Burden v. *The United Kingdom*, nos. 13378/05, 29 April 2008, (2008) ECHR 357

Case 'Relating to Certain Aspects of the Laws on the Use of Languages in Education in Belgium', nos. 1474/62; 1677/62; 1691/62; 1769/63; 1994/63; 2126/64; 23 July 1968, Series A, No. 6; (1979–80) 1 EHRR 252

Chapman v. *The United Kingdom*, no. 27238/95, 18 January 2001, (2001) 33 EHRR 18

Chassagnou and Others v. *France*, nos. 25088/94, 28331/95 and 28443/95, 29 April 1999, (2000) 29 EHRR 615

Cobzaru v. *Romania*, no. 48254/99, 26 July 2007, (2008) 47 EHRR 10

Cyprus v. *Turkey*, no 25781/94, 10 May 2001, (2001) 35 EHRR

D.H. and others v. *The Czech Republic*, no. 57325/00, 7 February 2006, (2007) ECHR 922

D.H. and others v. *The Czech Republic* [GC], no. 57325/00, 13 November 2007, (2006) 43 EHRR 41

Dudgeon v. *United Kingdom*, 23 September 1981, Series A, No.45; (1982) 4 EHRR 149

Folgerø and Others v. *Norway* [GC], no. 15472/02, 29 June 2007, (2008) EHRR 47

Fredin v. *Sweden*, no. 12033/86, 18 February 1991, Series A, No.192, (1991) 13 EHRR 784

Gaygusuz v. Austria, no. 17371/90, 16 September 1996, (1997) 23 EHRR 364

Gillow v. *United Kingdom*, no. 9063/80, 24 November 1986, Series A, No. 109; (1986) 11 EHRR 355

Hoogendijk v. *The Netherlands*, no. 58641/00, 6 January 2005, 40 EHRR 22

Hugh Jordan v. *United Kingdom*, no. 24746/94, 4 May, 2001, (2003) 37 EHRR 52

Inze v. *Austria*, no. 8695/79, 28 October 1987, Series A, No. 126, (1988) 10 EHRR 394

Ireland v. *The United Kingdom*, 18 January 1978, 2 EHRR 25
Keenan v. *United Kingdom*, no. 27229/95, 3 April 2001, (2001) ECHR 242
Krasnov and Skuratov v. *Russia*, nos. 17864/04 and 21396/04, 19 July 2007, (2007) ECHR 638
L. and V. v. *Austria*, no. 39392/98; 39829/98, 9 January 2003, (2003) ECHR 20
Lithgow v. *United Kingdom*, 8 July 1986, Series A, No. 102, (1986) 8 EHRR 329
M.S. v. *Sweden*, 20837/92, 27.08.1997, 28 EHRR 313
Moldovan and Others v. *Romania*, nos.41138/98 and 64320/01, 12 July 2005, 44 EHRR 16
Nachova and others v. *Bulgaria*, nos. 43577/98 and 43579/98, 26 February 2004 39 EHRR 37
Nachova and others v. *Bulgaria* [GC], nos.43577/98 and 43579/98, 6 July 2005, 42 EHHR 43
National Union of Belgian Police v. *Belgium*, 22 October 1975, Series A, No.19; (1979–80) 1 EHRR 578
Okpisz v. Germany, nos.59140/00, 25 October 2005, (2006) 42 EHRR 32
Oršuš and others v. *Croatia* [GC], no. 15766/03, 16 March 2010
Petropoulou – Tsakiris v. *Greece*, no 44803/04, 6 December 2007, 48 EHRR 48
Phinikaridou v. *Cyprus*, no. 23890/02, 20 December 2007
Rainys and Gasparavicius v. *Lithuania*, nos. 70665/01 and 74345/01, 7 April 2005
Roche v. The United Kingdom, no. 32555/96, 19 October 2005, 42 EHRR 30
Rotaru v. *Romania*, no. 28341/95, 4 May 2000, 8 BHRC 43
S.L. v. *Austria*, no 45330/99, January 2003, 37 EHHR 505
Salgueiro da Silva Mouta v. *Portugal*, no. 33290/96, 21 December 1999, (2001) 31 EHRR 1055
Savez crkava "Riječ života" and Others v. *Croatia*, no. 7798/08, 9 December 2010
Schmidt and Dahlström v. *Sweden*, 6 February 1976, Series A No. 21, (1979–80) 1 EHRR 632
Sejdić and Finci v. *Bosnia and Herzegovina*, nos. 27996/06 and 34836/06, 22 December 2009, (2009) ECHR 2122
Sheffield and Horsham v. *United Kingdom*, nos.22885/93 and 23390/94, 30 July 1998, (1999) 27 EHRR 163

Sidabras and Dziautas v. *Lithuania*, nos. 55480/00 and 593300/00, 27 July 2004, 42 EHRR 6
Silver v. *United Kingdom*, 25 March 1983, Series A, No.61, (1983) 5 EHRR 347
Smith and Grady v. *United Kingdom*, nos. 33985/96 and 33986/96, 27 September 1999, (2000) 29 EHRR 493
Stoica v. *Romania*, no. 42722/02, 4 March 2008, ECHR 191
Sunday Times v. *United Kingdom*, 26 April 1979, Series A, No.30, 2 EHHR 245 (1979–80)
Sunday Times v. *United Kingdom* (No.2), 26 November 1991, Series A, No.217, (1992) 14 EHHR 229
Timishev v. *Russia*, nos. 55762/00 and 55974/00, 13 December 2005, (2005) ECHR 858
Thlimmenos v. *Greece*, no.34369/97, 6 April 2000, (2001) 31 EHRR 411
Van Raalte v. *The Netherlands*, no. 20060/92, 21 Feb. 1997, 24 EHRR 503
Willis v. *United Kingdom*, no. 36042/97, 11 June 2002, 35 EHRR 547
Yiğit v. *Turkey* [GC], no. 3976/05, 2 November 2010
Zarb Adami v. *Malta*, no.17209/02, 20 June 2006, 44 EHRR 3

Human Rights Committee

Althammer v, *Austria*, Communication No 998/01, 8 August 2003
Araujo-Jongen v. *The Netherlands*, Communication No. 418/1990, 22 October 1993
Aumeeruddy-Cziffra and 19 other Mauritian women v. *Mauritius*, Communication No. 35/1978, 9 May 1981
Blaga v. *Romania*, Communication No 1158/2003, 30 March 2006
Broeks v. *The Netherlands*, Communication No 172/1984, 9 April 1987
Danning v. the *Netherlands*, Communication No 180/1984, 2 April 1987
Derksen and Bakker v. *The Netherlands*, Communication No 976/2001, 1 April 2004
Drda v. *The Czech Republic*, Communication No. 1581/2007, 27 October 2010
Gueye et al. v *France*, Communication No. 196/1985, 3 April 1989
Haraldsson and Sveinsson v. *Iceland*, Communication No. 1306/2004, 24 October 2007
Jacobs v. *Belgium*, Communication No. 943/2000, 7 July 2004
Karnel Singh Bhinder v. *Canada*, Communication No. 208/1986, 9 November 1989

Kavanagh v. *Ireland*, Communication No. 819/1998, 4 April 2001
Länsman et al v. *Finland*, Communication No. 671/95, 30 October 1996
Lindgren et al v. *Sweden*, Communication No. 298/1988, 9 November 1990
Love et al v. Australia, Communication No. 983/2001, 25 March 2003
R.T. v. *France*, Communication No. 262/87, 30 March 1989
Simunek, Hastings, Tuzilova and Prochazka v. *The Czech Republic*, Communication No. 516/1992, 19 July 1995
Süsser v. *Czech Republic*, Communication No. 1488/2006, 25 March 2008
Toonen v *Australia*, Communication No. 488/1992, 31 March 1994
Tsarjov v. *Estonia*, Communication No. 1223/2003, 26 October 2007
Vicente et al v. *Colombia*, Communication No. 612/95, 29 July 1997
X v. *Colombia*, Communication No. 1361/2005, 30 March 2007
Zwaan-de Vries v. *The Netherlands*, Communication No. 182/1984, 9 April 1987

Committee on the Elimination of All forms of Racial Discrimination
Adan v. *Denmark*, Communication No. 43/2008, 13 August 2010
A.W.R.A.P. v. *Denmark*, Communication No. 37/2006, 8 August 2007
B.M.S. v. *Australia*, Communication No. 8/1996, 12 March 1999
Diop v. *France*, Communication No. 2/1989, 10 May 1991
Durmic v. *Montenegro, Serbia* Communication No. 29/2003, 8 March 2006
Gelle v. *Denmark*, Communication No. 34/2004, 6 March 2006
Jama v. *Denmark*, Communication No. 41/2008, 21 August 2009
Jewish Community of Oslo et al v. *Norway*, Communication No. 30/2003, 15 August 2005
L.K. v. *The Netherlands*, Communication No. 4/1991, 16 March 1991
L.R. et. al. v. *Slovakia*, Communication No. 31/2003, 7 March 2005
Ms. M.B v *Denmark*, Communication No. 20/2000, 13 March 2002
Quereshi v. *Denmark*, Communication No. 33/2003, 10 March 2005
Yilmaz-Dogan v. *Netherlands*, Communication No. 1/1984, 29 September 1988
Z.U.B.S. v. *Australia*, Communication No. 6/1995, 26 August 1999
Ziad Ben Ahmed Habassi v. *Denmark*, Communication No. 10/1997, 17 March 1999

European Committee of Social Rights

Autism-Europe v. *France*, Complaint No. 13/2002, 4 November 2003

Centre on Housing Rights and Evictions (COHRE) v. *Italy*, Complaint No. 58/2009, 25 June 2010

European Roma Rights Centre v. *Bulgaria*, Complaint No. 31/2005, 18 October 2006

European Roma Rights Centre v. *Italy*, Complaint No. 27/2004, 7 December 2005

Sud Travail et Affaires sociales v. *France*, Complaint No. 24/2004, 16 November 2005

Syndicat national des Professions du Tourisme v. *France*, Complaint No. 6/1999, 10 October 2000

Domestic Courts of Law

United Kingdom

Aina v Employment Service [2002] DCLD 103D

Carrington v. *Helix Lighting Ltd* [1990] ICR 125

Mandla (Sewa Singh) v. *Dowell Lee* [1983] 2 WLR 620, [1983] ICR 385, [1983] IRLR 209

Marshall v F Woolworth & Co. Ltd COIT 1404/80, ET

Panesar v Nestlé Co Ltd, [1980] IRLR 482

Singh v. *British Rail Engineering Ltd., June 25, and July 29 1985*, [1986] ICR 22

West Midland Passenger Transport Executive v Singh [1988] ICR 614

United States Supreme Court

Brown v. *Board of Education*, 17 May 1954, 347 U.S. 483 (1954)

Plessy v. Ferguson, No.210, 18 May 1896, 163 U.S. 537, 16 S. Ct. 1138, 41 L.Ed.256

Canadian Supreme Court

Canada (Attorney General) v. *Lavell*, [1973] S.C.R. 1349

BIBLIOGRAPHY

Adorno, Theodor W. et al. *The Authoritarian Personality*, Abridged edition. New York: Norton, 1982.

Alemu, Fitsum. *Testing to prove racial discrimination: methodology and application in Hungary*. An internet article available at: http://www.errc.org/cikk.php?cikk=1016

Alexander, Larry. 'What makes wrongful discrimination wrong? Biases, preferences, stereotypes, and proxies'. In Christopher McCrudden (ed.) *Anti-Discrimination Law*. Aldershot: Dartmouth, 2004.

Alfredsson, Gudmundur. 'Article 4.' In Marc Weller (ed.). *The Rights of Minorities: A Commentary on the European Framework Convention for the Protection of National Minorities*. Oxford: Oxford University Press, 2005.

Alfredsson, Gudmundur. 'A Frame an Incomplete Painting: Comparison of the Framework Convention for the Protection of National Minorities with International Standards and Monitoring Procedures'. *International Journal of Minority and Group Rights* 7: 291–304, 2000.

Allasino, E. et al. *Labour market discrimination against migrant workers in Italy*. International Migration Papers 67. Geneva: International Labour Office, 2004.

Allen, Anita. 'Can Affirmative Action Combat Racial Discrimination? Moral Success and Political Failure in the United States.' In Erna Appelt –Monica Jarosch (eds.) *Combating Racial Discrimination: Affirmative Action as a Model for Europe*. Oxford: Berg, 2000.

Alvarez, Michael R. – Lisa García Bedolla. 'The Revolution against Affirmative Action in California: Racism, Economics, and Proposition 209.' *State Politics and Policy Quarterly*, Vol 4, No 1, Spring 2004.

Andersen, Susan M. et al. 'Automatic Thought.' In E. T. Higgins – A. W. Kruglanski (eds.), *Social psychology: Handbook of basic principles*. 2nd ed. New York : Guilford Publications, 1996.

Anderson, Alan B. 'The Complexity of Ethnic Identities: A Postmodern Reevaluation' *Identity: An international journal of theory and research* 1(3) 2001.

Appelt, Erna. 'Affirmative Action: a Cross-National Debate.' In Erna Appelt –Monica Jarosch (eds.) *Combating Racial Discrimination: Affirmative Action as a Model for Europe*. Oxford: Berg, 2000.

Appelt, Erna –Monica Jarosch (eds). *Combating Racial Discrimination: Affirmative Action as a Model for Europe*. Oxford: Berg, 2000.

Arrijn, Peter et al. 'Discrimination in access to employment on grounds of foreign origin: the case of Belgium'. International Migration Papers 23. Geneva: International Labour Office, 1998.

Artemjeff, Panu – Kirsi Henriksson (eds.). *Mainstreaming Equality and Non-discrimination in Theory and Practice*. Helsinki: Cosmoprint, 2006.

Artemjeff, Panu. 'Mainstreaming Equality: Conceptual Development and Mainstreaming Model of the Join In Project.' In Panu Artemjeff – Kirsi Henriksson (eds.), *Mainstreaming Equality and Non-discrimination in Theory and Practice*. Helsinki: Cosmoprint, 2006.

Asbrock, Frank et al. 'The Road to Negative Behaviour: Discriminatory Intentions in the German Population.' *International Journal of Conflict and Violence* Vol 1(1) 2007.

Asscher-Vonk, Irene P. "Towards One Concept of Objective Justification." In Titia Loenen & Peter Rodrigues (eds.), *Non-Discrimination Law: Comparative Perspectives*. The Hague: Kluwer Law International, 1999.

Bainbridge, David. *EC Data Protection Directive*. Butterworths: London, 1996.
Balibar, Etienne – Immanuel Wallerstein. *Race, Nation, Class: Ambiguous Identities*. London: Verso, 1992.
Banakar, Reza – Max Travers. 'Critical Approaches.' In Reza Banakar – Max Travers (eds.): *An Introduction to Law and Social Theory*. Oxford: Hart, 2002.
Banks, Cyndi. *Criminal Justice Ethics: Theory and Practice*. Sage 2004.
Banton, Michael. 'The causes of, and remedies for, racial discrimination'. E/CN.4/1999/WG.1/BP.6
Banton, Michael. *Discrimination*. Buckingham: Open University Press, 1994.
Banton, Michael. *International action against racial discrimination*. Oxford: Clarendon Press, 1996.
Barker, Martin. *The New Racism*. London: Junction Books, 1981.
Barry, Eilís. 'Strategic Enforcement – From Concept to Practice.' In Janet Cormack (ed.) Strategic Enforcement and EC Equal Treatment Directives. Migration Policy Group, 2004.
Barth, Fredrick. *Ethnic Groups and Boundaries: The Social Organization of Culture Difference* Bergen: Universitetsforlaget, 1969.
Bauman, Zygmunt. *Modernity and Ambivalence*. Cambridge: Polity Press,1991.
Baumann, Gerd. *The multicultural riddle: rethinking national, ethnic and religious* identities. New York: Routledge, 1999.
Baumeister Andrea. *Liberalism and the 'Politics of Difference'*. Edinburgh: Edinburg University Press, 2000.
Beck, Ulrich. *Risk society*. London: Sage, 1992.
Beger, Nico J. 'Putting Gender and Sexuality on the Agenda: Queer Theory and Legal Politics.' In Reza Banakar – Max Travers (eds.) *An Introduction to Law and Social* Theory, 2002.
Bell, Derrick. *Silent Covenants: Brown v. Board of Education and the Unfulfilled Hopes for Racial Reform*. New York, Oxford University Press, 2004.
Bell, Mark. *Anti-Discrimination Law and the European Union*. Oxford: Oxford University Press, 2002.
Bell, Mark. 'Combating Structural Racism through Law.' *ENARgy Issue* 17, July 2006
Bell, Mark et al. *Developing Anti-Discrimination Law in Europe: The 25 EU Member States compared*. Luxembourg: Office for Official Publications of the European Communities, 2007.
Bell, Mark. 'Direct discrimination.' In Dagmar Schiek – Lisa Waddington – Mark Bell. *Non-Discrimination Law: Cases, Materials and text on National, Supranational and International Non-Discrimination Law*. Oxford, Hart Publishing, 2007.
Beqiri, Nexhat. *Toiveena monipuolinen asukasrakenne*. Sisäasiainministeriön julkaisuja 30/2008.
Berger, Peter – Thomas Luckmann. *The Social Construction of Reality: A Treatise in the Sociology of Knowledge*. New York: Anchor Books, 1966.
Berlin, Isaiah. *Two Concepts of Liberty*. Oxford: Clarendon Press, 1958.
Berry, John W. et al. *Cross-cultural psychology: Research and applications*, 2nd ed. Cambridge: Cambridge University Press, 2002.
Borking, John. Privacy-Enhancing Technologies (PET) - Darf es ein Bitchen weniger sein?' *Datenschutz und Datensicherheit*, Volume 25, Number 10, October 2001.
Bossuyt, Marc. *The concept and practice of affirmative action*. Preliminary report by Mr. Marc Bossuyt, Special Rapporteur to the Commission on Human Rights, 19 June 2000. E/CN.4/Sub.2/2000/11.
Bossuyt, Marc. 'Comprehensive examination of thematic issues relating to racial discrimination: The concept and practice of affirmative action', Commission on Human Rights 19 June 2000, E/CN.4/Sub.2/2000/11.
Bovenkerk, Frank. *A Manual for International Comparative Research on Discrimination on the Grounds of "Race" and Ethnic Origin*. Geneva: International Labour Office, 1992.

Boyle, Kevin and Anneliese Baldaccini. 'A Critical Evaluation of International Human Rights Approaches to Racism.' In Sandra Fredman (ed.) *Discrimination and Human Rights*. Oxford: Oxford University Press, 2001.
Brosnan, Sarah F. & Frans B.M. de Waal. 'Monkeys reject unequal pay.' *Nature*, Vol. 425, 18 September 2003.
Brown, Rupert. *Prejudice – Its Social Psychology*. Oxford: Blackwell, 1995.
Brownlie, Ian. *Principles of Public International Law*, 4th ed. Oxford: Clarendon Press, 1990.
Buergenthal, Thomas. 'State obligations and permissible derogations.' In Louis Henkin (ed.) *The International Bill Of Rights: The Covenant on Civil and Political Rights*. New York: Columbia University Press, 1981.
Bukovska, Barbora. 'Ethnic Statistics and Data Protection: The Czech Case.' In Andrea Krizsán (ed.) *Ethnic Monitoring and Data Protection*. Budapest: CPS Books, 2001.
Bulmer, Martin – John Solomos (eds). *Racism*. Oxford: Oxford University Press, 1998.
Bulmer, Martin – John Solomos. 'Introduction: Re-thinking Ethnic and Racial Studies' *Ethnic and Racial Studies*, Vol. 21, No 5, 1998.
Bygrave, Lee A. *Data Protection Law: Approaching its Rationale, Logic and Limits*. The Hague: Kluwer, 2002.
Börzel, Tanja A. et al. *Conceptualizing New Modes of Governance in EU Enlargement*. Research Paper 12/D1, Free University of Berlin, 7 February 2005.
Çalı, Başak – Alice Wyss. 'Authority of International Institutions: The Case for International Human Rights Treaty Bodies' (4 October 2009). Electronic copy available at: http://ssrn.com/abstract=1278582
Cediey, E. – F. Foroni. *Les discriminations á raison de 'lórigine dans les embauches en France: Une enquête nationale par tests de discrimination selon la méthide du bureau international du travail* (2007). Available at: http://www.ilo.org/public/french/bureau/inf/download/discrim_france.pdf
Chalmers, Damian. 'The Mistakes of the Good European.' In Sandra Fredman (ed.) *Discrimination and Human Rights*. Oxford: Oxford University Press, 2001.
Chalmers, Damian – Adam Tomkins. *European Union Public Law: Text and Materials*. Cambridge: Cambridge UP, 2007.
Chateauvert, Melinda. 'Using Historical and Sociological Evidence to Defend Anti-Discrimination Policies.' In Erna Appelt – Monica Jarosch (eds.) *Combating Racial Discrimination: Affirmative Action as a Model for Europe*. Oxford: Berg, 2000.
Cholewinski, Ryszard. 'The Racial Convention and the Protection of Cultural and Linguistic Ethnic Minorities.' *Revue de Droit International* (69) 1991.
Clapham, Andrew. *Human rights and the European Community: A Critical Overview*. Baden-Baden, Nomos, 1991.
Clark, Mary E. *In search for human nature*. London: Routledge, 2002.
Coenders, Marcel – Marcel Lubbers – Peer Scheepers. *Majorities' attitudes towards minorities in the old 15 EU Member States: results from the standard Eurobarometers 1997–2000–2003*. Vienna: EUMC, 2005. Available at: http://www.fra.europa.eu/fraWebsite/attachments/Report-2.pdf (accessed 1.7.2009).
Cohen, Barbara. 'The Stephen Lawrence Inquiry – lessons to be learned' in *ENARgy* Issue 17, July 2006. Available at: http://www.enar-eu.org/en/enargy/ENARgy_17_EN.pdf
Cohen, Philip. 'It's Racism What Dunnit.' In Martin Bulmer – John Solomos, *Racism*. Oxford: Oxford University Press, 1999.
Colectivo IOE. Labour market discrimination against migrant workers in Spain, International Migration Papers 9. Geneva: International Labour Office, 1995.
Collins, Francis – Karin G. Jegalian. 'Genomics and the Future', *Scientific American*, December 1999.
Commission for Racial Equality. *Ethnic Monitoring. A guide for public authorities*. CRE 2002.

Cooper, Bob. 'The Fair Employment Commission in Northern Ireland.' In Martin MacEwen (ed.), *Anti-Discrimination Law Enforcement*. Ashgate 1997.

Correll, Shelley – Cecilia L. Ridgeway. 'Expectation States Theory' in Delamater, John (ed.), *Handbook of Social Psychology*. New York: Kluwer, 2003.

Corsaro, William A. – Laura Fingerson. 'Development and Socialization in Childhood.' In John Delamater (ed.), *Handbook of Social Psychology*. New York: Kluwer, 2003.

Cotterrell, Roger. *The Sociology of Law*. 2nd ed. London: Butterworths, 1992.

Council of Europe. *Filling the Frame: Five years of monitoring the Framework Convention for the Protection of National Minorities*. Strasbourg: Council of Europe Publishing, 2004.

Craig, Paul – Gráinne de Búrca. *EU law: text, cases, materials*. Oxford: Oxford University Press, 2007.

Crenshaw, Kimberle. 'Mapping the margins: Intersectionality, Identity Politics and Violence Against Women of Color' *Stanford Law Review*, Vol. 43, No 6 (1991).

Crisp, Richard J. – Sarah R. Beck. 'Reducing Intergroup Bias: The Moderating Role of Ingroup identification.' *Group Processes & Intergroup Relations*, 2005 Vol. 8 (2)

Cunningham, Frank. 'Positive Action and Democracy.' In Erna Appelt –Monica Jarosch (eds.) *Combating Racial Discrimination: Affirmative Action as a Model for Europe*. Oxford: Berg, 2000.

Darwin, Charles. *The Descent of Man: and selection in relation to sex*. 2nd Ed, London, 1887.

Dawkins, Richard. *Selfish Gene*. Oxford: Oxford University Press, 2006.

de Búrca, Gráinne. 'New Modes of Governance and the Protection of Human Rights.' In Philip Alston – Olivier de Schutter (eds.) *Monitoring fundamental rights in the EU: the contribution of the fundamental rights agency*. Oxford: Hart, 2005.

de Schutter, Olivier. *Prohibition of discrimination under European Human Rights Law*. Luxembourg: Office for official Publications of the European Communities, 2005.

de Schutter, Olivier. 'European Union Legislation and the Norms of the Framework Convention for the Protection of National Minorities' Strasbourg 23 October 2006, DH-MIN(2006)019

de Schutter, Olivier. 'Three models of equality and European anti-discrimination law.' *NILQ* Vol 57, No 1, 2006.

de Schutter, Olivier. 'Chapter Seven: Positive Action.' In Dagmar Schiek – Lisa Waddington – Mark Bell, *Non-Discrimination Law: Cases, Materials and text on National, Supranational and International Non-Discrimination Law*. Oxford: Hart Publishing, 2007.

de Vos, Marc. 'Beyond Formal Equality: Positive Action under Directives 2000/43/EC and 2000/78.' Luxembourg: Office for Official Publications of the European Communities, 2007.

Deitch, Elizabeth A. 'Subtle Yet Significant: The Existence and Impact of Everyday Racial Discrimination in the Workplace' *Human Relations*, Vol. 56, No. 1, 1299–1324 (2003).

Delamater, John (ed.). *Handbook of Social Psychology*. New York: Kluwer, 2003.

Delgado, Richard. 'The Ethereal Scholar: Does Critical Legal Studies have What Minorities Want?' *Harvard Civil Rights – Civil Liberties Review* 22 (1987).

Dex, Shirley and Kingsley Purdam. *Equal Opportunities and Recruitment. How Census data can help employers to assess their practices*. York: York Publishing Services, 2005.

Dhami, Ravinder Singh – Judith Squires – Tariq Modood. *Developing positive action policies: learning from the experiences of Europe and North America*. Department for Work and Pensions, Research Report No 406. Corporate Document Services, 2006.

Dingwall, Robert. 'Ethnomethodology and Law.' In Reza Banakar – Max Travers (eds.) *An Introduction to Law and Social Theory*. 2002.

Donnelly, Jack. *Universal Human Rights in Theory and Practice*. 2nd ed, Ithaca, N.Y.: Cornell University Press, 2003.

Douglas-Scott, Sionaidh. *Constitutional Law of the European Union*. Harlow: Person, 2002.

Döring, Jan. 'Influences of Discriminatory Incidents on Immigrant's Attitudes Toward German Society'. *International Journal of Conflict and Violence* Vol 1(1) 2007.

Doyle, Brian. 'Disability discrimination and enforcement in Britain: future prospects.' In Martin MacEwen (ed.), *Anti-Discrimination Law Enforcement*. Aldershot: Avebury, 1997.

Drzewicki, Krzysztof. 'The Right to Work and Rights in Work.' In Asbjørn Eide et al (eds.) *Economic, social and cultural rights: A textbook*. Dordrecht: Martinus Nijhoff, 2001.

Duckitt, John. *The Social Psychology of Prejudice*. London: Greenwood, 1994.

Dumont, Jean-Christophe (OECD) – Georges Lemaître (OECD). *Counting immigrants and expatriates in OECD Countries: A New Perspective*. OECD Social, Employment and Migration Working Papers No. 25 (2005).

Dworkin, Ronald. *Taking Rights Seriously*. London: Duckworth, 1978.

Dworkin, Ronald. *Sovereign Virtue: the theory and practice of equality*. Cambridge: Harvard University Press, 2002.

Eder, Donna – Sandi Kawecka Nenga. 'Socialization in Adolescence.' In John Delamater (ed.), *Handbook of Social Psychology*. New York: Kluwer, 2003.

Eide, Asbjørn – Allan Rosas "Economic, Social and Cultural Rights: A Universal Challenge." In Eide et al. (eds.) *Economic, Social and Cultural Rights: a Textbook*. The Hague: Kluwer Law International, 1995.

Eide, Asbjørn et al (eds). *Economic, social and cultural rights: A textbook*. Dordrecht: Martinus Nijhoff, 2001.

Eide, Asbjørn. 'Economic, Social and cultural rights as Human Rights.' In Asbjørn Eide et al (eds.) *Economic, social and cultural rights: A textbook*. Dordrecht: Martinus Nijhoff, 2001.

Eide, Asbjørn. 'The Framework Convention in Historical and Global Perspective.' In Marc Weller (ed.) *Rights of Minorities: Commentary on the European Framework Convention for the Protection of National Minorities*. Oxford: Oxford University Press, 2006.

ERRC – Interights – MPG. *Strategic Litigation in Europe: From Principles to Practice*. Nottingham: Russell Press ltd, 2004.

Essed, Philomena – David Theo Goldberg (eds.). *Race Critical Theories*. Oxford: Blackwell, 2002.

Essed, Philomena. 'Everyday Racism: A new approach to the study of racism.' In Philomena Essed – David Theo Goldberg (eds.). *Race Critical Theories*. Oxford: Blackwell, 2002.

EU Network of Independent Experts on Fundamental Rights. *Combating Racism and Xenophobia through Criminal Legislation: The Situation in the EU Member States*. Opinion No 5-2005, 28 November 2005.

EU Network of Independent Experts on Fundamental Rights. *Commentary of the Charter of Fundamental Rights of the European Union*. 20 June 2006.

EU Network of Independent Experts on Fundamental Rights. *Ethnic Profiling*. Opinion No 4-2006, December 2006.

EUMC. *Racism and Xenophobia in the EU Member States – trends, developments and good practice. Annual Report 2005 – Part 2*. EUMC 2005.

European Commission. *Critical review of academic literature relating to the EU directives to combat discrimination*. European Communities, 2004.

European Monitoring Centre on Racism and Xenophobia. *Migrant's Experiences of Racism and Xenophobia in 12 EU Member States: Pilot Study*, May 2006.

Fish, Stanley E. 'The Annual John Randolph Tucker Lecture – Force.' In Thomas Morawetz (ed.), *Law and Language*. Aldershot: Ashgate, 2000.

Fitzpatrick, Barry. 'The Effectiveness of Equality Law Remedies: A European Community Law Perspective.' In Bob Hepple and Erika Szyszczak (eds.), *Discrimination: The Limits of Law?* London: Mansell, 1992.

Fix, Michael – Margery Turner. 'Testing for Discrimination: The Case for a National Report Card' *Civil Rights Journal*, Fall 1999.

Foster, Morris W. – Richard R. Sharp. 'Classifications as Proxies of Biological Heterogeneity' *Genome Res.* 2002 12:844–850.

Fredman, Sandra (ed.). *Discrimination and Human Rights: The Case of Racism*. Oxford: Oxford University Press, 2001.

Fredman, Sandra. *Discrimination Law*. Oxford: Oxford University Press, 2002.

Fredman, Sandra – Sarah Spencer. 'Beyond Discrimination: It's Time for Enforceable duties on Public Bodies to Promote Equality Outcomes' *E.H.R.L.R.* Issue 6 (2006).

Frostell, Katarina – Martin Scheinin. 'Women.' In Asbjørn Eide, Catarina Krause and Allan Rosas (eds.), *Economic, Social and Cultural Rights: A Textbook*, 2nd revised Edition. The Hague: Kluwer Law International, 2001.

Fullinwider, Robert K. *The Reverse Discrimination Controversy*. New Jersey: Rowman and Littlefield, 1981.

Gachet, Isil. 'The Issue of Ethnic Data Collection From the Perspective of Some Council of Europe Activities'. In Andrea Krizsan (ed.) *Ethnic Monitoring and Data Protection: The European Context*. Budapest: Central European University Press, 2001.

Gardner, John. 'Private Activities and Personal Autonomy: At the Margins of Anti-discrimination Law.' In Bob Hepple and Erika Szyszczak (eds.) *Discrimination: The Limits of Law?* London: Mansell 1992.

Gastwirth, Joseph L. 'Statistical Evidence in Discrimination Cases.' *J. R. Statist. Soc.* A (1997).

Gerards, Janneke. 'Protocol No. 12 – the Dutch Debate.' In Stéphanie Lagoutte (ed.), *Prohibition of Discrimination in the Nordic Countries: The Complicated Fate of Protocol No. 12 to the European Convention on Human Rights*. Copenhagen, the Danish Institute for Human Rights, 2005.

Gervais, Marie-Claude. *The Drivers of Black and Asian people's perceptions of racial discrimination by public services: A qualitative study*. West Yorkshire: Communities and Local Government Publications, 2008.

Gijzen, M.H.S. *Selected issues in equal treatment law: a multi-layered comparison of European, English and Dutch law*. Antwerpen: Intersentia, 2006.

Gilbert, Geoff. 'The protection of minorities under the European convention on human rights.' In Janet Dine & Bob Watt (eds.), *Discrimination Law: Concepts, Limitations, and Justifications*. London: Longman, 1996.

Gilroy, Paul. 'The End of Antiracism.' In Philomena Essed – David Theo Goldberg (eds.) *Race Critical Theories: Text and Context*. Wiley-Blackwell, 2001.

Glazer, Nathan. 'Affirmative Action and "Race" Relations: Affirmative Action as a Model for Europe.' In Appelt, Erna – Monica Jarosch (eds.) *Combating Racial Discrimination: Affirmative Action as a Model for Europe*. Oxford: Berg, 2000.

Goldberg et al, Labour Market Discrimination against foreign workers in Germany. International Migration Papers 7. Geneva: International Labour Office, 1996.

Goldberg, David Theo – Philomena Essed. 'Introduction: From Racial Demarcations to Multiple Identifications.' In Philomena Essed – David Theo Goldberg (eds.) *Race Critical Theories*. Blackwell, 2001.

Goldhagen, Daniel. *Hitler's Willing Executioners: Ordinary Germans and the Holocaust*. London: Little, Brown and Company, 1996.

Goldschmidt, Jenny. 'Enforcement of equal treatment: The role of the Equal Treatment Commission in the Netherlands' in Martin MacEwen (ed.), *Anti-Discrimination Law Enforcement*. Ashgate 1997.

Goncalves-Ho Kang You, Lilian – Louise Mulder. 'Positive Action: the Dutch Experience' in Erna Appelt – Monica Jarosch (eds.) *Combating Racial Discrimination: Affirmative Action as a Model for Europe*. Oxford: Berg, 2000.

Greer, Steven. 'What's Wrong with the European Convention on Human Rights', *Human Rights Quarterly* 30 (2008).

Grief, Nicholas. 'Non-Discrimination under the European Convention on Human Rights: a critique of the United Kingdom Government's refusal to sign and ratify Protocol 12.' *27 E.L.Rev. Human Rights Survey*, 2002.

Griffiths, John. 'The Social Working of Anti-Discrimination Law.' In Titia Loenen – Peter Rodrigues (eds.) *Non-Discrimination Law: Comparative Perspectives*. The Hague: Kluwer, 1999.

Griffiths, Lowri. 'Positive Duties to Promote Equality.' In Soraya Obura – Fiona Palmer (eds.) *Strategic Enforcement: Powers and Competences of Equality Bodies*. Brussels: Equinet, 2006.

Guillaumin, Colette. 'Race and Nature: The system of Marks. The Idea of Natural Group and Social Relationships' *Feminist Issues* 8, No. 2 (1998).

Haapanen, Ari. *Monimuotoisuusbarometri 2007 - ikä ja monikultuurisuus haasteena ja voimavarana*. Espoo: Frenckell, 2007.

Habermas, Jurgen. *Knowledge and Human Interests*. Cambridge: Polity Press, 1987.

Habermas, Jurgen. 'Private and Public Autonomy, Human Rights and Popular Sovereignty.' In Obrad Savic (ed.). *The Politics of Human Rights*. London: Verso, 2002.

Hall, Stuart. *Identiteetti*. Tampere: Vastapaino, 1999.

Hampton, Mary B. and John S. Heywood. 'Do workers accurately perceive gender wage discrimination?' *Industrial and Labour Relations Review*, Vol. 47, No.1 (Oct., 1993), 36–49.

Hannikainen, Lauri. *Peremptory norms (jus cogens) in international law: Historical development, criteria, present status*. Helsinki: Finnish Lawyers' Publishing Company, 1988.

Hannikainen, Lauri – Eeva Nykänen (eds.). *New trends in discrimination law – international perspectives*. Turku: Grafia, 1999.

Hart, H.L.A. *The Concept of* Law (Oxford: Clarendon Press, 1994).

Harwood, Rupert. 'Race Back from Equality: Has the CRE been breaching race equality law and has race equality law been working?' Public Interest Research Unit, 2007. Available at: http://www.piru.org.uk/wordpress/wp-content/uploads/PIRU_Race_Back_From_Equality.pdf

Heintze, Hans-Joachim. 'Article 1.' In Marc Weller (ed.) *The Rights of Minorities: A Commentary on the European Framework Convention for the Protection of National Minorities*. Oxford: Oxford University Press, 2005.

Heitmeyer, Wilhelm. *Deutsche Zustände - Folge 1*. Frankfurt am Main: Suhrkamp Verlag, 2002.

Henkel, Kristin E. et al 'Institutional Discrimination, Individual Racism, and Hurricane Katrina.' *Analyses of Social Issues & Public Policy* Dec 2006, Vol. 6 Issue 1.

Henkin, Louis. 'National and International Perspectives in Racial Discrimination.' *Human Rights Journal 4* (1971).

Henkin, Louis (ed.). *The International Bill Of Rights: The Covenant on Civil and Political Rights*. New York: Columbia University Press, 1981.

Henkin, Louis. 'Introduction.' In Louis Henkin (ed.) *The International Bill Of Rights: The Covenant on Civil and Political Rights*. New York: Columbia University Press, 1981.

Henkin, Louis. *International Law: Politics and Values*. Dordrecht: Martinus Nijhoff, 1995.

Henrard, Kristin. 'The Impact of International Non-Discrimination Norms in Combination with General Human Rights for the Protection of National Minorities: The European Convention on Human Rights'. Paper prepared for the Committee of Experts on Issues Relating to the Protection of National Minorities (DH-MIN), DH-MIN(2006)020.

Henrard, Kristin. *Devising an Adequate System of Minority Protection: Individual Human Rights, Minority Rights, and Self-Determination*. The Hague: Kluwer, 2000.

Hepple, Bob – Erika Szyszczak (eds.). *Discrimination: The Limits of Law?* London: Mansell 1992.

Hepple, Bob. 'Have Twenty-five years of the race Relations Acts in Britain Been a Failure?' In Bob Hepple and Erika Szyszczak (eds), *Discrimination: The Limits of Law?* London: Mansell 1992.

Hepple, B., M. Coussey and T. Choudhury. *Equality: A New Framework*. Report of the Independent Review of the Enforcement of UK Anti-Discrimination Legislation. Cambridge: University of Cambridge, 2000.

Hepple, Bob. 'Race and Law in Fortress Europe' *Modern Law Review*, Vol 67, No 1, January 2004.

Heringa, Aart Willem. 'Standards of review for discrimination: The scope of review by the Courts.' In Loenen - Rodriquez (eds.) *Non-Discrimination Law: Comparative Perspectives*, 1999.

Hernández-Truyol, Berta. "Human Rights Through a Gendered Lens: Emergence, Evolution, Revolution." In Askin & Koenig (eds.) *Women and International Human Rights*. New York: Transnational Publishers, 1999.

Hoffman, Rainer. 'The Framework Convention for the protection of National Minorities: An Introduction' in Marc Weller (ed.). *The Rights of Minorities: A Commentary on the European Framework Convention for the Protection of National Minorities*. Oxford: Oxford University Press, 2005.

Hoffman, Rainer. 'The Impact of International Norms on the Protection of National Minorities in Europe: The Added Value and Essential Role of the Framework Convention for the Protection of National Minorities' Strasbourg, 5 December 2006.

Hogan, Des. 'Inquiries within a wider functional strategy.' In Janet Cormack (ed.) *Strategic Enforcement and EC Equal Treatment Directives*. Migration Policy Group, 2004.

Holmberg, Lars - Britta Kyvsgaard. 'Are Immigrants and their Descendants Discriminated against in the Danish Criminal Justice System?' *Journal of Scandinavian Studies in Criminology and Crime Prevention* Vol. 4, No 2 (2003).

Holtmaat, Rikki. *Catalysts for Change: Equality bodies according to directive 2000/43/EC - existence, independence and effectiveness*. Luxembourg: Office of the Official Publications of the EC, 2006.

Holzer, Harry - David Neumark. 'Assessing Affirmative Action' *Journal of Economic Literature*, Vol 38, No 3 (Sep. 2000).

Home Office. *Crime in England and Wales 2006/07*. Edited by Sian Nicholas, Chris Kershaw and Alison Walker, 4th Edition, July 2007. http://www.homeoffice.gov.uk/rds/pdfs07/hosb1107.pdf

Hooghe, Marc et al. 'Ethnic Diversity, Trust and Ethnocentrism and Europe: A Multilevel Analysis of 21 European Countries'. Paper presented at the 102nd Annual Meeting of the American Political Science Association, Philadelphia, August 31–September 3, 2006.

Howard, Judith A. - Daniel G. Renfrow. 'Social Cognition.' In John D. DeLamater (ed.), *Handbook of Social Psychology*. New York: Kluwer-Plenum, 2003.

Hoy, David Couzens. 'Interpreting the Law: Hermeneutical and Poststructuralist Perspectives', in Tom Morawetz (ed.), *Law and Language*. 2000.

Ilzkovitz, Fabienne - Adriaan Dierx - Viktoria Kovacs - Nuno Sousa. *Steps towards a deeper economic integration: the Internal Market in the 21st century:* A contribution to the Single Market Review, European Commission Economic Papers No 271, January 2007.

Inglehart, Ronald. 'Globalization and Postmodern Values' *The Washington Quarterly*, 23:1 Winter 2000.

Jaakkola, Magdalena. *Suomalaisten suhtautuminen maahanmuuttajiin vuosina 1987 – 2003*. Työpoliittinen tutkimus 286. Helsinki: Työministeriö, 2005.

Jacobs, Francis G. - Robin C.A. White. *The European Convention of Human Rights*. third Edition, Clarendon Press, Oxford, 2002.

Jasinskaja-Lahti, Inga - Karmela Liebkind - Tiina Vesala. *Rasismi ja syrjintä Suomessa: Maahanmuuttajien kokemuksia*. Helsinki: Gaudeamus, 2002.

Jasinskaja-Lahti, Inga – Karmela Liebkind – Riku Perhoniemi. 'Perceived ethnic discrimination at work and well-being of immigrants in Finland: The moderating role of employment status and work-specific group-level beliefs' *International Journal of Intercultural Relations* 31 (2007).

Jay, Rosemary – Angus Hamilton. *Data Protection Law and Practice*. Second edition. London: Sweet & Maxwell, 2003.

Joseph, Sarah – Jenny Schultz – Melissa Castan *The International Covenant on Civil and Political Rights: Cases, Materials and Commentary*. Oxford: Oxford University Press, 2000.

Kalev, Alexandra – Frank Dobbin – Erin Kelly. 'Best Practices or Best Guesses? Assessing the Efficacy of Corporate Affirmative Action and Diversity Policies' *American Sociological Review*, 2006, Vol. 71 (August 589–617).

Kalev, Alexandra – Frank Dobbin. 'Enforcement of Civil Rights Law in Private Workplaces: The Effects of Compliance Reviews and Lawsuits Over Time.' *Law & Social Inquiry*, Volume 31, Issue 4, 855–903, Fall 2006.

Kamminga, Menno T. – Martin Scheinin. *The Impact of Human Rights Law on General International Law*. Oxford: Oxford University Press, 2009.

Kant, Immanuel. *Über die verschiedenen Rassen der Menschen (On the Different Races of Man)* 1775.

Karim, Razia. 'A legal Strategy to Combine and coordinate Different Tools Available' in Janet Cormack (ed.) *Strategic Enforcement and EC Equal Treatment Directives*. Migration Policy Group, 2004, p. 31–32.

Kennedy, David. *The Dark Sides of Virtue: Reassessing International Humanitarianism*. Princeton: Princeton University Press, 2004.

Kennedy, Duncan. 'Form and Substance in Private Law Adjudication.' *Harvard Law Review* Vol 89, (1975/1976), 1685–1778.

Kenrick, Douglas et al. 'Evolutionary Social Psychology: Adaptive Predispositions and Human Culture.' In John Delamater (ed.) *Handbook of Social Psychology*. New York: Kluwer Academic, 2006.

Keränen, Tuunia. *Poliisin tietoon tullut rasistinen rikollisuus Suomessa 2004*. Helsinki: Edita 2005.

Klabbers, Jan. *The Concept of treaty in International Law*. The Hague: Martinus Nijhoff, 1996.

Klabbers, Jan. 'Constitutionalism and the making of international law' *No Foundations* No. 5, 9 April 2008.

Knabb, Richard D. et al. *Tropical Cyclone Report: Hurricane Katrina* (National Hurricane Center, 20 December 2005, updated in 10 August 2006). http://www.nhc.noaa.gov/pdf/TCR-AL122005_Katrina.pdf

Koppelman, Andrew. *Anti-Discrimination Law and Social Equality*. New Haven: Yale University Press, 1996.

Korff, Douwe. *EC Study on Implementation of Data Protection Directive. Comparative Summary of National Laws*. September 2002, available at: http://ec.europa.eu/justice_home/fsj/privacy/docs/lawreport/consultation/univessex-comparativestudy_en.pdf (visited 1 May 2006).

Koskenniemi, Martti. 'Human Rights, Politics, and Love' *Mennesker & rettigheter* (4/2001).

Koskenniemi, Martti. *Gentle Civilizer of Nations: The Rise and Fall of International Law 1870–1960*. Cambridge: University of Cambridge Press, 2002.

Koskenniemi, Martti. *From Apology to Utopia. The Structure of International Legal Argument* (Cambridge: Cambridge University Press, 2005, reissue with new epilogue).

Koskenniemi, Martti. *Fragmentation of International Law: Difficulties Arising from the Diversification and Expansion of International Law*, Report of the Study Group of the International Law Commission, Finalized by Martti Koskenniemi, 13 April 2006, UN Doc. A/CN.4/L.682.

Kymlicka, Will. *Multicultural citizenship: a liberal theory of minority rights*. Oxford: Clarendon Press, 1995.

Lagoutte, Stéphanie (ed.). *Prohibition of discrimination in the Nordic Countries: The Complicated fate of Protocol No. 12 to the European Convention on Human Rights*. Copenhagen: The Danish Institute for Human Rights, 2005.

Lange, Anders. *Migrants on Discrimination II*. Edsbruk 1997.

Lappalainen, Paul. *Det blågula glashuset – strukturell diskriminering i Sverige, 2005*. SOU 2005:56. Stockholm: Elanders Gotab AB, 2005.

Lappalainen, Paul. 'Stimulating leadership to promote positive action.' In European Commission, *Putting Equality to Practice: What role for positive action?* Luxemburg: Office for the Official Publications of the EC, 2007.

Latraverse, Sophie. *Report on Measures to Combat Discrimination. Country Report – France*. December 2004. European Network of Legal Experts in the non-discrimination field. Available at http://ec.europa.eu/employment_social/fundamental_rights/pdf/legnet/frrep05_en.pdf (visited 1 September 2006).

Lauren, Paul Gordon. *The Evolution of International Human Rights: Visions Seen*. Philadelphia: University of Pennsylvania Press, 1998.

Leighninger, Matt. *The Next Form of Democracy: How Expert Rule is Giving Way to Shared Governance… and Why Politics Will Never Be the Same*. Nashville, Vanderbilt University Press, 2006.

Lerner, Natan. *Group Rights and Discrimination in International Law*. Dordrecht: Martinus Nijhoff, 1991.

Lerner, Nathan. *Group rights and discrimination in international law*. Dordrecht: Nijhoff, 1991.

Levy, Jacob T. *The Multiculturalism of Fear*. Oxford: Oxford University Press, 2000.

Lewontin, Richard. *Human Diversity*. W.H. Freeman & Co, 1995.

Lieberman, Matthew D et al. 'An fMRI investigation of race-related amygdala activity in African-American and Caucasian-American individuals'. *Nature Neuroscience*, Vol 8 No 6 June 2005.

Liebkind, Karmela. 'Some problems in the theory and application of cultural pluralism: the complexity of Ethnic Identity.' In Juha Pentikäinen – Marja Hiltunen (eds.) *Cultural Minorities in Finland: An Overview towards Cultural Policy*. Helsinki: Sivén, 1995.

Liebkind, Karmela – Sonja Nyström – Eeva Honkanummi – Anders Lange. 'Group Size, Group Status and Dimensions of Contact as Predictors of Intergroup Attitudes' *Group Processes & Intergroup Relations* 2004 Vol 7(2) 145–159.

Liebkind, Karmela – Juha Haaramo – Inga Jasinskaja-Lahti. 'Kannattaa tutustua paremmin.' In Karmela Liebkind (toim.) *Monikulttuurinen Suomi: Etniset suhteet tutkimuksen valossa*. Helsinki: Gaudeamus, 2000.

Locke, John. *Two Treatises*. Cambridge: Cambridge University Press, 1988.

Loenen, Titia – Peter Rodrigues (eds). *Non-Discrimination Law: Comparative Perspectives*. The Hague: Kluwer, 1999.

Lundström, Birgitta et al. *Yhdenvertaisuuslain toimivuus. Tutkimusraportti viranomaisten käsityksistä sekä oikeus-, laillisuusvalvonta- ja lainvalvontakäytännöstä*. Työ- ja elinkeinoministeriön julkaisuja 11/2008.

MacEwen, Martin. 'Concluding remarks.' In Martin MacEwen (ed), *Anti-Discrimination Law Enforcement*. Aldershot: Avebury, 1997.

MacEwen, Martin. 'Promoting equal opportunity: the enforcement agency', in Martin MacEwen (ed.), *Anti-Discrimination Law Enforcement*. Aldershot: Avebury, 1997.

MacEwen, Martin. *Tackling Racism in Europe: An Examination of Anti-Discrimination Law in Practice*. Oxford: Berg, 1995.

Macpherson of Cluny, Sir William. *The Stephen Lawrence Inquiry: Report of an Inquiry by Sir William Macpherson of Cluny*. London: The Stationery Office 1999.

Makkonen, Timo. *Good as far as it goes, but does it go far enough? A report on Norway's anti-discrimination laws and policies* (Migration Policy Group, 2008).

Makkonen, Timo. "Minorities' Right to Maintain and Develop Their Cultures: Legal Implications of Social Science Research." In Martin Scheinin and Francesco Francioni (eds.) *Cultural Rights as Human Rights*. Leiden: Martinus Nijhoff, 2008.

Makkonen, Timo. *Identity, Difference and Otherness: The Concepts of 'People', 'Indigenous People' and 'Minority' in International Law*. Eric Castrén Institute Research Reports 7/2000. Helsinki: University Press, 2000.

Makkonen, Timo. *Measuring Discrimination: Data collection and EU Equality Law*. Thematic Report of the Group of Independent Experts. Luxembourg: Office of the Official Publications of the EC, 2007.

Makkonen, Timo. *European Handbook on Equality Data*. Luxembourg: Office of the Official Publications of the EC, 2007.

Malloy, Tove H. 'The Title and the Preamble' in Weller, Marc (ed). *The Rights of Minorities: A Commentary on the European Framework Convention for the Protection of National Minorities*. Oxford: Oxford University Press, 2005.

Martin, David L. 'The Limburg Principles Turn Ten: An Impact Assessment' Sim special 20, p. 200. Available at: http://www.uu.nl/uupublish/content/20-09.pdf

McClintock, Michael *Everyday Fears: A Survey of Violent Hate Crimes in Europe and North America*. Human Rights First, 2005.

McCrudden, Christopher (ed.). *Anti-Discrimination Law*. Aldershot: Dartmouth, 1991.

McCrudden, Christopher. 'Merit Principles' *Oxford Journal of Legal Studies*, Vol 18, Winter 1998.

McCrudden, Christopher. 'Regulating Discrimination: Advice to a Legislator on Problems Regarding the Enforcement of Anti-Discrimination Law and Strategies to Overcome Them.' In Loenen, Titia – Peter Rodrigues (eds.) *Non-Discrimination Law: Comparative Perspectives*. The Hague: Kluwer, 1999.

McCrudden, Christopher. 'International and European Norms Regarding National Legal Remedies for Racial Inequality.' In Sandra Fredman (ed.) *Discrimination and Human Rights*. Oxford: Oxford University Press, 2001.

McCrudden, Christopher. 'The New Concept of Equality' (2003) 3 ERA-Forum 9.

McCrudden, Christopher (ed.). *Anti-Discrimination Law*. 2nd ed. Aldershot: Dartmouth, 2004.

McCrudden, Christopher. 'Mainstreaming Human Rights.' In Colin Harvey (ed.). *Human Rights in the Community: Rights as Agents of Change*. Oxford: Hart, 2005.

McCrudden, Christopher – Haris Kountouros. 'Human Rights and European Equality Law.' In Helen Meenan (ed.) *Equality Law in an Enlarged European Union*. Cambridge: Cambridge University Press, 2007.

McCrudden, Christopher. 'Consociationalism, Equality and Minorities in the Northern Ireland Bill of Rights Debate: The Role of the OSCE High Commissioner on National Minorities.' In John Morison – Kieran McEvoy – Gordon Anthony (eds). *Judges, Transition and Human Rights Culture*. Oxford: Oxford University Press, 2007.

McCrudden, Christophe et al. 'Affirmative Action without Quotas in Northern Ireland.' *The Equal Rights Review*, Vol. Four, 2009.

McGoldrick, Dominic. *The Human Rights Committee: Its Role in the Development of the International Covenant on Civil and Political Rights*'. Oxford: Clarendon Press, 1991.

McKean, Warwick. *Equality and Discrimination under International Law*. Oxford: Clarendon Press, 1983.

Mclaughlin, Etienne. 'From Negative to Positive Equality Duties: The Development and Constitutionalisation of Equality Provisions in the UK' *Social Policy & Society* 6:1, 111–121.

McLeod, Jane D. – Kathryn J. Lively. 'Social Structure and Personality', in John Delamater (ed.) *Handbook of Social Psychology*. New York: Kluwer, 2003.

Melander, Göran. 'Article 8'. In Asbjørn Eide et al (eds.) *The Universal Declaration of Human Rights: A Commentary*. Oslo: Universitetsforlaget, 1992.

Merrills, J.G. *The development of international law by the European Court of Human Rights*. Manchester: Manchester University Press, 1993.
Merrills, J.G. – A.H. Robertson. *Human rights in Europe: A study of the European Convention on Human Rights*. 4th ed. Manchester: Manchester University Press, 2001.
Miles, Robert. *Racism*. London: Routledge, 1989.
Milgram, Stanley. *Obedience to Authority: An Experimental View*. London: Printer and Martin, 2005.
Mill, J.S. *On Liberty*. London: John W. Parker and Son, 1859.
Miller-Loessi, Karen – John Parker. 'Cross-Cultural Social Psychology.' In John Delamater (ed.), *Handbook of Social Psychology*. New York: Kluwer, 2003.
Mills, C. Wright. *The Sociological Imagination*. Oxford: Oxford University Press, 1959.
Møller, Birgit – Lise Togeby. *Oplevet Diskrimination: En undersøgelse af etniske minoriteter*. København: Nævnet for Etnisk Ligestilling, 1999.
Möller, Jacob Th. 'Article 7.' In Asbjørn Eide et al (eds.) *The Universal Declaration of Human Rights: A Commentary*. Oslo: Universitetsforlaget, 1992.
Moon, Gay. 'Chapter Eight: Enforcement Bodies' in Dagmar Schiek – Lisa Waddington – Mark Bell, *Non-Discrimination Law: Cases, Materials and text on National, Supranational and International Non-Discrimination Law*. Oxford, Hart Publishing, 2007.
Morawetz, Thomas. 'Introduction.' In Thomas Morawetz (ed.), *Law and Language*. Aldershot: Ashgate, 2000.
Morawetz, Thomas (ed). *Law and Language*. Aldershot: Ashgate, 2000.
Morsink, Johannes. *The Universal Declaration of Human Rights: Origins, Drafting and Intent*. Philadelphia: University of Pennsylvania Press, 1999.
Muenz, Rainer. *Europe: Population and Migration in 2005*. Hamburg Institute of International Economics and Erste Bank.www.migrationinformation.org, June 1, 2006
Mukhopadhay, C.C. – Y.T. Moses. 'Reestablishing 'Race' in Anthropological Discourse.' *American Anthropologist* 99(3) (1997).
National Research Council. *Measuring Racial Discrimination. Panel on Methods for Assessing Discrimination*. Washington DC: National Academies Press, 2004.
Niessen, Jan. 'The Starting Line and the promotion of EU anti-discrimination legislation: The role of policy-oriented research.' *Journal of International Migration and Integration* Vol. 1, No 4, December 2000.
Niessen, Jan. 'Making the Law Work. The Enforcement and Implementation of Anti-Discrimination Legislation.' *European Journal of Migration and Law* 5: 249–257, 2003.
Niessen, Jan – Thomas Huddleston – Laura Citron. *Migrant Integration Policy Index*. Brussels: British Council and the MPG, 2007.
Laura Beth Nielsen et al. *Contesting Workplace Discrimination in Court: Characteristics and Outcomes of Federal Employment Discrimination Litigation 1987–2003*. Chicago: American Bar Foundation, 2008.
Norris, Pippa – Ronald Inglehart. *Sacred and Secular: Religion and Politics Worldwide*. Cambridge University Press, 2004.
Nousiainen, Kevät. 'Utility based equality and disparate diversities – from a Finnish perspective.' In Schiek – Chege (eds.) *European Union Non-Discrimination Law: Comparative perspectives on multidimensional equality law*. Oxon: Routledge-Cavendish, 2009.
Novitz, Tonia. 'Remedies for violation of Social Rights within the Council of Europe: The Significant Absence of a Court.' In Claire Kilpatrick, Tonia Novitz and Paul Skidmore (eds.). *The Future of Remedies in Europe*. Oxford: Hart, 2000.
Nowak, Manfred. *U.N. Covenant on civil and political rights: CCPR Commentary*. Kehl: N.P. Engel, 1993.

Nowak, Manfred. 'The Right to Education', in Asbjørn Eide et al (eds.). *Economic, Social and Cultural Rights: A textbook*. Dordrecht: Martinus Nijhoff, 2001.

O'Cinneide, Colm. 'The Racial Equality Directive as a Basis for Strategic Enforcement' in Janet Cormack (ed.) Strategic Enforcement and EC Equal Treatment Directives. Migration Policy Group, 2004.

O'Flaherty, Michael. 'The UN Committee on the Elimination of All forms of Racial discrimination as an implementation agency' in Martin MacEwen (ed.), *Anti-Discrimination Law Enforcement*. Aldershot: Avebury, 1997.

Obura, Soraya – Fiona Palmer (eds). *Strategic Enforcement: Powers and Competences of Equality Bodies*. Brussels: Equinet, 2006.

OECD. International Migration Outlook: Sopemi 2007 edition. Paris: OECD publishing, 2007.

Ojanen, Tuomas. *Johdatus perus- ja ihmisoikeusjuridiikkaan*. Helsinki: Yliopistopaino, 2009.

Omi, Michael and Howard Winant. 'Racial Formation.' In Philomena Essed – David Theo Goldberg (eds.) *Race Critical Theories: Text and Context*. Oxford: Wiley-Blackwell, 2001.

Owens, Timothy. 'Self and Identity.' In John Delamater, *Handbook of Social Psychology*. New York: Kluwer, 2003.

Pan, Christoph – Beate Sibylle Pfeil. *National minorities in Europe*. Handbook, Ethnos Series Vol. 63, Vienna.

Paradies, Yin Carl. *Race, Racism, Stress and Indigenous Health*, PhD study, Department of Public Health, The University of Melbourne (July 2006).

Pellonpää, Matti. *Euroopan ihmisoikeussopimus*. Helsinki: Talentum, 2005.

Petrova, Dimitrina. 'The Denial of Racism.' In Claude Cahn (ed.) *Roma Rights: Race, Justice, and Strategies for Equality*. Amsterdam: IDEA, 2002.

Petrova, Dimitrina. 'A Right to Equality Integral to Universal Human Rights' *The Equal rights review*, Vol. One (2008).

Pettigrew, T. F., – Tropp, L. R.. 'Does intergroup contact reduce prejudice? Recent meta-analytic findings.' In Stuart Oskamp (ed.), *Reducing Prejudice and Discrimination* (pp. 93–114). Hillsdale, NJ: Lawrence Erlbaum, 2000.

Peutere, Laura. *Rasistisia piirteitä sisältävät rikosepäilyt rikosprosessissa*. Tampere: Poliisiammattikorkeakoulu, 2008.

Phillips, Anne. 'Multiculturalism, Universalism and the Claims of Democracy' M. Molyneux and S. Razavi (eds.) *Gender Justice, Development and Rights*. Oxford: Oxford University Press, 2002.

Pierce, Jennifer L. 'A Raced and Gendered Organisational Logic in Law Firms', in Reza Banakar – Max Travers (eds.), *An Introduction to Law and Social Theory*. Oxford 2002.

Pitt, Gwyneth. 'Madame Butterfly and Miss Saigon: Reflections on Genuine Occupational Qualifications.' In Janet Dine & Bob Watt (eds.), *Discrimination Law: Concepts, Limitations, and Justifications*. London: Longman, 1996.

Platt, Lucinda. *Poverty and Ethnicity in the UK*. Bristol: Policy Press, 2007.

PLS Ramboll Management. *Study of the Use of Equality and Diversity Considerations in Public Procurement: Final Report*. Available at: http://ec.europa.eu/employment_social/fundamental_rights/pdf/stureps/pubproc_en.pdf

Pound, Roscoe. 'The limits of effective legal action' 27 *Int'l J. Ethics* 150 (1917).

Putnam, Robert D. '*E Pluribus Unum*: Diversity and Community in the Twenty-first Century. The 2006 Johan Skytte Prize Lecture.' *Scandinavian Political Studies* Vol. 30 –No 2, 2007.

Pääbo, Svante. 'Genomics and Society: The Human Genome and Our View of Ourselves.' *Science* Vol 291. No 5507, pp. 1219–1220 (16 February 2001).

Ramcharan, B.G. 'Equality and non-discrimination.' In Louis Henkin (ed.) *The International Bill of Rights: The Covenant on Civil and Political Rights*. New York: Columbia U.P., 1981.

Rawls, John. *A Theory of Justice*. London: Oxford University Press, 1973.

Rawls, John. 'The law of Peoples.' In Obrad Savic (ed.) *The Politics of Human Rights*. London: Verso, 2002.

Raz, Joseph. *Human Rights Without Foundations* (March 2007). Oxford Legal Studies Research Paper No 14/2007. Available at SSRN: http://ssrn.com/abstract=999874 (accessed 1.7.2009).

Reuter, Niklas – Timo Makkonen – Olli Oosi. *Study on Data Collection to measure the extent and impact of discrimination in Europe. Final Report 7.12.2004*. Helsinki: NetEffect, 2004.

Riach, P.A. – J. Rich. 'Field Experiments of Discrimination in the Market Place.' *The Economic Journal* 112, November 2002.

Riach, P.A. – J. Rich. 'Deceptive Field Experiments of Discrimination: Are they Ethical?' *Kyklos*, Vol. 57, No 3, pp. 457–470, August 2004.

Risch, Neil et al. 'Categorization of humans in biomedical research: genes, race and disease.' Opinion, *Genome Biology* 2002:3 (1 July 2002).

Rodrigues, Peter R. 'The Dutch experience of enforcement agencies: current issues in Dutch anti-Discrimination law' in Martin MacEwen (ed), *Anti-Discrimination Law Enforcement*. Ashgate 1997.

Romualdi, Chiara et al. 'Patterns of Human Diversity, within and among Continents, Inferred from Biallelic DNA Polymorphisms.' *Genome Res*. 2002 12:602–612.

Rosas, Allan – Martin Scheinin. "Implementation Mechanisms and Remedies". In Asbjørn Eide – Catarina Krause – Allan Rosas (eds.), *Economic, Social and Cultural Rights: A Textbook*, pp. 425–453. (2nd revised edition) Dordrecht: Martinus Nijhoff Publishers, 2001.

Roseberry, Lynn M. *The Limits of Employment Discrimination Law in the United States and European Community*. Copenhagen: DJOF Publishing, 1999.

Rühl, Stefan – Gisela Will. *National Analytical Study on Racist Violence and Crime*. European Forum for migration studies, Institute at the University of Bamberg. Available at: http://www.fra.europa.eu/factsheets/Multimedia/Documents/2007/CS-RV-NR-DE.pdf

Sachar, Ayelet. *Multicultural Jurisdictions: Cultural Differences and Women's Rights*. Cambridge: Cambridge University Press, 2001.

Salentin, Kurt. 'Determinants of Experience of Discrimination in Minorities in Europe' *International Journal of Conflict and Violence* Vol 1(1) 2007, pp. 32–50.

Salmenhaara, Perttu. 'From Horizontal to Vertical Divides: Immigrant' Employment in Finland in the 1990s'. *Finnish Journal of Ethnicity and Migration*, Vol. 3, No1/2008.

Savic, Obrad (ed.). *The Politics of Human Rights*. London: Verso, 2002.

Schachter, Oscar. 'The obligation to implement the covenant in domestic law' in Henkin (ed.) *The International Bill of Rights: The Covenant on Civil and Political Rights*. New York: Columbia U.P., 1981.

Scheinin, Martin. 'International Human rights in National Law.' In Raija Hanski & Markku Suksi (eds.), *An Introduction to the International Protection of Human Rights: A Textbook*. Turku: Åbo Akademi University Institute for Human Rights, 1999.

Scheinin, Martin. "Women's Economic and Social Issues of Practical Implementation." In Hannikainen & Nykänen, *New Trends in Discrimination Law – International Perspectives*. Grafia, Turku, 1999.

Scheinin, Martin and Catarina Krause. "The Rights not to be Discriminated Against: The Case of Social Security" in T. Orlin and M. Scheinin, *The Jurisprudence of Human Rights Law: A Comparative Approach*. Jyväskylä: Gummerus, 2000.

Scheinin, Martin. 'Economic and Social Rights as Legal Rights.' In Asbjørn Eide et al (eds.) *Economic, social and cultural rights: A textbook*. Dordrecht: Martinus Nijhoff, 2001.

Scheinin, Martin – Reetta Toivanen (eds.). *Rethinking non-discrimination and minority right*. Turku: Institute for Human Rights, Åbo Akademi University, 2004.

Scheinin, Martin. 'Experiences of the application of article 26 of the International Covenant on Civil and Political Rights' in Council of Europe, *Non-discrimination: A human right*. Proceedings of the Seminar marking the entry into force of Protocol No 12 to the European Convention on Human Rights, Strasbourg, 11 October 2005. Council of Europe, 2006.

Scheinin, Martin. 'Human Rights treaties and the Vienna Convention on the Law of Treaties – Conflicts or Harmony?' In Venice Commission (ed.), *The status of international treaties on human rights*. Strasbourg: Council of Europe Publishing, 2006.

Schiek, Dagmar – Lisa Waddington – Mark Bell. *Non-Discrimination Law: Cases, Materials and text on National, Supranational and International Non-Discrimination Law*. Oxford, Hart Publishing, 2007.

Schiek, Dagmar – Victoria Chege (eds). *European Union Non-Discrimination Law: Comparative perspectives on multidimensional equality law*. Oxon: Routledge-Cavendish, 2009.

Schiek, Dagmar. 'From European Union non-discrimination law towards multidimensional equality law for Europe' in Dagmar Schiek – Victoria Chege (eds), *European Union Non-Discrimination Law: Comparative perspectives on multidimensional equality law*. Oxon: Routledge-Cavendish, 2009.

Schokkenbroek, Jeroen. 'A New European Standard Against Discrimination: Negotiating Protocol 12 to the European Convention on Human Rights.' In Stéphanie Lagoutte (ed.), *Prohibition of discrimination in the Nordic Countries: The Complicated fate of Protocol No. 12 to the European Convention on Human Rights*. Copenhagen: The Danish Institute for Human Rights, 2005.

Selmi, Michael. 'The Price of Discrimination: The Nature of Class Action Employment Discrimination Litigation and its Effects.' *Texas Law Review* Vol 81, 2003.

Selzer, William – Margo Anderson. *After Pearl Harbor: The Proper Role of Population Data Systems in Time of War*. 2000. A research paper available at: http://www.uwm.edu/~margo/govstat/newpaa.pdf

Selzer, William. *On the use of Population Data Systems to Target Vulnerable Population Subgroups for Human Rights Abuses. Coyuntura Social* No. 30, 2005.

Shauer, Frederick. *Playing by the Rules: A Philosophical Examination of Rule-Based Decision-Making in Law and in Life*. Clarendon Press, 1992.

Shelton, Dinah. *Remedies in International Human Rights Law*. Oxford: Oxford University Press, 2006.

Skogly, Sigrun. 'Article 2.' In Asbjørn Eide et al (eds.) *The Universal Declaration of Human Rights: A Commentary*. Oslo: Universitetsforlaget, 1992.

Smith, Peter B. – Michael Harris Bond. *Social Psychology Across Cultures* (Essex: Pearson Education Limited, 1998).

Sohn, Louis B. 'The Rights of Minorities.' In Louis Henkin (ed.) *The International Bill Of Rights: The Covenant on Civil and Political Rights* (New York: Columbia University Press, 1981).

Sommers, Samuel R. et al. 'Race and Media Coverage of Hurricane Katrina: Analysis, Implications, and Future Research Questions' *Analyses of Social Issues & Public Policy* Dec 2006, Vol. 6 Issue 1.

Sowell, Thomas. 'From Equal Opportunity to "Affirmative Action." In Francis J. Beckwith –Todd. E. Jones (eds.) *Affirmative Action: Social Justice or Reverse Discrimination*. New York: Amherst, 1997.

Sowell, Thomas. *Affirmative Action Reconsidered: Was it Necessary in Academia*. Washington: American Enterprise Institute for Public Policy, 1975.

Stanfield II, John H. 'Methodological Reflections: An Introduction.' In John H. Stanfield – M. Dennis Ruthledge (eds.) *Race and Ethnicity in Research Methods*. California: Sage Publications, 1993.

Steeh, Charlotte – Maria Krysan. 'The Polls – Trends: Affirmative Action and the Public, 1970–1995' *Public Opinion Quarterly* Vol 60:128–158 (1996).

Strauss, David A. 'The Law and Economics of Racial Discrimination in Employment: The Case for Numerical Standards' in McCrudden (ed.) *Anti-Discrimination Law*. 2004.

Szyszczak, Erika. 'Race Discrimination: The Limits of Market Equality?' In Bob Hepple and Erika Szyszczak (eds), *Discrimination: The Limits of Law?* London: Mansell 1992.

Taguieff, Pierre-Andre. 'New Cultural Racism in France' *Telos* Spring 90, Issue 83.

Tajfel, Henri. *Human Groups and Social Categories*. Cambridge: Cambridge University Press 1981.

Taylor, Paul. 'Positive Action in the United Kingdom' in Appelt, Erna –Monica Jarosch (eds.) *Combating Racial Discrimination: Affirmative Action as a Model for Europe*. Oxford: Berg, 2000.

Thornberry, Patrick. *International Law and the Rights of Minorities*. Oxford: Oxford University Press, 1991.

Triandis, Harry C. *Culture and Social Behaviour*. New York: McGraw-Hill, 1994.

Tropp, Linda R. 'The Psychological Impact of Prejudice: Implications for Intergroup Contact' *Group Processes & Intergroup Relations*, 2003 Vol 6 (2).

Tuori, Kaarlo. *Critical Legal Positivism*. Aldershot: Ashgate, 2002.

Turton, David – Julia González (eds). *Ethnic Diversity in Europe: Challenges to the Nation State*. Bilbao: University of Deusto, 2000.

Tyson, Adam. 'The Negotiation of the European Community Directive on Racial Discrimination, *European Journal of Migration and Law* 3, 2001.

Tzanou, Maria – Tuomas Ojanen. *Thematic EU/International Legal Study on assessment of data protection measures and relevant institutions*. EU Fundamental Rights Agency, forthcoming.

Ucellari, Paola. 'Multiple Discrimination: How Law can Reflect Reality' *The Equal Rights Review*, Vol One (2008).

van Boven, Theo. 'The Committee on the Elimination of Racial Discrimination: Trends and Developments.' In *Roma Rights* 1–2, 2003.

van Dijk, Teun A. 'Theoretical Background.' In Ruth Wodak – Teun A. van Dijk (eds.) *Racism at the Top. Parliamentary Discourses on Ethnic Issues in Six European States*. Klagenfurt: Drava, 2000.

van Dijk, Theun A. 'Denying Racism: Elite Discourse and Racism.' In Philomena Essed – David Theo Goldberg (eds.) *Race Critical Theories: Text and Context*. Oxford: Blackwell, 2001.

Verkuyten, Maykel. *The Social Psychology of Ethnic Identity*. Hove: Psychology Press, 2005.

Waks, Jay W. et al. 'The Use of Statistics in Employment Discrimination Cases'. *The Trial Lawyer*, Vol. 24 (2001).

Wal, Jessica ter. 'Conclusions.' In EUMC, *Racism and cultural diversity in the mass media. An overview of research and examples of good practice in the EU Member States, 1995–2000*. Vienna: EUMC, 2002.

Weller, Marc (ed.). *The Rights of Minorities: A Commentary on the European Framework Convention for the Protection of National Minorities*. Oxford: Oxford University Press, 2005.

Weller, Marc. 'The Contribution of the European Framework Convention for the Protection of National Minorities to the Development of Minority Rights.' In Weller (ed) *The Rights of Minorities: A Commentary on the European Framework Convention for the Protection of National Minorities*. Oxford: Oxford University Press, 2005.

Weller, Marc. 'Preface' in Weller (ed.) *The Rights of Minorities: A Commentary on the European Framework Convention for the Protection of National Minorities*. Oxford: Oxford University Press, 2005.

Wellman, David T. 'Toward a sociology of white racism.' In Martin Bulmer – John Solomos (eds.) *Racism*. Oxford: Oxford University Press, 1999.

Wheatley, Jonathan. 'The Economic Status of National Minorities in Europe: a Four-Case Study.' *Journal on Ethnopolitics and Minority Issues in Europe* 1/2007.

White, James Boyd. 'Law as an Expression: Thinking about our language.' In Tom Morawetz (ed.), *Law and Language*. 2000.

Wiley, Maya – John A. Powell. 'Tearing Down Structural Racism and Rebuilding Communities', *ENARgy* Issue 17.

Wilkie, Meredith. 'Australia's Human Rights and Equal Opportunity Commission.' In Martin MacEwen (ed.), *Anti-Discrimination Law Enforcement*. Ashgate, 1997.

Williams, David R. 'Race, Socioeconomic Status, and Health: The Added Effects of Racism and Discrimination' *Annals New York Academy of Sciences* 1999, 896:173–88.

Williams, Melissa S. 'In Defence of Affirmative Action: North American Discourses for the European Context?' In Erna Appelt -Monica Jarosch (eds.) *Combating Racial Discrimination: Affirmative Action as a Model for Europe*. Oxford: Berg, 2000.

Winant, Howard. 'Racism today: Continuity and change in the post-civil rights era', *Ethnic and Racial Studies* Vol 21, No 4 (1998).

Wodak, Ruth – Martin Reisigl. 'Discourse and Racism.' In Ruth Wodak – Teun A. van Dijk (eds.) *Racism at the Top. Parliamentary Discourses on Ethnic Issues in Six European States*. Klagenfurt: Drava, 2000.

Wodak, Ruth – Teun A. van Dijk (eds.). *Racism at the Top. Parliamentary Discourses on Ethnic Issues in Six European States*. Klagenfurt: Drava, 2000.

Wrench, John – Tariq Modood. *The Effectiveness of Employment Equality policies in Relation to Immigrants and Ethnic Minorities in the UK*. International Migration Papers 38. Geneva: ILO, 2000.

Wrench, John. 'Combating Employment Discrimination in Europe: National Variation and the Dawn of 'Good Practice.'' In Appelt, Erna -Monica Jarosch (eds.) *Combating Racial Discrimination: Affirmative Action as a Model for Europe*. Oxford: Berg, 2000.

Wrench, John. *Diversity Management and Discrimination: Immigrants and Ethnic Minorities in the EU*. Aldershot: Ashgate, 2007.

Yanow, Dvora. *Constructing "Race" and "Ethnicity" in America: Category-Making in Public Policy and Administration*. New York: M.E. Sharpe, 2003.

Yeung, Karen. 'Private Enforcement of Competition Law' in Christopher McCrudden (ed.) *Regulation and Deregulation: Policy and Practice in the Utilities and Financial Services Industries*. Oxford: Clarendon Press, 1999.

Ziemele, Ineta (ed). *Reservations to Human Rights Treaties and the Vienna Convention Regime*: Conflict, Harmony or Reconciliation. Leiden: Martinus Nijhoff, 2004.

INDEX

Advisory Committee on the Framework Convention for the Protection of National Minorities 202–208, 240, 270, 309, 332
Affirmative action. *See* positive action
Anthropology 16–20
Anti-semitism 129, 138, 268
Apartheid 6, 37, 60, 62, 71, 92, 117, 119, 129, 144, 151–152, 240, 247, 264, 268, 340
Awareness raising 23, 78, 126, 266, 272, 296, 311–312, 321

Biases, unintentional 57, 80–83, 89
Burden of proof 7, 147, 180, 181, 184, 201, 233, 249, 273, 304, 390, 397, 399

Charter of Fundamental Rights 96, 217–218, 220–222
Charter of United Nations 3, 43, 96, 116–117, 121, 146, 267
Civil rights movement 43
Collective agreements 125, 200
Colonialism 11, 12, 42, 62, 71, 129, 348
Committee of Experts on the Application of Conventions and Recommendations 123–126, 240
Committee on Economic, Social and Cultural Rights 166–173, 240, 242, 308, 334
Committee on the Elimination of All forms of Discrimination (CERD) 130–149, 182, 183, 238, 240, 248, 257, 259, 269, 270, 271, 309, 333
Communism 173
Comparators 147, 224, 231, 247, 306–307
Conflict theory 64
Constitution of the United States 120
Convention against Discrimination in Education 127–128, 153
Convention against Torture or other Cruel, Inhuman or Degrading Treatment or Punishment 210–211
Convention No 111 on Discrimination 96, 123–127, 153, 219
Critical Race Theory 60

Data collection 11, 24, 49, 126, 181–182, 226, 227, 240, 241, 293, 296, 301–341, 386, 398
Declaration of Principles on Equality 299
Declaration of the Rights of Man and of the Citizen 114
Democracy 45–47, 173, 253, 269, 290, 322, 326, 375
Discrimination 31–39, 77, 82, 90–92, 96–98, 118–124, 131–134, 150–156, 167–169, 174–182, 197–199, 223–228, 277, 304, 313
- by association 230
- causes of 57–83, 266, 301, 313
- direct discrimination 34, 154, 168, 197, 224, 230, 254, 305
- effects of 39, 83–90, 266, 301, 313
- empirical evidence of 49–57, 274–275
- everyday discrimination 34–35, 84, 98, 237, 247, 264
- indirect discrimination 34, 100, 132–133, 154–155, 168, 173–183, 198, 223, 225, 237, 240, 244, 254, 255, 259, 264, 265, 387
- institutional discrimination 35–38, 90, 99, 224, 225; 264, 265, 295, 299, 348
- structural discrimination 35–36, 38–39, 90, 224, 225, 237, 264, 265, 295, 299, 313, 348, 387
- statistical discrimination 78–80

Directive 2000/43/EC 7, 96, 179, 181, 217–218, 222–236, 238, 240, 244, 245–248, 259, 266–270, 273, 283, 310, 355, 388, 394
Diversity 11–15, 18, 28–30, 254, 293
Dualism 104
Durban declaration and programme of action 4, 257, 282, 283, 310, 334

Enforcement of law; individual rights model of enforcement 7, 249, 251, 272–277, 281, 368, 369, 392
Equality 31–33, 40–47, 115, 204–206, 220, 228, 235, 242, 250, 254, 283, 287–292, 297, 345, 356, 368, 377

cultural equality 45–46, 205, 250, 254, 288, 295
market equality 44–45, 247, 256, 288, 295, 346, 356, 368
material equality 44–45, 121, 250, 254, 256, 288, 346
moral equality 41–43
political equality 46–47, 205–207, 235, 288
civil rights equality 43–44, 288, 356
Equality data. *See* data collection
Essentialism 28–30, 59, 76, 245, 270–272, 282, 337, 360, 383
Ethnic minorities. *See* minorities
Ethnicity 17, 18, 24–29, 100, 158, 169, 179, 183–184, 199, 229, 231, 244, 245, 246, 263, 271, 309, 339, 360, 365, 383
European Commission against Racism and Intolerance 182, 183, 212, 269, 270, 320, 334, 391
European Committee on Social Rights 196–201, 238–240, 259
European Convention for the Protection of Human Rights and Fundamental Freedoms 96, 173–195, 197, 217, 219–222, 248, 325, 326
European Court of Human Rights 111, 174–196, 198, 238–245, 259, 325, 326, 354, 354
European Court of Justice 106, 111, 217–219, 225, 228, 327, 354
European Social Charter 96, 196–201, 219, 244, 257
European Union 11–13, 49–51, 55, 215–236
European Union Agency for Fundamental Rights 4, 49–52, 274, 320
Expectation states theory 81–82

Far-right movements 60, 67–68, 71, 223, 268, 358
FRA. *See* European Union Agency for Fundamental Rights
Framework Convention for the Protection of National Minorities 201, 237, 242, 243

Group rights 240, 281

Harassment 7, 35, 87, 89, 98, 200, 224, 227, 230, 237, 238, 242, 264, 266, 360, 370, 373
Harm principle 240, 251
Human Rights Committee 150–162, 238, 242, 259, 270, 308, 326, 333

Identity politics 45, 293, 383, 386
Immigration 11–14, 227, 268, 289
Indeterminacy of law 105–111, 239, 253, 254, 258–260
Indigenous and Tribal Peoples Convention 210, 242
International Convention on the Elimination of All forms of Racial Discrimination 3, 23–24, 41–42, 96, 128, 167, 238, 242, 248, 264, 269, 271, 273, 279, 338, 356
International Convention on the Protection of the Rights of All Migrant Workers and Members of their Families 208–209, 257
International Court of Justice 117
International Covenant on Civil and Political Rights 41, 96, 118, 140, 149–165, 167, 169, 171, 193,195, 219, 237, 242, 243, 248, 326
International Covenant on Economic, Social and Cultural Rights 41, 96, 118, 140, 149–150, 166–172, 237, 248
International Labour Organisation 54, 123–126
Interpretation of law 105–111, 259, 260, 261
Intersectional discrimination. *See* Multiple discrimination

Jews 62, 322

League of Nations 116
Legal certainty. *See* Indeterminacy of law
Liberalism. *See* political liberalism
Limburg Principles 167, 168, 171, 173

Maastricht Guidelines 167, 171, 173
Macpherson inquiry 38
Margin of appreciation 176–177, 186, 205
Merit principle 261, 262, 288, 351–353
Minorities 11–14, 62–63, 85, 88–89, 121, 178, 182, 202–208, 221, 239, 268, 269, 289, 290, 292, 309, 322, 324, 332, 335–338, 344, 347, 352, 357–365, 377, 382
Minority rights 133–134, 163–164, 179, 201–210, 243, 255, 268
Minority treaties 114–116
Monism 104

Monitoring 101, 202, 258, 261, 265, 308, 311, 318, 328–329, 334, 371, 376, 378, 380
Multiculturalism 46, 64
Multiple discrimination 100, 138, 158, 169, 231, 237, 244, 246, 247, 365
Muslims 63, 70, 92

Nation 26, 29; nation building, 11, 16, 17–18, 292
Nazism 57, 60, 67–69, 71, 76, 92, 116, 129, 173

Organisation for Security and Co-operation in Europe 212–213

Paris Peace Conference 114
Permanent Court of International Justice 115
Political liberalism 18, 249–254, 261, 279, 360
Positive action 144, 155–156, 177, 228, 242, 252, 253, 258, 271, 299, 343–366, 372, 377, 387
Positive duties 281, 298, 367–387, 391
Prejudices 57, 60, 61, 72–78, 80, 87–89, 91, 126, 146, 191, 258, 278, 280, 290, 292, 295, 297, 301, 346, 356–359, 362, 370, 387, 392, 405
Privacy (protection of) 159, 160, 252, 321, 324–334, 339, 340
Procurement 367, 372, 377–378, 385

Race 17, 18–22, 26, 29, 30, 65, 100, 113, 121–122, 127, 134–139, 157, 169, 179, 182–184, 199, 221, 229, 239, 244–246, 263, 271, 288, 309, 339, 360, 365, 370, 383
Racial Equality Directive. *See* Directive 2000/43/EC
Racialism 20, 21, 22, 57–58, 69–70, 191, 271, 282, 360–361
Racism 17, 20, 57–72, 129, 278, 279, 283, 348, 387
Racist violence 35, 68–69, 85
Remedy 101–102, 122–123, 126, 146, 160–163, 171, 180, 189–190, 201, 203, 207, 222, 232, 248, 272, 273, 275, 281, 287, 298, 301, 390, 392
Roma 4, 5, 11, 51, 52, 56, 180, 187, 198, 211, 264, 322, 337, 338

Sami 11, 210
Segregation 6, 62, 129, 142, 144, 145, 148, 263, 309, 348
Self-identification 138–139
Skinheads 67–69, 71
Slavery 42, 62, 71, 113, 292, 348
Social construction 16–17, 30, 33, 250, 288, 289, 297, 337
Social identity theory 64–65
Special measures 128, 133–134, 143–144, 168, 252, 253, 258. *See* also positive action
Specialized bodies 50, 201, 235, 249, 273, 310, 315, 371, 387, 388, 393, 395–396, 399
Statistical evidence. *See* data collection
Stereotypes 17, 57, 73, 80–81, 88–89, 126, 258, 278, 280, 290, 295, 297, 299, 346, 356–359, 362, 382–389
Strategy of avoidance 86

Trade unions 170, 197, 201, 395
Treaty of Lisbon 217, 220
Treaty of Rome 215–216
Treaty on European Union 218, 221

Unintentional biases 80–83, 278, 295
Universal Declation on Human Rights 3, 41, 118–119, 140, 149–150, 152, 171, 237, 242, 248, 267
United Nations Educational, Scientific and Cultural Organisation (UNESCO) 19, 20, 96, 127, 131, 153
United States Declation of Independence 113–114

Victimization 7, 148, 234, 249, 273, 373, 393
Vienna Convention on the Law of Treaties 107, 108

www.ingramcontent.com/pod-product-compliance
Lightning Source LLC
La Vergne TN
LVHW081514300926
849161LV00006B/1169
* 9 7 8 9 0 0 4 2 1 7 0 5 8 *